IBM Cognos 8 Business Intelligence: The Official Guide

Dan Volitich

New York   Chicago   San Francisco
Lisbon   London   Madrid   Mexico City
Milan   New Delhi   San Juan
Seoul   Singapore   Sydney   Toronto

The McGraw·Hill Companies

Cataloging-in-Publication Data is on file with the Library of Congress

McGraw-Hill books are available at special quantity discounts to use as premiums and sales promotions, or for use in corporate training programs. To contact a special sales representative, please visit the Contact Us page at www.mhprofessional.com.

IBM Cognos 8 Business Intelligence: The Official Guide

4567890   DOC DOC   019

ISBN   978-0-07-149852-4
MHID   0-07-149852-4

Sponsoring Editor
Lisa McClain

Editorial Supervisor
Janet Walden

Project Manager
Vasundhara Sawhney,
International Typesetting
and Composition

Acquisitions Coordinator
Mandy Canales

Copy Editor
Lisa Theobald

Technical Editors
Pam Neeley
Oliver Bergmann
Lori Pitcher
Dean Harrington
Dan Wagemann
Armin Kamal

Proofreaders
Erin Morris
Mary Gido
Steven P. Gaghan

Indexer
WordCo Indexing
Services, Inc

Production Supervisor
James Kussow

Composition
International Typesetting
and Composition

Illustration
International Typesetting
and Composition

Art Director, Cover
Jeff Weeks

About the Author

Dan Volitich is president and owner of John Daniel Associates, which he cofounded in 1996 to serve the business intelligence market. Dan's extensive experience with business intelligence (BI) began in the mid-1980s (before the market coined the term BI) at a large commercial real estate firm in Fairfax, Virginia. As their IT director, he successfully delivered enterprise business intelligence solutions, streamlining mission-critical business functions for every department in the company.

Upon his return to Pittsburgh in the early '90s, Dan again found himself chartered with empowering end users. Dan's background has given him tremendous insight into the value of empowering end users with business critical data, and that insight is invaluable in the delivery of BI solutions to John Daniel clients today.

With more than 24 years of experience in planning and delivering successful BI solutions to Fortune 500 and mid-market companies, Dan believes superior product knowledge and outstanding customer support are essential components to maintaining a leadership role in the BI market. That combination has been a significant factor in the continued growth of John Daniel Associates. Dan is a Penn State graduate with a Bachelor's degree in accounting with a heavy emphasis in IT.

Contents at a Glance

Contents

Part II   Accessing and Using IBM Cognos 8 Business Intelligence

Acknowledgments

The idea for this book was presented to me at a meeting in Burlington, Massachusetts, by Peter Malandra and Paul Hufford. Jacqueline Coolidge joined the project shortly after the effort was underway and we were off. I live this technology every day, and I thought, "How difficult could it be to put it into words and diagrams so that others may benefit by this great technology in their businesses?" So off I went to my team to get their buy-in. "Sure," they said. "We will help you do this without interruption to our clients." And they did. But I know they interrupted other aspects of their lives: most importantly, time with their families and sleep—lots of sleep. For that, I am extremely grateful. While I have the byline for this book, this book would not have been possible without the assistance of my team. The Cognos 8 solution is very deep. Since the 8.3 version was just released in the fourth quarter of 2007, it was impossible to think that one person could compile this information in a way that would have comprehensive value to its readers.

A heartfelt thank you to the following individuals on my team: Rob Kovacevic, my executive VP of quality and the foundation of my technical team; Gerard Ruppert and Susan Boyles, both principal associates on my team; Bryan Townsend, Alicia Scappe, and Susie Bann, all associates who also contributed content to the book; Erin Morris and Mary Gido, thank you for your endless hours of editing, screen capture, and insight; Janet Amos Pribanic, executive VP of sales, thank you for encouraging the rest of us to keep plugging forward and reminding us how much celebrating would be in line when we were complete. And to the rest of my team, I say thank you for your commitment to excellence over the years. You are the best.

Because of the aggressive publication schedule, and the fact that we were writing the book in addition to our full-time professional obligations, I partnered with a local firm, i-Squared, to act as our project manager. i-Squared is an enterprise content management and development firm. Val Tassari was my main contact there. She kept the information moving and the documents organized, and she even helped edit and review the chapters before passing them on to McGraw-Hill. This book would not have been possible without the help of Val and her great team at i-Squared.

Cognos, an IBM Company, is a first-class organization. I have been working with this technology for more than 17 years, and we have been an exclusive partner with Cognos for more than 12 years. I wish to thank the Cognos executive team that has supported this effort and trusted us as a partner to deliver this book. Peter Malandra, thank you for recognizing the quality of our partnership and internally supporting our endeavor. Jacque Coolidge and the technical reviewers at Cognos: Oliver Bergmann, Dean Harrington, Armin Kamal, Pam

Neeley, Lori Pitcher, and Dan Wagemann. Thank you for your expertise and input to help make this an excellent product.

The individuals at McGraw-Hill are some of the most patient folks I've met in quite some time. Lisa McClain and Mandy Canales did a great job of keeping me on task and guiding me forward one step at a time. Janet Walden, the editorial supervisor, Lisa Theobald, our copy editor, and Vasundhara Sawhney, the project manager at ITC—all of you did a great job of making sure that those deadlines (for the most part) were never missed. Thank you all for your patience and for understanding that excellent technology people are not necessarily prepared to be excellent authors and process people; somehow you helped me bridge that gap quite well. I am sure you all have several nicknames for me by now, but all I can say is thank you.

Last, but certainly not least, I would like to thank the tremendously talented development team under the direction of Peter Griffiths. For more than 12 years I have represented only the Cognos solution. I do that because I truly believe that Cognos is the best solution in this space. Writing this book has been a reminder of just how good it is. Enjoy.

Introduction

O nce I was on board with the idea of writing a book to communicate the functionality and value of Cognos 8, it became clear to me that many of the chapters in this book could, indeed, be their own individual books. The depth of Cognos 8 is just that substantial: Cognos 8 brought about significant improvement and a brand new architecture as well as a unified user platform. This release introduced the ability to deliver *reporting, analytics, scorecards, dashboards,* and *office of finance solutions* under one architecture.

My first glimpse into Cognos 8 was in the spring of 2005. I thought it was so great that I went out and bought cognos8.com, pointed it to my web site, and promptly heard from the Cognos lawyers. But that is another story. We realized immediately that the changes in the product would warrant significant planning and education, not only for our own team, but for our clients and prospects as well. The change in reference from administrative "catalogs" to a Framework Manager "model" made us realize that our deep understanding of this solution would benefit our clients immensely. These changes and my desire to communicate the value of this solution evolved with this book into a realistic objective, not just an idea.

Who Should Read This Book?

The audience for this book includes end users of the Cognos 8 solution, power users, administrators, and even executives who are stakeholders in a performance management or BI initiative. If you are new to Cognos 8 as a user or administrator, it is a great time to be coming on board. If you are a client using previous versions of the software and considering migration to Cognos 8, it is a great time to be coming on board. This book does not, in any way, replace any formal training offering on the Cognos solution. It will, however, augment your knowledge and present real examples and context of applicability with Cognos 8 inherent with the experiences we have had with the solution.

Approach and Organization of the Book

This book is organized a little differently from some of the technology books we have read. My approach was to lay the foundation for an introduction to Cognos 8 and the definitions of performance management and business intelligence so that you, the reader, would have that understanding up front while moving through subsequent chapters of the book.

Cognos 8 functionality is defined by user roles, and as such, those roles increase in technical depth and functionality. The user roles in Cognos 8 are defined by a user's need, leveraging specific studios that enable that role. My intent is to enable you to progress through the content of the book and increase the functionality extended in the solution as you go along. For example, we discuss performance management concepts early on so that you can gain insight to the purpose of a performance management initiative within your organization. Furthermore, the book focuses on aspects that an organization might need to consider when taking on such an endeavor by way of people, process, and technology.

Many of our clients ask us how best to deploy Cognos 8 for their organization. It is my hope that you will find value in the insight and tips and techniques that we have learned along the way with our clients, and I hope that it will have value to you in your Cognos 8 deployment.

We have witnessed confusion in the market between dashboards and scorecards. The business user community may communicate the need for multiple facets of their business on one page, and understanding these differences when describing their information needs to a development team will translate to a conversation around what is possible with their current data and if, indeed, a dashboard satisfies that requirement. The development team will be required to discern whether a user is describing a scorecard or dashboard. This unity in understanding these concepts will yield higher returns for your business.

The Cognos 8 technology leads this industry in delivering better decision-making tools for its users. But, no doubt about it, it requires smart, diligent people and a cohesive plan and commitment to that plan. Your technical expertise and business insight are both solid requirements for successful deployment of Cognos 8. Whether you're an IT administrator responsible for the delivery of the Framework Manager model or an end user who is performing analytics for your organization through Analysis Studio, this book will help you elevate your skills and leverage this powerful technology for the betterment of your organization.

Following is a glimpse at what's inside this book.

Part I: Introduction to Performance Management and IBM Cognos 8 BI

The definitions of *performance management* and *business intelligence* are discussed, as well as the various perspectives of business intelligence. IT administrators play a critical role in this solution. We discuss the IT perspective in such an initiative. The business user's role is empowered by use of effective information in the Cognos 8 solution. Whether consuming a report as an Cognos 8 consumer or performing analytics as a business analyst, the Cognos 8 user roles provide flexibility for information delivery. Additionally, we describe the difference between a scorecard and a dashboard, so that you can understand the place of each solution in your business. We provide insight into and definition of the roles and studios within Cognos 8. These definitions will help identify *how* and *what* to deploy to *whom*. As mentioned, the office of finance has become an integral component of performance management, and in this part we discuss integration, reporting, setup, and configuration of the planning, budgeting, and forecasting solution.

Part II: Accessing and Using IBM Cognos 8 Business Intelligence

We move into the access and use of IBM Cognos 8 BI in Part II. The Cognos Connection portal helps you organize information for your business. We share insight about Cognos Connection and how users run reports using filters, options, and settings for report properties. Additionally, we provide information for creating a portal page and viewer options. Cognos 8 brings brand new functionality to the stage by way of IBM Cognos 8 Go! and its integration with Microsoft Office and search mode. Cognos 8 can now push reporting right to your mobile Blackberry device.

Part III: Authoring IBM Cognos 8 Business Intelligence Content

IBM Cognos 8 BI content and authoring provides tremendous insight to self-service report authoring in Query Studio. We discuss relational versus multidimensional data sources as well as use of the Query Studio Wizard. We move on to advanced report authoring within Report Studio. Creation of reports, grouping, filtering, adding calculations, and formatting reports are included. Additionally, in this section we present analytics using the Analysis Studio to enable analysis versus reporting. Within Analysis Studio, Cognos 8 introduces complex filtering, top and bottom 10, nesting, and calculations, to name a few features.

Cognos 8 introduces the ability to deliver dimensional reporting, and we discuss the advantages of dimensional authoring as well as the application of dimensional function and navigation and much, much more. To help you dive even deeper into an understanding of your business, Part III provides information for the creation of scorecards and metrics and the extensive functionality within the Metrics Studio.

Event management is also a new functionality within Cognos 8. We share the definition of an event and business uses for event management as well as the tasks needed for creating agents, executing tasks, and scheduling agents.

Part IV: Administration of IBM Cognos 8 Business Intelligence

The foundation of Cognos 8 administration is Framework Manager. Part IV provides the insight and definitions needed for creating a Framework Manager model, creation of objects, setting properties, and adding query subjects. The administrator responsible for the Framework Manager model can read and learn about adding query subjects, namespaces and folders, calculations, filters, and creating and publishing a page.

Part IV also addresses modeling practices and how to avoid traps along the way. How do we know about this? Let's just say we've learned a few things in the past 12 years. We also share advanced modeling techniques to include maintenance of a model, use of macros, navigation, and query traps.

Security of Cognos 8 is paramount for every organization. Authentication, authorization, and access permissions and the setup capabilities for roles, which is a new functionality in 8.3, are included in this section.

Cognos Connection management addresses content administration, data sources, schedule management, and server administration to name a few hot spots in this section.

Cognos 8 is a powerful solution that yields tremendous benefit to its clients. The journey is extensive and the return is great. We are committed to excellence in the implementation of this solution and hope that you find the content in the chapters that follow that will prove helpful in your quest for excellence in your organization.

Introduction to Performance Management and IBM Cognos 8 BI

PART

I

Introduction to Performance Management and IBM Cognos 8 BI

Performance Management

Performance management, business performance management, corporate performance management, business intelligence—each of these terms identifies a way to measure and manage performance within your organization.

IBM Cognos 8 Business Intelligence (BI) is technology that supports performance management by providing better visibility in business performance. In order for your Cognos 8 implementation to provide maximum benefit to your organization, your organization needs to understand BI's potential to change the way in which decisions are made. The more your organization is aligned with the performance management objectives and willing to change, the more significant the impact. In many cases, change happens in stages. We call this progression through stages a *journey*.

Your initial Cognos 8 implementation will evolve as your organization becomes more competent in both the process and the technology. Changes in corporate positioning, strategy, or point of view can be implemented quickly and easily allowing for better, faster decision-making. Failure to implement a performance management solution may put your organization at risk of being at a competitive disadvantage.

This chapter describes performance management and provides insight into how a strategic implementation can affect your organization.

Your first meeting with many prospects and clients begins with them telling you, "We have the data that we need in our ERP.... We just can't get it out as usable information." Sales managers often want better and timelier information about how they are performing against their forecasts. The operations team has no coordinated view of the organization and often learns of closed sales opportunities long after the opportunities have passed. Finance managers want better financial reporting and the ability to deliver accurate, yet critical information to key stakeholders and executive management.

As you continue to learn about business objectives for better information, you find that the process used to collect the needed information often exceeds business cycles, leaving no time to analyze or assess what has happened or to determine what corrective measures may be necessary to improve the company's performance.

Every aspect of a business is connected to every other aspect, and performance management helps you connect the dots and align the organization. For example, optimized supply chain performance provides vendors a means for executing effectively through the supply chain so that orders may be fulfilled in a timely and quality-driven manner. This impacts customer satisfaction. Objectives of improved profitability, projected growth, and better overall performance are all impacted by the performance of the supply chain. The performance goals of the organization cannot be realized unless the organization has the means of aligning information and business process to produce results. The promise delivered by this alignment is enhanced business performance or performance management.

Defining Performance Management

Let's start by identifying how to define *performance management*. It's not as simple as you might think. An Internet search conducted in July 2007 on the term *performance management* returned 23,000,000 results. Out of the gate, the search for the "answer" begins and we find ourselves digging through disparate data sources to identify the right answer. With some initial investigation, we find that the term *performance management* is used and referred to as both *business performance management* (BPM) and *corporate performance management* (CPM).

BPM is a set of processes that helps organizations optimize their business performance. It is a framework for organizing, automating, and analyzing the business methodologies, metrics, processes, and systems that drive business performance. BPM helps businesses efficiently use their financial, human, material, and other resources. Organizations may take components of the performance management spectrum and deliver solutions specific to the business area seeking better decision-making. Performance management then can be the next generation of BI.

CPM has been defined as "a set of processes that help organizations optimize their business performance. It is a framework for organizing, automating, and analyzing business methodologies, metrics, processes, and systems that drive business performance." Sound familiar?

The Cognos 8 Solution comprises three coordinated segments of performance management that answer questions such as those shown in Figure 1-1:

- **Measuring and monitoring**   Businesses seek the answer to "How are we doing?" Most people find the answers to this question by going to a number of different sources or tools. They pick up the phone, send e-mails, review the last presentation, and check spreadsheets. Some companies have home-grown systems or tools that are focused at the executive level. The answers get pulled together from various sources and are often manually entered into tools.

- **Reporting and analysis**   Decision-makers want to find answers to the question "Why?" In most organizations, this means consulting a number of reports and analysis tools to pull together a picture of why they are on or off track. Analysis tools use a variety of systems and pool data to get the answers. It sometimes requires calling on an IT department to understand elements of the puzzle—When did this happen? Was it consistent across the board or limited to a couple of regions? Was it all products or just a few? Answers to these questions, and likely many others, are found via data analysis that is used to identify trends, high or low performance, and a deeper understanding through greater insight to the data.

- **Planning, budgeting, and forecasting**   Plan for the future and identify a reliable means to gather that plan across your organization. The answer to "What should we be doing?" begins with planning where you want to go. It is the process of allocating resources to achieve goals with planning, budgeting, and forecasting and includes making course corrections when changes occur to reallocate resources. Companies often do not have such plans in place. In most companies, these answers come from thousands of individually created spreadsheets.

How are we doing?

Scorecarding & Dashboarding

Why?

Reporting & Analysis

What should we be doing?

High-frequency Planning

Figure 1-1   Finding answers to the questions that drive performance

The questions How?, What?, and Why? can be mapped to the Cognos 8 software that enables and automates answers—scorecards and dashboards for "How are we doing?" and reports and analyses for "Why?" (usually automated with pieces of BI). The challenge with BI in many organizations is that the tools have grown up regionally and functionally, creating a patchwork of different applications and tools. The result is that, from a business user perspective, the organization ends up with different interfaces, different time periods, and even gaps in information, creating a lack of confidence in the numbers.

Many factors influence a company's performance. One critical factor is the decisions made throughout the organization from top to bottom and across functions and divisions. All those decisions are based on the information on hand, and they depend on the accuracy, timeliness, and completeness of the information. Once you identify where your organization can yield the greatest benefit, you can begin to plan your initial phase of the business performance journey. If you are like most organizations, finding answers to these fundamental questions is difficult.

As companies dig through data looking for answers, it becomes clear that they need a means to gain insight from this information. But don't be fooled—selecting some cool technology that will yield great graphs and highly formatted reports will not necessarily solve this problem. The tools are only part of the solution. Many companies make the mistake of thinking that the tools will solve data problems when the single largest challenge is not the tools, infrastructure, or data, but actually the people. Organizations need to ask themselves the following questions:

- Do we have the people and culture that truly understand our business and who are willing to make fact-based, not gut-based, decisions? Fact-based decisions do not always "feel good."
- Do we have the process and methodology that will take what we have learned from our BI insight and apply it to new business decisions and processes?
- Will our culture enable, embrace, and execute change?

Answers to these questions require executive input, executive direction, and a commitment to the plan for execution. More important, if the answer to the questions is "No," then save your budget, time, and sanity and do not embark on this journey. Should that be your choice, however, you must know that your competition is likely figuring out how to make this work to gain a competitive advantage through insights to their market, customers, and profits.

The IT Perspective of BI

From an IT perspective, implementing and maintaining a host of different tools can be inefficient and expensive. It costs money, it takes time, it requires people, and it has significant inefficiencies. Resources or report objects cannot be shared, and you need a help desk for every tool or class of users.

Businesses often seek assistance from IT to find the answer to these problems, to make the solution easy to use, to leverage applications which are easy to maintain, and most importantly, to solve the problems. Businesses seek the "big button" that they can press to get what they want. IT gets a new project, evaluates tools, writes up the RFP, sends it out to vendors, and then months later claims they have done what they were asked to do. However, the business has not adopted the solution and finds that it is still using disparate spreadsheets. The project is deemed successful by IT, but a failure by the business because the manual processes are still in place and the business is spending exorbitant amounts of time trying to solve the same problems that existed prior to IT's decision for a solution. How did this happen? Let's break it down.

Countless experts have made statements on the value of BI in the market and how "good data" is required to make BI successful. The IT department is tasked with participation in a BI solution because the mounds of data that the company has collected need to be organized in a manner that can be presented to the business. But is it really about IT and the technology it brings? In part, yes. IT has been responsible in most global and small/medium business markets for gathering the operational data. IT has built sophisticated systems that enable organizations to collect information about all aspects of business, and companies have evolved from legacy systems to enterprise resource planning (ERP) (well, most have) to help make use of data to increase knowledge and profitability.

Because IT has been charged with data collection, it has historically been viewed by business as the group that "owns" the data. And because the resources that collect the data must be knowledgeable about the organization of that data, they have built and taken ownership of the systems that house the data. While the talent and resources necessary to manage data are significant, business units are created to specialize in data. But how does one know that the data being collected can be used to improve performance for tomorrow, next quarter, next year, or five years from now? More importantly, have insights been made into "how" data is collected so that it can be transformed into usable information by typically non-technical business users? These questions can be challenging to answer because IT often does not understand why the business cannot understand the information they have provided.

Because BI solutions bring use of "information" together with business performance, we need a bridge that will give IT comfort that the information they are gathering for the business is accurate and that will provide the business with the confidence that the "information" can be used easily to make important decisions.

To use this information, IT must do the following:

- *Provide "good data."* We have all heard the saying "garbage in—garbage out." It is very true. IT must adhere to strict data planning that provides, for example, a common definition of a customer and clean delivery of that definition as defined within the business.

  Business Case   At a client site, we were charged with the deployment of a data warehouse for sales and market forecasting. When we pulled the data from their point-of-sale (POS) system, the data contained multiple instances of customer names, misspelled customer names, and varying opinions about whose responsibility it was to clean them up. The client knew this problem existed in their data, but a manual process of correcting the problems in a spreadsheet versus in the data source masked the insight to their business that was really needed to make informed decisions about the product mix. The lesson in such a case is to make sure a solid plan is in place so that data can be easily maintained as necessary—this will benefit the organization as a whole, and you may become an IT hero along the way.

- *Work with your business to understand the benefit of your role in the BI journey.* This is not an "IT versus Business User" undertaking. If you attack it that way, the project will fail. Do not take it personally if the business requires IT to change or add a field in the database or the DBA is asked to adjust the access rights to the data.

  Business Case   On a recent Balanced Scorecard Initiative project, we provided plant managers with the ability to see real shipment data for the first time. The shipment data was stored in the data warehouse along with other financial data, so access was prohibited for the Cognos users. During the project, issues arose regarding access to the data warehouse. The need for and use of the data was neither communicated nor explained to the DBA, who refused to change the access rights. As a result, the project missed milestones and deadlines, and the ability to troubleshoot issues with the implementation was almost impossible. This ultimately impeded the progress of the project and increased the cost of the effort. The solution to this impasse was to obtain executive management involvement and direction. However, the problem with the DBA continued to linger throughout the entire project.

- *Educate yourselves and ask for help from a trusted source who has embarked on this journey before, even if you partner with them for a short time.* We have a saying in our organization when getting new resources up to speed: "It is always easier the tenth time." This does not mean that it takes 10 times to get it right; it means we have potentially found ways that are clearly not right before nailing the right one.

Business Case   One client was sincerely attempting to roll out new metrics functionality with Cognos 8 and was having a horrible time of it, spending months of effort that resulted in personnel being unavailable for other internal projects. The client's frustration with Metric Studio stemmed from having wrong expectations for this Studio's capabilities. By leveraging our knowledge of the application with their knowledge of their business, we were able to bring resolution to the issue within a shorter period of time. After placing the data into Metric Studio, we had the customer back on track and completed the project within a few weeks. This led to greater value and return to the business and a shorter deployment period.

The BI Business Perspective

Have you ever balanced your checkbook after writing your monthly financial obligations and thought that you should adjust your budget so that you have more cushion from month to month? Do you begin your day with a check-and-balance of your initiatives at hand? How do you prioritize tasks on your To-Do list? How do you adjust to a shortage in your checkbook? Perhaps you transfer funds from another account. In essence, you adjust your monthly plan, knowing that if you do not, you will fall short on next month's obligations.

Businesses are the same. They need a solid plan with visibility so they know if they need to "adjust." Better yet, they need to have visibility into "why" the business might need to adjust. For example, a new product line might be exceeding sales expectations—therefore, the organization may need to adjust its supply chain so that it can have adequate inventory to fulfill orders. In doing so, managing cash becomes critical to such growth, and on, and on.

How does BI help with all of this? BI provides high-level checks and balances that allow a business to react to resolve problems or priority changes. Because IT controls the data and monitors the data integrity, they are often tasked with the selection and implementation of the data warehousing solution. Sometimes, IT departments build requirements without talking with the users and understanding their needs. For companies with healthy BI processes, BI becomes a bridge between IT and the business. Business users have visibility and insight into the technical details behind the business, and the IT engineers gain an understanding of the business drivers and issues. In addition, if users are given permission to create reports, IT's workload lessens and business users have access to what they need, when they need it. A win, win!

A BI solution is safe. All data extracted from a data source is organized and wrapped within a security package. The data in the data source cannot be touched, manipulated, or destroyed. Business users may have a lot of data to thrash through using Microsoft Excel, but where does that data come from? Usually, IT extracts the data from a database to a file format that Excel can understand. Before you know it, you might have multiple spreadsheets containing multiple versions of the same data. Who owns the correct data? Wouldn't an automated process be better for the user?

What does the data mean? Using a BI solution, you can analyze what is happening in your business. You have heard that customer complaints are increasing. Using dashboards, you can see that the number of calls coming into the data center is higher than normal. As you drill-through the dashboard, the results show that shipments have not been leaving the plant on time. Upon further drill-through, you see that one of the largest machines in the plant has not produced your company's product for more than a week. A phone call to that department indicates that the machine is under repair. The BI solution brings a level of validity to performance measurements and a basis upon which to make adjustments. Your plant cannot argue with the numbers. They are what they are.

Create a BI Competency Center

A BI Competency Center (BICC) does not have its own building or office space, but it does need to be staffed by result-oriented individuals within your organization and an executive sponsor(s) dedicated to ensuring that your performance management implementation is successful. The value realized by a successful BICC extends to both the IT and business segments of your organization. Some organizations call it a Center of Excellence, as it can help drive a lower total cost of ownership to your BI solution, enable a faster adoption rate of the BI solution across the enterprise, and introduce and enforce BI standards across your organization. It is the bridge between all divisions, departments, and organizational groups.

At a minimum, the BICC team should include a business director, who ensures success within your organization; a business analyst, who understands and can communicate the needs of your users; and a technical consultant, an IT group advocate for the technical implementation teams. There is no "ideal" or "perfect" model for a BICC. This concept is based on your specific organizational objectives, process, culture, and technology infrastructure. The team is chartered with developing a repeatable process and a set of best practices for the BI implementation. And while there is no "perfect" recipe for a BICC that will work for all organizations, there are best practices for developing a BICC.

Once best practices and standards are established, the BICC will provide the means to educate key stakeholders and avoid a "silo approach" to implementation. The BICC guides new users on potential new uses of performance management within your company, teaches internal users how to use the application to review information, and markets the solution internally to promote additional interest or knowledge about the BI application. Having a BICC coordinates the data challenges possible by including knowledgeable IT staff, gives business users the voice that they need, and documents the guidelines for future performance management application development.

Paramount to the success of your BICC is the requirement to set clear roles and responsibilities for those involved in the BICC. Guidelines for implementing a successful BI project are included in the following section.

The Pursuit of Performance Management

You can apply numerous strategies as you pursue a performance management solution for your organization. The goal of the pursuit is to get better at measuring and managing your business. For example, if the re-engineering of a raw material formula in a product recipe, which makes the product significantly better, causes the recipe to be too expensive for one of your customers to purchase, do you want to revert to the old recipe or do you want to stop supplying that customer?

Performance management is a strategic endeavor that demands support from senior management. This point may seem obvious, but its importance cannot be understated. Many performance management initiatives are led by the CEO and/or CFO. Initiatives at client sites can fall by the wayside or get lost in budget shuffles or turf wars due to a lack of commitment from the executives. On the opposite end of that spectrum, many companies have benefited by truly changing the way they do business by leveraging the Cognos 8 Performance Management Solution to their strategic and competitive advantage with senior executives who were committed to fact-based and analytical decision-making. The CEO of one successful organization presented his information strategy, which included a BI initiative, and stated to his staff, "You are either on this bus with me, or the door is that way." He directly attributes 20 percent bottom line growth to the success of his BI initiative. To date, it has been a six-year journey.

Performance management is about linking strategy to execution. It starts with the strategy. Strategy management is an emerging trend touted by leading organizations, such as the Balanced Scorecard Collaborative. This group set the standard for providing best practice balanced scorecard deployment and proven methodology. The role of strategy management is to help the company establish strategy, adapt it when necessary, and ensure that it stays focused on the successful execution of that strategy.

Equally critical is ensuring that everyone in the organization has regular visibility into the strategy and is aligned with the strategy. This initiative may be communicated through regular meetings, executive newsletters, technology portals, or by any means that enables the strategy to be communicated to employees to allow them to access the strategy and understand where they are on or off track and what the successful execution means to them.

The following steps are required for delivery of Performance Management:

1. Choose a segment of your business that will have the greatest return to your organization's information needs.   The chosen segment should have value to the company, but perhaps not great visibility. What if you were able to see, in an instant, how well you were meeting product needs for your customer? How valuable would it be to see how quickly a new product is gaining market share? With visibility into critical areas of your business, important decisions can be made more quickly and corrective actions can be put in place sooner to help your business become more agile in the face of change.

In addition, once they become more confident with the information that the solution provides, users will be happier employees. No more late nights crunching numbers when forecasts are due. No need to have employees pulling their hair out when spreadsheets don't balance or the numbers don't add up the way they should. And users will become empowered to use the information for the benefit of the business.

NOTE *Performance management is a journey. It cannot be implemented overnight. Attack it in increments, starting with the highest priority areas.*

---

2. Gather information for the selected segment.   What data sources exist that contain the information needed to support the chosen segment? Do you have databases containing shipment information, POS figures, or safety information? If the data resides in a database or ERP system, it is likely more reliable than data created by hand. Do you have access to the data? If the data resides on a departmental desktop instead of a network server, the location of the data will need to be changed. Is the data clean? Having data entered that does not adhere to specific naming conventions, for example multiple iterations of a customer name, will cause problems when the data is extracted for display. The customer picture will be fuzzy instead of clear.

Data sources bring value to your solution because they eliminate as much risk as possible and avoid erroneous outcomes. How many times have numbers been transposed when input manually? We have all heard of the corporate accounting scandal charges against Enron, Adelphia, WorldCom, and others, where numbers were fudged by top executives to misuse or misdirect funds, overstate revenues, understate expenses, overstate the value of corporate assets, or underreport the existence of liabilities. Having the data extracted from the data source and displayed directly on the scorecard, dashboard, or report reduces the accessibility to the raw data and almost eliminates the possibility of scandalous acts. The key is to incorporate business logic when displaying the information from the data source, to ensure that the business information is not compromised.

3. Build a prototype and review the data.   Executives might not buy into the solution until they can see the benefit the solution brings. So provide a mechanism for data review. Start with a small concept that will likely provide insight into performance indicators. Discuss this potential solution with the key users and gather as many requirements from them as possible. Developing the prototype is an iterative process. How close is the data shown to target? Make adjustments and try again. Is the data getting better or worse? Are you hitting or exceeding the target? Does it impact the supply chain? Your executives will know for sure.

BI enables organizations to look at targets and year-over-year comparisons. Performance management will enable you to adjust the business strategy and goals to optimize the business.

Gather executives and run through the prototype with them. Focus on the business in the performance management solution. Use metrics, analytics, and reports to show different results and views of the data from the data source. After some time, executives will begin to provide valuable feedback and insight into how data should be structured. This provides the perfect opportunity for them to articulate ideas for improvement or to express concerns regarding the implementation. Be ready for their surprise should the reports show a glaring sea of red flags or their delight when they receive confirmation of something going right that they previously had a gut feeling about.

Here are a few examples of actual business cases: A client wanted to see if its plants were meeting production performance objectives. They had been reviewing performance figures in a spreadsheet, which became a nightmare to create because the data was not all stored in one place. When the report was complete and presented to the executives, they were surprised to see that the results were so bad. And they could easily pinpoint where the problem(s) began.

Another company continually adjusted its production capacity to meet the demands of one customer. This customer purchased a large quantity of product on a regular basis, but the company feared that the constant change requirements were eating into its profit margins. The first report produced confirmed their fears. They were then faced with the decision of whether to continue to meet the demands of this customer and modify their production or to cut their losses and move on.

The beauty of the Cognos 8 application is that you can easily make changes based on user requirements. By dragging and dropping new data dimensions into the report template, you can make additional information available for review, and the report is improved—from the executive's point of view. Because the implementation is iterative, executives can review and suggest changes as many times as needed until they are satisfied with the outcome.

4. Deploy the solution.   The way in which the solution is deployed is as important as the implementation effort. Pick a date for the live deployment. Identify the personnel who will use the application, develop a training plan—either formal or informal—and train personnel prior to their first use. Proper training results in a high probability of success that personnel will use the solution. Technology can be intimidating. Companies waste thousands of dollars on implementation because they forget to add training to the project goals.

NOTE *Proper training results in a high probability of success that personnel will use and receive value from the solution.*

Part of deployment includes monitoring. Review the performance of the solution regularly. Evaluate its success based on user feedback. Do the users have enhancement suggestions? If so, build them into a plan for Phase 2 or 3, if it makes sense to do so. Use a coordinated approach to build upon the successes found in Phase 1.

Summary

In summary, the performance management journey will require planning, corporate commitment, and technical perseverance. The most successful organizations that have deployed BI and then progressed to a strategic performance management–driven enterprise have initiated best practice deployment and clear measurement of their success.

Align business and technology objectives closely. Remember that everyone benefits in a well-performing company. Insight to that performance is critical and will enable you to make adjustments as necessary—quicker, better, and faster than your competition. Your internal (and external) clients depend on a proficient means to get the information they need to make sound, well-supported decisions. These decisions will drive insight to the performance of the organization and provide a sustainable model for moving forward with subsequent areas of your business.

As you implement, focus on establishing clear and measurable value from each step before embarking on the next step of the journey. This will assure success over the long term and consistent management support as you move forward. Good luck on a successful performance management journey!

CHAPTER 2

Monitoring Performance Using Dashboards and Scorecards

Dashboards are created using Report Studio, which is a standard component installed with IBM Cognos 8 Business Intelligence (BI). Scorecards, on the other hand, are created using Metric Studio. Companies sometimes struggle when implementing either dashboards or scorecards because they are unclear of which studio to use. Or they hear words and phrases from users that might indicate the use of dashboards or scorecards, when, in actuality, what they need is a report. This chapter explains the differences between dashboards and scorecards and provides the information that will help you decide which studio you should use to meet your goals. It also offers hints you can use to achieve success with your dashboard or scorecard implementation.

Monitoring performance can be a daunting, but necessary, task. Once your organization's vision is cast and all objectives are communicated, monitoring to ensure the objectives are being met can be all-consuming. You need to be immediately aware of critical shortfalls and other related objectives, and you must focus your energies on those that most need to be addressed. Performance monitoring is daunting when your data is inconsistent and difficult to obtain. Do you use multiple applications, each having its own structure and architecture? Do you need to switch back and forth between applications to grasp the big picture? Can you easily access the information that you need to understand the pulse of your organization? Each of these problems can be solved using Cognos 8's measuring and monitoring mechanisms: dashboards and scorecards.

Dashboards provide at-a-glance summaries of critical information that is captured during an established time period using sophisticated graphical data representations, such as graphs, charts, gauges, maps, and so on. From these graphical images, you can drill-up or drill-down to see either the bigger picture or essential data. The images are personal—you determine what information is shown. They are fairly easy to create and are not subject to rules and regulations for creation. S*corecards*, on the other hand, display performance metrics to determine company health. They show visual representations of actuals, targets, and variances and can provide the same drill-through to the details that are used with dashboards. Most likely, you will need to use one or the other during your Cognos 8 implementation.

One or both of these may suit your needs. It is important early on in the development that you get the terminology correct and that you know the differences between the two.

Dashboards Show Current Information

Suppose that Oprah Winfrey's latest show highlighted the effectiveness of your product. Without any advance notice, Oprah-mania hits your business head-on. Your product sales have jumped enormously. The next thing you know, your warehouse manager sends a message saying they cannot fill orders. You are losing money by the hour because your organization was late to react to the sales influx. Your customers are placing orders with your competitors, who are happy that your business has faltered.

Now consider the same situation with the use of a dashboard. Whether or not you knew of the Oprah show, you actively monitor the status of your company. At a set time increment, your dashboard updates incoming sales, outgoing orders, and level of production. Sales are up. Inventory is down. You increase production to keep up with the demand. Your warehouse continues shipping product as the orders come in. Your customers are happy, because you are meeting their needs. The dashboard allowed you to see and immediately react to a serious problem that could have negatively impacted your bottom line. The company that reacts the quickest is the most successful!

Dashboards are sexy. Everyone wants one. Corporate executives, sales directors, and parts and inventory managers each need a different view of perhaps the same information, and each benefit from having vital information at their fingertips. Dashboards are reports created using graphs and charts as a mechanism for presenting information. Dashboards communicate complex information quickly. They translate information from your various corporate systems and other supplemental data into visually rich presentations that show multiple results together. They allow you to unite data from different core areas of your business—such as sales, finance, HR, logistics, and distribution—to view a complete, multi-department picture.

When our customers ask for a dashboard, we ask them to explain their vision. We must understand what they are looking for to determine the best deployment option. Some customers envision hundreds of numbers on a dashboard, which contains links to other dashboards also containing hundreds of numbers. This vision is not a dashboard; it is a series of reports linked together. If you have to work hard to understand the contents of a dashboard, it is probably not designed properly or, at the very least, is not a dashboard.

On the dashboard of your car, you see a variety of gauges and images that visually identify signals from your car, including the measurement of gasoline remaining in your tank, your engine's temperature, and the speed at which you are traveling. Each status is current. You see how fast you are going now, not how fast you drove last month. You see how much gas you have now, not how much gas you had yesterday. You see immediately whether your car is performing as expected. What would happen if each of those graphical representations on your car's dashboard were precise numerical values? Gasoline remaining would be shown in gallons, engine temperature would be in degrees Fahrenheit (at what temperature does the car overheat?), and wait, how many tire revolutions equals 60 miles per hour? Understanding the state of your car would become much more difficult. What if this information didn't exist at all? Driving your car could be disastrous!

TIP   *How current should your dashboard's information be? If current means "to the minute," then you should consider purchasing Cognos NOW! This add-in provides continuously updated information that can be personalized to contain up-to-the-second metrics, graphs, and indicators and is presented at the "right time" for your needs.*

Take a look at the Employee Satisfaction dashboard, shown in Figure 2-1, which is part of the installed Cognos 8 demo. This dashboard has three regions. At the upper left, a scatter chart shows the results of an employee survey with indications of satisfaction across a variety of topics. At a glance, you can see that the majority of the employees indicate that communication and feedback needs to improve. At the upper right, the same survey results are charted against industry norms and corporate targets. Again, communication is shown as an area needing improvement, which affects the employee's overall satisfaction. Finally, the table shows the actual rankings as percentages and how these rankings reflect employee attrition. All provide valuable information when evaluating the health of an organization.

So, what makes a good dashboard? A good dashboard is personalized to the needs of an individual user. Some users will not be happy until they see all the detail that the charts and graphs hide. These users absolutely hate charts and graphs, and that's okay. But keep in mind that delivering a dashboard that they will not use does not denote success.

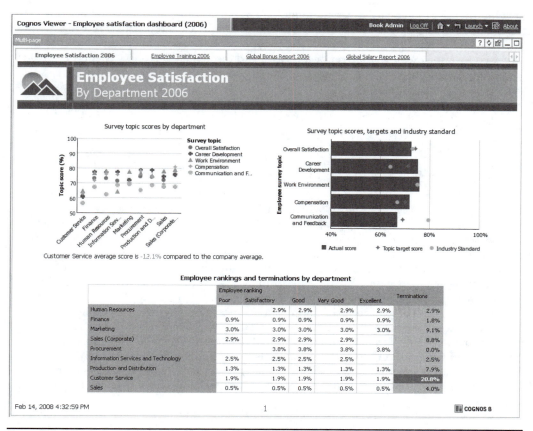

FIGURE 2-1   Employee Satisfaction dashboard

Viewing Metrics with Scorecards

Most companies measure success by meeting financial expectations. Their financial data generally reflects past accomplishments (or the lack thereof). They use forecasting to predict the future and budgeting to control expenditures. In many companies, this data is disparate. Data is stored in many different systems or forms, such as enterprise resource planning (ERP), customer relationship management (CRM), spreadsheets, legacy data, and so on. Calculating metrics on this data causes executives and managers to spend time gathering and trying to understand the validity of the results instead of actually being able to use the data to manage performance. And then you have issues understanding where the problems are located and who is responsible for resolving them—that is, if everyone can agree that a problem exists at all. This leaves your company making strategic business decisions based on gut feeling and best guesses.

Enter scorecards. Scorecards are a proven approach for monitoring, measuring, and managing performance at a tactical and strategic level within the entire organization. Their development is based on a proven methodology for managing and enhancing performance. Automated scorecards gather data from the disparate sources and organize it using metrics. The metrics tell you three fundamental things: your actual measurement (current), the target you want to achieve (budget or forecast), and the actual-to-target variance. If linked with analytics and reports, scorecards can provide visibility and accountability for performance problems that may span multiple departments or functional areas at all levels. Scorecards are always on, always current, and always factual.

Figure 2-2 depicts a typical scorecard. Colored indicators on the scorecard show how the metrics are performing currently and whether the metric is on an upward or downward trend.

***

NOTE *Scorecard indicators are shaped differently to assist those who are color blind. For more information about scorecards, refer to Chapter 13.*

***

Scorecards provide consistency, which is achieved when everyone agrees to and works toward accomplishing the same goals. Along with identifying the goals, everyone must have a consistent view of what denotes organizational success. With scorecards, goal-driven metrics can be delivered to each desktop, so everyone in the organization from managers to CFOs can see how their performance and decisions are impacting the goals of the company. Users can see at a glance whether their performance is trending up, down, or remaining stable based on color schemes or graphics used, or both.

Implementation of a scorecard is more of a business challenge than a technical challenge. Executives need to identify which metrics should be tracked to provide visibility into the company's performance. Metrics are not one-size-fits-all, and they can change over time. The implementation can take several trials to get right—which is perfectly normal. Companies may start small by identifying key metrics and applying indicators to those metrics. From there, additional metric attributes, such as impacted/impacting relationships, can be added.

Cognos 8.3 creates scorecard metric relationships of the same metric type automatically. For example, if your scorecard has a corporate sales metric, Cognos 8.3 provides tracking to allow the VP of sales to view how divisional and branch sales have impacted corporate sales.

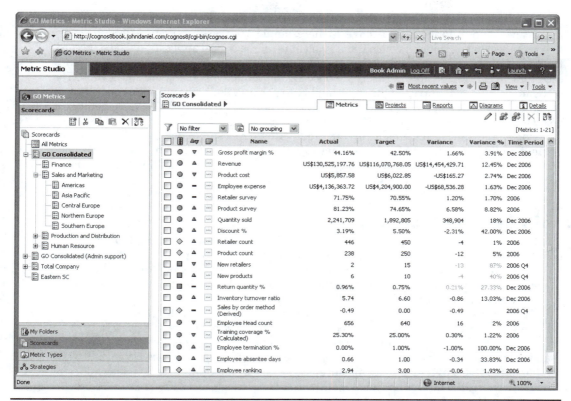

FIGURE 2-2   Typical scorecard

Sales managers reviewing the metrics for these relationships can see how their efforts impact those above them in the organization. The VP of sales may also want to see how other metrics impact corporate sales. For instance, if the product quality is poor or if shipments are not sent when expected, they may be able to see a drop in sales. These relationships are added to the scorecard by the Cognos 8 BI Business Manager.

Let's look at a scorecard example. A company spent a significant amount of money implementing a critical business software application. The users were extremely satisfied with the performance of this application and the time savings it provided for their daily tasks. Several months later, the users were unable to access vital data in the application. Upon investigation of the problem, the database administrator, the network administrator, and the server administrator all verified that their pieces of the application were working as expected. The three administrators worked in different departments, and possibly different locations, all reporting up to different managers and, unfortunately, that was how they were being monitored. The database was running, the network was up, and the server was operable—three green indicators. From their three individual perspectives, the application should have been operable. But it was not working. From an application standpoint, the scorecard was measuring the wrong things or not enough things.

Coordination and alignment between all the responsible parties in the vertical organization makes an Cognos 8 application effective. In this example, your task would be to find the metric that provides that alignment, which is the availability of the critical application. The scorecard for this application should be flagged with the highest priority—a huge red indicator—until the problem is resolved and the users are once again productively using the application. The software being down impacted the users' ability to perform their jobs, which impacted the company's ability to ship products to fill orders. An aligned organization works together to resolve issues, which results in better overall performance.

Scorecards allow you to ensure accountability down to a single-person level by keeping a finger on the pulse of your business. They identify where your company is currently and where it is going. Managers and executives can easily access the information they need to practice excellent decision-making.

Value of a Balanced Scorecard

The key to a balanced scorecard is accountability. The balanced scorecard methodology enables business users to better understand what will be their future financial performance. It provides the means for employees at all levels and across multiple departments to manage their own performance. What makes this methodology unique and different from forecasting is that it is accomplished without a "crystal ball."

The balanced scorecard methodology was created by Drs. Robert Kaplan and David Norton and an article describing it was published in the *Harvard Business Review* in 1992. Kaplan and Norton write that the interplay between people and processes are dynamics that, when aligned with company strategy, can be measured using metrics. Scorecard implementation is governed by the Balanced Scorecard Collaborative, which determines whether it meets the minimum functional standards necessary in a software solution to meet the Kaplan/Norton methodology. Companies that do not understand the balanced scorecard methodology have great difficulty implementing scorecards to measure the metrics of their organization.

Let's take a look at the value balanced scorecarding brings to an organization. Balanced scorecarding is grouped into four major perspectives: financial, customer, internal, and learning and growth. All four perspectives are dependent upon each other. The real trick is to figure out what to monitor today so that next week or next month your financial performance is somewhat guaranteed or predictable.

All companies report and analyze financial data. This data is represented in Figure 2-3 in the Finance segment. Depending on how quickly your organization closes its books and publishes financial information, the information you see can be several days old. Financial data is generally backward-looking or a view of the past. The challenge for all companies is how to prepare today for solid financial performance tomorrow.

The customer perspective is a view of your company as your customers see it. This is represented in the Sales and Marketing segment of Figure 2-3. Satisfied customers are a critical component of financial success. If you ensure that your customers are happy today, then next week or next month you should have customers paying their invoices and making repeat orders, which leads to financial performance.

How do you make certain your customers are happy today to ensure your financial performance tomorrow? You do this by monitoring your internal perspective. The internal perspective is how you view and measure yourselves, which is shown in the Production

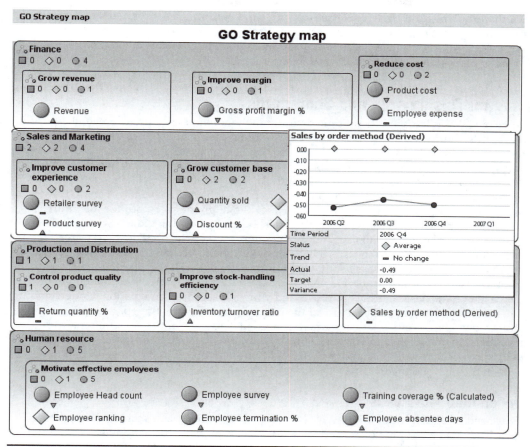

FIGURE 2-3   Strategy Map

and Distribution segment in Figure 2-3. Are you shipping on time today? Are you shipping complete orders on time? Do you have in stock what your customers want to buy? You can see where this is going. If you manage your internal perspective (operations) today, then next week or next month your customer satisfaction will be high and the following week or month your financial performance will be on target.

Learning and growth are the foundations of the entire process. This perspective includes training and mentoring new and existing employees. Investing in your team, making sure everyone is trained to perform his or her job, and making sure that workers understand safety measures assures internal perspective performance next week, which assures customer satisfaction the following week, which assures financial performance after that. HR is often responsible for this task, as Figure 2-3 depicts.

An example of a company that has successfully used the balanced scorecard methodology is Southwest Airlines. Southwest Airlines used performance perspectives to improve business. Company representatives measured the amount of time passengers were waiting to board

Southwest planes and recognized this as a potential performance improvement that would provide a benefit to customers. The airline instituted a new procedure to reduce the turnaround time at the gate. As an effect, Southwest Airlines was able to increase its ridership, fly more planes, and improve its financial performance.

Planning for Dashboards and Scorecards

Some businesses have a difficult time determining what metrics to use to create their scorecards. During our interview processes, we often pick some metrics, put in some simple targets, and show them the result. This is usually enough to get the creative juices flowing and spur some lively conversation about what can be done. Don't worry about conquering all four balanced scorecard perspectives initially. If your company is like most, you will have financial and internal data available to you. Use what you have to get started. Your organization can build upon this sample to plan and align the scorecard for the future.

Customers also struggle when creating dashboards. They don't know what graphs and charts to use or how many to use. We use the same interview process to get the creative juices flowing for their dashboards that we use with the scorecards. The key is to get started.

Once you have some ideas about what information would be helpful to monitor, gather all of the users of the application to help you determine the amount of information to be displayed on the dashboard, its purpose, and your goals for implementation. Understanding what metrics provide a clear picture of the performance of your entire organization allows scorecards to be developed. Involvement is needed across the entire corporation, from executives, to mid-management, to the IT staff, to the distribution center, for an implementation to be successful. A well executed, well-thought-out plan provides the tools needed to be agile in the face of danger.

Understand Your Needs

Your needs will determine whether you implement a dashboard, a scorecard, or perhaps both. They will also help you to understand how current the information needs to be. The responses provided to questions posed in the initial interview are valuable to help design your Cognos 8 implementation.

> **NOTE** *Cognos 8 provides the tools needed to implement what you want to see. It does not provide turnkey metrics or magic buttons that gather and display the information. You must have a clear understanding of what information will help you to manage your company's performance.*

Corporate executives provide valuable information and insight into the company's inner workings. At the beginning of your project, engage the top executives in a meeting to help you understand the needs and direction of the organization. Extend your interviews to the directors and managers reporting to the executives to identify the information they need to see to manage effectively. Some example questions to ask during your interviews include the following:

- What is important to monitor?
- What is your goal?
- What numbers interest you?

- What information helps you to manage?
- What are your targets?
- How do you calculate to reach your target?
- What corrective actions do you take when problems exist?
- What departments impact your ability to meet your goals?
- Who is impacted by your performance?
- How frequently do you need this information?

When all of your interviews are complete, you will understand the information to be gathered, which will help you to determine whether to produce a dashboard or a scorecard.

Choose Metrics

Suppose you've decided to implement a scorecard. For your scorecard to be successful, you need to select the appropriate metrics to be evaluated. And you need to be ready to react to what the metrics tell you. The metrics provided by the application may do the following:

- *Identify weaknesses in your organization down to the person or task creating the weakness.*

    Business Case   One organization measured the productivity of all similar machines located in geographically disbursed factories. The indicator on the scorecard for one particular machine was red. The manager initially thought this indicator was wrong because all of the machines were recently serviced. Upon investigation, the manager discovered that workers had reduced the speed of a machine, which affected the productivity of the machine and the group, and caused the red indicator to display.

- *Cause an organizational change to take place.*

    Business Case   When the Cognos 8 implementation at one company went live, it showed one of their distribution centers had more than $1 million in excess inventory that had been carried over several months. Upper management went on a fact-finding trip to verify the accuracy of this number. An action plan was decided and entered into the actions area of Metric Studio to improve the metric by reducing excess inventory.

TIP   *Linking actions to a metric provides a written record of what changes will be made or are expected to improve the metric. The action is visible from the Action tab.*

- *Change over time.*

    Business Case   An equipment manufacturer understands that its business is cyclical. During winter months, its product sales drop. Using a scorecard, the business owner monitored the situation closely and changed the metrics to reflect the current sales trend.

The phrase "What gets measured, gets done" applies. What gets done can be negative or positive depending on how the measurement is implemented. One company that was

---

Help Available for Metrics

If you are unsure of which metrics to use to evaluate your business, help is available. The book *The Performance Manager: Proven Strategies for Turning Information into Higher Business Performance,* written by Roland Mosimann, Patrick Mosimann, and Meg Dussault, can be ordered online from Cognos or from a bookseller. It provides an incremental approach to building a scorecard. It describes decision areas within the major functional areas of a company and identifies the goals, metrics, and dimensions that allow you to review information from various standpoints. The book takes into account the need to understand data and to plan and monitor performance.

Every decision-making cycle depends on finding the answers to three main questions:

1. *How are we doing?* Monitor your business using dashboards or scorecards.

2. *Why?* Use BI reports and metrics to measure history against the future to see and understand both anomalies and trends.

3. *What should we be doing?* Review budgets, plans, and forecasts to see a reliable view of the future and to respond to changes happening in your business.

The Performance Manager provides helpful insight into applying performance perspectives in your organization along with examples and case studies of successful implementations.

---

concerned about invoices being sent in a timely manner added metrics that measured the amount of time from the last client contact until the invoice was sent. After receiving more red indicators than were desired, the employees found a way to "touch" the account and thereby avoid the red indicator. The company needed to change the metric to enforce the invoice rule. The moral of this story is this: If what you measure can be manipulated, expect it to be manipulated unless you put the right amount of protection in place. Everyone implementing metrics runs into this scenario at least once during the life of a project. Do not be alarmed if it happens. It is human nature to try to avoid being caught in a negative spotlight.

If the performance captured by metrics falls below a certain threshold, people are alerted and can take immediate action. They can review additional reports and collaborate with others in their organization to find the solution. If performance measurements are in the red, and remain red, change needs to occur. On the other hand, if a department's metrics are always green, perhaps bonuses, pay raises, or promotions are appropriate for the workers in that department.

Benefits of a Successful Implementation

Your application is always running, always current, and providing visibility into your company's operations. It provides an easy way to drive performance by allowing you to measure, monitor, analyze, and plan for optimal organizational behavior. This is accomplished by the following:

- Focusing on key issues that affect financial stability
- Providing immediate access to reliable, consistent, and current data from disparate sources

- Using dashboards or scorecards to show at-a-glance views of performance
- Evaluating business processes, inter-departmental relationships, and strategic goals against target values
- Allowing drill-through to reports providing details of trouble areas
- Facilitating visibility, accountability, and collaboration between and within departments
- Encouraging continuous review of the company's strategy and goals

What should you take away from this chapter? Our goal was to provide enough information about dashboards and scorecards so that, regardless of whether you are a business user or an IT implementer, you are able to communicate with each other using the same language. You have knowledge about what dashboards and scorecards are and know which studio to use in Cognos 8.

The main ingredient in a successful Cognos 8 implementation is communication. Business users need to explain their needs clearly in terms of the amount of graphical information versus numerical information to be seen. Implementers need to listen to the business users to understand their needs without any preconceived ideas. Do not get caught in the trap of implementing what you *thought* you heard. Business user requirements may contain the word *metrics*, but what they need is, in actuality, a *report*.

When should you use a dashboard? Dashboards provide a graphical view of the state of the organization at a point in time. Use them when you want to review status at a glance. What about using scorecards? When you are ready to begin your journey into creating a balanced scorecard, following the methodology put in place by the Balanced Scorecard Collaborative, use scorecards to view metric measurements and relationships to other metrics that encourage alignment and coordination across your organization.

Introduction to IBM Cognos 8 Business Intelligence

Your organization has invested in the Cognos 8 software and has obtained licenses for user roles. After installing Cognos 8, users often ask two questions: "What do these roles mean, and what can I do with them?" This chapter tries to answer these questions. Successfully implementing Cognos 8 begins with an understanding of the native user roles and responsibilities, as well as the various IBM Cognos 8 studios. IBM Cognos 8 users will have the permissions to interact with IBM Cognos 8 and studios based on the roles and the privileges assigned to them. This chapter describes the user roles and the studios.

NOTE *For information on defining roles and permissions, refer to Chapter 17.*

Typically, an organization's employees comprise executives, financial accounting staff, IT architects, IT developers, sales managers, part/product managers, and so on. Each employee has a specific role in a specific segment of the organization and the need to access data to support that role. Sometimes, he or she may need to view data from within and across organizational segments to make decisions, understand trends, or view performance statistics. Certain data is protected, such as financials, and only those with a need to know are granted access.

When you implement your Cognos 8 application, you must keep users' needs in mind. Does the user need to be able to interact with the data or is a view of the data sufficient? Will the user review the same information month after month, or does the user need to create ad hoc reports during the month to keep track of the company's progress? Does the user need simply to view data or run reports? The answers to these questions determine how you will configure the Cognos 8 license roles in which you have invested.

These questions also help you to determine which Cognos 8 studio will be made available to the user. If a user reviews information monthly and does not need to create reports, you can assign the Recipient role, which allows the user to view reports created by another member of the organization. If the user needs to drill-through the data to create reports or scorecards, assign that user a role that provides access to one or more of Cognos 8 studios, such as Query Studio, Report Studio, or Metric Studio—just to name a few.

Cognos 8 User Roles

If you are in the process of implementing roles and are confused, do not be alarmed. Cognos 8 user roles have some amount of overlap. Each of the roles described in this section has a specific set of access permissions. You have the option of using the predefined roles or creating roles of your own.

NOTE *For more information on customizing roles, refer to Chapter 17.*

Cognos 8 user roles are grouped according to the amount of control the user should have over the application. The first grouping, *non-author roles*, allows users access to reports generated from Cognos 8 via various mechanisms such as e-mail, a portal, or direct access to a studio. The second grouping, *author roles*, allows users to create reports using one or more studios. Also, discussed within author roles are the *administration roles* of the BI Professional and the BI Administrator.

Non-Author Roles

Cognos 8 has three non-author roles that provide all users with the ability to view stored reports, and in the case of the consumer, to run reports. The three roles are the Remote Recipient, Recipient, and Consumer.

Remote Recipient

As a Remote Recipient, you can receive reports that have been generated by Cognos 8 and that have been released to you through various outlets (such as e-mail, wireless devices, or paper). Users can view reports without access to any Cognos software.

Recipient

As a Recipient, you have access to the Cognos Connection portal to select and view stored reports. Additionally, you can set the default language, time zone, and other personal preferences in Cognos Connection. You can view the same reports that Remote Recipients can, but you can view them directly on the portal. The following example shows a typical view of a Recipient's Cognos Connection screen.

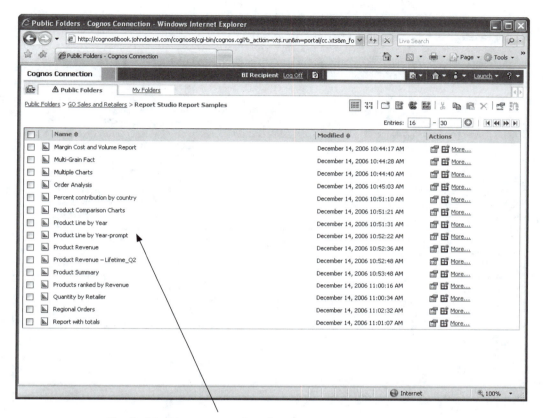

The Recipient has access only to these reports

NOTE *For more information about Cognos Connection, refer to Chapters 5 and 6.*

Consumer

Consumers have access to the Cognos Connection portal to select and view stored reports in the same way that the Recipient does. As a Consumer, you can consume any content in Cognos Connection by running reports, responding to prompts, and scheduling reports.

Additionally, you can consume report output inside the Microsoft Office environment with the IBM Cognos 8 Go! Office component. This allows you to access your business intelligence (BI) content directly from your Microsoft document. You can receive Event Studio notifications (such as status changes, updates about priority customers, and so on). Finally, you can set preferences and create folders in the Cognos Connection portal.

NOTE *For more information on IBM Cognos 8 Go! Office, refer to Chapter 7.*

The next example shows a typical view of a Consumer's Cognos Connection screen. Unlike the Recipient's screen, the Consumer's Cognos Connection screen shows Run With options displayed in the Actions column for each applicable report. This gives you the ability to execute reports using a variety of options.

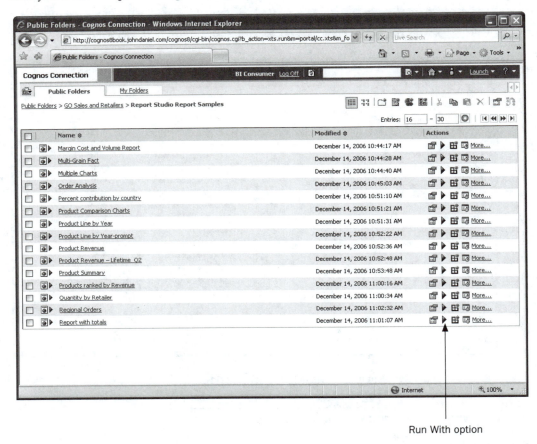

Run With option

Note *For more information about Cognos Connection, refer to Chapters 5 and 6.*

Author Roles

Cognos 8 offers many author roles that give users varying levels of access to studios and applications in Cognos 8. This chapter covers the five most common roles that give you access to Query Studio, Report Studio, Event Studio, Metric Studio, and Analysis Studio. The following sections provide a brief description of each role and to what studios each role has access.

Business Author

The Business Author role is designed for business users who need fast answers to business questions. It has all of the capabilities of the Consumer role but also includes ad hoc query and reporting capabilities. Users can create simple queries or access and edit existing queries. All queries and analysis can be saved in folders in Cognos Connection.

The next example shows a typical view of a Business Author's Cognos Connection screen. Notice that any query that the Business Author can modify displays the Query Studio action in the Actions column.

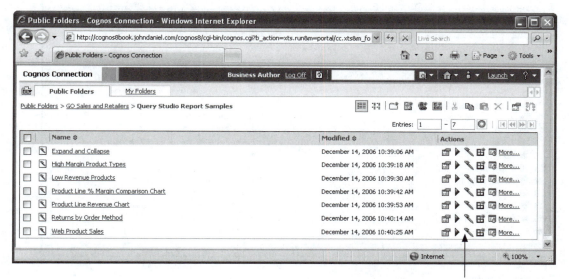

Open with Query Studio to modify display

Business Analyst

As a Business Analyst, you have the same rights as the Consumer. You also have access to Analysis Studio and all of its functionality to perform interactive analysis on your organization's BI content. You can also see trends and identify anomalies to help keep your organization ahead of the competition.

The following example shows a typical view of a Business Analyst's Cognos Connection screen and Launch menu.

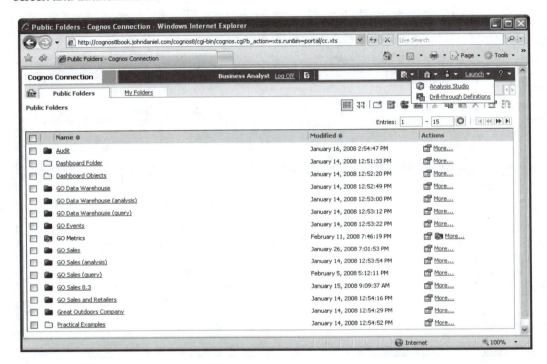

Business Manager

The Business Manager role is designed for business managers who need a cross-functional view of the business in the perspective of key performance indicators. Business Managers have the same rights as the Consumer and also have access to Metric Studio and Metric Designer and all of their functionality to set up and manage scorecards and scorecard security.

The next example shows a typical view of a Business Manager's Cognos Connection screen and Launch menu.

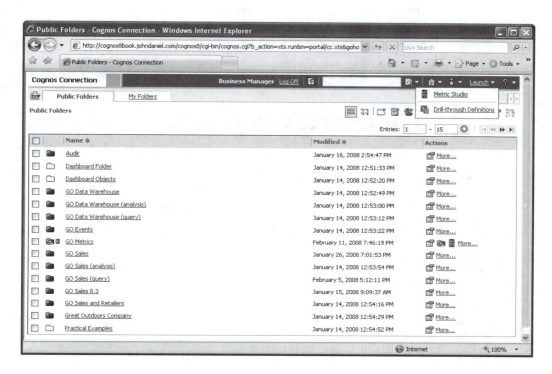

Professional Author

Professional Authors are generally people who create reports for others to consume. They have a greater requirement for professional quality output. As a Professional Author, you have the same rights as the Consumer. You also have access to Query Studio, where you can create ad hoc queries and edit saved queries, and Report Studio, where you can create and test new reports, edit existing reports, and publish the reports for consumption by your organization. As an added level of quality assurance and quality control, the Administrator can require that two Professional Authors are needed to publish a report where the first Professional Author creates the report and the second Professional Author audits and publishes the report. Finally, different Professional Authors may have access only to the reports pertinent to their department. For example, one Professional Author may have access only to financial reports, while another may have access only to sales reports.

The next example shows a typical view of a Professional Author's Cognos Connection screen and Launch menu.

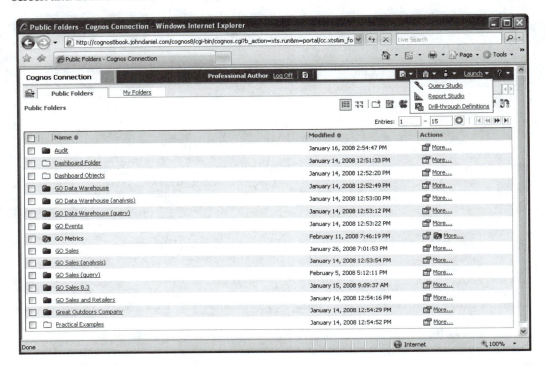

BI Professional

The BI Professional spends a great deal of time creating BI content for the rest of the organization to use. As a Professional, you have access to all five studios: Query Studio, Report Studio, Analysis Studio, Metric Studio, and Event Studio, as well as Metric Designer, Transformer, and all deployed packages. You have nearly the same abilities as the Administrator with the exception of Framework Manager and Map Manager. A Professional can create reports and scorecards, perform analysis, or set up notifications. Typically, an organization has only one or two Professionals.

The next example shows a typical view of a Professional's Cognos Connection screen and Launch menu.

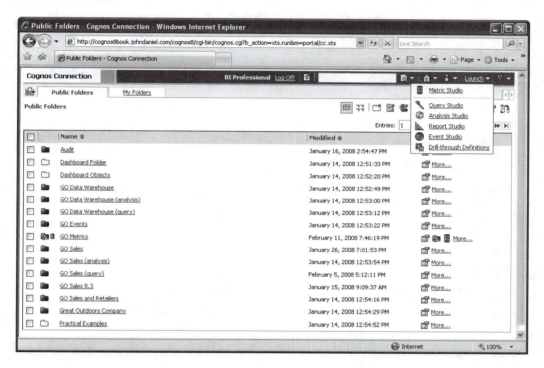

BI Administrator

As a BI Administrator, you have access to all five studios. In addition, you have access to Framework Manager to model metadata and publish packages, and Map Manager to create maps, add attributes to maps, and manage maps. You are the creator and manager of how Cognos 8 collaborates with your BI content.

The next example shows a typical view of a BI Administrators' Cognos Connection screen and Launch menu.

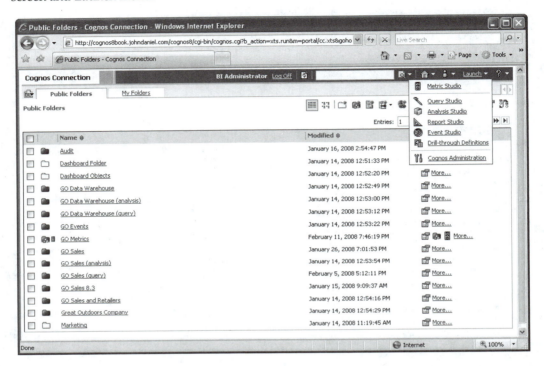

NOTE *With the Administrator and Professional roles, you are licensed for each of the five studios. This can be useful for running a pilot on one of the studios that you have not deployed. For example, if scorecarding is not deployed in your organization, one person has access to Metric Studio to create a mock-up scorecard. When the decision-makers see the value in Scorecard, you can purchase additional Business Manager licenses for the people who would need to access Metric Studio to consume the scorecards.*

Cognos Connection and Cognos 8 Studios

All of the roles discussed in this chapter, with the exception of the Remote Recipient, give you access to Cognos Connection. The studios to which you have access depends on the role you have been assigned. As discussed, each role allows different access rights. Using Query Studio, Report Studio, Event Studio, Metric Studio, and Analysis Studio, you can create ad hoc reports, detailed reports, and notifications based on data, and you can monitor and analyze your data. Table 3-1 provides a graphical depiction of what roles have access to Cognos Connection and the studios.

	Remote Recipient	Recipient	Consumer	Business Author	Business Analyst	Business Manager	Professional Author	BI Professional	BI Administrator
Cognos Connection		X	X	X	X	X	X	X	X
Query Studio				X			X	X	X
Report Studio							X	X	X
Event Studio								X	X
Metric Studio						X		X	X
Analysis Studio					X			X	X

TABLE 3-1   A Matrix of Roles and How They Relate to Cognos Connection and the Studios

Cognos Connection

Cognos Connection is the web portal by which users access Cognos 8 and the studios. Depending on the role that you have been assigned, you can use the Cognos Connection portal to retrieve, view, publish, manage, and organize your organization's reports, scorecards, and agents. The Administrator also uses the Cognos Connection portal to establish roles and user permissions and manage the Cognos Connection content.

All Cognos Connection users can personalize how Cognos Connection displays for them. Users can modify personal preferences, such as the language and regional settings. They can also change the format (PDF, Excel, HTML) in which they receive content, such as queries, reports, and analyses.

NOTE *For more information on Cognos Connection, refer to Chapters 5 and 6.*

Query Studio

Query Studio, shown next, is an easy-to-use authoring tool with which you can quickly create simple queries from the data stored in your database without having the skills of a professional report writer. With a few clicks of the mouse, you can view, filter, sort, and format the data; modify the query layout; and add charts. Finally, you can save and share the queries you created with other people in your organization.

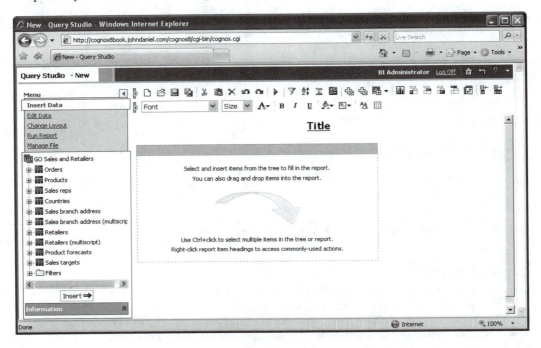

NOTE *For more information about Query Studio, refer to Chapter 8.*

Report Studio

With Report Studio, shown next, you can create and format reports easily using two authoring modes: the Professional authoring mode and the Express authoring mode. The difference between these modes lies in the functionality they provide in Report Studio.

NOTE *For more information about Report Studio, refer to Chapters 9 and 10.*

Professional Authoring Mode

Professional authoring mode gives you access to all of Report Studio's functionality. You can create charts, maps, lists, repeaters, or any other available report types using static data from relational or multi-dimensional data sources. The Professional authoring mode has all of the features that the Express authoring mode has and then some.

Express Authoring Mode

Express authoring mode provides a scaled-down version of Report Studio. The average report writer can access relational and multi-dimensional data sources and create financial and management statement reports. In the Express authoring mode, you can create crosstab reports and access live data. You can view a report that was created in Professional authoring mode; however, you cannot modify objects available only in Professional authoring mode (such as charts, maps, and lists).

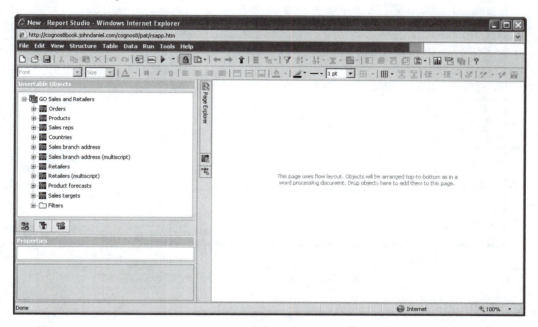

Event Studio

With Event Studio, shown next, you can establish a threshold or assign a specific event that sends a notification to the decision makers in your organization. You create agents that monitor your thresholds or event, and when the threshold is reached or event occurs, the agent sends the notification. Notifications can include an e-mail, adding information to the portal or running reports.

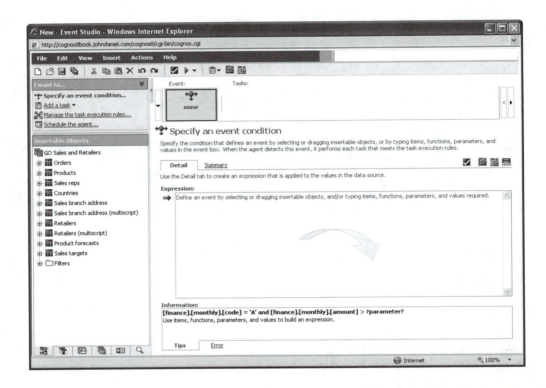

NOTE *For more information about Event Studio, refer to Chapter 14.*

Metric Studio

With Metric Studio, shown next, you can monitor and analyze your organization's business metrics by creating a scorecarding environment. Metric Studio allows you to establish criteria and then monitor your organization to see how it is responding as the criteria changes.

NOTE *For more information about Metric Studio, refer to Chapter 13.*

Analysis Studio

Analysis Studio, shown next, enables business users to get fast answers to business questions so the organization can better understand product, customer, and organizational needs to react swiftly and stay ahead of the competition. Analysis Studio is best for exploring information in multiple dimensions and for deep comparative analysis.

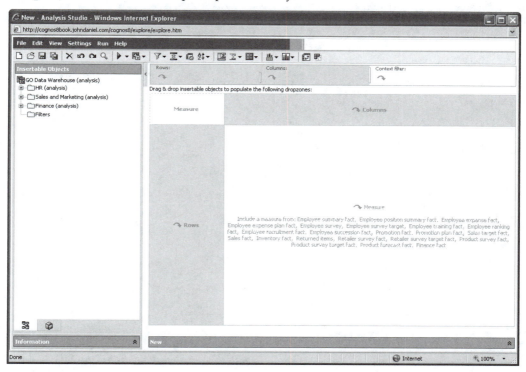

NOTE *For more information about Analysis Studio, refer to Chapter 11.*

Planning, Budgeting, and Forecasting for the Finance Office

IBM Cognos 8 BI provides all the components your organization needs to implement performance management. As mentioned in Chapter 1, performance management planning is a key component. IBM Cognos 8 Planning can be a data source in IBM Cognos 8 Business Intelligence (BI). Although this book does not go into planning design concepts, you should understand how planning can be defined as a data source so that the plan can be reported and even merged with other corporate data using IBM Cognos 8 BI.

Options for Integrating

The IBM Cognos 8 Planning application is a powerful tool for streamlining the planning, budgeting, and forecasting processes. It has many advantages, including gathering data in a central location, managing the process via the Workflow screen in Cognos Contributor, versioning control, and other features such as Breakback. However, the solution has one disadvantage, which is the number one reason and need for integrating Cognos Planning with IBM Cognos 8 BI: the Enterprise Planning Tool is limited in the types of reports it can output. You are probably already aware of this disadvantage because it has been a challenge in the past.

Often times, you need to present reports to senior level management, middle management, co-workers, colleagues, investors, and others, but the Enterprise Planning Tool is not designed for highly formatted, professional reports. To create these reports, you can export data to Microsoft Excel and format the spreadsheet to meet reporting requirements. This process can be inefficient and cumbersome, and you run the risk of lacking standardization.

You are now in luck, however, and this goes far beyond the abilities of exporting data to Excel. You can now choose from several options to make your contributor data available for Cognos 8 Reporting Studios. Once you allow the contributor data to be a source for the IBM Cognos 8 BI tools, you will have all of the Cognos 8 Reporting Studios and Cognos Connection functionality available for formatting, scheduling, and distributing your contributor data.

Options for Reporting Enterprise Planning Data

Four options can be used for reporting Enterprise Planning data in Cognos 8:

- Create a package when running Go To Production (GTP) on the Planning application
- Select Planning Contributor as a data source in Framework Manager
- Use Generate Framework Manager model extension
- Create a Framework Manager model based on a publish container data source (refer to Chapter 9 to see how to set up a Framework Manager data source)

NOTE *For Enterprise Planning versions prior to version 8.2, only the last three options are available.*

Create Package when Running GTP on Planning Application

In Enterprise Planning version 8.2, you can create an Cognos 8 package when you run a GTP on your Enterprise Planning application. You can turn this option on or off by selecting or clearing the Create Planning Package checkbox on the Go To Production Wizard's Options screen in Contributor Administration, as shown next. This option creates an Cognos 8 package.

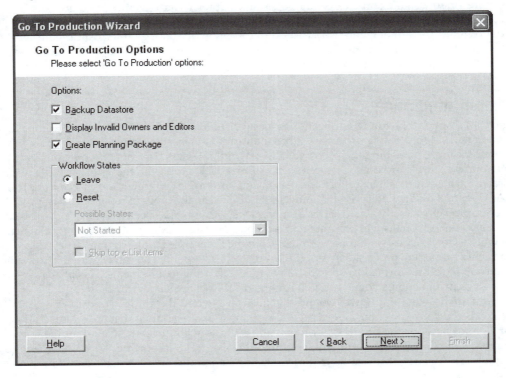

Since this package is linked directly to the Enterprise Planning application's datastore, via the Cognos 8 Planning Data Service (PDS), it will support real-time reporting on your contributor data. There is no Framework Manager model behind this package; therefore, if you make structural changes to the Enterprise Planning application, you run the risk of breaking any Cognos 8 reports created from this package. For this reason, this reporting option is suggested to be used for ad-hoc reporting and not for standardized reporting from your contributor application.

Select Planning Contributor as a Data Source in Framework Manager

You can use the Cognos 8 PDS server to connect directly to your Enterprise Planning application datastore. When creating a new Framework Manager model, you will create a new data source by selecting Cognos Planning Contributor as your data source type. You are then presented with a listing of your Enterprise Planning cubes, as shown next:

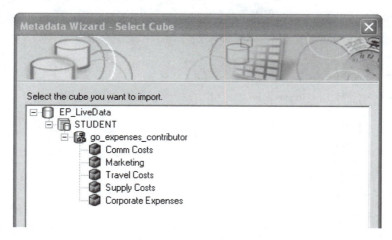

Select the cube you want to include in your Framework Manager model. If you want to include multiple cubes in the same Framework Manager model, you must first select the Run Metadata Wizard option in Framework Manager.

NOTE   *Chapter 15 contains information on setting up a new data source, as well as running the Metadata Wizard in Framework Manager.*

By choosing to use the Planning Contributor option as a data source in Framework Manager, you will also be able to create real-time reports from your Enterprise Planning application.

CAUTION   *When reporting from live (real-time) contributor applications, you will not be able to use text data fields in reports.*

Use Generate Framework Manager Model Extension

You can create a Framework Manager model for data published from your planning application by using the Generate Framework Manager Model Extension option in Contributor Administration. This option is the recommended proven practice for creating standard reports from your enterprise planning data. This extension allows you to select which Enterprise Planning cubes you want to make available for reporting in Cognos 8. You access the Generate Framework Manager Model Extension option from the Admin Extensions folder in Contributor Administration, as shown here:

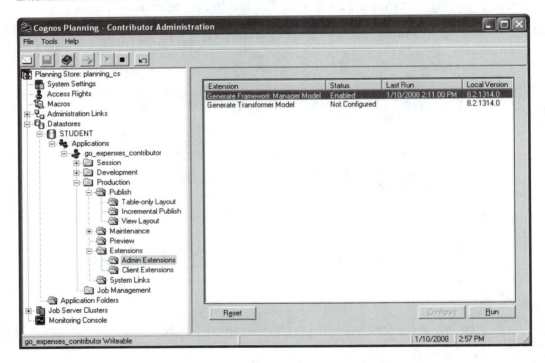

Setup Prior to Running the Generate Framework Manager Model Extension

Several factors must be in place before you can configure the Generate Framework Manager Model Extension option. This section discusses what you need to do before configuring the extension, how to configure the extension, and how to maintain your Framework Manager Model when changes are made to your contributor application.

Table-only Publish Layout

To make your contributor data available in Cognos 8 for highly formatted reporting, you will publish the data using the Table-only Layout option in Contributor Administration. The Table-only Publish Layout container is set up and populated with your contributor data.

CAUTION *You cannot run the Generate Framework Manager Model Extension option against data published to the View Only Publishing option in Contributor Administration.*

To publish your contributor data to a Table-only Publish Layout container, you must be able to answer "Yes" to each of the following questions:

- Has a GTP been run and completed successfully on your contributor application?
- Have all e.list items been reconciled?
- Have you selected the d-cubes to be included in the Table-only Publish Layout container?
- Have you selected a Dimension for Publish for each d-cube?
- Have you selected the e.list items to be published?
- Have you selected the necessary options for the Table-only Publish Layout container?

  The Table-only Publish Layout container options are listed here:

  - Create data items based on the dimension for publish?
  - Create columns for specific data types?
  - Include rollups?
  - Include zero or blank values?
  - Prefix column names with data type?
  - Include user annotations?
  - Include audit annotations?

Including Cubes in the Table-only Publish Layout Container

The Table-only Publish Layout container must be able to create reports from your Enterprise Planning database. You should include any planning cubes that hold data that you want to be included in the report.

Selecting Dimension as the Dimension for Publish

One of the d-lists most often used as the Dimension for Publish is the primary calculation d-list, or the number 1 d-list for the Enterprise Planning d-cube. However, sometimes you need to select a different Dimension for Publish. When trying to decide which dimension to select, keep in mind your reporting needs. For instance, you may be asked to produce a list report showing the calculations as the rows of your report, while showing the periods as columns. In this case, you would want to select the time scale dimension, or the number 4 d-list, as your Dimension for Publish.

You might consider using a d-list as the Dimension for Publish for the following reasons:

- The d-list contains a combination of text, numeric, and date items (mixed data types).
- The d-list contains numeric items with different display formats, such as ##% and #,###.##.
- Report(s) will require additional calculations between items in the d-list.
- You need to treat some of the d-list items separately.

Your decisions should be considered carefully and made prior to running the Generate Framework Manager Model Extension option. If you need to make modifications to the Table-only Publish Layout container after generating the Framework Manager model, you can update your model by re-running the Wizard and/or by manually making changes to the Framework Manager model.

CAUTION *If you change the Dimension for Publish after generating the Framework Manager model, any reports using the current structure need to be re-created.*

Dimension for Publish in the Table-only Publish Layout Container   The d-list that you select to use as the Dimension for Publish is reflected in the Table-only Publish Layout container with the *et_* prefix. This d-list will be published as the Measures Table within the Table-only Publish Layout container. Depending on the options you select when publishing the data, this table will contain each item as one or all of the following data types: Numeric, Varchar, and Date-Time.

Include Annotations in the Table-only Publish Layout Container
If you want to be able to generate reports against the comments that users enter into the Enterprise Planning application, you should include user's annotations in your Table-only Publish Layout container.

TIP *Remember that you must add the Table-only Publish Layout container to a job server in order for the publish job to run.*

Configure and Run the Generate Framework Manager Model Extension

Now that you have prepared your contributor application for the Generate Framework Manager Model Extension, you are ready to begin gathering information needed for configuring and running the extension. Your first step will be to gather information for the Generate Framework Manager Model Wizard. Next, you can successfully run the extension. You need to know the following to run the Wizard successfully:

- Location for the Framework Manager model
- A name for your package
- Which Enterprise Planning cubes you want to make available for reporting
- The type of list(s) you want to include in the model
- Whether or not to make annotations available for reporting

NOTE *For Enterprise Planning versions prior to version 8.2, you will also need to know the Cognos 8 Dispatcher URI. The URI can be located in Cognos Configuration by selecting the Environment Node. It will display in the Dispatcher URI for external applications text box in the right pane of Cognos Configuration.*

You always have the option of modifying the Framework Manager model by re-running the Wizard and selecting to update the existing model (as discussed later in this chapter).

CAUTION *For Enterprise Planning versions prior to version 8.2, the user who runs the Generate Framework Manager Model Extension option must be a member of a user class higher than the highest user class that is included in the Enterprise Planning application. For Enterprise Planning version 8.2, any user belonging to the Planning Rights Administrator role or who has been granted the appropriate rights within the Access Rights screen of the Contributor Administration Console will have the ability to run the Generate Framework Manager Model Extension.*

Framework Manager Model Location

The location you choose for your Framework Manager Model should simply be a folder on your network or server where anyone who needs to make modifications to the Framework Manager model has read and write access. Additional folders to hold the base model and log files will be created via the extension to hold the related files.

Package Name

You need to name the package to be published to Cognos Connection when you run the Generate Framework Manager Model Extension option. This will be the name that users see and are able to access in Cognos Connection.

List Types

You can include three types of lists in your Framework Manager model, which you select in the Wizard:

- Unformatted lists
- Derived hierarchy lists
- Complete hierarchy lists

Unformatted Lists

Unformatted lists are the items in your Published Table-only Database prefixed with *it_*. These d-lists do not include any roll-up information. When you choose to use the unformatted lists in your Framework Manager model, the wizard will create an Unformatted List Tables folder. This folder will hold a query subject for each of the d-lists in the publish container. These query subjects will contain the following data items:

- **itemid**   The Enterprise Planning item GUID
- **dimensionid**   The Enterprise Planning dimension GUID
- **itemname**   The Enterprise Planning item unique name
- **displayname**   The name displayed in the Enterprise Planning application
- **disorder**   The order in which the items are displayed in the Enterprise Planning application
- **itemiid**   The Enterprise Planning item IID

The wizard will create any necessary relationships between the query subjects for the unformatted lists and the query subjects for the cube tables. The wizard decides what relationships are necessary based on what d-lists are included in the Enterprise Planning d-cubes.

Business Case: Include Unformatted Lists   If you are asked to create a report in which text fields are part of the data cells in Cognos Contributor, you should include unformatted lists in your model. Since Cognos Contributor allows text data within the data cells of the model, you may be asked to produce a report with the text item and a total associated for that row across multiple e-list items. This can be accomplished by using the data stored in an unformatted list.

Derived Hierarchy Lists

Derived hierarchy lists are the items in your Published Table-only Database prefixed with *sy_*. These d-lists are also referred to as *simple hierarchies* and include hierarchy information that is derived from the Enterprise Planning d-lists. The derived hierarchy lists are intended to be used when the d-list contains simple parent-child relationships between d-lists items. Derived hierarchy lists allow the reporting tools to generate the summaries automatically for each level of the hierarchy.

When you choose to include derived hierarchy lists in the Framework Manager model, the wizard will create a dimensionally modeled relational model. The model will include a dimensional definition of the d-lists, as well as a star schema grouping for each published cube.

Complete Hierarchy Lists

Complete hierarchy lists are the items in your Published Table-only Database prefixed with *cy_*. The complete hierarchy lists are intended to be used when the d-list contains complex calculations between the d-list items. These tables will hold the calculated values you see in Cognos Contributor at each level of the hierarchy. You can use complete hierarchy lists to avoid having to re-create calculations in your Cognos 8 report, which are already in the Enterprise Planning application.

When you choose to include complete hierarchy lists in the Framework Manager model, the wizard will again create a dimensionally modeled relational model. The model will include a dimensional definition of the d-lists, as well as a star schema grouping for each published cube.

Annotations

Select the Include Annotations checkbox if you want users to be able to create reports that include any annotations users have entered into the Cognos Contributor application.

Generate Framework Manager Model Extension Wizard

Now that you know what you need in place for the Generate Framework Manager Model Extension option, you can configure and run the wizard.

To configure and run the wizard, do the following:

1. The Generate Framework Manager Extension option is located in the Admin Extensions folder for your planning application in Contributor Administration. To configure the extension, click the Admin Extensions folder.

2. Click the Generate Framework Manager Extension from the list of extensions.

3. Click Configure. The Welcome To The Generate Framework Manager Model Wizard screen appears.

NOTE *If you have already configured the extension and need to rerun it, select Run instead of Configure.*

4. Click Next. The Create Or Update Model screen appears:

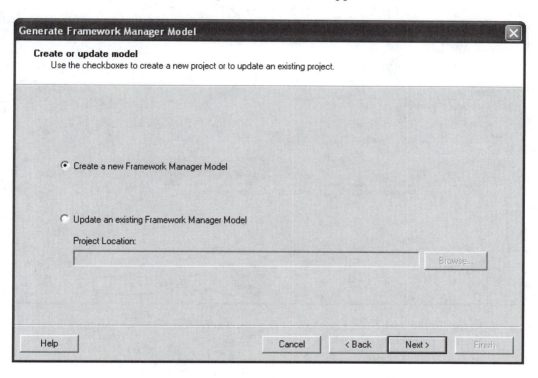

5. Select whether you want to create a new Framework Manager Model or update an existing Framework Manager Model. Note that if you belong to more than one user class, you will be prompted to select the user class you want to log into to run the Generate Framework Manager Model.

CAUTION *In versions prior to 8.2, you must choose a user class that is above all of the Cognos Contributor user classes that exist in the application. In version 8.2, you must choose a user/ group that belongs to the Planning Rights Administrator role or a user/group that has been given access via the Contributor Administration Console Access Rights screen.*

6. Click Next. If you select to update an existing Framework Manager Model, the extension will run and update the selected model. If you are creating a new Framework Manager model, the Business Intelligence Package screen displays, as shown next. (Note that in versions prior to Enterprise Planning version 8.2, this screen is named Framework Manager Settings in Contributor Administration.)

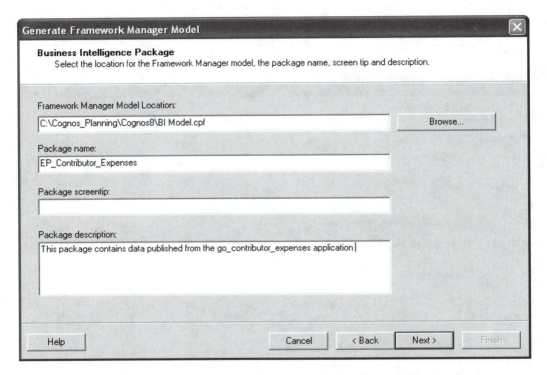

7. In the Framework Manager Model Location text box, enter a location for the Framework Manager Model.

8. In the Package Name text box, enter a name for the package.

CAUTION *In versions prior to Enterprise Planning version 8.2, in the Cognos 8 Dispatcher URI text box, enter a URI, and in the Location of the Framework Manager BMT ScriptPlayer Location text box, enter the location of the Framework Manager BMT ScriptPlayer. The Cognos 8 Dispatcher URI can be found in Cognos Configuration in the External Dispatcher URI field of the Environment node. The BMT ScriptPlayer Location is located in the bin folder of your installation directory.*

9. Click Next. The Select Contents Of Model screen displays:

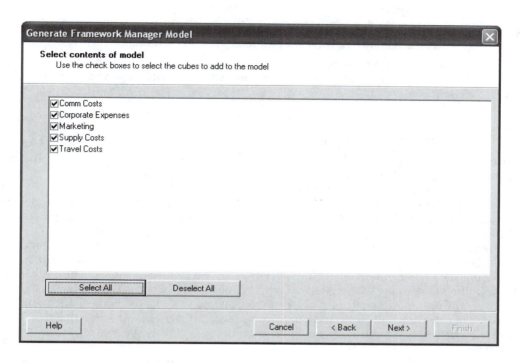

10. Select the check box(es) of the cube(s) you want to include in the Framework
    Manager Model. Note that the selection contents shown are only the cubes that you
    had selected to be included as part of the Table-only publish container.

11. Click Next. The Select Data Source Query Subjects screen displays:

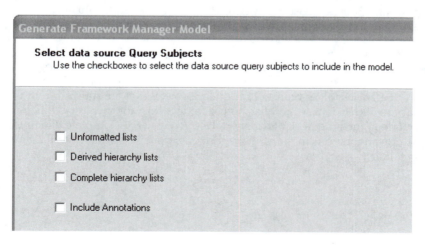

12. Select the checkbox(es) of the query subject(s) you want to include in the Framework Manager model. Then click Next. A summary of the configuration displays.

13. Review the items on the screen. If you need to make modifications to the configuration, click Back. If you are satisfied with the configuration, click Finish. The configuration is complete.

Inside the Framework Manager Model

Once the Generate Framework Manager Model Wizard has completed, you can immediately open and use the package in Cognos Connection. You are also able to open the model in Framework Manager to review it and make any necessary modifications.

It is a good idea to get familiar with what is included in the Framework Manager model so that you can provide additional customization to the model as required for your users. This section discusses what is included in your Framework Manager model.

By running the extension, you will create two Framework Manager models. The first model is the base model, which contains all of the definitions for the objects contained in your Published Enterprise Planning datastore. The second is the user model, which serves as the buffer between the base model and what is published to Cognos Connection in the package. The user model contains all of the modifications made by the Framework Manager model. The extension will create and publish a package to Cognos Connection that will always be created and published from the user model. You will also be able to use the Framework Manager model extension in conjunction with the Synchronize feature in the Framework Manager model to update your model(s) when you have structural changes to your planning application.

Physical and Business View

The Framework Manager model contains two top level folders. The first folder, Physical View, contains all of the database query subjects. The second folder, Business View, contains the dimensions and star schema grouping objects.

Physical View: Top Level Folder

The Physical View folder, shown next, contains all the data source query subjects. The query subjects are held in folders describing the type of table by which the query subject is sourced. A Cube Tables folder holds all the query subjects that are sourced from the d-lists you chose as the dimensions for publish. Other folders exist for each type of hierarchy you chose to include in the model—Unformatted, Derived, and/or Complete. Finally, if you chose to include annotations in the model, those query subjects will be held in an Annotation folder.

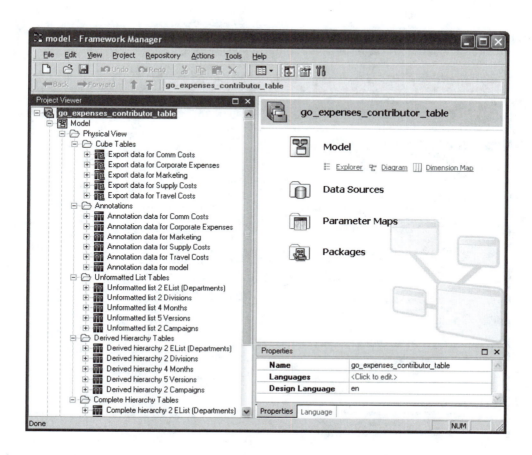

Business View: Top Level Folder

The Business View folder, showed next, contains a folder for all derived dimensions and complete dimensions included in the model. Other folders are named after each of the published d-cubes. The Derived and Complete Dimensions folders contain the regular dimension objects for each of the d-lists in the Table-only Publish Layout container.

The levels for the regular dimension objects are determined by the summaries and/or calculations created in the Enterprise Planning Analyst d-lists.

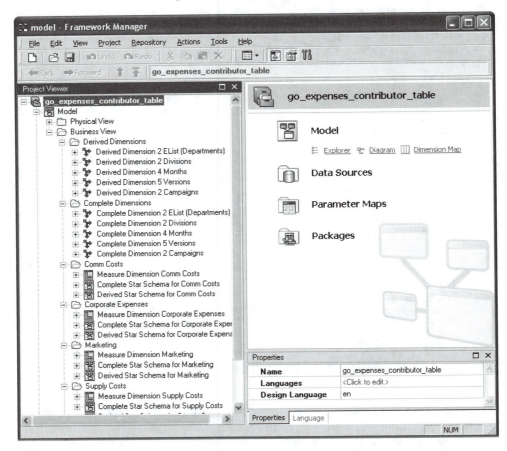

The additional folders within the Business View folder hold the complete star schema grouping and the derived star schema grouping for the published d-cubes. This folder also contains a measure dimension object based on the d-list you chose for the Dimension for Publish in Contributor Administration. Each star schema grouping will hold shortcuts that link back to the measure dimension objects and the regular dimension objects.

Relationships Created

The Generate Framework Manager model extension creates relationships within the model for you. The relationships are created between all related tables of the Table-only Publish Layout container. This means that all d-lists for each cube will have the necessary relationships between each other. The extension understands that the dimensional tables should be joined to each cube export table (Dimension for Publish d-list) if the dimension is a d-list in the Enterprise Planning d-cube.

Security Filters

Security filters will be set up in the Framework Manager model based on the contributor e.list security. Therefore, any user within a user group that has access to the Enterprise Planning application will also have access to the Framework Manager model, as well as the package published from the model. The security will also take into consideration the view level assigned to the e.list items in Contributor Administration.

NOTE *If you add a subtotal or calculation to your analyst d-list, you will alter the levels of the regular dimension object. You must rerun the Generate Framework Manager Model Extension option, synchronize within Framework Manager, and republish the package.*

Package Ready for Publishing

The Framework Manager model will contain a package for publishing to Cognos Connection. By default, all items within the model will be published in the package. However, the Framework Manager modeler does have the ability to customize which objects are published. Refer to Chapter 15 for additional information for customizing your Framework Manager model.

Data Source to Table-only Layout Container

Finally, the Generate Framework Manager model extension will create a data source in Cognos Connection. This data source can be used to create additional Framework Manager model packages without running the Generate Framework Manager Model Extension option.

PART

Accessing and Using IBM Cognos 8 Business Intelligence

Cognos Connection I

C ognos Connection is a web-based portal that allows users (such as executives, sales associates, finance managers, IT departments, and consumers) to run reports, queries, metrics, and analyses; perform administrative functions; and access other Cognos 8 content. Cognos Connection gives users a single access point to application-specific data available in Cognos 8 for their corporation. Users can customize Cognos Connection and the appearance of data in a variety of ways—by organizing content within folders, selecting separators in list view, setting a default home page, and changing the default language, to name a few. In this chapter, you will learn how to set and use these options and others.

NOTE *This chapter presumes that readers have basic access permissions in Cognos Connection. If you do not have access to a specific location, contact your Cognos 8 administrator.*

About Cognos Connection

Executives, managers, associates, consumers, and others access their company's data (such as, packages, reports, dashboards, scorecards, and so on) using Cognos Connection. A user can interact with Cognos Connection by clicking commands, folders, and links to perform various actions.

At the top of the Cognos Connection interface, in the bar with the Cognos username shown in the following illustration, are commands that you can use to log out of the application, refresh the screen, perform searches, set and return to a home page, set preferences, view and manage run activities, launch studios, and access online help.

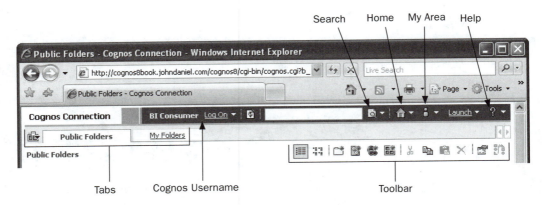

Under the bar with your username, you can navigate within Cognos Connection using the Public Folders and My Folders tabs. You can use the commands on the toolbar to create and order folders, set a view, create new jobs or pages, set properties, and perform basic cut, copy, paste, and delete actions. In addition, paging commands are provided to view entries in the list under the toolbar (see Table 5-1).

Toolbar Icons	Description
	List View
	Details View
	New Folder
	New Job
	New URL
	New Page
	Cut
	Copy
	Paste
	Delete
	Set Properties
	Order

TABLE 5-1   Toolbar Icon Descriptions

The entries list contains links to all of the packages, folders, and reports to which you have access, along with links to the actions that you can perform on each of the entries. The color of the package and folder icons is a visual aid for administrators.

Customizing Cognos Connection

You can easily customize Cognos Connection to your preferences to help you quickly locate your company's data. All changes that you make take effect immediately. The settings are stored and can be used for future sessions until they are changed again.

Set a Home Page

Upon launching Cognos 8, the Welcome page displays by default. A checkbox with the text "Show this page in the future" located at the bottom left of the Welcome page allows you to determine whether this page should be presented by Cognos 8 each time the application is launched. To enter Cognos 8 from this page, click My Home or Cognos Content.

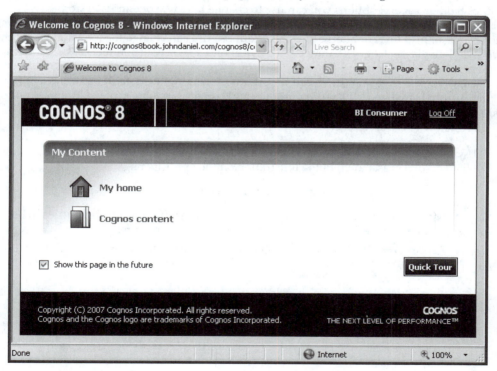

Cognos Connection displays the Public Folders tab. You can set any location in Cognos Connection as your default home page.

Here's how to set a home page:

1. Navigate to the screen you want to use as your default home page.

2. Click Home Options, as shown next, and then click the Set View As Home link. The current location is now set as your default home page.

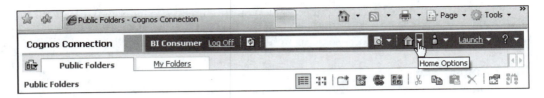

Set Preferences

Cognos 8 offers several options you can use to change the view of entries in Cognos Connection. You can set your preference for the number of entries to display before scrolling and the use of grid lines or alternating backgrounds. You can change the look and feel of the layout and display in Cognos Connection by applying a style (Corporate, Classic, Modern, Contemporary, and so on).

Increasing or decreasing the screen refresh rate, changing the default report format (for example, from HTML to PDF), setting product and content languages for multilingual users, and specifying a time zone for users in different locations can also be easily set.

Here's how to set preferences:

1. On the blue bar, click My Area and then click the My Preferences link. The General tab displays, as shown in the illustration on the opposite page.

   The following settings appear on this screen:

   - **Number Of Entries In List View**   Sets the maximum number of entries to be displayed when using List View before scrolling is required.

   - **Report Format**   Changes the default report format (for example, from HTML to PDF).

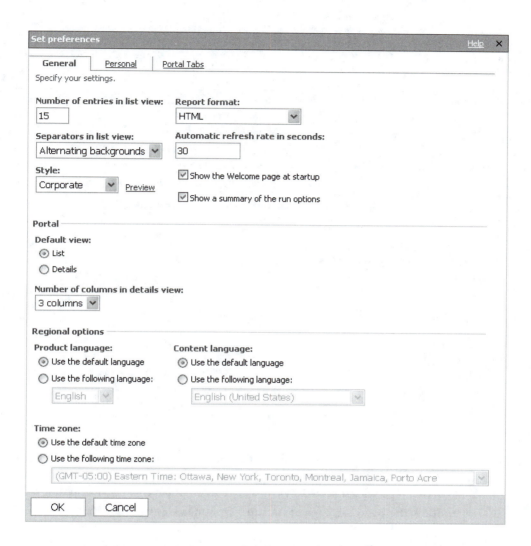

- **Separators In List View**   Displays grid lines or alternating backgrounds when using List View. Sample screen captures of these options are shown in the following two illustrations.

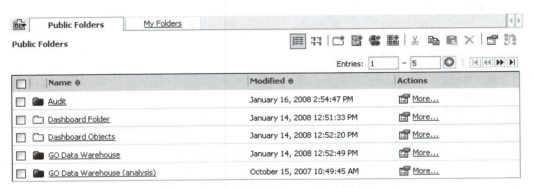

Cognos Connection List View with alternating background

Cognos Connection List View with grid lines

- **Automatic Refresh Rate In Seconds**   Sets the amount of time Cognos 8 waits before refreshing the interface.
- **Style**   Applies a specified style to all of the components of the Cognos 8 application.
- **Show the welcome page at startup**   Option to show or hide the Welcome page at start of session.
- **Show a summary of the run options**   Option to show a summary of the run actions for reports not run interactively.
- **Default View**   Sets the default view (List or Details) of Cognos Connection.
- **Product / Content Language**   Changes the language for the Cognos 8 interface (Product), including Cognos Connection, Cognos Viewer, and Report Studio, or the language displayed in Cognos 8 (Content), including report data, entry descriptions, names, and so on.

2. Specify your applicable settings and then click OK. Your changes take effect immediately.

TIP *To modify the Cognos Connection tab sequence, click Tab Menu and select the Modify the sequence of tabs link.*

Tab Menu

Run Reports

Cognos 8 reports can be set up to generate when selected, thereby retrieving the latest information from the source database, or to display a pre-generated version of the report. The icon to the left of the report title indicates the report's display settings.

Here's how to execute a report:

Click on a report link (as seen in the following illustration).

If a blue arrow is displayed to the right of the report format icon, the report is executed and retrieves the current data from the data source. This action may take several minutes to execute. If a blue arrow is not displayed to the right of the report format icon, this indicates a saved report. A saved report displays the output from the last execution of the report.

The Modified date and time, shown in the following illustration, is the most recent date and time that the entry was modified. It is not the date and time that the entry was created.

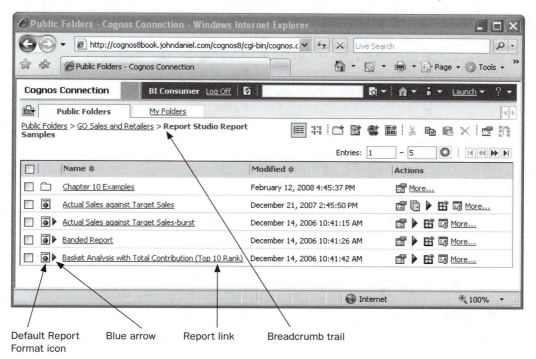

Default Report   Blue arrow   Report link   Breadcrumb trail
Format icon

TIP *To determine your location within the application, view the breadcrumb trail below the Tabs.*
To open a specific folder, click the folder name link on the breadcrumb trail.

Organize Information

You can organize the entries in Cognos Connection to suit your preferences. You can create
folders, change the layout view, change languages and permissions, and set the name and
descriptions for each folder.

NOTE *This section presumes that most readers are not able to modify the content in Cognos*
Connection Public Folders. To perform the actions in this section, click the Cognos Connection
My Folders link and then complete the following steps.

Create a New Folder

You can create new folders to organize entries, such as reports and links, in Cognos Connection.
Folders enable you to find and view information quickly and are typically named with
detailed and meaningful descriptions. For example, a Sales Forecasting folder would contain
entries for increased revenue to use when forecasting.

Here's how to create a new folder:

1. In Cognos Connection, navigate to the location where you want to create a new
   folder. On the toolbar, click New Folder. The Specify A Name And Description
   screen appears, as shown next:

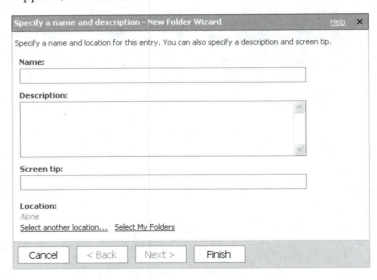

2. Enter a name for the folder in the Name text box.

3. Optionally, in the Description box, enter a description of the folder that displays in
   Details View.

4. Optionally, in the Screen Tip box, enter text that will display when the mouse pointer
   is moved over the folder icon. The Screen Tip text box is limited to 100 characters.

TIP *To change folder locations, under Location, click either the Select Another Location link or the Select My Folders link.*

---

5. Click Finish. The new folder displays.

6. Click the folder name link. The folder opens, displaying the entries it contains.

Set the Default View

Cognos 8 offers two views of the data viewed using Cognos Connection. List View shows the name, modified date, and available actions for the entry, and Details View shows the same information but also provides the description of the entry. You can choose which view you prefer by clicking a radio button on the General tab under the Default View section in My Preferences.

Here's how to set the default view:

1. Click My Area, and then click the My Preferences link. The General tab displays, as shown next:

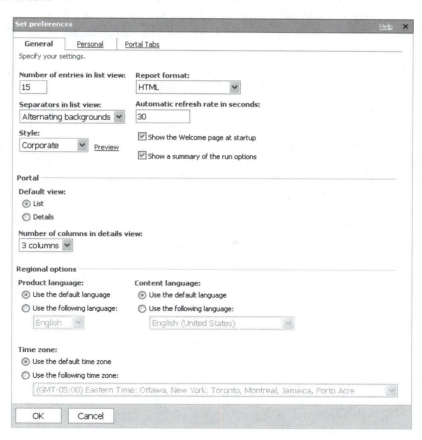

2. In the portal preferences under Default View, select List or Details and then click OK. If you select Details, you can select the number of columns per row to display in the Number Of Columns In Details View list. Your changes take effect immediately.

Sample screen captures of these options are shown next.

Tip *To switch between views, on the toolbar, click List View or Details View, as shown in the following two Illustrations*

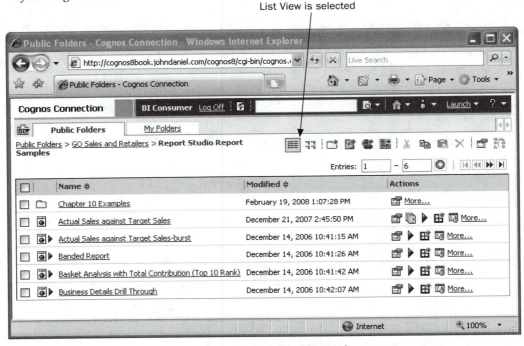

Cognos Connection in List View mode

Details View is selected

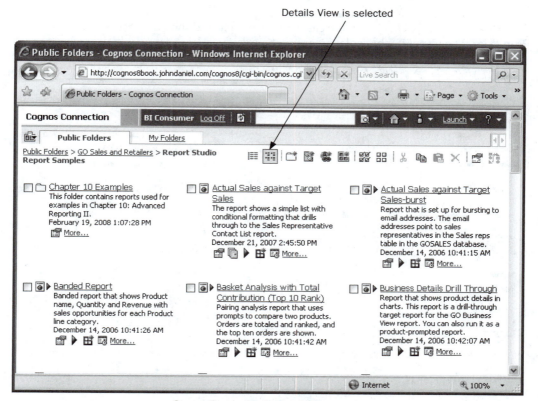

Cognos Connection in Details View mode

Set Properties

You can change the appearance, behavior, and properties of entries in Cognos Connection. Language and permissions can be modified for an entry and the name and descriptions of an entry can be changed (for example, from *Sales* to *Sales Forecasting*). An individual can be assigned responsibility for an entry by setting a contact, and entries that are no longer used can be disabled.

A *contact* is an individual who is responsible for the content of an entry and is typically a liaison to the owner of the entry. Contacts do not have access permissions to change the entry. If you have feedback regarding the content of an entry, you speak with the contact. The contact then informs the owner of the feedback. The owner has access permissions to change the entry and to modify the content, permissions, and security for the entry.

Here's how to set the properties for an entry:

Select an entry by clicking in the checkbox next to it, and then from the toolbar, click Set Properties. The General tab displays, as shown next:

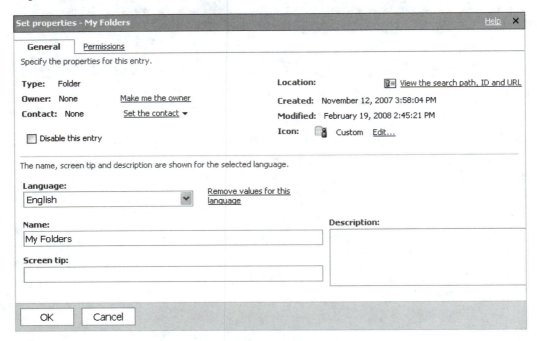

The settings on this tab include the following:

- **Set The Contact**   Specifies an individual responsible for the content of the entry.
- **Disable This Entry**   Disables the entry and displays a disabled icon next to the entry, as shown next:

Disabled Entry icon

- **Language**   Sets the language for the individual entry, screen tip, and description.
- **Name**   Sets the name that appears on the entry.
- **Screen Tip/Description**   Sets the screen tip and description of the entry.

Specify your applicable settings and then click OK. The properties are immediately set. For users with access permissions for the Permission tab, as shown next, the settings on the tab include the following:

- **Override the Access Permissions Acquired From The Parent Entry**   Overrides the access permissions (read, write, execute, set policy, and traverse) for users of the entry.

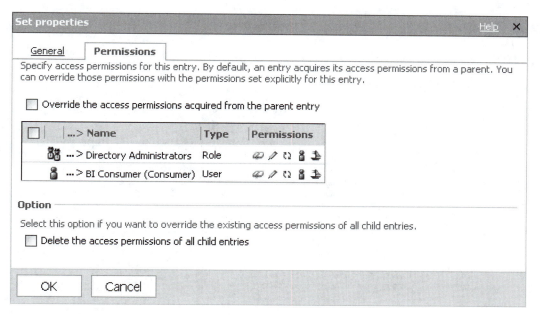

> **NOTE**   *By default, an entry acquires its access permissions from a parent.*

Manage Reports

Reports are managed in Cognos Connection. They can be scheduled to run at a convenient time or can be removed from the schedule completely.

> **NOTE**   *To schedule an entry, you must have run permissions for that entry.*

Save Report Views

A Report View, shown next, is a reference to another report that has its own properties, such as prompt values, schedules, and results. You use report views to share a report specification instead of making copies of it. You can specify a name, description, screen tip, and location for the new report view.

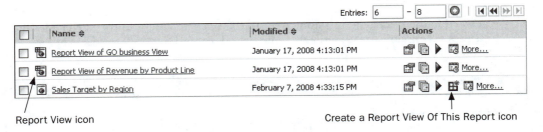

Report View icon

Create a Report View Of This Report icon

Here's how to save a Report View:

1. Click the Create a Report View Of This Report icon. The Specify a Name And Description—New Report View Wizard screen displays.

2. Optionally, you can enter a name, description, and location for the Report View, as shown next:

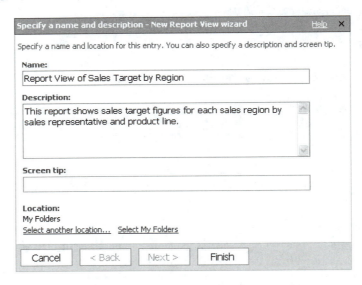

3. Click Finish. The new Report View is created, as indicated by the icon displayed next to the entry.

Schedule Reports

You can schedule the entries in Cognos Connection to run at a specific time or a recurring date and time (for example, by day, week, month, year, or trigger). You can use the default values, or specify your own options by using the Schedule action. For example, you may have a large report that takes several hours to run. By scheduling the report or modifying the schedule of the report, you can run the report during non-working hours to utilize faster performance times. You can also remove the schedule.

NOTE *Each entry in Cognos Connection can have only one schedule.*

Here's how to schedule a report:

1. Click Schedule, as shown next.

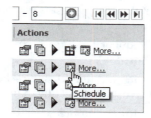

2. The Schedule screen displays:

Schedule - Report View of Conditional Display   Help   ✕

Schedule this entry to run at a recurring date and time. You can run using the default values or specify the options. You can disable the schedule without losing any of its details.

☐ Disable the schedule   **Priority:**   **Start:**
                                3   Feb 19, 2008   ▦▾
                                                       4 : 21   PM   ▲▼

Frequency: **End:**
Select the frequency by clicking on a link.   ◉ No end date
                                                       ○ End by:
By Day   ✔ **By Week**   By Month   By Year   By Trigger   Feb 19, 2008   ▦▾
                                                       4 : 21   PM   ▲▼

Every 1   week(s) on:
☐ Monday   ☑ Tuesday   ☐ Wednesday   ☐ Thursday
☐ Friday   ☐ Saturday   ☐ Sunday

Options
☐ Override the default values
   Formats:
   Default
   Languages:
   Default
   Delivery:
   Save the report

Prompt values
☐ Override the default values
   No values saved

[OK]   [Cancel]

The settings on this screen include the following:

- **Disable The Schedule**   Disables the entry without losing the scheduling information.

- **Priority**   The default value is 3. If more than one entry contains the same priority setting, the entry placed in the queue first runs first. As a consumer, you will not be able to edit this setting. Users responsible for managing the Cognos queue will be able to modify the priority.

- **Frequency**   Sets the frequency of the schedule (for example, to run by week on every Monday and Thursday).

- **Start/End**   Sets the dates and times for the schedule to start and finish. The Calendar wizard can be used to select the date.

3. Specify your applicable settings and then click OK. The schedule is created and the report will run at the next scheduled date and time.

Here's how to modify or remove the report schedule:

Click the More link for the entry you want to edit. The Perform An Action Screen displays. Then do the following:

- To remove the schedule, click the Remove The Schedule link and then click OK. The schedule is removed for the report.

- To modify the schedule, click the Modify The Schedule link. The Schedule screen displays, as shown earlier. Repeat the steps used to schedule a report, as discussed earlier.

Create a New Job

A *job* is a group of executable entries, such as reports, that are executed as a batch. They share the same schedule settings. When the job executes, all of the entries in the job execute. This option saves you valuable time when you want to modify the schedule of several reports.

For example, suppose you created 10 report views that are set to execute every day at 10 A.M. Because they take a lot of time to execute, you want to change the execute time to 7 P.M., when fewer users are on the system. To do this, you can modify the schedule for each Report View separately. However, if you create a job and add the reports to it, you can modify the schedule once.

Here's how to create a new job:

1. From the toolbar, click New Job. The Specify A Name And Description screen of the New Job Wizard displays, as shown in the illustration on the opposite page.

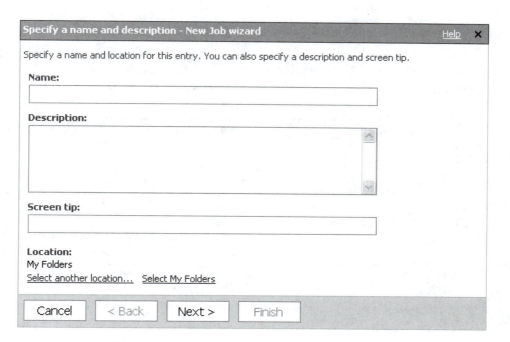

2. In the Name box, enter a name for the entry.

3. Optionally, you can enter a Description of the entry that will display in Details View.

4. Optionally, you can also enter a Screen Tip that will display when the pointer is moved over the job icon.

5. Optionally, to change folder locations, in the Location group, click either the Select Another Location link or the Select My Folders link.

6. Click Next. The Select The Steps screen displays.

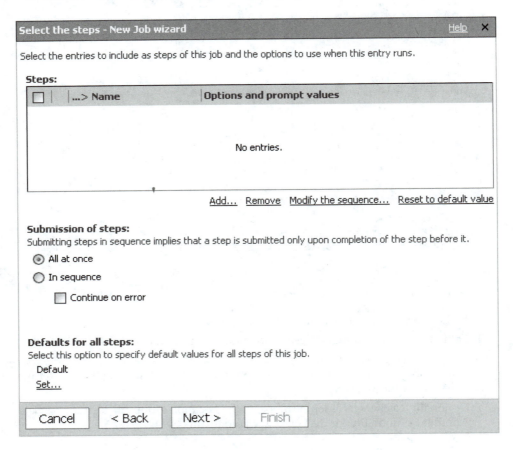

7. Click the Add link. The Select Entries (Navigate) screen displays:

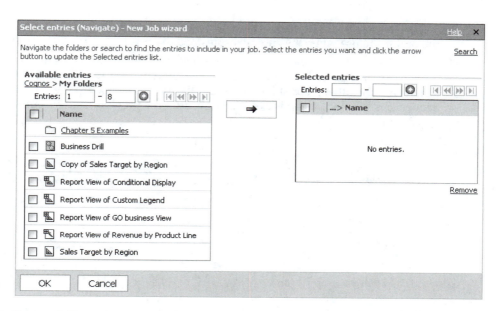

8. Optional: To navigate to another location, click the applicable folder name link on the breadcrumb trail.

9. In the left pane, select the checkboxes of the entries that you want to add to the job. Then click the add arrow to move the entries to the right pane, and click OK. The Select The Steps screen displays again, with the entries you selected:

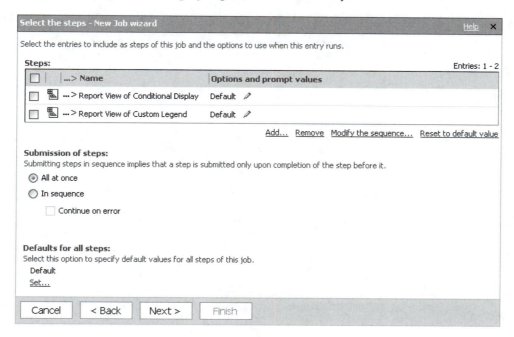

10. Select the checkboxes for the entries that you want to include as steps in the job and the options to use when the entry executes.

11. Determine how steps should be sequenced in the job by making selections under Submission of Steps: All At Once or In Sequence. When All At Once is selected, if a step fails, the other steps still execute and the job has a Failed status. When In Sequence is selected, a step is executed only after the previous step executes successfully.

12. Click Next. The Select An Action screen displays:

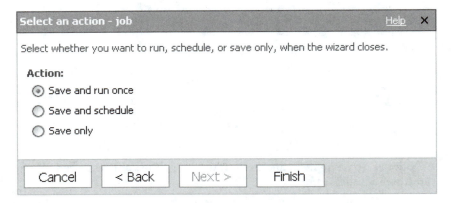

13. Select an action (Save And Run Once, Save And Schedule, or Save Only), and then click Finish.

- If the Save And Run Once action is selected, the Run With Options screen displays:

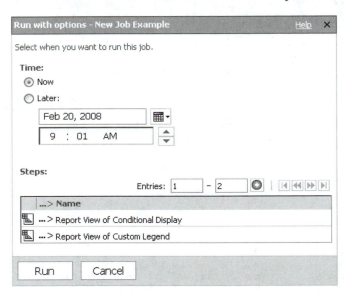

Select when you want the job to execute and then click Run. Click OK. The new job displays in the entries list. Optionally, you can select the View The Details Of This Job After Closing This Dialog checkbox and then click OK to view the job details.

- If the Save And Schedule action was selected, the Schedule screen displays:

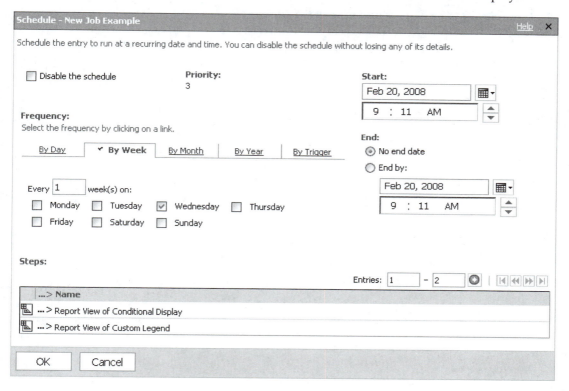

To disable the schedule temporarily, select the Disable The Schedule checkbox. The schedule will be disabled without losing the scheduling information.

The Priority is set to 3 by default, specifying the order that the entry will execute. Priority values are from 1 to 5. The lower the number, the higher the priority is. If more than one entry contains the same priority setting, the entry that arrives in the queue first executes first. Priority can only be set by users with permissions to manage the queue.

In the Frequency group, click the applicable link to set the frequency of the schedule (for example, to execute by week on every Monday and Thursday) and then select the applicable options.

In the Start and End text boxes, set the start and end dates and times for the schedule to start and finish and then click OK.

The schedule is created for the job and the report will execute at the next scheduled date and time.

TIP *The Calendar Wizard can be used to select the date easily.*

- If the Save Only Action was selected, the schedule for the job is saved without scheduling or executing.

Cognos Connection II

ognos 8 allows users to specify various options for running reports, managing report versions, and organizing reports. New pages and portal tabs can be created to house commonly used reports in one location, saving you from having to open multiple pages. The portal tabs have advanced options, which are also discussed in this chapter, that are commonly used by Cognos 8 users. Users can also access detailed historical information of an entry, if needed.

NOTE *This chapter assumes that most readers have basic access permissions in Cognos Connection. If you do not have access to a specific location, contact your administrator.*

View Output Versions

Cognos 8 supports several output versions: HTML, PDF, Excel 2007, Excel 2002, Excel 2000 Single Sheet, delimited text (comma-separated values, or CSV), and XML. In Cognos Connection, you can tell that a different output version is created for a report in two ways:

- View the report format icon to see if a saved report format (such as PDF, Excel, XML, and so on) other than the default HTML format exists.

- View the Actions column to see if a View Report Output Versions icon appears, which indicates that saved versions of this report exist.

The following illustration shows Default Report Format icons and View Report Output Versions icon.

		Name ⇕	Modified ⇕	Actions
☐		Employee Profile	January 4, 2007 3:43:34 PM	
☐		Sales Target by Region	January 11, 2008 12:14:00 AM	
☐		Tool Tips	January 4, 2007 3:44:30 PM	

Report Format icons   View Report Output Versions icon

TIP *To control the number of output versions for a report, click on Set Properties and set the Number Of Occurrences option under Report Output Versions.*

Cognos 8 also allows you to download a report for future reference, and administrators can delete older versions of reports or versions that contain erroneous data using the Manage Versions link within the View Report Output Versions option. These options will be discussed later in this section.

Here's how to view output versions of a report:

1. In the Actions column of the report that you want to view, click the View Report Output Versions icon. (Or, in the Actions column, click the More link and then click View Report Output Versions.) The View Report Output Versions screen displays, listing the most recent version of the report:

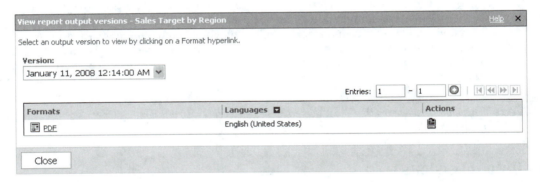

2. From the Version drop-down list, select the version of the report you want to view.

3. In the Formats column, click the applicable format (PDF, HTML, and so on). The report opens within the browser.

Download

You can download a copy of the report and open it within its respective program. You may want to use the download option to send the information in a report to an individual outside the organization who does not have access to Cognos Connection.

TIP *If you are using Internet Explorer 6 or 7, ensure that Automatic Prompting For File Downloads and File Download are enabled. Access this option from Internet Options in the Control Panel. Then open the Security tab and click the Custom Level button. Scroll down to Downloads and make sure Automatic Prompting For File Downloads and File Download are set to Enable.*

Here's how to download a report:

1. In the Actions column, click the View Report Output Versions icon. The View Report Output Versions screen displays, listing the most recent version of the report.

2. In the Actions column, click the Download icon. A message displays with an option to download the report.

3. Click Save. The Save As dialog opens.

4. Navigate to the location in which you want to save the report, and click Save. The report is saved in the selected location.

Manage Versions

When using the View Report Output Versions option, authorized users can delete older versions of content items or versions of content items that contain erroneous data. For example, suppose you run several reports and notice that they contain incorrect data. You can simply delete these reports to prevent any confusion that might occur if individuals within your organization viewed this data.

Here's how to manage report versions:

1. In the Actions column, click the View Report Output Versions icon. The View Report Output Versions screen displays, listing the most recent version of the report:

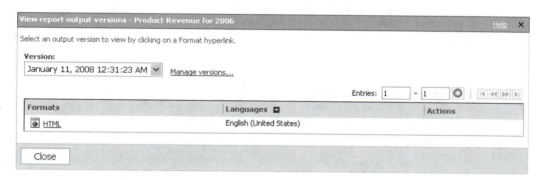

2. Click the Manage Versions link. The Manage Report Output Versions screen displays, listing all the versions of the report:

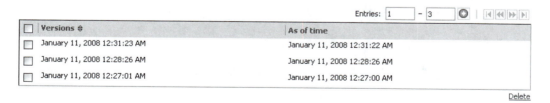

3. Select the applicable item's checkbox(es), and then click Delete. A confirmation message displays.

4. Click OK. The report is deleted and removed from the list.

NOTE *Only individuals assigned to the Professional Author, BI Professional, and BI Administrator roles have access to the Manage Versions option in Public Folders. By default, all users have access to the option under My Folders.*

Run with Options

Running with options allows you to specify how you want to run and receive a report. For example, you can receive a report in PDF format instead of HTML format, and save the report after running it as users have different needs for reports. A sales person may want to output the report to an Excel format to use during a customer visit, whereas a sales manager may want to save the report after running it for quick and easy retrieval.

The Advanced Options are accessed through Run With Options and allow you to specify how the report is delivered (for example, saving, e-mailing, or printing the report), the output format, and the time the report is run, to mention a few.

Here's how to run a report with options:

1. In the Actions column of the report, click Run with options, as shown on the right. (Or, in the Actions column, click the More link and then click Run With Options.)

   The Run With Options screen displays:

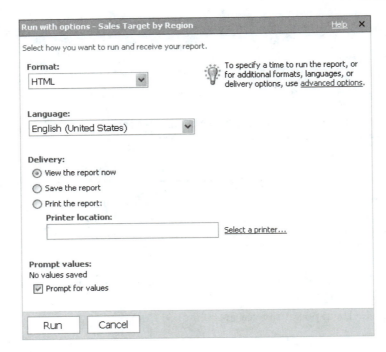

2. In the Format list, select the desired format.

3. In the Language list, select the language in which you want the report to display.

4. In the Delivery area, select the applicable delivery method. You can choose View the Report Now, Save the Report, or Print the Report. If you select the Print The Report option, specify a printer in the Printer Location text box.

NOTE *By default, users assigned to the Consumer role can save items only in My Folders.*

5. Optionally, in the Prompt Values area, select the Prompt For Values checkbox to specify the prompt values. Select this option to require that the user running the report respond to any prompts in the report. (You need to select this option only if the content item has default prompt values saved and you do not want the content item to run with those values.)

6. Optionally, click the Advanced Options link. The Run With Advanced Options screen displays:

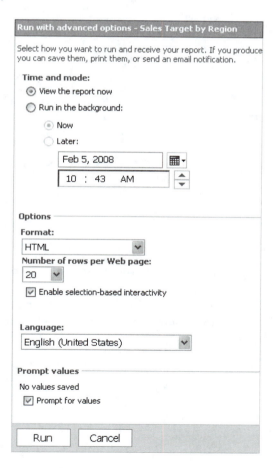

7. In the Time And Mode area, select the applicable option for viewing the report. You can choose to View The Report Now or Run In The Background. The Run In The Background option allows you to set a specific date and time to run the report, as well as the display format, the delivery method, and the language, and whether to require the user respond to prompts. When running in the background, multiple outputs can be selected. Format becomes a list of checkboxes to allow for multiple selections. If the Run In The Background option is selected, the Delivery area displays, as shown next:

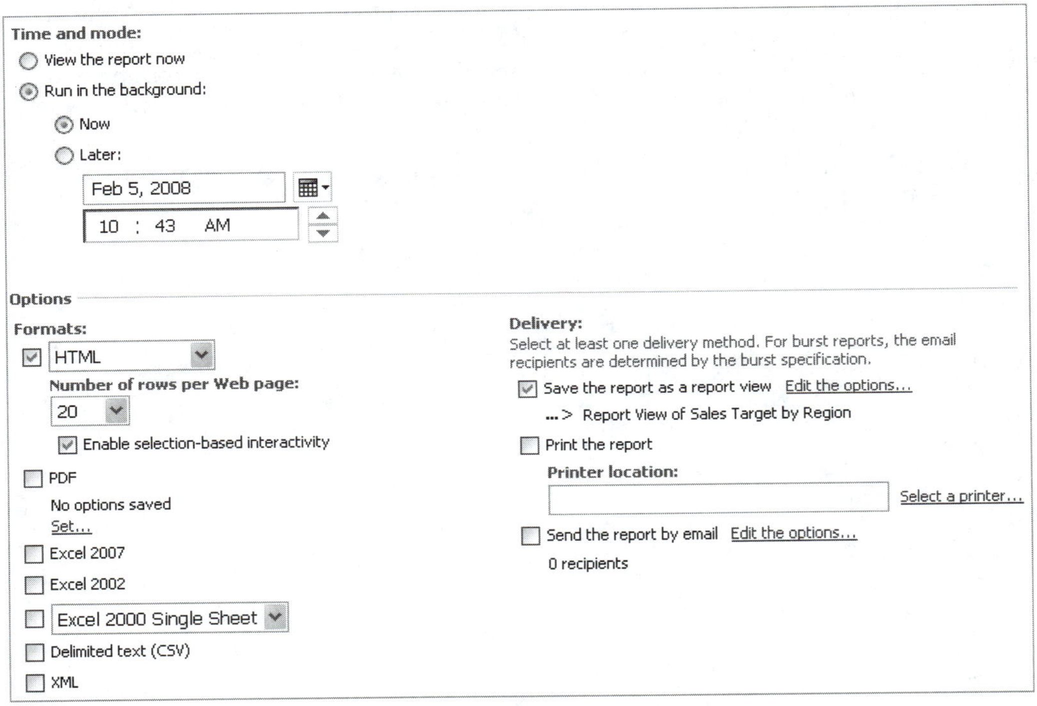

8. Select an option for when you want to run the report in the background and a delivery method.

9. If you select the PDF checkbox, click the Set link as seen in the last illustration. The Set The PDF Options screen displays, as shown in the illustration on the opposite page.

Set the PDF options - Sales Target by Region   Help   ✕

Specify the orientation and paper size to use for PDF reports. You can also specify that passwords are
needed to open PDF reports, use PDF options or both.

Orientation:
(Default) ▼

Paper size:
(Default) ▼

Access control

☐ Requires a password to open the report
   Password:
   [   ]
   Confirm Password:
   [   ]

☐ Requires a password to access options
   Password:
   [   ]
   Confirm Password:
   [   ]

   Allow printing:
   High-level Representation ▼

   Allow changes:
   ☑ Modify the document's content
   ☑ Add or modify text annotations
   ☑ Fill in forms and sign the document
   ☑ Assemble the document (insert, delete or rotate pages and create navigation elements)

   Allow content extraction:
   ☑ Extract text for screen reader devices
   ☑ Copy of text, images, and other content

[OK]   [Cancel]

10. Set the applicable options, such as requiring a password to open the report, allowing modification of the document content, and so on.

11. Click OK. The Run With Advanced Options screen displays again.

12. Click Run. Depending on the options you selected, you are either returned to Cognos Connection or the report runs.

View Historical Information

Each time an entry runs in the background, Cognos 8 tracks information, such as start time, completion time, and status. This information can be easily viewed for each entry in Cognos Connection by using the Run History and Run History Details options. The Run History option shows you top-level information for an entry, such as request time, start time, and status.

The Run History Details option displays more detailed information for a specific entry, such as error and warning messages, and actions that you can take. This information is extremely useful if a report does not complete when expected or if the report fails.

View Run History

You can view the request, start, and completion date and times to show the amount of time it took for a report to run, as well as the status of the item.

You can filter the entries by status (canceled, executing, failed, pending, succeeded, and suspended) to limit the number of entries displayed and access the View Run History Details and View Output screens from the View Run History screen.

Here's how to view the run history:

1. In the Actions column of the content item, click the More link. The Perform An Action screen displays.

2. Click View Run History. The View Run History screen displays, as shown next:

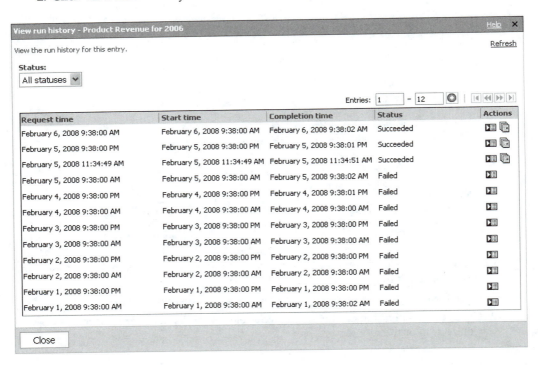

3. From the Status list, select the applicable status. The screen refreshes and displays all the entries with the selected status, as shown next:

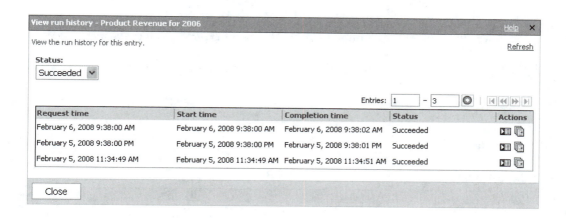

View Run History Details

The View Run History Details action allows you to view the details for a particular run of an entry (for example, query options, general, error, and warning messages, report outputs, and so on). The e-mail delivery status is also listed if an e-mail is associated with the entry. The View Run History Details option is a great starting point to see why a content item failed before you contact the adminstrator.

Here's how to view run history details:

1. In the Actions column of the report, click the More link. The Perform an Action screen displays.

2. Click View Run History. The View History screen displays.

3. In the Actions column of the entry that you want to view, click View Run History Details, as shown next:

View Run History Details icon

The View Run History Details screen displays the details of the individual content item that was run. An option to Rerun the report is provided if the report failed.

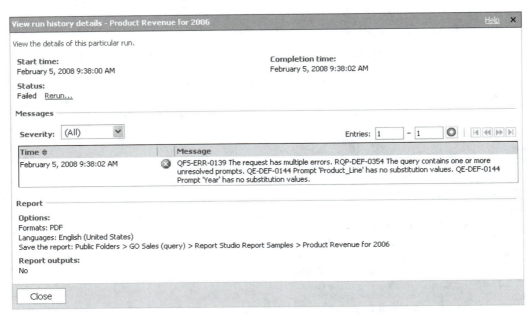

4. Optionally, from the Severity drop-down list, select the severity (All, Warning, Information, Fatal, Error, or Debug) to filter the messages list on for the entry.

Set Properties

The Set Properties option allows users to edit the report name that displays in Cognos Connection; the language; screen tip; and description.

NOTE *To change the title of a report, you must edit the report in the studio in which it was created.*

Users can also edit the number of occurrences and the duration for the run history and report output versions using these options. Packages can also be linked to a report, although caution is advised when using this option since the links can be broken.

NOTE *Properties are specific to an object. For example, changing the properties for the parent report does not change the properties for the target drill-through report.*

Cognos Connection provides additional options such as the ability to inform you when a new report version is generated, disable access to reports, and view the default URL of the report. You can also change the report output formats.

Here's how to set properties:

1. In the Actions column of the report whose properties you want to set, click Set Properties as shown here:

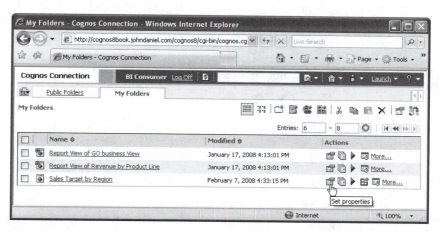

2. The Set Properties screen displays three tabs: General, Permissions and the tab for the type of content you are viewing, such as Report, Query, Analysis, and Permissions. In this example, you see the General tab:

Set properties - Sales Target by Region   Help ×

| General | Report | Permissions |

Specify the properties for this entry.

Type: Report
Owner: BI Consumer
Contact: None   Set the contact ▾

☐ Disable this entry

Location: My Folders   📄 View the search path, ID and URL
Created: July 17, 2005 4:04:09 PM
Modified: February 7, 2008 4:33:15 PM
Icon: 📄 Standard   Edit...

The name, screen tip and description are shown for the selected language.

Language:
| English (United States)   ▾ | Remove values for this language

Name:
| Sales Target by Region |

Description:
| |

Screen tip:
| |

Run history:
◉ Number of occurrences: 5
◯ Duration: [   ] Day(s) ▾

Report output versions:
◉ Number of occurrences: 1
◯ Duration: [   ] Day(s) ▾

Package:
GO Data Warehouse   Link to a package...

| OK | | Cancel |

3. From the Language drop-down list, select the language in which you want the report to display.

4. In the Name text box, you can type a new name for the report.

5. In the Run History area, specify the amount of run history to save by selecting the following options:

   - **Number Of Occurrences**   Enter the number of occurrences of the report to be saved.
   - **Duration**   Enter a number and select Day(s) or Month(s).

6. In the Report Output Versions area, specify the versions of the report to be saved by selecting the following options:

   - **Number Of Occurrences**   Enter the number of occurrences of the report to be saved.
   - **Duration**   Enter a number and select Day(s) or Month(s).

7. In the Package area, click Link To A Package to link the report to a different package.

CAUTION *This is an extremely powerful feature. You should understand the consequences of linking a report to a different package. Use extreme caution when using this option as the data underlying model must match what is in the report. For example, all of the query items in the report must match the package to which you plan to link.*

---

8. Set any other required options and then click OK. Your changes are saved and Cognos Connection displays.

My Watch Items

My Watch Items allows you to add alerts that inform you when a new output version of a report is available. You can also add a user-defined rule based on a value within the report that alerts you if that value meets the criteria defined. Rules can be added only to reports that are in the HTML output format. To add a watch item, the report for which you are adding the alert must have watch items enabled by the administrator or report owner.

TIP *To access My Watch Items from Cognos Connection, click My Area, and then click My Watch Items.*

Enable Alerts for Watch Items

In the Set Properties screen, the administrator or report owner must set the Enable Alerts About New Versions option and Enable Enhanced User Features In Saved Output Versions option in the Advanced Options area for the report to allow users to set watch items for the report.

Here's how to enable alerts for watched items:

1. In the Actions column for the report on which you want to set watch items, click Set Properties.

2. Click the Report tab.

3. Click Advanced Options. The Advanced Options area expands, as shown next:

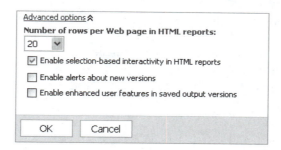

4. To allow users to enable alerts, select the Enable Alerts About New Versions checkbox.

5. To allow users to enable rules, select the Enable Enhanced User Features In Saved Output Versions checkbox.

6. Click OK.

Set an Alert for My Watch Items

Through My Watch Items, you can view and manage alerts for new versions of a report. Once this option is set, every time a new version of the selected report is generated you receive an e-mail notification message.

Here's how to set an alert for My Watch Items:

1. In Cognos Connection, click My Area, as shown next. The My Watch Items, My Preferences, and My Activities and Schedules options display:

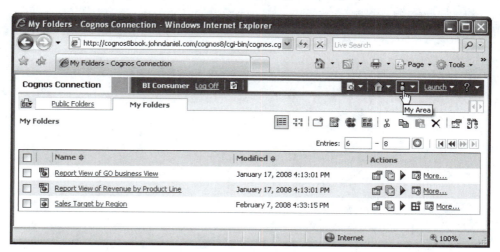

2. Click My Preferences. The Set Preferences screen displays with the General tab, Personal tab, and Portal Tabs tab:

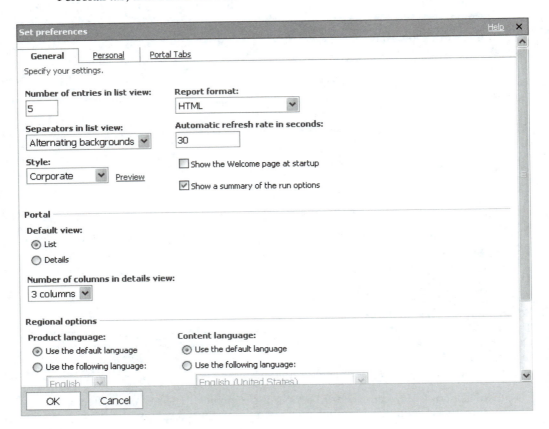

3. Click the Personal tab. You'll see a summary of your authentication information and credentials.

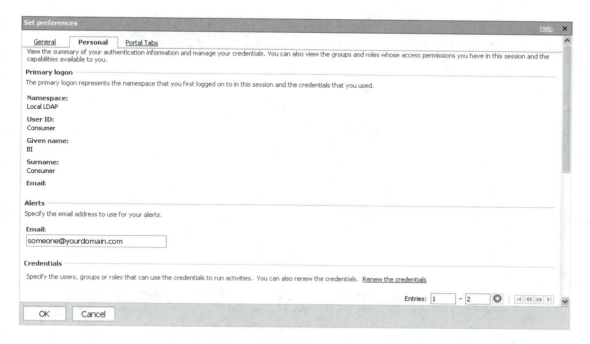

4. In the Alerts area, in the Email text box, enter an e-mail address of where to send the alert.

5. Click OK. Cognos 8 saves your changes and returns you to Cognos Connection.

6. Click a report link to open a saved report, which can be identified by not having a blue arrow next to the report format icon. The report displays in Cognos Viewer, shown here:

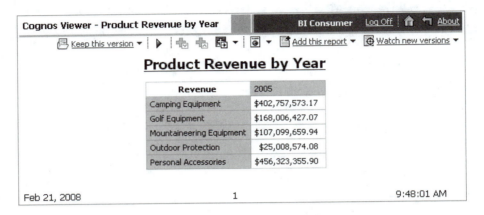

7. Click the arrow next to Watch New Versions, and then click Alert Me About New Versions. A message displays, as shown here:

Tip *If the Watch New Versions menu is not visible, the report output is not a saved version.*

8. Click OK. The e-mail address is added to the alert list, and Cognos 8 returns you to the Cognos Viewer screen.

Every time a new version of the report is created, Cognos 8 sends an e-mail to the recipients on the alert list.

Tip *As an alternative to steps 6 through 8, in the Actions column of a report, click the More link and then click Alert Me About New Versions. To remove an e-mail from an entry alert list, in the Actions column for the entry, click the More link, and then click Do Not Alert Me About New Versions.*

Set a Rule for My Watch Items

Rules determine when a user is notified about a new version of the report. When the condition is met, an alert is sent. A rule can be set only on an item that is in HTML output format.

Here's how to set a rule for reports in My Watch Items:

1. Click a report link to open a saved report, which can be identified by not having a blue arrow next to the report format icon. The report opens in Cognos Viewer.

2. Select an item in the report.

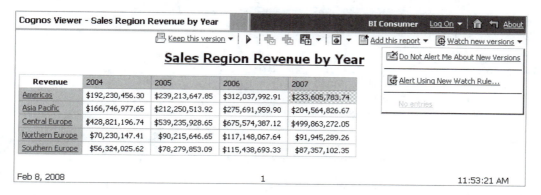

3. Click the arrow next to Watch New Versions, and then click Alert Using New Watch Rule. The Specify The Rule screen displays, as shown here:

4. Optionally, from the Send An Alert When The Report *[Report Name]* Contains area, select the applicable condition (greater than, less than, equal, between, and so on).

5. Optionally, specify a new value in the text box. Cognos 8 sends the alert when the criteria for steps 4 and 5 have been met. For example, if you selected greater than in step 4 and entered 23360783.74 in step 5, Cognos 8 sends the alert when the selected report contains a value greater than 23360783.74.

6. In the For The Selected Context area, select or clear the applicable checkbox(es). The example in step 3 shows the Americas and 2007 checkboxes. If both boxes are selected, the rule evaluates the cell where *Americas* and *2007* intersect. If only one is selected, the rule evaluates all the cells in the row or column for the selected item. If neither is selected, the rule evaluates all cells within the report.

7. Click Next. The Specify The Alert Type screen, shown next, displays with the Send The Report By Email option and the Publish A News Item option. The Send The Report By Email option sends the report as part of an email. The Publish A News Item option creates a news item with a headline, text, and link to additional information that is displayed in Cognos Connection. We go over the Send The Report By Email option beginning at step 8 and the Publish a news item option starting at step 12.

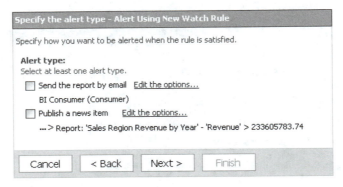

8. Select the Send The Report By Email checkbox.

9. Click the Edit The Options Link. The Set The Email Options screen displays:

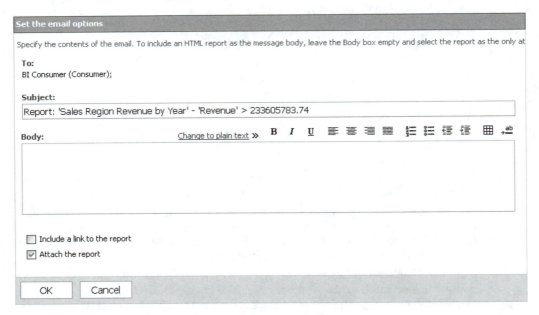

10. Set the applicable options such as the Subject, enter a message in the Body text box, and select Include A Link To The Report, or make other appropriate selections.

NOTE *If you want to include an HTML report as the message, leave the Body text box empty and select the Attach The Report checkbox. Cognos 8 sends the report as the body of your e-mail.*

11. Click OK. The Specify The Alert Type screen displays again. If you do not want to publish a news item, skip to step 16. Otherwise, continue to step 12.

12. Select the Publish A News Item checkbox.

13. Click the Edit The Options link. The Newsletter Options screen displays:

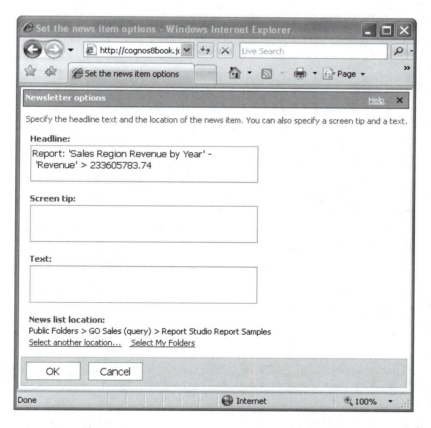

14. Set the applicable options such as the Headline, Screen tip, and Text for the news item. You can also change the News List Location by clicking on Select Another Location or Select My Folders.

15. Click OK. The Specify The Alert Type screen displays again.

16. Click Next. The Specify A Name And Description screen displays with the Name, Description, and Screen Tip text boxes and the option of selecting a folder in which to save the alert, as shown next. By default, Cognos 8 saves the alert in My Watch Items.

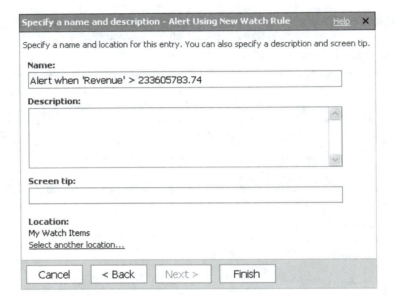

17. Set the applicable options such as entering a new name or description for the alert and selecting a new location for the alert.

18. Click Finish. Cognos 8 saves the rule and returns you to the Cognos Viewer.

Each time the criteria for the rule are met, Cognos 8 sends an e-mail to the recipients in the alert list and/or publishes a news item, depending on the alert type(s) chosen.

Disable an Entry

If you do not want users to access an entry (such as a report, page, or folder) you can disable that entry. Users who do not have write permissions will no longer see that entry in the portal. Users with write permissions will see a disabled icon to the right of the entry.

Here's how to disable an entry:

1. In the Actions column of the entry that you want to disable, click Set Properties.

NOTE *Consumers may or may not be able to edit properties of an entry. The Cognos administrator defines users' permissions.*

2. Select the Disable This Entry checkbox.

3. Click OK. A disabled icon displays to the right of the entry in Cognos Connection:

View the URL

When a report is created and saved, Cognos 8 assigns the item a URL based on where in Cognos Connection the report is saved. The URL is the web address where the report can be found. The URL is useful for Cognos 8 users who want to save that URL as a favorite so that they can access a report without having to navigate through the Cognos Connection content. You can view URL in the Set Properties screen.

Here's how to view the URL:

1. In the Actions column of an entry, click Set Properties.

2. Click View The Search Path, ID And URL. The View The Search Path, ID And URL screen displays:

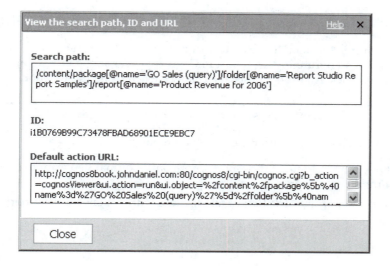

NOTE *The Default Action URL can be used to open the content item directly from a location where a hyperlink can be embedded, such as an e-mail, a desktop icon, or a favorite in your browser. When you click the URL, you are taken directly to the report for execution and/or viewing, if you are already authenticated. If you are not authenticated, you will be directed to the Log On screen first.*

Change Output Formats

Cognos 8 provides several output formats for reports to accommodate users with different viewing requirements. For example, the CEO may want to view a report in PDF format and the sales manager may want to view the reports in Excel format.

Each output format displays with a unique icon in Cognos Connection:

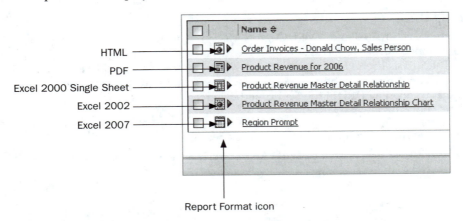

Report Format icon

Users can change the default output format for a report, the default behavior of the link (for example, instead of running the report in Cognos Viewer, it opens in Report Studio), and set prompt values. All users can see the changes when using these options.

TIP *You can also specify access permissions for an entry from the Permissions tab.*

Here's how to change the output formats for a report:

1. In the Actions column of the report whose ouput format you want to change, click Set Properties.

2. Click the Report tab. The Report tab displays with options for the report:

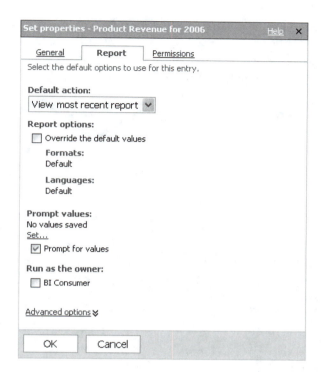

3. From the Default Action drop-down list, select the action you want to occur when the user clicks the link to the report. The default value is View Most Recent Report. Keep in mind users must have Professional Author or above permissions to edit the report when choosing Open With Report Studio.

NOTE *In Cognos Connection, a blue arrow located to the right of a report format icon indicates that the report link runs the report in real time.*

4. In the Report Options area, select the Override The Default Values checkbox. The default values for Report Options expand:

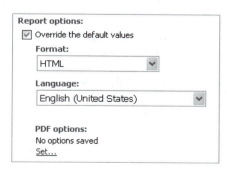

5. From the Format drop-down list, select the applicable output format. The default format is HTML.

6. If PDF is selected from the Format list, in the PDF Options area, click the Set link. The Set The PDF Options screen displays:

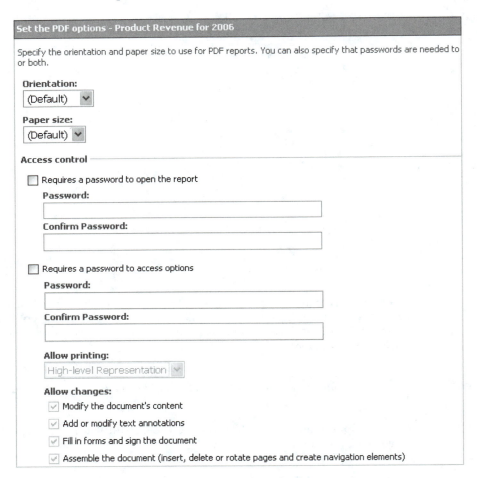

7. Set the applicable options (such as, changing the PDF layout or setting a password), and then click OK. Cognos 8 returns you to the Report tab of the Set Properites screen.

8. From the Language drop-down list, select the applicable language.

9. In the Prompt Values area, select the Prompt For Values checkbox to set prompt values.

10. Click Advanced Options. The Advanced Options expand:

11. Set the applicable options (such as the number of rows to display per web page in HTML reports) and then click OK. Your changes are saved and you are returned to Cognos Connection.

Use Report Viewer Options

Reports that run from Cognos Connection open in the Cognos Viewer. Cognos Viewer provides a report viewer options toolbar in the upper-right part of the screen:

Depending on your role, you can e-mail or save the report, save it as a report view, or open it in Report Studio. You can run the report, use the drill-through options, and view the report in different formats (for example, if it opened in HTML format, you can view it in Excel 2007 format). You can also add the report to My Folders or to a browser bookmark from the report viewer options toolbar.

Save As Report View

If you frequently use a particular entry, you can save that entry as a Report View in My Folders. This makes accessing the entry quicker. The Report View shares the same report specification as the source report. If the location of the source report changes, the Report View link is not broken. Prompt values that are important to you can be set so you do not have to answer the prompts each time you run the report. This feature comes in handy when scheduling.

Here's how to save a report as a Report View from the report viewer toolbar :

1. In Cognos Connection, click a report link to run the report. The report opens in Cognos Viewer.

2. From the Keep This Version drop-down menu, click Save As Report View. The Save As Report View screen displays:

3. In the Name text box, type a name for the report.
4. In the Location area, select a location for the report by doing one of the following:
   - Click Select Another Location. The Select A Location (Navigate) screen displays. Navigate to the folder where you want to save the entry. Select the option for the folder and then click OK.
   - Click Select My Folders.
5. Click OK. Cognos saves the report view in the specified location and returns you to the Cognos Viewer screen.
6. Navigate to the specified location. The report view that you saved is indicated by a Report View icon:

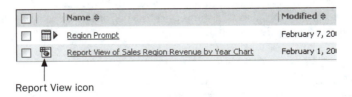

Report View icon

Use Drill-up and Drill-down

The drill-up and drill-down icons in the report viewer options are available when the column and/or row headings in a report are links. *Drill-up* and *drill-down* allow you to move through a column or row in the report. For example, if you click Product Line in the report, you could then drill-down to Product Type, which would display data about the Product Line. Drilling-down on Product Type would take you to Product and display detailed data regarding the selected product type. Drilling-up from Product displays data for the Product Type. If you drill-up on Product Type, the Product Line displays and takes you back to where you started. You can also drill-down or drill-up by right clicking on a row or column heading and choosing which you would like to do from the menu. Clicking on a row or column heading will also allow you to drill-down.

TIP *The ability to drill-up and drill-down in a report depends on the report being created from a dimensional source. Refer to Chapter 8 for more information on drilling capabilities.*

Use the Go To Link

When a report has *drill-through* access, the report is linked to another report by a common field. For example, if drill-through access is set up, you can drill through from a summary report to a more detailed report to help you answer business questions using Go To in Cognos Viewer.

TIP *Within Cognos Viewer, the Go To option allows you to drill through to another report regardless of the model source. The report must be set up for drill-through capability, and there must be a report setup as the drill-through target. For more information on drill-through access, refer to Chapter 10.*

New Pages

Creating a new page allows you to move a variety of content to a centralized location so you can personalize the page, showing only content that relates to your area of business or for which you are responsible. For example, you could create a dashboard within a page displaying reports that you access on a regular basis.

Create a New Page

You can group different types of content together on a new page in Cognos Connection. For example, suppose your company organized the sales folders according to year instead of product and you want to view all the reports for a specific product. You can create a new page with all of the product reports in one location. You can also search for reports using the Cognos Navigator portlet.

Here's how to create a new page:

1. In Cognos Connection, click New Page.

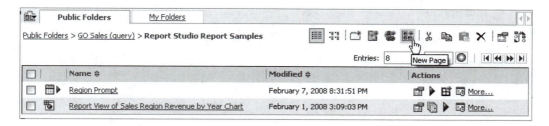

The Specify A Name And Description screen appears.

2. In the Name text box, type a name for the new page.

3. Optionally, in the Description and/or Screen Tip text box(es), type in a description for the new page.

4. Optionally, click Select Another Location to change the location for the new page.

5. Click Next. The Set Columns And Layout screen displays:

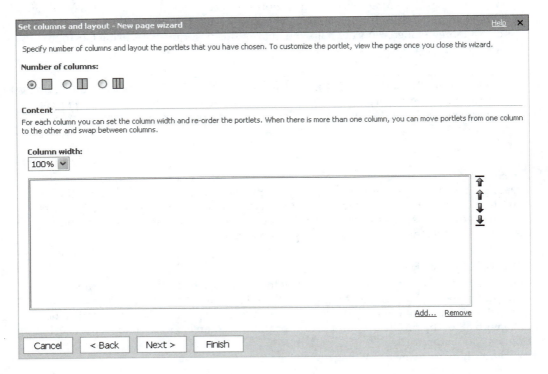

6. In the Number Of Columns area, select the option for the number of columns to display on the new page. Your selection displays the columns, as shown in the illustration on the opposite page.

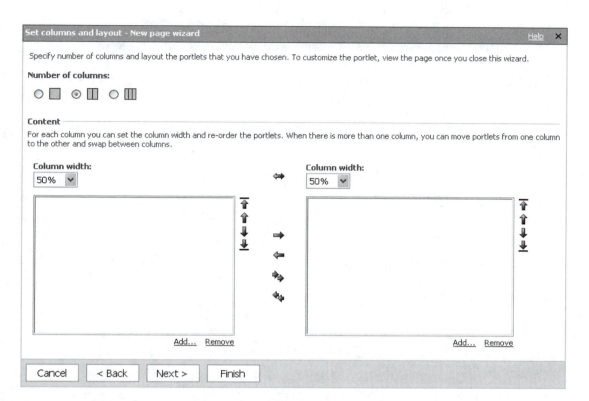

7. Optionally, from the Column Width drop-down list, select a column width.

8. In the column to which you want to add portlets, click Add. A *portlet* allows you to add content and functionality to your page. For example, you can use the Cognos Content portlet to browse folders in one section of your page and the Cognos Viewer portlet to view reports in another. You will not have navigated away from the page. The Select Portlets (Navigate) screen, shown next, displays, listing the available portlets:

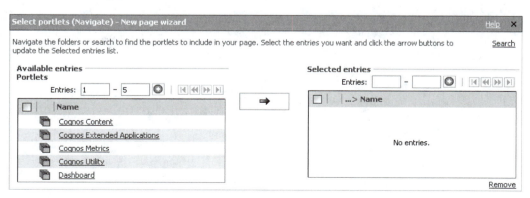

9. In the Available Entries area, click a folder to navigate to the portlets. The Select Portlets (Navigate) screen shows you the portlets contained within the selected folder.

10. From the Available Entries area, select the checkbox(es) of the portlet(s) that you want to add to the new page.

TIP *In the Actions column, click View This Portlet to view what the portlet does and how it will look on the page.*

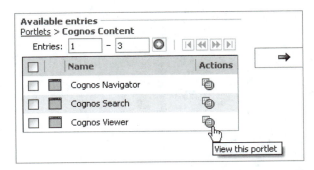

11. Click Add. The screen refreshes and Cognos 8 adds the portlet(s) to the Selected Entries box:

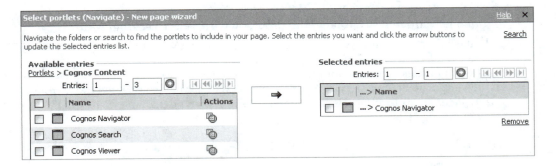

12. Repeat steps 9 through 11 to add multiple portlets. (Note that you can add the same portlet multiple times.)

13. Click OK. The Set Columns And Layout screen displays and the selected portlet(s) are added in the specified columns:

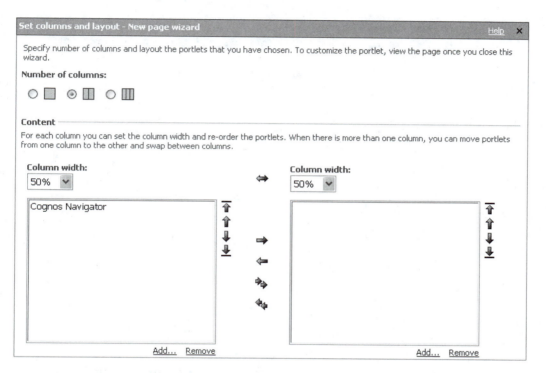

14. Optionally, repeat steps 8 through 13 to add portlets to the other column.

15. Click Next. The Set Page Style screen displays:

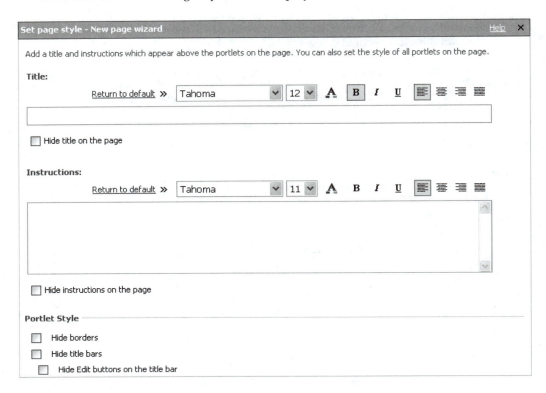

16. In the Title text box, type a name for the new page.

17. Select any other applicable options for the new page. For example, under the Instructions area, in the text box, you can add instructions for using the page. Under the Portlet Style area, you can hide the borders of the portlet, hide the title bars of the portlet, or hide the edit buttons on the title bar by selecting the appropriate checkbox.

18. Click Next. The Select An Action screen displays:

19. Optionally, from the Action After Closing The Wizard area, select the Add This Page To The Portal Tabs checkbox to add the page as a tab in Cognos Connection, and/or select the View The Page checkbox to view the page. For this example, we do not select either checkbox. We discuss adding the page as a portal tab later in this chapter. For more information, refer to the "Create a Portal Tab" section of this chapter.

20. Click Finish. Cognos 8 creates the new page in the specified location and returns you to the Cognos Connection screen.

21. To view the newly created page, navigate to the specified location. The new page is identified by a new Page icon:

Page icon

22. Click the link to run the page and view the layout. The Cognos Viewer opens and displays your page, as shown here:

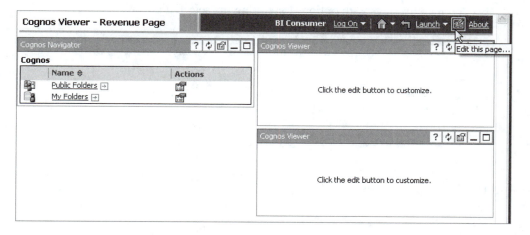

23. If changes are necessary, click Edit This Page. The Set Properties screen displays.

24. Make the necessary changes and click OK.

Add Content to a Portlet

You have created a new page that contains portlets; however, the portlets do not contain any content, such as names for title bars, reports or links to the reports, or pages. Now you add the content to the portlets.

NOTE *For this section, we assume that you followed the instructions in the "Create a New Page" section of this chapter and did not create a portal tab. If you did create a portal tab, click the tab for the page and go directly to step 3.*

Here's how to add content to a portlet:

1. Navigate to the location of the page containing the portlets for which you want to add content.

2. In Cognos Connection, click the applicable link to open the page. The page opens in Cognos Viewer.

3. In the title bar for the portlet, click Edit:

A screen displays with options for editing the selected portlet:

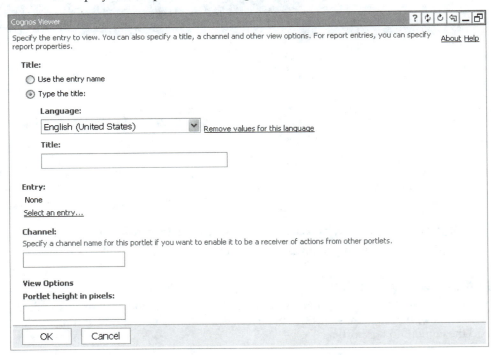

4. In the Title area, select the Use The Entry Name option to use the name of the portlet as the title or Type The Title option to add a custom title to the title bar.

5. If you select the Type The Title option, you must also select a language from the Language list and enter a title for the portlet in the Title text box.

6. In the Entry area, click Select An Entry. The Select An Entry (Navigate) screen displays:

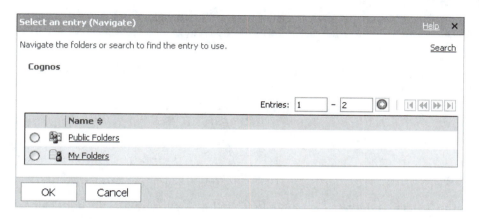

7. Navigate to the folder and select the report or folder that you want to add to the portlet.

8. Click OK. The options screen for the selected portal displays.

9. Click OK. The selected report or folder contents display within the portlet you modified. In this example, the Sales Region Revenue By Year report displays in a Cognos Viewer portlet titled the same as the report:

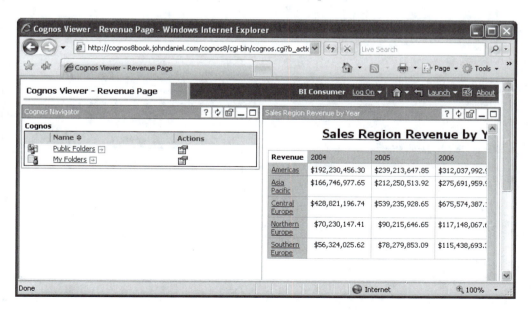

10. Repeat steps 3 through 9 to add content to additional portlets. The edit options that display are dependent on the type of portlet that you are editing.

Create a Portal Tab

You can access a page quickly by adding it as a tab to the Cognos Connection portal. If you did not choose to create a tab when you initially created a page, you can do so now.

Here's how to create a portal tab:

1. In the Actions column of the page for which you want to create a portal tab, click Add To My Portal Tabs.

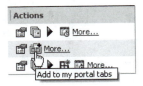

The tab is added to the portal. In the following illustration, the portal tab is named Revenue Page:

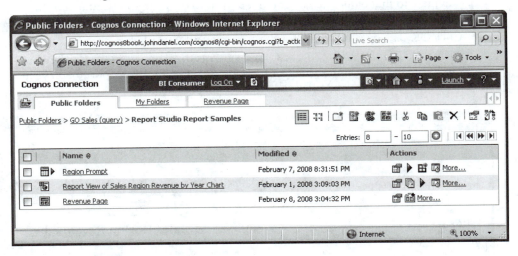

TIP *You can also remove tabs and modify their sequence using the Tab Menu option. When you remove a tab, only the tab is deleted; the entries and content that were on the tab remain in their specified locations.*

Tab Menu ——→

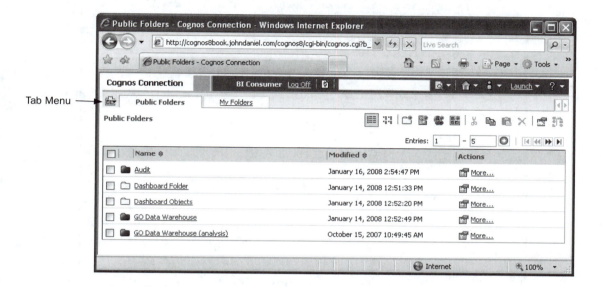

Advanced Portal Page Features

Cognos 8 offers several advanced features that can be added to a portal page. Portlet-to-portlet communication and passing report variables allows you to coordinate content between all portlets on a single portal page or tab.

Portlet-to-Portlet Communication

Portlet-to-portlet communication can be set up to allow portlets to interact. The actions from a source portlet display in the target portlet. For example, when you run a report from the source portlet, instead of opening the report in a new window, the target portlet can display the report within the portlet page. This is enabled by creating a channel name in the target portlet and referencing that channel name in the source portlet.

Here's how to set up portlet-to-portlet communication:

1. Navigate to the location of the page containing the portlets to which you want to add content. In this example, we use a page with two columns. The first column contains a Cognos Navigator portlet and a Cognos Search portlet. The second column contains two Cognos Viewer portlets.

2. In Cognos Connection, click the applicable report link to open the page. The page opens in Cognos Viewer, as shown next:

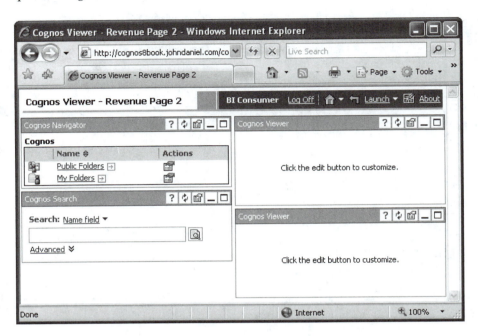

NOTE *If your page exists as a tab in Cognos Connection, you can click the portal tab.*

3. In the title bar of the source portlet, click Edit. In this example, we click Edit in Cognos Navigator. A screen displays with options for the selected portlet:

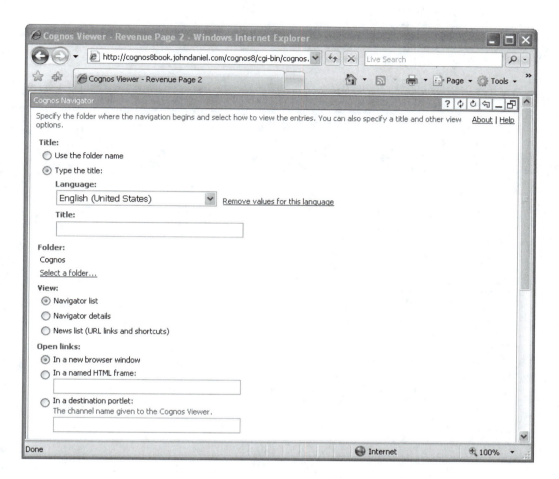

4. In the Open Links area, select the In A Destination Portlet option.

5. In The Channel Name Given To The Cognos Viewer text box, enter a name by which you can reference the channel.

NOTE *Channel names cannot contain spaces. You can use letters, numbers, and underscores (_), however.*

6. Click OK. Your page displays.

7. In the title bar of the target portlet, click Edit. In this example, we use a Cognos Viewer portlet as shown in step 2. A screen displays with options for a Cognos Viewer portlet:

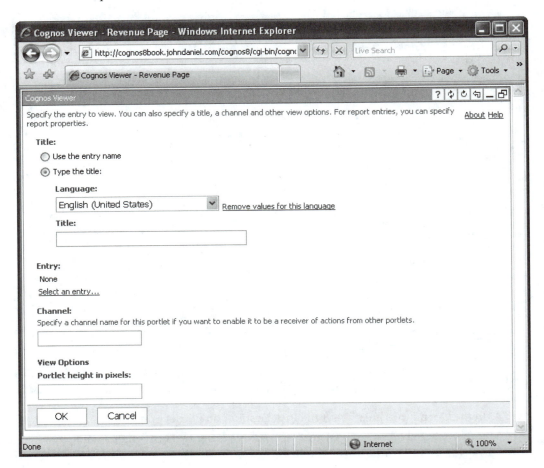

TIP The source and target portlets can be on different pages.

8. In the Channel text box, enter the same channel name that you entered for the source portlet in step 5.

9. Click OK. Your page displays.

10. Repeat steps 3 through 9 to add the communication between the other portlets on your page. In this example, we use a Cognos Search portlet as the source portlet and another Cognos Viewer portlet as the target portlet.

11. In the Cognos Navigator portlet, run or search for a report. The report displays within a Cognos Viewer portlet instead of a new web browser:

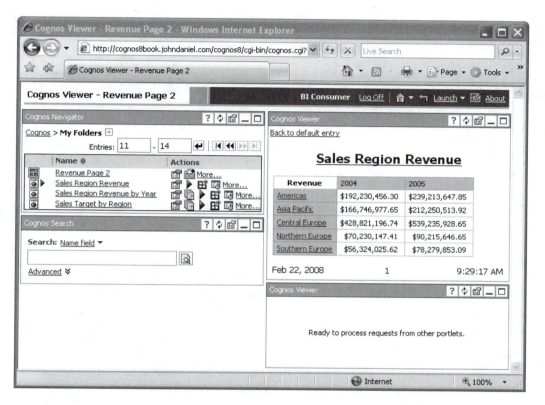

Portlet-to-Portlet Communication Using a Prompt

A prompt page can be used within a portlet to filter reports in other portlets on the same page. When you select a prompt item in one portlet, the screen refreshes and displays the filtered information in the other portlet(s) on the page.

Here's how to set up portlet-to-portlet communication using a prompt:

1. Navigate to the location of the page containing the portlets to which you want to add content. In this example, we use a page with two columns. The first column contains a Cognos Viewer portlet with a prompt. The second column contains two Cognos Viewer portlets with reports linked to the prompt in the first column's portlet.

2. In Cognos Connection, click the applicable link to open the page. The page opens in Cognos Viewer.

NOTE *If your page exists as a tab in Cognos Connection, you can click the portal tab.*

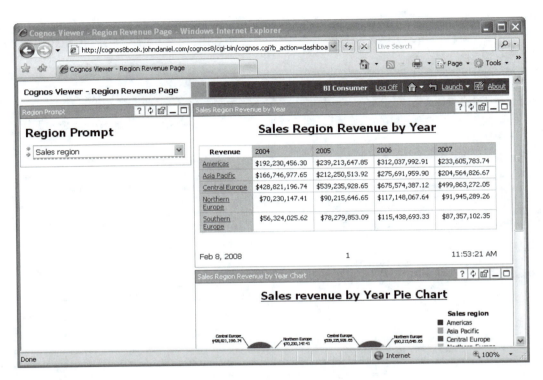

3. In the title bar of the source portlet, click Edit. In this example, we click Edit in the Region Prompt title bar. A screen displays with options for the selected portlet.

4. In the Channel text box, enter a name by which you can reference the channel.

NOTE *Channel names cannot contain spaces. However, you can use letters, numbers, and underscores.*

5. In the Entry area, click Edit Properties. The Advanced Properties Editor screen displays:

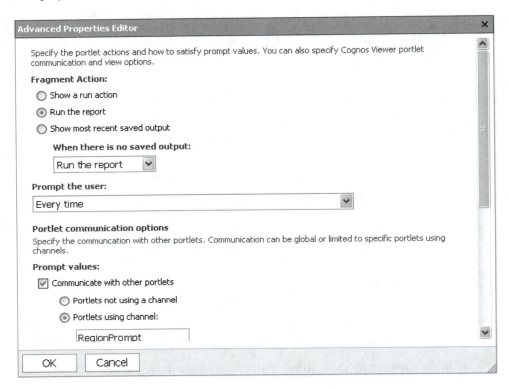

6. In the Fragment Action area, select the Run The Report option.
7. From the Prompt The User drop-down list, select Every Time.
8. In the Prompt Values area, select the Communicate With Other Portlets checkbox.
9. Click the Portlets Using Channel option.
10. In the Channel text box, enter the same channel name that you entered in step 4.
11. Click OK. The screen with the portlet options displays as shown in step 3.
12. Click OK. The page you are editing displays as shown in step 2.
13. In the title bar of the target portlet, click Edit. In this example, we use the Sales Region Revenue by Year portlet as shown in step 2. A screen displays with options for the selected portlet:

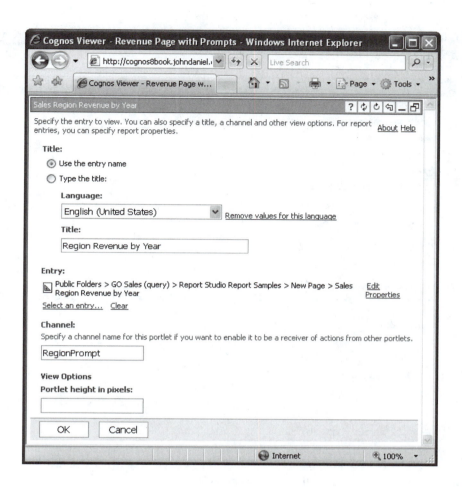

TIP   *The source and target portlets can be on different pages.*

14. In the Channel text box, enter the same channel name that you entered for the source portlet in step 4.

15. In the Entry region, click Edit Properties. The Advanced Properties Editor screen displays with options for the selected portlet:

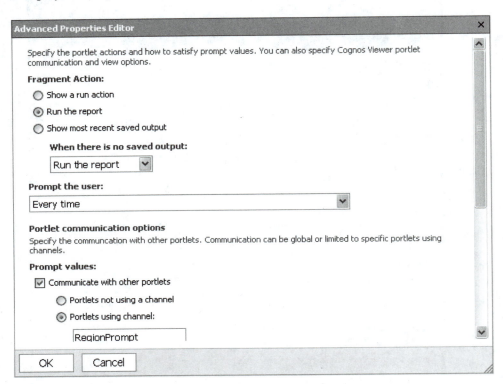

16. Under Fragment Action, select Run The Report.

17. In the Prompt The User list, select Every Time.

18. Under Prompt Values, select the Communicate With Other Portlets checkbox.

19. Click Portlets Using Channel.

20. In the Channel text box, enter the same channel name that you entered in step 4.

21. Click OK. The screen with the portlet options displays as shown in step 13.

22. Click OK. The page you are editing displays as shown in step 2.

23. Repeat steps 13 through 22 to add communication between the source portlet and any additional target portlets. In this example, we use Region Prompt as the source portlet and the Sales Region Revenue by Year Chart as an additional target portlet.

24. In the portlet containing the prompt, select an item. The page refreshes and the reports are filtered within the portlet page, as shown here:

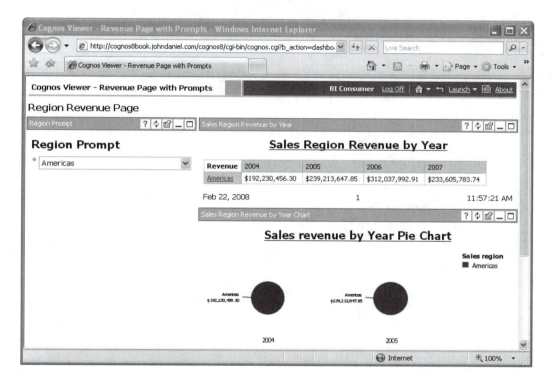

IBM Cognos 8 BI Consumer Modes

We live in a world where information changes constantly and everyone is on the go, where management wants information yesterday to make decisions now. You don't have time to sit down and eat lunch, let alone create presentations and spreadsheets; search through a great number of reports, queries, and analyses; or wait in your office to receive a report that you could view on the road. IBM Cognos 8 Go! provides the answer for these situations.

IBM Cognos 8 Go! comes in three flavors: IBM Cognos 8 Go! Office (Go! Office), IBM Cognos 8 Go! Search (Go! Search), and IBM Cognos 8 Go! Mobile(Go! Mobile). You can use one or any combination of the three. Go! Office installs an add-in to your Microsoft Office applications that lets you access and import Cognos 8 data into a Microsoft Word document, Excel spreadsheet, or PowerPoint presentation. Go! Search enhances the native search in Cognos Connection, giving you a more robust and user-friendly search engine. On top of that, Go! Search can be integrated with third-party enterprise search engines and portals. Go! Mobile lets you view your Cognos 8 reports and analyses anywhere your Blackberry has service. IBM Cognos 8 Go! Mobile Version 8.3 also supports symbian S60 3rd Edition, and Windows Mobile Version 5 and 6.

Using IBM Cognos 8 Go! Office

When you install Go! Office, Cognos 8 installs add-ins for Microsoft PowerPoint, Word, and Excel. These add-ins let you import some or all of your Cognos 8 content into your Microsoft Office documents.

NOTE *This chapter assumes that the PC you are using has the Go! Office add-in installed.*

How you want to present the content determines which Office application you will use. Following is an example of how you can use the same report you created in Report Studio across all three Office applications:

Every month you attend a sales meeting with the executives in your organization, and every month they want to know the status of sales. You could print the report you created in Report Studio and distribute copies to the executives in that sales meeting, and that would give them the information that they need—and maybe that was good enough in the past. But now you are on the move and you want to show them a presentation. It used to be that you had to create a PowerPoint presentation and laboriously create charts and lists; this would take hours that you did not have. With Go! Office, you can import the charts and lists quickly and easily and provide the executives with accurate and timely information.

You don't want to stop with just the presentation, though. You know from past experience that three days after your presentation, one or two of the executives are going to ask follow-up questions that you don't have time to answer. So you decide to create a hand-out in Microsoft Word that contains the same data that appeared in your presentation, with brief explanations for each of the charts and lists. You pass these out, and they practically throw the key to the executive washroom at you for your foresight. You have successfully used the same data in two different formats.

But that's not all. You found out an hour before your meeting that the CFO was in town and was planning to attend the meeting. You know that he likes to see specific financial information, but you do not include this data in your meetings on a regular basis. You don't have time to change your PowerPoint presentation or Word document. Besides, he is a financial person and likes spreadsheets. You create a financial report in Excel and add the calculations that the CFO likes to see all with time to spare to print copies for everyone. In a few days, you and the CFO will be having a dinner meeting to discuss your career and future advancement.

Will Go! Office advance your career? That depends on you. Go! Office provides the tools that you need to incorporate Cognos 8 content into Microsoft Office documents. The rest is up to you.

There is just one more thing—probably the coolest feature of all. You can reuse the same PowerPoint presentation, Word document, or Excel spreadsheet for a future meeting, because Go! Office makes that easy, too. Instead of having to re-create the document or even manually entering updated figures, you can refresh your data with the click of the mouse. To help you keep track of your documents, you can publish them to Cognos Connection along with the Cognos 8 content that they reference. You can even store them all in one folder if you like. With Go!, it's easy to create, store, refresh, and reuse a document.

NOTE *Throughout this section, we refer to the Cognos 8 toolbar. If you are a Microsoft Office 2007 user, the tools you need to access can be found in the Cognos 8 ribbon.*

Connect to Microsoft Office

Before you can begin using the powerful Microsoft Office add-ins, you need to connect your Office products with Cognos 8. The steps for accomplishing this are the same for all three Office products, and you have to take these steps only once. So you don't have to do it for all three Office products and you don't have to do it every time you launch one.

NOTE *The following illustrations feature Microsoft PowerPoint, but the steps are the same for Microsoft Word and Excel.*

Here's how to connect to Microsoft Office:

1. Launch the desired Office application, PowerPoint in this case, which opens and displays the Cognos 8 toolbar:

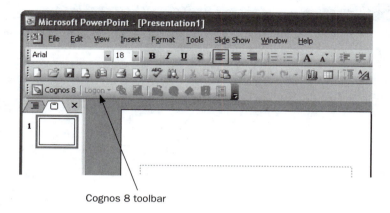

Cognos 8 toolbar

2. Click Cognos 8. PowerPoint activates the toolbar and displays the Cognos 8 for Office task pane:

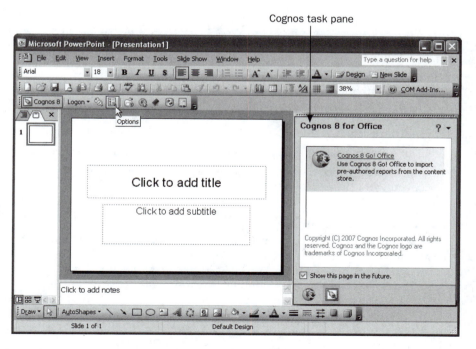

Cognos task pane

3. From the Cognos 8 toolbar, click Options. The Options window displays, as shown next, with the System Gateway URI and Friendly Name text boxes. The System Gateway URI is the web address, or URL, required to access the Cognos gateway.

The Friendly Name is a name you can use to help you to identify the gateway location.

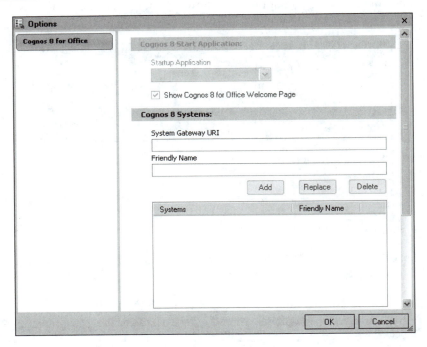

NOTE *You may need to obtain the System Gateway URI from your system administrator.*

4. In the System Gateway URI text box, enter the gateway location.

5. In the Friendly Name text box, enter a name for the gateway location.

6. Click Add. The gateway location and the name display in the Systems box.

7. Click OK. Go! Office is now ready to use the existing Cognos 8 Business Intelligence (BI) content within Microsoft Office.

Log on to Cognos 8 Through Microsoft Office

If security is applied to the Cognos 8 server, you must be logged on to Cognos 8 to import data into your Microsoft Office documents. You can log on through Cognos 8, or you can log on through Office.

Here's how to log on to Cognos 8 through Microsoft Office:

1. Launch the Microsoft Office application, which opens and displays the Cognos 8 toolbar.

2. From the Cognos 8 toolbar, click Cognos 8. The Office application activates the toolbar.

3. From the Cognos 8 toolbar, click Log On. The Log On dialog displays:

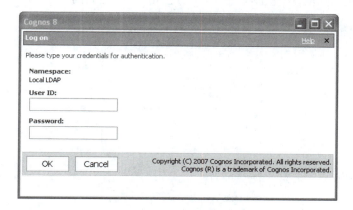

4. If you have more than one authentication provider, from the Namespace list, select a namespace and click OK.

5. Enter your Cognos 8 user ID and password in the appropriate text boxes.

6. Click OK. You are logged on to Cognos 8 and can begin importing Cognos 8 content.

Import Cognos 8 Content into an Office Application

Importing Cognos 8 content into an Office application is a quick and easy way to use data, charts, and lists. Regardless of the Office application that you use, the steps are the same.

NOTE *The following illustrations feature PowerPoint; however, the steps are the same for Word and Excel.*

Here's how to import Cognos 8 content into an Office application:

1. Launch the Office application, which opens and displays the Cognos 8 toolbar.

2. From the Cognos 8 toolbar, click Cognos 8. The Office application activates the toolbar and displays the Cognos 8 for Office task pane.

NOTE *If you are not logged onto Cognos 8, you can log on from the Cognos 8 toolbar. For more information, refer to the "Log on to Cognos 8 Through Microsoft Office" section in this chapter.*

3. From the Cognos 8 Go! Office task pane, click Cognos 8 Go! Office link. Two Cognos content tabs display in the task pane, as shown next. One tab shows the Cognos 8 content residing in Cognos Connection to which you have access. The other tab shows the Cognos content that you have saved locally. Your next steps are dictated

by where you select to pull your Cognos 8 content. The more common way is to pull content directly from Cognos 8, so that is covered here.

4. From the Cognos 8 Go! Office task pane, click the plus sign to navigate to the Cognos folder in which the content resides, and then select the report to import.

5. From the Cognos 8 Go! Office pane, click Import Content. The Select Report Properties of the Import Content screen displays with a Name text box, Report Pages area, and Report Version area, as shown here:

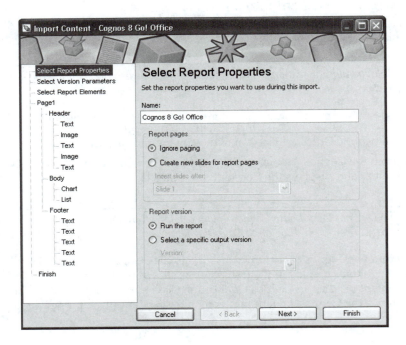

NOTE *The options that display on the Import Content screen differ slightly for PowerPoint, Word and Excel, but the concepts are the same across all three products.*

The Name text box contains the name of the content to be imported. The Report Pages area gives you the options of distributing content with multiple pages over multiple slides, or having all of the content imported on a single slide. The Report Version area gives you the options of running the content prior to importing to have the most current data, or importing a version of the content that you have saved.

TIP *As an alternative to step 5, from the Cognos 8 Go! Office task pane, navigate to the content and drag-and-drop the content into your presentation. Go! Office imports the content in its entirety and you are not presented with the options outlined in steps 6 through 21. If you use this method, skip to step 22.*

6. From the Report Pages area, select Ignore Paging or Create New Slides For Report Pages. If you select the Create New Slides For Report Pages option, the Insert Slides After drop-down list becomes active, and PowerPoint inserts the slide after the slide you choose from the list.

7. From the Report Version area, select Run The Report or Select A Specific Output Version. If you select the Select A Specific Output Version option, the Version drop-down list becomes active and PowerPoint imports the version of the content that you choose from the list.

8. Click Next. The Select Report Elements of the Import Content screen displays with a list of the selected content's elements. You can select to import some or all of the elements contained within the content, as shown next:

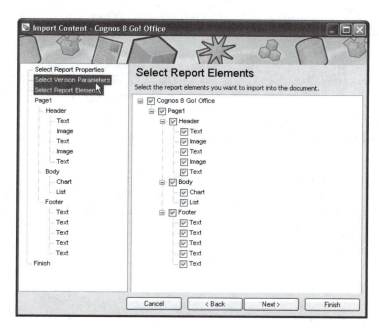

9. Clear the checkboxes of the elements that you do not want to import. For example, you may want to import only the chart and list that you created in Cognos 8 and leave out the header and footer. In that case, you would clear the Header and Footer checkboxes.

10. Click Next. Your next steps depend on the elements that you chose to import. Go! Office displays a dialog where you define how the selected elements are imported. To continue with the example from step 9, the following illustrations and discussion focus on the steps for importing a chart and list. In our example, the Chart dialog of the Import Content screen displays with a Name text box, Location list box, and option to Add New Slide:

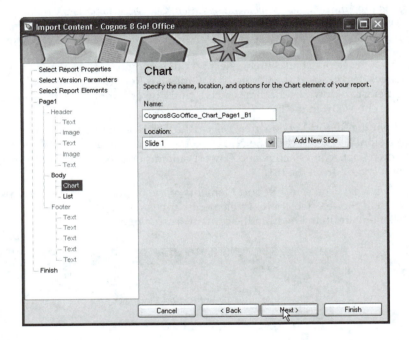

11. Optionally, in the Name text box, enter a new name for the chart to be imported. By default, Go! Office names the chart based on the elements of the content.

12. From the Location list, select the slide for which you want the chart to be imported.

13. Optionally, click Add New Slide to import the chart into a new slide.

14. Click Next. In our example, the List dialog of the Import Content screen displays with the Name text box, Location drop-down list, Add New Slide button, Import As

A Chart Object checkbox, Number Of Rows To Display list, and Number Of Columns To Display list:

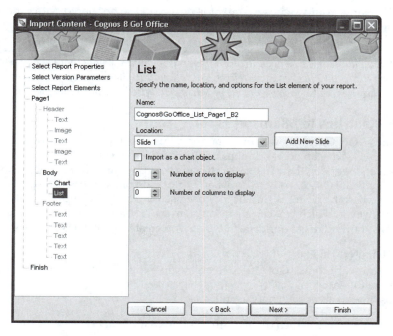

15. Optionally, in the Name text box, enter a new name for the chart to be imported. By default, Go! Office names the list based on the elements of the content.

NOTE *Do not include spaces in the name. Use the underscore in place of a space.*

16. From the Location drop-down list, select the slide on which you want the list to be imported, or click the Add New Slide button to import the chart into a new slide.

17. Optionally, select the Import As A Chart Object checkbox. When selected, Go! Office imports the list as an object into the Microsoft Office application that you are using.

18. From the Number Of Rows To Display list, specify the number of rows in your list to be displayed on the slide. By default, all the rows in your list are displayed.

19. From the Number Of Columns To Display list, specify the number of columns in your list to be displayed on the slide. By default, all the columns in your list are displayed.

20. Click Next. The Finish screen displays. You can go back and make changes to any of your import settings by clicking Back or by choosing the screen to display from the tree structure located on the left side of the screen.

21. Click Finish. Go! Office imports the selected elements based on the import options you selected.

22. Optionally, move and resize the objects.

23. Repeat steps 4 through 22 to add content to your document.

24. Save the document in the appropriate format for the Office application that you are using. Your Cognos 8 content is now ready to be shared with others in your organization.

NOTE *If you plan to use this document from month to month, you do not have to re-create it every month. With Go! Office, you can refresh the data within the document. For more information, refer to the "Refresh Cognos 8 Content in Microsoft Office" section of this chapter.*

Using BI Analytics in Microsoft Excel

IBM Cognos 8 Go! Office allows you to perform Business Intelligence (BI) analytical actions in Microsoft Excel. You can access dimensionally modeled data or cubes from your Cognos 8 installation and work on them in Excel as though the application were a slicer and dicer for data. With Cognos 8 Go! Office, you can create an exploration or a cell-based analysis. An *exploration* provides a crosstab and tools similar to those used in Analysis Studio, but it also somewhat restricts the way in which you can create an analysis. A *cell-based analysis* requires that you have a little more knowledge of your data, but it lets you create a more customized analysis.

Access BI Analysis in Excel

Whether you want to use Go! Office to create an exploration or a cell-based analysis, the steps are the same.

Here's how to access BI analysis in Excel:

1. Launch Excel, which displays the Cognos 8 toolbar.

2. From the Cognos 8 toolbar, click Cognos 8. Excel activates the toolbar and displays the Cognos 8 for Office task pane:

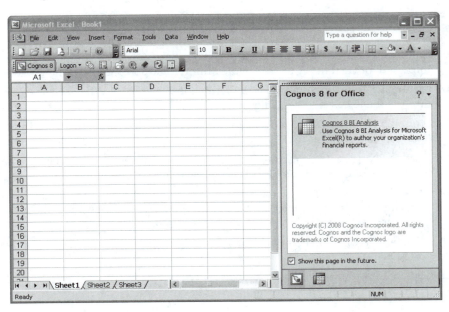

3. From the Cognos 8 for Office task pane, click Cognos 8 BI Analysis. The Cognos 8 BI Analysis task pane displays, as shown next:

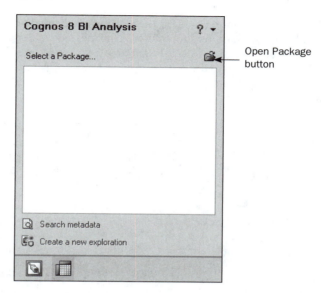

4. From the Cognos 8 BI Analysis task pane, click the Open Package button. The Select Package dialog displays with two options of folders in which to retrieve the package, Public Folders or My Folders, or you can choose from recently used packages:

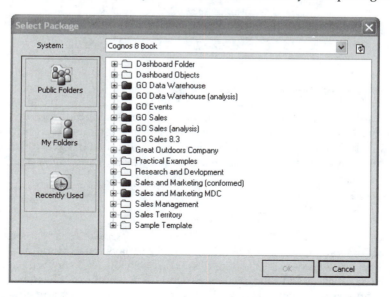

5. Navigate to the folder containing the package to which you would like to analyze in Excel.

NOTE *You must select a dimensionally modeled relational data source or OLAP cube to use BI Analysis.*

6. Click OK. The Source tree for the selected package displays in the Cognos 8 BI Analysis task pane, as shown next. Your next steps depend on whether you want to create an exploration or cell-based analysis. For more information on creating an exploration, refer to the "Create an Exploration" section. For more information on creating a cell-based analysis, refer to the "Create a Cell-based Analysis" section a little later in this chapter.

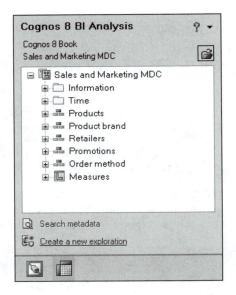

Create an Exploration

An exploration lets you create an analysis in Excel where you are able to interact with data in a way similar to how you interact with data in Analysis Studio. You can drill-through data, suppress zeros, and nest items. You can perform these functions with data that is pulled directly from Cognos 8. You can also convert this data in Excel formulas, which lets you use the tools available in that application. All these features make creating an exploration a great way to develop financial reports.

Here's how to create an exploration:

1. Access Cognos 8 BI Analysis in Excel.

2. From the Cognos 8 BI Analysis task pane, click Create A New Exploration. Cognos 8 BI Analysis creates a new worksheet and displays the exploration toolbar, overview area, and work area, as shown next. The overview area shows a list of items that have been added to the exploration and the functions that have been applied (such as zero suppression). The work area contains a crosstab where you can drag-and-drop items from the Source tree to create the exploration. The crosstab has a

Measure section, Columns section, and Rows section, in which you can drag-and-drop items from the Source tree:

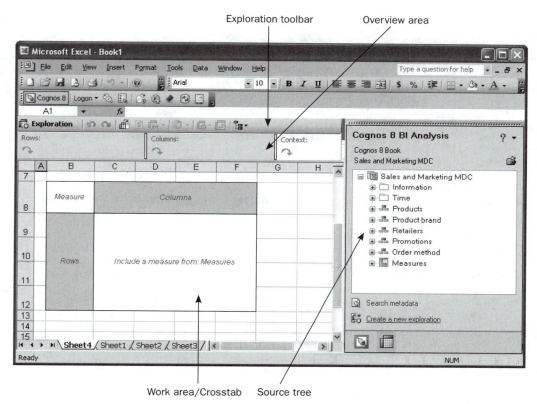

Exploration toolbar   Overview area

Work area/Crosstab   Source tree

3. Add an item(s) to the Columns section from the Source tree. Cognos 8 BI Analysis adds the selected item(s) as columns in the crosstab.

4. Add an item(s) to the Rows section from the Source tree to create your rows. Cognos 8 BI Analysis adds the selected item(s) as rows in the crosstab.

NOTE   *You can also drag-and-drop items from the Source tree into the overview area for the Rows and Columns.*

5. Add a measure(s) to the Measure section from the Source tree. Cognos 8 BI Analysis adds the selected measure to the crosstab and creates a subtotal column and row for the selected items added to the crosstab. In the example shown next, we added Time to the Columns section, Products to the Rows section, and Revenue to the Measure section. As you add items to crosstab, lists are added to the overview area, and you can use these lists to drill-through data and apply filters. Your next steps

depend on what you want to do with your data. The following steps highlight some common functions that people use with their data.

	Revenue	2004	2005	2006	2007	Time
9	Camping Equipment	356,295,381.72	430,950,603.29	535,409,192.43	377,614,053.07	1,700,269,230.51
10	Personal Accessories	419,062,390.16	488,265,990.81	635,590,067.01	474,751,991.34	2,017,670,439.32
11	Outdoor Protection	38,697,107.54	26,759,174.27	11,073,618.15		81,313,896.99
12	Golf Equipment	164,302,620.55	179,766,876.96	246,217,989.49	186,972,676.64	777,260,163.64
13	Mountaineering Equipment		114,596,636.14	172,312,610.89	151,427,095.18	438,336,342.20
14	Products	978,357,499.98	1,240,339,281.47	1,600,603,477.96	1,195,549,813.25	5,014,850,072.67

Rows: Products   Columns: Time   Context:

6. Optionally, drill-through your data to see what is above or below a selected item. Double-click a cell at the top of a column, far left of a row, or at the intersection of a column and row to drill-down.

7. Double-click a subtotal to drill-up.

NOTE *As an alternative, you can use the lists from the overview area to drill-down or drill-up.*

8. To nest an item, select an item from the Source tree and drag that item in the work area. Cognos 8 BI Analysis nests the item in the crosstab. In the next example, we drilled-through Camping Equipment to get to the TrailChef Water Bag and nested the heading "Order method." The results show which sales method generated what revenue for all TrailChef Water Bags that were ordered from 2004 through 2007:

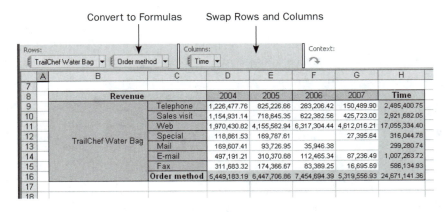

Convert to Formulas   Swap Rows and Columns

Rows: TrailChef Water Bag | Order method   Columns: Time   Context:

		Revenue	2004	2005	2006	2007	Time
9		Telephone	1,226,477.76	825,226.66	283,206.42	150,489.90	2,485,400.75
10		Sales visit	1,154,931.14	718,645.35	622,382.56	425,723.00	2,921,682.05
11		Web	1,970,430.82	4,155,582.94	6,317,304.44	4,612,016.21	17,055,334.40
12	TrailChef Water Bag	Special	118,861.53	169,787.61		27,395.64	316,044.78
13		Mail	169,607.41	93,726.95	35,946.38		299,280.74
14		E-mail	497,191.21	310,370.68	112,465.34	87,236.49	1,007,263.72
15		Fax	311,683.32	174,366.67	83,389.25	16,695.69	586,134.93
16		Order method	5,449,183.19	6,447,706.86	7,454,694.39	5,319,556.93	24,671,141.36

9. To swap the positioning of your rows and columns, from the exploration toolbar, click Swap Rows and Columns. Cognos BI Analysis swaps your rows and columns.

10. You also have the option of converting your Cognos 8 data to Microsoft Excel formulas. From the exploration toolbar, click Convert to Formulas. By default, the data in your crosstab is pulled from Cognos 8. Cognos 8 BI Analysis breaks the link between your exploration and Cognos 8 and converts the data in your crosstab to formulas to which you can apply standard Excel formatting.

NOTE *If you choose Convert to Formulas, you will no longer be able to drag-and-drop items from the Source tree for this particular exploration.*

11. To create a filter, drag-and-drop an item from the Source tree into the Context section of the overview area. For example, you can drag-and-drop the name of a specific country (United States) into the Context section and the crosstab displays only the items that were sold in the United States.

12. To suppress zeros, on the exploration toolbar click the suppression button and from the suppression list, choose one of the following: No Suppression, Apply To Rows Only, Apply To Columns Only, or Apply To Rows And Columns. Suppression removes empty cells that do not contain data:

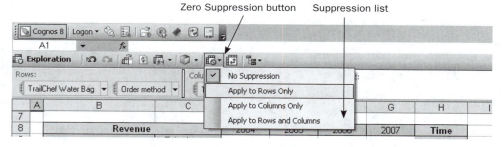

Also, a suppression icon displays in the overview region for the appropriate tag:

13. You can open your exploration in either Analysis Studio or Report Studio. From the exploration toolbar, from the Open Report in Analysis Studio button, click Analysis Studio or Report Studio. Cognos 8 prompts you for your login and launches the studio, provided you have access to the selected studio. You can use all of the tools available in the selected studio to work with your data:

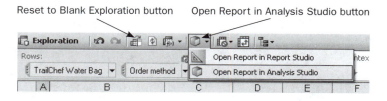

14. From the Excel toolbar, click Save. Excel saves the exploration. You can publish the exploration to Cognos 8. For more information on publishing to Cognos 8, refer to the "Publish Microsoft Office Documents in Cognos 8" section later in this chapter.

15. Optionally, from the exploration toolbar, click Reset to Blank Exploration to clear your work area and start over.

Create a Cell-Based Analysis

Like an exploration analysis, the cell-based analysis lets you interact with your data from Cognos 8. However, the cell-based analysis lets you use specific items from the Source tree to build a highly customized analysis without the use of a crosstab. You can drill-through your data, and use all the tools available in Excel or you can compare two data sources side by side in the same worksheet. Once you created your cell-based analysis, you can convert it to an exploration.

Here's how to create a cell-based analysis:

1. Access Cognos 8 BI Analysis in Excel. The Cognos 8 toolbar and work area display, as shown next. The work area provides space for you to drag items from the Source tree to create your analysis. For more information, refer to the "Access BI Analysis in Excel" section of this chapter.

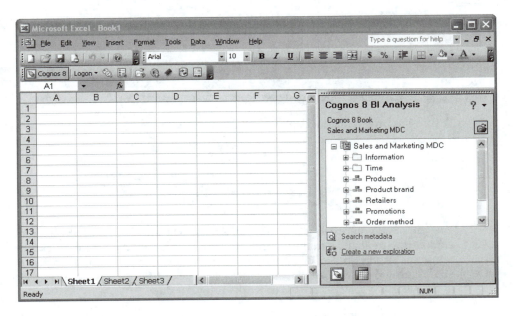

2. Add items for the column(s) from the Source tree. Drag your selections to the work area and then press and hold down the CTRL key as you drag your selections into place. Pressing CTRL while dragging selections over the work area flips selections from rows to columns. Cognos 8 BI Analysis adds the item(s) as column(s) in your analysis.

TIP *To select noncontiguous items, press and hold down the CTRL key while selecting items from the Source tree.*

3. Add item(s) for the row(s) from the Source tree. Make selections from the Source tree and then drag your selections to the work area. Go! Office adds the item as a row in your analysis.

4. Add a measure from the Source tree by dragging an item to the intersection cell directly to the left of your column header and directly above your rows. Cognos 8 BI Analysis processes the data from Cognos 8 and displays your analysis, as shown next:

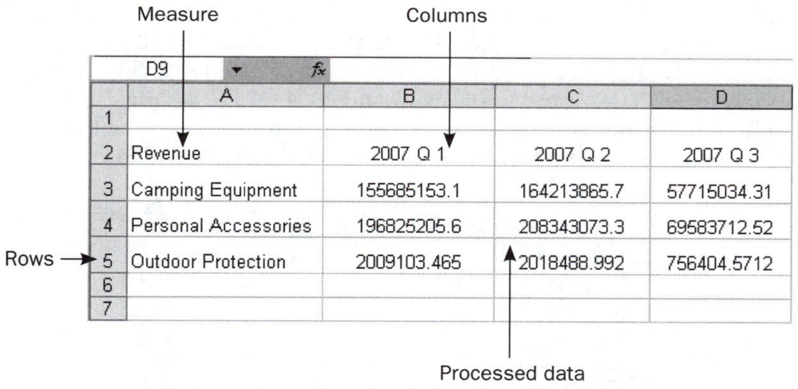

Measure		Columns	

	A	B	C	D
1				
2	Revenue	2007 Q 1	2007 Q 2	2007 Q 3
3	Camping Equipment	155685153.1	164213865.7	57715034.31
4	Personal Accessories	196825205.6	208343073.3	69583712.52
5	Outdoor Protection	2009103.465	2018488.992	756404.5712
6				
7				

Rows → 5

Processed data

5. Optionally, expand an item to show the components of that item. You can expand an item left, right, up, or down. Right-click the cell containing the item to be expanded. In the context menu that appears, choose Cognos 8 BI Analysis | Expand. An expand submenu displays. Cognos 8 BI Analysis inserts the components of the item based on your selection. Expand Left inserts the components to the left of the selected item. Expand Right inserts the components to the right of the selected item. Expand Up inserts the components above the selected item. Expand Down inserts the components

below the selected item. The following illustration shows the results of expanding the Camping Equipment item down:

	A	B	C	D
1				
2	Revenue	2007 Q 1	2007 Q 2	2007 Q 3
3	Camping Equipment	155685153.1	164213865.7	57715034.31
4	Cooking Gear	26816616.67	26320725.78	9258423.925
5	Tents	50322629.32	54647244.74	17731572.28
6	Sleeping Bags	30023125.46	31122530.57	12395452.71
7	Packs	35864569.95	39272641.14	13841631.7
8	Lanterns	12658211.68	12850723.45	4487953.698
9	Personal Accessories	196825205.6	208343073.3	69583712.52
10	Outdoor Protection	2009103.465	2018488.992	756404.5712
11				

6. Optionally, you can drill-through your data to see what is above or below a selected item from a cell containing a number value, right-click in the cell, and from the context menu choose Cognos 8 BI Analysis | Drill. A Drill dialog displays with the detailed data that lies below the item in the selected cell. For example, if you had an analysis with Camping Equipment and 2004 for the year and you selected to drill-down in the intersecting cell of the two, you would see all of the items under Camping Equipment broken down by quarter, as shown here:

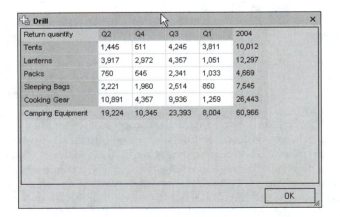

7. Optionally, open a new data source to compare data from different data sources on the same analysis. From the Cognos 8 BI Analysis task pane, click Select A Package. The Select Package dialog displays.

8. Navigate to the folder containing the package to which you would like to analyze in Microsoft Excel.

9. Click OK. The data source replaces the former Source tree with one for the selected data source.

10. Drag items in the same way that you did for steps 2 through 4. Cognos 8 BI Analysis creates the analysis in the same worksheet, using two different data sources.

11. Optionally, insert Excel formulas to compare the data from the two analyses.

12. From the Microsoft Excel toolbar, click Save. Excel saves the exploration. You can publish the exploration to Cognos 8. For more information on publishing to Cognos 8, refer to the "Publish Microsoft Office Documents in Cognos 8" section of this chapter

13. To view the analysis as an exploration, right-click in the cell containing the information for which you would like to create the exploration, choose Cognos BI Analysis | Explore. Cognos 8 BI Analysis creates an exploration in a new Excel worksheet, as shown next. From here, you can work with the data as needed. For more information on explorations, refer to the "Create an Exploration" section earlier in this chapter. The original analysis is still available from the worksheet on which it was created.

Rows: Camping Equipment		Columns: 2007 Q 1			Context:
	B	**C**	**D**	**E**	**F**
7					
8	**Revenue**	2007/Jan	2007/Feb	2007/Mar	**2007 Q 1**
9	Cooking Gear	8,322,969.99	8,866,544.58	9,627,102.10	26,816,616.67
10	Tents	15,215,080.31	16,201,994.76	18,905,554.25	50,322,629.32
11	Sleeping Bags	9,115,382.15	9,695,430.99	11,212,312.32	30,023,125.46
12	Packs	10,555,770.78	11,529,596.41	13,779,202.75	35,864,569.95
13	Lanterns	3,840,941.16	4,186,208.06	4,631,062.45	12,658,211.68
14	**Camping Equipment**	47,050,144.40	50,479,774.80	58,155,233.87	155,685,153.07
15					

Publish Microsoft Office Documents in Cognos 8

When you publish Office documents in Cognos 8, you are actually exporting your files. This allows you to share Office documents through Cognos Connection in either Public Folders or My Folders. For example, suppose you create a presentation for a monthly sales meeting with your colleagues and supervisors, and your supervisor wants to use that same presentation for a monthly meeting with the board. Rather than e-mailing him the presentation every month, you can publish it to Cognos Connection and he will know where to find it.

Here's how to publish Microsoft Office documents in Cognos 8:

1. Launch the Office application for the type of document that you want to export to Cognos 8.

2. Open the document to be exported.

3. From the Cognos 8 toolbar, click Cognos 8. The Office application activates the toolbar and displays the Cognos 8 Go! Office task pane.

4. From the Cognos 8 toolbar, click Publish. The Publish screen displays with the name of the document in the Name text box:

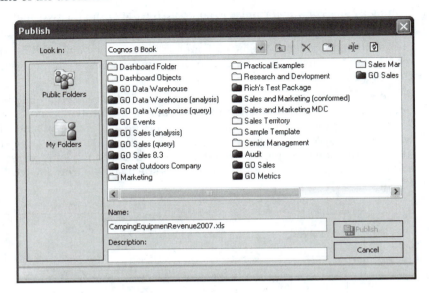

5. Navigate to the location in which you would like to save the Office document.

6. Optionally, in the Name text box, change the name of the document.

NOTE *If you change the name of the document, be sure that you include the period and file extension in the new name. For example, if you change the name of the document from Top Ten Sales Reps in Word.doc to Top Ten.doc, be sure to include the .doc file extension.*

---

7. Optionally, in the Description text box, enter a description for the document.

8. Click Publish. Go! Office exports the document to the selected location in Cognos Connection, as shown next. Other Cognos 8 users with access to the folder in which you saved the document and with the appropriate Office application installed on their computer can now access the document through Cognos Connection.

Refresh Cognos 8 Content in Microsoft Office

You have successfully imported all the Cognos 8 data that you need for your Office documents, or you have created an analysis using BI Analysis for Microsoft Excel for this month. Now, the next month comes and goes and it is time for you to give your presentation or share your analysis. Go! Office makes refreshing that data simple and easy. As with the other functions mentioned throughout this chapter, the steps to refresh your Cognos 8 content are the same for all three applications.

Here's how to refresh Cognos 8 content in Microsoft Office:

1. Launch the Office application in which you want to refresh your Cognos 8 content. The Cognos 8 toolbar displays.

2. Open the Office document.

3. From the Cognos 8 toolbar, click Cognos 8. The Office application activates the toolbar and displays the Cognos 8 Go! Office task pane.

4. From the Cognos 8 toolbar, click Refresh. Go! Office updates the data in your document to reflect your current Cognos 8 content. Your Office document is ready to be shared in less than a minute.

5. Save the document in the appropriate format for the Office application that you are using.

Using IBM Cognos 8 Go! Search

IBM Cognos 8 Go! Search allows users to use a single search engine for all their search needs. Go! Search enhances the search capabilities of Cognos Connection and can be easily integrated with third-party enterprise search engines such as Autonomy IDOL Server or Google OneBox for Enterprise, or third-party portals such as IBM WebSphere or Plumtree. On top of all of this, search results from Go! Search shows users only the content they have permission to view in Cognos Connection. So Dan's search results display only the reports that Dan has permission to see, Sue can only see Sue's reports, and so on.

What kind of robust search capabilities does Go! Search provide to its users? Instead of just looking at titles, as you can with some search engines, Go! Search looks at every bit of content in the document. This expands the search results, so that a user who does not remember the exact name of a document but knows some keywords in the document can now access the elusive document.

The most common use for Go! Search is within Cognos Connection, and this focuses on that function. To find out more about integrating Go! Search with your enterprise search engine or portal, contact your IBM Cognos 8 representative.

Create a Search Index

Creating a search index indexes all of the content in Cognos 8. The index is easy to create and enables Go! Search to perform in-depth searches of the title, body, and description of your Cognos 8 content.

Here's how to create a search index:

1. In Cognos Connection, choose Launch | Cognos Administration.

2. Click the Configuration tab, and then click Content Administration from the menu. Content Administration displays with toolbar options at the top-right of the screen and a list of entries in the middle of the screen:

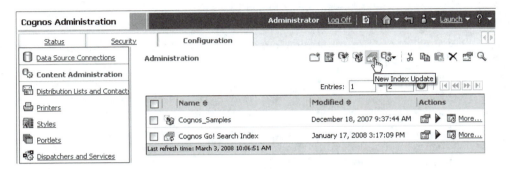

3. From the toolbar, click New Index Update. The New Index Update Wizard launches and displays the Specify A Name And Description screen:

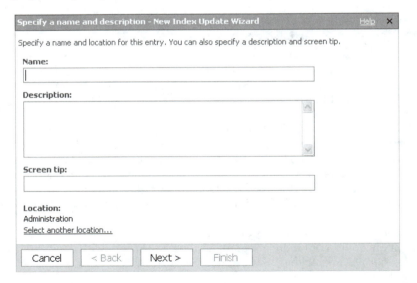

4. In the Name text box, enter the name by which to reference your index update.

5. Optionally, in the Description text box, enter a description of the index update.

6. Optionally, in the Screen Tip text box, enter a ScreenTip that displays when the user moves the pointer over the index update.

7. Optionally, click Select Another Location to designate a new location in which to save the index update. By default, Cognos 8 saves the index update in Public Folders.

8. Click Next. The Select An Action screen displays with options to Save And Run Once, Save And Schedule, and Save Only, as shown next. The latter option saves only the index update job, does not create an index of your content, and requires that you go back and either run the job or create a schedule for the job at a later time. If you are ready to create the index, choosing the Save And Run Once or Save And Schedule option is better. We recommend that you Save And Schedule the index update because you are indexing all of your content, and it may take some time to create the index update and create a drain on system resources. Additionally, creating a schedule that repeats now helps to ensure that the index updates periodically to include new content.

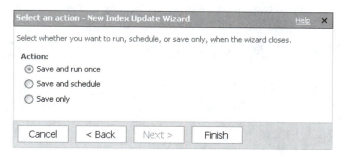

9. Select the desired save option and then click Finish. Content Administration displays and the index update is added to the list of entries:

NOTE *If you did select only to save the job, do not forget either to run or schedule the index update.*

10. Optionally, from the Actions column, click the More link to view the run history of the index update to confirm that the job was successful. The Perform An Action screen displays with the Available Actions area.

11. Under Available Actions, click View Run History. The View Run History screen displays the Request Time, Start Time, Completion Time, and Status for the index job.

12. Click Close. Content Administration displays. When the index has updated, Go! Search is ready to be used within Cognos Connection and Content Administration.

NOTE *If you did not create a repeating schedule for the index, it is a good idea to do so as soon as possible to ensure that the index is updated periodically to include new content.*

Access Search Mode

Creating a search using Go! Search is no different from using any other search engine. However, there is an enormous difference in the quality of the search results. Because an index of your Cognos 8 content was created, Go! Search performs an in-depth search, not the cursory search you get with some search engines. For example, if you search for the word *Sales*, Go! Search looks at the title, body, and description and returns all of the content with the word *Sales* in any or all of those fields.

Here's how to perform a search using Go! Search:

1. Launch Cognos Connection.

2. In the Search text box, shown next, enter the item for which you want to search:

Search text box

3. Click Search. Cognos 8, by default, uses the newly created index and displays the search results and relevancy ranking. The results include all instances of the search value within the document including the name, heading, and body of all content included in the search index, as shown next:

Refine By pane   Advanced options link   New Search link

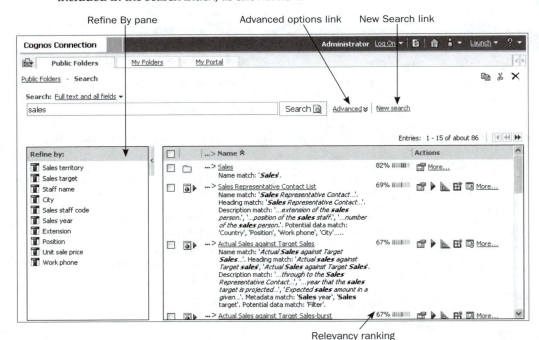

Relevancy ranking

The Search screen also includes the following search features:

- **Search Options drop-down**   Contains a list from which you can select to refine your search. The options are Full Text And All Fields, Name Field, Description Field, and Name Or Description Fields.

- **Refine By pane**   Contains a list of report fields that can be included in the search results. Move the pointer over the icon of one of the report fields to display the item description from the Framework Manager model and the metadata source.

- **Advanced options link**   Displays a list from which you can select a specific type of content in which to search (such as an Agent, Query, or Metric).

- **New Search link**   Starts a brand new search.

4. Optionally, from the Refine By pane, select an item to narrow your search further to include content from the initial search value and an item from the tree. The results of the search display:

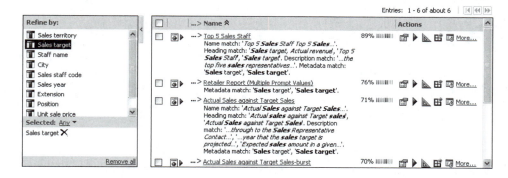

5. Optionally, click Advanced from the Search screen. The Type list displays with various types of content on which you can narrow your search (such as a Query or Report):

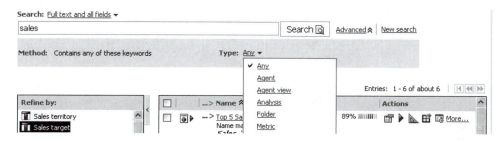

6. From the Type list, click the type of content on which to conduct the search. Cognos 8 narrows down the search results based on your selection.

7. Optionally, from the Search list, click an item that limits the search to the selected item. Cognos 8 narrows down the search results based on your selection.

8. Optionally, click New Search to begin a fresh search.

Using IBM Cognos 8 Go! Mobile

IBM Cognos 8 Go! Mobile provides the ultimate access to your Cognos 8 reports and analyses. You can view your content anywhere your Blackberry mobile device has service. Instead of having to wait in the office for that report to finish running, you can have it pushed to your Blackberry. You can be on time for that business meeting and ready to share up-to-date data with a client while your competitor is rummaging through his stack of papers.

How do you get this kind of mobility for Cognos 8 content? Your administrator needs to install Go! Mobile in addition to the Cognos 8 installation. The Go! Mobile rich client components need to be installed on your Blackberry as well. For more information on both installations, refer to the *IBM Cognos 8 Go! Mobile Installation and Administration Guide*.

Once the installation is complete, your administrator can set up schedules so that you receive the reports or analyses that you want, when you want. Don't worry about your data if your Blackberry is lost or stolen, because your administrator can pull back the content stored on your Blackberry or set up expiration dates so that the content is deleted at specific dates and times.

Authoring IBM Cognos 8 Business Intelligence Content

CHAPTER 8

Self-Service Query Authoring

Query Studio is a simple query authoring interface designed for business people who know their business, but don't know how or have the time to write complex reports. Using Query Studio, you can retrieve data from a source and put it into query format. After you create queries, Query Studio provides the tools you need to dress up the query using the same type of formatting tools you would use in any of the Microsoft Office products. Finally, you can share queries with licensed Cognos 8 users such as management, co-workers, colleagues, and investors who have access to Cognos Connection.

Throughout this chapter, you will see different features from the Query Studio menu and toolbars. Most of the options available in the menu are also available as icons from the toolbars at the top of the work area. As you become more familiar with Query Studio, you may decide that it is just as easy to access what you want by simply clicking one of these icons.

In this chapter, reports created in Query Studio are called *queries* for two reasons: to help you understand the ease with which you can create a report in Query Studio without thinking of it as a report, and to help you differentiate between reports created in Query Studio and those created in other studios. From this point forward in the book, you can think of everything created in Query Studio as a *query*.

About Query Studio

Query Studio allows a user with average computer skills to author ad hoc queries that provide answers to business questions. This section provides a brief introduction to Query Studio, the types of data available, and the way that data may be presented to you.

Types of Data

Query Studio can pull data from *relational* or *dimensional* data sources. The Cognos administrator determines whether the data that you see is from a relational or dimensional data source when he or she sets up your package in Cognos 8. Whether using relational and dimensional data, you create a query in the same way, enhance the query using the same features, and manage the query using the same tools. However, there are differences between relational and dimensional data. The icons are displayed differently for each type of data source, and the ability to drill-down or drill-up through the dimensions defined in the package is only available with a dimensional data source.

Icons

In Query Studio, the Menu displays on the left side of the screen with the Source tree of the selected data source in it, as shown next. You use the items in the Source tree to create queries, regardless of whether you are working with a relational or dimensional data source. The difference is in what the items in the Source tree are called.

Relational data sources consist of query subjects. Within each query subject lay query items and measures. Your relational data source may also include folders that group query items and measures. You use query items and measures to create a query.

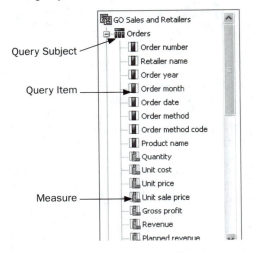

Dimensional data sources typically consist of multiple namespaces. Within each namespace are dimensions, measures, levels, and level attributes. All of the levels and level attributes are members that make up a dimension. You use levels, level attributes, and measures to create your query.

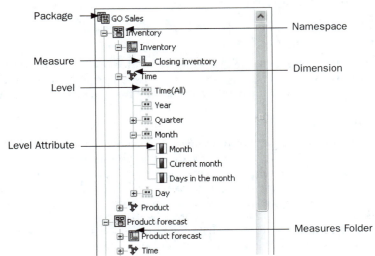

NOTE *When this chapter discusses creating a query, it refers to creating queries with query subjects, query items, and measures to simplify things a bit. For readers using dimensional data sources, a query subject is analogous to a level, a query item is analogous to a level attribute, and a measure is a measure regardless of the data source type.*

Drilling Capabilities

Drill-up and drill-down capability is available only when you are using dimensional data sources. Users can drill-down or drill-up the defined hierarchy. As mentioned, the icons in the Source tree for dimensional data sources display differently than the icons for relational data sources. The same is true for the items once they have been added to the query. Items from dimensional sources that have been added to the query are underlined and act as hyperlinks that you can use to drill-up or drill-down. This allows you to view all the members of a particular level.

Consider the following illustration, for example. Suppose you have a query containing the Product (All) level from the Product dimension. The Product (All) level contains Product Line, and underneath that is the Product Type. When you drill-down on Product (All), the query displays all of the Product Line items under Product (All). If you drill-down on one of the Product Line items, your query displays all of the Product Type items that are within that Product Line in the data source.

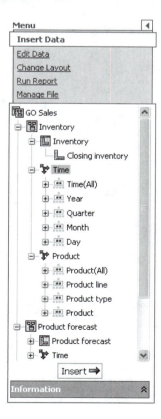

When you drill-up, you see the data of the level of which the selected item is a member. For example, when you drill-up on Product Type, the query displays the items of the level of which Product Type is a member, which is the Product Line level.

Data Views

When creating queries, the query in the work area can display with all of the data present, limited data present, or no data present. Your Cognos administrator determines the default view of the package. The data view being used can be modified by clicking the Run Report link in the Menu and choosing Run With All Data, Preview With Limited Data, or Preview With No Data from the options.

When Run With All Data is selected, the query displays with all of the data from the data source. This is useful in that all of the data is available for the selected Query Items and Measures. However, it can possibly be cumbersome as Query Studio is processing the data while you are creating the query.

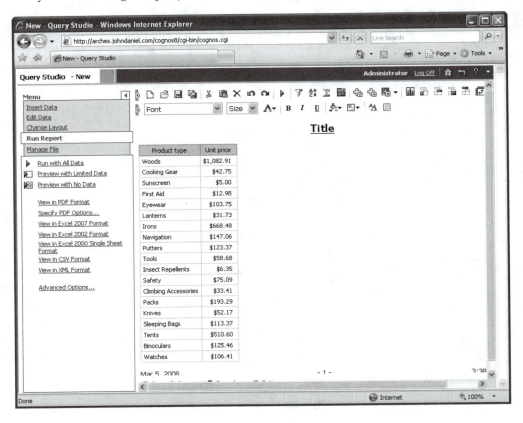

When Preview With Limited Data is selected, the query retrieves and displays only a portion of the data as defined in the package. With limited data retrieval, the data is processed faster. Query Studio indicates you are working with limited data by lining the top and bottom of the work area with a torn border labeled "Limited Data."

NOTE *The Preview With Limited Data option only retrieves limited data if design mode filters were set in Framework Manager.*

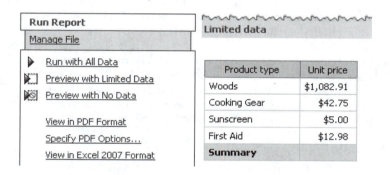

NOTE *Limited data paints only part of the picture and should not be used to make any business decisions.*

When Preview With No Data is selected, the query retrieves no data and displays generic placeholders instead of actual data. This data view is useful when you are making formatting changes or designing your report and do not want Query Studio to process data with every change you make. Query Studio indicates you are working with no data by lining the top and bottom of the work area with a torn border labeled "Data is turned off."

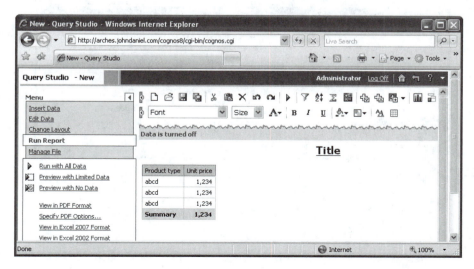

Create a Query

With Query Studio, you can author queries using different methods. You can highlight a query item or measure and click Insert, double-click a query item or measure, or you can drag a query item or measure to the work area. You can even drag a query subject into the query to view all query items and measures in that query subject. Additionally, Query Studio provides some easy-to-use tools that enable you to filter, sort, format, calculate, and group data. After you create the query, you can review the data prior to sharing the query. Once you have created the query and applied some initial enhancements, you can further enhance it in various ways, as discussed in the "Enhance a Query" section later in the chapter. Finally, your query is ready to be managed.

This section also discusses some of the features available once you have opened Query Studio, chosen your package, and added query items. The most commonly used features are discussed here. The features listed in this section only brush the surface of what you can do with Query Studio. After you have finished this section, refer to the "Enhance a Query" and "Manage a Query" sections for even more features available in Query Studio. Consider this section somewhat of a "quick start" for creating a query in Query Studio.

Open Query Studio

Query Studio launches in the same web browser as Cognos Connection so that you do not have to jump back and forth between pages or tabs. Everything that you need to run Query Studio is on the same page.

Here's how to open Query Studio:

1. Log in to Cognos Connection. If the Welcome screen displays, click Cognos content.

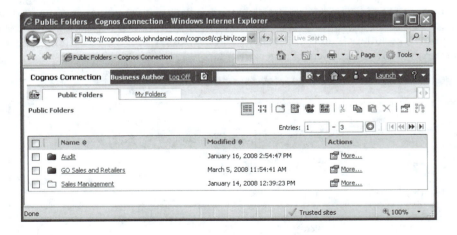

2. From the Launch menu located in the upper right of the screen, click Query Studio. The Select a Package screen displays.

3. Click on a package link.

   The Query Studio screen displays, as shown next. You are ready to begin developing queries.

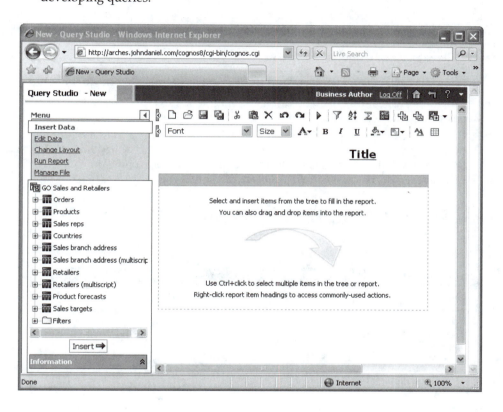

Add Query Items

You have launched Query Studio and selected a package. Your next step is to add query items and measures to the work area to create your query.

NOTE *Query items that have been added to your query are referred to as* report items *in the Cognos User Guide. To keep the query theme running throughout this chapter, we refer to items that have been added to the query as* query items.

Here's how to create a query:

1. From the Insert Data menu, expand a query subject to display the query items, measures, and folders associated with that subject.

2. Select a query item or measure and drag the item to the work area.

3. Continue to add any query items or measures to your query. In this example, we have added the Product Line query item from the Products query subject of the Go Sales and Retailers package. We have also inserted the Revenue and Gross Profit measures from the Orders query subject.

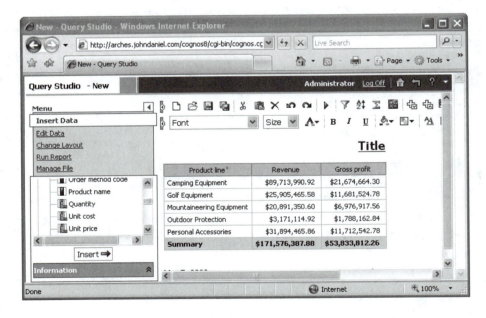

NOTE *Query Studio has an Auto-Aggregation feature. As you add query items and measures to the query, Query Studio aggregates the measure as defined by the Cognos 8 administrator and adds a summary line. As more detailed query items are added, the aggregation of the measure adjusts to the lowest level of detail in the query.*

A query has been created and can be shared in its current form.

Move Columns

You can rearrange the order of the query items in your query. Rearranging may be necessary if you need to change the order in which your data displays in the query.

Here's how to move a column:

1. Highlight the column to be moved. Using the query from the previous illustration, we want to move the Gross Profit column to the left of the Revenue column. We highlight the Gross Profit column.

2. From the standard toolbar, click Cut.

3. Highlight the column to the right of where you want the column to appear. We highlight the Revenue column.

4. From the standard toolbar, click Paste. Query Studio inserts the column.

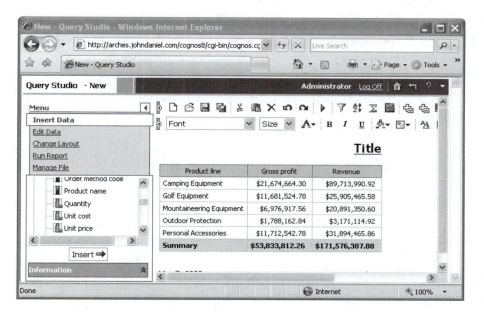

Filter Data

The query you created could be pulling more data from the data source than necessary. For the purposes of your query, you may not need or want to display all of that data. A filter allows you to establish criteria for the data to be displayed. Only data meeting the criteria displays in the query. You can create your own filter or use predefined filters.

Create a Filter

Creating a filter in Query Studio can be accomplished with a few clicks of the mouse. Query Studio requires that the query item(s) or measure(s) on which you want to filter are visible in the query before you can apply the filter. For example, if you want to filter on the Product Type, that query item must be included in the query. Once you apply the filter, you can remove that particular query item or measure from the query and the filter remains intact.

You can filter on query items or measures. Both of these processes are discussed in this section.

Apply a Filter to a Query Item

Applying a filter to a query item allows you to filter out data that you do not want to display in your query.

Here's how to create a filter for a query item:

1. Highlight the column containing the value to be filtered. We select the Product Line column in a query that contains the Product Line query item from the Products query subject and the Revenue measure from the Orders query subject of the Go Sales and Retailers package.

2. From the Edit Data menu, click the Filter link. The Filter pane displays with options for the filter:

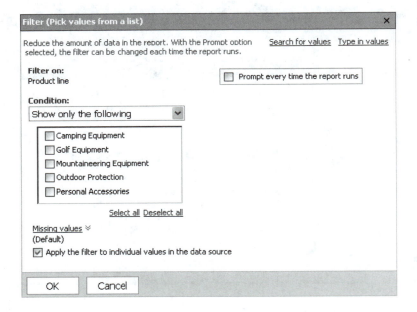

3. From the Condition drop-down list, select the condition by which the filter is to be applied. For this example, we select Show Only The Following.

4. Select the checkbox(es) for the item(s) for which to apply the filter. In addition, you can select filter items in two optional ways: You can click the Search For Values link to search for filter values using keywords, or you can click the Type In Values link to define a specific filter value. For this example, we select Camping and Golf Equipment.

5. Optionally, select the Prompt Every Time The Report Runs checkbox to prompt users to choose the item(s) for which the filter applies every time the report is run.

6. Click the Missing Values link to display a list of options that determine how the filter handles any data that is missing. Choose to Include Missing Values, Leave Out Missing Values, and Show Only Missing Values by clicking the appropriate checkbox.

7. Click OK to apply the filter. Query Studio applies the filter and displays an icon with the name of the filter above the query.

Product line: Camping Equipment, Golf Equipment

Product line	Revenue
Camping Equipment	$89,713,990.92
Golf Equipment	$25,905,465.58
Summary	**$115,619,456.50**

Query Studio requires that the query item on which you are applying the filter be present in the query while creating the filter. In some cases, you may not want that query item to be included in the final query. Query Studio allows you to remove that item and still retain the filter.

8. Optionally, remove the column containing the query item on which the filter is based. Highlight the column and then click the Delete button on the standard toolbar. A Delete dialog box displays to let you know there is a filter associated with the item.

9. To keep the filter and remove the query item, clear the checkbox and then click OK.

TIP *If you use or plan to use a filter on a regular basis, ask your Cognos administrator to add the filter to your package.*

Apply a Filter to a Measure

As with applying a filter to a query item, applying a filter to a measure filters out data you do not want to display in the query. Also, when filtering on a measure, you can apply the filter to the details, summaries, or individual values of the measure.

Here's how to create a filter for a measure:

1. Highlight the column containing the measure to be filtered. We select the Revenue column in a query that contains the Product Line and Product Type query items from the Products query subject and the Revenue measure from the Orders query subject of the Go Sales and Retailers package. The Product Line query item is grouped in our query.

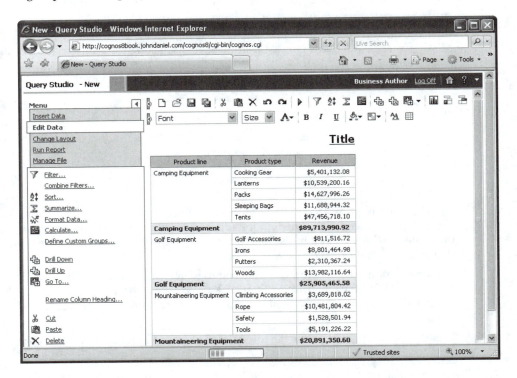

2. From the Edit Data menu, click the Filter link. The Filter pane displays with options for the filter:

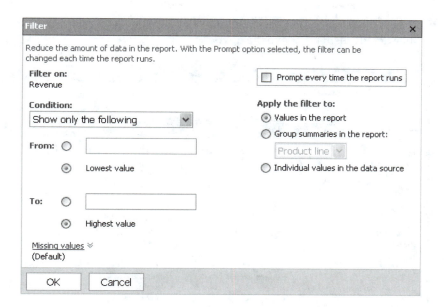

3. From the Condition drop-down list, select the condition by which the filter is to be applied. For this example, we select Show Only The Following.

4. In the From text box, enter a starting value on which to base your filter, or select the Lowest Value radio button. For this example, we enter the value 10000000.

5. In the To text box, enter an ending value on which to base your filter, or select the Highest Value radio button. For this example, we select the Highest Value option.

6. Optionally, select the Prompt Every Time The Report Runs checkbox to prompt users to choose the item(s) for which to apply the filter every time the report is run.

7. Click the Missing Values link to display a list of options that determine how the filter handles any data that is missing. Choose to Include Missing Values, Leave Out Missing Values, and Show Only Missing Values by clicking the appropriate checkbox.

8. Optionally, from the Apply The Filter To options, select to what values in the query to apply the filter. The Values In The Report option applies the filter only to the values that are currently displayed that you can see in your query. The Group Summaries In The Report option applies the filter to subtotal values displayed in the summary in your query. The Individual Values In The Data Source option applies the filter to the actual data rows found in the data source. Refer to next section for more details on the Apply The Filter To options. For this example, we select Values In The Report.

9. Click OK. The query displays with the filter applied and a filter icon displaying the filter details displays above the query.

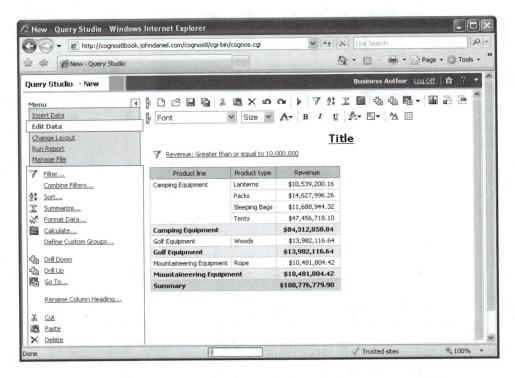

TIP   *To edit a filter that you have applied, click the name of the filter directly above the query. If you choose a filter from the Edit Data menu, Query Studio resets the Apply The Filter To option to Values In The Report.*

Query Studio requires that the measure on which you are applying the filter be present in the query while creating the filter. In some cases, you may not want that measure to be included in the final query. Query Studio allows you to remove that item and still retain the filter.

10. Optionally, remove the column containing the measure on which the filter is based. Highlight the column and then click the Delete button on the standard toolbar. A Delete dialog box displays to let you know there is a filter associated with the item.

11. To keep the filter and remove the query item, clear the checkbox and then click OK.

TIP   *If you use or plan to use a filter on a regular basis, ask your Cognos administrator to add the filter to your package.*

The following examples show how Query Studio handles the Apply The Filter To options. For these examples, our query contains the Product Line query item from the Products query subject and the Order Number query item and the Quantity measure from the Orders query subject of the Go Sales and Retailers package. The query is grouped on the Product Line query item, and we have already added a filter on the Order Number query item to limit the query to ten orders. We then add a second filter on the Quantity measure to show orders with quantities greater than 200 units to demonstrate the Apply The Filter To options. By default, Query Studio is set to automatically suppress duplicate entries in queries. (Refer to the "Modify Advanced Options" section for details on how to modify this option.) Because of this suppression, rows with duplicate order numbers are summarized into one row.

The next illustration shows the query before applying the second filter to the Quantity measure.

▼ Order number: Between 1,150 and 1,160

Product line	Order number	Quantity
Camping Equipment	1153	672
	1154	240
	1155	300
	1156	158
	1157	118
	1158	454
	1159	226
	1160	132
Camping Equipment		**2,300**
Outdoor Protection	1153	728
	1155	516
	1156	332
	1157	488
	1158	178
	1160	154
Outdoor Protection		**2,396**
Personal Accessories	1155	30
	1158	52
	1160	70
Personal Accessories		**152**
Summary		**4,848**

In the next illustration, the second filter has been added with the Values In The Report option selected. Notice that for Camping Equipment, Query Studio filtered out order numbers

1156, 1157, and 1160, and the summary total dropped from 2,300 to 1,892. The Values In The
Report option filtered on the summarized query data shown in the previous illustration.

| ▼ Order number: Between 1,150 and 1,160 |
| ▼ Quantity: Greater than or equal to 200 |

Product line	Order number	Quantity
Camping Equipment	1153	672
	1154	240
	1155	300
	1158	454
	1159	226
Camping Equipment		**1,892**
Outdoor Protection	1153	728
	1155	516
	1156	332
	1157	488
Outdoor Protection		**2,064**
Summary		**3,956**

In the next illustration, the filter has been modified so that the Group Summaries In The
Report option is selected. Notice that Personal Accessories is filtered out as it is the only
group with a summary less than 200.

| ▼ Order number: Between 1,150 and 1,160 |
| ▼ Quantity summary for Product line: Greater than or equal to 200 |

Product line	Order number	Quantity
Camping Equipment	1153	672
	1154	240
	1155	300
	1156	158
	1157	118
	1158	454
	1159	226
	1160	132
Camping Equipment		**2,300**
Outdoor Protection	1153	728
	1155	516
	1156	332
	1157	488
	1158	178
	1160	154
Outdoor Protection		**2,396**
Summary		**4,696**

In the next illustration, the filter has been modified so that the Individual Values In The
Data Source option is selected. Notice that for Camping Equipment, Query Studio filtered
out all order numbers with the exception of 1153 and the summary total dropped to 254.

The Individual Values In The Data Source option filtered on the non-summarized data from the data source.

▽ Order number: Between 1,150 and 1,160 AND Quantity: Greater than or equal to 200

Product line	Order number	Quantity
Camping Equipment	1153	254
Camping Equipment		**254**
Outdoor Protection	1153	728
	1155	376
Outdoor Protection		**1,104**
Summary		**1,358**

The next illustration shows the query with the automatic summarization of details and duplicate suppression disabled. This shows to which data Query Studio applies the filter when using the Individual Values In The Data Source option. Notice the duplicate entries for Order Number, and that only one entry under Quantity exceeds 200.

▽ Order number: Between 1,150 and 1,160

Product line	Order number	Quantity
Camping Equipment	1159	126
	1154	122
	1153	100
	1155	58
	1158	80
	1160	54
	1156	64
	1157	44
	1160	78
	1157	74
	1158	52
	1158	32
	1154	14
	1159	100
	1153	254
	1154	104

Apply a Predefined Filter

Using predefined filters from your package is a quick way to apply a filter that you use on a regular basis. There is no need to add the query item on which you are filtering to the query, create the filter, and then remove the query item. Additionally, using predefined filters ensures that you are filtering by the same criteria each time. Ask your Cognos administrator to add filters you use on a regular basis to your package.

Query Studio offers three ways to apply a predefined filter to your query. You can highlight the filter and click Insert, drag the filter into the query, or double-click the filter as discussed next.

Here's how to apply a predefined filter:

1. From the Source tree on the Insert Data menu, expand the Filters folder. A list of the available filters for the package displays, as shown here:

2. Double-click a filter to apply it to the query. Query Studio filters the data and displays a link to the filter above the query. In this example, we have applied the Americas filter to a query containing the Product Line query item from the Products query subject and the Revenue measure from the Orders query subject of the Go Sales and Retailers package.

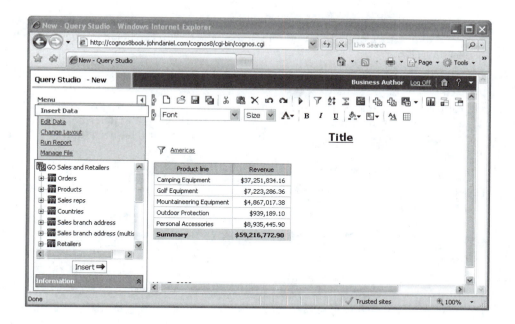

Sort Data

In Query Studio, you can sort the columns in a query alphabetically or numerically. You can select the column to be sorted and then click the Sort button on the standard toolbar. Query Studio sorts the column in ascending order the first time you click the Sort button, in descending order the second time, and removes the sort the third time you click the Sort button. Another way to sort data provides you with more specific control over how the data is sorted and is described here.

Here's how to sort data:

1. From the Edit Data menu, select Sort. The Sort pane displays at the bottom of the window:

2. Select Ascending or Descending and then click OK. Query Studio sorts the query A to Z, Z to A, 1 to 9, or 9 to 1 based on your selection. You can also remove sorting by selecting Don't Sort.

Group Data

You can group data so that a query displays similar items together. This proves useful when a query item is repeated row after row after row. You can group by that item making the query easier to consume. Grouping also inserts summary rows for the query item by which you are grouping.

Here's how to group data:

1. Highlight the column you want to group. In this example, we select the Product Line column.

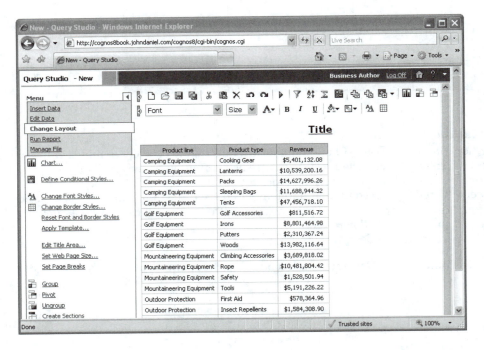

2. From the Change Layout menu, select Group. Query Studio groups the data in your query, and adds a summary line for each data grouping, as shown next. You can group multiple query items to organize your data further.

Product line	Product type	Revenue
Camping Equipment	Cooking Gear	$5,401,132.08
	Lanterns	$10,539,200.16
	Packs	$14,627,996.26
	Sleeping Bags	$11,688,944.32
	Tents	$47,456,718.10
Camping Equipment		**$89,713,990.92**
Golf Equipment	Golf Accessories	$811,516.72
	Irons	$8,801,464.98
	Putters	$2,310,367.24
	Woods	$13,982,116.64
Golf Equipment		**$25,905,465.58**
Mountaineering Equipment	Climbing Accessories	$3,689,818.02
	Rope	$10,481,804.42
	Safety	$1,528,501.94
	Tools	$5,191,226.22

Chart Data

Charts help you graphically visualize data that a query provides. Query Studio has bar, pie, line, column-line, area, and radar charts available for your use. Additionally, any charts you insert using Query Studio can be modified using Microsoft Excel.

Here's how to add a chart:

1. From the Change Layout menu, select Chart. The Chart pane displays with options for inserting a chart:

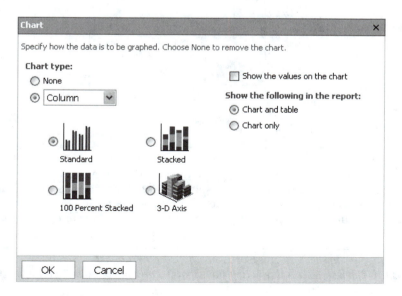

2. In the Chart Type list, select the type of chart to be inserted. Configurations for the selected chart type display. In this example, we choose Bar. Our query contains Product Line and Revenue from the Go Sales and Retailers package.

3. Click a chart configuration. In this example, we select standard.

4. Optionally, you can show the values on the chart by selecting the Show The Values On The Chart checkbox.

5. In the Show The Following In The Report region, click Chart And Table to display the chart and the table with the data, or click Chart Only to display only the chart.

6. Click OK. The chart displays.

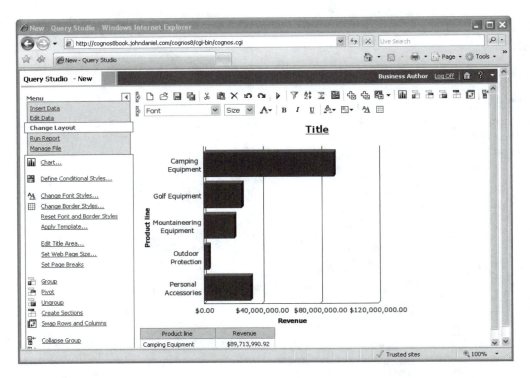

7. To export the chart to Excel, navigate to the Run Report menu. Options for running, viewing, and exporting your data display. Query Studio exports to three versions of Excel: 2007, 2002, and 2000. Click the appropriate link for the Excel format. A File Download dialog box opens and displays the option to save or open in Excel.

TIP *If you are using Internet Explorer 6 or 7, ensure that the Automatic Prompting For File Downloads is enabled. Access this option from Tools | Internet Options | Security | Custom Level | Downloads.*

You have created your query. What should you do next? Review your data. This is especially important if your Cognos administrator has set your default view with limited or no data present. You want to make sure that the data is displaying properly prior to sending it out for review by your colleagues.

TIP *If your Cognos administrator has set up your default view to display all of the data, you still want to review the data to ensure that your query is rendering the data properly.*

To review the data, select Run With All Data from the the Run Report menu. The query runs and populates the work area with the resulting data. If the displayed data is what you were aiming for, you can save or print your query. If the data does not quite look the way that you expected or wanted it to, you may need to revisit the portion of this section where you think things went wrong, or you can forge ahead to "Enhance a Query" or "Manage a Query." Perhaps the answers to your issues lie there.

Save a Query

You have completed all the basic steps for creating a query, and you certainly don't want to lose all of your hard work. You can save the query. The permissions you have been granted determine where you can save the query.

NOTE *You are not saving the resulting data of your query. To save the results you must export the results. For more information, refer to the "Export and View Queries" section later in this chapter.*

Here's how to save a query:

1. From the Manage File menu, choose Save As. The Save As pane displays.

2. In the Name text box, enter a name for your query.

3. Optionally, in the Description text box, provide a brief description of the query.

4. Optionally, in the Screen Tip text box, enter a screen tip that displays when you drag your mouse over the icon for your saved query.

5. Optionally, click Select Another Location to choose an alternative place in which to save your query. Location shows the path of where your query will be saved.

6. Click OK. Query Studio saves your query in the selected location.

Print Data

If the data in your query is accurate and it looks good, you are ready to print. You have several options for getting your query into printable format. You can print using the web browser, but this prints the whole screen as you see it and is therefore not as printer-friendly as other options. The most common way to print is to export to Excel or to PDF, as discussed next, and print in one of these formats.

Here's how to print your data in PDF:

1. From the Run Report menu, choose View In PDF Format. A new browser window opens and displays the query results.

2. Click Print. Your query results print and are ready to be shared with others.

Enhance a Query

The query you created is ready to be shared with your colleagues. It is a perfectly respectable looking query with some nice formatting, and most importantly, good data. However, Query Studio provides tools you can use to edit and refine the look of your data. You can also use these tools to make an average looking query red-carpet ready. You can change your formatting, apply a template, combine filters, summarize your data, create a crosstab, modify advanced options, and calculate data.

Format a Query

Query Studio provides several formatting tools that help you set the look of your query results apart from the crowd. You can change things like the appearance of fonts and numbers, the number of rows that display in the resulting data, and the title of the query, as well as add conditional styles and custom grouping.

Modify Font Appearance

Queries created in Query Studio have a default font as defined in the package. You can change the font of an individual query item or of multiple query items at one time. You can also apply numerous fonts to different items in the query.

Here's how to modify font appearance:

1. Select the item(s) for which you would like to change the font.

2. From the Change Layout menu, select Change Font Styles. The Change Font Styles pane displays at the bottom of the window with options to change the type of font

to be used along with the size, weight, color, effects, style, background color, and text alignment:

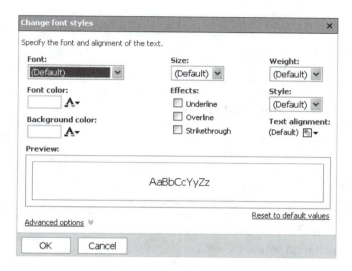

3. Make the desired changes to the font style. As you make changes to the font styles, your changes display in the Preview box.

4. Optionally, click Advanced Options for font style options, as shown next. Two options display: Apply Styles To The Current Selection applies your changes to the column or row in your query that is currently highlighted; Apply Styles Only To The Selections Below applies your changes to the specific categories selected.

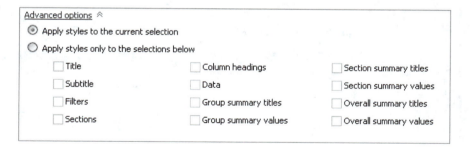

5. Optionally, click Reset To Default Values to restore font appearance back to the default settings.

6. Click OK. Query Studio modifies the font appearance.

Format Numbers

Query Studio displays number values based on the default setting as defined in the package. You can easily change how Query Studio displays number formats without changing the data so that they display as a number, currency, a percentage, or a scientific number.

Here's how to change the number appearance:

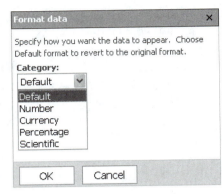

1. From the Edit Data menu, select Format Data. The Format Data pane showing the Category list displays, as shown here.

   Depending on which option you choose from the drop-down list, more options appear in the Format Data pane. For example, if you choose Currency, five additional lists display that include currency display options for the number of decimal places, the scale, multiple countries' currency, whether to display a negative sign or parenthesis for negative numbers, whether or not to use a thousands separator, and whether to display a currency symbol or international code.

2. Choose an item from the Category list and set the desired options from the lists that are available. The following examples show the available options that display as you select each of the available categories.

   This illustration shows the options for the Number category:

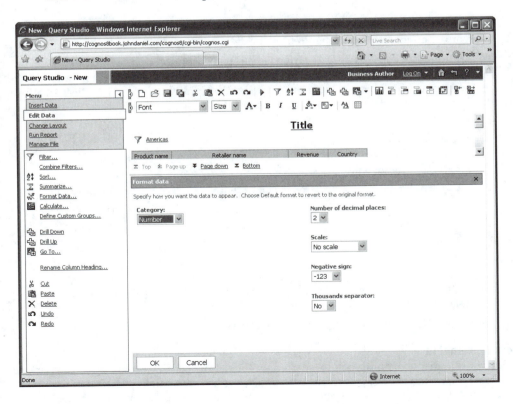

This illustration shows the options for the Currency category:

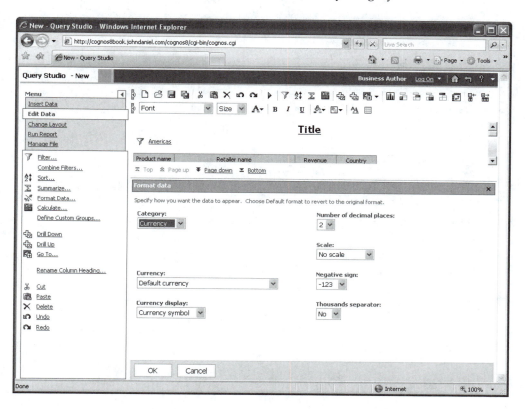

This illustration shows the options for the Percentage category:

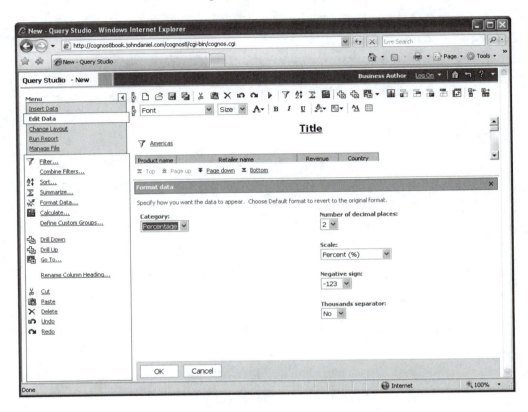

This illustration shows the options for the Scientific category:

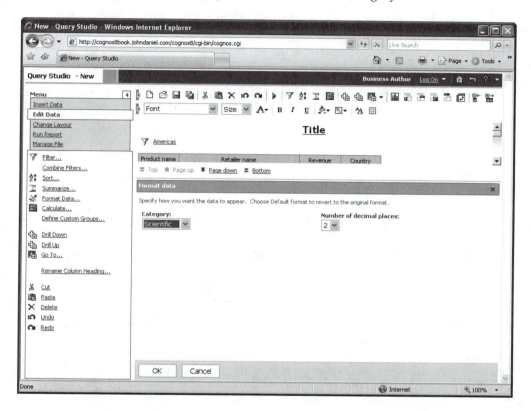

3. Click OK. Query Studio updates the format of your numbers accordingly.

Specify the Number of Rows per Page

By default, Query Studio displays 20 rows of data per page when you run your query. The number of rows that displays can be increased or decreased. Increasing the number of rows that displays reduces the amount of times that you have to page up or page down the query; however, it also increases the amount of data that Query Studio must retrieve to display the query results. Increasing the number of rows is helpful if you want to scroll through more of the query instead of paging up or down.

NOTE *This option does not affect the number of rows that displays when your query is printed.*

Here's how to change the number of rows:

1. From the Change Layout menu, select Set Web Page Size. The Set Web Page Size pane displays:

2. From the Number Of Rows list, select number of rows to be displayed in your web browser. The options range, in various increments, from 4 rows to 1000 rows.

3. Optionally, select the Show Row Numbers checkbox. When selected, this option assigns row numbers to the individual rows in the resulting data.

4. Click OK. Query Studio updates the number of rows displayed on the page.

Change the Title

When you create a Query Studio query, a default title of *Title* displays at the top of the query. For some users, this may be sufficient. Users who are going to be printing the resulting data might want to change the title or add a subtitle to the query. Additionally, you can choose whether or not to show what filters and sorts have been applied to the query.

Here's how to change the title:

1. From the Change Layout menu, select Edit Title Area. The Edit Title Area pane displays, as shown here:

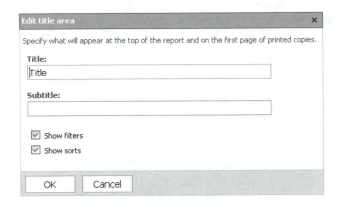

2. In the Title and Subtitle text boxes, enter the new title and optional subtitle.

3. Optionally, choose whether the query shows what filters and sorts have been applied to the query. A checkmark means that the filters or sorts will be displayed. If you choose not to show filters or sorts, this will not affect your query. The data will still maintain its filter or sort.

4. Click OK. Query Studio updates your query based on your entries.

Add Conditional Styles

Conditional styles enable the user to establish criteria on which Query Studio highlights (brings to the attention of readers) specified ranges or values. You can use conditional styles with numeric data, text data, and date values. You can establish range thresholds that require certain criteria to be met. If the data exceeds or falls short of the threshold, the query displays the resulting data in a specified color.

For example, suppose your query shows the revenue for all the product types your company has sold. You can set ranges that make sense for your business, such as revenue above 10,000,000 is excellent, revenue above 1,000,000 is average, and revenue below 1,000,000 is poor. Query Studio applies the conditional highlighting based on where your data falls within your thresholds. You can also add conditional styles to values. Conditional styles are added to query items and measures differently.

Here's how to add conditional styles:

1. Select the column for which you would like to apply conditional styles. For this example, we select the Revenue column in a query containing Product Line, Product Type and Revenue from the Go Sales and Retailers package.

2. From the Change Layout menu, select Define Conditional Styles. The Define Conditional Styles pane displays:

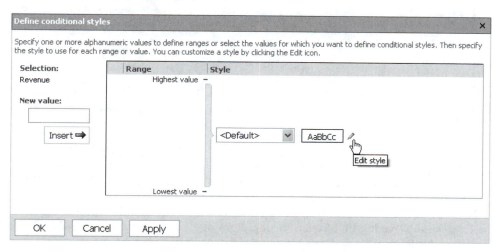

3. In the New Value text box, enter a value by which to establish the conditional highlighting and then click Insert. Query Studio adds the value to the Range column. For this example, we insert 10,000,000 as our first value.

4. From the Style list, select a style to apply to the range value. The available styles are Default, Excellent, Very Good, Average, Below Average, Poor, and Custom. All of the styles, with the exception of Custom, have defaults for the color and font style. For Custom, you establish the color and font style yourself. When data meets the established criteria, Query Studio styles the data accordingly. For this example, we select Excellent as the style for all values greater than or equal to 10,000,000.

5. Optionally, click the Edit Style button to edit the font style.

6. Optionally, to move the value above or below the threshold, click the arrow button that is next to the value. The threshold is the point at which the conditional highlight is applied. For this example, we move 10,000,000 above the threshold so that the condition for Excellent is "greater than or equal to 10,000,000" instead of "greater than 10,000,000."

7. Repeat steps 3 through 6 to add any values you would like. For this example, we add the value 1,000,000 and choose Average as the style for any values greater than or equal to 1,000,000 and less than 10,000,000 and Poor as the style for any values less than 1,000,000.

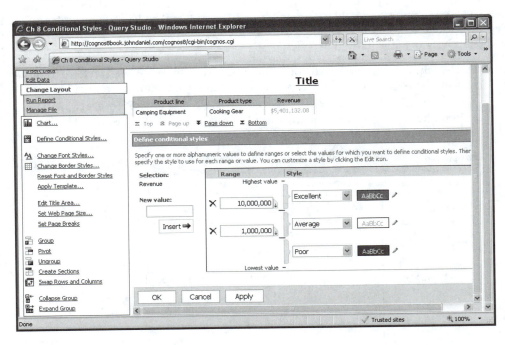

8. Optionally, click Apply to see a preview of how Query Studio applies the conditional highlighting. If the highlighting does not meet your needs, make the appropriate changes and then click Apply again.

9. Click OK. Query Studio applies the conditional highlighting.

Add Custom Grouping

Custom groups are a great way to create groupings that do not already exist in a query. You can group individual values together, or you can group values or measures that fall within a range. The values or measures that meet the established criteria are labeled with a group name or range name, respectively. Non-numeric items have the option of being grouped by defining individual values or a range, while numeric items can only be grouped by a range.

Customize Groups of Individual Values   You can group items based on individual values to see a total of that group. For example, you could group all of the countries in a query that are located in North America into one group. The resulting query displays the sum total of all the individual values under the North America grouping.

Here's how to create customized groups of individual values:

1. Highlight the column to which you want to add custom grouping. For this example, we highlight the Country column in a query containing the Product Line query item from the Products query subject, the Country query item from the Countries query subject and the Revenue measure from the Orders query subject of the Go Sales and Retailers package.

2. From the Edit Data menu, select Define Custom Groups. The Define Custom Groups screen displays:

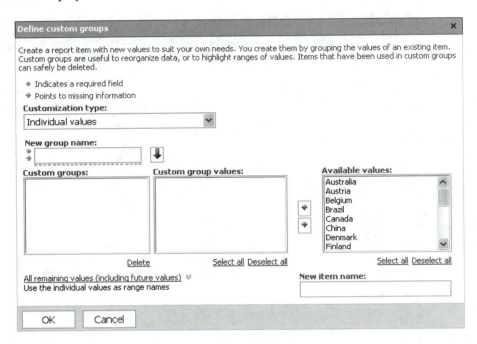

3. From the Customization Type drop-down list, select Individual Values.

4. In the New Group Name text box, enter the name by which you want to refer to this grouping. For this example, we enter North America.

5. Click Insert (the green arrow pointing down). The new group name displays in the Custom Groups box.

6. From the Available Values list, highlight values to be added to your custom group. For this example, we highlight Canada, Mexico, and United States.

7. Click Add (the green arrow pointing left). The values display in the Custom Group Values box.

8. Optionally, in the New Item Name text box, enter a new name for the column containing the custom grouping. If no new name is entered, the column retains the same name as the column on which it is based. For example, if you selected to create a custom group for the Product Name column, Query Studio names the new column Product Name (Custom).

9. Optionally, click the All Remaining Values (Including Future Values) link. Options for how Query Studio should label any values not included in the group display, as shown here:

10. You can select Use The Individual Values As Range Names, Do Not Show Range Names, or enter a New Range Name.

11. Click OK. The custom group for individual values is created. In our example, the original Country column was deleted. Canada, Mexico, and United States have been combined into a group named North America.

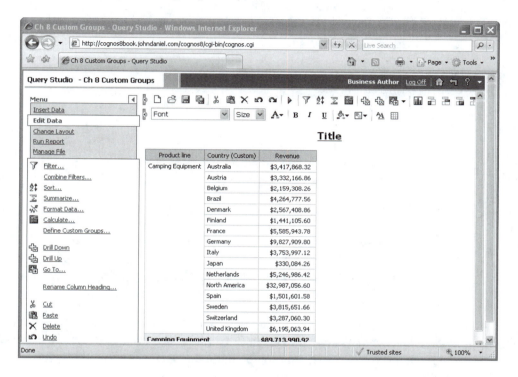

Customize Groups of Ranges   You can group ranges of items so that your query displays all of the items that fall within a specified range together. For example, you could create a group called Average Revenue that would group all of the items in a query that have a revenue between 1,000,000 and 10,000,000.

Here's how to create customized groups of ranges:

1. Highlight the column to which you want to add custom grouping. For this example, we highlight the Revenue column in a query containing the Product Line query item from the Products query subject, the Country query item from the Countries query subject and the Revenue measure from the Orders query subject of the Go Sales and Retailers package.

2. From the Edit Data menu, select Define Custom Groups. The Define Custom Groups screen displays.

3. From the Customization Type drop-down list, ensure Ranges is selected, as shown next.

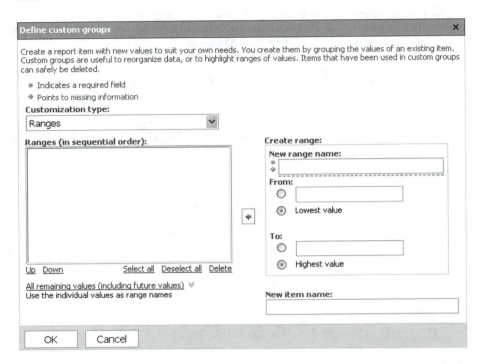

4. In the New Range Name text box, enter the name by which you want to refer to this grouping. For this example, we name our first grouping Excellent Revenue.

5. In the From text box, enter the starting point for the range, or select the Lowest Value option button to use the lowest value for the selected query item. For this example, we enter 10,000,000 for the starting point.

6. In the To text box, enter an ending point for the range, or click the Highest Value option button to use the highest value for the selected query item. For this example, we choose the Highest Value option.

7. Add any other ranges you would like to your custom grouping. For this example, we add a second grouping named Average Revenue that goes from 1,000,000 to 10,000,000.

8. Optionally, in the New Item Name text box, enter a new name for the column containing the custom grouping. If no new name is entered, the column retains the same name as the column on which it is based. For example, if you selected to create a custom group for the Product Name column, Query Studio names the new column Product Name (Custom).

9. Optionally, click the All Remaining Values (Including Future Values) link. Options for how Query Studio should label any values not included in the group(s) display.

10. You can select to Use The Individual Values As Range Names, Do Not Show Range Names, or enter a New Range Name. For this example, we choose New Range Name and enter Poor Revenue.

11. Click OK. Query Studio labels the values accordingly. In the next illustration, we have grouped the query on the column containing the custom group.

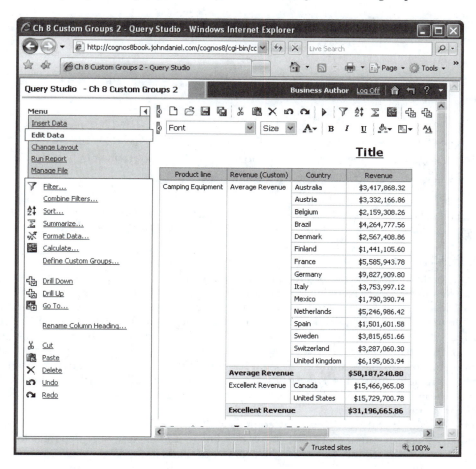

Apply a Template

You can apply templates created in Report Studio to your query. For example, you can use a Query Studio template to customize page headers and footers and to restyle layout objects. Applying the template does not change the way in which your query functions, only the look and feel. It can provide your organization with a unified look.

Here's how to apply a template:

1. From the Change Layout menu, select Apply Template. The Apply Template pane displays:

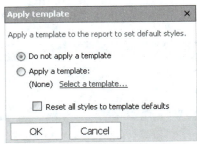

2. Click the Select A Template link. The Select A Template (Navigate) pane displays.

3. Navigate to the template you want to apply and click the name of the template.

4. Click OK. Query Studio applies the template.

TIP *Optionally, select the Reset All Styles To Template Defaults checkbox. This option resets all of the styles that you may have manually applied to the query to that of the template.*

Combine Filters

You can combine multiple filters and apply them to your query to create more complex filters. Creating filters to combine is not much different from the examples given in the "Filter Data" section. The way in which you apply them to the query changes, however.

Following is an example of how combining filters works for the Go Sales and Retailers package that contains data for a company that sells various products throughout the world. The end result that they want to see is how much mountaineering equipment has been sold in France or how much camping equipment has sold in the United States. They must create four filters to accomplish this. *Filter A* filters for products sold in France, *filter B* filters for mountaineering equipment, *filter C* filters for products sold in the United States, and *filter D* filters for camping equipment.

First, the Great Outdoors Company combines filters A and B to create *Combined Filter 1*. If applied by itself, Combined Filter 1 shows only the mountaineering equipment sold in France. The Great Outdoors Company then combines filters C and D to create *Combined Filter 2*. If applied by itself, Combined Filter 2 shows only the camping equipment sold in the United States.

When you set Query Studio to show the results of the Combined Filter 1 or Combined Filter 2, the query shows the amount of mountaineering equipment that sold in France and the amount of camping equipment that sold in the United States.

Here's how to combine filters:

1. Highlight the column containing the query item to be filtered. For this example, we highlight the Product Line column in a query containing Product Line, Quantity, Revenue and Country from the Go Sales and Retailers package.

Note that you do not have to highlight the column prior to accessing the Combine Filters feature, but you cannot apply a filter without highlighting one at some point.

2. From the Edit Data menu, select Combine Filters. The Combine Filters pane displays with Detail and Summary tabs:

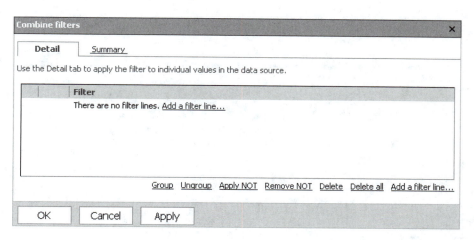

The Detail tab enables you to apply filters to the detailed data in the query. The Summary tab allows you to apply filters to the summarized data in the query. The technique of combining filters under the Detail tab and Summary tab are identical.

3. Click the desired tab. The selected Detail or Summary tab displays and lists any filters that you have created. For this example, we remain on the Detail tab.

4. To add any filters, click the Add A Filter Line link in the Combine Filters pane. Create any filters you would like. Refer to the "Filter Data" section earlier in this chapter for steps on creating a filter. After you have created all of the desired filters, you can begin combining them. For this example, we add filters to show only Camping Equipment and Mountaineering Equipment for Product Line and to show only France and United States for Country.

NOTE *When you add a filter in the Combine Filters pane, it is automatically preceded with AND. You can change the AND to OR by clicking on AND. A dialog opens and allows you to click AND or OR. The value of AND means that the criteria of both filters must be met. The OR value means that one or the other filter's criteria can be true, but not both.*

---

5. Highlight the rows containing the filters you want to combine by holding down CTRL and clicking the icons to the far left of the filter rows, and then click Group. Query Studio groups the filters together. For this example, we combine the filters for Mountaineering Equipment and France and the filters for Camping Equipment and United States.

6. You can apply an AND or an OR to grouped filters. ANDs and ORs function the same in groups as they do on separate filters. For this example, we change the AND

to OR for the combined filters so that our query displays quantity and revenue that falls under Mountaineering Equipment for France or Camping Equipment for United States.

7. Optionally, apply a NOT to your filter by highlighting the filter and then clicking Apply NOT.

8. Click OK. The query is filtered based on the combine queries.

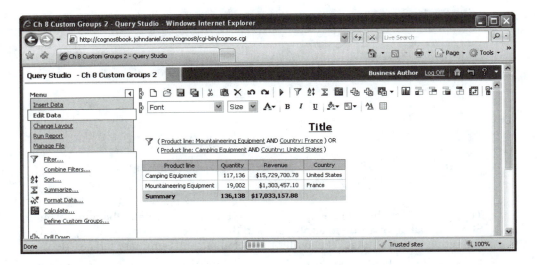

Summarize Data

Query Studio automatically summarizes all query items that contain a measure. You can add, change, or remove a summary. Your summary can be displayed as a total, average, maximum, minimum, median, standard deviation, variance, count distinct, count, calculated, or automatic. Query Studio also provides the ability to add, change, or remove the summary for cells.

Here's how to summarize data:

1. Highlight the column for which you want to change the summary data.

2. From the Edit Data menu, select Summarize. The Summarize pane displays, as shown here.

3. From the Summary For Footers drop-down list, select the function that you want to use to summarize your data and then click OK.

4. To change the Summary for cells, highlight the column containing the cells you want to summarize, access the Summarize pane, and

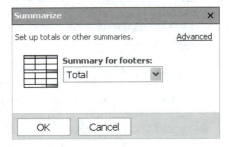

then click Advanced. The Summarize (Advanced) pane displays, as seen in this illustration.

5. From the Summary For Cells drop-down list, select the function that you want to use to summarize your data and then click OK. Query Studio updates the cells in the selected column.

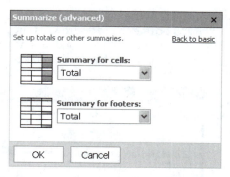

Pivot to Create a Crosstab

Query Studio provides the ability to pivot a column to create a crosstab. A crosstab is a way to show more information using less space. You can see the value of a measure at the intersection point of the rows and columns.

Here's how to pivot to create a crosstab:

1. Highlight the query item that you want to pivot to become the columns in a crosstab. In this example, Country is selected in a query that contains Product Line, Country, and Revenue from the Go Sales and Retailers package.

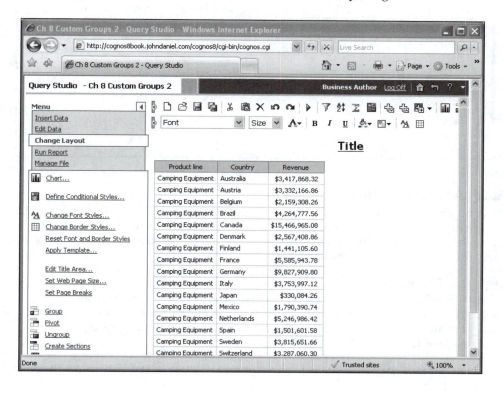

2. From the Change Layout menu, select Pivot. The selected column is pivoted and becomes a header row, as shown next. In this example, the items from the Country column are displayed as a header row and the revenue for each product line displays in the intersecting cells.

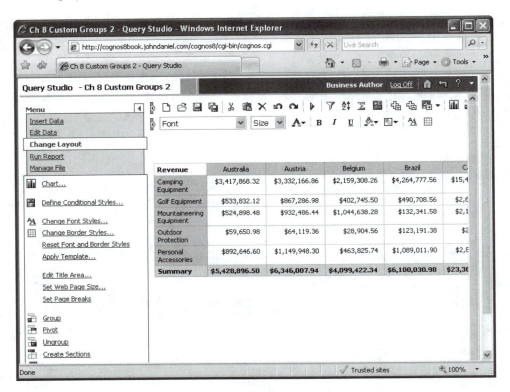

Modify Advanced Options

Query Studio provides access to advanced options. The Query Options and Drill Options provide further customization of your query. You can access both options by choosing Advanced Options from the Run Report menu. The option that users access the most is how Query Studio handles summary data.

Toggle Auto-Summarize

In Query Studio you can control two types of summary information: You can control whether your query automatically generates footer summaries for measures and whether your query automatically summarizes detail values, suppressing duplicates.

Here's how to toggle auto-summarize:

1. From the Run Report menu, click Advanced Options. The Advanced Options pane displays:

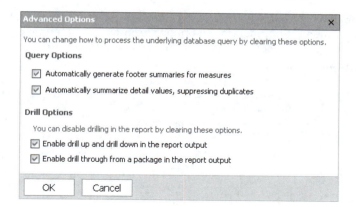

The Query Options area contains two settings associated with summary data. By default, both checkboxes are selected. The Automatically Generate Footer Summaries For Measures setting creates a summary row that contains the sum total for all of the entries for a given measure. The Automatically Summarize Detail Values, Suppressing Duplicates checkbox setting suppresses any duplicate items into a summary.

2. Optionally, clear the Automatically Generate Footer Summaries For Measures checkbox to remove the summary footer for measures.

3. Optionally, clear the Automatically Generate Summarize Detail Values Suppressing Duplicates checkbox to remove summarization of duplicate items.

4. Click OK. Query Studio updates your query according to the options you selected.

Calculate Data

Query Studio automatically calculates the summary total based on the sum of the data for the measure. By default, Query Studio uses the arithmetic operation. You can toggle the way Query Studio calculates summary data between Arithmetic, Percentage, and Analytic. Toggling the way in which Query Studio calculates data is the same for all options.

The following two examples show how to toggle the data calculation based on the percent of total and percent of group.

Example of Percent of Total

When calculating your data based on the percent of total, Query Studio displays the percent of the total for each item of the query item.

Here's how to calculate data based on percent of total:

1. Select the item for which you want to apply the calculation. For this example, we select Revenue in a query containing Product Line, Country, and Revenue from the Go Sales and Retailers package.

2. From the Edit Data menu, select Calculate. The Calculate pane displays.

3. From the Operation Type list, select Percentage, as shown next. The Operation drop-down list populates with options for how Query Studio calculates percentages: percent, percent of total, percent of footer, and percent of growth.

4. From the Operation list, select % Of Total.

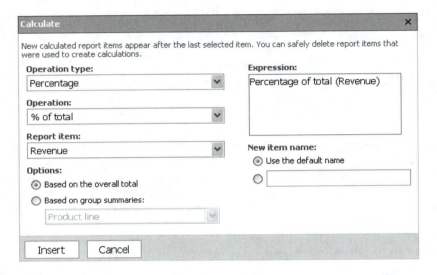

5. Under Options, select Based On The Overall Total.

TIP   *To calculate data based on the percent of a group, choose Based On Group Summaries under Options.*

6. Optionally, under New Item Name, enter a name for the calculation column inserted by Query Studio. If you do not enter a new name, Query Studio labels the column *% of total (Query Item)*.

7. Click the Insert button. Query Studio inserts a column displaying the percentage of the total for each item.

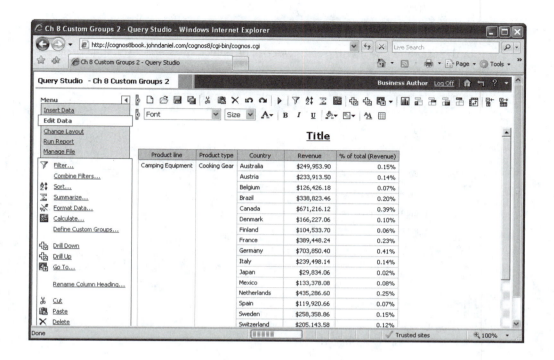

Manage a Query

Queries you create in Query Studio can be saved to be accessed at a later time. You can open an existing query to modify it, view the query, view the query definitions, or export the query data. As with all aspects of Query Studio, performing this function is easy.

Open an Existing Query

Query Studio allows you to open an existing query to change definitions or add further enhancements. You can open an existing query in two ways: You can access the query from either the Public Folders or My Folders, and then double-click the query name. This launches Query Studio and displays your query. Or, you can open Query Studio from Cognos Connection as discussed in the "Open Query Studio" section earlier in this chapter and open your query directly from Query Studio.

Here's how to open an existing query from Query Studio:

1. From the Manage File menu, select Open. The Select The Report (Navigate) screen displays:

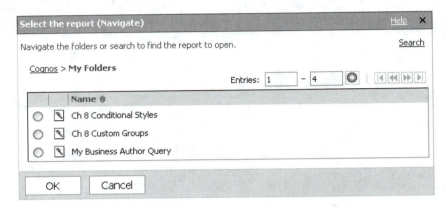

2. Navigate to the folder containing the query.

3. Select the query.

4. Click OK. The query opens.

Export and View Queries

Queries created in Query Studio can be viewed by colleagues who do not have access to Query Studio. You simply need to export your query in the format that works best for you and your colleagues. You can export your query into a variety of formats: PDF, three versions of Excel, CSV (comma-separated values), or XML. Accessing the export option is the same for all formats. It is the way that the data displays that differs depending on the format. The PDF and XML formats display in a new web browser, and the Excel and CSV formats display in Microsoft Excel. You access the Export option from the Run Report menu.

Report Definitions

You can view the building blocks of your query through report definitions, which show you all the query items and filters that make up your query. This is helpful if your package has similar query items in multiple query subjects, because the expression shows you the fully qualified path of the query item.

Here's how to view report definitions:

1. From the Manage File menu, select Report Definition. The Report Definition screen displays a list of all of the query items and the expressions that make up those items:

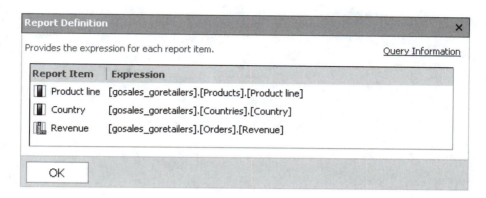

2. Optionally, click Query Information. The Query Information pane displays an XML version of the query.

3. Click OK to close the pane.

Advanced Reporting I

In this chapter, you will learn how to use Report Studio to create several different styles of reports. While creating these reports, you should become familiar with commonly used toolbar items, menu options, and other features within Report Studio. As in many applications, Cognos 8 gives you multiple ways of accomplishing a task. This chapter details the most commonly used ways to accomplish a single task and references alternative ways to achieve the same goal.

Today's decision-makers are looking for quicker, more efficient ways to view their business data for a competitive edge. Report Studio is a Web-based application that gives users the ability to create simple or complex reports that allow decision-makers to make quick and intelligent business decisions. Report Studio grants users the flexibility needed to create lists, crosstabs, charts, and dashboard style reports. Reports can be grouped, sorted, and formatted in a variety of ways to meet business requirements. Report output options include the industry standards HTML, PDF, and Microsoft Excel. Report Studio makes it easy to manipulate and present data with a wide array of report creation tools.

Opening Report Studio

Here's how to open Report Studio:

1. Log on to the Cognos 8 application. The Cognos 8 Welcome screen displays, as shown next:

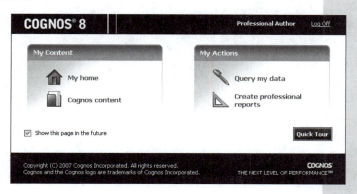

2. Click Cognos Content. The Cognos Connection Public Folders tab displays by default, as shown next.

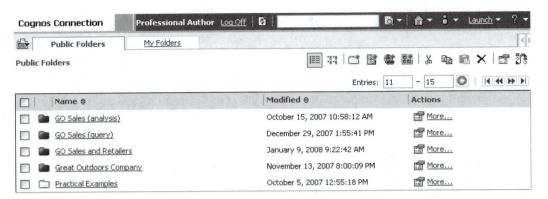

Within the Public Folders shown here, there is a package named Go Sales and Retailers that is used throughout this chapter.

3. From the Launch menu, click Report Studio. The Select A Package (Navigate) screen displays.

4. Click on a package. The Cognos 8 Report Studio Welcome dialog box displays:

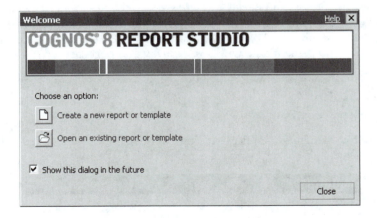

5. Click Create A New Report Or Template. The New dialog box displays, as shown next. Select one of the report templates as a basis for creating your report. Report styles are described in Table 9-1.

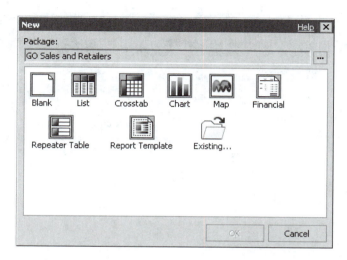

Report Style	Description
List	View detailed information in a tabular format.
Crosstab	View summarized information at the intersecting point of a column and row. For example, viewing Sales Reps figures for each month of the year. The Sales Reps would display in the rows and the months would display in the columns.
Chart	View graphically represented data. The available options are Column, Bar, Progressive, Pareto, Line, Pie, Donut, Area, Combination, Scatter, Bubble, Point, Radar, Polar, Gauge, and Metrics Range.
Map	Show tabular data in geographical means. For example, a map of the United States could be colored to show revenue for sales territories.
Repeater Table	Repeat blocks of data within a report. Repeaters are commonly used to create mailing labels.
Blank	Creates an empty template. Unlike the other templates, this template contains no objects at all (such as a headers, lists, crosstabs, or footers). Use this to create a report from scratch.
Financial	View data in a financial format. This template contains a crosstab, but it has a different style attached to it. The style gives the report a financial look.

TABLE 9-1 Report Studio Report Styles

6. Click OK. Report Studio opens, displaying the main user interface, which is made up of several sections: Standard toolbar, Style toolbar, Insertable Objects pane, Properties pane, Explorer bar, and work area as shown next:

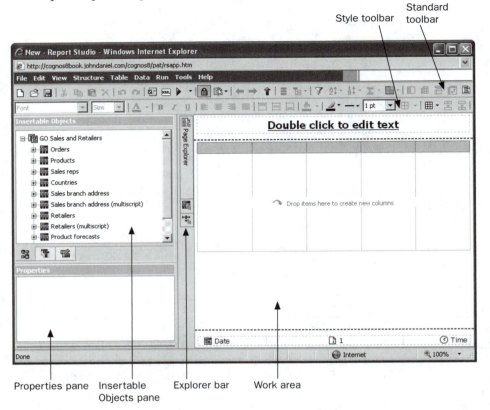

Standard Toolbar

Some commonly used features from the Standard toolbar are listed in Table 9-2.

Style Toolbar

Some commonly used features from the Style toolbar are listed in Table 9-3.

If a toolbar icon has a downward facing black arrow to the right of it, this indicates the toolbar button has a drop-down list associated with it.

Insertable Objects

The Insertable Objects pane is made up of the following tabs:

- **Source**   Contains the namespace, query items, and data items that make up the selected package.
- **Data Items**   Contains the data items that are being used in the current report.
- **Toolbox**   Contains other objects that can be added to reports, as listed in Table 9-4.

Icon	Name	Description
▷	Run Report	Runs the Report.
🔒	Lock / Unlock	Locks or Unlocks page objects.
▽	Filters	Opens the Filters dialog box where filters can be added and used to filter the report.
↕	Sort	Sorts the report in ascending or descending order.
Σ	Aggregate	List of Summary Functions that can be applied to the report.
▣	Group / Ungroup	Groups or Ungroups data in a report.
⊟	Section	Creates sections in a report with a data item appearing as a heading for the section.
▤	Headers & Footers	Creates page Headers and Footers.
⊞	Build Prompt Page	Creates a prompt page for the report.

TABLE 9-2 Standard Toolbar Objects

Icon	Name	Description
Size ▾	Font Size	Change the size of the selected text.
A	Foreground Color	Changes the color of the selected text.
🖌	Background Color	Changes the background color of an object.
🖌	Border Color	Changes the color of the border for an object.
—	Border Styles	List of border styles.
⊞	All Borders	Adds borders to the selected object.
%#	Data Format	Opens the Data Format dialog box to change the format of a data item.
▦	Conditional Styles	Allows you to apply style to cells dependent upon a conditional.

TABLE 9-3 Style Toolbar Objects

Object Type	Object Description
[ab] Text Item	Adds informational text to the report.
[:::] Block	Acts as a container to help organize other objects within the page.
[⊞] Table	Organizes objects in an HTML table within the report.
[▦] Query Calculation	Adds a calculation to the query or report.
[▨] Image	Adds a referenced image to the report or report page.
=⁺ Singleton	Adds a single queried item anywhere on the report page.
[▨] Conditional Blocks	Reports objects that can have conditions assigned to them—for example, conditionally hiding and showing the container and the objects inside.
[Html] HTML Item	Allows users to write HTML or Java scripts that render when the report runs.
[▾] Value Prompt	Retrieves data based on values selected from a list.

TABLE 9-4   Toolbox Objects

Explorer Bar

The options on the Explorer bar determine how the work area is used:

- **Page Explorer**   Allows you to manage report pages, prompt pages, and classes.
- **Query Explorer**   Allows you to manage queries that are in the report.
- **Condition Explorer**   Allows you to manage the variables that are being used in the report.

Work Area

The work area has three different modes. In the Page Explorer mode, you insert data items and other toolbox objects into the work area to create the layout for reports. In the Query Explorer mode, you can manipulate queries, data items, and filters. In the Condition Explorer mode, you can edit variables and values for those variables.

Properties Pane

The Properties pane lists the properties that you can set for an object in a report. These properties include text source type, data format, text source variables, and other types of information.

Business Case: Create a Gross Profit Margin Report

Suppose you have been asked to create a report that shows revenue, production cost, and gross profit for sales territory and product line. It must also display the gross profit percentage for each product line in a territory. The report must be well formatted and have the ability to be generated in PDF file format. Throughout this chapter, we will create a report that meets these requirements.

TIP *When you create a new report, it is good practice to assign it a name and save it before continuing to build the layout.*

List Report

A *list report* is a report that presents data in rows and columns. List reports are used to show detailed information from a data source in a list format.

Here's how to create a simple list report:

1. From the Source tab in the Insertable Objects pane, drag a data item to the work area and drop it where you would like to insert it. A flashing black bar displays where you can drop a data item to be added to the list. For this example, we are inserting the Sales Territory data item from the Countries query subject of the Go Sales and Retailers package:

2. Optionally, from the Source tab in the Insertable Objects pane, double-click a data item to add to the list. For this example, we double-click on the Product Line data item from the Products query subject. The new data item displays to the right of the first data item in the work area:

Sales territory	Product line
<Sales territory>	<Product line>
<Sales territory>	<Product line>
<Sales territory>	<Product line>

3. From the Insertable Objects pane, add any other data items you would like to your list. For this example, we added the Revenue, Production Cost, and Gross

Profit data items from the Orders query subject. Your list should now look similar to this:

Sales territory	Product line	Revenue	Production cost	Gross profit
<Sales territory>	<Product line>	<Revenue>	<Production cost>	<Gross profit>
<Sales territory>	<Product line>	<Revenue>	<Production cost>	<Gross profit>
<Sales territory>	<Product line>	<Revenue>	<Production cost>	<Gross profit>

4. From the Standard toolbar, click Run Report to view the report in Cognos Viewer.

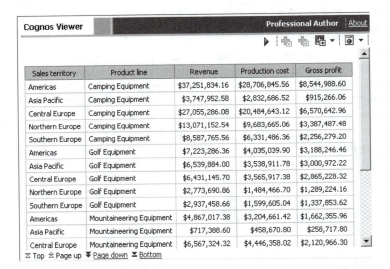

Report Studio displays the data in a simple, unformatted state. The sales territories are ordered alphabetically for each product line. You can make this report easier to read by grouping the data.

Group Data in Reports

Grouping data makes reports more visually appealing and makes it easier for the end user to locate and view the data. In this section, we group data in the report that was previously created.

Here's how to group data in a report:

1. Open the simple list report that was created in Report Studio.

2. In the list, select a column and then, on the standard toolbar, click Group/Ungroup. For our example, we select the Sales Territory column.

3. From the Standard toolbar, click Run Report to view the changes made to the report. By grouping data in the report, the report is easier to read, as shown here:

Sales territory	Product line	Revenue	Production cost	Gross profit
Americas	Camping Equipment	$37,251,834.16	$28,706,845.56	$8,544,988.60
	Golf Equipment	$7,223,286.36	$4,035,039.90	$3,188,246.46
	Mountaineering Equipment	$4,867,017.38	$3,204,661.42	$1,662,355.96
	Outdoor Protection	$939,189.10	$416,736.40	$522,452.70
	Personal Accessories	$8,935,445.90	$5,653,344.92	$3,282,100.98
Asia Pacific	Camping Equipment	$3,747,952.58	$2,832,686.52	$915,266.06
	Golf Equipment	$6,539,884.00	$3,538,911.78	$3,000,972.22
	Mountaineering Equipment	$717,388.60	$458,670.80	$258,717.80
	Outdoor Protection	$615,808.94	$257,885.36	$357,923.58
	Personal Accessories	$5,461,606.00	$3,385,802.90	$2,075,803.10
Central Europe	Camping Equipment	$27,055,286.08	$20,484,643.12	$6,570,642.96
	Golf Equipment	$6,431,145.70	$3,565,917.38	$2,865,228.32
	Mountaineering Equipment	$6,567,324.32	$4,446,358.02	$2,120,966.30
	Outdoor Protection	$796,312.94	$360,992.98	$435,319.96
	Personal Accessories	$9,818,473.90	$6,303,987.56	$3,514,486.34
Northern Europe	Camping Equipment	$13,071,152.54	$9,683,665.06	$3,387,487.48
	Golf Equipment	$2,773,690.86	$1,484,466.70	$1,289,224.16
	Mountaineering Equipment	$5,151,662.02	$3,410,216.42	$1,741,445.60

Filtering Reports

Filtering allows you to minimize the amount of data that is returned in the report. In the previous illustration, the data represents total amounts for 2004, 2005, and 2006. In this section, we add a filter to the report that only lists data for the year 2006.

Here's how to add a filter to a report:

1. From the Standard toolbar, click Filters. The Filters window displays, as shown here:

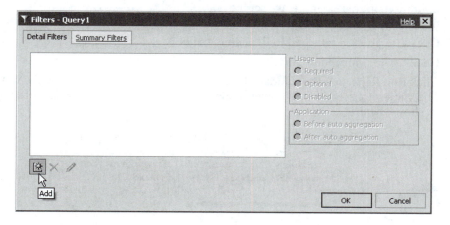

NOTE *The Detail Filters are used to filter detail level values within a report. The Summary Filters are used to filter summary level values within a report.*

2. From the Filters window, click Add. The Detail Filter Expression window displays, as shown here:

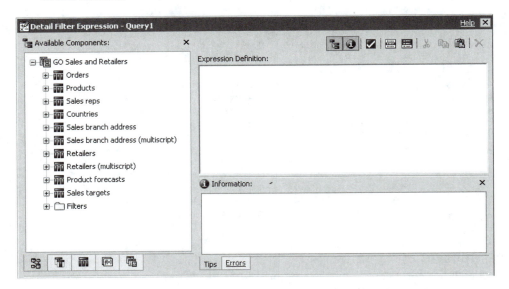

3. In the Available Components pane, double-click the data items to add them to the filter expression. In this example, we add the Order Year data item (*[gosales_goretailers]. [Orders].[Order year]*) to the Expression Definition pane by double-clicking on it.

4. Add necessary terms to your expression definition. In this example, we set the expression equal to 2006, as shown here.

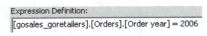

5. Click OK. You are returned to the Filters window.

6. Click OK to return to Report Studio.

7. Click Run Report on the standard toolbar to view the changes made to the report. The values are significantly lower than when the report was run without the filter, as shown next.

Sales territory	Product line	Revenue	Production cost	Gross profit
Americas	Camping Equipment	$15,037,083.06	$11,679,569.32	$3,357,513.74
	Golf Equipment	$2,815,742.12	$1,594,037.20	$1,221,704.92
	Mountaineering Equipment	$2,748,318.88	$1,816,961.72	$931,357.16
	Outdoor Protection	$184,973.22	$81,266.34	$103,706.88
	Personal Accessories	$3,544,178.56	$2,276,724.56	$1,267,454.00
Asia Pacific	Camping Equipment	$1,964,103.48	$1,481,507.28	$482,596.20
	Golf Equipment	$3,351,097.02	$1,837,572.32	$1,513,524.70
	Mountaineering Equipment	$375,502.46	$243,780.04	$131,722.42
	Outdoor Protection	$148,606.36	$60,949.64	$87,656.72
	Personal Accessories	$2,691,334.26	$1,697,455.28	$993,878.98
Central Europe	Camping Equipment	$11,315,114.20	$8,618,080.76	$2,697,033.44
	Golf Equipment	$2,344,760.38	$1,310,732.80	$1,034,027.58

TIP *You can use the Query Explorer work area to add filters.*

Adding Calculations to Reports

Adding calculations to a report allows the user to view additional data that does not exist in the package. In this section, we add a gross profit percentage calculation to a report as an example.

Here's how to add a calculation to a report:

1. In the Insertable Objects pane, click the Toolbox tab.

2. Double-click Query Calculation. The Create Calculation dialog displays.

3. In the Name box, type a name for the calculation. In this example, we use the name **Gross Profit %**.

4. Click OK. The Data Item Expression window displays to create the calculation, as shown next.

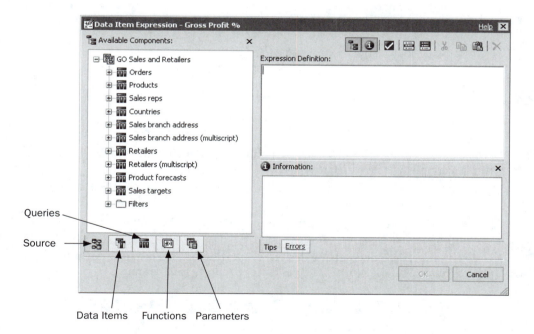

5. From the Available Components pane, add data items to your expression definition. In this example, we use data items that already exist in the report. We click the Data Items tab and double-click the Gross Profit data item. The Gross Profit data item is added to the Expression Definition pane (*[Gross profit]*).

NOTE *You are not limited to using these items; you can also use data items directly from the Source tab.*

6. In the Available Components pane, click the Functions tab to add functions to your expression definition. In this example, we expand the Operators folder, and then double-click the divide operator. The divide operator (/) is added to the Expression Definition pane.

TIP   *An alternative method is to type the appropriate characters in the Expression Definition pane instead of selecting them from the Available Components pane.*

7. From the Available Components pane, add any other necessary data items to your expression. In this example, we click the Data Items tab and then double-click the Revenue data item. The Revenue data item is added to the Expression Definition pane (*[Revenue]*).

8. Click OK to return to Report Studio.

9. Click Run Report on the Standard toolbar to view the report. The added calculation is formatted in the default style, as shown next. Calculations use the format of the data items that make up the calculation by default. You must manually change the format to the appropriate style, if need be.

In our example, Gross Profit % should be formatted to display as a percentage.

10. Click the column to be formatted to highlight the data item within the list report. In this example, we click on Gross Profit %.

11. In the Properties pane, click the Data Format property and then click the ellipsis. The Data Format box displays.

12. From the Format Type list, select the appropriate type. For our example, we select Percent.

13. In the Properties pane, set any desired properties for the Format Type. In this example, we set the No. of Decimal Places property to 2, as shown next.

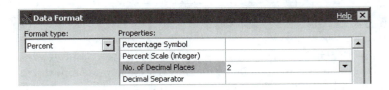

14. Click OK.

15. Click Run Report on the Standard toolbar to view the report. Your results display as shown here:

Sales territory	Product line	Revenue	Production cost	Gross profit	Gross Profit %
Americas	Camping Equipment	$15,037,083.06	$11,679,569.32	$3,357,513.74	22.33%
	Golf Equipment	$2,815,742.12	$1,594,037.20	$1,221,704.92	43.39%
	Mountaineering Equipment	$2,748,318.88	$1,816,961.72	$931,357.16	33.89%
	Outdoor Protection	$184,973.22	$81,266.34	$103,706.88	56.07%
	Personal Accessories	$3,544,178.56	$2,276,724.56	$1,267,454.00	35.76%
Asia Pacific	Camping Equipment	$1,964,103.48	$1,481,507.28	$482,596.20	24.57%
	Golf Equipment	$3,351,097.02	$1,837,572.32	$1,513,524.70	45.17%
	Mountaineering Equipment	$375,502.46	$243,780.04	$131,722.42	35.08%
	Outdoor Protection	$148,606.36	$60,949.64	$87,656.72	58.99%
	Personal Accessories	$2,691,334.26	$1,697,455.28	$993,878.98	36.93%

Adding Summary Lines to Reports

In Report Studio, you can add summary level data for the entire report, for one grouped data item, or for multiple grouped data items. Our example report has one Grouped data item (Sales Territory). In this section, we add summary data to the report and the Sales Territory grouped data item.

Here's how to add summary lines to a report:

1. Select the columns you would like to summarize by holding down CTRL while you click each of them. In our example, four columns are selected in the list (Revenue, Production Cost, Gross Profit, and Gross Profit %).

2. From the Standard toolbar, in the Aggregate list, click Total.

3. From the Standard toolbar, click Run Report. In this example, the report now contains a summary line for each Sales territory, as shown next. Click the Bottom link to navigate to the last page of the report to view the summary line for the entire report.

Sales territory	Product line	Revenue	Production cost	Gross profit	Gross Profit %
Americas	Camping Equipment	$15,037,083.06	$11,679,569.32	$3,357,513.74	22.33%
	Golf Equipment	$2,815,742.12	$1,594,037.20	$1,221,704.92	43.39%
	Mountaineering Equipment	$2,748,318.88	$1,816,961.72	$931,357.16	33.89%
	Outdoor Protection	$184,973.22	$81,266.34	$103,706.88	56.07%
	Personal Accessories	$3,544,178.56	$2,276,724.56	$1,267,454.00	35.76%
Americas		**$24,330,295.84**	**$17,448,559.14**	**$6,881,736.70**	**1.91432317**
Asia Pacific	Camping Equipment	$1,964,103.48	$1,481,507.28	$482,596.20	24.57%
	Golf Equipment	$3,351,097.02	$1,837,572.32	$1,513,524.70	45.17%
	Mountaineering Equipment	$375,502.46	$243,780.04	$131,722.42	35.08%
	Outdoor Protection	$148,606.36	$60,949.64	$87,656.72	58.99%
	Personal Accessories	$2,691,334.26	$1,697,455.28	$993,878.98	36.93%
Asia Pacific		**$8,530,643.58**	**$5,321,264.56**	**$3,209,379.02**	**2.00729545**

Setting the Rollup Aggregrate Function

Once summary lines are added to a report, you may need to change the Rollup Aggregate Function for the summary data. The Rollup Aggregate Function property defines the type of aggregation applied to summarized values. In our example, the Rollup Aggregate Function for the Gross Profit % calculated field is defaulted to Total because we chose Total as the aggregation for the columns we summarized. This property needs to be changed in order to correctly rollup the Gross Profit percentage calculation (*[Gross profit]/[Revenue]*) at the summary level. You may also need to modify data formats at the summary level to be consistent with the rest of the report.

Here's how to change the Rollup Aggregate Function:

1. Click the list cell for which you need to modify the Rollup Aggregation Function. We select <Total(Gross Profit %)> at the Sales Territory level.

2. In the Properties pane, click the Rollup Aggregate Function property.

3. Select the appropriate option. In this example, we choose the Calculated option.

4. Optionally, change the format of the data item.

5. Select the cells for which you want to modify the data format. In this example, we selected the <Total(Gross Profit %)> list cell at the Sales Territory level and the <Total(Gross Profit %)> list cell at the Summary level.

6. In the Properties pane, double-click the Data Format property. The Data Format box displays.

7. From the Format Type drop-down, select the appropriate type. In this example, we choose Percent.

8. In the Properties pane of the Data Format box, set any desired properties. In this example, we set the No. of Decimal Places property to 2.

9. Click OK.

10. From the Standard toolbar, click Run Report. The summary level data for the calculated column is now displayed as it was formatted, and the summary rows display the calculation correctly, as shown next.

Sales territory	Product line	Revenue	Production cost	Gross profit	Gross Profit %
Americas	Camping Equipment	$15,037,083.06	$11,679,569.32	$3,357,513.74	22.33%
	Golf Equipment	$2,815,742.12	$1,594,037.20	$1,221,704.92	43.39%
	Mountaineering Equipment	$2,748,318.88	$1,816,961.72	$931,357.16	33.89%
	Outdoor Protection	$184,973.22	$81,266.34	$103,706.88	56.07%
	Personal Accessories	$3,544,178.56	$2,276,724.56	$1,267,454.00	35.76%
Americas		**$24,330,295.84**	**$17,448,559.14**	**$6,881,736.70**	**28.28%**
Asia Pacific	Camping Equipment	$1,964,103.48	$1,481,507.28	$482,596.20	24.57%
	Golf Equipment	$3,351,097.02	$1,837,572.32	$1,513,524.70	45.17%
	Mountaineering Equipment	$375,502.46	$243,780.04	$131,722.42	35.08%
	Outdoor Protection	$148,606.36	$60,949.64	$87,656.72	58.99%
	Personal Accessories	$2,691,334.26	$1,697,455.28	$993,878.98	36.93%
Asia Pacific		**$8,530,643.58**	**$5,321,264.56**	**$3,209,379.02**	**37.62%**

Basic Report Formatting

Formatting a report, such as adding a header, changing a font size, and applying borders and backgrounds, organizes the data and makes it easier for end users to read. In this section, we continue using the same example report.

Add a Header to a Report

You can add a header to a report in Report Studio to make it easier to read.
Here's how to add a Header to a report:

1. Select the List Column Body in the column for which you want to create a header.

2. From the Standard toolbar, click Create Header. In this example, we selected the Sales Territory list column body. Report Studio creates a header for the Sales Territory column.

NOTE *A column has to be grouped before it can be made into a header.*

3. The column for which we have created a header is no longer necessary. With the column still selected, from the Standard toolbar, click Cut. Report Studio removes the selected column from the list report.

4. From the Standard toolbar, click Run Report. The results display as seen next.

Product line	Revenue	Production cost	Gross profit	Gross Profit %
Americas				
Camping Equipment	$15,037,083.06	$11,679,569.32	$3,357,513.74	22.33%
Golf Equipment	$2,815,742.12	$1,594,037.20	$1,221,704.92	43.39%
Mountaineering Equipment	$2,748,318.88	$1,816,961.72	$931,357.16	33.89%
Outdoor Protection	$184,973.22	$81,266.34	$103,706.88	56.07%
Personal Accessories	$3,544,178.56	$2,276,724.56	$1,267,454.00	35.76%
Americas	**$24,330,295.84**	**$17,448,559.14**	**$6,881,736.70**	**28.28%**
Asia Pacific				
Camping Equipment	$1,964,103.48	$1,481,507.28	$482,596.20	24.57%
Golf Equipment	$3,351,097.02	$1,837,572.32	$1,513,524.70	45.17%
Mountaineering Equipment	$375,502.46	$243,780.04	$131,722.42	35.08%
Outdoor Protection	$148,606.36	$60,949.64	$87,656.72	58.99%
Personal Accessories	$2,691,334.26	$1,697,455.28	$993,878.98	36.93%

In our example, the Sales Territory column is removed and the product line data is now organized by sales territory. To emphasize the header, you can modify its style, by increasing the font size and changing the background color of the list cell.

Change Font Size in a Report

You can change the font size of the objects in your report.

Here's how to change the font size in a report:

1. In the report, click the object for which you want to modify its font size to select it.

2. From the Style toolbar, click the Size drop-down box.

3. Select the desired font size. The object changes to the selected size.

TIP *As an alternative method, many styles can be applied by right-clicking an object and selecting the style.*

Add Background Color to an Object in a Report

You can add a background color to an object in a report.

Here's how to add a background color to an object in a report:

1. Click the object to select it.

2. From the Style toolbar, click Background Color.

3. Select a color to apply to the background. Click OK.

TIP *Move the pointer over a color box to display the hexadecimal value.*

4. From the Standard toolbar, click Run Report to view the report. The results display in the chosen color.

Add a Border to an Object

You can add a border to an object in your report. Adding a border can provide a visual separation between the groups and the summary levels in reports.

Here's how to add a border to an object in a report:

1. Click the first cell in the row for which you want to add a border.

2. In the title bar of the Properties pane, click Select Ancestor and then click List Row. The entire row is now selected.

3. Right-click the row, choose Style, and then choose Border. The Border window displays.

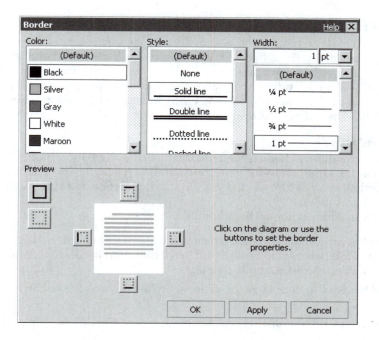

4. Add borders to any side of the row and choose the desired color, style, and width for the borders. In this example, we added a solid black 1pt bottom border.

5. Click OK.

6. From the Standard toolbar, click Run Report to view the report. The results display as shown next:

Product line	Revenue	Production cost	Gross profit	Gross Profit %
Americas				
Camping Equipment	$15,037,083.06	$11,679,569.32	$3,357,513.74	22.33%
Golf Equipment	$2,815,742.12	$1,594,037.20	$1,221,704.92	43.39%
Mountaineering Equipment	$2,748,318.88	$1,816,961.72	$931,357.16	33.89%
Outdoor Protection	$184,973.22	$81,266.34	$103,706.88	56.07%
Personal Accessories	$3,544,178.56	$2,276,724.56	$1,267,454.00	35.76%
Americas	**$24,330,295.84**	**$17,448,559.14**	**$6,881,736.70**	**28.28%**
Asia Pacific				
Camping Equipment	$1,964,103.48	$1,481,507.28	$482,596.20	24.57%
Golf Equipment	$3,351,097.02	$1,837,572.32	$1,513,524.70	45.17%
Mountaineering Equipment	$375,502.46	$243,780.04	$131,722.42	35.08%
Outdoor Protection	$148,606.36	$60,949.64	$87,656.72	58.99%
Personal Accessories	$2,691,334.26	$1,697,455.28	$993,878.98	36.93%
Asia Pacific	**$8,530,643.58**	**$5,321,264.56**	**$3,209,379.02**	**37.62%**

Conditional Highlighting

Conditional highlighting allows the end user to visually identify areas of interest within the business. One way this can be achieved is by changing the background and text color of a data item cell in a report when certain requirements are not met. In our example, we use several manually created conditions, a pre-canned condition, and pre-canned styles for the conditions. In this section, we use the **Gross Profit** % column for the conditionally highlighted field. The criteria and result for this example are shown in Table 9-5.

Cognos 8.3 and Above

This example of conditional highlighting uses features that were introduced in Cognos 8.3. You can achieve the same results for versions prior to 8.3 using the instructions that follow in the next section. You can also use the steps in the next section as an alternative method for versions 8.3 and above.

Here's how to add conditional highlighting to a report in Cognos 8.3 and above:

1. Select the list column body for which you want to set conditional highlighting. In this example, we use the Gross Profit % column from the example report we have been creating throughout this chapter.

2. From the Style toolbar, click Conditional Styles. The Conditional Styles window displays.

3. In the New Conditional Style list, select Advanced Conditional Style, as shown next:

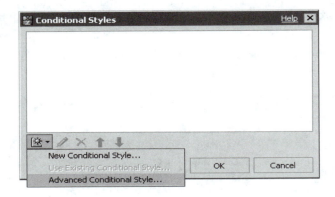

Gross Profit Criteria	Style/Value	Cell Color for Met Criteria	Text Color for Met Criteria
% >= 50%	Excellent	Green	White
% >= 25% and < 50%	Average	Yellow	Black
% < 25%	Poor	Red	White

TABLE 9-5 Conditions for Conditional Highlighting Example.

4. In the Name box, type in a name for the style. In this example, we use **Evaluate Gross Profit %**, as shown next.

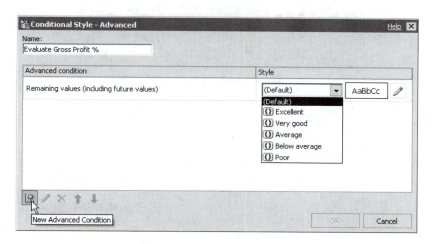

As you can see in the illustration, an advanced condition already exists. This condition is set to the default style of a white cell background and black text. This is a *pre-canned conditional style* to which changes cannot be saved. The Style list contains the existing pre-canned styles (that is, Excellent, Very good, Average, Below average, and Poor). You can click on each of these styles to see the background and/or text color changes on the button next to Style. You can also define a custom style by editing any of the pre-canned styles.

5. Click on New Advanced Condition.

6. In the Available Components pane of the Report Condition window, double-click any data items you want to add to the expression. We add the Gross Profit % data item to the Expression Definition pane (*[Query 1].[Gross Profit %]*).

7. In the Expression Definition pane, specify terms for the expression. We set the expression to *[Query1].[Gross Profit %] >= .50*, as shown next, and then click OK.

8. From the Style list, select a Style. The background and text colors chosen as the Style appear in the cells for which the condition was met. In this example, we use Excellent as the Style. When the Gross Profit % value is greater than or equal to 50%, the cell color is green and the text color is white.

9. Follow steps 5 through 7 to create any more conditions your column requires. In this example, we add another condition for when Gross Profit % is greater than or equal to 25% and less than 50%, as listed in Table 9-5.

10. To the right of Style, click Edit. The Style window displays, as shown here:

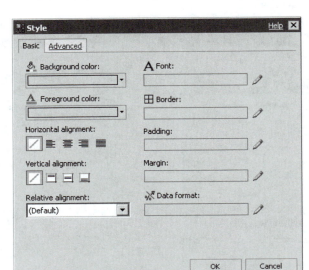

11. Change any desired properties to define a Custom Style. In this example, we set the Background Color to Yellow and the Foreground Color to Black.

12. Click OK.

13. You can change the Style of the Remaining Values (Including Future Values) condition to set how values that do not fall under the defined conditions appear. In this example, we set the Style of the Remaining Values to Poor.

14. Click OK twice to close the Conditional Styles windows.

15. From the Standard toolbar, click Run Report to view the report. The results display:

Product line	Revenue	Production cost	Gross profit	Gross Profit %
Americas				
Camping Equipment	$15,037,083.06	$11,679,569.32	$3,357,513.74	22.33%
Golf Equipment	$2,815,742.12	$1,594,037.20	$1,221,704.92	43.39%
Mountaineering Equipment	$2,748,318.88	$1,816,961.72	$931,357.16	33.89%
Outdoor Protection	$184,973.22	$81,266.34	$103,706.88	56.07%
Personal Accessories	$3,544,178.56	$2,276,724.56	$1,267,454.00	35.76%
Americas	**$24,330,295.84**	**$17,448,559.14**	**$6,881,736.70**	**28.28%**
Asia Pacific				
Camping Equipment	$1,964,103.48	$1,481,507.28	$482,596.20	24.57%
Golf Equipment	$3,351,097.02	$1,837,572.32	$1,513,524.70	45.17%
Mountaineering Equipment	$375,502.46	$243,780.04	$131,722.42	35.08%
Outdoor Protection	$148,606.36	$60,949.64	$87,656.72	58.99%
Personal Accessories	$2,691,334.26	$1,697,455.28	$993,878.98	36.93%
Asia Pacific	**$8,530,643.58**	**$5,321,264.56**	**$3,209,379.02**	**37.62%**

NOTE *The conditional style is not applied to the summary level. To show the conditional highlighting at the summary level, you have to create the same conditions for the summary level cells.*

Cognos 8.2 and Below

This is also an alternative method for Cognos versions 8.3 and above as well.

Here's how to add conditional highlighting to a report in versions of Cognos previous to 8.3:

1. Navigate to the Condition Explorer and then click the Variables link. You need to add the variable condition that is passed to make conditional highlighting work. In this example, the work area has changed to display the Condition Explorer work area, as shown next:

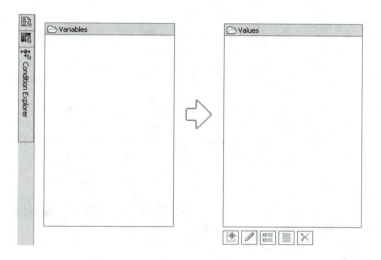

2. In the Insertable Objects pane, double-click the String Variable object. The Report Expression window displays.

3. In the Expression Definition pane, type the appropriate expression for the conditions you are setting. In this example, we use the following expression that returns a string value when one of the criteria is met:

```
Case
  when [Query1].[Gross Profit %] >= .50
  then 'Excellent'
  when [Query1].[Gross Profit %] >= .25 and [Query1].[Gross Profit %] < .50
  then 'Average'
  when [Query1].[Gross Profit %] < .25
  then 'Poor'
end
```

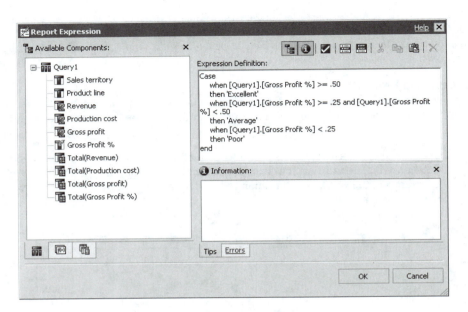

4. Click OK. The default name of the variable is String 1. To change the default to a more descriptive name, in the Properties pane, click in the Name property, and specify a new name. In this example, we use **Evaluate Gross Profit Margin %**. The name in the Variables work area is changed, as shown next:

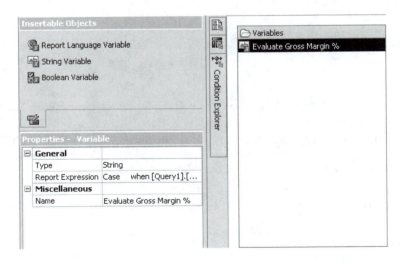

5. In the work area, under the Values box, click Add. The Add dialog displays.

6. In the Value box, type a name for the value to be added to the variable that was created. In this example, we add **Excellent** as a value to the Evaluate Gross Profit Margin % variable.

7. Click OK.

8. Repeat steps 5 and 6 to add other values to the variable. In this example, we add Average and Poor values. Our Values work area now contains the three values, as shown here:

NOTE *The values that you add for the variable must match exactly as you typed them in the Expression Definition of the variable.*

9. From the Page Explorer, navigate to the report page.

10. In the work area, click on the list column body for which you want to set the conditional style. We are using Gross Profit % column for this example.

11. In the Properties pane, click the Style Variable property and then click the ellipsis. The Style Variable window displays.

12. From the Variable list, select the variable that you created.

13. Click OK. In the Properties pane, the name of the variable displays in the Style Variable property.

14. From the Condition Explorer tab, click one of the values under your variable. The Explorer Bar turns green, as shown next, indicating that any changes you make apply only to the selected variable value.

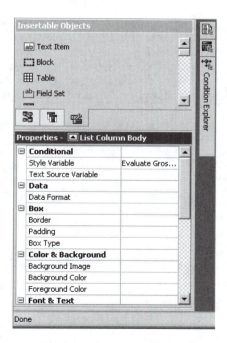

15. To change the background color of cells whose values meet the condition, click Background Color on the Style toolbar.

16. Select a color. You can also specify the background color from the Properties pane by clicking on the ellipsis for the Background Color property.

17. To change the text color, click Foreground Color on the Style toolbar.

18. Select a color. You can also specify the text color from the Properties pane by clicking on the ellipsis for the Foreground Color property.

19. Repeat steps 12 through 18 for the other values created for the variable. In our example, we set the colors for the values as specified in Table 9-5.

20. When finished, double-click the green Explorer bar to deactivate conditional formatting.

21. From the Standard toolbar, click Run Report. The results display as set:

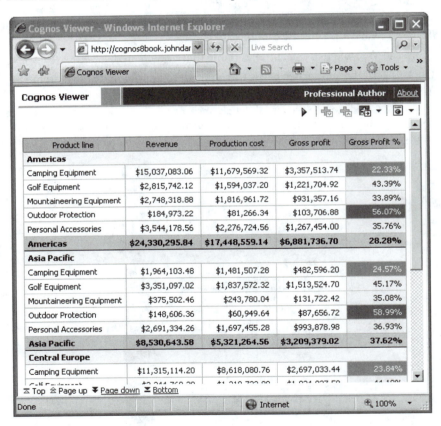

Prompting

You can add a prompt to a report to add interactivity for users. Prompts act as questions for specific areas of business that narrow the result set, making the report more manageable. Prompts can come in many styles such as text box prompts, value prompts, search and select prompts, and date prompts. Within each style, a variety of properties can be changed to alter its functionality. For example, you can set a value prompt to allow one or multiple items to be selected. Date prompts can prompt for a single date or a range of dates.

In this section, we add a prompt for product line to the example report we have been using throughout the chapter. With a prompt for product line added to the report, the user can choose which product line(s) display in the report.

Here's how to add a prompt to a report:

1. In the work area, select the column that contains the data item or the column header for which you want to add a prompt. In this example, we select the product line column.

2. From the Standard toolbar, click Build Prompt Page. This automatically creates a prompt page based on the column you selected.

3. From the Page Explorer, navigate to the new prompt page. The prompt page consists of a title for the prompt and the prompt itself, as shown next. Report Studio places each of these objects into a *block object*. This gives you the flexibility to align and space each object on the page.

4. From the Standard toolbar, click Run Report. The prompt screen displays.

5. From the prompt, make a selection.

6. Click Finish.

7. The report filters out the values not selected. In the example, we choose Golf and Mountaineering Equipment at the Product Line prompt. Therefore, the other lines are not displayed in the report as shown next:

Product line	Revenue	Production cost	Gross profit	Gross Profit %
Americas				
Golf Equipment	$2,815,742.12	$1,594,037.20	$1,221,704.92	43.39%
Mountaineering Equipment	$2,748,318.88	$1,816,961.72	$931,357.16	33.89%
Americas	**$5,564,061.00**	**$3,410,998.92**	**$2,153,062.08**	**38.70%**
Asia Pacific				
Golf Equipment	$3,351,097.02	$1,837,572.32	$1,513,524.70	45.17%
Mountaineering Equipment	$375,502.46	$243,780.04	$131,722.42	35.08%
Asia Pacific	**$3,726,599.48**	**$2,081,352.36**	**$1,645,247.12**	**44.15%**

PART III

Report Studio completed several actions when creating the prompt. To take a closer look, select Query Explorer from the Explorer bar. Report Studio created the Product line query, as shown here:

By opening the existing query (Query1 in this example), you can see a Detail Filter has been added to filter the query on the selections that were made at the prompt.

New Filter

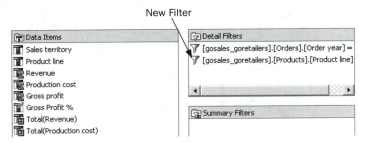

Double-click the new filter to view the filter in more detail. The Expression Definition displays as *[gosales_goretailers].[Products].[Product line] in ?Product line?*, in this example. The filter is a key component in creating prompts.

Cascading Prompt

With *cascading prompts*, the values in one prompt are driven by what is selected in another prompt. In our example, the Product Type prompt is driven by what is selected in the Product Line prompt. When a product line is selected, only product types within that product line are included in the Product Type prompt.

Here's how to create cascading prompts in a report:

1. Create a first prompt for your report to be used as the cascading source. In this example, we use the product line prompt we created in the last section. We have added the Product Type data item to the list between Product Line and Revenue. We have also grouped Product Line by selecting the column and clicking the Group/ Ungroup icon on the Standard toolbar.

2. Insert another prompt. The Prompt Wizard window displays. For this example, we first inserted two blocks from the Tools tab in the Insertable Objects pane: the first to add a text item to create a heading for the prompt; the second for a Value Prompt.

TIP   *Inserting items inside of blocks makes it easy to format the padding and alignment of the object.*

3. In the Create A New Parameter box, name the parameter.

4. Click Next. The Create Filter window displays.

5. Click the ellipsis button to the right of the Package Item property. The Choose Package Item window displays.

6. Choose a data item to which you want to link the prompt.

7. Click OK. In this example, we use Product Type from the Products query subject.

8. From the Operator list, select the appropriate operator. In this example, we choose the In operator.

9. Click Next. The Apply Filter window displays, allowing you to choose which queries are filtered by the prompt.

10. Select the appropriate checkbox. In this example, we select the Query1 checkbox.

11. Click Next. The Populate Control window displays.

12. In the Name text box, enter a name for the query.

13. From the Cascading Source list, select the prompt to be used as the source. In this example we select Product Line.

14. Click Finish.

15. Set any necessary properties of the first prompt from the Properties pane, as shown next. In this example, for the Product Line value prompt, we set the Multi-Select property to No and the Auto-Submit property to Yes. By setting Auto-Submit to Yes in the first prompt, options automatically appear in the second prompt when a selection is made in the first.

NOTE *The Multi-Select property defines whether a prompt allows you to select more than one item. Auto-Submit allows the prompt to automatically render the selection made, and can only be set to Yes if Multi-Select is set to No.*

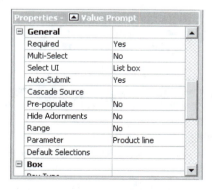

16. Set any necessary properties of the second prompt from the Properties pane. In this example, for the Product Type prompt, we set the Multi-Select property to Yes to allow the selection of multiple products.

17. From the Standard toolbar, click Run Report. The prompt screen displays.

18. From the first prompt, make a selection. The second prompt populates with options based on your selection at the source prompt. For this example, we choose Camping Equipment from the source prompt and select Cooking Gear, and Tents using CTRL-click at the Product Type prompt.

19. Click Finish. The report displays only the items that you selected at the second prompt, as shown next:

Product line	Product type	Revenue	Production cost	Gross profit	Gross Profit %
Americas					
Camping Equipment	Cooking Gear	$699,134.36	$502,868.96	$196,265.40	28.07%
	Tents	$8,931,122.62	$7,321,954.74	$1,609,167.88	18.02%
Americas		**$9,630,256.98**	**$7,824,823.70**	**$1,805,433.28**	**18.75%**
Asia Pacific					
Camping Equipment	Cooking Gear	$151,601.82	$103,855.76	$47,746.06	31.49%
	Tents	$1,020,742.12	$837,646.62	$183,095.50	17.94%
Asia Pacific		**$1,172,343.94**	**$941,502.38**	**$230,841.56**	**19.69%**

Adding Dynamic Titles

Adding *dynamic titles* to a report can allow users to see what was selected on the prompt screen. For our example, we continue to use the example report created throughout the chapter, to which we have added the title Gross Profit Margin.

Here's how to add dynamic titles to a report:

1. In the Insertable Objects pane, click the Toolbox tab.

2. Drag a Block object below the title of the report.

3. From the Insertable Objects pane, drag a Text Item to the block.

4. Click OK without adding any text. A text object displays in the block object, as shown next:

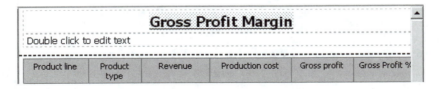

5. In the block object, click the Text Item.

6. In the Properties pane, set the Source Type property to Report Expression (by default it is set to Text).

7. Click the ellipsis at the right of the Report Expression property. The Report Expression window displays.

8. In the Available Components pane, click the Parameters tab.

9. Double-click a parameter to add it to the expression. In this example, we add Product line. The expression *ParamDisplayValue('Product line')* is added to the Expression Definition pane:

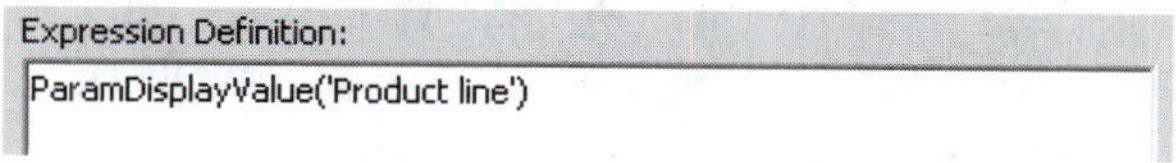

Expression Definition:
ParamDisplayValue('Product line')

10. Click OK. In this example, we repeat steps 1 through 9 to add a second dynamic title for the parameter for Product Type.

11. From the Standard toolbar, click Run Report. The prompt screen displays.

12. From the prompts, make your selections.

13. Click Finish. In this example, we select Camping Equipment at the Product line prompt, and from the Product Type list, we select Cooking Gear and Lanterns. The report displays the items that you selected in the prompt below the title and above the list report, as shown next:

Gross Profit Margin

Camping Equipment
Cooking Gear, Lanterns

Product line	Product type	Revenue	Production cost	Gross profit	Gross Profit %
Americas					
Camping Equipment	Cooking Gear	$699,134.36	$502,868.96	$196,265.40	28.07%
	Lanterns	$1,499,253.72	$1,060,521.26	$438,732.46	29.26%
Americas		**$2,198,388.08**	**$1,563,390.22**	**$634,997.86**	**28.88%**

Adding Formatting to Parameters

Adding formatting to parameters makes it easier for end users to locate and view data on the report. For this example, we continue to use the example report created throughout this chapter.

Here's how to add formatting to parameters in a report:

1. Select the Block objects that contain the title of the report and the dynamic title(s) created in the previous section.

TIP *Selecting multiple items at once can be accomplished holding the* CTRL *button while clicking on objects.*

---

2. In the Properties pane, click the ellipsis to the right of the Padding property. The Padding window displays.

3. Add padding to the objects. In this illustration, we add 7 pixels of padding to the Top and Bottom of the object and leave the Left and Right padding blank.

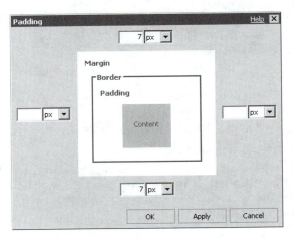

4. Click OK.

5. Select the Block object that contains the dynamic title.

6. In the Properties pane, double-click the Border property. The Border window displays.

7. Add any borders to the object you would like. In this example, we have two dynamic titles. We add a top border to the first and a bottom border to the second.

8. From the Toolbox tab in the Insertable Objects pane, drag a Text Item in front of the parameter in the Block that contains the dynamic title. The Text dialog box displays.

9. Type descriptive text for the parameter. Be sure to leave a space after the text so that the text and the parameter do not run together, and then click OK. We add the text Product Line: for our first parameter and then repeat steps 6 and 7 to add Product Type(s): for the second parameter.

10. From the Style toolbar, you can use features such as Bold, Foreground Color, and Font to format the text. We make our text Bold and change the Foreground color to Blue.

11. From the Standard toolbar, click Run Report. The results display:

Gross Profit Margin

Product Line: Camping Equipment

Product Type: Cooking Gear, Lanterns

Product line	Product type	Revenue	Production cost	Gross profit	Gross Profit %
Americas					
Camping Equipment	Cooking Gear	$699,134.36	$502,868.96	$196,265.40	28.07%
	Lanterns	$1,499,253.72	$1,060,521.26	$438,732.46	29.26%
Americas		**$2,198,388.08**	**$1,563,390.22**	**$634,997.86**	**28.88%**

The dynamic title stands out after the basic formatting we have applied to it. You can also use similar formatting techniques on the Prompt page to make it easier for the end user to read.

Creating Crosstab Reports

The crosstab report layout is quite different from a list report. Crosstab reports summarize data in a table format.

Here's how to create a crosstab report:

1. Open Report Studio.

2. From the Welcome dialog box click Create A New Report Or Template.

3. From the New dialog box, click Crosstab.

4. Click OK. The template for the crosstab report displays in the work area, as shown next:

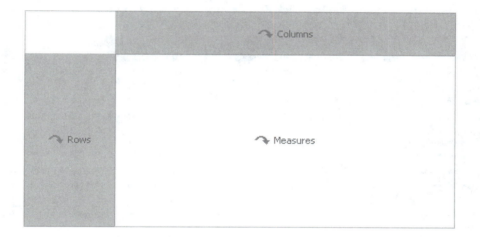

5. From the Source tab in the Insertable Objects pane, drag a data item to the Columns section of the work area. In this example, we add the Order Year query item from the Orders query subject of the Go Sales and Retailers package to the columns.

6. From the Source tab in the Insertable Objects pane, drag a data item to the Rows section of the work area. In this example, we add the Sales Territory query item from the Countries query subject to the rows.

7. Optionally, nest data items within the rows of the crosstab by dragging items from the Insertable Objects pane to the right of the Rows section in the work area. In this example, we drag the Product Line query item from the Products query subject and drop it to the right of Sales Territory in the Rows drop zone.

8. Optionally, nest data items within the columns of the crosstab by dragging items from the Insertable Objects pane to the bottom of the Columns section in the work area. In this example, we drag the Revenue measure from the Orders query subject and drop it below Order Year in the Columns section of the crosstab.

		<#Order year#>		<#Order year#>	
		<#Revenue#>	<#Gross profit#>	<#Revenue#>	<#Gross profit#>
<#Sales territory#>	<#Product line#>	<#1234#>	<#1234#>	<#1234#>	<#1234#>
	<#Product line#>	<#1234#>	<#1234#>	<#1234#>	<#1234#>
<#Sales territory#>	<#Product line#>	<#1234#>	<#1234#>	<#1234#>	<#1234#>
	<#Product line#>	<#1234#>	<#1234#>	<#1234#>	<#1234#>

9. From the Standard toolbar, click Run Report. The results display:

		2004		2005		2006	
		Revenue	Gross profit	Revenue	Gross profit	Revenue	Gross profit
Americas	Camping Equipment	$10,437,996.60	$2,463,558.02	$11,776,754.50	$2,723,916.84	$15,037,083.06	$3,357,513.74
	Golf Equipment	$1,978,245.94	$903,221.50	$2,429,298.30	$1,063,320.04	$2,815,742.12	$1,221,704.92
	Outdoor Protection	$492,499.26	$272,295.20	$261,716.62	$146,450.62	$184,973.22	$103,706.88
	Personal Accessories	$2,504,156.96	$953,578.58	$2,887,110.38	$1,061,068.40	$3,544,178.56	$1,267,454.00
	Mountaineering Equipment			$2,118,698.50	$730,998.80	$2,748,318.88	$931,357.16
Asia Pacific	Camping Equipment	$99,813.98	$28,089.00	$1,684,035.12	$404,580.86	$1,964,103.48	$482,596.20
	Golf Equipment	$852,136.08	$415,604.64	$2,336,650.90	$1,071,842.88	$3,351,097.02	$1,513,524.70
	Outdoor Protection	$242,884.38	$139,554.80	$224,318.20	$130,712.06	$148,606.36	$87,656.72
	Personal Accessories	$814,797.98	$319,422.36	$1,955,473.76	$762,501.76	$2,691,334.26	$993,878.98
	Mountaineering Equipment			$341,886.14	$126,995.38	$375,502.46	$131,722.42

Crosstab reports also allow you to aggregate both the rows and columns. You can add formatting to the report to make it more visually appealing for the end user, along with conditional highlighting, prompts, dynamic titles, and many of the same options that were used on the list report.

Creating Chart Reports

Charts are a graphical representation of tabular data. They can be used to quickly identify large numeric data for different areas of business. They are commonly used in dashboard style reports.

Here's how to create a simple chart report:

1. Open Report Studio.

2. From the Welcome dialog box, click Create A New Report Or Template.

3. From the New dialog box, select Chart.
4. Click OK. The Insert Chart dialog box displays:

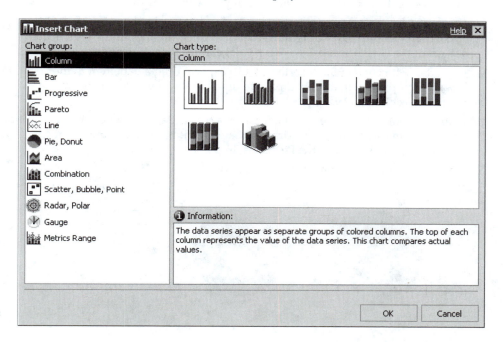

5. Under Chart Group, select a group. For this example, we select Pie, Donut.
6. In the Chart Type pane, select a type for your chart. We select Pie With 3-D Visual Effect.
7. Click OK. A blank chart displays in the work area:

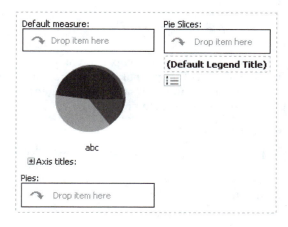

8. A pie chart has three drop zones: Default Measure, Pie Slices, and Pies. The Default Measure is the value that you want measured across each Pie and Pie Slice. Pies and Pie Slices can be the areas of business that you want to evaluate.

9. From the Source tab in the Insertable Objects pane, drag a data item to the Pies drop zone. In this example, we drag the Order Year query item from the Orders query subject of the Go Sales and Retailers package to the Pies drop zone.

10. From the Source tab in the Insertable Objects pane, drag a data item to the Default Measure drop zone. In this example, we drag the Revenue measure from the Orders query subject to the Default Measure drop zone.

11. From the Source tab in the Insertable Objects pane, drag a data item to the Pie Slices drop zone. In this example, we drag the Sales Territory query item from the Countries query subject to the Pie Slices drop zone.

12. From the Standard toolbar, click Run Report. The results display:

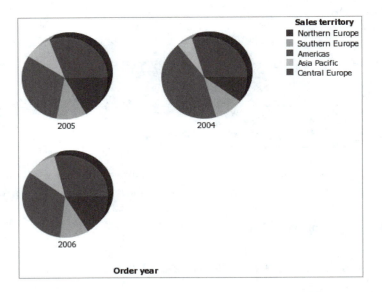

Our results graphically show a year-by-year comparison of revenue for each sales territory. You can see that Americas and Central Europe make up a large portion of the revenues. By default, you do not see how much revenue each sales territory generated.

Here's how to display the measure for each pie slice:

1. In Report Studio, select the chart.

2. In the Properties pane, the Values property is set to None by default. Set it to Inside Slices, Outside Slices, or Outside Slices With Lines. The Values property determines if and where values for the slices will display. In our example, we set the Values property to Outside Slices With Lines.

3. Set any other properties you want for the chart. In this example, we set the Tooltips property, which shows detailed information for the slices when you move your pointer over the slices, to Show (by default it is set to Hide), and then set the Value Representation property to Percent (by default it is set to Values). The Value Representation property determines whether the values are displayed as the actual values or as a percentage of the whole.

4. From the Standard toolbar, click Run Report. The results display, as shown next:

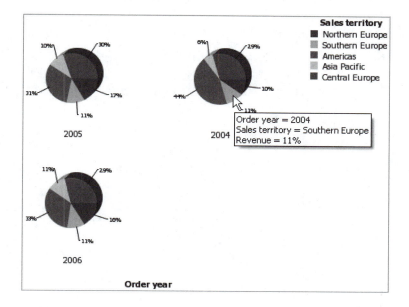

Our results show the percentage for each Sales territory. When you point to a pie slice, a screen tip appears, describing the order year, sales territory, and the revenue generated.

Advanced Reporting II

In Chapter 9, you learned how to create a report, add filters, group reports, and apply formatting, among other things. In this chapter, you will learn about some advanced features, including the variety of query types available, setting variables, and adding HTML items in reports. You will also learn how to create drill-through access, use advanced prompting, select ancestors, and create a table of contents (including entries for particular data items and bookmarks) to make navigating through reports and data easier for the user.

The No Data Contents option displays a message for the user when a report does not have data to display. The Master Detail Relationships option allows you to link separate data containers such as a list, crosstab, or chart within a report, and the Singleton object allows you to take a single query item and place it anywhere in the report layout; both options offer a high level of flexibility when you are creating advanced reports. Finally, the Bursting option distributes the contents of a report to specific recipients or groups via e-mail or to a directory in Cognos Connection.

Create a Drill-Through

Creating drill-through access within a report makes it easier for you to navigate through large reports or link separate reports containing related information. When you create drill-through access, you can create a bookmark that lets you navigate through a particular dimension of a report or pass a parameter from a source report to a target report. When the drill-through data item value in the source report is selected, the target report opens. The target report is filtered on the parameter that was passed from the source report. This allows you to link separate reports with related information. For the following example, we will set up drill-through access using two separate reports: a target report and a source report.

Set Up a Target Report for Drill-Through Access

The target report opens after you click a data item value in the source report. This report contains related or more detailed information about the source report. In the next section, we create a source report that contains revenue for all sales regions by year. In this section, sales region is set up as our drill-through text within the target report. When you click the sales region drill-through text, the target report opens, displaying revenue for sales staff for the sales region that was selected in the source report. Setting up drill-through access gives the user quick access to detailed information without having to navigate through folders to run another report.

Here's how to set up a target report for drill-through access:

1. Create or open a report to use as the target report. For this example, we use a crosstab with Sales Staff nested within Sales Region as the rows, Current Year as the columns, and Revenue as the measure.

2. Create a detail filter for the target report that uses the parameter on which you want to filter when drilling-through from the source report. For this example, we create a filter for Sales Region, as shown next. This filters the report based on which sales region is selected in the source report.

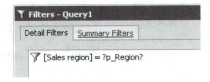

NOTE *For more information on adding a filter to a report, refer to Chapter 9.*

---

3. Save the target report. For this example, we save the target report as Sales Staff Revenue by Year.

TIP *You can run the target report to see that you are prompted for the value correctly to ensure that the filter is right.*

Set Up a Source Report for Drill-Through Access

The source report contains the data item value which a user can click to drill-through to the target report to view more detailed information. To set up the source report to contain the drill-through definition, you need to know the name and location of the target report and the parameter used in the filter of the target report.

Here's how to set up a source report for drill-through access:

1. Create or open a report to use as the source report that contains the item you want to use for the drill-through. For this example, we use a crosstab with Sales Region as the rows, Current Year as the columns, and Revenue as the measure. We are using Sales Region as the drill-through.

2. In the work area, select the item to be used as the drill-through. For this example, we select Sales Region in the rows of the crosstab.

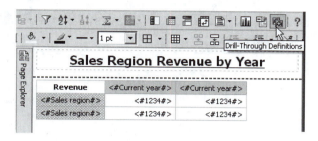

NOTE *To activate the Drill-Through Definitions option, you must first make a selection in the work area.*

3. Click the Drill-Through Definitions button on the standard toolbar. The Drill-Through Definitions screen displays:

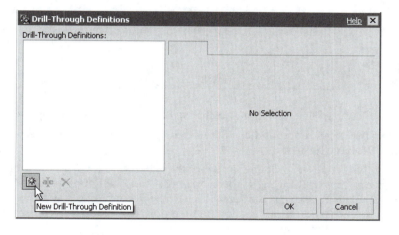

4. Click the New Drill-Through Definition button. The Drill-Through Definitions screen displays, as shown next.

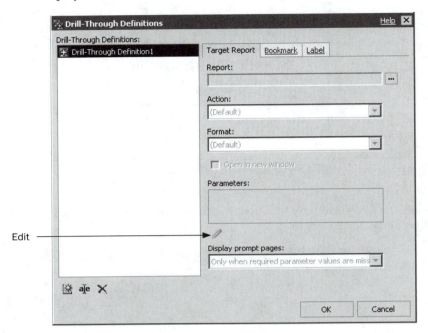

Edit

5. Under Report, click the ellipsis to choose the report to drill-through to.

6. Select the target report and click the Open button. For this example, we select Sales Staff Revenue by Year.

7. From the Action drop-down list, select the action for how the target report will render during drill-through. You can choose Run The Report, which runs the report and displays the most recent data; View Most Recent Report, which displays the most recent saved output version of the report; or Default, which uses the report action defined in Cognos Connection.

8. From the Format drop-down list, select the output format for the report when it runs. You can choose HTML, PDF, Excel 2007, Excel 2002, Excel 2000 Single Sheet, Delimited Text (CSV), XML, and Default, which uses the output format defined in Cognos Connection.

9. Optionally, select the Open In New Window checkbox to open the target report in a new window when it is accessed from the source report. If you do not select this checkbox, the target report replaces the source report in the Cognos Viewer.

10. Click Edit to display the parameters from the target report. The Parameters dialog displays with the details of the parameter(s) in the target report:

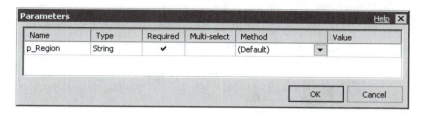

11. From the Method drop-down list, select the method for passing the parameter. You can choose from Do Not Use Parameter, which does not pass the parameter; Pass Data Item Value, which passes a value from a data item within the source report; Pass Parameter Value, which passes a parameter value from the source report; or Default, which does not pass the parameter. For this example, we select Pass Data Item Value.

12. From the Value drop-down list, select the Data Item value from the source report. In this example, we use Sales Region.

13. Click OK. The parameter(s) to pass to the drill-through definition display in the Parameters box on the Drill-Through Definitions screen.

14. From the Display Prompt Pages drop-down list, select an option for when to display the prompt pages. The available options are Always, Based On The Default Prompt Settings Of The Target Report, and Only When Required Parameter Values Are Missing. For this example, we use Only When Required Parameter Values Are Missing.

15. Click OK. Report Studio updates the report. The data item being used as a drill-through object becomes a hyperlink, and the drill-through icon displays, as shown next:

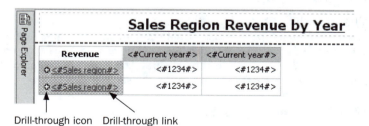

Drill-through icon   Drill-through link

16. Run the report to test the drill-through. The source report opens in Cognos Viewer and the data items containing the drill-through definition display as hyperlinks that allow you to drill-through to the target report, as shown next:

Sales Region Revenue by Year

Revenue	2004	2005	2006	2007
Americas	$192,230,456.30	$239,213,647.85	$312,037,992.91	$233,605,783.74
Asia Pacific	$166,746,977.65	$212,250,513.92	$275,691,959.90	$204,564,826.67
Central Europe	$428,821,196.74	$539,235,928.65	$675,574,387.12	$499,863,272.05
Northern Europe	$70,230,147.41	$90,215,646.65	$117,148,067.64	$91,945,289.26
Southern Europe	$56,324,025.62	$78,279,853.09	$115,438,693.33	$87,357,102.35

17. From the column containing the drill-through definition links, click a hyperlink. The drill-through target report displays with detailed information about the selected item. In this example, the target report opens and displays detailed information about the sales staff within the Central Europe region.

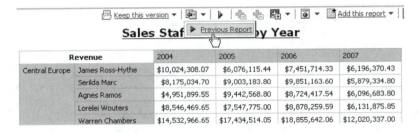

Revenue		2004	2005	2006	2007
Central Europe	James Ross-Hythe	$10,024,308.07	$6,076,115.44	$7,451,714.33	$6,196,370.43
	Serilda Marc	$8,175,034.70	$9,003,183.80	$9,851,163.60	$5,879,334.80
	Agnes Ramos	$4,951,899.55	$9,442,568.80	$8,724,417.54	$6,096,683.80
	Lorelei Wouters	$8,546,469.65	$7,547,775.00	$8,878,259.59	$6,131,875.85
	Warren Chambers	$14,532,966.65	$17,434,514.05	$18,855,642.06	$12,020,337.00

TIP *To return to the source report, click Previous Report on the Cognos Viewer toolbar and then click the source report link.*

Master Detail Relationship

Master detail relationships link information between two data containers (such as a list, crosstab, or chart) within a report: a master data container, and a detail data container. Using a master detail relationship, you can use a single report to display information that would normally take two reports. You can also link data from two separate data sources into one report, as long as the data sources are in the same package.

Create a Master Detail Relationship

Master detail relationships can be created for any data container within Report Studio (such as a list, crosstab, or chart). This section describes the steps required to link a crosstab, which will be the master data container, with a chart, which will be the detail data container. Here's how to create master detail relationships:

1. Create or open a report to use that has one data item container. For this example, we create a crosstab report with Product Type nested within Product Line as the rows, Current Year sorted in ascending order as the columns and Revenue as the measure.

2. From the Toolbox tab in the Insertable Objects pane, drag a container object next to the container in the work area. For this example, we insert a chart object and then choose Column chart from the Insert Chart dialog box.

3. Insert data items from the Insertable Objects pane into the container. For this example, we insert Revenue as the Default measure, Current Year as the Category and Product Type as the Series, as shown next:

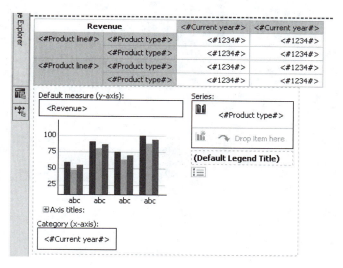

4. From the Standard toolbar, click Unlock (the padlock icon) to unlock page objects.

5. Select the second container object, and drag it into the first container where you want to place it. In this example, we drop the chart to the left of the Product Type data item in the rows of the crosstab. The chart displays embedded within the crosstab, as shown next:

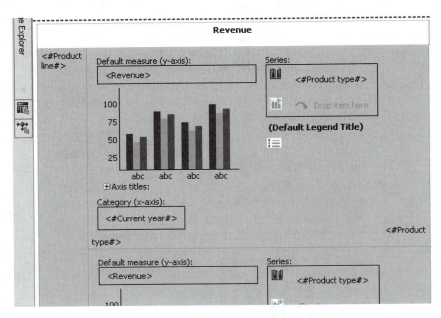

6. Click the embedded container object to select it.

7. From the Data menu, click Master Detail Relationships to create the master detail links. The Master Detail Relationships dialog displays the data items that make up the first container from Query1 and the data items that make up the second container from Query2:

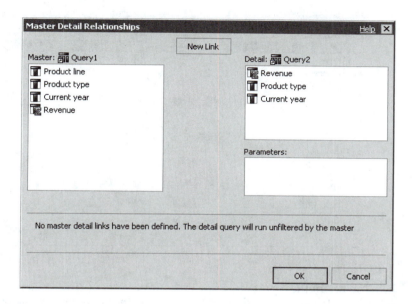

8. Click New Link to create a master detail link. Report Studio creates a link between the first data items from each query.

9. Select the data items from each query that you want to link for the master detail relationship. In this example, we select Product Type from both Query1 and Query2.

The selected data item in the Master area now links to the selected data item in the Detail area as shown by the arrow:

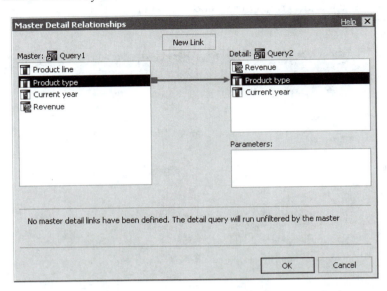

10. Click OK.
11. Click Run to run the report and view the output to ensure the master detail relationship displays properly. For this example, the chart displays nested in the crosstab and correctly shows the data for the Product Type that it is embedded within, as shown next:

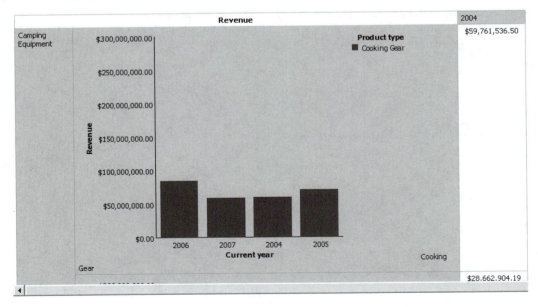

Although the master detail relationship is displaying properly within the report, it is a little difficult to digest, as the chart is very large within the crosstab. Properties of the chart can be modified to change the appearance of the chart.

With the chart selected, we modify the following features from the Properties pane:

- Legend, Y1 Axis, and Ordinal Axis are set to Hide so that these items do not appear with the chart.

- Relative Alignment is set to Middle of Text so that text in the cell with the chart is centered vertically.

- Height and Width for the Size & Overflow property are both set to 50 px so that the size of the chart is manipulated to 50 pixels by 50 pixels.

We run the report to view the results again. By using the master detail relationship to link the list to the chart, we now have a small graphical representation nested within each Product Type that shows how they have performed over four years, as shown next:

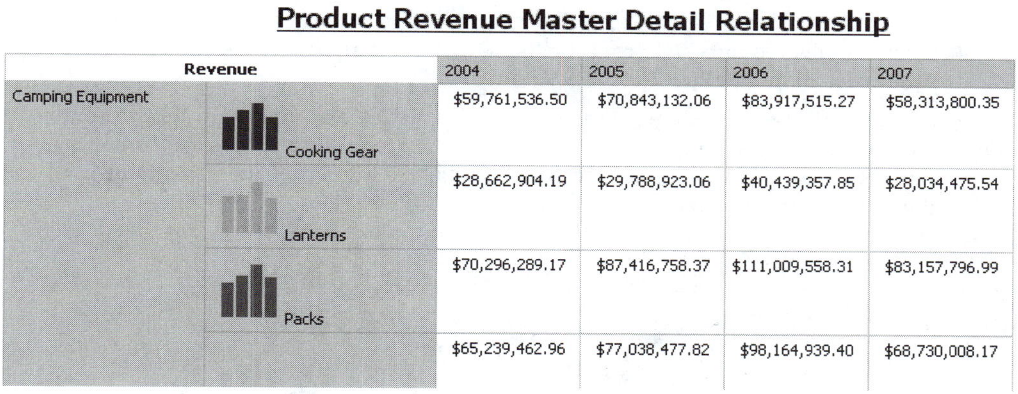

Product Revenue Master Detail Relationship

Revenue		2004	2005	2006	2007
Camping Equipment	Cooking Gear	$59,761,536.50	$70,843,132.06	$83,917,515.27	$58,313,800.35
	Lanterns	$28,662,904.19	$29,788,923.06	$40,439,357.85	$28,034,475.54
	Packs	$70,296,289.17	$87,416,758.37	$111,009,558.31	$83,157,796.99
		$65,239,462.96	$77,038,477.82	$98,164,939.40	$68,730,008.17

Selecting Ancestors

Ancestors are all of the containers that hold the currently selected container. Clicking the Select Ancestor button displays a list of ancestors for the currently selected container. This allows you to navigate quickly through the containers on a page or to select common containers of the page that you are not able to easily select in the work area, so that you can change their properties or apply styles to them.

For example, suppose you have created a report that has a heading and contents which are the same size and font, causing the information to blend together. The headings can be quickly modified by using the Select Ancestor button to select the appropriate data container. The properties of all headings can then be simultaneously edited to increase font size and perhaps make the heading text bold to distinguish the headings from the contents of the report.

Here's how to select ancestors:

1. Open a report. Report Studio displays the report in the work area.

2. Click the work area outside of any containers. The Page Body properties display in the Properties pane.

3. In the title bar of the Properties pane, click the Select Ancestor button. A context menu displays the available ancestors for the selected item. In this example, we click the Select Ancestor button to display the ancestors for Page Body, as shown next:

4. Click the desired ancestor from the list. For this example, we select Page. The page properties display in the Properties pane.

5. From the Properties pane, set the desired properties. For this example, we set the Horizontal Alignment property to Center. Report Studio displays the contents of the page with the settings you selected applied to the report in the work area. Here, the contents of the page are centered:

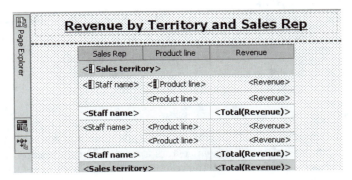

Modify the Style for Multiple Items

You can edit the properties of a style, such as list column title style, which modifies the style of all instances of that data container type. This method is faster than changing the style of items individually.

Here's how to modify the style of multiple items:

1. Click a cell whose style appears in multiple instances, and then click the Select Ancestor button. Here, List Column Body is chosen. A context menu displays the available levels of ancestors:

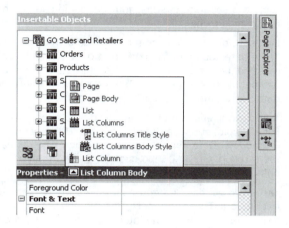

2. Choose the appropriate style for the data container item you want to edit.

3. In the Properties pane, set the desired properties.

Query Management

A *query* defines the data items and conditions that, when sent to the data source, determine the set of data that is returned for inclusion in the report. A Report Studio report can contain multiple queries, resulting in multiple sets of data being included in the report. They can be managed using Query Explorer, which gives you a great deal of control over the data that appears in a report.

Queries must be associated to the report layout in order for the data to appear in the report. You can associate your queries to the report layout in several ways. If you create the report by starting with a report template that contains a data container (such as a list, crosstab, or chart), a query is automatically associated with the layout. If you start with a blank report and drag a data container to the work area, a query is created and automatically associated to the layout. At any time, you can change the query that is associated to a data container by changing the Query property of the data container in the Properties pane.

Query Types

Report Studio provides several types of queries, such as Join, Union, Intersect, and others, which are described in detail in Table 10-1. These give you the flexibility to create complex reports and to create reports using query items from different data sources. The query types listed in the table are accessible by navigating to Queries from the Query Explorer menu.

Icon	Description
Query	Adds a single query to a report. Single query objects, single query items, and multiple data items can be added within this query to return one subset of data in the report.
Join	Joins two separate queries. You can manipulate the relationships between the queries using links.
Union	Links two queries into one subset of data. The two queries can be from the same data source or from different data sources. Note that the queries must contain the same number of data items, the data types must be compatible (for example, a Date is only compatible with a Date), and the data items must appear in the same order.
Intersect	Takes two queries and returns only the data that intersects in each query. For example, suppose Query1 contains 100 products and Query2 contains 3 products. Data item(s) are returned only when a match occurs between the two queries. So if 2 products in Query1 match 2 products in Query2, only 2 products are returned.
Except	Takes two queries and returns the data where no match occurs between each query. This query performs the opposite of the Intersect query. Using the example for the Intersect query, 98 products would be returned.
SQL	Writes a SQL statement manually or converts a regular query into a SQL query object. This query corresponds to relational models. Note that once a query item is converted into a SQL query object, you cannot pull data from your source model. Any additional data must be added manually.
MDX	Writes Multidimensional Expressions (MDX) code manually, which is the underlying SQL for dimensional models. Note that once a query item is converted into a SQL query object, you cannot pull data from your source model. Any additional data must be added manually.

TABLE 10-1   Cognos 8 Query Types

Creating a Join

Joins link two separate queries. This can allow you to perform a calculation between these queries that might not be possible without the join. For example, suppose you have created individual queries for each year that each return the revenue for retailers, and you want to measure the rate of growth from year to year for each retailer. Using joins, you can join the query that returns the first year's revenue with the query that returns the second year's revenue and measure the rate of growth between each year in a new query.

Here's how to create a join between two queries:

1. Create a new report using the blank template.

2. From the Query Explorer tab, click the Queries link. The available queries display in the work area.

3. From the Insertable Objects pane, drag a Join object into the work area. The Join object creates *Query1*, the Join relationship object, and two drop areas for the queries that you want to join, as shown next:

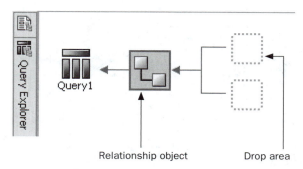

Relationship object   Drop area

4. From the Insertable Objects pane, drag a Query object into the first (upper) drop area in the work area. A shortcut to Query2 displays in the first (upper) drop area, and *Query2* displays on the page in the work area:

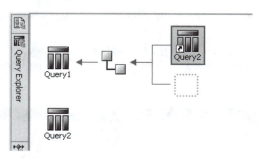

5. From the Insertable Objects pane, drag another Query object to the second (lower) drop area. A shortcut to Query3 appears in the join relationship and *Query3* displays in the work area.

6. Double-click one of the two queries that make up the join and add the desired data items to the query by dragging items from the Insertable Objects pane to the Data Items area in the work area. For this example, we add Retailer Name, Current Year, and Revenue to Query3.

7. From the Properties pane, set any desired properties for the data items, such as Type, Name, or Label. For this example, we set the Name property of Revenue to *2006 Revenue* and the Name property of Current Year to *Current year 2006.*

8. From the Data Items area, drag any desired data item(s) to use as a filter into the Detail Filters area and set the detail filter expression(s). For this example, we define a detail filter using the Current Year data item to limit data retrieved by this query to the year 2006.

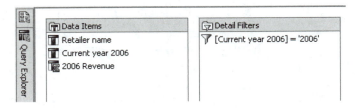

9. From the Query Explorer tab, open the other query that makes up the join and then add the desired data items to the query. For this example, we add Retailer Name, Current Year, and Revenue to Query 2.

10. Repeat steps 7 and 8 to set any properties of the data items or any detail filters for the query. For this example, we repeat these steps for Query2 using 2005 in place of 2006.

11. From the Query Explorer tab, click the Queries link. The available queries display in the work area.

12. In the work area, double-click the Join relationship object. The Join Relationships screen displays with the data items that make up each query listed in the Query2 and Query3 areas:

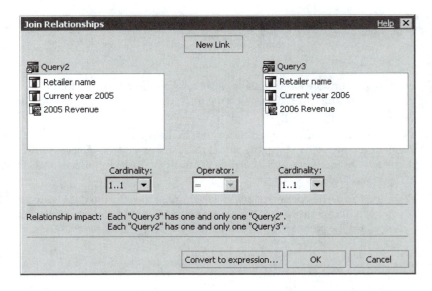

As an alternative, from the Properties pane, at the end of the Join Relationships property, you can click the ellipsis to work with the Join Relationships.

13. Click New Link to create a join relationship between two data items. Report Studio creates a link between the first data items from each query.

14. Select the data items from each query that you want to link for the join relationship. For this example, the Retailer Name data item from each query is what we want to link, because Retailer Name is the common attribute between the queries.

15. In both Cardinality drop-down lists, select the applicable relationship impact setting for the data items. The available options are 1..n, 1..1, 0..n, and 0..1. For this example, we select 1..1 so that the report displays the retailers that are the same from both queries.

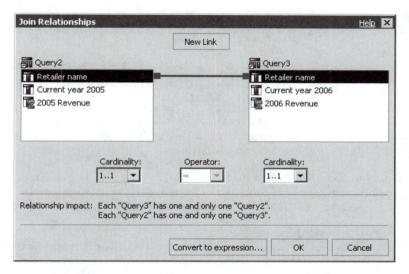

16. Click OK to save the specified join relationship settings.

17. Double-click the join query, and add the desired data items to the query. For this example, we add Retailer Name, 2005 Revenue, and 2006 Revenue to Query1:

At this point, the join query is complete and can be linked to from a data container in the layout. For this example, we create a list in the layout of the report and link it to the join query.

18. From the Page Explorer tab, open the page. Report Studio displays a blank template in the work area.

19. From the Toolbox tab in the Insertable Objects pane, drag a data container object into the work area. For this example, we use a List object to create a list report.

20. In the Properties pane of the data container, set the Query property to the join query. In this example, we set the Query property to Query1 for the List data container, as shown next. The data items within Query1 are now available for use:

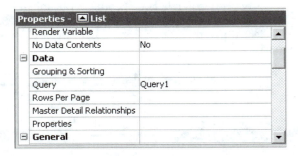

> **NOTE** *By default, when adding a data container, a new query is created for that container. In this example, Query4 was created when the list was added. When you set the Query property of the List data container to Query1, Report Studio removes Query4 as it did not contain data items.*

21. From the Data Items tab in the Insertable Objects pane, drag the data items from the join query into the data container in the work area. For this example, we add Retailer Name, 2005 Revenue, and 2006 Revenue to the list:

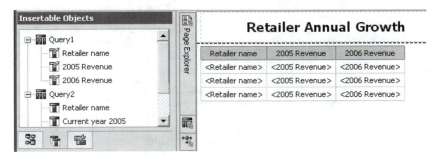

22. Add any other items to the report you want. For this example, to show the growth between the two years, we create a Query Calculation named Annual Growth that calculates the growth from year to year as the last column in the list, as shown next:

23. From the Properties pane, set the desired properties for any data items in the report, such as Source Type, Data Item Value, and Data Format. In this example, for the Annual Growth calculation, we set Format Type to Percent and No. of Decimal Places to 1 for the Data Format property.

24. Click Run to run the report and view the output. In this example, the growth between the revenue for each year displays in the Annual Growth column:

Retailer name	2005 Revenue	2006 Revenue	Annual Growth
1 for 1 Sports shop	$1,841,265.46	$1,715,812.95	-6.8%
4 Golf only	$1,667,634.53	$1,875,229.33	12.4%
Aarhus Sport	$1,214,820.52	$2,506,561.08	106.3%
Accapamento	$1,711,149.20	$2,613,580.91	52.7%
Accesorios Importados, S.A. de C.V.	$1,853,330.86	$2,650,667.17	43.0%
AcquaVerde	$2,084,544.22	$2,881,701.02	38.2%

Creating a Union

Unions let you link two separate queries into one result set. When using the Union object, two queries can come from the same data source or from separate data sources.

NOTE *For the Union to work properly, each query must have the same number of data items, the data types must be compatible, and the data items must appear in the same order.*

For example, suppose the Sales division of a large corporation has multiple territories that contain a different number of sales representatives within each territory. The corporation wants to create a sales report that shows the top five sales representatives and the bottom five sales representatives for all of the territories. To do this, the corporation creates a report that contains two separate queries. One query returns the top five sales representatives and the other query returns the bottom five sales representatives. The corporation pulls the two queries into one query, using the Union option and the same data source, to create the sales report.

Here's how to create a union between two queries:

1. Create a new report using the blank template.

2. From the Query Explorer tab, click the Queries link. Currently, no queries are available, so no queries appear in the work area.

3. From the Insertable Objects pane, drag the Union object into the work area. The Union query object creates *Query1*, the Union relationship object, and two drop areas for the queries that you want to link together in the work area, as shown next:

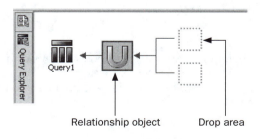

Relationship object   Drop area

4. From the Insertable Objects pane, drag a Query object into the first (upper) drop area in the work area. A shortcut to Query2 displays in the first (upper) drop area and *Query2* displays on the page in the work area:

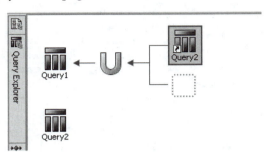

5. From the Insertable Objects pane, drag another Query object to the second (lower) drop area. A shortcut to Query3 displays in the union relationship and *Query3* displays in the work area.

6. Double-click one of the two queries that make up the union and add the desired data items to the query by dragging items from the Insertable Objects pane to the Data Items area in the work area.

   For this example, we add Sales Region, Staff Name, Current Year, and Revenue to Query3. We also create a new data item named Rank that calculates sales region rank by dragging a Data Item object from the Toolbox tab in the Insertable Objects pane to the work area. The rank is sorted in ascending order to determine the bottom reps.

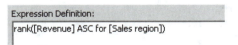

7. Edit the expression definitions of any data items you want by double-clicking on the data item. For this example, we edit the expression definition of Sales Region, so that the added text is concatenated onto the Sales Region data item in the report. We include a space before *Bottom* so that a space appears between the name of the region and the word Bottom in the report, as shown next:

8. From the Data Items area, drag any desired data item(s) to use as a filter to the Detail Filters area and set the detail filter expression(s). For this example, we define two detail filters. The first uses the Current Year data item to limit the data retrieved to 2006, as shown next:

Expression Definition:
[Current year] = '2006'

The second detail filter uses the Rank data item to retrieve representatives ranked less than or equal to 5:

> Expression Definition:
> [Rank] <= 5

9. From the Properties pane, set any desired properties, such as Type, Name, or Label. For this example, we set the Application property to After Auto Aggregation for the Rank detail filter, so that the rankings are determined before the filter is applied.

10. Repeat steps 6 through 9 for the other query that makes up the union. For this example, we repeat these steps for Query 2. We create a Rank data item sorting the rank in descending order to determine the top reps, and we edit the expression definition of Sales Region to include *Top 5 Reps*.

NOTE *Query2 must have the same number of data items in the same order as Query3. The data types must also be compatible.*

11. From the Query Explorer tab, click the Queries link to view the queries in the report.

12. From the Properties pane of the Union operator, set any properties you want. To retain all of the duplicate rows that are returned on the report, set the Duplicates property to Preserve. To change the order of the data items in the queries, set the Projection List property to Manual.

13. Double-click the union query, and add the desired data items that you want to the query. For this example, we add Sales Region, Staff Name, Current Year, Revenue, and Rank.

    At this point, the union query is complete and can be linked to from a data container in the layout. For this example, we create a list in the report layout and link it to the union query.

14. From the Page Explorer tab, open the page. Report Studio displays a blank template in the work area.

15. From the Toolbox tab in the Insertable Objects pane, drag a data container object into the work area. For this example, we use a List object to create a list report.

16. In the Properties pane of the data container, set the Query property to the union query. In this example, we set the Query property to Query1 for the List data container. The data items in Query1 are now available for use in this list.

NOTE *By default, when adding a data container, a new query is created for that container. In this example, Query 4 was created when the list was added. When the Query property is set to Query1, Report Studio removes Query4 as it did not contain data items.*

17. From the Data Items tab in the Insertable Objects pane, drag the data items from the union query into the data container in the work area. For this example, we add Sales Region, Staff Name, Revenue, and Rank to the list.

18. Format the report. For this example, we group Sales Region. We also aggregate a total for revenue, sort the Rank column in ascending order, and add a header for a title to the report.

NOTE *For detailed information on grouping data in reports, refer to Chapter 9.*

19. Click Run to run the report and view the output. In this example, the five top sales representatives and five bottom sales representatives display for each region and their corresponding revenue figures:

Top Reps vs. Bottom Reps for 2006

Sales region	Staff name	Revenue	Rank
Americas Bottom 5 Reps	Beatriz Couto	$905,704.48	1
	Morela Castro	$1,533,562.39	2
	Silvia Romero	$2,449,969.65	3
	Karly Millers	$3,392,973.85	4
	Samantha Pierce	$3,720,463.21	5
Americas Bottom 5 Reps		**$12,002,673.58**	
Americas Top 5 Reps	Charles Laurel	$20,681,527.49	1
	George Harrows	$17,924,373.12	2
	Lucía Reyna	$17,341,182.19	3
	Pascal Lanuit	$17,173,887.86	4
	Eduardo Guimarães	$15,262,238.60	5
Americas Top 5 Reps		**$88,383,209.26**	
Asia Pacific Bottom 5 Reps	Akira Hashimoto	$1,206,901.22	1

Specify What Appears when There Is No Data Available

When no data is available for a report, you can inform users that no data is available by defining what Report Studio displays. This can be defined for lists, crosstabs, charts, maps, repeaters, repeater tables, and table of contents objects. If a prompted value returns no data, a more specific message can be displayed for the users by informing them of the values entered that returned no data.

Setting up this feature can alleviate the confusion between a report that is still running and a report with no data to display. Without this feature, users may think a report is still running, unaware that the report has completed but no data is available.

NOTE *This option is not available in versions prior to 8.3.*

Here's how to set up the No Data Contents option:

1. Click a data container.
2. From the Properties pane, click the Select Ancestor button and choose the data container type. For this example, we choose Crosstab. (For information on selecting ancestors, refer to the "Selecting Ancestors" section of this chapter.)

3. From the Properties pane, set the No Data Contents property to Yes. Report Studio displays the No Data Contents tab in the work area with a place to create contents to display when no data is returned:

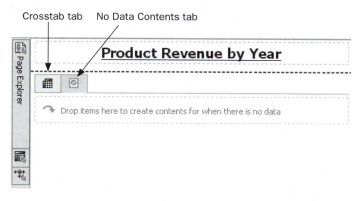

4. From the Toolbox tab in the Insertable Objects pane, drag the objects you want to display when no data is available. For this example, we use a Text Item and a Layout Calculation. The Layout Calculation is used to include the prompt value in the message to the user.

5. Click Run to run the report and view the output. The report displays in Cognos Viewer informing the user that no data is available. In this example, we chose 2008 at the prompt and the message "There is no data for 2008" displays:

Dynamic Data Formatting Using Variables

By using variables, you can change the format of values displayed in a report depending on what you choose at the prompt. For example, if you choose Quantity at the prompt, you could set the values to display in numeric form with no decimal places; but if Revenue is chosen, you could set the values to display as currency with two decimal places.

Here's how to set up dynamic data formatting using variables:

1. Create a new crosstab report. For this example, we use Product Line for the rows, Current Year for the columns, and Quantity as the measure.

2. Create a prompt page for the report that prompts the user to select a value. For this example, we use a value prompt with the parameter *p_Values* and static choices of *Quantity* and *Revenue* as the options.

3. From the Condition Explorer tab, click the Variables link. Report Studio displays a Variables area and a Values area in the work area:

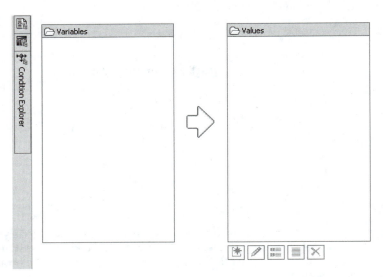

4. From the Insertable Objects pane, drag a variable into the Variables area.

   - If you select Report Language Variable, the Languages dialog displays. Select the applicable language checkboxes.

   - If you select String Variable or Boolean Variable, the Report Expression dialog displays. For this example, we use Boolean Variable. Set the expression definition for the variable. For this example, we use *ParamDisplayValue('p_Values') = 'Quantity'*.

5. Click OK. Report Studio adds *[Variable]1 (Report Language1, String1, or Boolean1)* in the work area.

6. From the Properties pane, set any desired properties, such as Type, Report Expression, or Name. For this example, we set the Name property to v_Values.

7. From the Query Explorer tab, open Query1.

8. Double-click a data item to set the expression definition to make the report dynamic based on what the user selects at the prompt. For this example, we use the Quantity data item and set the expression definition to a case statement. The case statement specifies the measure used in the crosstab based on the parameter used for the prompt. If the prompt returns 'Quantity', the data item is Quantity and if the prompt doesn't return 'Quantity' the data item is Revenue.

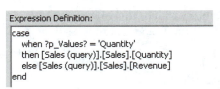

9. From the Page Explorer tab, open the report page.

10. Click a cell in the crosstab to set properties for the Crosstab Intersection.

11. From the Properties pane, set the Style Variable property to the name of the variable you created. For this example, it is set to v_Values.

12. From the Condition Explorer tab, click one of the values of your variable. For this example, we click Yes. The Explorer bar turns green, indicating that conditional formatting is turned on. Any changes that you make while the Explorer bar is green apply only to the variable value.

13. From the Properties pane, set the desired properties for the value, such as the Data Format. For this example, we set the Format Type to Number and the No. of Decimal Places to 0 for the Data Format property for the Yes value.

14. Repeat step 13 for the other variable value(s). For this example, we set the Format Type to Currency and the No. of Decimal Places to 2 for the Data Format property for the No value.

15. Click Run to run the report and view the output. The prompt dialog displays in Cognos Viewer with the specified prompt values. In this example, Quantity and Revenue display:

Prompt Page

Select a Value
⦿ Quantity
○ Revenue

Cancel	< Back	Next >	Finish

16. Select a value. For this example, we select Quantity.

17. Click Finish. The report displays in Cognos Viewer with the value you selected at the prompt. In this example, Quantity values display in a numeric format:

Quantity	2004	2005	2006	2007
Camping Equipment	5,895,053	6,903,764	8,399,156	6,103,176
Golf Equipment	1,092,982	1,297,793	1,536,772	1,186,154
Mountaineering Equipment		2,644,713	3,700,262	3,555,116
Outdoor Protection	5,614,356	4,111,058	1,599,585	689,446
Personal Accessories	7,572,339	8,567,357	10,706,015	8,061,994

18. Run the report again to select another value so that you can see the difference in the format of the values. The report displays in Cognos Viewer reflecting the new value

selected at the prompt. In this example, Revenue values display. Notice the format of the values now display in a dollar amount, as shown next:

Quantity	2004	2005	2006	2007
Camping Equipment	$332,986,338	$402,757,573	$500,382,423	$352,910,330
Golf Equipment	$153,553,851	$168,006,427	$230,110,271	$174,740,819
Mountaineering Equipment		$107,099,660	$161,039,823	$141,520,650
Outdoor Protection	$36,165,521	$25,008,574	$10,349,176	$4,471,025
Personal Accessories	$391,647,094	$456,323,356	$594,009,408	$443,693,450

Bursting Reports

Bursting lets you distribute the contents of a particular report that would be of interest or value to a recipient or group of individuals. For example, a sales report can have bursting applied for the individual sales representatives and the report can be distributed through e-mail showing only their individual sales; or the report can apply bursting to the sales representatives by territories showing their sales according to territory. A report can also be distributed to a directory and only those individuals who have access to that directory or report are able to access the report.

NOTE *For bursting to work properly, a recipient or group on which you want to burst the report (such as a territory or the individual users) must be specified in the report.*

Here's how to set up bursting in a report:

1. From the Query Explorer tab, open the query that retrieves the data you want to distribute.

2. From the Toolbox tab in the Insertable Objects pane, drag a data item into the Data Items area to add a recipient to receive the report. The Data Item Expression box displays. For this example, we want the report to burst to a group of Cognos users. We do the following:

   • From the Security tab in Cognos Administration, we open the Cognos Namespace:

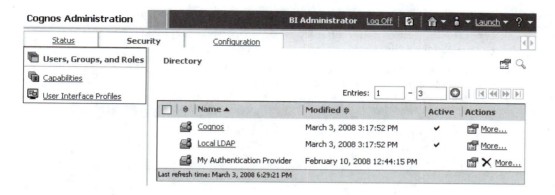

- In the Actions column, we select Set Properties for the consumer group.
- From the General tab, we click the View The Search Path, ID And URL link:

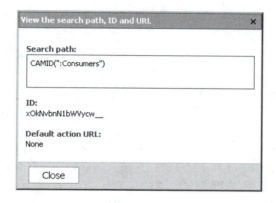

- Copy the text in the Search Path text box to insert into the expression definition in Report Studio.

3. In Report Studio, set the expression definition for the recipients of the report. For this example, we paste the Consumers group Search Path into the Expression Definition text box:

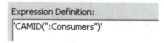

4. Click OK to save the expression definition for the new data item.

5. From the Properties pane, set any desired properties for the data item. For this example, we set the Name property to BurstRecipients.

6. From the File menu, select Burst Options. The Burst Options screen displays with a checkbox to make the report available for bursting:

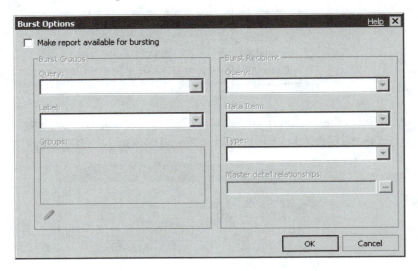

7. Select the Make Report Available For Bursting checkbox. Report Studio activates the Burst Groups and Burst Recipient areas.

8. From Query drop-down list in the Burst Groups area, select the query that you are using. For this example, we select Query1.

9. From the Label drop-down list, select the data item to be used to label each burst report. For this example, we use Sales Region.

10. Click the Edit button beneath the Groups area to specify the groups upon which the burst reports are based. The Grouping & Sorting dialog displays a list of available data items to select:

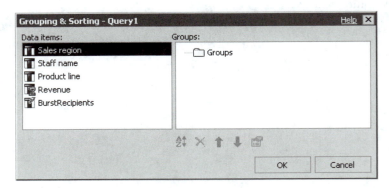

11. From the Data Items area, double-click the applicable data item by which you want the reports grouped and then click OK. For this example, we select Sales Region so that the reports are grouped by each region.

12. In the Burst Recipient area, in the Query drop-down list, select the query that you are using. For this example, we select Query1.

13. From the Data Item drop-down list, select the data item that you created for the recipients of the burst report(s). For this example, we select BurstRecipients.

14. From the Type list, select the applicable option to send the report. The available options are Automatic, Email addresses, and Directory entries. For this example, we select Directory entries.

15. Click OK to save the specified Burst Options.

16. From the standard toolbar, click Save to save the report. The report is ready for bursting.

17. In Cognos Connection, navigate to the saved report and click Run With Options from the Actions column of the entry to manually run the burst report.

18. On the Run With Options screen, click the Advanced Options link. The advanced options appear on the screen.

19. From the Time And Mode area, select the Run In The Background option to access the bursting option. The options update.

20. From the Bursting area, select the Burst The Report checkbox.

21. Click the Run button, and then click OK. Cognos Connection runs the report in the background.

22. From the actions column of the burst report entry, click View Report Output Versions. The output versions are displayed by the specified group. In this example, the report displays by sales region (Americas, Asia Pacific, Central Europe, and so on):

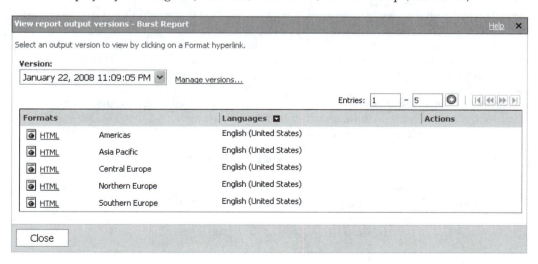

23. Click a report format link of a group. The report displays in Cognos Viewer with the items from the selected group. In this example, we select HTML for the Americas sales region:

Cognos Viewer - Burst Report   About

Keep this version ▼ ▶ | 🔲 🔲 🔲 ▼ | 🔲 ▼ | 🔲 Add this report ▼ | 🔲 Watch new versions ▼

Revenue by Territory

Sales region	Staff name	Product line	Revenue
Americas	Alexandre Pereira	Camping Equipment	$16,906,320.08
		Golf Equipment	$5,578,190.40
		Mountaineering Equipment	$7,156,071.19
		Outdoor Protection	$867,348.22
		Personal Accessories	$4,213,047.81
	Anna Valdez	Camping Equipment	$5,375,997.44
		Golf Equipment	$3,299,164.75
		Mountaineering Equipment	$5,263,513.55
		Outdoor Protection	$138,505.37
		Personal Accessories	$1,738,855.32
	Audrey Lastman	Camping Equipment	$25,066,705.70
		Golf Equipment	$7,592,276.74

NOTE *Bursting cannot be applied to a crosstab report by itself. However, you can do so if you drag a crosstab report into a list report and then link the two reports using master detail relationships. For more information on master detail relationships, refer to the "Master Detail Relationship" section of this chapter.*

Advanced Prompting

Prompts let you filter a report to return a subset of data that is geared toward the items that you want to see. For more information on prompts, refer to Chapter 9.

An *inline prompt* is a prompt embedded within a report. The user is not prompted at runtime. For example, a sales report that displays the top five sales representatives by default can contain a prompt within the report so that the number of representatives displayed for each sales region can be defined by the user. The user can simply change the value in the text box prompt, submit the change, and the requested number of sales representatives displays. The user does not have to exit the report to change the value.

Here's how to set up a report with an inline prompt:

1. In the work area of the report, add two block objects to the left of the data container. For this example, we use a list report containing Sales Region, Staff Name, Revenue, and Rank. The list is grouped by Sales Region and aggregated for Revenue totals. Rank is a created data item that calculates the rank for each sales region by revenue.

Expression Definition:
rank([Revenue] for [Sales region])

2. In the first block in the work area, add a text object. The Text dialog displays.

3. In the text box, enter instructional text for the prompt being created. For this example, we enter **Specify the Number of Rankings to View**.

4. From the Insertable Objects pane, drag a Text Box Prompt object to the second block in the work area. The Prompt Wizard displays with options to create a new parameter or use an existing parameter:

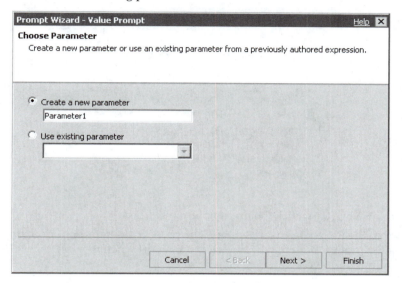

5. In the Create A New Parameter text box, enter a name for the parameter. For this example, we enter **p_Rank**.

TIP *It is good practice to preface the names of parameters with p_, such as p_rank. This helps to organize and identify your prompts.*

6. Click Finish to close the Prompt Wizard. Report Studio adds the text prompt to the second block in the work area, as shown here:

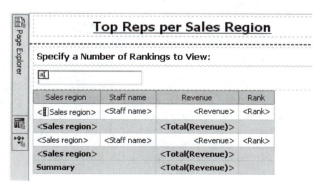

NOTE *Inline text prompts require a prompt button to submit changes. Value prompts contain an option in the properties to automatically submit the selection in the prompt when it is altered.*

7. From the Insertable Objects pane, drag a Prompt Button object to the right of the text prompt in the work area. Report Studio displays the Next prompt button in the work area:

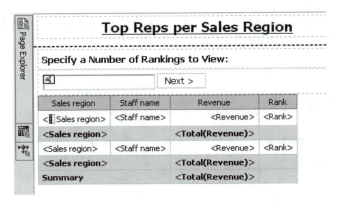

8. In the work area, click the prompt button to select it.

9. From the Properties pane, set the Type property to Reprompt to change the action of the prompt button, which re-runs the report when the user clicks the button. The prompt button displays *Reprompt* in the work area, shown next:

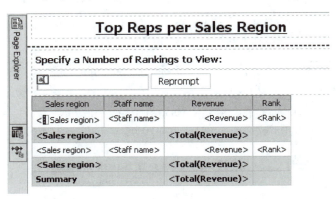

10. In the work area, click the Text prompt to select it.

11. From the Properties pane, set any properties for the Text Box prompt. Set the Required property to No so that the user is not prompted before the report runs. For this example, we also set the Numbers Only property to Yes and specify the number 5 for the Default Selections property.

12. From the Query Explorer tab, open the query to which you want to add a detail filter for the prompt value.

13. Add the applicable detail filter that includes the parameter created for the prompt. For this example, we add a detail filter for the rank parameter:

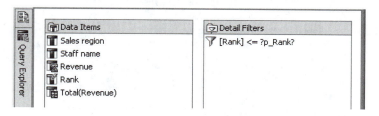

14. From the Properties pane, set the desired properties for the detail filter. For this example, we set the Application property to After Auto Aggregation so that rank is determined before the filter is applied.

15. Click Run to run the report and view the output. The report displays in Cognos Viewer with the Reprompt text box and button. In this example, the five top sales representatives for each region displays, with their corresponding Revenue values and Rank order:

Top Reps per Sales Region

Specify a Number of Rankings to View:

5		Reprompt	

Sales region	Staff name	Revenue	Rank
Americas	Charles Laurel	$59,406,874.73	1
	Eduardo Guimarães	$48,839,028.63	3
	George Harrows	$49,959,770.53	2
	Janice Thomas	$48,547,731.47	4
	Lucía Reyna	$47,438,275.14	5
Americas		**$254,191,680.50**	
Asia Pacific	Akemi Takahashi	$49,285,152.87	3
	Chang-ho Kim	$59,422,592.32	1
	Fang Chan	$47,820,429.34	4
	Fei Meng	$51,005,700.69	2
	Xiangyong Wang	$45,167,539.44	5
Asia Pacific		**$252,701,414.66**	

16. In the Reprompt text box, enter a value to reprompt the report. For this example, we use **3**.

17. Click the Reprompt button. The report displays the entered number of items. In this example, the three best sales representatives for each region display with their corresponding Revenue values and Rank order:

Top Reps per Sales Region

Specify a Number of Rankings to View:

3		Reprompt	

Sales region	Staff name	Revenue	Rank
Americas	Charles Laurel	$59,406,874.73	1
	George Harrows	$49,959,770.53	2
	Eduardo Guimarães	$48,839,028.63	3
Americas		**$158,205,673.89**	
Asia Pacific	Chang-ho Kim	$59,422,592.32	1
	Fei Meng	$51,005,700.69	2
	Akemi Takahashi	$49,285,152.87	3
Asia Pacific		**$159,713,445.88**	
Central Europe	Fausta Bruno	$79,955,838.92	1
	Roderick Albiñana	$75,976,074.43	2

HTML Items

You can add HTML items to your reports that allow you to insert anything that your browser can execute, such as images, links, multimedia, tool tips, or JavaScript. An HTML item is a container in which you can insert HTML code. For example, HTML items allow you to apply formatting to a page to maintain consistency with other pages in Cognos Connection (for example, displaying the same styles, borders, and so on) or to add JavaScript to a page to provide the user with interactivity, such as a ScreenTip that displays when the user moves the pointer over an item on the page.

NOTE *HTML Items appear only when the report is run in HTML format.*

Here's how to add HTML items:

1. From the Insertable Objects pane, drag the HTML Item object into the work area. The HTML item displays in the work area where inserted, as shown next. This is the container in which HTML code can be inserted.

2. In the work area, double-click the HTML item. The HTML dialog box displays.

   As an alternative, in the Properties pane of the HTML item, click the ellipsis in the HTML property.

3. Enter the HTML code in the dialog box. For this example, we enter code so that a date prompt displays the current date:

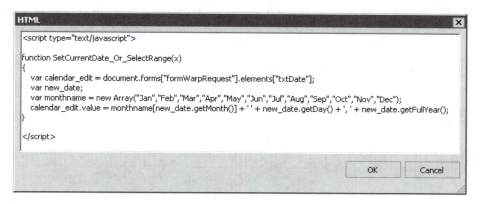

4. Click OK. The dialog box closes.

5. Click Run to run the report and view the prompt page. In this example, the prompt page displays in Cognos Viewer with the default of the current date in the Date prompt:

Singleton

A *singleton* object lets you insert a single data item anywhere in your report. Inserting a single data item is beneficial when you want to display a value that is independent from the rest of the values in the report or when an item will be used over and over. You can also include singleton items in a report that are drawn from multiple queries. For example, suppose your sales department has a report for the highest earning product and another report for the lowest earning product. The marketing director wants to view each of these in her Forecasting report. Using the singleton object, these two items can easily be added to her Forecasting report.

Insert a Singleton Object

You can add a singleton to a report in Report Studio in two ways: by dragging the Singleton object from the Toolbox tab in the Insertable Objects pane or by dragging a data item directly onto the report.

Here's how to insert a singleton object:

1. From the Toolbox tab in the Insertable Objects pane, drag the Singleton object to the work area, as shown next. For this example, we insert a Singleton object into a crosstab showing the revenue for products for each order year:

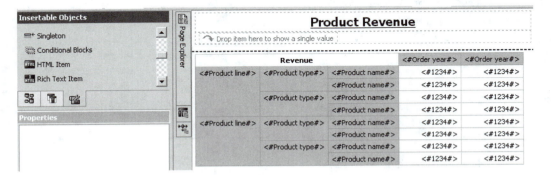

Report Studio creates an empty data container in the work area, and you can see a query in the Query Explorer tab.

2. From the Source tab in the Insertable Objects pane, drag a data item into the singleton container in the work area. The data item displays in the singleton container in the work area. In this example, Revenue is the data item:

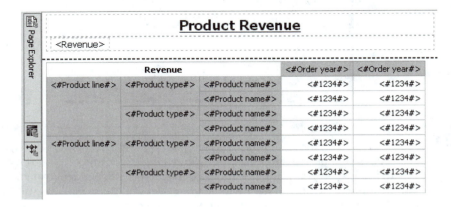

NOTE *You can also drag a data item anywhere within the report outside of a container to create a singleton.*

Edit a Query Associated with a Singleton Object

By default, the singleton object returns the first row of the query with which it is associated. As a result, you may need to filter the data that is retrieved by the query to see what you want. Here's how to edit a query associated with the singleton object:

1. From the Query Explorer tab, open the query the singleton object created. The data items associated with the query display. For this example, we open Query2 and see the Revenue data item in the query.

2. From the Insertable Objects pane, drag the desired data items to add to the query into the Data Items area. For this example, we add Product Name and Order Year and create a new data item called Maximum Revenue that returns the revenue for the highest grossing product, as shown next:

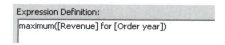

Expression Definition:
maximum([Revenue] for [Order year])

3. Add any detail filters to the singleton query. For this example, we want to see the product with the maximum revenue for the year 2006, so we added two filters:

TIP *To view the underlying data when editing a query, from the Query Explorer tab, right-click the applicable query, select View Tabular Data, and then click OK. A tabular view of the data for the query displays in Cognos Viewer.*

4. Click Run to run the report and view the output. The report displays in Cognos Viewer with the singleton. In this example, the Revenue singleton displays under the header, as shown next:

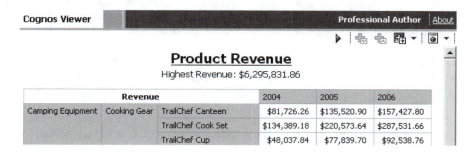

Associate Multiple Singletons to One Query

In some cases, you may need multiple singleton items displayed on a report. If that is the case, your singletons should be associated with the same query. This will help the performance of the report.

Here's how to associate multiple singletons to one query:

1. Create a singleton and edit its query by following the steps in the previous two sections.

2. From the Data Items tab in the Insertable Objects pane, drag a data item from the singleton query. In this example, we choose Product Name because we want the name of the product with the highest revenue to display with the amount.

3. Click Run to run the report and view the output. The report displays in Cognos Viewer with both singletons. This example shows the Product Name singleton, and the Revenue singleton with descriptive text in between:

Product Revenue

Star Dome has the highest revenue with: $6,295,831.86

Revenue			2004	2005	2006
Camping Equipment	Cooking Gear	TrailChef Canteen	$81,726.26	$135,520.90	$157,427.80
		TrailChef Cook Set	$134,389.18	$220,573.64	$287,531.66
		TrailChef Cup	$48,037.84	$77,839.70	$92,538.76
		TrailChef Deluxe Cook Set	$96,107.94	$161,787.44	$187,598.76
		TrailChef Double Flame	$416,684.44	$628,350.72	$806,600.22

Table of Contents

The Table of Contents option lets you create a report booklet of a PDF report (Adobe's Portable Document Format), which contains a table of contents page with hyperlinks to the different pages within the report. The report booklet can be distributed to recipients via e-mail. The table of contents provides a navigation method that helps the user quickly view a specific page within a multiple-page report. For example, suppose the CEO of a large production company receives a report booklet of more than 100 pages. Instead of having to sort through each page in the report, she can easily navigate to her desired location using the hyperlinks in the table of contents within the PDF file.

The Table of Contents option also lets you set up additional entries if a report spans across multiple pages and add bookmarks to the reports and table of contents within the report booklet for navigation purposes. All these options are discussed in the following sections.

Set Up the Table of Contents

When a report contains multiple entries, adding a table of contents to a report booklet makes viewing the entries easier for the user, as they display in one location.

Here's how to set up a table of contents in a report:

1. From the Page Explorer, click the Report Pages link and add pages from the Insertable Objects pane for each page you want in the report. These pages contain

the report pages to be used in the table of contents. Rename the pages, making the first "Table of Contents". In this example, we name the pages as shown next:

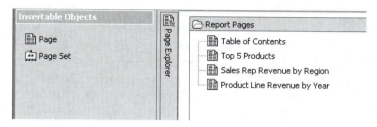

2. Add content to each page in the report. For this example, we create a crosstab for the Top 5 Products page, a list for the Sales Rep Revenue by Region page, and a chart for the Product Line Revenue by Year page.

3. From the Page Explorer tab, open the Table of Contents page. Report Studio displays the page in the work area.

4. From the Toolbox tab in the Insertable Objects pane, drag a Table of Contents object into the work area. The table of contents object displays in the work area, as shown next:

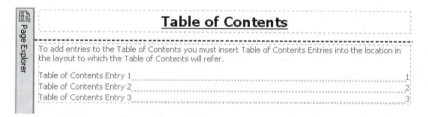

5. From the Page Explorer tab, open the first report page. Report Studio displays the page in the work area. For this example, we use the Top 5 Products page.

6. From the Toolbox tab in the Insertable Objects pane, drag a Table of Contents Entry object into the work area so that it is the first item on the page. A table of contents entry icon displays in the work area:

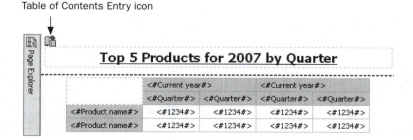

7. Repeat steps 5 and 6 for the remaining pages in your report.

8. From the Page Explorer tab, open the Table of Contents page:

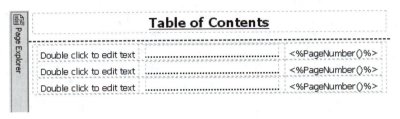

9. Add the page names for each page by double-clicking in the table of contents to edit text box. For this example, we add the names: Top 5 Products, Sales Rep Revenue by Region, and Product Line Revenue by Year, as shown next.

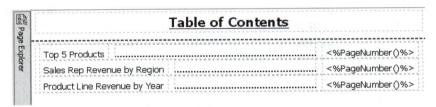

10. From the Run menu, select Run Report - PDF to run the report in PDF format and view the output. The report booklet displays in Adobe Reader in a Cognos Viewer window with a descriptive Table of Contents, which contains hyperlinks to the report pages within the PDF:

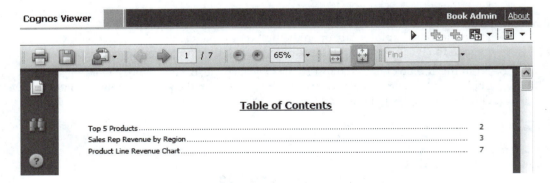

Add a Table of Contents Entry for a Particular Data Item

When a single report spans multiple pages, you can add a table of contents entry that is specific for a particular data item within the report. For example, suppose a company's Products report contains pages for its entire product line (Glasses, Plates, Silverware, and so on), referred to as *data items.* In the report, a table of contents entry was created for each data item because each product spanned multiple pages. The results are as follows: under Glasses are entries such as Wine, Water, Champagne, and Miscellaneous; under Plates are entries such as Salad, Entrée, and Dessert. These additional entries narrow down the location to find a specific product.

Continuing with the example from the "Set Up the Table of Contents" section, we will now add a table of contents entry for particular data items in the report.

Here's how to add a table of contents entry for a particular data item:

1. From the Page Explorer tab, open a page within the report (other than the Table of Contents page). For this example, we use the Sales Rep Revenue by Region page.

2. From the standard toolbar, click the Unlock button.

3. From the Toolbox tab in the Insertable Objects pane, drag a Table of Contents Entry object to the first cell in the first column. A table of contents entry icon displays in the column:

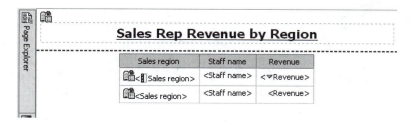

4. From the Page Explorer tab, open the Table of Contents page. Report Studio displays the Table of Contents page with a *<Column Name>* object in the table of contents. In this example, *<Sales region>* displays in the table of contents:

5. From the Run menu, select Run Report - PDF to run the report in PDF format and view the output. The report booklet displays in Adobe Reader in a Cognos Viewer window with a hyperlink for each data item. In this example, a hyperlink displays for each region in the Sales Rep Revenue by Region report:

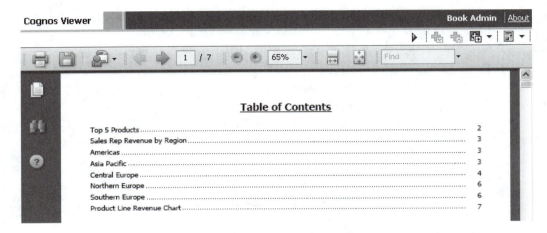

6. Optionally, format the Table of Contents to make the items easier for the user to read (for example, offsetting the data items entries, adding color to the entries, and so on).

NOTE *For more information on formatting, refer to Chapter 9.*

7. From the Run menu, select Run Report - PDF to run the report in PDF format and view the output. The report booklet displays in Adobe Reader in Cognos Viewer with the applicable formatting. In this example, the sales region hyperlinks are indented under the report entry and display in blue text:

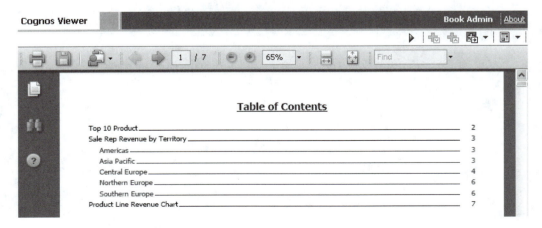

Add Bookmarks to the Table of Contents

Bookmarks take the user from the selected report within the report booklet back to the Table of Contents page. This is a quick navigation tool for the user instead of having to scroll through all of the pages within the booklet.

Continuing with the example from the "Add a Table of Contents Entry for a Particular Data Item" section, we now add bookmarks to the report booklet.

Here's how to add bookmarks to the table of contents:

1. From the Page Explorer tab, open the Table of Contents page.

2. From the toolbox tab in the Insertable Objects pane, drag a Bookmark object before the header in the work area. A bookmark object icon displays in the work area:

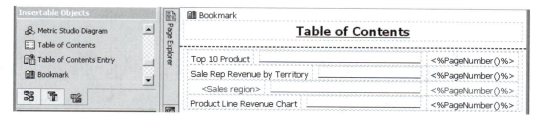

3. Click the bookmark to select it.

4. From the Properties pane, set the Label property to an appropriate name for the Table of Contents page. For this example, we use **Return to TOC**.

5. From the Page Explorer tab, open a page within the report. For this example, we open the Top 5 Products page.

6. From the Toolbox tab in the Insertable Objects pane, drag a Block object under the data container in the work area to add a hyperlink that returns the user to the bookmark on the Table of Contents page.

7. From the Toolbox tab in the Insertable Objects pane, drag a Text Item object into the block object in the work area. The Text dialog displays.

8. In the text box, enter descriptive text for the action, and then click OK. For this example, we use **Return to Table of Contents**:

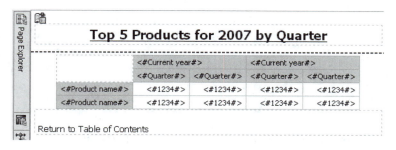

9. Right-click the text item, and from the context menu select Drill-Through Definitions. The Drill-Through Definitions screen displays:

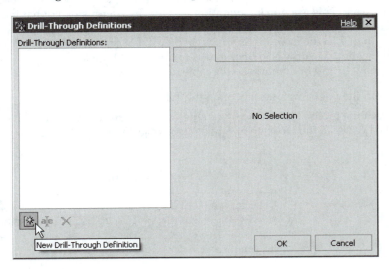

10. Click the New Drill-Through Definition button.
11. Click the Bookmark tab.
12. From the Source Type list, select Text. Report Studio displays a Text text box under the Source Type list:

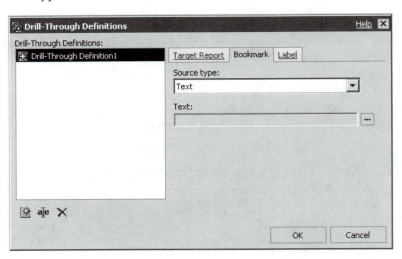

13. At the end of the Text text box, click the ellipsis. A Text dialog displays.

14. Enter the Label that was used for the Bookmark on the Table of Contents page you created in step 4. For this example, we use **Return to TOC**.

NOTE *The Text name must be the same name that was used for the bookmark.*

15. Click OK. The text item is now a hyperlink:

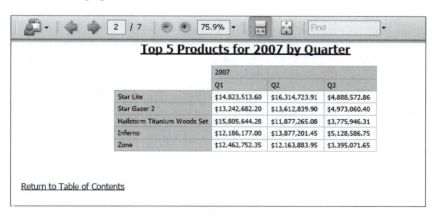

16. Click the block object to select it.
17. From the standard toolbar, click the Copy button.
18. Navigate to the page in the report where you want to insert the link, and after clicking the page to select it, click the Paste button on the standard toolbar to insert the block with the link.
19. From the Run menu, select Run Report - PDF to run the report in PDF format and view the output. The report booklet displays in Adobe Reader in Cognos Viewer with the hyperlinks for the report.
20. Click a report hyperlink to view the table of contents entry. For this example, we click the Top 5 Products link. The Return to Table of Contents hyperlink displays in the report, as shown next, and when clicked, this hyperlink returns the user to the Table of Contents page:

Analytics Using Analysis Studio

Why create an analysis and not a report? What's the difference? You create reports to answer a business question. If another business question arises from that report, you can create another report based on the new question, or you can search for reports that contain similar information. This can be a time-consuming process, however, and the data may not be as current as you need it to be.

Analysis is a more sophisticated process for users who don't know exactly what they are looking for. An analyst first looks at data to make sure everything is in order. While looking at the data, the analyst may notice that something is not quite right. The analyst's job is like a homeowner who walks into the house and smells something burning. She is not quite sure what it is or from where it is coming. But she now knows something is not right; so, she goes throughout the house searching for the source of the smell. She finds the source: somebody has left on the curling iron in the upstairs bathroom and closed the door. She has some options. She can continue to leave it on unattended, at which point the house may catch on fire, or she can turn off the curling iron and end any threat to the safety of her home.

Analysis is like this. You simply follow your nose to the source of the problem.

About Analysis Studio

To find the source of the smell in the preceding example, your tools would be your legs taking you from room to room, your arms opening and closing doors searching for the root of the problem, and your feet helping you to stand on your tippy toes to look deep into the cupboards.

Analysis Studio provides its own tools to help you dig through dimensional data to discover the source of problems and issues. These tools help you drill-through data, apply various types of filters, see the top and bottom percentages of the data, group data, insert charts and graphs, and apply templates. All the tools provided in Analysis Studio can be used separately or in conjunction with one another to answer your next business question.

Defining the Next Business Question

What is the *next business question*? The next business question is the question that you did not know existed until you began looking at data. That data may have been presented in a report at the monthly sales meeting or it may be raw data that has not yet been included in a report. You search for issues—you smell smoke, or you see that 98 stores are selling millions of dollars of Product A and 22 stores are not breaking even with the same product. The issues you uncover reveal that an important question (or questions) needs to be answered, and that is the next business question.

Understanding Dimensions and Measures

How do you sort through tons of data to answer the next business question? That has got to be a daunting task—right? In fact, Analysis Studio is a powerful and easy-to-use tool that makes sorting through data much less of a time-consuming chore. To understand how Analysis Studio works, you do need to understand what makes a dimensional data source.

Dimensional data sources consist of *measures* and *dimensions*. Measures are the quantifiable indicators that determine how your business is performing; they give you the numbers behind your business. Dimensions are groups of data that relate to one another— the who, what, when, where, and why of a measure. The groups of data that make up a dimension are called *members*. For example, suppose you have a dimension named Products. The Products dimension consists of the Golfing Equipment, Mountaineering Equipment, and Personal Accessories members. Each of those members consists of other members, and so on. For example, Golfing Equipment contains the Irons, Woods, Putters, and Golf Accessories members, and Irons contains specific types of irons. You can think of data members as a parent and child relationship, where a parent is made up of children. So Golfing Equipment would be a parent for the children: Irons, Woods, Putters, and Golf Accessories. If you select Irons, Irons becomes the parent and the specific type of irons becomes the children.

The dimensions and their components (the members) create a *data hierarchy* that allows you to look at varying levels of detail from your data source.

Create an Analysis

In Analysis Studio, you create an analysis by inserting data into a crosstab. Data can be inserted via two methods: you can right-click a dimension or a member to open a context menu from which you can insert the dimension or member into the analysis, or you can drag a dimension or member into a crosstab. You can insert an entire dimension and all its members or individual members.

After you have created the initial analysis, you can use the information in the rest of this chapter to understand and use the full potential of Analysis Studio to help you analyze the same data in different ways to arrive at the answer to your next business question.

Open Analysis Studio

You access Analysis Studio from Cognos Connection. Analysis Studio opens in a separate web browser window, which means you still have access to Cognos Connection if you need it.

Here's how to open Analysis Studio:

1. Log on to Cognos Connection. If the welcome screen displays, click Cognos content.
   The Public Folders tab displays:

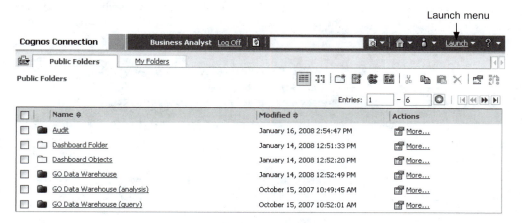

2. From the Launch menu located in the upper-right corner of the screen, click Analysis
   Studio. The Select A Package screen displays. Dimensional packages are listed as
   hyperlinks. Packages not listed as hyperlinks are *not* dimensional packages. Remember
   that some dimensional packages may be located within folders. In Cognos 8.3,
   packages can be published within folders.

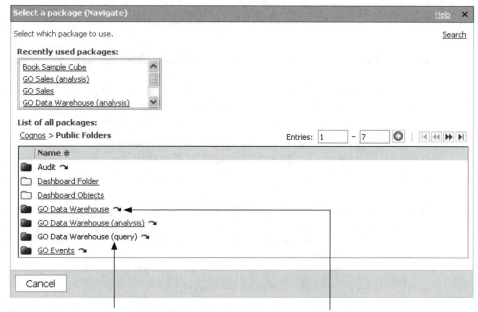

Relational package (not available for Analysis Studio)   Dimensional package

3. Select a package. The Analysis Studio Welcome screen displays, as shown next, and is where you can choose to create a blank analysis or a default analysis. A blank analysis lets you start from scratch by providing a blank crosstab in the work area. A default analysis lets you use the default analysis for the package. The default analysis is created by placing the first dimension on the rows, the second dimension on the columns, and the first measure in the cells where the rows and columns intersect.

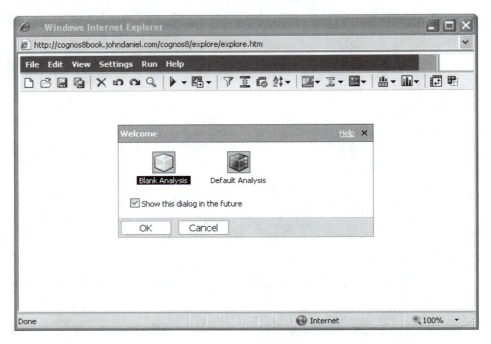

4. From the Welcome screen, select Blank Analysis or Default Analysis and click OK. Analysis Studio displays with the following items:

   - **Source tab**   Contains the source tree in the Insertable Objects pane.

   - **Source tree**   Located on the Source tab in the Insertable Objects pane contains items that you insert into the crosstab in the work area to create an analysis.

   - **Analysis Items tab**   Shows custom sets and other analysis items created in Analysis Studio.

   - **Overview area**   Shows an overview of what the analysis contains. The Rows and Columns areas show you the details of the items in the crosstab for the respective rows and columns. The Context Filter area shows you what context filters have been applied to the analysis.

- **Work area**   Contains a crosstab with a Rows drop zone, a Columns drop zone, and a Measure drop zone, into which you insert items from the Insertable Objects pane.

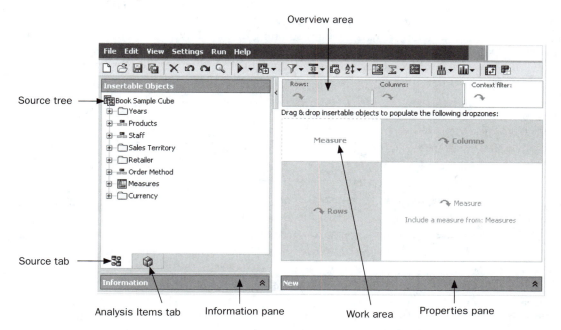

Add Dimensions and Measures

To begin using what Analysis Studio has to offer, you need to add items to the crosstab. Adding dimensions, members, or measures is simple as dragging items from the source tree to the crosstab. At least one dimension or member must be added to the Rows drop zone, at least one to the Columns drop zone and a measure added to the Measure drop zone.

NOTE   *More than one item can be added to each of the drop zones by nesting. For more information, refer to the "Nesting Items" section later in this chapter.*

Here's how to add dimensions or members and measures:

1. From the source tree, drag a dimension or member to the Columns drop zone in the work area. The dimension or member is added as the column headings of the crosstab. For this example, we add the Prior YTD, the YTD, and the YTD Change members from the All Dates dimension.

2. From the source tree, drag a dimension or member to the Rows drop zone in the work area. The dimension or member is added as the row headings of the crosstab. For this example, we add the Products dimension.

3. From the source tree, drag a measure to the Measure drop zone in the work area. The measure is added to the crosstab and the analysis is created. For this example, we add the Revenue measure. As shown next, you can see that from the prior year-to-date to the current year-to-date, overall revenue has increased by almost $12 million. However, revenue has decreased by more than $340,000 for Outdoor Protection. A potential question is beginning to unfold: Why is revenue down for Outdoor Protection? This is where you can begin to use some of the tools that Analysis Studio has to offer to see what might be happening. This generates the next business question that needs to be answered.

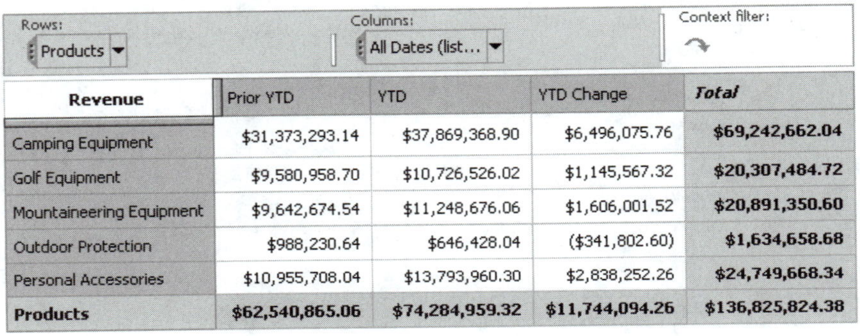

Rows: Products ▼	Columns: All Dates (list... ▼			Context filter:
Revenue	Prior YTD	YTD	YTD Change	*Total*
Camping Equipment	$31,373,293.14	$37,869,368.90	$6,496,075.76	**$69,242,662.04**
Golf Equipment	$9,580,958.70	$10,726,526.02	$1,145,567.32	**$20,307,484.72**
Mountaineering Equipment	$9,642,674.54	$11,248,676.06	$1,606,001.52	**$20,891,350.60**
Outdoor Protection	$988,230.64	$646,428.04	($341,802.60)	**$1,634,658.68**
Personal Accessories	$10,955,708.04	$13,793,960.30	$2,838,252.26	**$24,749,668.34**
Products	**$62,540,865.06**	**$74,284,959.32**	**$11,744,094.26**	**$136,825,824.38**

With Analysis Studio, you can use many tools to answer your business questions. One of the first things that you may want to do is navigate through your data. Navigating through a dimensional data source is a lot like accessing data in a filing cabinet: You keep digging through the folders until you get to the data you need. In a dimensional data source, this is called *drilling-down* and *drilling-up*.

Drill-Down and Drill-Up

When you drill-down or drill-up through data, you can see what items lie beneath other items, much like items stored in folders inside a filing cabinet.

When you drill-down, you see the children of the selected parent. Again, a child is the detailed information that lies beneath the current level, or parent, in the hierarchy. For example, suppose the Geography dimension of a package has been added to an analysis. Within the dimension, the first member and the highest level is Country, which contains all the countries in which the company sells products. If we click a country link in the analysis, the United States for example, the next level down, Provinces/States, displays in the analysis. This level contains the states in the United States in which the company sells products. If we now click a state link, Pennsylvania for example, the next level below that displays in the analysis, which is Cities. This level shows all of the cities in Pennsylvania in which the company sells products.

When you drill-up, you see less detailed information or the parent of the child that you are currently viewing. For example, if we drill-up on the Cities member, we see the Provinces/States, or if we drill-up on Provinces/States, we see Countries.

Here's how to drill-down or drill-up:

1. Navigate to the cell in the analysis that contains the item on which you want to drill-down or drill-up. For this example, we use an analysis with Products as the rows, Prior YTD, YTD, and YTD Change as the columns and Revenue as the measure.

2. Drill-down or drill-up on the item by performing one of the following actions:

   • Click a row or column heading to drill-down one level to the children of the selected member unless no more data is located beneath the member, in which case it drills-up one level.

   • Click a summary heading to drill-up one level for either the columns or the rows.

   • Click the intersection of a row and column to select the cell, and then click it again to drill-down one level to the children of both the selected row and column members unless no more data is located beneath the members, in which case it drills-up one level.

   • Click the intersection of a summary row heading and a summary column heading to select the cell, and then click it again to drill-up one level on both the row and column members.

   • Right-click on a cell to display a context menu and select Drill Down or Drill Up.

For this example, we drill-down on Outdoor Protection by right-clicking the row heading and selecting Drill Down from the context menu that displays.

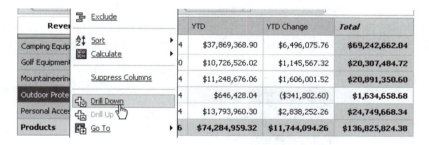

The analysis displays the members of the Outdoor Protection product line, as shown next. This example shows that each member of Outdoor Protection has a decrease in revenue:

Revenue	Prior YTD	YTD	YTD Change	Total
First Aid	$181,059.22	$108,805.06	($72,254.16)	$289,864.28
Insect Repellents	$494,608.50	$326,324.70	($168,283.80)	$820,933.20
Sunscreen	$312,562.92	$211,298.28	($101,264.64)	$523,861.20
Outdoor Protection	**$988,230.64**	**$646,428.04**	**($341,802.60)**	**$1,634,658.68**

Rows: Outdoor Protect... ▾   Columns: All Dates (list... ▾   Context filter:

Navigate Down or Up a Level

Navigating down a level or up a level provides access to levels within the hierarchy without being influenced by parents. This ability is useful when sorting or ranking levels within the hierarchy.

When navigating down a level, you see the children of all the parents from that level. When navigating up a level, you see the parents of all the children from that level. This differs from drilling-down or drilling-up because when you drill-down or drill-up the action is performed on a specific member, or specific parent and child relationship.

For example, the Outdoor Protection member contains three product types, as shown in the previous illustration. If you drill-down on one of the product types in the Outdoor Protection member, you see all the products within the selected product type. However, if you go down a level, you see the products of all product types within Outdoor Protection.

Here's how to navigate up or down a level:

1. Right-click the appropriate navigation bar, shown next, for the part of the analysis for which you want to view a different level.

Navigation bars

2. A context menu displays, with options to navigate down a level or up a level:

3. From the context menu, select Down A Level or Up A Level. The analysis displays the data that is below or above the selection, respectively. For this example, we choose Down A Level from the rows navigation bar menu, and all the products within Outdoor Protection display:

Revenue	Prior YTD	YTD	YTD Change	Total
Deluxe Family Relief Kit	$38,686.54	$17,439.00	($21,247.54)	$56,125.54
Aloe Relief	$21,907.76	$14,769.38	($7,138.38)	$36,677.14
Insect Bite Relief	$49,055.78	$31,150.88	($17,904.90)	$80,206.66
Compact Relief Kit	$39,735.40	$26,312.08	($13,423.32)	$66,047.48
Calamine Relief	$31,673.74	$19,133.72	($12,540.02)	$50,807.46
BugShield Extreme	$131,478.98	$79,713.26	($51,765.72)	$211,192.24
BugShield Natural	$81,579.06	$62,517.78	($19,061.28)	$144,096.84
BugShield Spray	$76,464.00	$45,586.84	($30,877.16)	$122,050.84
BugShield Lotion Lite	$106,850.24	$75,887.62	($30,962.62)	$182,737.86
BugShield Lotion	$98,236.22	$62,619.20	($35,617.02)	$160,855.42
Sun Blocker	$50,165.56	$34,190.92	($15,974.64)	$84,356.48
Sun Shelter Stick	$16,756.58	$10,280.74	($6,475.84)	$27,037.32
More				
Total	$988,230.64	$646,428.04	($341,802.60)	$1,634,658.68

The revenue from all Outdoor Protection products is down, as shown above. To analyze this example in the next section, we navigate Up A Level on the rows to return to the members of Outdoor Protection.

Slice and Dice an Analysis

You can use Analysis Studio tools to slice and dice the data to answer your next business questions. The next business question, in this instance, has been determined with a few simple clicks performed in the examples from the previous sections. We now want to see the revenue of Outdoor Protection for each Order Method to learn more about the decrease in revenue for Outdoor Protection.

This section provides an overview of slicing and dicing the analysis from the previous sections. The examples below show what you can do with Analysis Studio when you use a combination of several tools to analyze Outdoor Protection. Subsequent sections go into more detail about how to perform the actions shown in this section.

We drop the Order Method dimension onto the rows to look at the revenue for each order method with a context filter of Outdoor Protection. In the analysis, as shown next,

you can see the revenue is down for all order methods. In particular, the revenue of
telephone orders has decreased greatly:

Rows: Order Method	Columns: All Dates (list...)	Context filter: Outdoor Protect...		
Revenue	Prior YTD	YTD	YTD Change	*Total*
Fax	$53,224.76	$32,387.72	($20,837.04)	**$85,612.48**
Telephone	$246,964.74	$142,908.00	($104,056.74)	**$389,872.74**
Mail	$45,023.92	$22,686.90	($22,337.02)	**$67,710.82**
E-mail	$156,742.04	$112,951.26	($43,790.78)	**$269,693.30**
Web	$231,261.18	$175,267.48	($55,993.70)	**$406,528.66**
Sales visit	$226,981.80	$148,883.42	($78,098.38)	**$375,865.22**
Special	$28,032.20	$11,343.26	($16,688.94)	**$39,375.46**
Order Method	**$988,230.64**	**$646,428.04**	**($341,802.60)**	**$1,634,658.68**

We now want to see whether telephone sales are down for all retailers; so, we drill-down
on the Telephone order method, and drag the Retailer dimension onto the rows. The rows
now contain retailer types and the analysis has a second context filter of Telephone. This
means the analysis shows the revenue from telephone orders of products from the Outdoor
Protection product line for each retailer type, as shown next. You can see the greatest drop in
revenue is attributed to Outdoors Shop:

Rows: Retailer	Columns: All Dates (list...)	Context filter: Outdoor Protect...	Telephone	
Revenue	Prior YTD	YTD	YTD Change	*Total*
Department Store	$76,584.72	$57,403.64	($19,181.08)	**$133,988.36**
Direct Marketing	$6,502.32	$4,612.88	($1,889.44)	**$11,115.20**
Equipment Rental Store	$0.00	$610.00	$610.00	**$610.00**
Eyewear Store	$0.00	$0.00	$0.00	**$0.00**
Golf Shop	$0.00	$0.00	$0.00	**$0.00**
Outdoors Shop	$108,046.06	$54,234.22	($53,811.84)	**$162,280.28**
Sports Store	$43,313.58	$20,053.26	($23,260.32)	**$63,366.84**
Warehouse Store	$12,518.06	$5,994.00	($6,524.06)	**$18,512.06**
Retailer	**$246,964.74**	**$142,908.00**	**($104,056.74)**	**$389,872.74**

Now, we drill-down on the Outdoors Shop retailer type to see the retailers within Outdoors Shop where telephone sales are down. The members of Outdoors Shop display and you can see the difference in revenue from year to year for each retailer. Notice the word *More* at the bottom of the list of retailers, as shown next. This indicates that more shops are not currently being displayed:

Rows: Outdoors Shop ▼	Columns: All Dates (list... ▼		Context filter: Outdoor Protect... ▼	Telephone ▼
Revenue	Prior YTD	YTD	YTD Change	*Total*
Rock Steady	$0.00	$0.00	$0.00	**$0.00**
Outdoor-Fachgeschäft Müller	$2,434.78	$3,166.50	$731.72	**$5,601.28**
Caravanserai	$8,731.58	$2,576.08	($6,155.50)	**$11,307.66**
Jensen Mountaineering	$2,495.64	$4,358.64	$1,863.00	**$6,854.28**
Outdoor Experience	$9,603.18	$203.60	($9,399.58)	**$9,806.78**
Lan King Sports Co., LTD.	$11,181.50	$5,000.00	($6,181.50)	**$16,181.50**
Falcon Outfitters	$7,864.38	$4,136.86	($3,727.52)	**$12,001.24**
In die Berge!	$5,205.54	$4,665.38	($540.16)	**$9,870.92**
Extrem!	$4,504.82	$906.00	($3,598.82)	**$5,410.82**
Extreme Outdoors	$2,119.46	$1,398.80	($720.66)	**$3,518.26**
Trail Masters	$0.00	$0.00	$0.00	**$0.00**
Jack and Jill Climbing School & Supplies	$250.50	$0.00	($250.50)	**$250.50**
More				
Outdoors Shop	**$108,046.06**	**$54,234.22**	**($53,811.84)**	**$162,280.28**

The analysis we created here is a good example of what you can do with Analysis Studio using just a few features. From here, you have many more options. You can get deeper into your data using the tools described throughout this chapter. You can also dress-up your analysis by following the steps provided later in the "Modify the Layout" section of this chapter.

Save an Analysis

Once you have created an analysis, you can save it. Your permissions determine where you can save the analysis.

Here's how to save an analysis:

1. From the toolbar, click the Save As icon. The Save As dialog displays:

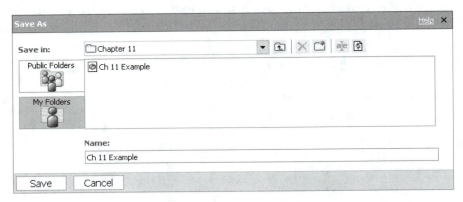

2. Select a location in which to save the analysis.
3. In the Name text box, enter a name for the analysis.
4. Click the Save button. The analysis is saved in the specified location.

Working with Large Data Sets

At times, you may be working with large amounts of data during an analysis, which can become daunting, and an abundance of data can cloud your vision. To help keep the important data at the top of the pile, you may want to consider the 80/20 rule: where 80 percent of your sales comes from 20 percent of your products. For example, 80 percent of the revenue is more than likely the result of sales from 20 percent of your products. The other 20 percent of the revenue is very important to the success of your business, but it is not the most important, nor will it have the greatest impact.

Analysis Studio provides tools that can help you sift through the 80 percent of the data to get to the 20 percent of your results.

NOTE *All of the following sections assume that you have already created an analysis. For more information on creating an analysis, refer to the "Create an Analysis" section earlier in this chapter.*

Showing Less Is More

By default, Analysis Studio displays the first 12 rows of data in an analysis. More often than not, this is all the data you need to see what is happening in your organization. Since the 80/20 rule means you can look at a small portion of the data to get the big picture, you don't necessarily need to see more data just because it is available.

However, Analysis Studio lets you know when more data is available than what is shown in the analysis. A *More* link at the bottom of the row headings list provides a visual cue that there is more data than displayed.

Here's how to view more data:

1. Click the More link at the bottom of the row headings list. A context menu displays with options for the number of rows of data you want to show:

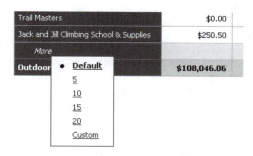

2. Select the number of rows you want to display, or select Custom and define the number of rows to display.

   • If you choose any of the numeric values, the analysis refreshes displaying the selected number of rows.

   • If you choose Custom, a dialog displays with Display, Filter, Context Filter, and Sort areas, as shown next. The Display area contains a Visible Items text box in which you can enter a custom number of rows to display. The Filter and Context Filter areas show any filters that have been applied to the analysis. The Sort area shows whether the analysis has been sorted and how it has been sorted:

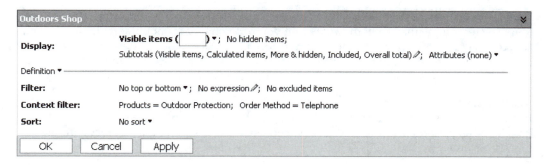

3. In the Visible Items text box, enter the number of rows you want to display in the analysis, and then click OK. The analysis refreshes and displays the number of rows you entered.

Applying Context Filters

Context filters refine the data that the analysis displays based on a dimension or member selected from the source tree. Instead of seeing all of the data from a dimension or member, you can limit the data so that the results relate to the dimension or member defined as a context filter. For example, the analysis from previous sections shows all the product types and the revenue for the year-to-date and prior year-to-date of the Outdoor Protection product line. You want to see if revenue is down for a certain order method. You can apply a context filter so that you see the revenue for only fax orders. If revenue looks good there, you can change the context filter to mail orders, and so on, until you determine the order method for which revenue is down the most.

Here's how to apply a context filter:

1. Drag a dimension or member into the Context Filter region of the overview area that you want to use to filter the analysis. Analysis Studio adds the selected dimension to the overview area, and filters the data based on the selection. In the following example, we use the Fax member from the Order Method dimension. We can see the revenue from fax orders for the Outdoor Protection product line:

Rows: Outdoor Protect... ▼		Columns: All Dates (list... ▼		Context filter: Fax ▼
Revenue	Prior YTD	YTD	YTD Change	**Total**
First Aid	$9,817.08	$2,203.00	($7,614.08)	**$12,020.08**
Insect Repellents	$24,755.46	$20,424.94	($4,330.52)	**$45,180.40**
Sunscreen	$18,652.22	$9,759.78	($8,892.44)	**$28,412.00**
Outdoor Protection	**$53,224.76**	**$32,387.72**	**($20,837.04)**	**$85,612.48**

TIP *You can also create a context filter of the item currently inserted in the rows of an analysis by dropping a different item onto the rows to replace the existing one.*

Create and Edit Calculations

You can create a calculation in the analysis if you need one that is not inherently in the data source. The calculation that you create is not stored in the data source itself but rather saved as part of the analysis. That means if the data in the data source has changed and you open a saved analysis, Analysis Studio reruns the calculation and displays the new data.

Create a Calculation

In Analysis Studio, you can create a calculation to reveal more information about the data. For example, you might want to see the percentage of total sales of the product with the highest revenue.

NOTE *If you find that you are creating the same calculation over and over, contact your Cognos 8 administrator to see if the calculation can be added to the data source so you do not have to re-create it continuously.*

Here's how to create a calculation:

1. Select the rows or columns for which you want to create a calculation. SHIFT-click to select contiguous items, or CTRL-click to select non-contiguous items. For this example, we select Camping Equipment and Golf Equipment in an analysis with the Products dimension as the rows; Prior YTD, YTD, and YTD Change as the columns; and Revenue as the measure.

2. On the toolbar, click the Calculate button, as shown next. A context menu displays with options for using a predefined calculation or creating a custom one. If you choose a predefined calculation, Analysis Studio inserts a row based on your selection. The following steps create a custom calculation.

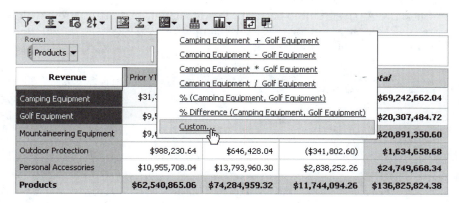

3. From the context menu, choose Custom. The Calculate screen displays, as shown next, with options to create the calculation.

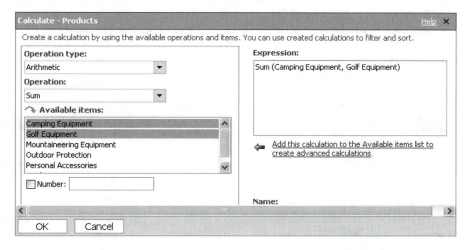

4. From the Operation Type drop-down list, select the type of calculation you want to create. Your selection dictates the available options. For our example, we select Arithmetic.

5. From the Operation drop-down list, select the operation to perform. For our example, we select Sum.

6. From the Available Items box or drop-down list, select the item(s) on which you want to base the calculation. For our example, we select Camping Equipment and Golf Equipment.

7. Set any other available options for the chosen operation.

8. Optionally, in the Name area, select the option to enter a custom name and enter a name for the heading of the row or column that contains the calculation. For this example, we use the custom name *Two Types of Equipment*.

9. Click OK. Analysis Studio performs the calculation and inserts a row with the results. You can see in the following example a row has been added in the analysis containing the calculations:

Revenue	Prior YTD	YTD	YTD Change	Total
Camping Equipment	$31,373,293.14	$37,869,368.90	$6,496,075.76	$69,242,662.04
Golf Equipment	$9,580,958.70	$10,726,526.02	$1,145,567.32	$20,307,484.72
Two Types of Equipment	$40,954,251.84	$48,595,894.92	$7,641,643.08	$89,550,146.76
Mountaineering Equipment	$9,642,674.54	$11,248,676.06	$1,606,001.52	$20,891,350.60
Outdoor Protection	$988,230.64	$646,428.04	($341,802.60)	$1,634,658.68
Personal Accessories	$10,955,708.04	$13,793,960.30	$2,838,252.26	$24,749,668.34
Products	$62,540,865.06	$74,284,959.32	$11,744,094.26	$136,825,824.38

Calculations can be used to create additional calculations. For example, we may want to see what the percentage *Two Types of Equipment* (the calculation we just created) is of the total. To do this, follow the steps in this section to create a calculation choosing the appropriate options. In this example, we choose Percentage as the Operation Type, % of Total as the Operation, and *Two Types of Equipment* from the Available Items drop-down list. Analysis Studio adds the calculation, as shown next:

Revenue	Prior YTD	YTD	YTD Change	Total
Camping Equipment	$31,373,293.14	$37,869,368.90	$6,496,075.76	$69,242,662.04
Golf Equipment	$9,580,958.70	$10,726,526.02	$1,145,567.32	$20,307,484.72
Two Types of Equipment	$40,954,251.84	$48,595,894.92	$7,641,643.08	$89,550,146.76
% of Total ((Two Types of Equipm	65.48%	65.42%	65.07%	65.45%
Mountaineering Equipment	$9,642,674.54	$11,248,676.06	$1,606,001.52	$20,891,350.60
Outdoor Protection	$988,230.64	$646,428.04	($341,802.60)	$1,634,658.68
Personal Accessories	$10,955,708.04	$13,793,960.30	$2,838,252.26	$24,749,668.34
Products	$62,540,865.06	$74,284,959.32	$11,744,094.26	$136,825,824.38

Edit a Calculation

After you have created a calculation and look at the resulting data, you may decide that is not exactly what you wanted. Analysis Studio allows you to edit calculations. This ability is useful when you have multiple calculations in an analysis and you want to change a calculation on which other calculations are based.

For example, in the previous section, we created two calculations in the same analysis. The first shows the sum of Camping Equipment and Golf Equipment, and the second shows the percentage that sum is of the total. Suppose you want to change the first calculation from Camping Equipment and Golf Equipment to Camping Equipment and Mountaineering Equipment. Changing that calculation changes the result of the second calculation. In previous versions of Cognos 8, you had to re-create the first calculation and then re-create the second calculation and delete the original calculations. With Cognos 8.3, you can edit the first calculation and Analysis Studio automatically updates any calculation that refers to the first, which is the behavior that most users would expect.

Here's how to edit a calculation:

1. Right-click the calculation to be edited.

2. From the context menu, click Edit this Calculation. The Calculate screen displays with the same options available as when you created the calculation.

3. Make the desired changes to the calculation. For our example, we change the available items from Camping Equipment and Golf Equipment to Camping Equipment and Mountaineering Equipment.

4. Click OK. Analysis Studio updates the calculation(s) according to your changes. In the example, you can see that we are now calculating the sum of Camping Equipment and Mountaineering Equipment, and this has changed the percentages in the second calculation:

Revenue	Prior YTD	YTD	YTD Change	*Total*
Camping Equipment	$31,373,293.14	$37,869,368.90	$6,496,075.76	**$69,242,662.04**
Golf Equipment	$9,580,958.70	$10,726,526.02	$1,145,567.32	**$20,307,484.72**
Mountaineering Equipment	$9,642,674.54	$11,248,676.06	$1,606,001.52	**$20,891,350.60**
Two Types of Equipment	$41,015,967.68	$49,118,044.96	$8,102,077.28	**$90,134,012.64**
% of Total ((Two Types of Equipm	65.58%	66.12%	68.99%	**65.88%**
Outdoor Protection	$988,230.64	$646,428.04	($341,802.60)	**$1,634,658.68**
Personal Accessories	$10,955,708.04	$13,793,960.30	$2,838,252.26	**$24,749,668.34**
Products	**$62,540,865.06**	**$74,284,959.32**	**$11,744,094.26**	**$136,825,824.38**

Display Top or Bottom Values

If you are analyzing a dimension with many members, you may want to add a Top or Bottom filter to narrow your analysis down to what you want to see. In Analysis Studio, you can choose to display the top or bottom values in the data by number, percentage, or a cumulative sum. For example, a number could be the top 10 sales representatives in your organization, a percentage could be the stores with the bottom 20 percent in sales, and a cumulative sum could be a group of customers that helped you reach $1 million in sales.

For this example, we return to the analysis used in the "Slice and Dice an Analysis" section, earlier in this chapter. This is an analysis of the Revenue of Outdoors Shop retailers for Prior YTD, YTD, and YTD Change with context filters of Outdoor Protection and Telephone. There are more retailers available than displayed in the analysis. We would like to see the 10 percent of retailers with the least revenue.

NOTE *When you choose to display the top or bottom values of the analysis, potentially important data is not removed from the analysis as it may be when suppressing zeros.*

Here's how to display the top and bottom values:

1. Select the column or row for which you want to show the top or bottom values. For this example, we select one of the rows.

2. From the toolbar, click Top or Bottom. A submenu displays with the option to choose No Top or Bottom, Top, or Bottom, as shown next. For either Top or Bottom there is a submenu with the options for choosing 5, 10, 20, or Custom. For this example, we choose Custom from the Bottom submenu:

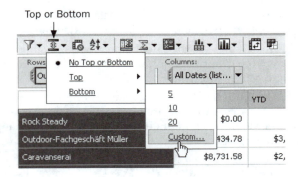

3. Choose an option from the submenu. If you choose 5, 10, or 20, Analysis Studio refreshes the analysis and displays only the top or bottom 5, 10, or 20 rows of data. If you choose Custom, Analysis Studio displays the Define Top Or Bottom Filter screen, as shown next, with options for customizing the Top or Bottom filter. The Number Of Items area has text boxes where you can set a numeric value, percent value, or sum value. The By Measure drop-down list contains all the measures available in the data source you are using. The For Row and For Column drop-down lists contain all the available items in the rows and columns for the analysis:

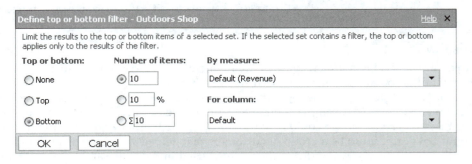

4. Under the Top Or Bottom heading, select None, Top, or Bottom. For this example, Bottom is selected.

5. Under the Number Of Items heading, select whether you want to see a number of items, a percentage of items, or a cumulative sum, and then enter a value for the selection in the text box. For this example, percentage is selected and 10 is entered as the value.

6. From the By Measure drop-down list, select the measure from which the filter is calculated. The default is the measure in the analysis.

7. From the For Column or For Row drop-down lists, select an item on which the filter is to be calculated. The default is the item that you selected in step 1 of this process.

8. Click OK. Analysis Studio applies the Top or Bottom filter to the analysis. In this example, we show the prior year-to-date and the year-to-date revenue for the bottom 10 percent of retailers for the Outdoor Protection product line from Telephone orders:

	Rows:	Columns:	Context filter:	
	🍃 Outdoors Shop ▼	All Dates (list... ▼	Outdoor Protect... ▼	Telephone ▼

Filters are applied. See the Properties pane for more details.

Revenue	Prior YTD	YTD	YTD Change	*Total*
Rock Steady	$0.00	$0.00	$0.00	**$0.00**
Trail Masters	$0.00	$0.00	$0.00	**$0.00**
Jack and Jill Climbing School & Supplies	$250.50	$0.00	($250.50)	**$250.50**
By A Thread	$788.88	$210.00	($578.88)	**$998.88**
Altitudes extrêmes	$1,719.68	$0.00	($1,719.68)	**$1,719.68**
Artículos de Campismo El Aquila, S.A. de C.V.	$459.90	$1,857.30	$1,397.40	**$2,317.20**
Weston Outfitters	$1,921.44	$490.00	($1,431.44)	**$2,411.44**
Kanga Kampers	$1,895.42	$668.04	($1,227.38)	**$2,563.46**
Extreme Outdoors	$2,119.46	$1,398.80	($720.66)	**$3,518.26**
Extrem!	$4,504.82	$906.00	($3,598.82)	**$5,410.82**
Subtotal (included)	**$13,660.10**	**$5,530.14**	**($8,129.96)**	**$19,190.24**
Outdoors Shop	**$108,046.06**	**$54,234.22**	**($53,811.84)**	**$162,280.28**

TIP *You can create a context filter that has a Top or Bottom filter applied to it by dropping a dimension or member onto the rows of an analysis after the Top or Bottom filter has been created.*

Applying Zero Suppression

By using *zero suppression*, you can prevent Analysis Studio from displaying data with zeros. This is beneficial so that the analysis is not cluttered with zeros that you do not need to see. It cleans up the data and lets you get to the point.

Suppression does not change the subtotals in the analysis. It changes only the data that is displayed. For example, if you suppress zeros on the Prior YTD column of an analysis,

Analysis Studio removes each row that has a zero where it intersects with the Prior YTD column, even if there is data in other columns. Aggregations (subtotals, totals, and so on) in the analysis remain the same and still account for any values not shown.

Continuing to use the example from the last section, you can see that there are columns in the analysis that contain zeros. We want to suppress the zeros in these columns.

Set Suppression

Prior to applying suppression, you have to set how Analysis Studio applies the suppression. You can choose to suppress *Empty Cells Only*, which hides any cells that do not contain data, or you can suppress *Zeros and Empty Cells*, which suppress any cells that do not contain data and any cells containing zeros.

Here's how to set suppression:

1. From the Settings menu, select Suppress. A Suppression submenu displays with the options to choose the suppression behavior. You can suppress Empty Cells Only or Zeros And Empty Cells:

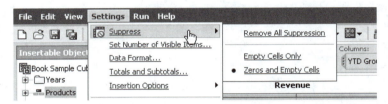

2. Click Empty Cells Only or Zeros And Empty Cells. Analysis Studio stores the selection.

Apply Suppression

After you have set your suppression, you are ready to apply it to your analysis and clean up the data that is displayed.

Here's how to apply suppression:

1. Highlight the row or column to be suppressed. For this example, we select the YTD column in an analysis that shows the bottom 10 percent of Outdoor Shops retailers with the least revenue for Outdoor Protection from Telephone orders. Refer to the "Display Top or Bottom Values" section in this chapter for the illustration.

2. From the toolbar, click the Suppress Rows or Columns icon. Analysis Studio suppresses the specified row or column and adds a note above the analysis alerting

you that suppression has been applied. In this example, the rows that had zeros in the YTD column have been removed. However, the subtotal and total remains the same.

Suppress Rows or Columns   Suppression note

Revenue	Prior YTD	YTD	YTD Change	*Total*
By A Thread	$788.88	$210.00	($578.88)	**$998.88**
Artículos de Campismo El Aquila, S.A. de C.V.	$459.90	$1,857.30	$1,397.40	**$2,317.20**
Weston Outfitters	$1,921.44	$490.00	($1,431.44)	**$2,411.44**
Kanga Kampers	$1,895.42	$668.04	($1,227.38)	**$2,563.46**
Extreme Outdoors	$2,119.46	$1,398.80	($720.66)	**$3,518.26**
Extrem!	$4,504.82	$906.00	($3,598.82)	**$5,410.82**
Subtotal (included)	**$11,689.92**	**$5,530.14**	**($6,159.78)**	**$17,220.06**
Outdoors Shop	**$108,046.06**	**$54,234.22**	**($53,811.84)**	**$162,280.28**

Suppressing zeros may hide potentially valuable information contained in other cells of the row that have been removed from the analysis. In the previous example, two retailers with data in the Prior YTD column were removed during suppression because these rows had zeros in the YTD column. Applying suppression to the Prior YTD column as well takes the values of both columns into consideration. The following illustration shows suppression applied to both columns.

NOTE *Attempting to apply suppression to multiple rows or columns simultaneously will produce an error. Suppression must be applied one row or column at a time.*

Revenue	Prior YTD	YTD	YTD Change	*Total*
Jack and Jill Climbing School & Supplies	$250.50	$0.00	($250.50)	**$250.50**
By A Thread	$788.88	$210.00	($578.88)	**$998.88**
Altitudes extrêmes	$1,719.68	$0.00	($1,719.68)	**$1,719.68**
Artículos de Campismo El Aquila, S.A. de C.V.	$459.90	$1,857.30	$1,397.40	**$2,317.20**
Weston Outfitters	$1,921.44	$490.00	($1,431.44)	**$2,411.44**
Kanga Kampers	$1,895.42	$668.04	($1,227.38)	**$2,563.46**
Extreme Outdoors	$2,119.46	$1,398.80	($720.66)	**$3,518.26**
Extrem!	$4,504.82	$906.00	($3,598.82)	**$5,410.82**
Subtotal (included)	**$13,660.10**	**$5,530.14**	**($8,129.96)**	**$19,190.24**
Outdoors Shop	**$108,046.06**	**$54,234.22**	**($53,811.84)**	**$162,280.28**

Managing Custom Sets

Sets give you the ability to group dimensions or members for use in the current analysis, or you can share custom sets with other analyses. The other side to that is other analysts in your organization can share their sets with you for use in an analysis.

Creating Custom Sets

Creating a custom set allows you to group items that you frequently use. This saves you from continually dragging various groups of dimensions or members into the analysis.

For example, we have created an analysis that shows the Outdoor Shops retailers with the least revenue for Outdoor Protection products from Telephone orders. We may want to create a custom set of this group of retailers to be able to use them in other analyses to keep an eye on them.

NOTE *When creating a custom set, the members in the set do not have to be on the same level, but must be within the same dimension.*

Here's how to create a custom set:

1. From the analysis, select the members to be used to create the custom set. For this example, we select the retailers in an analysis that shows the bottom 10 percent of Outdoor Shops retailers with the least revenue for Outdoor Protection from Telephone orders.

2. Right-click on the selection. A context menu displays.

3. Select Save As Custom Set. The Save As Custom Set screen displays, as shown next. The Existing Custom Sets box lists any custom sets already created. In this example, no custom sets currently exist:

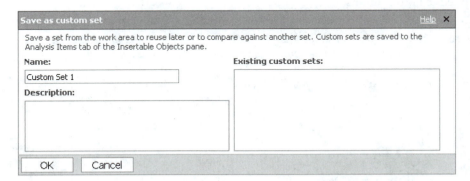

4. In the Name text box, enter a name for the custom set. For this example, we name the set Bottom Outdoor Shops.

5. Optionally, in the Description text box, enter a description for the custom set.

6. Click OK. Analysis Studio creates the custom set and displays the Analysis Items tab in the Insertable Objects pane. In the Custom Sets folder of the source tree, the

new custom set displays, as shown next. You can share the custom set with other analysts in your organization or retrieve it the next time you create an analysis.

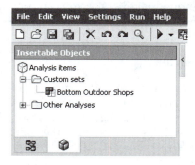

Insert Sets

You can use custom sets in the analysis that you have created or sets that have been created by other analysts in your organization. Using sets saves you from having to navigate through the source tree to find groups of members that you use often. This is especially helpful if you use members that are on different levels.

Here's how to insert sets:

1. In the Insertable Objects pane, click the Analysis Items tab.

2. From the Analysis Items source tree, navigate to the set to be added to the analysis.

3. Drag the set into the analysis. Analysis Studio adds the set to the analysis:

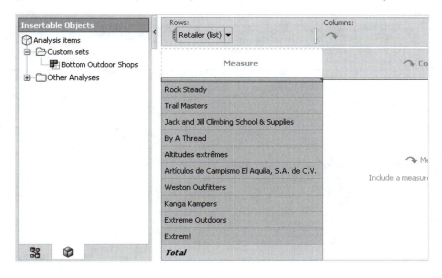

Applying Complex Filters

Complex filters allow you to add multiple filters to the analysis to break down the data even more. You can create individual filters or you can combine filters so that multiple filters work together.

Apply Custom Filters

Here's how to apply a custom filter:

1. In the analysis, highlight the row or column on which you want to apply a filter. In this example, we highlight the rows in an analysis that contains the Irons member from the Products dimension as the rows, the Prior YTD, YTD, and YTD Change members from the All Dates dimension as the columns and Revenue as the measure.

2. From the toolbar, click Filter. A submenu displays with two options: No Filter or Custom.

3. Select Custom. The Filter pane displays with options to add and delete filters on the analysis:

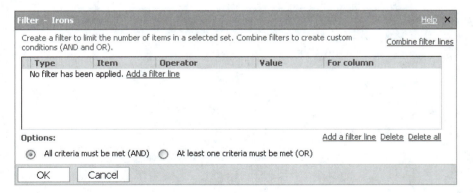

4. Click the Add A Filter Line link. The Filter pane refreshes with options for creating a filter:

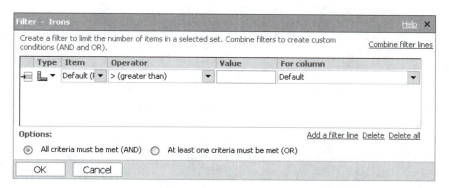

5. From the Type drop-down list, select the type of data on which to apply the filter: measure, label, or attribute. This selection determines the other available options. For this example, we select Measure.

6. From the Item drop-down list, select a measure. The measure in the analysis is the default. However, you can select any measure in the data source. For this example, we select the Quantity Sold measure.

7. From the Operator list, select an operator for the filter expression. For this example, we select *greater than or equal.*

8. In the Value text box, enter a value for the filter expression. For this example, we enter 600, as we only want to see products whose Quantity Sold is greater than or equal to 600.

9. From the For Column or For Row list, select the column or row on which to base the filter. The default is the summary column or row. For this example, we select the Prior YTD column.

10. Click OK. Analysis Studio applies the filter. Notice that Analysis Studio added a Subtotal (included) row that provides a subtotal of the filtered data and maintains the total of all the data included in the analysis:

Rows: ⟨Irons ▼⟩   Columns: ⟨All Dates (list... ▼⟩   Context filter: ↻

Filters are applied. See the Properties pane for more details.

Revenue	Prior YTD	YTD	YTD Change	*Total*
Hailstorm Steel Irons	$1,130,059.86	$1,268,556.30	$138,496.44	**$2,398,616.16**
Lady Hailstorm Steel Irons	$366,901.52	$391,060.18	$24,158.66	**$757,961.70**
Lady Hailstorm Titanium Irons	$390,326.64	$413,882.02	$23,555.38	**$804,208.66**
Hailstorm Titanium Irons	$1,367,045.96	$1,563,038.78	$195,992.82	**$2,930,084.74**
Subtotal (included)	**$3,254,333.98**	**$3,636,537.28**	**$382,203.30**	**$6,890,871.26**
Irons	**$3,254,333.98**	**$3,636,537.28**	**$382,203.30**	**$6,890,871.26**

Apply Additional Filters

You can see from the example in the previous section that nothing was filtered out of the analysis by the custom filter created. All products displayed must have met the criteria of having 600 units sold for the prior year-to-date. Now we may want to create additional filters to further analyze the data. Applying multiple filters to an analysis is where the filters become complex.

Here's how to apply additional filters:

1. In the analysis, highlight the row or column on which you want to apply a filter. For this example, we select the rows to apply an additional filter to the Irons in the analysis.

2. From the toolbar, click Filter, and then select Custom from the submenu. The Filter pane displays and shows any filters already created in the analysis.

3. Click the Add A Filter Line link. Follow the steps from the section above to create any additional filters you want to apply to the analysis. For this example, we add the filters: (*Gross profit > 500000*) and (*Revenue > 1000000*).

4. Under the Options heading, select the All Criteria Must Be Met (AND) option or the At Least One Criteria Must Be Met (OR) option.

5. Click OK. Analysis Studio applies the additional filter(s) to the analysis and displays the results, as shown next. Repeat this process to add as many filters as you need.

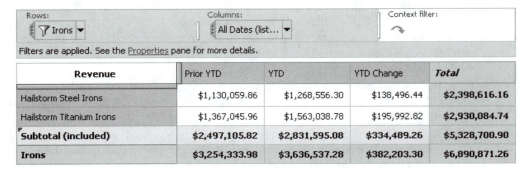

Combine Filters

You can create even more complex filters by combining multiple filters. You can use the combined filters in conjunction with other filters in the analysis so that they work with one another. When only two filters are applied, there are two options available for how Analysis Studio applies them to the analysis. The filters can be set so that either both must be met or one of the two must be met. When a third filter is introduced to the party, the options increase. For example, suppose you have Filter A, Filter B, and Filter C. You want the criteria for Filter A and Filter C to be met, or the criteria of Filter B to be met. Analysis Studio can display the data in the analysis that meets the criteria established by Filter A and Filter C, as well as the data that meets the criteria for Filter B.

Here's how to combine filters:

1. In the analysis, highlight the row or column on which you want to combine filters. For this example, we select the Irons row from the analysis created in the previous section.

2. From the toolbar, click Filter, and then select Custom from the submenu.

3. The Filter pane displays showing the existing filters and a link to Combine Filter Lines:

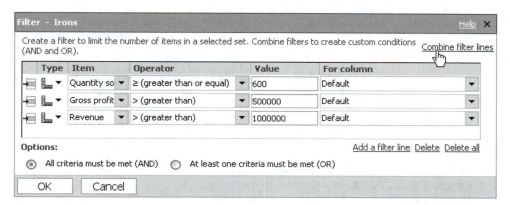

4. Click the Combine Filter Lines link. The Combine Filter Lines pane displays and lists all the filters currently applied to the analysis:

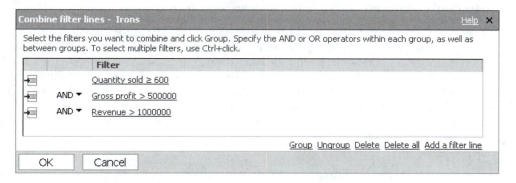

5. Select the filters to combine by CTRL-clicking the row of each filter you want to combine. For this example, we select the (*Quantity Sold >= 600*) and (*Gross Profit > 500000*) filters.

6. Click the Group link to combine the selected filters.

7. Optionally, change the operators between any filters. Click the AND or OR operator you want to change and select an operator from the options that display. For this example, we change the second operator to OR, as shown next:

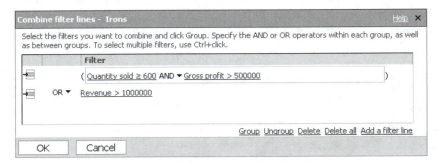

8. Click OK. Analysis Studio applies the combined filters to the analysis.

Nesting Items

Dimensions, members, and measures can all be nested in rows or columns in multiple ways. Nesting gives you a way to group items in the analysis.

Nesting dimensions or members in a row or column is useful when you want to see items grouped in a hierarchy. For example, if you have an analysis with the Products dimension as the rows and the YTD Grouped member from the All Dates dimension as the columns and Revenue as the measure, you could nest the Order Method member with the Products to see how each product line compares for order method.

Here's how to nest items in an analysis:

1. From the Source tree, drag the item to nest to the desired position in the rows or columns drop zone. To nest in the rows drop zone, position the item to the left or right of the already inserted item. To nest in the columns drop zone, position the item above or below the already inserted item. Analysis Studio indicates where the dimension or member will be nested with a flashing black bar. For this example, we drag the Order Method dimension to be nested to the left of the Products dimension in the rows drop zone:

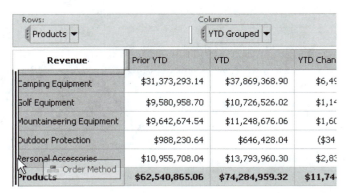

Analysis Studio updates the analysis to include the nested item. The overview area also updates to accommodate any additions. In this example, you see the revenue of each order method for each product line. Subtotals have been added for each grouping of order method:

Rows: Order Method ▼ Products ▼	Columns: YTD Grouped ▼		Context filter:

Revenue		Prior YTD	YTD	YTD Change	YTD G
Fax	Camping Equipment	$1,522,878.58	$1,836,400.30	$313,521.72	20
	Golf Equipment	$508,769.58	$635,590.76	$126,821.18	24
	Mountaineering Equipment	$662,612.52	$557,716.86	($104,895.66)	-15
	Outdoor Protection	$53,224.76	$32,387.72	($20,837.04)	-39
	Personal Accessories	$598,985.66	$566,175.82	($32,809.84)	-5
	Products	**$3,346,471.10**	**$3,628,271.46**	**$281,800.36**	**8.**
Telephone	Camping Equipment	$7,880,932.52	$9,280,845.86	$1,399,913.34	17
	Golf Equipment	$2,410,111.66	$2,454,580.78	$44,469.12	1
	Mountaineering Equipment	$2,524,028.34	$2,855,944.64	$331,916.30	13
	Outdoor Protection	$246,964.74	$142,908.00	($104,056.74)	-42
	Personal Accessories	$2,938,441.44	$3,468,271.58	$529,830.14	18

Now that you have items nested in the analysis, you can use Analysis Studio tools to view data in the analysis. You can drill-down or drill-up on the nested items. Nested items can be deleted from an analysis by right-clicking on the item in the overview area and selecting Delete from the context menu

---

NOTE *You can nest multiple dimensions and/or members, as well as measures, in the same analysis.*

Stacking Items

Stacking lets you insert multiple items into an analysis for side-by-side comparison. Dimensions, members, and measures can each be used for stacking.

For example, suppose the analysis has the Products dimension as the rows, the YTD Grouped member as the columns, and Revenue as the measure. You also want to see how the sales territories performed while maintaining the YTD Grouped member for the columns and Revenue as the measure. Stacking enables you to look at the Products and Sales Territory dimensions as they relate to the YTD Grouped member and Revenue measure on the same analysis.

Here's how to stack items in an analysis:

1. From the source tree, drag the item to stack to the desired position in the rows or columns. To stack in rows, position the item above or below the already inserted item. To nest in columns, position the item to the left or right of the already inserted item. Analysis Studio indicates where the item will be stacked with a flashing black bar. For this example, we drag the Sales Territory dimension to be stacked beneath the Products dimension in the rows of an analysis.

Revenue	Prior YTD	YTD	YTD Ch.
Camping Equipment	$31,373,293.14	$37,869,368.90	$6,·
Golf Equipment	$9,580,958.70	$10,726,526.02	$1,:
Mountaineering Equipment	$9,642,674.54	$11,248,676.06	$1,6
Outdoor Protection	$988,230.64	$646,428.04	($3
Personal Accessories	$10,955,708.04	$13,793,960.30	$2,8
Products	**$62,540,865.06**	**$74,284,959.32**	**$11,7·**

Sales Territory

Analysis Studio updates the analysis to include the stacked item(s). You can now view data from the two analyses in one crosstab without having to jump back and forth between crosstabs:

Rows: Combination

Columns: YTD Grouped

Context filter:

Revenue	Prior YTD	YTD	YTD Change	YTD Growth	**YTD Grouped**
Camping Equipment	$31,373,293.14	$37,869,368.90	$6,496,075.76	20.71%	**$0.00**
Golf Equipment	$9,580,958.70	$10,726,526.02	$1,145,567.32	11.96%	**$0.00**
Mountaineering Equipment	$9,642,674.54	$11,248,676.06	$1,606,001.52	16.66%	**$0.00**
Outdoor Protection	$988,230.64	$646,428.04	($341,802.60)	-34.59%	**$0.00**
Personal Accessories	$10,955,708.04	$13,793,960.30	$2,838,252.26	25.91%	**$0.00**
Products	**$62,540,865.06**	**$74,284,959.32**	**$11,744,094.26**	**18.78%**	**$0.00**
Americas	$19,473,578.30	$24,330,295.84	$4,856,717.54	24.94%	**$0.00**
Asia Pacific	$6,542,364.12	$8,530,643.58	$1,988,279.46	30.39%	**$0.00**
Central Europe	$19,024,195.38	$21,436,647.58	$2,412,452.20	12.68%	**$0.00**
Northern Europe	$10,499,696.46	$11,886,569.84	$1,386,873.38	13.21%	**$0.00**
Southern Europe	$7,001,030.80	$8,100,802.48	$1,099,771.68	15.71%	**$0.00**
Sales Territory	**$62,540,865.06**	**$74,284,959.32**	**$11,744,094.26**	**18.78%**	**$0.00**

Now that you have items stacked in the analysis, you can use Analysis Studio tools to view data in the analysis. You can drill-down or drill-up on the stacked items. Stacked items can be deleted from an analysis by right-clicking on the item in the overview area and selecting Delete from the context menu

Nesting and Stacking Items

Items can be both nested and stacked in an analysis. Nesting and stacking measures lets you see how multiple measures relate to the dimensions or members in the analysis. For example, if you have an analysis with the Products dimension as the rows, the YTD Grouped member from the All Dates dimension as the columns, and Revenue as the measure, you could nest the Revenue measure and then stack the Quantity Sold measure to see how the two compare to one another.

Here's how to nest and stack measures:

1. From the source tree, drag the measure already in the analysis to the bottom of the columns drop zone, as shown next. Analysis Studio indicates where the measure will be nested with a flashing black bar. For this example, we drag the Revenue measure to be nested just below the YTD Grouped column headings:

Revenue	Prior YTD	YTD	YTD Change
Camping Equipment	$31,373,293.14	$37,869,368.90	$6,496,075
Golf Equipment	$9,580,958.70	$10,726,526.02	$1,145,56;
Mountaineering Equipment	$9,642,674.54	$11,248,676.06	$1,606,00:
Outdoor Protection	$988,230.64	$646,428.04	($341,802
Personal Accessories	$10,955,708.04	$13,793,960.30	$2,838,25;
Products	**$62,540,865.06**	**$74,284,959.32**	**$11,744,094**

2. From the Source tree, drag a second measure to be stacked to the right or the left of the first nested measure. Analysis Studio indicates where the measure will be inserted with a flashing black bar:

Revenue	Prior YTD	YTD	YTD Change	YTD Growth
	Revenue	Revenue / Quantity sold	Revenue	Revenue
Camping Equipment	$31,373,293.14	$37,869,368.90	$6,496,075.76	20.71%
Golf Equipment	$9,580,958.70	$10,726,526.02	$1,145,567.32	11.96%

Analysis Studio adds the measure to the analysis, so you can compare how the dimensions or members reflect the two selected measures:

Revenue	Prior YTD		YTD		YTD Change
	Revenue	Quantity sold	Revenue	Quantity sold	Revenue
Camping Equipment	$31,373,293.14	306,566	$37,869,368.90	377,846	$6,496
Golf Equipment	$9,580,958.70	38,692	$10,726,526.02	41,796	$1,145
Mountaineering Equipment	$9,642,674.54	139,562	$11,248,676.06	162,396	$1,606
Outdoor Protection	$988,230.64	171,182	$646,428.04	112,022	($341,
Personal Accessories	$10,955,708.04	133,674	$13,793,960.30	169,912	$2,838
Products	**$62,540,865.06**	**789,676**	**$74,284,959.32**	**863,972**	**$11,744,**

NOTE *If you want to nest a dimension or member with only part of a stacked analysis, you must first nest the dimension or members and then stack them.*

Modify the Layout

Analysis Studio is a straightforward tool used to display the data for you to examine; it's not about making the data look pretty. As a result, Analysis Studio does not provide the formatting capabilities available in Report Studio or Query Studio. However, there is some flexibility in the way in which you can display the analysis. You can rank items from best to worst or vice versa, you can sort the data from A to Z or Z to A, you can exclude categories and subtotals, you can insert charts and graphs, and you can apply templates.

NOTE *The following sections begin with you having already created the analysis. For more information on creating an analysis, refer to the "Create an Analysis" section earlier in this chapter.*

Sorting Data in an Analysis

Sorting the data in an analysis is no different from sorting rows or columns in Report Studio or Query Studio. You can sort in ascending or descending order.

Here's how to sort rows and columns in an analysis:

1. Select the row or column to be sorted.

2. From the toolbar, click Sort. A submenu displays with the No Sort, Ascending, and Descending options:

3. From the submenu, select Ascending or Descending. Analysis Studio sorts the selection of the analysis accordingly.

Excluding Categories

Excluding categories lets you eliminate a category from being displayed in the analysis while still including the excluded categories in the appropriate summaries. For example, suppose you have an analysis displaying all product types within Camping Equipment: Cooking Gear, Sleeping Bags, Packs, Tents, and Lanterns. You want to exclude Tents from your analysis because that product type always performs well and you don't need to see it. You can exclude that row from displaying in the analysis, but the data from that row will still be included in the product line totals. A subtotal row will also be added to the analysis with a subtotal for all included categories.

Here's how to exclude a category:

1. From the analysis, right-click the category to be excluded. A context menu displays with the option to exclude the category. For this example, we want to exclude the Tents product type:

2. From the context menu, select Exclude. Analysis Studio removes the selected category from the analysis and adds a Subtotal (included) row. This new row includes data only for those dimensions or members that are currently displayed in the analysis:

Revenue	Prior YTD	YTD	YTD Change	*Total*
Cooking Gear	$1,871,272.24	$2,341,848.56	$470,576.32	**$4,213,120.80**
Sleeping Bags	$4,094,981.02	$4,987,198.60	$892,217.58	**$9,082,179.62**
Packs	$5,095,093.26	$6,273,583.42	$1,178,490.16	**$11,368,676.68**
Lanterns	$3,741,719.36	$4,405,840.74	$664,121.38	**$8,147,560.10**
Subtotal (included)	**$14,803,065.88**	**$18,008,471.32**	**$3,205,405.44**	**$32,811,537.20**
Camping Equipment	**$31,373,293.14**	**$37,869,368.90**	**$6,496,075.76**	**$69,242,662.04**

Manage Totals and Subtotals

Analysis Studio lets you determine what totals and subtotals to display in the analysis. This feature gives you additional control over the layout of the analysis. The selections you make do not affect the data in the data source, only how the data is displayed.

Here's how to manage totals and subtotals:

1. From the Settings menu, select Totals And Subtotals. The Subtotals screen displays with options for presenting the totals and subtotals in the analysis:

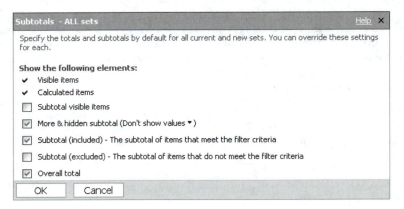

2. Select the checkbox(es) next to the appropriate option(s).

3. Click OK. The totals and subtotals display in the analysis based on your selections.

Inserting Charts and Graphs

You can add charts and graphs to an analysis to depict the resulting data graphically. Analysis Studio offers a variety of charts and graphs. You can also choose to show a chart and the crosstab, or just the chart.

Here's how to insert a chart or graph:

1. From the toolbar, click Chart Type. A submenu displays with chart options, as shown next:

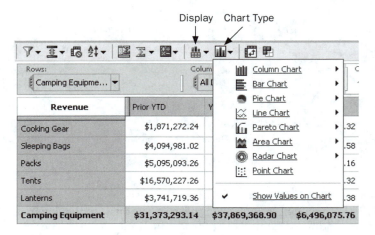

2. Click the type of chart you want to insert into the analysis. A submenu of chart styles for the selected chart type displays with the exception of Point Chart. If you click Point Chart, Analysis Studio inserts the chart into the analysis.

3. Click the style of chart to be inserted into the analysis. The selected chart type and style display in the analysis. For this example, we choose Standard from the Bar Chart submenu to create a chart for the revenue of the Camping Equipment product types.

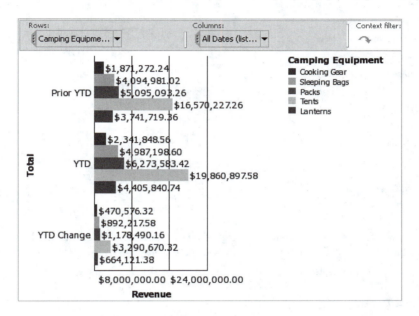

4. Optionally, show the numeric values on the chart.

5. From the toolbar, click Chart Type.

6. Click on the Show Values On Chart option at the bottom of the menu to change the setting.

7. Optionally, display only the chart.

8. From the toolbar, click Display. A submenu displays with options to display Crosstab, Chart, or Crosstab and Chart. Select Chart to display the chart only.

Modify Data Format

You may find that the analysis does not display data for some dimensions or members when used in conjunction with other dimensions or members. Typically, this is a result of missing or incomplete data from the data source. The resulting analysis displays blank cells, errors, or a divide-by-zero symbol (/0). This does not necessarily affect the data, but it does affect the way the analysis looks. You can change the format of what displays for these and other items.

Here's how to modify data format:

1. From the Settings menu, select Data Format. The Data Format screen displays options to format the data in an analysis:

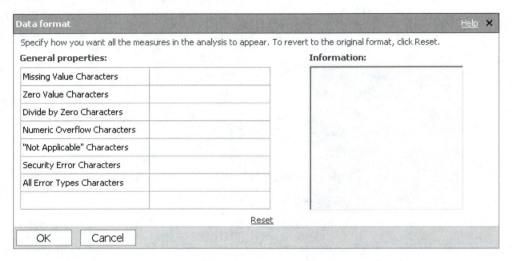

2. Enter values for the desired properties. For example, you can enter the number 0 in the Divide by Zero Characters text box to display a 0 in the analysis instead of /0.

3. Click OK. Data format changes are saved for this analysis.

Apply Templates

You have created an analysis that is worth saving and sharing with other members of your organization. You can apply a template to the analysis to give it your organization's look and feel.

NOTE *You can apply only Report Studio templates to an analysis.*

Here's how to apply a template:

1. From the Run menu, select Report Options. The Report Options screen displays with the Title, Display, Paper, Report Template, and Output Purpose tabs. These tabs let you set different report options.

2. Click the Report Template tab. Template options display, as shown next. You can use a default template as established by your Cognos administrator, or you can select a template to apply from Public Folders or My Folders:

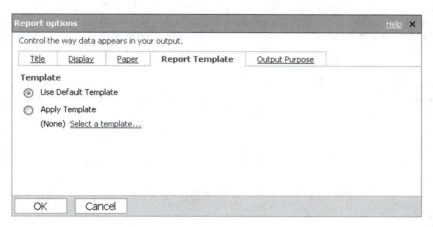

3. Select the Apply Template option.

4. Click the Select A Template link. The Select A Template pane displays, where you can navigate to a Report Studio template:

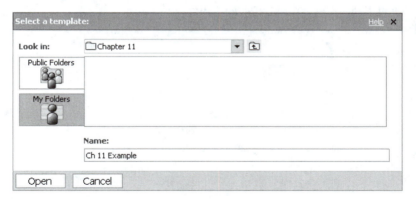

5. Navigate to a template saved either in Public Folders or My Folder.

6. Click Open to select the template.

7. Click OK to apply the template to the current analysis. You will not, however, see the template until you run the analysis in one of the available formats. From the Run menu, run the analysis in the desired format. Analysis Studio runs the analysis and displays it with the selected template.

Beyond Analysis Studio

Well, that's it right? You have created the analysis. You have defined business questions. There is nothing left to do. That is not exactly true. If you have created an analysis that you think is worth saving because it does answer business questions, then at least two options remain: You can open that analysis in Report Studio and use all of the tools available for use on dimensional data sources, or you can use the analysis with IBM Cognos 8 Go! Office.

View Analysis in Report Studio

Take your analysis to the next level. You can open an analysis in Report Studio that you created in Analysis Studio and take full advantage of all of the tools available for reports created from dimensional data sources.

NOTE   *To open an analysis in Report Studio, you must have access to Report Studio.*

Here's how to view an analysis in Report Studio:

1. From Cognos Connection, navigate to the analysis you want to open in Report Studio.

2. Under the Actions column, click More. The Perform An Action screen displays and lists different actions that can be performed on the analysis, as shown next. The actions include opening the analysis in Analysis Studio or Report Studio, running the analysis, and setting properties, to name a few.

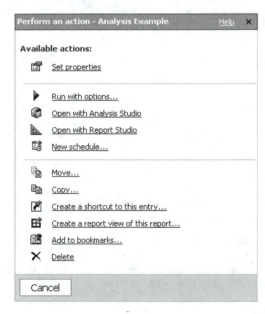

3. Click the Open With Report Studio link. Report Studio launches and the analysis opens in Report Studio, as shown next.

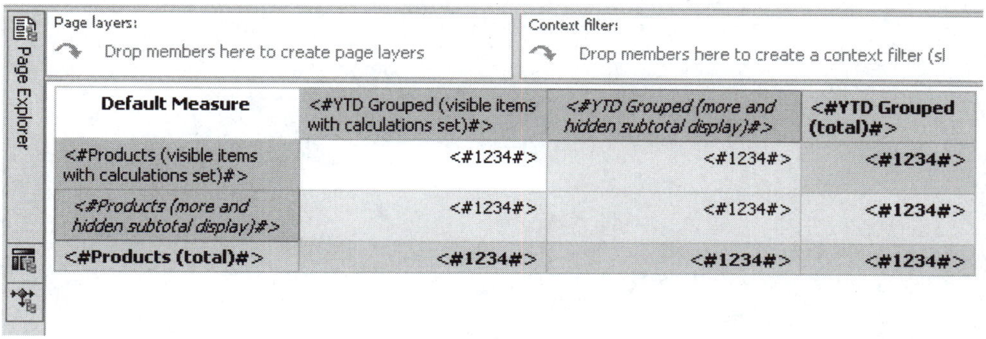

	Page layers: Drop members here to create page layers		Context filter: Drop members here to create a context filter (sl
Default Measure	<#YTD Grouped (visible items with calculations set)#>	<#YTD Grouped (more and hidden subtotal display)#>	<#YTD Grouped (total)#>
<#Products (visible items with calculations set)#>	<#1234#>	<#1234#>	<#1234#>
<#Products (more and hidden subtotal display)#>	<#1234#>	<#1234#>	<#1234#>
<#Products (total)#>	<#1234#>	<#1234#>	<#1234#>

NOTE *For more information on using all of the tools available to dimensional reports in Report Studio, refer to Chapter 12.*

IBM Cognos 8 Go! Office Analysis

Go! Office allows you to access analyses created in Analysis Studio in a Microsoft Excel spreadsheet. This can be very useful if you want to include your analysis as a chart or graph within a financial report that you have created and share with the management team.

Go! Office is an additional feature that needs to be installed separately from IBM Cognos 8 BI. When installed, Go! Office installs add-ins into Microsoft Excel. For more information on Go! Office, refer to Chapter 7 or contact your IBM Cognos 8 BI representative.

Advanced Reporting III

In Chapter 11, you learned how to create an analysis in Analysis Studio to help users answer the next business question. Now you need to share the information regarding that business question with others in your organization. You could share the analysis in its present form, but many more formatting options are available in Report Studio that allow you to take that analysis to the next level of distribution and consumption by other users.

Report Studio offers many ways to view and structure report data to fulfill a report's requirements. When you incorporate *dimensional structures* into your reports in Report Studio, you turn the analysis report into a highly formatted presentation. This chapter describes how to use the advanced features in Report Studio to create effective dimensional reports. You'll learn about dimensional structures and their uses and important functions that will help you leverage the dimensional data structures. This chapter also introduces you to the Express Authoring Mode feature that lets you generate statement style reports, which can be a great environment for financial authors.

Differences Between Relational and Dimensional Models

Dimensional models differ from relational models in a number of ways. The two types of models present different types of information and offer different advantages. Relational models contain more detailed data than dimensional models. For example, you may be able to see invoice line item descriptions in a relational model, but dimensional models generally contain summary data, so it is unlikely that you would be able to see this level of detail in a dimensional model.

Dimensional models have inherent drill-down capabilities in Analysis Studio and Query Studio due to the dimensional structures (hierarchies) that are defined. It is important to note that the drill-down capability is available in Report Studio, but it must be enabled by the report author.

Model Types and Dimensional Structure

Two types of models are used in Report Studio: relational and dimensional. Earlier chapters on Report Studio discussed reporting using relational data sources. This chapter discusses dimensional data structures and how to write a report using them as the source.

Dimensions contain members that can be structured into hierarchies and levels. *Dimensions* are the highest level of descriptive data. They tend to deal with the major aspects of the business. From a business modeling perspective, dimensions contain data that answers questions such as who, what, when, where, why, and how.

Below dimensions are *hierarchies*, which provide context to the structured levels of data that they contain. A dimension can contain multiple hierarchies that provide alternative views of the information included in the dimension. Hierarchies can contain several structured levels of information. Each subordinate level in a hierarchy contains increasingly detailed information that relates to the dimension.

NOTE *A hierarchy need not contain any defined levels. A parent-child hierarchy depends on the relationships between members rather than stratifying the members into distinct levels.*

Members are data entities that provide context to cell values. They are made up of a *member key* to identify the member, a *caption* that describes the member, and possibly *attributes* that provide additional information about the member. The following illustration shows an example of a dimensional structure and the data entities that display within that structure. The dimensional structure contains dimensions, hierarchies, levels, members, and attributes:

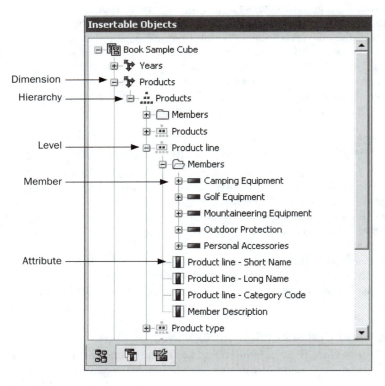

Navigating Dimensional Structures

The top level of the dimensional structure shown in the preceding illustration is the Products dimension. This dimension contains only one hierarchy, which is also named Products. It also contains information at many levels that relate to the products sold within the organization—information about specific products, product lines, and product models.

Below the Products dimension is the Products hierarchy. You can see the hierarchy Members folder and several levels related to the Products dimension, such as Products, Product line, Product type, and Product name. These items represent the core structures that define the graduation of detailed information in the Products hierarchy.

Under the Product line level is a Members folder and some Product line attributes. As mentioned, this attribute provides additional details about the members in the Product line level. In this example, the attribute is a product line category code associated with each member. You can tell that this is an attribute by the icon that appears next to the Product line–Category code and by its position in the hierarchy. Attributes appear at the same level as the Members folder. Within the Members folder are several members of the Product line level. The Members folder contains Camping Equipment, Mountaineering Equipment, Personal Accessories, and more.

Generating a Report from a Dimensional Model

Dimensional structures behave differently than relational structures in reports. When you create reports that contain data in a dimensional structure, a number of different features and options become available that allow you to input and manipulate data in a report in different ways. This section explains some of the options and features you encounter when creating a report with a dimensional model.

Inserting Hierarchies into Reports

When you insert a hierarchy into a report, Report Studio prompts you with a dialog that appears only when dimensional data is inserted. The Insert Hierarchy dialog allows you to insert Root Members or All Members, as shown next:

If you choose the Root Members option, only the members from the top of the hierarchy that display in the selected level display in the report. For example, if you insert the Products hierarchy into a report, only the highest level member displays in the report. If you choose the All Members option, the highest level member and all of the child members from each of the levels in the Products hierarchy display in the report.

Here's how to insert hierarchies into reports:

1. From the Insertable Objects pane, as shown next, drag a hierarchy into a report. The Insert Hierarchy dialog displays:

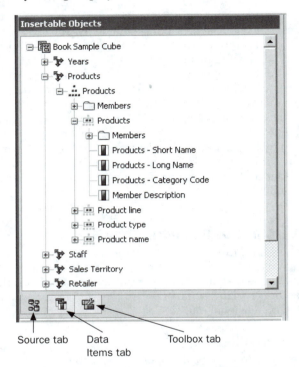

Source tab   Data   Toolbox tab
               Items tab

2. From the Insert Hierarchy dialog, select either Root Members or All Members.

3. Click OK to insert the selected dimensional structure into the report. Report Studio inserts the hierarchy. In this example, the inserted hierarchies display in the work area:

4. To configure which data is included in the report after you insert the hierarchy, select the hierarchy in the report, and in the Properties pane, set the Root Members Only property to Yes or No, as shown next:

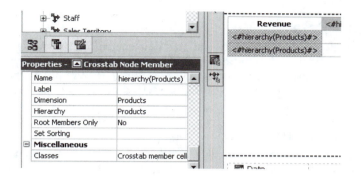

Attributes in Reports

Attributes can be included in a report to provide additional descriptive data for report users. Adding attributes to a report can be helpful for users who are unfamiliar with the data.

Here's how to insert an attribute into a report:

1. From the Insertable Objects pane, drag an attribute into the report. The Insert Member Property dialog displays:

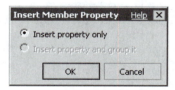

2. Select the Insert Property Only option to insert the attribute into the report.

3. Click OK.

4. Run the report. The attribute that you added displays next to the member heading to which it belongs. The following example shows a report with the Product line— Category Code attribute. The attribute displays to the right of the product name under the Revenue column heading.

Revenue		Years
Camping Equipment	1	$89,713,990.92
Golf Equipment	5	$25,905,465.58
Mountaineering Equipment	2	$20,891,350.60
Outdoor Protection	4	$3,171,114.92
Personal Accessories	3	$31,894,465.86

NOTE *Members also contain a descriptor known as the* member unique name *or MUN. A MUN describes a member's position in a dimensional structure and is referenced in the expression definition. If a MUN is changed or altered, then any report that references that MUN will no longer render. See the Cognos documentation for information on how to monitor this; it is something that you can avoid.*

Focus Dimensional Data

Dimensional data offers an extension to relational data structures, providing several ways to view and manipulate data. It is important that you understand how dimensional data structures behave and how to use the tools in Report Studio to manipulate these structures. This section explains how to use Report Studio to focus dimensional data to meet the requirements of your reports.

Dimensional Query Behavior

Dimensional queries return all members, whether they have measure values or not. Therefore, large dimensional structures without proper filtering can lead to large, inefficient reports. The key to creating efficient reports is limiting the items rendered in the queries to ensure that users get only the data they need to meet the report's requirements.

Efficient Dimensional Queries

One way to create dimensional queries that return only necessary data is to add information to a table by selecting individual members directly from the Insertable Objects pane. This can become a tedious task, however, if you want to include many members in a report, and it still may leave information in your reports that you do not need. To ensure that your dimensional queries return the most efficient reports, you need to use Report Studio options such as Set Functions, Filter Functions, Except Functions, Slicers, Dimensional Prompt Expressions, and Tree Prompts. These topics are explained in the following sections so that you can learn how to create efficient and effective reports.

Set Functions

The *Set Function* is used to gather specific members from within a dimensional structure. For example, if you have a data hierarchy called Football Equipment that contains the members Footballs, Shoulder Pads, and Helmets, and you want to retrieve only Footballs and Shoulder Pads, you can use the Set Function to create a data item that returns only these two child levels from the parent, Football Equipment.

Here's how to create a Set Function:

1. From the Toolbox tab in the Insertable Objects pane, drag a Query Calculation into the Rows drop zone.

2. The Create Calculation dialog displays, as shown next:

3. In the Name text box, enter a name for the Set Function calculation, and click OK. The dialog closes and the Data Item Expression–Set Function screen displays:

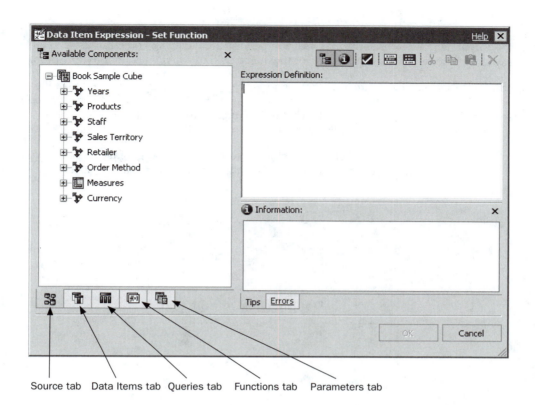

Source tab   Data Items tab   Queries tab   Functions tab   Parameters tab

4. From the Functions tab, expand the common functions folder, and then expand the R-Z folder.

5. From the R-Z folder, drag the Set Function into the Expression Definition pane, or type the calculation in the pane. The Set Function displays in the Expression Definition text box.

6. From the Source tab in the Available Components pane, drag the desired members into the Expression Definition pane, and close the expression with a parenthesis. The member aliases display in the Expression Definition pane, as shown next:

> Expression Definition:
> set([Americas], [Central Europe])

NOTE *To use the Set Function, the list of members selected must be from the same hierarchy.*

7. Click OK. The screen closes and Report Studio enters the selected members into the report.

This example shows a Set Function using the Americas and Central Europe members from the parent member Sales Territory. Once you define a Set Function, you can reuse it in other expressions to return the results only for the members that you defined in the expression.

Use a Set Function in an Aggregate   You can reuse a Set Function in an aggregate of the report. In this example, we create the aggregate using the Set Function from the preceding section. Additionally, we view and edit the Set Function expression.

Here's how to view the Set Function expression as it displays in an aggregate report:

1. From the Aggregate list on the standard toolbar, select Aggregate. The Aggregate displays at the bottom row in the table in the work area, as shown next:

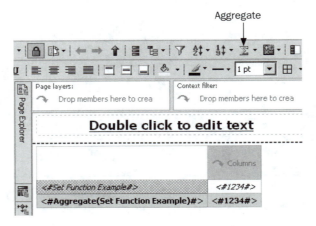

2. From the work area, double-click the Aggregate row heading. The Data Item Expression screen displays, as shown next, where you can view or edit the expression:

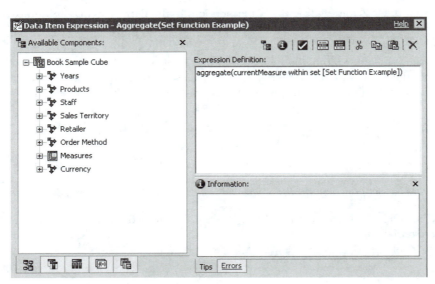

In this example, an alias to the Set Function used in the Aggregate expression displays as [Set Function Example]. This alias can be reused in other expressions to create more complex reports based on the two members included in the set.

3. Only the members of the Set Function are used for the aggregate. If you run the report created in this example, you will see that the aggregate returns the sum of only the members included in the Set Function:

Revenue	2004	2005	2006
Americas	*$15,412,898.76*	*$19,473,578.30*	*$24,330,295.84*
Central Europe	*$10,207,699.98*	*$19,024,195.38*	*$21,436,647.58*
Aggregate(Set Function Example)	**$25,620,598.74**	**$38,497,773.68**	**$45,766,943.42**

Filter Functions

Filter functions and detail filters are used to filter measure values in reports. This section explains how to use filter functions in reports. For more information on detail filters, refer to Chapter 9.

The *Filter function* returns a set of members in a query that is created by filtering a larger set of members based on a Boolean (that is a yes or no) condition. Filter functions are applied only to the members returned by the expression that you create. Filter functions are especially useful when the data for your reports is sparse, where you may not have measure values for all members, or it contains unnecessary data that does not meet the requirements of your report. Including unnecessary information can slow down the rendering of your reports, and they will typically be much larger than necessary.

The following illustration shows an example of an inefficient, unfiltered report. The report includes the Retailer name level within the Staff name level on the rows, the Years level on the columns, and the Revenue as the measure. When a report like this runs without filters, it takes a long time to generate because it returns every member. Additionally, the report contains many zero values. The Filter function can be used to remove zero values from the reports and ensure that only useful information is included in the reports.

Cognos Viewer		Professional Author	About

Revenue		2004	2005	2006
Humphrey Willoughby	Grand choix	$0.00	$0.00	$0.00
	Ausrüstungshaus Globetrotter	$0.00	$0.00	$0.00
	VIP Department Stores	$0.00	$0.00	$0.00
	Hartman's	$0.00	$0.00	$0.00
	Leisure Land	$57,940.06	$74,215.32	$73,006.52
	Connor Department Store	$0.00	$0.00	$0.00
	Chen Yu Enterprise Co.,	$0.00	$0.00	$0.00
	Sport & Freizeit	$0.00	$0.00	$0.00
	The Marketplace	$0.00	$0.00	$0.00
	Edward's Department Store	$0.00	$0.00	$0.00
	American Home	$0.00	$0.00	$0.00
	MER-KA-DOS, S.A. de C.V.	$0.00	$0.00	$0.00
	Chuei Hyakkaten	$0.00	$0.00	$0.00

≍ Top ≚ Page up ⯯ Page down ≍ Bottom

Here's how to create a Filter function:

1. From the Toolbox tab in the Insertable Objects pane, drag a Query Calculation into the Rows drop zone. The Create Calculation dialog displays.

2. Enter a name for the Calculation in the Name text box.

3. Click OK. The Data Item Expression screen displays.

4. Click the Functions tab.

5. From the Available Components pane, expand the Common Functions folder, expand the D-G folder, and drag the Filter function into the Expression Definition pane. The Filter function displays in the Expression Definition pane.

6. In the expression, include the information sources that you want to view in the report.

7. From the Source tab in the Available Components pane, drag the items that you want to include in the filter into the Expression Definitions pane. The item's path displays in the Expression Definition pane. In the example below, we select the Retailer name level.

8. Type a comma at the end of the expression.

9. From the Data Items tab in the Available Components pane, drag a measure into the Expression Definition pane. The measure path displays in the Expression Definition pane. In this example, we drag the Revenue measure.

10. At the end of the expression, type: **<> 0)**. The greater and less than signs translate to "not equal to": you are asking Report Studio to return all retailers with revenue not equal to zero. The parentheses are used to close the equation. You can view the complete expression in the Expression Definition pane, as shown next:

Expression Definition:

```
filter([PowerCube].[Retailer].[Retailer].[Retailer name],
[Revenue] <> 0)
```

The Data Item Expression dialog features the complete expression that removes Retailer names from the report with a Revenue value of zero.

11. Run the report. When the Filter function is applied to the data used to create the inefficient report, as shown next, the rows with all values of 0 are removed from the report.

Revenue		2004	2005	2006
Humphrey Willoughby	Leisure Land	$57,940.06	$74,215.32	$73,006.52
	Browns Opticals	$6,543.32	$2,402.40	$0.00
	Hurst Ironmongers	$61,985.58	$189,882.00	$16,159.60
	Jensen Mountaineering	$256,405.42	$127,016.40	$680,065.08
	Outdoor Experience	$260,139.36	$124,626.86	$299,750.80
	Beck's Sports Store	$245,154.58	$46,634.44	$175,906.22
James Ross-Hythe	Leisure Land	$77,975.00	$9,459.90	$45,701.24
	Browns Opticals	$7,334.72	$1,633.68	$9,560.00

Except Functions

The *Except function* returns the members of one Set function that are not in a second Set function. This means that the Except function excludes a set of members from a larger defined set. A common use for this is to combine it with the Top Count function or Bottom Count function, which are discussed later in this chapter.

The following example shows how to apply the Except function using the same crosstab data described earlier in the Filter functions section.

Here's how to create an Except function:

1. From the Toolbox tab in the Insertable Objects pane, drag a Query Calculation into the Rows drop zone. The Create Calculation dialog displays.

2. In the Name text box, enter a name for the calculation.

3. Click OK. The Data Item Expression screen displays.

4. Open the Functions tab.

5. From the Available Components pane, expand the Common Functions folder, and expand the D-G folder.

6. Drag the Except function into the Expression Definition pane. The Except function displays in the Expression Definition pane.

7. In the expression, include the information sources that you want to view in the report.

8. On the Source tab in the Available Components pane, navigate to the level that you want to include in the report.

9. Drag the selected level into the Expression Definition pane. The level path displays in the Expression Definition pane. In this example, we select the Product Line level.

10. Place a comma at the end of the expression in the Expression Definition pane.

11. From Functions tab in the Available Components pane, expand the Common Functions folder and expand the R-Z folder.

12. Drag the Set function into the Expression Definition pane. The Set function displays in the Expression Definition pane.

13. On the Source tab in the Available Components pane, navigate to the level that you selected in step 9.

14. Select the members that you want to exclude from the report.

15. Drag the selected members into the Set function in the Expression Definition pane. The members that display in this Set function are the exceptions that will be excluded from the report. In this example, we select the members Camping Equipment and Mountaineering Equipment.

16. Close the expression with two parentheses. This illustration shows the entire expression:

Expression Definition:

```
except([PowerCube].[Products].[Products].[Product line], set
([Camping Equipment],[Mountaineering Equipment]))
```

17. Run the report. The report displays in Cognos Viewer, and the two items included in the Set function are excluded from the report:

Revenue		2004	2005	2006
Humphrey Willoughby	Golf Equipment	$139,245.82	$212,818.52	$74,957.20
	Outdoor Protection	$31,897.90	$18,872.20	$12,489.16
	Personal Accessories	$193,131.66	$60,860.38	$276,084.90
James Ross-Hythe	Golf Equipment	$122,085.28	$70,508.86	$270,287.24
	Outdoor Protection	$30,587.22	$21,959.02	$13,149.14
	Personal Accessories	$331,678.12	$322,590.12	$278,558.10
Walter Taylor	Golf Equipment	$0.00	$0.00	$0.00

Slicers

A *Slicer* filter affects the cell value. Slicers are used to reduce the data included in measure rollups. Slicers are applied to the cells of the crosstab, not the row or column edges. This means that slicers are useful if you want some data in a report to be hidden and other data to be visible. You can create more than one slicer to filter across two or more dimensions, but you cannot create two slicers from the same dimension.

NOTE *You typically create slicers from a dimension that is not already referenced in a report. You can create slicers using items from a dimension that is referenced in a report, but often the results will not make sense.*

Let us use slicers in an example before diving into the procedure used to apply a slicer. The next illustration contains a crosstab with the member Product Type level on the rows, the Order Method level on the columns, and the Quantity Sold as the measure:

Quantity sold	<#Order Method#>	<#Order Method#>
<#Product type#>	<#1234#>	<#1234#>
<#Product type#>	<#1234#>	<#1234#>

The report generated from this Crosstab, shown next, shows Quantity Sold for all product types, for all order methods, and for all years:

Quantity sold	Fax	Telephone	Mail	E-mail	Web	Sales visit	Special
Cooking Gear	10,966	51,764	10,484	31,152	42,396	48,210	3,704
Sleeping Bags	4,030	25,582	4,218	15,534	22,224	22,878	1,780
Packs	5,138	23,542	5,446	14,516	22,356	22,410	2,144
Tents	7,720	32,074	7,352	21,566	28,658	31,138	2,156
Lanterns	14,718	89,886	17,680	55,464	73,752	86,108	7,488
Irons	812	3,228	860	2,140	3,336	3,616	252

Create a Simple Slicer We could use a slicer to make this report display only results for 2006. The following example describes how you would create a slicer that would result in this outcome.

Here's how to create a simple slicer:

1. From the Query Explorer tab, open Query 1 to modify the query:

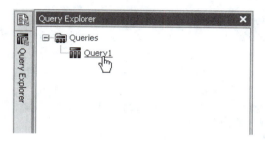

2. From the Insertable Objects pane, drag the 2006 member into the Slicer pane in the work area. The member displays in the Slicer pane:

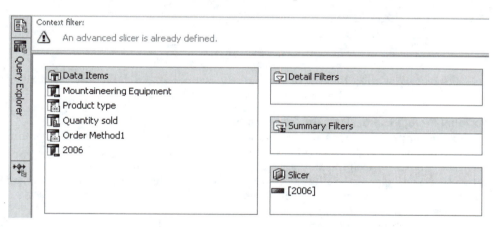

3. Run the report. The results are displayed in the following example. You can see that the results are considerably lower, because the slicer has included data only for the year 2006:

Quantity sold	Fax	Telephone	Mail	E-mail	Web	Sales visit	Special
Cooking Gear	4,652	20,272	3,346	12,950	23,578	20,914	700
Sleeping Bags	1,216	10,526	950	6,928	12,158	10,206	328
Packs	2,040	8,742	1,122	6,656	12,488	9,832	622
Tents	2,658	13,586	1,240	8,798	15,894	14,438	410
Lanterns	5,408	36,000	3,906	24,806	39,844	38,664	1,968
Irons	378	1,390	242	790	1,606	1,670	94
Putters	204	1,996	306	1,414	2,820	2,658	374

Create a Compound Slicer   After creating a simple slicer, you may want to move on to create *compound slicers.* A compound slicer contains more than one element in the Slicer pane. Here's how to create a compound slicer:

1. Repeat the steps for creating a simple slicer.

2. Add the desired members to the slicer pane. In this example, we add the members Fax, Telephone, and E-mail.

3. Click Run Report on the standard toolbar. The report displays, as shown next:

Quantity sold	Fax	Telephone	Mail	E-mail	Web	Sales visit	Special
Cooking Gear	4,652	20,272		12,950			
Sleeping Bags	1,216	10,526		6,928			
Packs	2,040	8,742		6,656			
Tents	2,658	13,586		8,798			
Lanterns	5,408	36,000		24,806			
Irons	378	1,390		790			
Putters	204	1,996		1,414			
Woods	390	1.400		850			

The slicer does not affect the row or column edges appearing in the report, but it affects the data itself and displays null values where no data is returned.

Dimensional Prompt Expressions and Tree Prompts

Dimensional prompt expressions and tree prompts allow you to create reports that prompt the user to select between different sets of data to determine what information will be visible in the report. For example, if your report contained the member Camping Equipment, and you wanted to allow users to generate separate reports that display results for specific brands of equipment, you could create a prompt that allows users to select which brands they want to display in the report.

The most common prompt expressions are based on a level or a hierarchy. The following sections explain how to create prompts using a crosstab report.

Create a Dimensional Prompt Expression

Dimensional prompt expressions allow users to select a member to include in a report. Here's how to create a dimensional prompt expression:

1. From the Toolbox tab in the Insertable Objects pane, drag a Query Calculation into the Rows drop zone. The Create Calculation dialog displays.

2. In the Name text box, enter a name for the Calculation.

3. Click OK. The Data Item Expression dialog displays.

4. On the Source tab in the Available Components pane, navigate to the level that you want to include in the report.

5. Drag the selected level into the Expression Definition pane. The level path displays in the Expression Definition tab. In this example, we select the Product Line level.

6. At the end of the expression, enter a parameter name, as shown next. In this example, we enter the following text: **->?p_Product_Line?**:

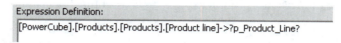

Expression Definition:
[PowerCube].[Products].[Products].[Product line]->?p_Product_Line?

NOTE *If you are using a different data item than Product Line, enter a parameter name that makes sense for the expression, such as the referenced data item name, in the place of p_Product_Line for this step.*

7. From the Data Item Expression dialog, click OK. The dialog closes.
8. Run the report. A value prompt displays in the Cognos Viewer:

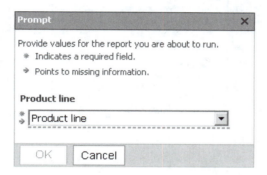

NOTE *Versions prior to Cognos 8.3 may interpret this example as a multi-select prompt control.*

9. From the list in the value prompt, choose a value for the parameter. Notice that you are able to select only one member from the list.
10. Click OK. The report displays in the Cognos Viewer. In this example, we selected Camping Equipment from the prompt:

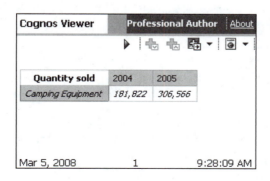

11. Optionally, manipulate the dimensional prompt expression to enable the selection of specified multiple prompt expressions to create reports.

12. Include the dimensional prompt expression in a Set function, as shown next:

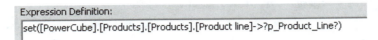

Expression Definition:
set([PowerCube].[Products].[Products].[Product line]->?p_Product_Line?)

13. Run the report. A value prompt displays that allows you to select multiple members at the prompt, as shown next:

14. Click OK. The report generates and displays only the members that you selected from the prompt.

Create a Tree Prompt   A tree prompt can also be used to filter data on a report. A tree prompt returns a set of members and their descendents from within a single hierarchy. The following instructions demonstrate how to create a tree prompt using the Products hierarchy from the example used in the preceding section.

NOTE *Tree prompts work only with dimensional data, as they rely on the hierarchical structure to build the member tree.*

Here's how to create a tree prompt:

1. From the Toolbox tab in the Insertable Objects pane, drag a Query Calculation onto the Rows drop zone. The Create Calculation dialog displays.

2. In the Name text box, enter a name for the Calculation.

3. Click OK. The Data Item Expression dialog displays.

4. On the Functions tab in the Available Components pane in the dialog, expand the Common Functions folder, and then expand the R-Z folder.

5. Drag the Set function into the Expression Definitions pane, or enter the text in the pane.

NOTE *The Set function is not mandatory for a tree prompt. If the Set function is omitted, the tree prompt will still be generated because it is referencing a hierarchy. However, the tree prompt will be only a single-select prompt.*

6. On the Source tab in the Available Components pane, navigate to the item that you want to include in the report.

7. Drag the selected item into the Expression Definition pane after the Set function. The path displays in the Expression Definition tab. In this example, we select the Products hierarchy.

8. At the end of the expression, enter a parameter name. In this example, we enter: **"->?p_Products?"**.

NOTE *If you are using a hierarchy other than Products, enter a parameter name that makes sense for the expression, such as the referenced data item name, in place of p_Products in this step.*

9. Close the expression with a closing parenthesis at the end, as shown next:

```
Expression Definition:
set([PowerCube].[Products].[Products]->?p_Products?)
```

10. Run the report. Report Studio prompts you with a tree prompt control, from which you can select checkboxes to determine what data displays, as shown next:

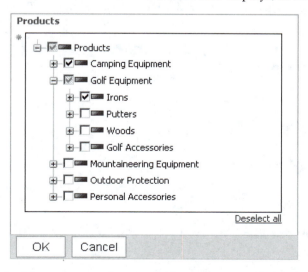

11. Select the checkboxes next to data items that you want to include in the report.

12. Click OK. The report displays in the Cognos Viewer, containing the data that you
    selected:

Quantity sold	2004	2005
Camping Equipment	181,822	306,566
Golf Equipment	18,912	38,692
Irons	2,692	5,382

Limit Data Shown in Tree Prompts   You can also limit what users see in tree prompts. This
example explains how to restrict what data users can see in a tree prompt.

Here's how to limit data shown in tree prompts:

1. From Page Explorer on the Explorer bar, click the Prompt Pages link. A Prompt
   Pages pane displays in the work area, as shown next:

2. From the Insertable Objects pane, drag the Page icon into the Prompt Pages pane in
   the work area.

3. Double-click the newly inserted page from the Prompt Pages pane. The page opens
   in the work area.

4. From the Toolbox tab in the Insertable Objects pane, drag the Tree Prompt icon into
   the work area. The Prompt Wizard Choose Parameter screen displays, as shown next:

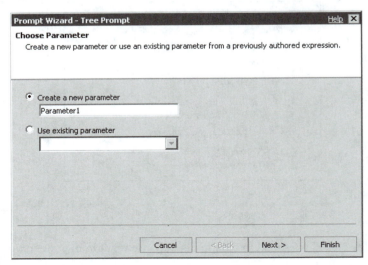

5. Select the Use Existing Parameter option, and choose a parameter from the drop-down list. For this example, we select the p_Products parameter we created in the previous section.

6. Click Next. The Populate Control screen displays.

7. In the Name text box, enter a name for the Query, or use the default name, as shown next:

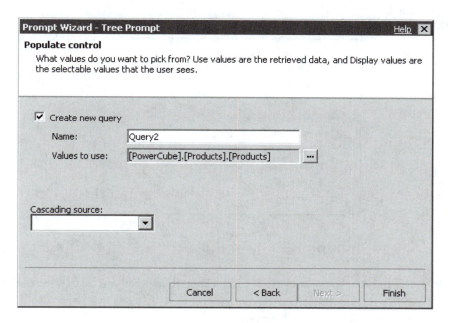

8. Click Finish. The wizard closes and the prompt page displays.

9. From Query Explorer on the Explorer bar, select the new query. The new query displays in the work area.

10. Double-click the data item in the Data Items pane. The Data Item Expression dialog displays.

11. Delete the current expression.

12. On the Functions tab in the Available Components pane, expand the Common Functions folder, and then expand the R-Z folder.

13. Drag the Set function into the Expression Definitions pane, or enter the text in the pane.

14. On the Source tab in the Available Components pane, navigate to the items that you want to include in the report.

15. Drag the selected items into the Expression Definition pane to the right of the Set function. The expression displays in the Expression Definition pane.

16. Close the expression with a closing parenthesis, as shown next, and click OK:

Expression Definition:
set([Golf Equipment],[Mountaineering Equipment])

17. Run the report. The tree prompt displays, containing only the members specified in the Set function:

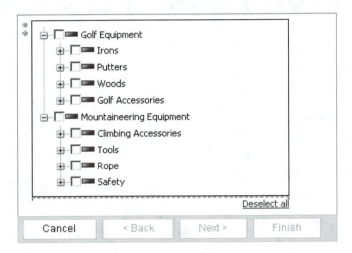

18. Select the checkboxes next to the individual items that you want to display in the report.

19. Click Finish to generate the report.

Navigation with Dimensional Functions

Dimensional functions make a report dynamic. You can create reports that prompt users to select a member to be featured in the report, and that member can be used to select other members based on its relationship in the dimensional function. Many dimensional functions are used to navigate through dimensional data in Report Studio. This section highlights some of the more important Family functions, Relative functions, and Complex functions used to navigate through those structures.

Family Functions

Family functions allow you to navigate through a dimensional data hierarchy both vertically and horizontally to retrieve members that are relative to a selected member. You can use Family functions to retrieve members. The functions are *ancestor, children, cousin, descendants, firstChild, firstSibling, lastChild, lastSibling, parent, siblings,* and many others. A variety of Family functions are available in Report Studio. This section will explain parent, children, ancestor, and cousin functions.

The following illustration shows a dimensional structure and the family relationships among the members in the structure. This dimensional structure contains revenue data included in members that represent specific periods of time, such as the year, quarter, and month.

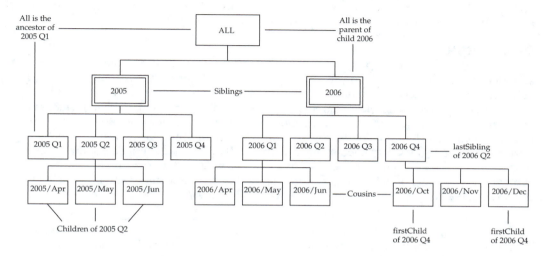

Children and Parent Functions

The *children* function navigates one level down in the dimensional structure to retrieve the child members of the selected member. For example, imagine that you have a parent member called Camping Equipment, and you want to retrieve the types of equipment that are children to the Camping Equipment member. You can use the children function to retrieve these Camping Equipment types. If you look at the Insertable Objects pane in the next illustration, you see a member named 2006. If you apply the children function on member 2006, it will return all the child members at the next level down, or members 2006 Q 1, 2006 Q 2, 2006 Q 3, and 2006 Q 4. Here's the expression: *children([2006])*.

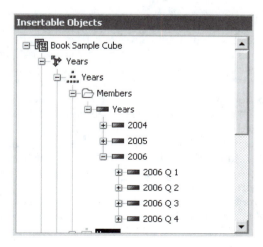

The *parent* function performs the opposite action of the *children* function. You can use the parent function to retrieve the member one level up in the hierarchy from the selected member. The parent function is useful if you want to know the context of the data with which you are working or if you need to navigate up a level in the dimensional structure. If you applied the parent function to member 2006 Q 1 from the preceding illustration, it will retrieve the member 2006. Here's the expression: *parent([2006 Q 1])*

Cousin Function

The *cousin* function retrieves a member in the same position relative to a member that you specify in the expression. This cousin function asks you to enter both the member for which you want to retrieve a cousin and the relative ancestor member from which you want to locate that cousin. For example, imagine that you are browsing through sales information in member 2006/Jun, or June 2006. Now imagine that you want to compare this sales information to that from June of the previous year. You can use the cousin function to retrieve that data. You would need to enter member 2006/Jun in the first half of the cousin function expression and enter the relative parent member 2005 in the second half of the expression. This function will navigate through the 2005 parent member and retrieve the cousin member 2005/Jun. Here's the expression: *cousin([2006/Jun],[2005])*

NOTE *The cousin member is determined based on the position in the collection of descendants from the ancestor at the same level as the selected ancestor member. For example, if your expression was* cousin([2006 Q 1], [2005]) *and 2005 Q 1 was not present in the hierarchy, then 2005 Q 2 would be the cousin (assuming 2005 Q 2 was the first member in the descendants of 2005).*

Ancestor Function

The *ancestor* function retrieves a parent member several levels up in the hierarchy, based on either the number of levels up or an ancestor level that you specify in the expression. If you applied the ancestor function to member 2006/Jun in the preceding example, and you specify that the expression is to navigate up two levels, the ancestor function looks up one level to the yearly quarter member (2006 Q 2), and then looks up again to the year member to return the member 2006. Here's the expression: *ancestor([2006/Jun],2)*

Relative Functions

Relative functions navigate horizontally in a level to retrieve members in the dimensional structure. Relative functions include *currentMember*, *lag*, *lead*, *nextMember*, and *prevMember*. These functions are not bound to the parent-child relationships of the hierarchy as the family functions are.

Lag and *lead* functions retrieve sibling members that are a specified number of places before (*lag*) or after (*lead*) the selected member. The number of positions before or after the selected member is specified by the report author in the expression. If you applied a lead function to the member, such as 2005/Apr, and you entered 2 in the lead function expression, it returns the member 2005/Jun: *lead([2005/Apr],2)*. It does not make sense to use the lag function on member 2005/Apr because it is the first child element at that level, and there are no members before it to retrieve. The *prevMember* function and *nextMember* function behave similarly to lead and lag functions, but they can retrieve only the previous or next sibling member. This means that you are not required to enter a number of places to move in their expressions.

NOTE *Applying the* lag *or* lead *function to the first or last respective member of the level won't return any member for the expression.*

Relative Time Functions

Relative time functions are typically used with the time dimension. This group includes functions such as *closingPeriod*, *lastPeriods*, *openingPeriod*, *parallelPeriod*, and *periodsToDate*. The *closingPeriod* function returns the last sibling of a level, which can optionally be restricted to the descendants of a specified member. In our example, the closing period of member 2006 Q 2, at the month level, would be member 2006/Jun. The *openingPeriod* function behaves in the same way as the closingPeriod function, but it returns the first time period in the level. For our example, the opening period of 2006 at the quarter level would be 2006 Q 1. Here's the expression definition: *closingPeriod([PowerCube].[Years].[Years].[Month], [2006 Q 2]).*

The *parallelPeriod* function returns a member from a period in the same relative position as the specified member in the expression. This means that it works similarly to the *cousin* function; however, where the cousin function requires that the new ancestor member be defined explicitly, the parallelPeriod function allows you to define the new ancestor based on a lag or lead at the same level of the ancestor of a specified member. For comparison purposes, this makes the parallelPeriod function more dynamic than the cousin function as the new ancestor will always be relative rather than a fixed reference. For example, imagine that you are reviewing sales information in a report at the end of the month of May 2006, and you want to review sales information from May of the year before so that you can get an idea of how sales information changed. You can retrieve this data by creating a parallelPeriod function. Continuing with our example, you will need to create the function and enter the *Years level* as the first part of the expression, enter *2006/May* as the parent member in the expression, and then enter the number *1* as the number of periods to move. This retrieves member 2005/May: *parallelPeriod([PowerCube].[Years].[Years].[Year],1,[2006/May]).*

NOTE *Positive and negative numbers behave differently in the parallelPeriod function than they do in most other functions. In most functions, a positive number would indicate a movement forward through the members of the level, but in this function, positive numbers move backward, or toward the first period in the level. Negative numbers cause the function to navigate forward to the next period in the level, or toward the last period in the level.*

The *periodsToDate* function can be used to retrieve all the descendants of a given member at a level up to a selected member or period. This function is commonly used to define sets such as the months of a "Year to Date," where the individual months are bound by a common ancestor, the year, but do not share a common parent member at the quarter level. For example, if you selected the *Years level*, and the member two levels down named 2006/Apr, the function would retrieve 2006/Jan, 2006/Feb, 2006/Mar, and 2006/Apr (January through April 2006). As you can see from this example, the periodsToDate function retrieves sibling members regardless of their parent as long as they are at the same level as 2006/Apr and included underneath the ancestor 2006: *periodsToDate([PowerCube].[Years].[Years].[Years], [2006/Apr]).*

Complex Functions

You can combine many of the navigational functions mentioned to create complex navigational functions. These functions can be used to navigate to and retrieve members that would normally require many steps to locate. The next example explains how to use complex functions and dynamic data to create a report that contains revenue information for a specific month and for the year-to-date up to a selected month. The data item This Year Selected Period can be seen in the first column heading:

Revenue	<#This Year Selected Period#>	<#Last Year Selected Period#>	<#2 Years Ago Selected Period#>	<#This Year YTD#>	<#Last Year YTD#>	<#2 Years Ago YTD#>
<#Staff name#>	<#1234#>	<#1234#>	<#1234#>	<#1234#>	<#1234#>	<#1234#>
<#Staff name#>	<#1234#>	<#1234#>	<#1234#>	<#1234#>	<#1234#>	<#1234#>

This column contains revenue information for a selected month this year, which is 2006 in this example. Double-click the column heading to display the Data Item Expression screen. In the Expression Definition pane, you can view the expression, as shown next:

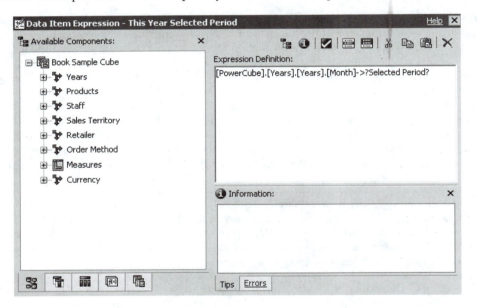

NOTE *Syntax instructions display below the Expression pane in the Expression Definition screen any time you select a function that requires you to add members or additional data to the expression.*

The expression in the preceding illustration creates a single selection prompt that asks the user to supply the month for the report. All the other data items that reference this data item retrieve their information based on the user's selection. This means that This Year Selected Period is a dynamic data item, and it is determined by what is selected in the prompt. For purposes of our example, let's assume that September 2006 (2006/Sep) has been selected here.

Now look at the column heading Last Year Selected Period; the second column heading in our example. This column contains revenue information for a selected month last year. Double-click this column heading to view the expression in the Expression Definition pane of the Data Item Expression screen:

Expression Definition:

```
parallelPeriod([PowerCube].[Years].[Years].[Year],1,[This Year Selected Period])
```

To better illustrate complex functions (multiple functions, as well as nesting), we use the expression in the next illustration. It returns the same results as the previous expression.

Expression Definition:

```
cousin([This Year Selected Period],lag(ancestor([This Year Selected Period],2),1))
```

This complex expression contains three functions as well as nesting. All of these functions reference the data item This Year Selected Period. Therefore, these functions navigate through the dimensional structure to retrieve certain members based on the prompt selection. As mentioned, for our earlier example, the member 2006/Sep was selected at that prompt.

The function that is nested the deepest in this complex function is the *ancestor* function. This function tells Report Studio to give us the ancestor 2006/Sep, two levels up. This returns the year member 2006.

The next function nested in this complex function is a *lag* function. This function looks back one member from 2006 to the member 2005.

The final function in this complex function is a *cousin* function. This function retrieves the cousin of 2006/Sep, but for the year 2005. This gives us the member in the same relative position, which is 2005/Sep.

The third column in our report is 2 Years Ago Selected Period. This column contains revenue information for a selected month two years ago. Double-click this column heading to view the following expression:

parallelPeriod([PowerCube].[Years].[Years].[Year],2,[This Year Selected Period])

NOTE *To better illustrate complex functions (multiple functions as well as nesting), the following expression was used. It returns the same results:*
cousin([This Year Selected Period],lag(ancestor([This Year Selected Period],2),2))

The 2 Years Ago Selected Period basically works the same way as Last Year Selected Period, except that the lag function has changed from one to two members back (the *parallelPeriod* function has also been changed from 1 to 2). This means that the lag function (*parallelPeriod* function) returns 2004 and the entire complex function returns 2004/Sep.

Our example also contains three columns that have not yet been discussed: This Year YTD, Last Year YTD, and 2 Years Ago YTD. These columns return an aggregate, or sum, of all of the revenue in their respective year leading up to the dynamic data item selected in This Year Selected Period.

To create an aggregate of each month to populate these YTD columns, you first need to use data items that retrieve all the members leading up to This Year Selected Period. This example shows a Query Explorer screen that contains the data items needed to retrieve this information. The data items are This Year Periods To Date, Last Year Periods To Date, and 2 Years Ago Periods To Date.

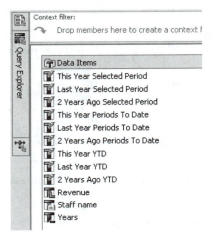

Double-click any of these data items to open the Data Item Expression screen. If you double-click This Year Periods To Date, the expression displays in the Expression Definition pane, as shown next:

Expression Definition:

periodsToDate([PowerCube].[Years].[Years].[Years],[This Year Selected Period])

This expression uses the data item This Year Selected Period to retrieve all the members from the beginning of the year through the period selected in the prompt in This Year Selected Period. Last Year Periods to Date and 2 Years Ago Periods To Date use Last Year Selected Period and 2 Years Ago Selected Period, respectively, as follows:

Last Year Periods to Date:

periodsToDate([PowerCube].[Years].[Years].[Years],[Last Year Selected Period])

2 Years Ago Periods to Date:

periodsToDate([PowerCube].[Years].[Years].[Years],[2 Years Ago Selected Period])

These expressions return the entire set of members from the period to date, which is not necessary if you want to view the sum of the revenues up to a particular month in a given year. The aggregate expressions used in the YTD columns solve this problem by rolling these values for each year into a single value.

Double-click one of the YTD column headings to see one of the following expressions:

This Year YTD:

aggregate(currentMeasure within set [This Year Periods To Date])

Last Year YTD:

aggregate(currentMeasure within set [Last Year Periods To Date])

2 Years Ago YTD:

aggregate(currentMeasure within set [2 Years Ago Periods To Date])

In these aggregate expressions, you will notice that the data items This Year Periods to Date, Last Year Periods to Date, and 2 Years Ago Periods To Date are aggregated to create a sum value for all months in the year leading up to the selected period in the year.

> **NOTE**   The aggregate *function relies on the aggregation defined within the cube to determine the rollup type. If the rollup is different from what is required for the report, then the relevant member summary function should be used instead of aggregate. For example, if the rollup type is set to average, then you should use the* total *member summary function.*

Express Authoring Mode

Express Authoring Mode offers a simplified interface that is helpful for non-technical report authors. It offers a statement-type of reporting, that allows for report standardization, and a quicker method of creating reports. Once you create a report, you can toggle between Express Authoring Mode and Professional Authoring Mode at your discretion without changing or losing data.

To toggle between Express Authoring Mode and Professional Authoring Mode, choose Authoring Mode from the View menu, and then select the authoring mode, as shown next. A loading dialog displays, and then the screen refreshes to the authoring mode that you selected.

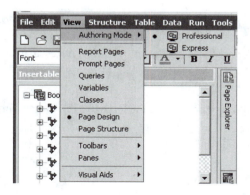

A noticeable difference between the two authoring modes is that the Express Authoring Mode contains live data that can be continuously updated. Any data that you add or remove from the work area in Express Authoring Mode immediately displays in the work area. This allows you to preview your reports before you run them. The work area in Express Authoring Mode is shown next:

Page layers:

➥   Drop members here to create page layers

Context filter:

➥   Drop members here to create a context filt

Express Authoring Mode

Revenue	2004	2005	2006
Products	$34,750,563.50	$62,540,865.06	$74,284,959.32
Camping Equipment	$20,471,328.88	$31,373,293.14	$37,869,368.90
Golf Equipment	$5,597,980.86	$9,580,958.70	$10,726,526.02
Mountaineering Equipment	$0.00	$9,642,674.54	$11,248,676.06
Outdoor Protection	$1,536,456.24	$988,230.64	$646,428.04
Personal Accessories	$7,144,797.52	$10,955,708.04	$13,793,960.30

While the live data offered by Express Authoring Mode is very useful while creating a report, it is important to note that this authoring mode also contains a number of altered or enhanced features, interface changes, and even some limitations. When you first encounter Express Authoring Mode, you will probably notice that the page, query, and variable explorers are not available, along with the Toolbox tab, List, Chart, and a variety of other options. Only crosstab reports are available. Express Authoring Mode differs in the way that it handles package tree settings, options for inserting data, parent member location, context and page layer filters, prompting, transferring reports to Analysis Studio, and drill-down capabilities. The differences between the authoring modes are explained in the following sections.

Package Tree Settings

In Express Authoring Mode, you can change package tree settings. These settings allow you to decide what members, levels, and properties are available to include in your report, so you can ensure that the report displays the information necessary to meet the requirements of the report.

Here's how to change package tree settings:

1. Right-click the data tree and select Package Tree Settings. The Package Tree Settings screen displays:

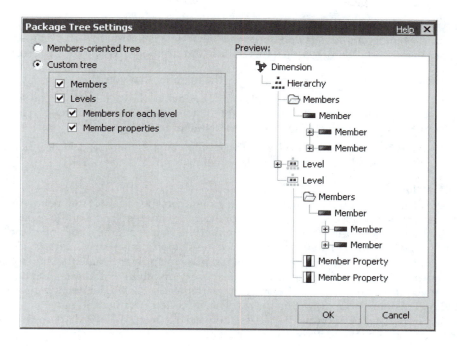

2. Select one of the two options:

   - **Member-Oriented Tree**   Creates a simplified view of data. This option is selected by default and is an ideal option if you are not a technical report author.

   - **Custom Tree**   Constructs the meta-data available to be displayed in the report. This option is useful for more technical report authors who have a good understanding of the dimensional structures.

3. Below the Custom Tree option, you can select several checkboxes to choose the metadata that displays in the report. A preview of the updated tree is shown as the options are changed in this screen.

4. Click OK to save the settings.

Advanced Options for Inserting Data Objects

You have several options to insert data in an Express Authoring Mode report. Two buttons in the Actions bar can be used to determine how data is inserted: Set Selection and Insert Member. Also, options for inserting child members when the parent member is already present on the report are available.

Insert Member

The Insert Member button lets you determine what data is inserted when you insert a member in a report. When you click this button, three options display on the screen:

- **Insert Single Member** Inserts only the member that you selected.
- **Insert Children** Inserts all child members below the member that you selected into a table. This is useful if you want to include all child members at a certain level, but you do not need to see the parent member in the report.
- **Insert Member with Children** Inserts the member that you selected, as well as all of the direct child members one level below.

Set Selection

The Set Selection button is useful for inserting members into a report that behave as a group when functions or measures are applied. For example, suppose you want to create a report that displays sales information for each month of the year separately, but you want to be able to apply functions to the report that affect these months as yearly quarters. If you insert the months as individual members, you would have to apply the same function to each of the three months in the yearly quarter to affect every month in that quarter. On the other hand, if you insert the three months in each quarter as a set, a single function affects each individual member (month) within the set. This helps to save time and effort.

The Set Selection button can be toggled between settings. When it displays surrounded by brackets, members inserted into the report at the same time will be grouped together as sets. When brackets are not displayed around the Set Selection button, members inserted into the report will be treated as individuals.

Insert Child Members when Parent Member Is Present on Report

When a parent member is present on the report, the immediate child members can be inserted by double-clicking on the report member. By double-clicking, the report member is expanded and the next lowest level of members appear on the report. By default, the newly added members are indented and appear after the report member. The report author is able to set the Double click insertion location from After, which is the default, to Off, Before, or Nest.

Here's how to change the default Double click insertion location:

1. From the Tools menu, select Options. The Options dialog displays.
2. Click the Edit tab to open it (see illustration at top of opposite page).
3. From the Double Click Insertion Location drop down list, select Off, Before, or Nest.
4. Click OK to close the Options dialog.

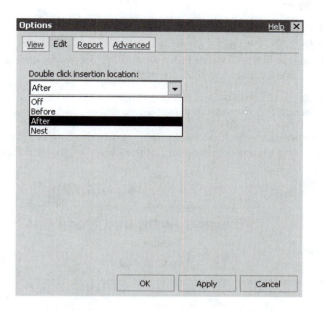

NOTE *Changing the double click insertion location does not change the current appearance of members already on the report.*

You are able to override this default on an as-needed basis. For instance, if you have the default set to After, the child members display after the parent when you double-click on the parent member. You may have a need for the child members to be shown before or nested with its parent member.

Here's how to override the default location on an as-needed location:

1. Select the report member that you want to expand.

2. From the Data menu, select Insert Children. The Insert Children submenu displays.

3. Choose Before or Nested. The child members display on your report, as shown next:

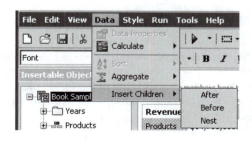

Context Filters

The Context filter allows you to use a member to filter or focus the data contained in the report. Drag a member into the Context Filter area in the work area and that member and all of its children become available to filter the report.

NOTE   *More than one context filter can be used.*

As shown next, Order Method has been dragged into the Context Filter area. This means that you can filter the report using any of the Order Methods available:

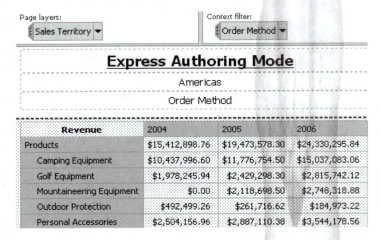

Here's how to select one of the members to filter by:

1. Click the down arrow of the member in the Context filter.
2. Select one of the child members to be used to filter the data.

NOTE   *When you select a member in the Context filter, the name of that member displays in the header in the work area. The header is automatically updated when the filters of the report are changed.*

Page Layers

Page layers can be added to a report to create separate pages for each of the included members. In the previous example, the Sales Territory hierarchy has been dragged into the Page Layers area. You can see that *Americas* displays in the header of the work area. *Americas* is the first member in the Sales Territory hierarchy so it is the first page displayed in this report. You can use the Top, Page Up, Page Down, and Bottom buttons at the bottom of the work area to cycle through each of the pages.

NOTE   *As you change pages, the member displayed in the header of the work area is automatically updated to reflect the page layer you are currently viewing.*

Pick Up and Apply Styles

You can copy the formatting of members or value cells and reuse it to format other areas of your report with fonts, colors, borders, and number formats. Picking up styles saves time because you do not have to create the same format multiple times.

Here's how to copy and apply formatting:

1. Select the member or cell formatting you wish to copy.
2. Click the Pick Up Style button (see the following illustration).
3. Select the member or cell area you wish to format.
4. Click the Apply Style button as shown next:

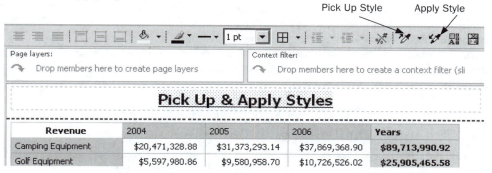

NOTE *You can make changes to the copied style. Click the down arrow to the right of the Pick Up Style icon, click Edit Dropper Style, edit the formatting, and click OK.*

Prompting

Prompting allows users to choose what data is visible and invisible each time the report is run. Enabling prompting is easy in Express Authoring Mode. Click the Context Filter list, and choose Prompting. In the menu that displays, choose one of the following values:

- **No Prompt**   Selected by default, it will not create a prompt.
- **Prompt On Hierarchy**   Creates a tree prompt in your report.
- **Prompt On Level**   Creates a value prompt that allows you to select values from the level of the assigned member.
- **Single Value**   Allows only one member to be selected from a list. This option is available only once a prompt is selected.

Calculations

Express Authoring Mode also contains a limited calculation feature. These calculations allow you to apply simple operations to one or more members in your report. You can select between predefined calculations or simple custom calculations.

Apply Predefined Calculations

With predefined calculations, you can use calculations already established in Cognos 8. Here's how to apply a predefined calculation in Express Authoring Mode:

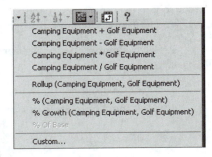

1. Click or CTRL-click the member(s) to which you want to apply a calculation.

2. From the Standard toolbar, click Calculate.

3. Select a predefined calculation to apply to the members, as shown here. The calculation you chose displays as a row in the report.

As an alternative, you can right-click a selected member and then mouse over the Calculate icon in the menu that displays, as shown next. A submenu displays simple, predefined calculations for the members you selected, and a Custom option. The available predefined options are context-sensitive and are adjusted based on the number of members that have been selected.

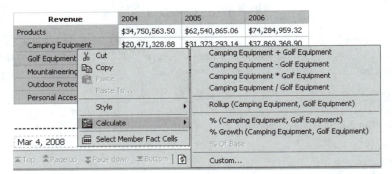

Create Custom Calculations

Custom calculations allow you to apply calculations to a report that specifically meet your needs. Here's how to create a custom calculation in Express Authoring Mode:

1. Click or CTRL-click the member(s) to which you want to apply a calculation.

2. On the standard toolbar, click Insert Calculation, and then select Custom from the submenu. The Insert Custom Calculation dialog displays a variety of operations that you can perform to the members that you selected. If you selected more than one member, you can apply those operations to two or more members.

3. Optionally, in the Number field, enter a value to apply a number and an operator to the member. For instance, you could select the multiply operator and enter 2 in the Number field to multiply the member data by 2.

4. Enter a name for the new custom calculation in the Name field.

5. Click OK. The new calculation displays as a row in the report.

NOTE *For more information on calculations, refer to Chapter 9.*

Analyze Intersections in Analysis Studio

Report Studio reports can be used in Analysis Studio to perform a more detailed analysis of the data.

Here's how to launch Analysis Studio from a report:

1. Right-click an intersection (table cell) in the report.
2. From the context menu, click Analyze, as shown next. This launches Analysis Studio. For more information on Analysis Studio, refer to Chapter 11.

Revenue	2004	2005	2006
Products	$34,750,563.50	$62,540,865.06	$74,284,050.33
Camping Equipment	$20,471,328.88	$31,373,29	
Golf Equipment	$5,597,980.86	$9,580,95	
Mountaineering Equipment	$0.00	$9,642,67	
Outdoor Protection	$1,536,456.24	$988,23	
Personal Accessories	$7,144,797.52	$10,955,70	

Context menu items: Override Default Text…, Cut, Copy, Paste, Paste To…, Style ▶, Select Fact Cells, Analyze…

Mar 4, 2008   1

▲ Top   ▲ Page up   ▼ Page down   ▼ Bottom

TIP *As an alternate method of opening Analysis Studio, you can click an intersection, and then select Analyze from the Tools menu.*

Drill-Down Capabilities

You can set drill-down capabilities in Express Authoring Mode, but you must configure these options in the Professional Authoring Mode. Switch back to Professional Authoring Mode and select Drill Behavior from the Data menu to open the Drill Behavior dialog, shown next, and configure these options. Once they are configured, you can return to the Express Authoring Mode. For more information on drills, refer to Chapter 10.

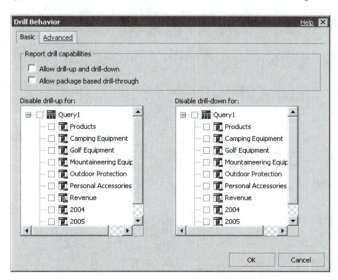

Scorecards and Metrics

Organizations embracing the Balanced Scorecard methodology use *scorecards* to view performance metrics of their organization at different levels. Cognos 8 provides the mechanisms for you to gather and load metrics to be used to measure performance. To develop a scorecard, you must familiarize yourself with and use both Metric Designer and Metric Studio. You use Metric Designer to gather metrics from import sources and prepare them for use in Metric Studio. Metric Studio enables users to monitor the business using key metrics and, when necessary, begin to understand more about the performance of the metric by easily reviewing reports created with Report Studio that are linked to the scorecards and metrics. You will find information about the Balanced Scorecard methodology in Chapter 2. Read this chapter to understand how to load data quickly to begin your journey to creating a balanced scorecard.

Introduction to Metric Designer

Cognos 8 Metric Designer exploits the power of the query subjects in the published packages in Cognos Connection, leveraging their design and behavior to generate metrics predictably for the organization. You use Metric Designer to gather metrics from your import source to be transferred into Metric Studio. This client application is installed on the business manager's (or the person responsible for working with Metric Studio) desktop.

You interact with Metric Designer using the Metric Extract Wizard. The wizard displays several screens used to identify metrics to be extracted, define scorecards and the metrics to be displayed on each scorecard, map time periods, identify default currency, and optionally filter the data.

Create Metrics

Perhaps the biggest stumbling block in using Metric Studio is loading the metrics. Loading metrics is a two-step process:

1. *Create a metrics extract.* Identify and extract the metrics from a data source package or PowerPlay cube to be used with Metric Studio. The metrics extract is stored in a staging area or in flat files that can be ported to other computers using Cognos 8 or other metrics applications that understand the file structure.

2. *Import metrics.* Import the extract from staging tables or from flat files into the metric store.

You use two Cognos 8 components to accomplish these steps. First, Metric Designer is used to extract the metric data from the import source. Then, Cognos Connection is used to import the data from the staging area into Metric Studio. After initial development and testing, the extract is published to Cognos Connection, with the entire process managed from Cognos Connection. You use Metric Designer only to modify or add new metrics as business requirements change.

Metric Types

A *metric type* defines how metrics are grouped and the behavior of all metrics of that type. You must define all metric types to be used in Metric Studio. To define a metric type, you provide values for metric type attributes. Figure 13-1 shows metrics of the same type grouped together in Metric Studio.

NOTE   *The items discussed in this section are found in Metric Studio, which is accessed through Cognos Connection.*

Common Metric Type Attributes

From Metric Studio, you can view the attributes of a metric type by clicking the metric type in the Metric Types region, clicking the Details tab, and then clicking the Set Properties icon, as shown next:

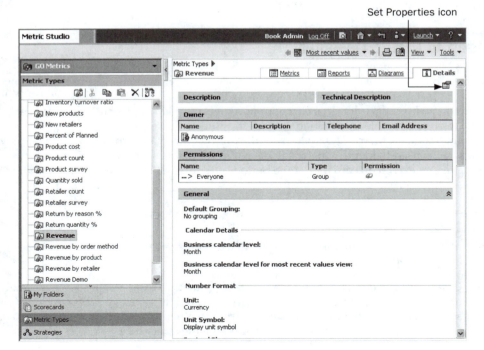

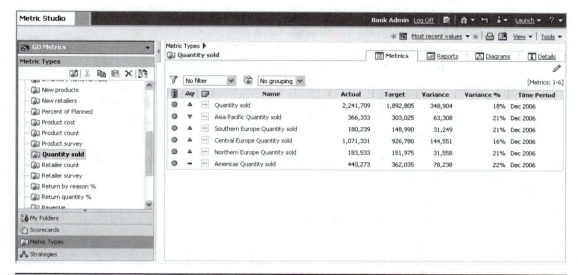

FIGURE 13-1   Metrics Grouped by Type

On the General tab of the Metric Types Details screen, you will find the most common attributes as shown next:

- **Business Calendar Level**   The values can be Monthly, Quarterly, or Yearly. This value identifies how often the metric is updated, also known as the *metric scope*, and is displayed as the Time Period on the Metric Types page.

- **Unit Of Measure**   Choose between General (the default), Currency, and Percent.

- **Unit Symbol**   If you chose Currency or Percent for the Unit Of Measure, this setting controls whether you see the dollar sign or percent sign with the number.

- **Decimal Places**   Choose how many decimal places should be included with the number when displayed.

On the Columns and Calculations tab of the Metric Types Details screen, you determine how values are handled, as shown next:

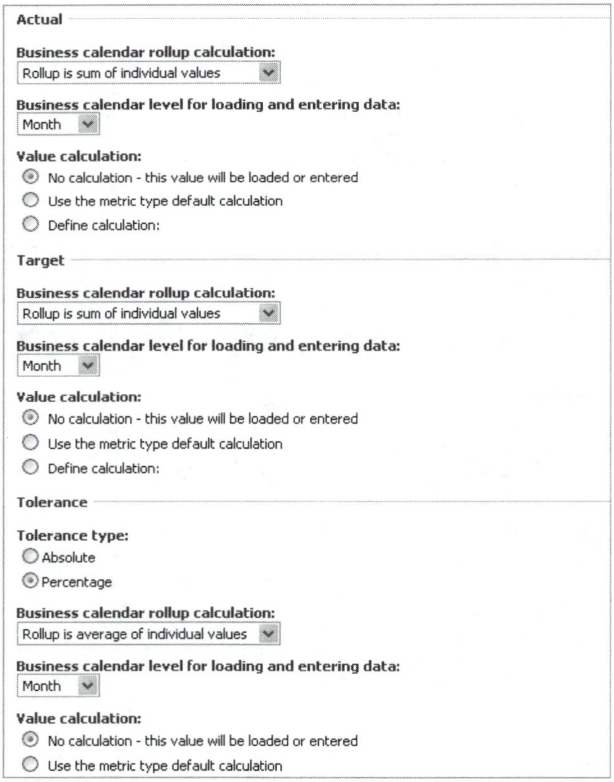

```
Actual

Business calendar rollup calculation:
Rollup is sum of individual values     ▼

Business calendar level for loading and entering data:
Month   ▼

Value calculation:
  ◉  No calculation - this value will be loaded or entered
  ○  Use the metric type default calculation
  ○  Define calculation:

Target

Business calendar rollup calculation:
Rollup is sum of individual values     ▼

Business calendar level for loading and entering data:
Month   ▼

Value calculation:
  ◉  No calculation - this value will be loaded or entered
  ○  Use the metric type default calculation
  ○  Define calculation:

Tolerance

Tolerance type:
  ○  Absolute
  ◉  Percentage

Business calendar rollup calculation:
Rollup is average of individual values   ▼

Business calendar level for loading and entering data:
Month   ▼

Value calculation:
  ◉  No calculation - this value will be loaded or entered
  ○  Use the metric type default calculation
```

- **Business Calendar Rollup Calculation**   When loading metrics from Metric Designer, most of the time this value should be set to Rollup Is Supplied By Client, which defaults to the values provided in the dimensional data source. You must select one of the Value Calculation settings for the Actual, Target, and Tolerance values.

On the Status Indicator tab of the Metric Types Details screen, you identify what makes a value positive, as shown next:

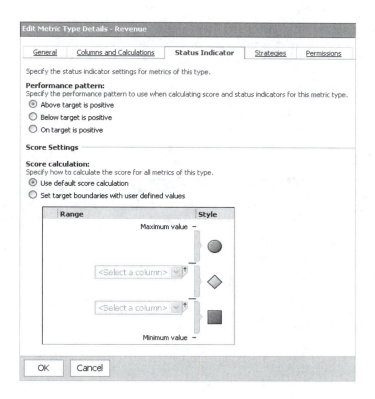

- **Performance Pattern**   Identifies when the target value is positive, which provides a green indicator for the value. For example, revenue above target is positive; safety below target is positive; marketing expenditures on target are positive.

On the Permissions tab of the Metric Types Details screen, you set user permissions, as shown next:

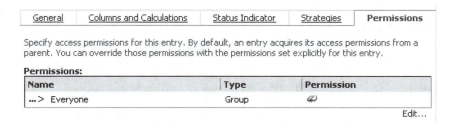

- **Permissions**   Identifies which metrics users can see this metric type.

Create a Metric Type

Metric Types can be created in either Metric Designer or in Metric Studio. In this section, we will use Metric Studio to quickly create two new Metric Types for use in the rest of this chapter, a Revenue Metric Type and a Percent Metric Type.

Here's how to create the Revenue Metric Type from Metric Studio:

1. From the Metric Types pane, click the New Metric Type icon. The New Metric Type screen displays, as shown next:

New Metric Type icon

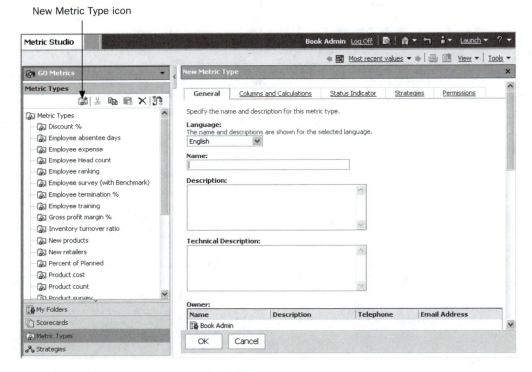

2. Enter the Metric Type Name (Revenue).

3. Click OK to accept the defaults for all other attributes and create the Revenue Metric Type.

Here's how to create the Percent Metric Type from Metric Studio:

1. From the Metric Types pane, click the New Metric Type icon.

2. Enter the Metric Type Name (Percent).

3. In the Number Format section of the General screen, change Unit to Percent, as shown next:

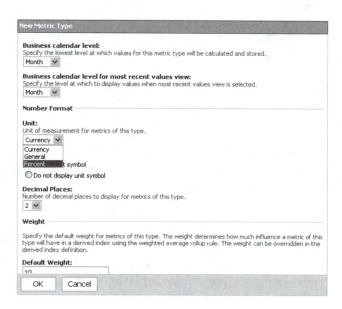

4. Click the Columns And Calculations tab.

5. In the Actual area, from the Business Calendar Rollup Calculation drop-down menu, select Rollup Is Supplied By Client, as shown next:

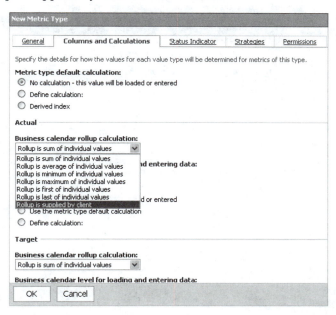

6. In the Target and Tolerance areas, from the Business Calendar Rollup Calculation drop-down menus, select Rollup Is Average Of Individual Values.

7. Click OK to create the Percent Metric Type.

Metric Types are typically the least confusing part of Metric Studio and Metric Designer, which is why we are not covering this topic in any great detail. The intent at this point is to make sure the two Metric Types used in later examples have been created.

Create a Metrics Extract from a Dimensional Source

Now that you have two of the more common metric types available, we can move on to creating and loading the metrics, in other words, we can create our metric extract.

NOTE *You must have created a metric package prior to attempting to extract metrics for use with Metric Studio. Instructions for creating a metric package are available in the Cognos user manual. You may create more than one metric package for use to measure performance.*

A *metric extract* contains all relevant information gathered from a dimensional data source to be used to create scorecards and metrics.

Here's how to create a metric extract from dimensional sources using Metric Designer:

1. Choose Start | All Programs | Cognos 8, and then click Cognos Metric Designer. The Metric Designer window opens, displaying all recent projects as well as commands to create or open projects:

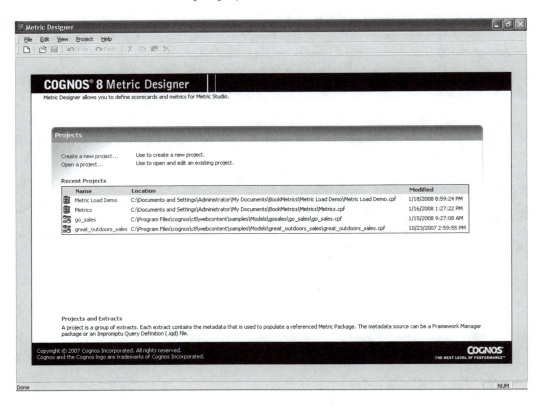

NOTE *Cognos 8 provides two options to access the New Project dialog. In addition to, using the Create A New Project link on the Metric Designer window, you can use the New command from the Metric Studio toolbar.*

2. Click on the Create A New Project link and then in the Project Name text box, enter the name for the project. The project file is used to store the definitions related to the extract. You will set the definitions in this procedure.

3. Click the folder to the right of the Location text box. The Select Project Location dialog opens.

4. Choose a location to be used to store the project file and click OK twice. The Logon dialog displays, as shown next. You must pass authentication by logging on before you can create a project.

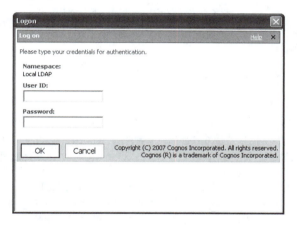

5. Enter your User ID and Password in the Logon dialog and click OK. The Create Metric Package Reference dialog opens:

6. Click the folder to the right of the Metric Package Location In The Content Store text box. The Select Metric Package In Content Store dialog opens, as shown next. The dialog displays all metric packages available for use with Metric Studio. If none of the packages can be selected, then you may not have created the Metric Package.

7. Select the metric package that you created and click OK. The Select Metric Package In Content Store dialog closes and the Location Entry box displays the path to the project file location in the Create Metric Package Reference dialog.

8. Click OK. Cognos 8 displays a message indicating the metric package reference was successfully created. You have the option to open the Metrics Extract Wizard to identify the metric to be created.

9. Click Yes. The Create Extract screen of the Metric Extract Wizard opens, as shown next. The Metric Extract Wizard steps you through the process of identifying the metrics to be extracted and imported into the data store. Using the wizard, you also map time periods, identify default currency, and can optionally filter the data.

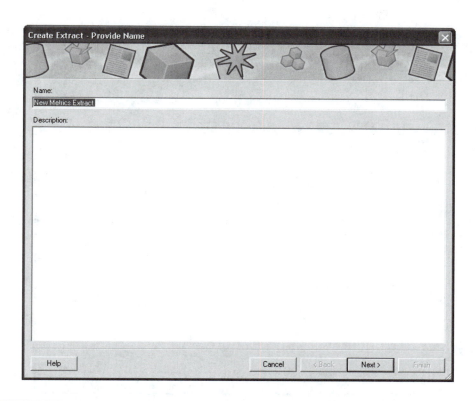

NOTE *You can also access the Create Extract screen of the Metric Extract Wizard by opening an existing project from the Metric Designer main page, expanding the hierarchy, right-clicking the metrics store in the Metric Designer Project Explorer, and selecting Create Metrics Extract from the menu that displays.*

10. In the Create Extract - Provide Name screen's Name text box, enter the name to be given to the extract. This names the metric extract.

11. Click Next. The Create Extract - Select Import Source screen displays, as shown next.

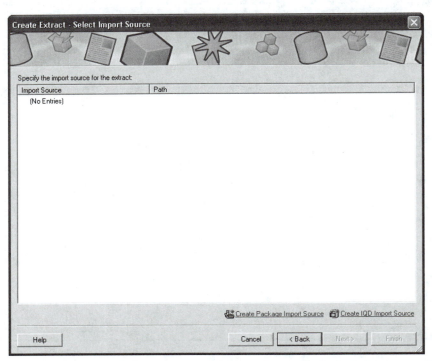

12. Click Create Package Import Source. The Create Import Source - Name window opens. Enter a Name to be assigned to the import source and click Next. The Create Import Source - Select Package screen displays:

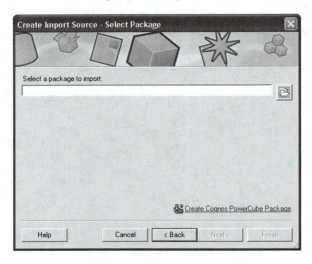

TIP *We recommend that you give the import source the same name used for your package. This helps you identify the import source in the list when required.*

13. Click the folder to the right of the text box. The Select Metric Package In Content Store screen opens, as shown next, with a list of import sources from which you can choose. All packages created for use with Metric Designer display in this screen:

NOTE *You can extract more than one metric from a single data source, and you can extract as many metrics as needed at one time.*

14. In the Select Metric Package In Content Store screen, select a metric package and click OK. The screen closes.

15. Click Finish. The Create Import Source screen closes, and Metric Designer displays a message indicating the package is being accessed. You have named the metric extract and identified the import source to be used to import data.

16. Click Next. The Create Extract - Scorecard Mapping screen displays, as shown next. Using the Available Objects, New Scorecard Levels, and Level Attributes panes, you build your scorecard hierarchy.

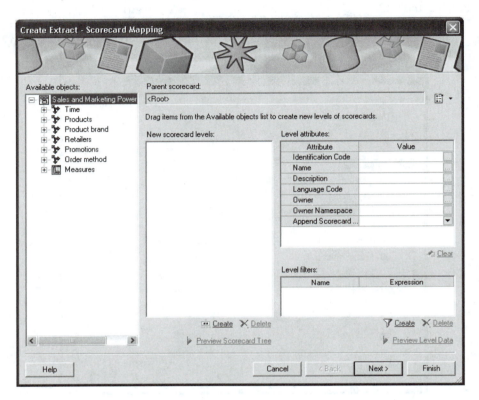

17. From the Create Extract - Scorecard Mapping screen, drag the objects to be used in the scorecard from the Available Objects pane into the New Scorecard Levels pane. In this example, we use Products, Product line, and Product type as shown next:

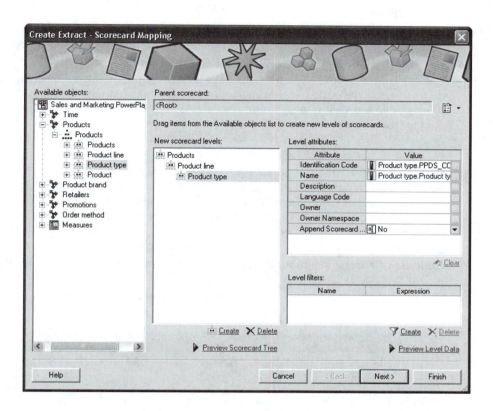

The objects nest themselves in a hierarchy in the New Scorecard Levels pane based on how they are dragged into the pane. The Identification Code attribute indicates the name assigned to the scorecard level. If you are not sure that your internal naming conventions ensure unique names, you should set the Append Scorecard attribute to Yes. For more information about this attribute, refer to the "Ensure Scorecards Have Unique ID Codes" section later in this chapter.

NOTE *All scorecard identification codes (or category codes) must be unique and cannot be used anywhere else in the data store. When you load metrics from any data source, you must have a consistent, predictable, and repeatable scorecard ID so that your metrics are displayed in the correct scorecard. In older versions of PowerPlay cubes, the identification (category) code was not as important as it is in Cognos 8. This code ties all components of Cognos 8 together and ties Metric Studio and all of the scorecards together particularly when importing data using Metric Designer. Use extreme care when creating the model to ensure the identification code's uniqueness. Note also that you can verify the identification code for each level in the hierarchy in the Preview Scorecard Tree window. Click Preview Scorecard Tree at the bottom of the New Scorecard Levels pane to open this window. The identification code displays preceding the metric name.*

18. Click Next. The Create Extract - Time Periods Filtering screen displays, as shown next, in which you identify the time periods to be extracted from the data source. Use the time period options as follows:

- **Use All Time Periods**   All time periods of data contained in the dimensional import source are loaded, including future time periods that may be in the dimensional source for budgets and forecasts. This option is ideal for loading data for the first time because it pulls all history. Once the metric store has been populated, this option is less desirable as you typically do not need to load history every time you run an extract.

- **Use The Current Time Period**   Retrieves metrics only for the current time period, which is based on your computer's system date. So, for example, if the system date is 1/1/2008, then data for 1/1/2008 will be loaded into Metric Studio. If you have an inventory of PowerPlay cubes, this has nothing to do with the PowerPlay Current Period.

- **Use The Last Completed Period**   Retrieves data for the period that includes the computer's system date minus one period. So if the system date is 1/1/2008, this would load 12/31/2007 data.

- **Use The Selected Time Periods**   Allows you to capture history manually for specified time periods.

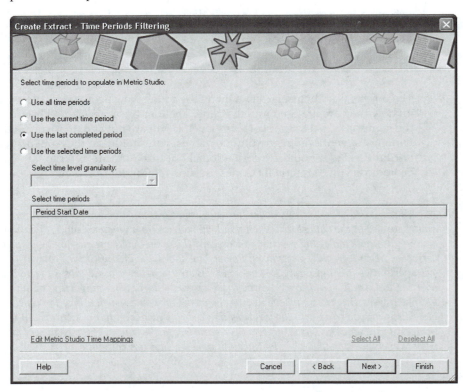

19. From the Select Time Periods pane, select the time period on which to filter your metrics. For our example, we use the Use The All Time Periods option since this is the first time we are loading the data.

20. Click the Edit Metric Studio Time Mappings link at the bottom of the window. The Time And Currency Mappings window opens with the Specify Business Calendar Mappings screen, as shown next. For each of the Business Calendar Levels at the left, the list of members (dates) available in Metric Studio is shown in the Business Calendar Members pane. You must map the Metric Studio calendar to the data in the dimensional data source. In this example we are mapping the Year, Quarter, and Month levels.

NOTE *You need to complete the time mappings only one time per dimensional import source. However, you need to complete the time mappings for every time level that you want to include in your scorecard.*

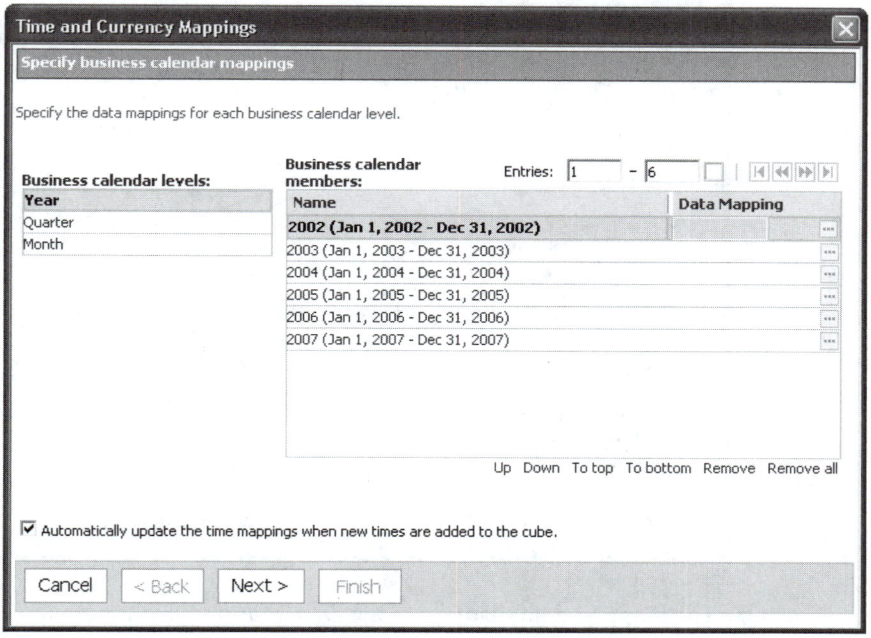

NOTE *It is acceptable for time and date ranges to be in the Business Calendar Members pane that are not mapped to the data source. The non-mapped ranges are not included in the scorecard. In this illustration, 2003 is a year in Metric Studio, but not in this dimensional data source. That is OK.*

21. Click the ellipsis to the right of an unmapped date range. The screen displays the available objects in the data source.

22. Expand the tree in this screen to navigate to the entry in the data source that matches the Metric Studio range, as shown next:

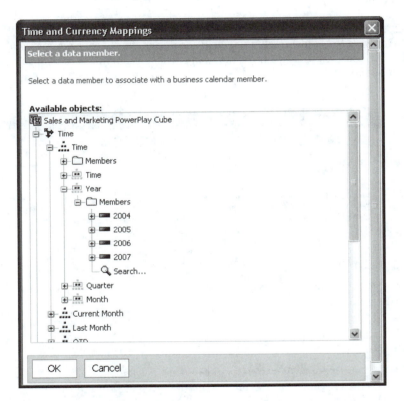

23. Click OK. The mapped data displays in the Data Mapping cloumn to the right of the Business Calendar Members cloumn.

24. Repeat steps 21 through 23 to map the data in the data source for all levels available in the Business Calendar Levels pane, such as the Year, Quarter, and Month. Your metric package may include weeks and days.

25. When you have completed mapping all levels and members, click Next. The Specify Currency Mappings screen displays, as shown next. Use this screen to specify currency to be used in Metric Studio. The default is US Dollars.

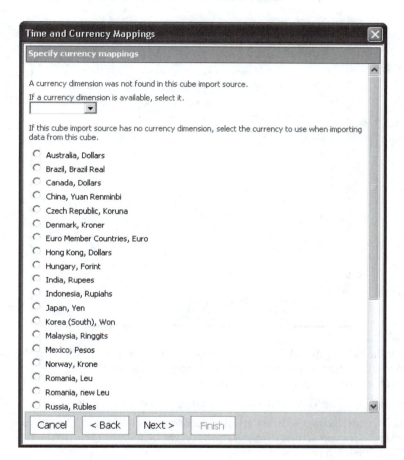

26. Click Next. The Select Dimensions screen displays, as shown next, where you identify which standard reports should be created. By default, none of the reports are checked. We recommend that you select all reports to see which are beneficial to your business. You can delete the reports you will not use from Metric Studio. It is a great way to review some of the default reports.

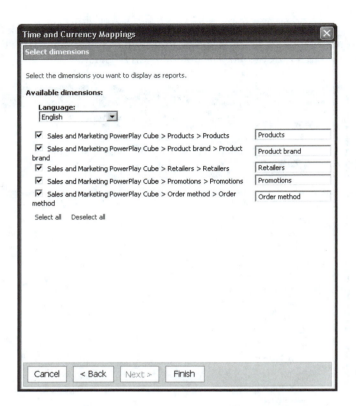

27. Click the Select All link at the bottom of the list of reports to identify the dimensions you want to display as reports in the scorecard; optionally, click the checkbox next to each report to identify them individually.

28. Click Finish. The Time and Currency Mappings window closes.

29. In the Create Extract - Time Periods Filter screen, click Next. The Create Extract - Metrics Mapping screen displays. You use this screen to identify the true metric value to be used in the scorecard.

30. From the Available Objects pane, drag measures into the Metric Mappings pane, as shown next. In this example, we use the Revenue measure.

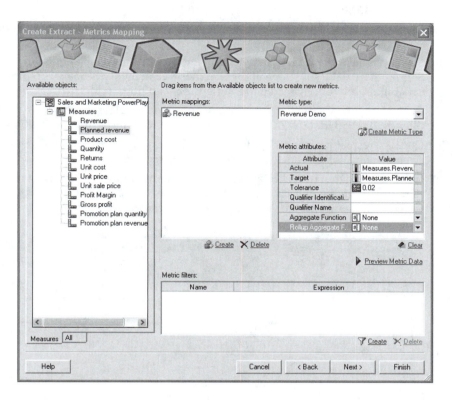

31. From the Metric Type drop-down list, you must select a metric type for each metric. As discussed above, a metric type defines many default characteristics of the metrics that belong to that type. Metric Designer displays defined metric types to be used when identifying the metric for the scorecard. Metric types control how the metric is displayed. They allow you to create links to reports and diagrams that link to all metrics using the selected type. All metrics inherit the settings for the selected metric type. See the section "Metric Types" for more information.

32. From the Available Objects pane, drag a measure into the Target field of the Metric attributes pane for each metric. The target determines the indicator displayed in the scorecard. By default, Cognos 8 uses three indicators to identify the status of your metric: green for excellent, yellow for caution, and red for needs attention. Green indicators are the goal and display depending on how you meet your target. For example, with Finance, you always want to meet or exceed your target. With Safety, you want to be below target. With Marketing, you want to meet your target.

33. For each metric, click the ellipsis to the right of the Tolerance attribute. The Expression Editor screen opens. The Tolerance is the allowed range above or below the target, which can be a percent or absolute depending on your requirements. Whether to use percent or absolute is defined on the metric type.

34. In the Expression Definition pane, enter a percentage in decimal format.

35. Click OK. Metric Designer saves the percentage and closes the Expression Editor screen.

36. Set the value of the Aggregate Function and Rollup Aggregate Function to None. Setting these values to None allows Cognos 8 Framework Manager rollup capabilities to work instead of defining the capabilities in Metric Designer.

37. Click Next. The Create Extract - Filter Data screen displays, as shown in the next illustration. You identify the values to be included in the scorecard in this screen.

38. Click Refresh at the bottom of the screen. The Assign Metric Values To Scorecards pane displays the objects to be included in the scorecard.

39. Expand the hierarchy to verify the objects and optionally deselect an object to remove it from the metrics extract. To deselect an object, click the arrow to display the context menu and then choose Exclude Metric Value.

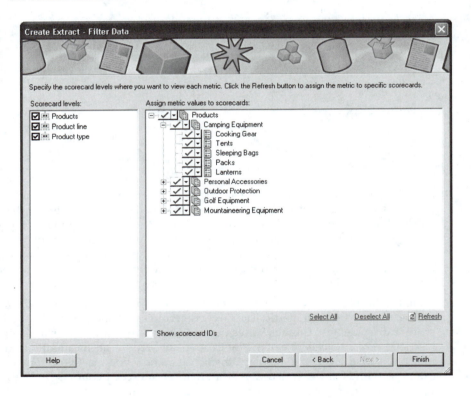

CAUTION *If you exclude objects from the metrics extract in Metric Designer, the metrics displayed in the scorecard in Metric Studio reflect only the included data and this does not provide a complete picture of your organization. For instance, if you choose to include 3 product lines out of 5, you cannot review the metrics on your entire product line. We recommend you extract all data and filter the metrics using Metric Studio.*

40. Click Finish. A dialog prompts you to validate the metric extract definition.

41. Click Yes. Metric Designer checks the metric extract definition for errors and displays a dialog identifying whether or not errors have been located.

42. Click OK. Metric Designer closes the dialog and displays an Object Diagram showing the data source where the data originates, the name of the data extract, and the name of the package to receive the data:

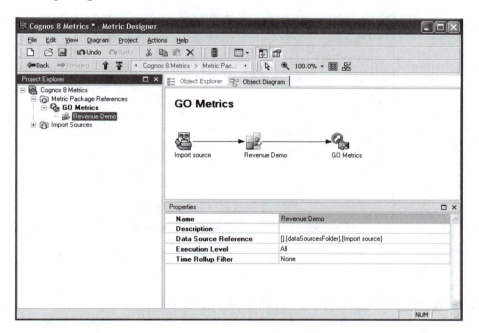

43. Right-click the name of the metric extract (depicted as Revenue Demo in the preceding illustration) to display a context menu.

44. From the context menu, choose Execute. The Execute Extract window opens. In this window, identify the location where the data extract should be stored. You can choose from the following options:

- **Write To Metric Staging Area**   Choose to write database files used to load the data directly into Metric Studio.

- **Write To Files**   Choose to create flat files of a specific format that can be moved to any location and uploaded into Metric Studio or any other metric system. The files are given several different extensions. CMV (Cognos Metric Values) is one of them. See the Cognos manual for information about the different file formats.

NOTE *Extracting prepares the metric data for import. The process reads the data source; reviews, collects, and breaks apart the metrics; sorts the metrics based on the time mapping and currency settings for all components; pulls in actuals and targets; calculates the variance; and separates the results into Metric Studio database files.*

45. Select the Write To Metric Staging Area option, as shown next. The metrics extract is saved to the staging area.

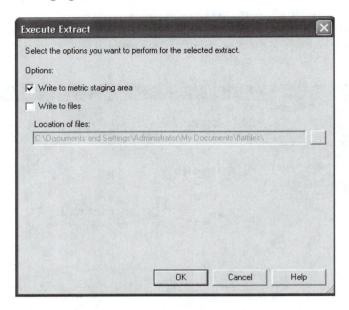

46. Click OK to the extraction complete message. The Create Extract window closes, which denotes the end of the wizard.

Create a Metric Extract from Relational Packages

Metric Studio can also be used to leverage packages created for reporting. The steps for using Metric Designer with a reporting package are mostly the same as the steps used when a PowerPlay cube is the metric source. This section shows another example of gathering metrics quickly for use.

Here's how to create an extract using packages:

1. In Metric Designer, open a project, right-click the metric package, and click Create | Metrics Extract, as shown next. The Create Extract screen of the Metrics Extract Wizard opens.

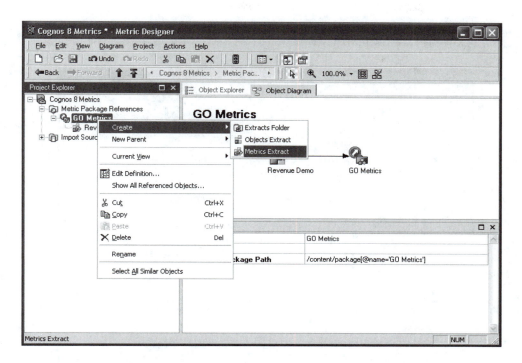

2. In the Name text box, provide a name for the relational metric extract.

3. Click Next. The Create Extract - Select Import Source screen displays.

4. Click Create Package Import Source. The Create Import Source - Name window opens. Enter a Name to be assigned to the relation import source and click Next. The Create Import Source - Select Package screen displays.

5. Click the folder to the right of the text box. The Select Metric Package In Content Store screen opens with a list of import sources from which you can choose. All packages available for use with Metric Designer display in this screen.

6. In the Select Metric Package In Content Store screen, select a reporting package and click OK.

7. Click Finish. Metric Designer displays a message indicating the package is being accessed. You have added a relational import source to be used to import data.

8. Click Next. In the Create Extract - Scorecard Mapping screen, click the Create link below the New Scorecard Levels pane:

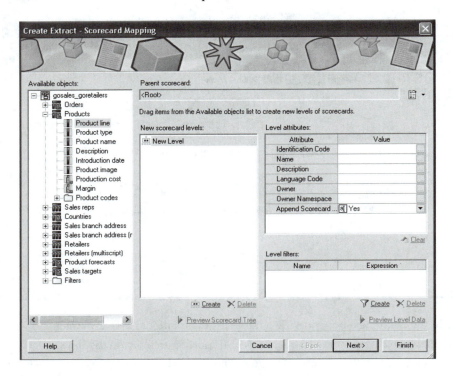

An object entitled New Level is added to the New Scorecard Levels pane. This action creates a top-level scorecard to be used to envelop all metrics contained on lower level scorecards that are not necessarily stored in the database. This step ensures that you can create a company-wide view of your metrics, which is necessary to create a scorecard for the company. For example, the total Company Sales figure does not really exist in the database. This value is almost always the sum of all products. For the next level down, we can use the Product Line and Product Type query items to create the scorecards using the data in the database.

CAUTION *When creating a metric extract using a package, you must be particularly careful that the package has a unique, predictable, and repeatable identification code for the scorecard. Otherwise, your metrics display on the wrong scorecard or a totally new one.*

9. In the Level Attributes pane, click the ellipsis to the right of the Identification Code. The Expression Editor screen opens.

10. In the Expression Editor screen, enter an identification code for the new level in the Expression Definition pane:

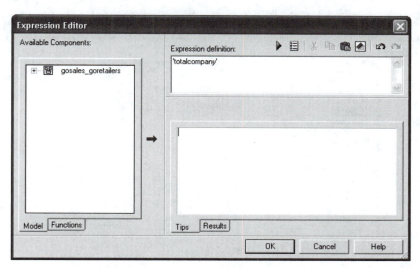

NOTE *When entering text values in the Expression Definition pane, enclose the value within single quotation marks.*

11. Click OK. Metric Designer saves the value and closes the Expression Editor screen.

12. Repeat steps 9 through 11 for the Name attribute. Enter a well-formatted name for the Name attribute. This is the name that displays as the title for your scorecard.

13. From the Available Objects pane, drag objects into the New Scorecard Levels pane to build the metric hierarchy. For every scorecard level, you must drag two query items from the package on the left. The first creates the scorecard ID and the second creates the scorecard name. If you have a unique code, such as product line code or product type code, you should drag this code into the Identification Code attribute.

14. Click Next. The Create Extract - Time Hierarchy Mapping screen displays:

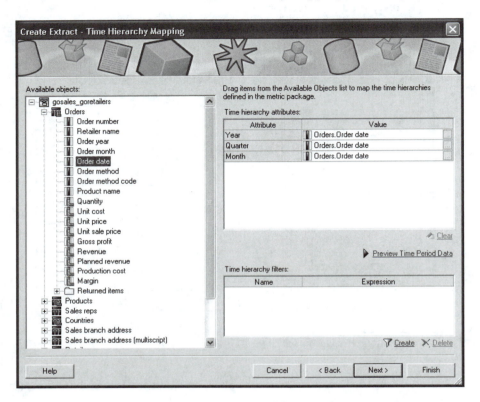

15. In the Available Objects pane, drag the Order Date object into the Value field of each entry in the Time Hierarchy Attributes pane: Year, Quarter, and Month. If your metrics package has lower level time, you may see Week and/or Day attributes as well.

16. Click Next. The Create Extract - Metrics Mapping screen displays.

17. In the Available Objects pane, expand the tree and drag a metric object into the Metric Mappings pane, as shown next:

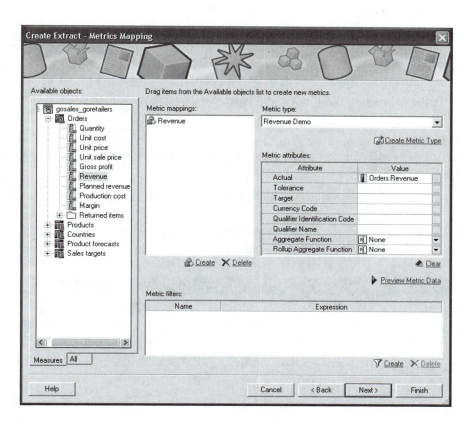

18. From the Metric Attributes pane, for the selected metric, set the Aggregate Function and Rollup Aggregate Function attributes to None. Setting these values allows the behavior of the package to be used when the query runs instead of overriding the behavior from Metric Designer.

19. From the Available Objects pane, drag an object into the Target attribute in the Metric Attributes pane to identify the target.

20. From the Metric Attributes pane, click the ellipsis to the right of the Tolerance attribute. The Expression Editor screen opens.

21. In the Expression Definition pane, enter a percentage in decimal format.

22. Click OK. Metric Designer saves the percentage and closes the Expression Editor screen.

23. From the Metric Attributes pane, click the ellipsis to the right of the Currency Code attribute. The Expression Editor screen opens.

24. In the Expression Definition pane, enter the abbreviation for the currency to be used.

NOTE   *Metric Studio supports multiple currencies. If you fail to enter the currency to be used, Metric Designer displays a warning message indicating the currency type was not identified. The abbreviation for US currency is USD.*

---

25. Click OK, Metric Designer saves the currency type and closes the Expression Editor screen.

26. Repeat steps 17 through 25 to add as many metrics as needed for this metric extract.

27. Click Next. The Create Extract - Filter Data screen displays, as shown next:

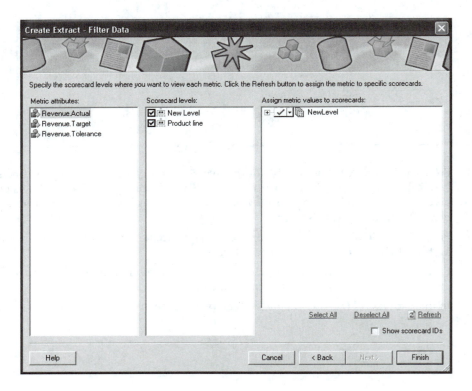

28. Click Finish. Metric Designer displays a window asking to validate the extract.

29. Click Yes. Metric Designer displays a message after validation indicating whether any errors were found in the extract instructions. These instructions were created as

you stepped through the various screens in the Metrics Extract Wizard. For example, if you did not select a currency type, the message would indicate that you missed that step.

30. Click OK to dismiss the message. Metric Designer closes the message box and displays an Object Diagram showing the data source where the data originates, the name of the data extract, and the name of the package to receive the data.

The remaining steps to create the metric extract are available in the "Create a Metrics Extract from a Dimensional Source" section earlier in this chapter.

Figure 13-2 depicts the metrics that were extracted as they are displayed in Metric Studio.

Add Multiple Metrics to a Single Scorecard

When creating scorecards in Metric Designer, you can identify multiple metric mappings to be shown on one scorecard.

Here's how to add multiple metrics to a scorecard:

1. In the Metric Designer Project Explorer, double-click a metrics package. The Edit Extract window opens with the Scorecard Mapping tab in view.
2. Click the Metrics Mapping tab. All metrics created for this scorecard display in the Metric Mappings pane of the Edit Extract screen, as shown below. Remember that

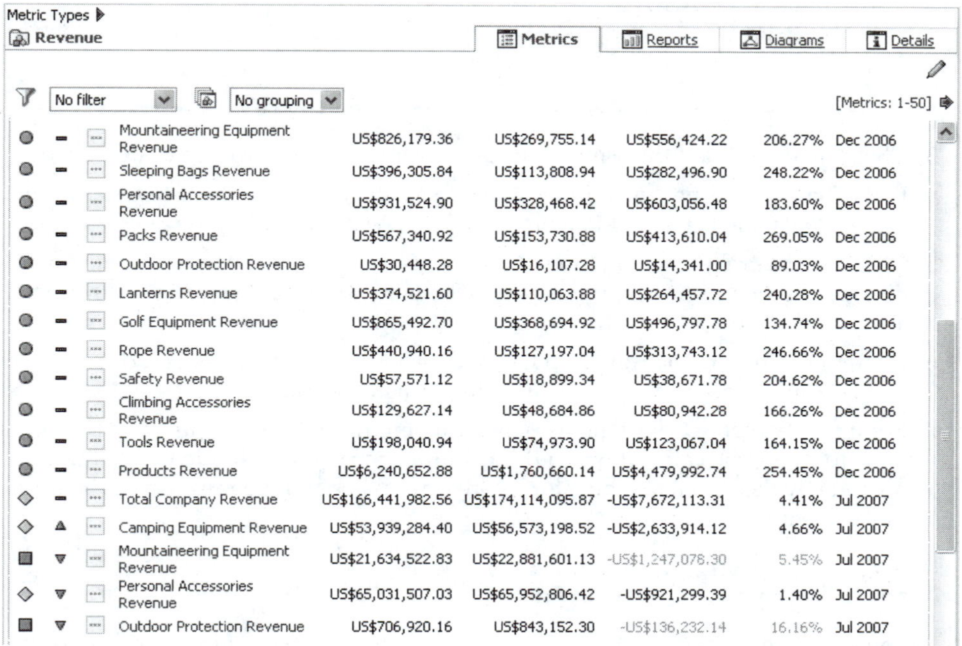

Mountaineering Equipment Revenue	US$826,179.36	US$269,755.14	US$556,424.22	206.27%	Dec 2006
Sleeping Bags Revenue	US$396,305.84	US$113,808.94	US$282,496.90	248.22%	Dec 2006
Personal Accessories Revenue	US$931,524.90	US$328,468.42	US$603,056.48	183.60%	Dec 2006
Packs Revenue	US$567,340.92	US$153,730.88	US$413,610.04	269.05%	Dec 2006
Outdoor Protection Revenue	US$30,448.28	US$16,107.28	US$14,341.00	89.03%	Dec 2006
Lanterns Revenue	US$374,521.60	US$110,063.88	US$264,457.72	240.28%	Dec 2006
Golf Equipment Revenue	US$865,492.70	US$368,694.92	US$496,797.78	134.74%	Dec 2006
Rope Revenue	US$440,940.16	US$127,197.04	US$313,743.12	246.66%	Dec 2006
Safety Revenue	US$57,571.12	US$18,899.34	US$38,671.78	204.62%	Dec 2006
Climbing Accessories Revenue	US$129,627.14	US$48,684.86	US$80,942.28	166.26%	Dec 2006
Tools Revenue	US$198,040.94	US$74,973.90	US$123,067.04	164.15%	Dec 2006
Products Revenue	US$6,240,652.88	US$1,760,660.14	US$4,479,992.74	254.45%	Dec 2006
Total Company Revenue	US$166,441,982.56	US$174,114,095.87	-US$7,672,113.31	4.41%	Jul 2007
Camping Equipment Revenue	US$53,939,284.40	US$56,573,198.52	-US$2,633,914.12	4.66%	Jul 2007
Mountaineering Equipment Revenue	US$21,634,522.83	US$22,881,601.13	-US$1,247,078.30	5.45%	Jul 2007
Personal Accessories Revenue	US$65,031,507.03	US$65,952,806.42	-US$921,299.39	1.40%	Jul 2007
Outdoor Protection Revenue	US$706,920.16	US$843,152.30	-US$136,232.14	16.16%	Jul 2007

FIGURE 13-2 Package extract displayed in Metric Studio

the Metrics Mapping screen is used to identify the true metric value to be used for the scorecard. Metric mappings are, in essence, the actual metrics.

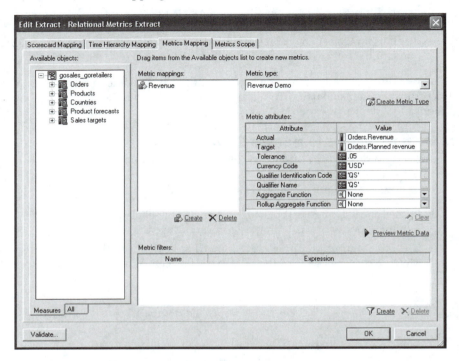

3. Click Create beneath the Metric Mappings pane. The New Metric dialog opens.

4. In the Name pane, type a name and select a Metric type from the list. In this example, we use the name Percent of Planned and the Percent Metric Type created earlier.

5. Click OK. Metric Designer closes the New Metric dialog. The newly named metric displays in the Metric Mappings pane. The metric type and settings for the metric attributes also display on the screen.

6. Click the ellipsis to the right of the Actual property. The Expression Editor screen opens. You define the metric calculation in this window.

7. From the Available Components pane, drag metrics into the Expression Definition pane to create the calculation. In this example, we want to divide the planned revenue by the actual revenue, for a percent of planned revenue metric. The formula looks like this:

```
total ( [gosales_goretailers].[Orders].[Revenue] ) /
total ( [gosales_goretailers].[Orders].[Planned revenue] )
```

You build the metric calculation using mathematical symbols, functions, and formulas. For example, to divide one metric by another, use the slash (/) mark as the division symbol. The list of available mathematical functions to be used can be viewed by clicking the Functions tab beneath the Available Components pane.

8. Set the Target value. In this example, we set the value to 1 for 100%.

9. Set the Tolerance value. In this example, we set the value to 0.1 for 10%.

10. Set the Aggregate Function and Rollup Aggregate Function to None.

11. Repeat steps 3 through 10 to create additional metrics for the current scorecard.

12. Click OK. Metric Designer saves your work and closes the Edit Extract window.

Helpful Hints for Working with Metrics

We want you to be successful using Cognos 8. Through our many projects and efforts creating scorecards using Metric Studio, we have uncovered the following tips and tricks that can prove helpful for a successful project.

> **TIP** *Dimensional data sources, such as PowerPlay cubes, are the perfect data source to be used to load historical data quickly.*

Ensure Scorecards Have Unique ID Codes

If you discover that newly transferred metric data is not displayed on the intended scorecard, nine times out of ten, the problem lies with the identification (or category) code. The identification code must be unique. If it is not, you will run into the problems described in this chapter. You can either have Cognos 8 ensure unique naming or you can name the scorecard yourself. Both of these activities are performed from Metric Designer's Create Extract - Scorecard Mapping screen.

Here's how to have Cognos 8 ensure unique naming:

1. From Metric Designer, double-click the metric extract to open the Edit Extract window.

2. In the New Scorecard Levels pane, select the metric.

3. In the Level Attributes pane, click the drop-down arrow at the right of the Append Scorecard attribute.

4. From the list, select Yes. Cognos 8 automatically concatenates the object names beginning with the top-most object to ensure unique scorecard naming.

Choose the Best Time Setting

When creating your metric extract from a dimensional source, you are asked to identify what time period of data to gather. Although the choices might seem obvious, we have found that you do not always get what you expect unless you understand what the various choices can do. The following descriptions should help you determine which to select:

- **Use All Time Periods** This setting is great for loading historical data quickly. The caveat is that you might get too much data. If your data source contains forecasts or budget information for periods in the future, this data will be included in the extract. When displayed in the scorecard, the Time Period value may not be what you expect.

- **Use The Current Time Period** The current time period is based on your computer's system date. The Current period from the PowerPlay cube is not used as you might expect. Metric Studio uses the time period in which the computer's system date falls.

This setting is helpful when tracking actual activity against planned activity to see if the actual is meeting the plan.

- **Use The Last Completed Period**   The last completed period is the period prior to the current time period (as defined above). This setting is recommended for use when viewing financial information and ensures all information from the previous month is gathered.

- **Use The Selected Time Periods**   Use this setting if you need to specify a time period of metrics to reload. You can use this setting for troubleshooting and updating specific time periods from a dimensional source. This setting is usually not used for production.

Verify Metric Data Extracted from Packages

Query Studio provides a great way to validate the metrics coming from a package into Metric Studio. Using the same data source, users with access to Query Studio can drag metric data into the work area and build a quick view of the metrics. You can create a crosstab to have Query Studio total values in columns. The values shown in the work area should be identical to the values shown in Metric Studio. If not, ensure that the Aggregate Function and Rollup Aggregate Function attributes on the metric mapping are set to None. Let the package do the work. For more information on creating queries in Query Studio, refer to Chapter 8.

Introduction to Metric Studio

Metric Studio is an add-on component to Cognos 8. As you can see in the next illustration, the words *Metric Studio* are visible in the title bar. The My Folders pane includes links for the Watch List and your personal folder. The Watch List displays by default. You use the Watch List to review metrics of interest from various scorecards in one location. This allows you to view specific information daily without having to navigate the folder list to find the scorecard.

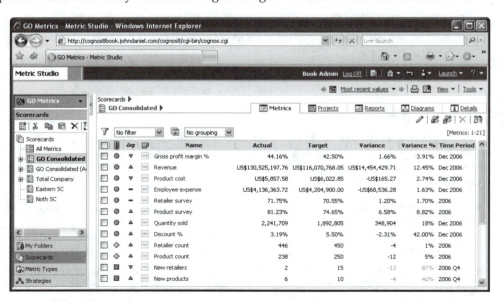

Selecting Scorecards at the bottom-left of the screen displays all available scorecards in the pane. The GO Consolidated Scorecard has multiple related scorecards—for example, Finance—which are viewed by expanding the hierarchy. *Scorecards* are a collection of metrics. The number of visible scorecards depends on your security permissions.

At a glance, you can tell how your organization is performing for each metric. The first column includes circle, triangle, and square symbols indicating excellent, average, and poor performance, respectively. The second column includes up arrow, horizontal line, and down arrow symbols, indicating whether the performance is better, the same, or worse, respectively, in comparison to the prior month by default. Each symbol is color-coded using green, yellow, and red, respectively (color meanings were described in the "Create a Metrics Extract from A Dimensional Source" section of this chapter). If you move your pointer over the name of a metric, a chart displays showing the trend between the target and the actual value.

The tabs at the upper-right of the screen let you display other views of the scoredcard information:

- **Metrics**   By default, provides access to all metric reports available for your security login.

- **Projects**   Create a project and assign metrics for tracking the project.

- **Reports**   View selected Cognos 8 reports that are linked to a scorecard, providing an overview of related data.

- **Diagrams**   Create strategy maps to bring all metrics together as needed to achieve corporate strategy. For more information on strategy maps, refer to Chapter 2. As on the main Metric Studio screen, you can move your pointer over any of the strategies to view details of each.

- **Details**   Provides extra information about each scorecard, including a detailed description, technical description, owners, permissions, and the path to the location of the data required to create the scorecard.

Upon selecting a metric from the list, two other tabs become available. The name of the selected metric is displayed at the top of the main area.

- **History**   Provides historical information about the metric. History can be viewed as a diagram or a list. The list provides more details about the metric.

- **Actions**   Allows you to create an action on an issue that can be recorded, tracked, and viewed for improvement in the metric.

Accessing Metric Studio

You access Metric Studio from Cognos Connection. Metric Studio opens in the same web browser as Cognos Connection so that you do not have to jump back and forth between pages or tabs.

Here's how to open Metric Studio:

1. Log on to Cognos Connection. If the Welcome screen displays, click Cognos Content. The Public Folders tab displays, as shown next. In Cognos 8, packages contain a single model and all the related entries and are designated by the blue folder. Folders contain related entries, such as reports, jobs, shortcuts, and so on, and are designated by the yellow folder. Metrics packages are represented by a blue folder with a metric symbol on top and a traffic light to the right of the folder. By default, clicking a metrics folder link will launch Metric Studio.

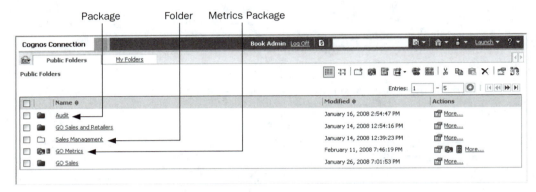

Tip   *If you have the Cognos 8 Welcome screen enabled, you can launch Metric Studio when logging into Cognos 8 by clicking Manage My Metrics. You can also open Metric Studio by clicking the Metric Studio link on the Launch Menu in Cognos Connection.*

2. Click on the Metric Package Link to access that package and launch Metric Studio.

Note   *You can set the properties of the metric folder either to launch Metric Studio or view the package content. By default, clicking the folder launches Metric Studio.*

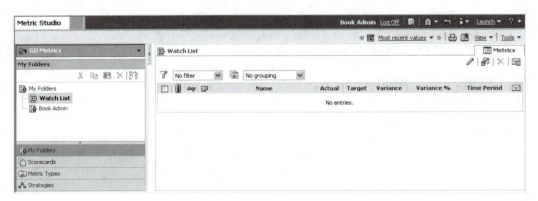

Transfer Metrics

Having launched Metric Studio, the next step is to transfer the data extracted with Metric Designer into Metric Studio to update your scorecards. When creating the metric extract, the metrics can be extracted to a staging area or to a set of flat files.

Transfer Metrics from the Staging Area

Metrics that have been written to the metric staging area are loaded into Metric Studio using Cognos Connection. The staging area is a location where metric files are stored until they are transferred into Metric Studio. You must identify and extract metrics from the data source and store them in the metric staging area prior to executing the following steps. For more information on extracting metrics, refer to the "Create Metrics" section earlier in this chapter.

Here's how to load metrics into Metric Studio:

1. Launch Metric Studio.

2. From the Tools menu, choose Metric Maintenance. All actions within the Metric Maintenance folder display, as shown next. The Metric Maintenance folder is located in Cognos Connection Public Folders.

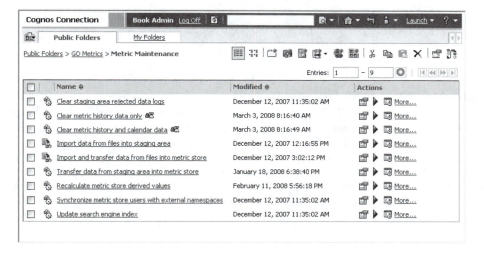

3. Click the Transfer Data From Staging Area Into Metric Store link. A message displays stating that the activity is running. When the transfer is complete, Cognos 8 displays a message.

NOTE *You can choose to have this activity run in the background while performing other actions in Cognos 8. Click Run In The Background. Optionally, you can schedule the activity to run in the evening, over the weekend, or monthly depending upon customer needs. For more information on scheduling activities, refer to Chapter 5.*

4. Click Close. Cognos Connection displays.

5. From the Launch menu, choose Metric Studio. Metric Studio displays. Perform the next two steps to verify that the information loaded into Metric Studio.

6. Click the Scorecard tab to the left to display all loaded metrics.

7. Click a metric to view the details of the metric in the display area.

Be Careful When Using Clear Metric History Data

The Clear Metric History Data Only and the Clear Metric History And Calendar Data functions *delete all of the metric data* in Metric Studio. These functions are located in Cognos Connection Metric Maintenance. When you select either of these functions, Cognos does not display the "Are you sure?" prompt. Imagine how catastrophic it would be to click this link and delete all of your work with no Undo command! We recommend that you disable these functions to avoid loss of information or change the permissions. The Disable This Entry setting is located in the Properties for each function.

Here's how to disable these functions:

1. Click Properties for the Clear Metric History Data Only function.

2. In the Set Properties screen, select the Disable This Entry checkbox.

3. Click OK.

4. Repeat steps 1 through 3 for the Clear Metric History And Calendar Data function.

Transfer Metrics from Flat Tables

Cognos 8 uses a specific file format when extracting metrics to flat tables. This file format is explained in the Cognos user guide. You can use flat tables to transfer metrics to another desktop or server running Cognos 8.

The most common use of the flat table load is to enable Cognos 8 to access data that is in a very old legacy file structure. Routines can be written to output the legacy data to a flat file in the specified format, for importing into Metric Studio. Flat files are also used to assist long time Cognos Metric users who have old extracts. Cognos 8.3 can import file formats from earlier versions of Metric Studio and even CMM (Cognos Metrics Manager).

Work with Scorecards

After metrics have been transferred into Metric Studio, you can create new relationships between the metric data or add new metrics to existing scorecards. Both of these activities help you create a balanced scorecard.

Create Impacting/Impacted Relationships

Depending on the data source or how the scorecard was formed, relationships are displayed for metrics within the metric hierarchy on the Diagrams tab after you select a metric. Two diagram views are available for a given metric; the Summary Impacts diagram, new for Cognos 8.3, and the Functional Impacts diagram. The Summary Impacts diagram shows the impacting/ impacted relationship of a metric type as it relates to the scorecard hierarchy. If we take Revenue as an example, this means that Summary Impacts diagrams will show how a revenue metric from the lowest level scorecard impacts the same revenue metric of the next level up, and so on all the way to the parent scorecard.

By default, you will see one level to the right or one level to the left of the selected metric, or if somewhere in the middle of the hierarchy, both impacting and impacted metrics, left and right. The diagram, as shown next, is created automatically in Cognos 8 and allows you to click through the diagram to see other related metrics.

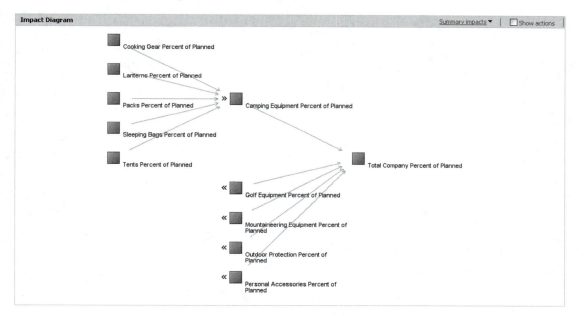

Functional Impacts diagrams are used to create relationships between metrics of different types. The metric types of Revenue, On-Time Shipments, and Customer Satisfaction are clearly different metric types but, functionally, they all impact your bottom line. The ability to show how metrics of different types interact in a diagram is required for the implementation of a corporate balanced scorecard and allows you to take full advantage of strategy mapping to coordinate and align your organization. For instance, you can use this feature to set the On-Time Shipment metric to affect Customer Satisfaction, or set the Customer Satisfaction or On-Time Shipments metrics to affect Revenue. The purpose is to identify leading indicators that affect financial performance.

Here's how to create a new relationship:

1. Launch Metric Studio.
2. Click Metrics Types at the bottom left of the screen to display all existing metric types.

3. In the Metric Types pane, click a metric type. The Metric Types pane displays all available metric types for the scorecard.

4. Click the Diagrams tab.

5. Click the pencil (edit) icon, at the bottom right of the page, to edit the diagram. The metric type selected in the Metric Types pane displays in the Edit Impact Diagram pane to the right, as shown next:

NOTE *If the pencil icon is not visible, click the up arrow to display the icon.*

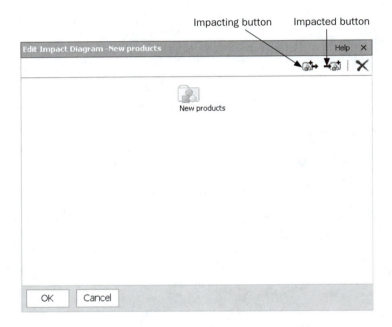

6. Click the Impacted or the Impacting button to edit the diagram. The Select Metrics - Impact Diagram window opens.

7. Navigate to the appropriate metric and select the checkbox next to the item to be used as the impacted or impacting metric type.

8. Click OK. Metric Studio closes the Select Metrics - Impact Diagram window, and updates the diagram to show the new relationship between the two metric types.

9. Repeat steps 6 through 8 to edit the diagram as desired.

10. Click OK. Metric Studio closes the Edit Impact Diagram screen. The result of creating the relationship between these metrics can be seen throughout the scorecard. The new Impact Diagram screen displays:

Metric Types pane

New Diagram button

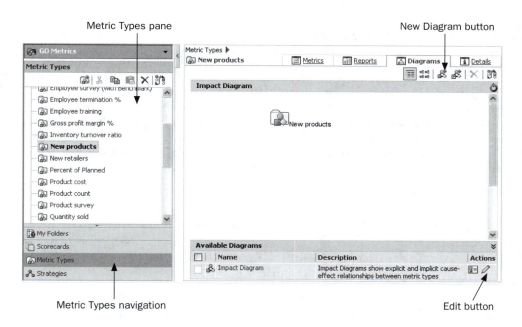

Metric Types navigation

Edit button

Add Metrics to Scorecards in Metric Studio

In its simplest form, a scorecard is a collection of metrics. At times, you will find it necessary to create a scorecard with a unique collection of metrics. You can do this by creating a scorecard and adding shortcuts to metrics.

Here's how to create a scorecard:

1. From the Scorecards pane, click New Scorecard. The New Scorecard pane displays the General tab.

New Scorecard button

New Metric Studio Security Model

The security model for Metric Studio changed considerably in Cognos 8. Be aware of this change. Earlier versions of the security model enabled you to set security at the scorecard level allowing metrics and metric shortcuts to inherit security from the scorecard. The current Cognos 8 security model only passes scorecard security to metrics, not to metric shortcuts. To be safe you must review the metrics that a user can view. Double check the All Metrics scorecard and the Metrics Type navigation area. It is possible for a user to see metrics that you do not want them to see.

In Cognos 8, for the tightest security, you must also consider security at the metric level especially if you are using metric shortcuts on scorecards.

2. In the Name text box on the General tab, enter a name for the scorecard.

3. Click OK. The new scorecard displays at the highest level in the hierarchy in the Scorecards pane. You must identify the metrics to be added to the scorecard.

4. Click the scorecard to select it to add metrics.

5. Click the Metrics tab. A screen displays in which you can add metrics.

6. Click the Add Shortcuts to Metrics button. The Select Metrics window opens.

7. Navigate to the appropriate metric.

8. Select the check box next to one or more metrics to be added to the scorecard.

9. Click OK. The Scorecard pane updates to display all metrics selected.

Create Scorecard Strategies

Metric Studio allows strategies and strategy elements in a complex strategy to be created. Metrics are assigned to a strategy to track whether the balanced scorecard perspectives are being improved. Strategy elements provide more detail for the perspective and can have metrics assigned to them as well. For example, strategy elements created to measure the development of new markets, the growth of the customer base, and improved customer experience all provide more detail for the sales and marketing perspectives.

Strategy maps are developed graphically by selecting strategy "shortcuts" and determining how the strategies relate to each other, as shown next. You can bring the strategy map into play at the metric level, the metric type level, or the scorecard level to see the strategy of the organization.

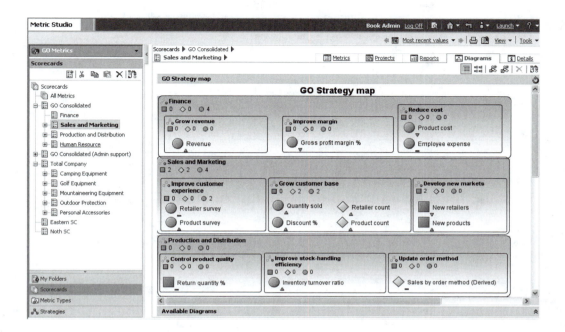

Develop Watch Lists

Watch lists are used to gather metrics of interest in one location so that they can be "watched" and potentially corrected. You can set alerts on the metric so that you are notified of changes to the metrics in the watch list via e-mail. The metrics added to the watch list can be those for which you are accountable or those that impact a perspective that is failing and needs additional oversight.

Add Cognos 8 Reports to Metrics

Reports can be added to a scorecard, a metric, or a metric type to display details of a selected metric. We recommend that reports be added at the metric type level. Doing so ensures the report is available for all metrics of that type. Reports are displayed on the Report tab in Metric Studio. When setting up reports having a prompt, you must be sure to select the Uses A Metric Item setting found in the Actions area of the Available Reports screen so that the report displays properly.

Metric Studio Success!

You should now be able to load metrics into Metric Studio with the help of Metric Designer. Using Metric Studio is fairly straight forward. As was stated at the beginning of this chapter, most newcomers to Metric Studio struggle loading metrics. Please take your time and follow the detailed examples to load metrics from Metric Designer. Once you understand that process, you will be on your way toward balanced scorecard success before you know it.

Event Management

Many organizations require up-to-date notification of data changes to drive business decisions. For these organizations, it is important that the information be delivered promptly so that decisions enhance the value of the business. With Cognos 8, event notifications can be sent based on business rules that define areas that need attention. Event Studio allows you to create *agents* that identify critical information and quickly deliver it to the business.

Event Studio is useful for different types of users in an Cognos 8 application. With Event Studio, your organization can be alerted to events as they happen to make effective and timely business decisions. Event Studio is driven by agents that look at data you specify, to detect specific events that may occur within your business. An *event* is triggered when specific actions occur, or when data conditions previously defined are met. You specify the event condition or the change in data, and when the agent detects this change, Event Studio performs a set of tasks, such as sending an e-mail notification, adding information to a portal, running reports, and starting other Cognos 8 administrative jobs.

An agent is made up of events, conditions, and a list of tasks. Suppose, for example, that you are part of the sales team for a sporting goods company. You want to be the sales manager for a specific product line, but before that happens, you have to prove that you can sell. A new product is about to hit the market and you think it's a great one. In fact, you believe this is the product that will get you the promotion you have been working toward. You tell your manager that you can sell $1 million worth of this product every month for the next three months, and that if you do this, you want the promotion. Your manager agrees, and off you go. You do all the things a sales person does, and you wait for the monthly sales results to arrive.

In this example, the event of interest to you, the ambitious salesperson, is the monthly sales reports, specifically the numbers for your product. The condition, in English, is this: Did my product produce at least $1 million in sales this month? Finally, the task will be to send an e-mail to the manager when sales are $1 million or more.

In your organization, the events, conditions, and tasks that you create will depend on what is important to you. No matter what that is, once you understand the basics, you will find that Event Studio is a flexible tool that allows you to monitor anything found in your data.

Accessing Event Studio

You access Event Studio from Cognos Connection. Event Studio opens in a separate web browser, which means you still have access to Cognos Connection if you need it.

Here's how to open Event Studio:

1. Log on to Cognos Connection. If the Welcome screen displays, click Cognos content. The Public Folders tab displays.

Tip *If you have the Cognos 8 Welcome screen enabled, you can also launch Event Studio from this screen by clicking Manage My Events.*

2. From the Launch menu located in the upper right of the screen, click Event Studio. The Select a Package screen displays.

3. Click on a package link. The Event Studio screen displays, as shown in the next illustration.

Navigation in Event Studio

The Event Studio screen is split into four areas: I Want To, Insertable Objects, Summary, and Content, as shown here:

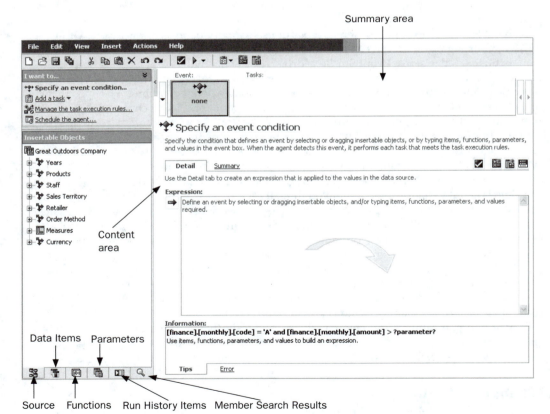

The I Want To area shows the tasks and functions available when you are creating an agent. You can specify an event condition, add additional tasks, manage the task execution rules, and schedule the agent from this area.

The Insertable Objects area is divided into six tabs: Source, Data Items, Functions, Parameters, Run History Items, and Member Search Results. The tabs are similar to those in Report Studio and Query Studio and contain the following:

- **Source tab**   Displays a hierarchical list of the source items, relational or dimensional, from your Framework Manager package.

- **Data Items tab**   Provides a quick reference to a list of the data items and calculations contained in the agent.

- **Functions tab**   Displays a list of functions, such as operators and summaries, which you can use in event conditions and to create calculated data items.

- **Parameters tab**   Displays a list of the defined parameters, indicated by the parameter icon. Parameters are used when specifying an event condition.

- **Run History Items tab**   Lists system environment variables that you can include in On Error events. These items include the date/time of the error, the person who ran the task, and other information.

- **Members Search Results tab**   Shows search utility results. The search utility displays at the bottom of the tree when a level has more members than can be displayed due to space constraints.

The Summary area shows the basic sequence for your agent, consisting of the event and the tasks to be executed when the event is triggered.

The Content area displays the details of the item in focus. When specifying an event condition, the expression entered displays here. When viewing tasks, the details of each task display in this area.

What Is an Event?

Events are the driving force behind the agent; they look for conditions in the data that meet the specifications required for an action to occur. When a condition is met, the event tells the agent to trigger the list of actions defined within the agent.

Events are made up of event instances, an event list, an event key, and task execution rules. An *event instance* is a row of data that meets the criteria of the event condition.

An *event list* shows the events that have been processed by the agent and are categorized by the following statuses:

- **New**   This is the first time the event has occurred.

- **Ongoing But Changed**   The event occurred before but the results are different this time.

- **Ongoing And Unchanged**   The event occurred before and the results are the same this time.

- **Ceased**   The event has stopped occurring.

An *event key* is a unique combination of fields from your data source that identifies an event and is used to determine the status of an event.

Task execution rules define the event status for which each task is executed.

When an agent executes, it looks at the data for any event instances. The agent uses the event key at runtime to compare the most recent event instances to the event instances from the previous run. From the comparison, the agent allocates a status to each event and stores the event in the event list. The task execution rules then determine which tasks are executed.

Business Uses for Event Management

The business uses for Event Management will be different not only among businesses but also among departments within a business. For example, the quality assurance manager at a manufacturing company might want to receive a text message on his cell phone any time the number of defective parts being produced reaches a specified threshold. Within the same company, a sales person might want to have a report e-mailed to her anytime the sales of her product reach more $1 million. These are two very different events, but the actions that make the events trigger are the same: new information is added to a data source, expressions are checked, results are evaluated, and an action either does or does not occur.

Creating an Agent

Agents monitor data to find instances of an event, and then they perform tasks associated with the event. These tasks can provide immediate notification of these events to businesses. When an agent runs, it checks the data for occurrences of the event and, if detected, performs the tasks using the task execution rules. Tasks can be run at the same time or in the order that you have specified.

Agents can be set to accept prompts, which provide the flexibility to reuse an agent for multiple users or business cases. Prompt values can be provided through the schedule or by passing in the values of a source item from the events of another agent.

Within Cognos Connection, you can create a view of the agent. Views are used to share the specifications of an agent to be used in another agent. With an agent view, different prompt values or an alternative schedule can be set.

The source for an Event Studio agent is a package published in your Cognos Connection environment. Event Studio uses the package, whether it is relational, dimensionally modeled relational (DMR), or a cube, to specify the event condition with data from the source, and then this data is monitored by the agent. Items from the source can also be used to define calculations and/or parameters to be included in the event condition.

NOTE *Event Studio looks at data sources from your Cognos 8 application. If you use a cube or materialized view from your data warehouse, Event Studio results will be triggered only after the data is refreshed in the cube or materialized view.*

Specify a Condition

In the following example, you will specify an event condition for an agent. To specify the event condition, you can use a combination of data items, functions, calculations, parameters, and run history items.

NOTE *An event condition is driven from a specified package that is chosen when opening Event Studio.*

Here's how to specify a condition:

1. In Event Studio, click either the Detail or the Summary tab in the content area. Click Detail if you are defining an event condition that applies to individual values in the data source. Click Summary if you are defining an event condition that applies to aggregate values.

2. In the Expression text box, shown next, create a query expression by dragging items and/or functions from the Insertable Objects pane or by typing directly in the Expression text box. For this example, we define "[Revenue] > 1000000" as the expression.

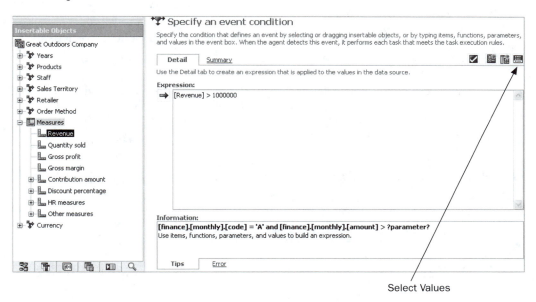

Select Values

TIP *To select from a list of values for the selected item, click Select Values. Move the values you want from the Select Value box to the Selected Items box, and then click OK.*

3. Optionally, from the Actions menu, select Preview to check the event list to ensure that you have specified the event condition correctly.

4. Optionally, from the Actions menu, select Count Events to view the number of event instances for the event condition you have specified.

Define a Parameter

Parameters can be defined to be used within an event condition. When the agent is manually run, the user will be prompted to enter a value for the parameter. Likewise, when you set up a schedule to run the agent automatically, you define the prompt value(s) and save it into the schedule. Parameters can also be used to accept the results from a previous agent.

Here's how to define a parameter:

1. From the Insert menu, select Parameter. The Define The Parameter screen displays.

2. In the Parameter Name text box, type a name for the parameter.

3. Click OK. The parameter displays on the Parameters tab in the Insertable Objects pane, as shown next:

Define a Calculation

A calculation uses multiple data items to derive a single value.

Here's how to define a calculation:

1. From the Insert menu, select Calculation. The Define The Data Item screen displays.

2. In the Name text box, type a name for the calculation. For this example, we name the calculation Gross Profit %.

3. In the Expression text box, define the calculation by dragging items and/or functions from the Insertable Objects pane or by typing directly in the Expression text box. For this example, we define the expression for the calculation as Gross Profit divided by Revenue, as shown next:

TIP *When typing directly in the Expression text box, you must include the full path of each data item.*

TIP *Click on a function in the Insertable Objects pane to view its meaning in the Information box.*

4. Click OK. The calculation displays in the Data Items tab. You can include the calculation when specifying an event condition or task. For this example, we add the Gross Profit % calculation to the event condition, as shown next:

Test an Agent

It is a good idea to test your agent as it is being developed. Early testing allows you to find and fix any errors while they are still easy to identify. If you develop the entire agent and then test it, you could spend a lot of time trying to locate the problem. There are two types of errors: logic and syntax. The Validate option in Cognos 8 will check the syntax of the agent. This test confirms that any functions being used have the correct number of parameters, the correct data types, available requested parameters, and so on. Testing the logic is performed by selecting Preview All from the Actions menu. This link displays the steps that the agent will take and what the outcome would be if it were run. It is up to you to determine whether the steps taken are logical or not.

Here's how to test an agent:

1. From the Actions menu, select Validate. If any syntax errors are found in the agent, they display in the View The Validation Results dialog after the validation is complete.

2. From the Actions menu, select Preview All. A new window displays each task in the agent. Examine the steps to determine whether they are correct.

Adding a Task

Once the condition has been specified, you can add tasks to be completed when the condition is met. Multiple tasks can be added to an agent, but only one condition can be defined per agent. Tasks can be used for things such as sending a notification to the business as data changes, providing automation to workflow, or running administrative tasks.

The list of tasks assigned to an agent displays in the Summary area. Tasks can be set up to perform in sequence or all at once. The following tasks are available:

- Send an email
- Publish a news item
- Run a report
- Run a job
- Run an agent
- Advanced
- Update a database
- Call a web service
- Run an export
- Run an import
- Run a content maintenance task

- Run a metric task
- Run a migration task

As you set up tasks and specify the event condition, it is important that you keep in mind how often tasks are performed. The following tasks are performed once:

Publish a news item	Run a report
Run a job	Run an agent
Run an export	Run an import
Run a content maintenance task	Run a metric task

Update A Database or Call A Web Service occurs once per event instance. Send An Email and Run A Migration Task varies depending on the criteria of the event.

The most commonly used items within Event Studio are notifications. Notifications are used to alert people to the results of an agent. An e-mail can be sent directly to the recipients or a news item can be published to a folder frequently viewed by people who need the information. The notification you select should contain all relevant information regarding the event and should be visible to your audience.

An important feature of notifications is that they can contain dynamic information; data items from the package can be inserted directly into notifications. The values are not retrieved until the agent is run. You can include any level of detail you find necessary for the recipients.

NOTE *The dynamic content in e-mail notifications can be applied to the list of recipients, the subject, and the body of the message. The dynamic content in news item notifications can be applied to the headline, the screen tip, and the text.*

E-mail notifications can be used through the Run A Report task or the Send An Email task. Depending on the purpose of the notification, the Run A Report task sends a single report that is built separately from the agent, while the Send An Email task sends a text based e-mail that can include dynamic content from your package. Dynamic content cannot be included in the Run A Report task.

NOTE *If only one HTML report is attached to the notification and the body of the e-mail is left blank, the report will appear in the body of the e-mail for both a report task and an e-mail task.*

E-mailing reports from Event Studio is useful since you can tailor the report to a specific event. If a report is viewed on a regular basis and is not tied to a specific event, then there is no need to create an agent to schedule it. The best method is to set up a schedule through Cognos Connection.

When using e-mail notifications with dynamic content, the outcome of the e-mail will differ depending on the number of event instances that are within the agent. Data items serve as placeholders for the content. When the agent is run, the placeholders turn into data. If the agent detects several events that satisfy the event condition, the size of the message can increase, or when the subject or the address lines contain data items, multiple e-mails may be generated. If the data items appear only in the message body, then a single e-mail is sent with the information for all of the details. A dynamic subject will generate an e-mail for each different subject, and a dynamic recipient list will generate an e-mail for each different e-mail address.

News items are published to a headline within a folder. The content in the folder is viewable in your Cognos Connection portal page. When the user clicks a news item headline, they can open Cognos 8 content or view a web page.

Send an E-mail

Add an e-mail task to an agent to send an e-mail regarding an important business event. E-mail tasks let you send an e-mail with the content you want to the appropriate recipients. You can also include dynamic content in the Send An Email task.

Here's how to add a Send An Email task:

1. In the I Want To area, click Add A Task.

2. Click Send An Email. The Specify The Email To Send screen displays:

3. In the To text box, drag data items from the Source tab or the Data Items tab in the Insertable Objects pane and click the Select The Recipients link to enter the e-mail addresses of the recipients. You can also type the name directly into the text box.

4. Optionally, in the Cc and/or Bcc text boxes, enter the e-mail addresses of the recipients using a method provided in step 2.

5. In the Subject text box, type the subject of the e-mail. You can also drag items from the Source tab or the Data Items tab in the Insertable Objects pane to create a dynamic subject.

6. In the Body text box, enter the body of the e-mail by typing in the text box or dragging data items from the Source tab or the Data Items tab in the Insertable Objects pane.

TIP *To change the message from HTML to plain text or vice versa, click the Change To Plain Text link or the Change To HTML Format link.*

7. Optionally, click Attach or Add Links to add attachments or links.

8. Click Save. The agent is saved with an e-mail task. When the e-mail task is executed, the agent retrieves values for any source items and sends the e-mail to the selected recipients.

Publish a News Item

Add a news item task to an agent to publish a headline to a folder in Cognos Connection. Here's how to add a Publish A News Item task:

1. In the I Want To area, click Add A Task.

2. Click Publish A News Item. The Specify The News Item To Publish screen displays:

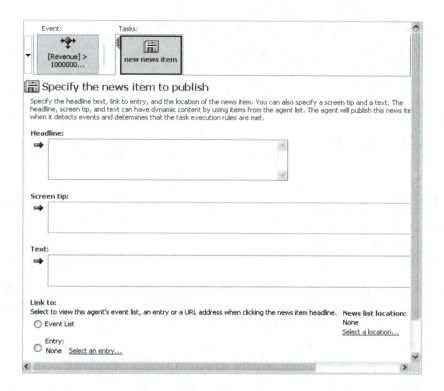

3. In the Headline text box, type the headline for the folder. You can also drag items from the Source tab or the Data Items tab in the Insertable Objects area to the text box.

4. Optionally, in the Screen Tip and Text text boxes, type a description of the entry. The Screen Tip text box has a 100-character limit.

5. In the Link To area, select the option for the item that you want to appear when the user clicks the headline.

6. In the News List Location area, click Select A Location to specify a location for the headline.

7. Click Save. The agent is saved with a news item task. When the news item task is executed, the agent publishes the headline to the location specified.

Run a Report

Add a report task when you want a report to run dependent on an event. For example, if an event condition is "January sales > 1,000,000," the sales manager might want a report that lists which sales representatives sold which products to which customers.

Here's how to add a Run A Report task:

1. In the I Want To area, click Add A Task.

2. Click Run A Report. The Select The Report screen displays:

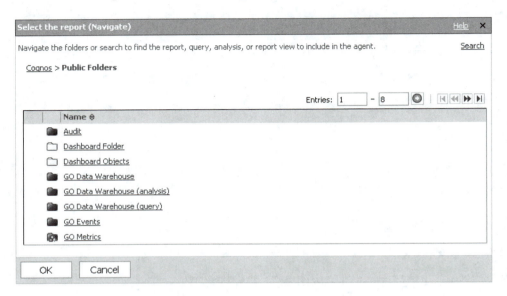

3. Navigate to the appropriate report.

4. Select the radio button next to the report.

5. Click OK.

6. Click Save. The agent is saved with a report task. When the report task is executed, the agent runs the report and delivers it according to the delivery options.

Customize a Run a Report Task   The report that you associated with an event may not have the default settings that you need—for example, the report defaults to HTML format but you would like the format to be PDF. You can customize the report setting specifically for your task.

Here's how to customize a report task:

1. In the Summary area, click the report task that you want to customize. The report task displays:

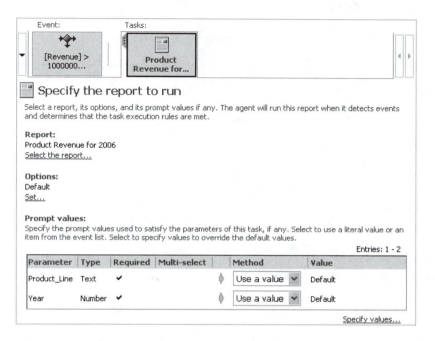

2. Under Options, click the Set link. The Select The Report Options screen displays showing the default values for the report:

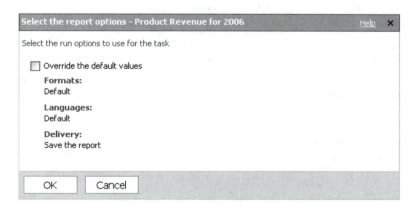

3. Select the Override The Default Values checkbox. The Select The Report Options screen displays with report options that can be modified:

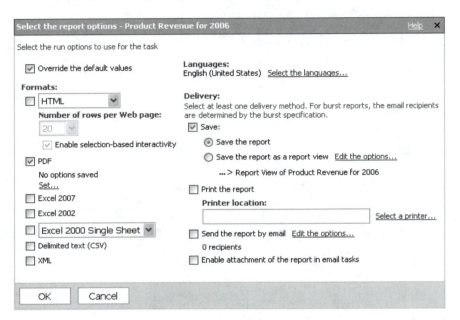

4. Make any necessary changes for the report.

5. Click OK to save the report options you have set.

6. Under Prompt Values, you can specify the values used when the task is executed for any prompts associated with the report.

7. When finished customizing the report task, click Save. The agent is saved with the customized report task. The next time the report task runs it will use these settings.

Run a Job

Add a job task whenever you want the agent to run a job. A *job* is a group of executable entries, such as reports, that are executed as a batch and share the same schedule settings.

Here's how to add a Run A Job task:

1. In the I Want To area, click Add A Task.

2. Click Run A Job. The Select The Job (Navigate) screen displays:

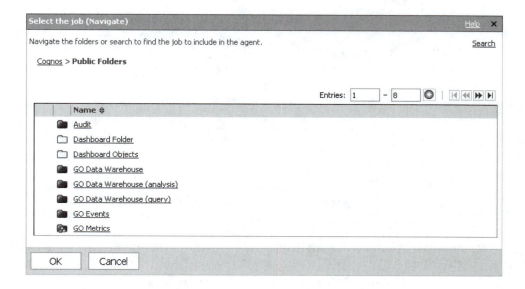

3. Navigate to an existing job that you want to run and select the radio button next to the job.

4. Click OK. The Specify The Job To Run screen displays.

5. Click Save. The agent is saved with a job task. When the task is executed, the job will run.

Run an Agent

Add an agent task when you would like the agent to run another agent. Running more than one agent in sequence allows the output from one agent to be used as the input for another agent. An agent task can also be used to allow agents pulling from different data sources to interact.

Here's how to add a Run An Agent task:

1. In the I Want To area, click Add A Task.

2. Click Run An Agent. The Select The Agent (Navigate) screen displays:

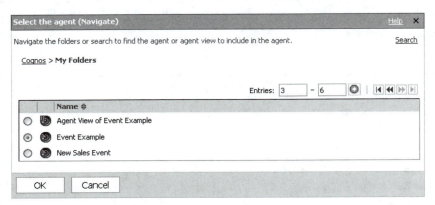

3. Navigate to the saved agent that you want to run and select the radio button next to the agent.

4. Click OK. The Specify The Agent To Run screen displays.

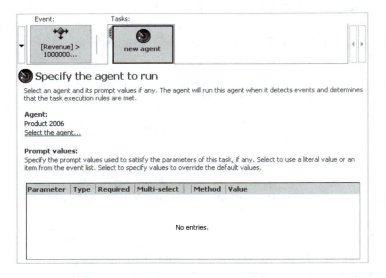

5. Optionally, in the Prompt Values area, specify the prompt values to be used to satisfy any parameters of the agent.

6. Click Save. The agent is saved with an agent task. When the task is executed, the agent that you specified runs.

Update a Database

Add a database task to update the information in a database by executing an existing stored procedure that is part of the database. Databases that have a package in the Cognos environment based on them are available for this task. Stored procedures must be marked as a data modification stored procedure in Framework Manager to be available in Event Studio.

Here's how to add an Update A Database task:

1. In the I Want To area, click Add A Task.

2. Move your pointer over Advanced. The Advanced submenu displays.

3. Click Update A Database. The Specify The Database To Update screen displays, as shown in the next illustration.

4. From the Package drop-down list, select the Framework Manager package that contains the stored procedure that you need.

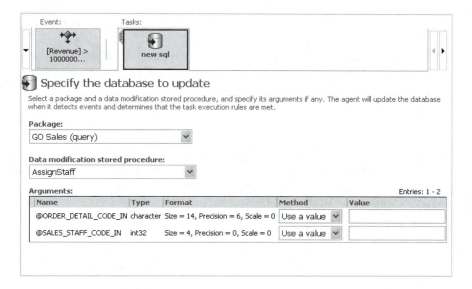

5. From the Data Modification Stored Procedure drop-down list, select the stored procedure to use.

6. Click Save. The agent is saved with a database task. When the task is executed, the agent executes the stored procedure, updating the database.

Call a Web Service

Add a web service task to run applications on either internal or external web servers using standard Internet protocols.

Here's how to add a Call A Web Service task:

1. In the I Want To area, click Add A Task.

2. Move your pointer over Advanced. The Advanced submenu displays.

3. Click Call A Web Service. The Specify The Web Service To Use screen displays:

4. In the Web Service URL text box, enter the URL to the web application that you want to run.

5. Click Retrieve. A list of parameters that the web application requires displays.

6. Enter the applicable information.

7. Click Save. The agent is saved with a web service task. When the task executes, the web service is used.

Run an Export

You can use an agent to run a saved content export process. This is useful when different installations of Cognos 8 are used for your development and production environments and you want an export to be deployed dependent upon a specific event.

Here's how to add a Run An Export task:

1. In the I Want To area, click Add A Task.

2. Move your pointer over Advanced. The Advanced submenu displays.

3. Click Run An Export. The Select The Export (Navigate) screen displays:

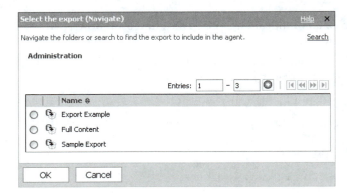

4. Navigate to the saved export that you want to deploy and select the radio button next to the export.

5. Click OK. The Specify The Export To Run screen displays:

6. Click Save. The agent is saved with an export task. When the task executes, the export is deployed.

Run an Import

The import task goes hand-in-hand with the export task. You can use an agent to run a saved import task; this will move migrated content from an export file into the target environment.

NOTE *The agent will not physically move the export file from the development server to the production server. The Content Administrator is responsible for performing this task.*

Here's how to add a Run An Import task:

1. In the I Want To region area, click Add A Task.

2. Move your pointer over Advanced. The Advanced submenu displays.

3. Click Run An Import. The Select The Import (Navigate) screen displays:

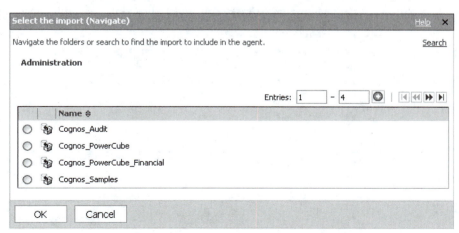

PART III

4. Navigate to the saved import that you want to transfer and select the radio button next to the import.

5. Click OK. The Specify The Import To Run screen displays:

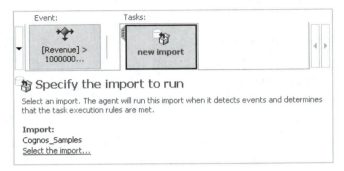

6. Click Save. The agent is saved with an import task. When the task executes, the specified file is imported.

Run a Content Maintenance Task

You can use an agent to run a previously defined Content Maintenance task. The Content Maintenance tasks do one of two things: a consistency check or a report upgrade. A consistency check can confirm that each Cognos 8 user defined in the Cognos namespace is a valid user in the Authentication namespace. Report upgrade attempts to upgrade any reports in the defined location to the currently installed version of Cognos 8. Report upgrades should be done only for very simple reports, as the conversion process can be complex and usually requires some sort of manual intervention.

Here's how to add a Run A Content Maintenance task:

1. In the I Want To area, click Add A Task.

2. Move your pointer over Advanced. The Advanced submenu displays.

3. Click Run A Content Maintenance Task. The Select The Content Maintenance Task (Navigate) screen displays:

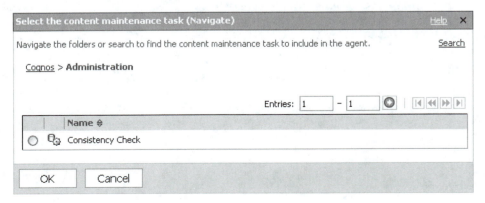

4. Navigate to a previously saved content maintenance task and select the radio button next to the task.

5. Click OK. The Specify The Content Maintenance Task To Run screen displays:

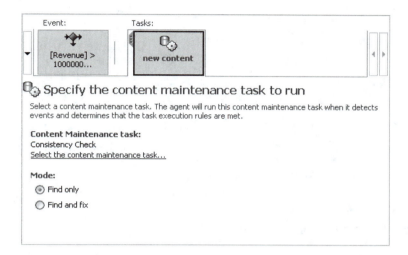

6. Click Save. The agent is saved with a content maintenance task. When the task executes, the specified content maintenance task runs.

Run a Metric Task

Add a metric task if you want metrics to run dependent upon an event.

Here's how to add a Run A Metric task:

1. In the I Want To area, click Add A Task.

2. Move your pointer over Advanced. The Advanced submenu displays.

3. Click Run A Metric Task. The Select The Metric Task (Navigate) screen displays:

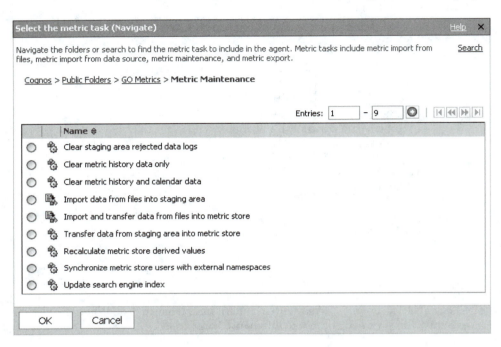

4. Navigate to the metric task that you want to use and select the radio button of the metric task.

5. Click OK. The Specify the Metric Task to Run screen displays:

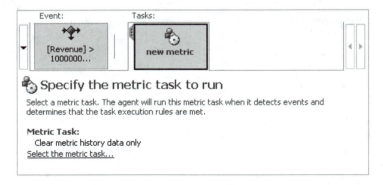

6. Click Save. The agent is saved with a metric task. When the task is executed, the specified metric task runs.

Specify the Task Execution Rules

Task execution rules define the event status for which each task is executed. By default, tasks are executed for all new and all ongoing instances of events. You can modify this behavior through the Manage The Task Execution Rules option in the I Want To area. This option allows you to define when a specific task will or will not run based on the status of the event.

NOTE *Task execution rules can only be modified one task at a time.*

The event key is set by comparing the event instances detected in each execution of the agent with those from the previous run. Next, the event key is used to establish the status for each event in the event list. The event list is then analyzed against the task execution rules for each task in the agent. Finally, a task is executed for each event that meets the rules.

An event key must be defined to ensure that the event list can be updated after each agent is run. The event key definition is set by a combination of items that uniquely identifies each event instance.

Using the example from earlier in the chapter, an agent has been created to provide the salesperson feedback on sales of her product. The event condition is set to the cumulative monthly revenue is greater than 1,000,000 for her product. The event key for the agent is the product number and the date of the last day of the month. Each time this agent executes, the event key is used to determine the status of the event. The task execution rules are set to execute the task if the status of the event is New. The agent is scheduled to run on the first of each month.

For example, the first time the agent is executed, on February 1, the event key is 107113:20080131, which consists of product number 107113 and the date of January 31, 2008. The event status is New. If the agent is executed on February 2, the event key is 107113:20080131, because there is only one event that meets the condition. This event status is Ongoing but unchanged. When the agent executes as scheduled on March 1, the event key is 107113:20080229 and the event status for this event is New. There are now two events that meet the event condition. In the event list, the first is categorized as Ongoing but unchanged and the second is categorized as New.

The agent checks the status of the event and performs the task if the execution rules are met. The salesperson is interested in receiving an e-mail only when the event key is New, so we select only New Events within the task execution rules.

Here's how to specify the task execution rules:

1. In the I Want To area, click Manage The Task Execution Rules. The Set The Task Execution Rules screen displays:

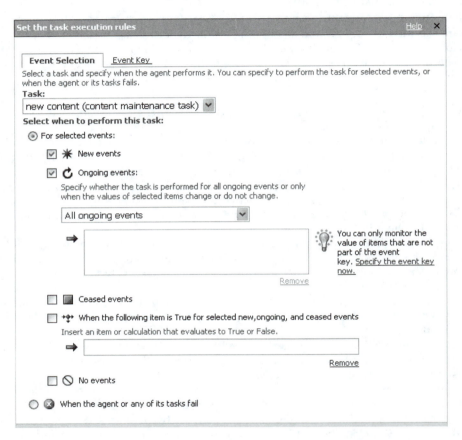

2. From the Task drop-down list, select the task for which you want to modify the execution rules.

3. From the Select When To Perform This Task area, select the For Selected Events option to specify under what circumstances to perform the task, or select the When The Agent Or Any Of Its Tasks Fail option to perform the task when the agent or a task fails.

4. If the For Selected Events option is selected, select or clear the checkboxes for the following options to specify the situation(s) in which to perform the task: New Events; Ongoing Events; Ceased Events; When The Following Item Is True For Selected New, Ongoing, And Ceased Events; and/or No Events.

TIP *When the For Selected Events option is selected, most users typically select the New Events and Ongoing Events checkboxes, along with the All Ongoing Events option in the Ongoing Events drop-down list.*

5. Click the Event Key tab in the content area. The Event Key screen displays, where you can specify the items that uniquely identify the event:

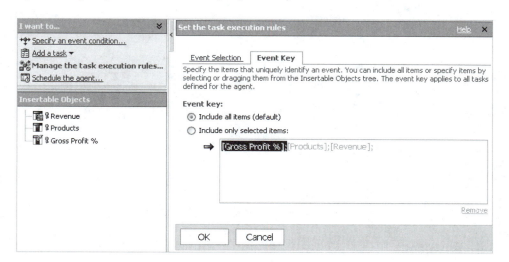

6. From the Event Key area, select the Include All Items (Default) option to include all items or the Include Only Selected Items option to select the items that you want to include.

TIP *When first setting the event key, start with the Include All Items (Default) option. You can modify the key later if the default does not meet your needs.*

7. If the Include Only Selected Items option is selected, select or drag the items from the Insertable Objects pane to the text box.

TIP *To remove an item, select the item and then click Remove.*

8. Click OK. The Event Studio screen displays.
9. Click Save. The agent is saved with the task execution rules as set.

Preview the Data

You can use the Preview option in Event Studio to see what conditions would be met if you were to run the agent. The Preview All option shows you the status of each item in the agent. The Preview option shows you the results of the event condition.

Select Preview from the Actions menu to view the results of the event condition. You can also select Preview All from the Actions menu to view the status of every item in the agent. The Cognos Viewer window displays, as shown next. When you are finished examining the results, close the results window.

Save an Agent

You should save your agent periodically throughout the process of creating it so that no modifications made to the agent are lost.

Here's how to save an agent:

1. From the File menu in Event Studio, select Save As. The Save As dialog opens.

2. In the Name text box, enter a name for the agent.

3. In the Location area, click Select Another Location to navigate to a different location to save the agent, or click Select My Folders to save the agent in My Folders.

4. Click OK. The agent is saved.

Scheduling an Agent

Setting a schedule for an agent allows you to set the agent to run at a later date and time or on a recurring basis. The agent monitors data and performs tasks according to its schedule and does not need to be run manually. Only one schedule can be associated with an agent.

Here's how to schedule an agent in Event Studio:

1. In the I Want To area, click Schedule The Agent. The Set The Schedule screen displays:

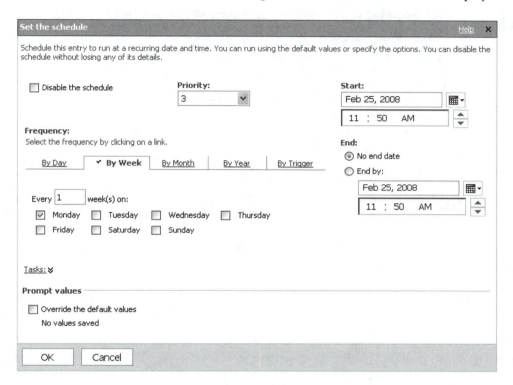

2. Set the schedule according to your needs.
3. Click OK. The agent is scheduled.
4. Click Save. The agent is saved along with the schedule.

NOTE   Refer to Chapter 5 for a detailed discussion on how to schedule items in Cognos 8.

Maintaining an Agent

Requirements for your agent may change over time. The event condition may need to be updated or additional tasks may need to be removed from the agent. Listed here are steps for some of the most common actions performed for an already created agent.

Modify an Event Condition

It is likely that an event condition can change, especially early in the life of a new agent. You might find that a logical condition is not quite what you thought or that the threshold on a condition is set too high or too low. In this case, you can update your condition.

Here's how to modify an event condition:

1. In Event Studio, open the agent that you would like to change.

2. Click Event in the summary area. The event displays in the content area:

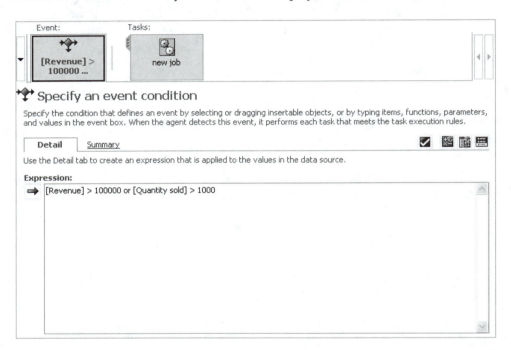

3. In the Expression text box, update the condition.

4. Click Save. The agent is saved with the updated event condition.

Modify a Task

When you want to make changes to a task, you can modify the task. For example, you might need to update the recipient list in an e-mail task or change options on a report task.

Here's how to modify a Task:

1. In Event Studio, open the agent that you would like to change.

2. In the summary area, click the task that you want to modify.

3. Change any applicable options you want.

4. Click Save. The agent is saved with the task modifications.

Delete a Task

If you no longer want or need a task within an agent, you can simply delete it.

Here's how to delete a task:

1. In Event Studio, open the agent that you would like to change.
2. In the summary area, click the task that you want to delete.
3. Click the Delete button on the toolbar or select Delete from the Edit menu.

Change the Order to Run Tasks

In an agent, you can either run tasks all at the same time or in sequence. You can define the order in which tasks are run only when you set them to run in sequence. You should specify tasks to run in sequence whenever a task in the sequence is dependent upon the outcome of a task earlier in the sequence. For example, if you have a database update task that changes the information that will be included in a report, you would want that task to execute completely before the report task executes.

Here's how to change the order in which to run tasks:

1. In the I Want To area, click Reorder The Tasks. The Reorder The Tasks screen displays:

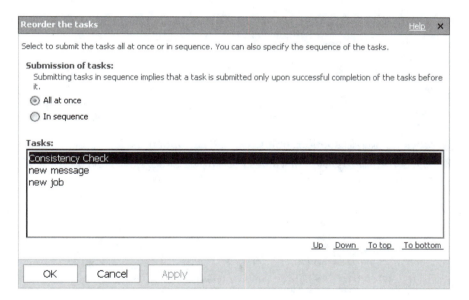

2. In the Submission Of Tasks area, select the All At Once or In Sequence option.
3. Move the tasks into the appropriate order by highlighting each task and then clicking the Up, Down, To Top, and To Bottom links.
4. Click OK. The tasks are listed in the specified order in the summary area.
5. Click Save. The agent is saved.

Specify Default Options for Tasks of an Agent

You can control the default behavior of report and import options for all tasks of an agent. When set in this location, these options apply to the defaults for any report or import tasks created in the agent.

Specify Default Options for Report Format

You can set the output format (PDF, HTML, Excel, and so on), define bursting options, and define delivery options (for example, send to a printer, e-mail, save, and so on). Report options can also be set individually on each report task.

NOTE *Refer to Chapter 6 for a detailed discussion on the report options available in Cognos 8.*

Here's how to specify default options for report tasks:

1. From the Actions Menu, select Set Default Options for All Tasks. The Select Default Options screen displays:

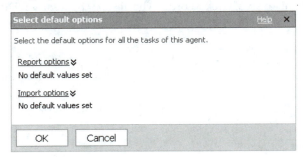

2. Click the Report Options link to expand the options.

3. Select the Specify Default Values For All The Reports Of This Job checkbox. The options expand:

4. Set any report options you want.

NOTE Bursting *allows you to specify which recipients receive which parts of a report. Consider this example: A large company has an All Sales report that displays all of the divisions of the company (cars, boats, motorcycles, vans, and so on). Bursting allows the company to send the CEO the entire sales report, and each division manager (cars, boats, vans, and so on) each of their respective division's sales for the report. You must organize or group the report on the company divisions (cars, boats, motorcycles, and so on) as bursting uses the logical order of the report to distribute, break, or burst apart the report. Refer to Chapter 10 for additional information on bursting.*

    5. Click OK. The specified report options are set as the default options for any report task created in this agent.

    6. Click Save. The agent is saved with the specified report options set as default.

Specify Default Options for Import Tasks

You can select to Upgrade All Report Specifications To The Latest Version or to Keep The Existing Report Specification Versions for all import tasks created in the agent.

    Here's how to specify default options for import tasks:

    1. From the Actions menu, select Set Default Options For All Tasks. The Select Default Options screen displays.

    2. Click the Import Options link to expand the options.

    3. Select the Specify Default Values For The Imports Of This Job checkbox. The available options expand:

    4. Set the appropriate report specification upgrade option.

    5. Click OK. The specified import option is now set for any import tasks added to this agent.

    6. Click Save. The agent is saved with the specified import option set as default.

Agents in Cognos Connection

Common Cognos Connection actions such as cut, copy, paste, delete, set properties, run, schedule and so on can be performed on agents.

Run an Agent Manually

Once an agent has been saved, you can run it either manually or on a schedule within Cognos Connection. Running an agent manually can be helpful in verifying that it runs properly.

Here's how to run an agent manually:

1. In Cognos Connection, navigate to the saved agent.

2. In the Actions column of the agent you want to run, click the Run With Options icon. The Run With Options screen displays.

3. Select the time you want to run the agent.

4. Click Run. The agent runs at the next occurrence of the selected time.

Schedule an Agent in Cognos Connection

Most agents will run on a schedule because the events that you are checking for might happen only once a day or once a month.

Here's how to schedule an agent from Cognos Connection:

1. In Cognos Connection, navigate to the saved agent.

2. In the Actions column of the agent you want to schedule, click the Schedule icon. The Schedule screen displays.

3. Set any properties for the schedule you want.

4. Click OK. The agent runs at the next occurrence of the selected date and time.

NOTE *Agents can also be scheduled from within Event Studio by selecting Schedule the Agent from the I Want To area. Refer to Chapter 5 for a detailed discussion on how to schedule items in Cognos 8.*

Create an Agent View

An agent view can be created of an agent to share the agent specification. This can be useful when you want different agents with the same event condition and tasks set with different sets of prompt values or set on varying schedules.

Here's how to create an agent view:

1. In Cognos Connection, navigate to the saved agent for which you would like to create an agent view.

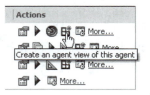

2. In the actions column, click the Create an Agent View of This Agent icon. The Specify A Name And Description screen displays.

3. Edit any properties you want and then click OK. The agent view has been created in the specified location.

4. Optionally, in the actions column of the agent view, click the Schedule icon to specify a different schedule than the original agent or to select alternate prompt values.

Administration of IBM Cognos 8 Business Intelligence

IV

PART

Building the Model with Framework Manager

As an Cognos 8 BI modeler, you need to know how to create and work with a model from which report writers will be able to develop reports. This chapter explains how to create, modify, organize, and publish a relational model from Framework Manager, the Business Intelligence (BI) modeling tool for Cognos 8.

This chapter assumes you have a working knowledge of relational database concepts such as tables, columns, and joins. If you don't, it would be beneficial to get that background knowledge before proceeding. This chapter also assumes that the PC you are using has Framework Manager installed and configured correctly to access your IBM Cognos 8 BI environment. If this is not the case, you will not be able to perform many of the actions described in this chapter, because Framework Manager will generate errors when trying to talk to the Cognos 8 BI Server to authenticate you as a user, access data source connection information, or publish packages. This book does not provide an in-depth explanation of installation and configuration, but the "environment" node in Cognos Configuration must be configured with the correct URIs that point to your Cognos 8 BI Server.

One final note before you proceed: Learning to model in Framework Manager is a somewhat holistic concept. It pays to understand all the major parts of the modeling process before you dive in. Putting the information in book form requires that it be presented in a serial manner, but that raises a number of chicken-and-egg situations. If topic X requires knowledge of topic Y, and Y requires knowledge of topic X, which should be presented first? Our advice, then, is not to use this chapter as a recipe book. Do not start reading the chapter while creating your model and counting on having a complete, correct, and best-designed model by the time you finish the chapter. Instead, treat this as a cooking class. Read through the whole chapter, understand the concepts and the components of modeling, and then start your model, using this chapter as a reference if necessary. You will get more out of it.

What Is a Model?

When you create a report in Cognos 8 Report Studio or Query Studio, how does IBM Cognos 8 BI know about your data? How does it know how to connect to your databases, and how does it know what the tables and data items are and how they relate to each other? That is the purpose of the Framework Manager model. The model, created by the BI Administrator using Framework Manager, is the framework that exposes the metadata that describes your source data to the Cognos Studio users.

Before we delve into the process of creating the model, we will try to clarify some terminology. We say "try" because the terminology invariably gets confusing because it changes as you move through the creation process. For starters, even though the tool we use to create the model is called Framework Manager, there is no entity referred to as a *framework* within the Cognos documentation. What you start with in Framework Manager is a *project*. The project is composed of a .cpf file and some XML files organized within a folder. The .cpf file is the one that you open with Framework Manager when accessing an existing project. The model is what you create within the project, but since there is generally only one model per project (you can debate this if you start linking models—more on that in the next chapter), it is common to refer to the project as the *model*. Once you have developed the content within the model, you need to make it available to the studio users. You do this by creating a *package*, so named because you can package up just the parts of the model you want to expose to the end users. Everything else will remain excluded, or at least hidden from the end user. Because more than one package can be created for a model (that is, within a project), the terminology is pretty clear—that is, until you publish the package and the end users start referring to it within Cognos Connection as a *model*, or a *package*, or even a *folder*. Clear now? Okay, let's move on.

Creating a New Model

To create a basic, but thorough, Framework Manager model from a relational database source, you will need to do the following:

- Create a data source connection (or reference an existing one).
- Create data source query subjects.
- Create model query subjects to resolve modeling challenges, if necessary.
- Set query item properties.
- Relate the query subjects (define the joins).
- Create model query subjects to present a business view.
- Create a package of the items to present to the studio users.
- Publish the package.

Beyond that list, other tasks can be performed in the model, including setting security, dealing with multilingual implementations, and adding calculations and filters. There is also the whole process of dimensionally modeling a relational data source. We will get to all of that in later chapters. The goal of this chapter is to enable you to create a basic, functional, relational model that can be used by Query Studio, Report Studio, or Event Studio, and that can also serve as a source for building metrics or PowerPlay PowerCubes.

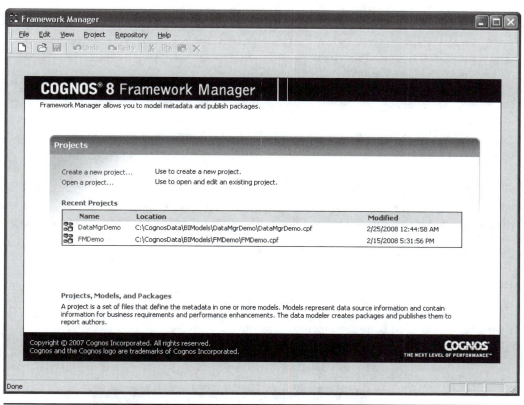

Figure 15-1   The Framework Manager opening splash screen

Starting a New Project

When you first open Framework Manager, you see the splash screen from which you can create a new project or open an existing one, as shown in Figure 15-1. The splash screen also shows a most-recently-used list of up to four projects.

Clearing the MRU List

If your list of most-recently-used projects is no longer applicable and you want to clear one or more entries in the list, you can do so by editing the following file and removing the references to the unwanted projects:

<*install location*>\c8\configuration\bmt.ini.

Make sure that your editor (Notepad will work) is set to save the file with UTF-8 encoding. If you don't know how to do that, you might want to leave the MRU list as is and let time take care of changing which projects appear on it.

Here's how to create a new Framework Manager project:

1. From the splash screen, click the Create A New Project link. If you already closed the splash screen, you can also start by choosing File | New Project, or by clicking the New Project icon on the toolbar.

2. Framework Manager pops up the New Project dialog, shown in Figure 15-2. Enter the project name and location. Note that the project name and location are linked in this dialog. If you change the project name, the end of the location changes, and vice versa. This is because the project is composed not just of the .cpf file, but the entire project folder in which the .cpf file of the same name resides.

3. Click OK.

Once you have clicked OK to the New Project dialog, you will be asked to log on to the Cognos 8 environment, unless your environment is configured to use single signon, in which case you will be authenticated without having to enter you user name and password. This login dialog is actually a small web page containing the same login screen that you see when logging into the Cognos Connection portal.

The Metadata Wizard

Once you're logged in, the Metadata Wizard will launch. You can exit out of the wizard and create everything manually, and you can even launch the wizard later from an existing project. But the wizard is quite helpful when starting a project, so we will use it to start our project.

FIGURE 15-2
New Project dialog

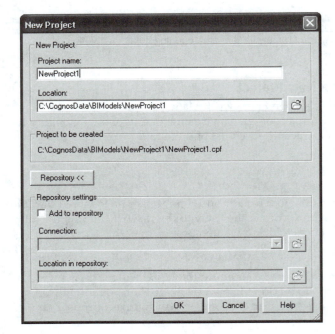

When the Metadata Wizard opens, it displays a prompt that asks the users to select the design language for the Project. Cognos 8 supports development in a number of languages.

Next, you must select the metadata source that will be used to provide metadata content for the model, as shown in Figure 15-3. The option at the top of the list, the most common one, is Data Sources, which is what we will be using now. Note that you can also use metadata exported from a variety of Cognos applications, such as Impromptu, Data Manager, or another Framework Manager model. You can also use metadata from a variety of third-party applications, including some modeling tools and some related or competing BI and data warehousing applications. If you are curious, now is a good time to select Third Party Metadata Sources and take a look at the list to see if any apply to you. You can always click the back button in the wizard to go back and select Data Source.

NOTE *The other Cognos metadata sources are interesting if they apply to you. The Impromptu and Architect options allow you to try to preserve any modeling work that you have invested in those older Cognos tools, but beware that the model it imports may not be the preferred way to model within the newer Cognos 8 environment. The options to use Data Manager or its predecessor, DecisionStream, allow you to move rather seamlessly from those Cognos data warehousing tools to a model of the data warehouse, or a portion thereof, that they produced. This gives you a great head start on a model, complete with a dimensionally modeled relational component, which we will address in the following chapter.*

FIGURE 15-3
Metadata Wizard -
Select Metadata
Source

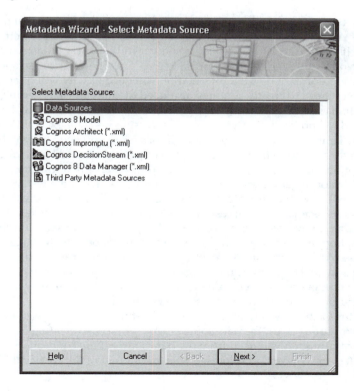

Start with a Data Source

If you think of the model as a hose, a conduit by which you will allow end users to access data for their reports, you can think of the data source as the spigot to which you must connect the hose. IBM Cognos 8 BI models can reference multiple data sources, but for now, we will keep it simple and create our initial model from just one source, which is all the wizard will accommodate at one time anyway.

When you select the Data Source option, the next dialog in the wizard asks which data source you want to use. The list comes from the data sources defined in your Cognos BI Server environment—that is, Cognos Connection. You can also create a new data source. Creating the source here in Framework Manager and creating it in Cognos Connection are equivalent operations. In fact, they use the same web interface: the screens you see when creating a new data source from the wizard are the same screens you see when creating the source in Cognos Connection.

NOTE *To create the data source from Cognos Connection in version 8.3 (assuming you have permission to do so), from the Launch menu, select Cognos Administration. On the Administration page, click the Configuration tab, and then select Data Source Connections. If you are using Cognos BI 8.2, choose Tools | Directory, and then select the Data Sources tab. In either version, once on the Data Sources page, click the button in the toolbar at the top right to create a new data source. The New Data Source wizard starts, so the rest is the same as if you launched that wizard from the Framework Manager Metadata Wizard.*

If you think you need a new data source, make sure the one you need is not defined already. Avoid cluttering the data source collection with multiple definitions of the same source. If you are creating a new data source, you will first need to know the type of data source you want, such as Oracle or IBM DB2. You will also need to specify the connection and logon information. What information you need exactly will depend on the type of data source you need to create. You may also need to know the manner in which you will access your database. For instance, if your source database is Microsoft SQL Server, then you will also need to know whether you plan on accessing it via ODBC, OLE-DB, or SQL 2005 Native Client. If you are not sure what information you need for your source database, you can run the wizard to the point at which you would need to know, and then record the information for which you are prompted. You can take that information to your database administrator to get the answers that you need to enter in the wizard.

You will also need to determine how Cognos will log on to the database for you when running the report. The simplest, which we will assume is sufficient for now, is to create a signon that the Everyone group can use. A *signon* is just a user name and password combination that can be attached to a data source to be used for logging on to the associated database. When permissions are given to the Everyone group to use a signon, then all reports and queries being run through this connection would log on as the user specified in that signon. As such, we recommend that you use a database user for this signon that has only read privileges on the database, not create, update, or delete. That way, no one can ever accuse the Cognos system of changing or deleting data from the source database.

Make sure you test the data source before you finish creating it. You will not be able to get the information you need from the data source if the connection definition is incorrect. A link to test the connection is located near the bottom of the New Data Source screen.

Whether you just created a new data source definition or were going to use an existing definition, you end up back at the Select Metadata Source screen in the Metadata Wizard. Select your data source, and then click Next.

Selecting the Objects to Include in the Model

Once you provide a data source and the correct information to connect to that data source, Framework Manager will query the source for the metadata information that describes the available objects in that source. The available objects are presented in a tree, from which you can select the objects that you want to include in the model. You do this by selecting the checkbox next to the components you want brought in, as shown in Figure 15-4. In this screen, the selection was made to include all the tables in the data source by selecting the checkbox next to the Tables folder. Unless you have a small number of tables and you know you will need all of them in the model, we recommend that you select specific objects to bring in at this point. You can select the desired tables, which is usually what you do, or just selected fields from tables and sometimes views. Views are queries that select from one or more tables. Views are stored on and executed by the database server when data is selected from them. Sometimes, a view is the best option, but unless there is a valid, compelling reason to use a view, stick with bringing in tables only. (See "To View or Not to View.")

FIGURE 15-4
Selecting all tables in the data source from the Metadata Wizard

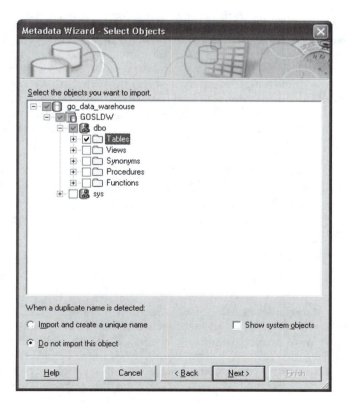

Don't worry about getting all the tables that you might eventually want in the model at this point. Just shoot for getting those you are sure you will need. You can always rerun the wizard later or create a data source query subject manually to bring in additional tables.

NOTE *Remember that in this discussion of using the wizard we are dealing with a relational database source. Other source types, such as a PowerPlay cube, will cause different behavior from the wizard.*

To View or Not to View

You can include tables and/or views from your source relational database in your model. You should opt for the tables as your preferred source objects, and not views. You may be wondering why we recommend you use tables instead of views. You may have been challenged by your database administrator (DBA) for a good reason not to use the custom views that he poured his heart, soul, and significant expertise into creating. Those would be the views that in his estimation bring together all the fields you might need to answer a particular question about the data.

You can take the smart-alecky approach and remind him that it is no longer the 1980s. Or you can call him names and threaten to rearrange the stickers on his Rubik's Cube, rendering it unsolvable. Whatever you end up doing, here is the explanation of why we prefer tables over views. You can share this with your DBA.

The beauty of a toolset like Cognos 8 is that it writes the database query for you based on what was included in the report. Cognos 8 includes only the fields, tables, and joins required to get the desired result from the database server. When you pull a view into the model, assuming the view is anything more complicated than just a selection of all fields in a single table, the database server must execute the view to get that result set before it can do anything required of the data based on your report definition. If you want to relate data from separate views (that is, joining the views), then each view is executed and the result sets are then joined. This will result in one or more of the following problems:

- No access to fields that are in the underlying tables, but not included in the views.

- Additional, unwanted fields and even tables accessed on your behalf by the view, even if you didn't want or need them in your report.

- Database indexing can be rendered useless by the view, resulting in poor performance when running your reports.

- You are at the mercy of the logic used to create the view, which could mean you experience problems such as dropping records that you want (think of missing outer joins, if that means something to you).

Think of the tables as baking ingredients such as flour, sugar, salt, butter, eggs, and baking powder. Think of a view as a particular kind of cake—let's say a carrot cake. If you always want carrot cake (just like the result set received from a particular view in the database), then the view is fine. But if you want the flexibility to make all kinds of cakes, breads, waffles, and cookies (just like the many different reports that will be written against your model), then you want the baking ingredients (such as the tables themselves) not that same old carrot cake (such as the view).

Are there times when a view makes sense? While rare, there can be times when a view seems to be what is needed. This can happen if the modeling tool does not support the logic needed in the view to get the proper data. But, frankly, Cognos 8 Framework Manager is sophisticated and flexible enough that you can probably write the necessary SQL into a Framework Manager query subject to get the desired results, so you could maintain it in the model rather than use a view. One notable exception is materialized views, which are really pre-aggregated summary tables supported by some database types and which should be treated as tables when modeling.

If that doesn't convince your DBA, then stay late one night and rearrange the stickers on his Rubik's Cube. He deserves nothing less.

Generating Relationships Automatically—or Not

Having selected the objects to include, click Next to progress to the Generate Relationships screen of the wizard. This screen is used to establish relationships among the tables we are bringing into the model. After all, what good is a relational data source without relationships? These relationships create a logical link between tables when one table references data in another table. For instance, a Sales table referencing a Product Code might be related to the Product table, linked by the Product Code, so that we can write a report with the revenue from the Sales table and the product name from the Product table and get the desired result.

Cognos 8 Framework Manager is offering to help us by trying to create relationships among the tables in our model based on the rules you choose in this screen. Remember, though, that the purpose of the wizard is to save you time by performing some steps for you. If you are not careful with what you allow Framework Manager to do in this step, you may spend more time looking for and cleaning up bad relationships that it created for you than you would have spent creating only the right ones manually. The safest option is the default option to Use Primary And Foreign Keys, which means only integrity constraints defined between tables in your source database will be imported in the model as joins. While not always completely correct, and while rarely complete, this is usually a good starting point. Then again, selecting this option might give you no automatically created relationships because the source database does not need to have the primary-foreign key relationships defined. In fact, if your source is a data warehouse, integrity constraints are often missing. This means only that you will need to create all the relationships manually, but, as we will soon explain, that is a pretty quick operation.

As shown in Figure 15-5, the other options are to use column name matching, either only on uniquely indexed columns or on all columns. These require a bit more knowledge of the naming conventions of your database. If every table has an indexed field generically named ID or CODE, then even when using only uniquely indexed columns, all of them will be joined to each other, which would be bad. If they are consistently named something like PRODUCT_CODE in both the Product table and in all the tables that refer to it, such as Sales and Inventory, then this option for the uniquely indexed columns might work for you. Using just matching query item names is almost never a good idea, lest you end up with something like the DESCRIPTION field in the Product table linked to the DESCRIPTION fields in the Customer table and every other table with a DESCRIPTION field. And that would be awful.

FIGURE 15-5
Metadata Wizard
options for
automatically
creating
relationships

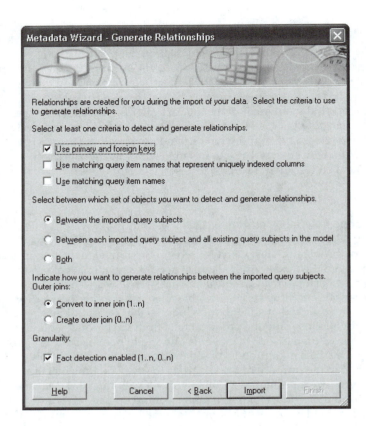

In the Generate Relationships screen, you also have options for telling Framework Manager among which tables it should look for relationships. You can choose to look for them only among the tables being imported at this time, or between the imported tables and the ones that already exist in the model, or both. Because we are just creating the model, nothing exists in the model yet in our case, but recall that we can run the wizard later, after we have some query subjects in the model, which would make this option mean more.

You also have options for converting outer joins to inner joins (read more on that in the sidebar "Inner Joins vs. Outer Joins" later in the chapter), and for detecting *granularity*, which means it will attempt to determine where the relationships have a "many" side. That is, in a many-to-one relationship, like many sales orders that refer to the same product, the relationship will be specified as "1..1" on the product side, and "1..n" on the sales order side. Leave the Fact Detection Enabled (1..n, 0..n) checkbox checked. Otherwise, you might find bad queries being generated as the result of incorrect cardinalities on the generated relationships. More on that in the section "How Cognos Uses Relationships to Generate Queries" later in this chapter.

Once you have made your selections in the Generate Relationships screen, click Import and let the wizard do its thing. It will bring in your selected tables from the data source you specified, and it will attempt to create the relationships based on the rules you specified. When the import is complete, take note of the report the wizard shows you regarding the number of tables, relationships, and so on, that it has imported based on your selections. Most importantly, this will tell you how many, if any, relationships were automatically generated for you.

That's it. You have a model, or more correctly a start of a model. At this point, you could create a package and publish it to the server, and you would be able to write reports from it. But you probably expected your model to have more and to do more for you, so we will not stop here with this new model. We will look at creating more of the model and refining it without using the wizard. First, however, let's get our bearings.

The Application and Its Objects

Before we get too far into the process of working with the model, we should look at the objects that make up the model and the layout of the Framework Manager interface.

Navigating Framework Manager

When you create a model in Framework Manager, you get a default view of the application, as shown in Figure 15-6.

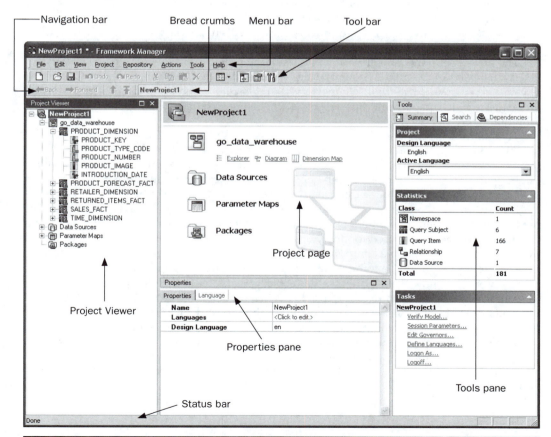

FIGURE 15-6 The default view of a project in Framework Manager

Framework Manager, like most applications, has a menu bar, toolbar, and status bar, plus a navigation bar that helps the user navigate around the model. The default view displays one main window, the *project page,* and three other optional and movable windows, or panes, that appear around it: the Project Viewer, the Properties pane, and the Tools pane. The project page appears in the middle of the application. If you have a project open, then you are viewing the project page. This screen shows the project and allows you to work with the project using one of three main views: the explorer, the diagram, or the dimension map, all of which we will soon discuss. As you navigate around the project page, say drilling into the project in the diagram, the "bread crumbs" in the navigation bar (see Figure 15-6) will show a trail of how you got there. To go up one or more levels, you can click the appropriate bread crumb in this area. The project page can also be used to access the data sources, parameter maps, and packages, but there is an easier way to access those objects in the project.

The Project Viewer is a handy tree structure that is easier to navigate than the explorer view of the Project page. The Project Viewer shows up by default on the left side of the Project page. Because it is so handy, we recommend that you always keep the Project Viewer open. With the Project Viewer, you can easily get to any object in the model with the exception of the relationships. Double-clicking a container object (container objects include namespaces and folders, including top-level folders such as those that hold data sources or packages) changes what is displayed in the project page—that is, the contents of the container selected are shown in the project page area.

The Properties pane appears at the bottom of the project page by default. Since every object that exists in the model has properties associated with it, this is an important pane to always keep displayed, as well. Whenever you single-click an object in the Project Viewer or in the main project page, the Properties pane will change to show the properties of that now-highlighted object.

The pane on the right side of the project page is the Tools pane. The Tools pane has three tabs: The Summary tab shows project language information, context-sensitive statistics (counts of objects contained in that part of the project) and context-sensitive tasks that you might want to perform. The Search tab helps you find objects by name, or part of a name. Note that if you are using the search facility, you can click the More button on the Search tab to get more options for narrowing your search, such as choosing the class (type of object) or the property you want to search. The third tab, Dependencies, is available in Cognos 8.3 but not in prior versions. It is used for analyzing dependencies between objects, which is done by dragging-and-dropping a component along with its child components from the Project Viewer and highlighting the component of interest in the upper panel. The lower panel on that tab will then show the list of dependent objects that refer to the highlighted object, such as relationships, determinants, and query items in a model query subject. You can then click the dependent object to access it as you would in the Project Viewer pane. This facility can help you to understand the impact of changes you might be making to objects in the model.

While the Tools pane is useful at times, it may be the least important of the panes for many of the typical modeling tasks, so you can hide it if you need the real estate on the screen to view and navigate the project. You can always get back any pane that you hide if you need to access it.

TIP   *To close any of the panes, click the "X" in the upper-right corner of the pane's title bar—or, choose View from the menu bar and then click the pane's name to clear it. To view a pane that is not visible, choose View and then click the pane's name to select it, and it will reappear as it was before you hid it. Or you can use the toggle buttons on the right side of the toolbar to turn these panes on and off.*

Note that in addition to being able to close the panes, you can detach a pane and move it around and outside of the application window by double-clicking its title bar, by clicking the little window icon in the title bar to the left of the "X," or by clicking the title bar and dragging-and-dropping it somewhere. You can re-anchor the pane by double-clicking its title bar or by dragging-and-dropping it to the top, bottom, left, or right of the project page. You can shuffle these panes around to arrange them as you wish, anchored or not, wherever you prefer them.

Objects that Make Up the Model

The model comprises a number of objects of different classes. The difference between a class and an object, as in a number of object-oriented environments, is simply that the class refers to the type of entity—like folders, query subjects, and packages—and an object, on the other hand, is a specific instance of a class—like the Addresses folder, the Products query subject, or the Sales Analysis package. Following are the major classes:

Project   The top-level object that contains all the other objects in your model.

Folder   A container to improve the organization of your model. It appears as a folder for report-writers using the published model but does not offer the naming protection of namespaces. Objects in different folders directly within the same namespace cannot have the same name. Generic folders can hold query subjects and a number of other objects. Query item folders and measure folders are used specifically to organize those types of objects within a query subject or measure dimension, respectively.

Namespace   Not to be confused with a security namespace, a Framework Manager namespace is a folder that also adds a level of naming to protect you if you try to give two separate objects the same name. If the objects are in different namespaces, they can have the same name; if they are directly in the same namespace, objects cannot have the same name. This works well because, for example, you may have a Sales namespace and a Shipments namespace, and you might want to use a Countries query subject in each, which would be okay. It would not make sense and would cause an error if you tried to have two query subjects named Countries in the same Sales namespace. For report-writers using the published model, a namespace acts like a folder.

Query Subjects   The heart of the model, query subjects define the data from your data source that you are making available to your query and report writers. Think of it as a definition that gets you a resulting set of data. It could be as simple as all the columns of a single table, or it could be more complex, with columns from multiple tables, filters, calculations, and even complex SQL logic. The three types of query subjects are discussed separately: data source, model, and stored procedure.

A *data source query subject* is really a SQL select statement that specifies the columns and the table(s) to be pulled into the model. Most of the data source query subjects take the following form:

```
SELECT * FROM DATABASE.TABLE
```

That definition will get all the columns from the table and make them available to you, making it easy to update the object to pull in new columns that may have been added to the table since the query subject was first defined (more on that later). Data source query subjects can have more complex definitions, but try not to do too much in the way of writing SQL here. We will discuss good and bad practices in query subject definitions later in the chapter in the section "Creating and Editing Query Subjects."

A *model query subject* refers to query items already in the model. These query items can come from data source query subjects or other model query subjects. In addition, you can add filtering and calculations to the model query subject definition.

Finally, you can create a *stored procedure query subject*. This is simply a definition that specifies a stored procedure coded within your data source that returns a table-like result set. If you are not sure what a stored procedure is, do not worry; this is by far the least used of the query subject types. But if you need it, it comes in handy.

Query Item   A column in a query subject, which can be an actual column or a calculation.

Shortcut   A reference to a query subject. See the sections on "Aliasing" and "Star Schema Groupings and Reference Shortcuts."

Relationship   If query subjects are the heart of the model, relationships are the soul. Admittedly, that's corny, but you get the idea: relationships are really important. A relationship defines how two query subjects are related. These are, in effect, the join definitions between tables. Relationships specify which fields in the two query subjects are related, how they are related (equals, greater than, and so on), and the cardinality of the join. The cardinality tells Cognos 8 if one of the tables is expected to have more than one matching record in the other (many-to-one relationships), or if a matching record is not required at all (outer joins). We will get more in depth with cardinality in the section "Creating Relationships" later in this chapter.

Data Source   A connection definition that tells the model how to connect to the source database. The data source definition allows Framework Manager to connect to the database and query it for the available metadata—that is, the tables and columns that can be accessed from the database. When a report is written against the model, the data source definition tells Cognos 8 where to connect to query for the data that will go into the report. The data source definition in Framework Manager actually references a data source definition in Cognos Connection. This fact allows you to re-point a Framework Manager data source to an alternative Cognos Connection data source to access a different instance of a database of the same design—for instance from a development version to a production version of the database.

Parameter Map   A simple, two-column table that is stored in the model and used in conjunction with the Framework Manager macro facility to substitute values in the model at runtime of a report to get the desired results. This facility can be used for implementing row-level security or dynamic database selection, for example. A parameter map can be populated manually or via a query. This will be covered in the "Macros" section in Chapter 16.

Package   Determines how you specify what in the model should be seen by the end user. You can declare a component of the model, such as a query subject, as included, excluded, or hidden. Included elements can be selected by report writers. Hidden elements are available to the report, but they cannot be selected explicitly by report authors. Excluded elements are not available to reports. Note that if an included element references an excluded element, Framework Manager is smart enough to hide the excluded element rather than truly exclude it and allow a report to receive an error for an indirect reference to an element that is not really there.

Calculation   Formulas for creating a new data item from zero or more other data items, which can be constants, simple constructs such as function calls or mathematical operations, or complex constructs with conditional logic. Calculations often exist within a query subject definition as just another query item, but you can create stand-alone calculations that you can place directly in a folder or namespace.

Filter   You can create two types of filters in a model. One is an embedded filter that is applied as part of and can only be accessed via a query subject definition. We cover creating embedded filters in the section "Completing Your Query Subject Definition." The other filter type, the stand-alone filter, is the one we discuss here because it will appear as its own object in the model. That filter type is a filter definition that can be included in a package and accessed by report authors. Stand-alone filters are a great way to provide consistent business-rule filters for authors to include selectively in a report.

Those are the major objects, all of which, with the exception of relationships, can be seen as nodes on the tree in the Project Viewer pane of the Framework Manager interface.

Creating New Objects in Your Model

Now that you know more about the objects that will be in your model, and how to navigate around the interface to access those objects, let's look at how to create and work with those objects in your relational model.

We already demonstrated how to create some of the objects using the Metadata Wizard when we created a new project. Using the wizard, we created data source query subjects with their query items, and possibly a data source and some relationships. Now we will start to examine how to create those and other objects manually in an existing model.

If you click the top-level namespace (go_data_warehouse, in our example), and then choose Actions | Create, the submenu will display all the objects that can be created, as shown in Figure 15-7.

Note that not all the objects are enabled for creation; some of them are grayed out. This is because the creation options are context-sensitive. That is, what is available for you to insert depends on which object is selected in the Project Viewer. Because we selected the top-level namespace before accessing the Actions menu, the objects enabled for creation can be inserted into a namespace because that is where the new object will be placed. Those enabled objects in this case are another Namespace, Folder, Query Subject, Relationship, Filter, Calculation, Measure Dimension, and Regular Dimension. The disabled objects—Query Item Folder, Measure Folder, Data Source, Parameter Map, and Package—can be created in the model, just not within a namespace object.

Using the Actions | Create submenu is a convenient way to see all the possible objects that you can create, and it is a viable way to create objects. But since you had to select the object within which you wanted to create the new object in order to create it anyway, you can save time by right-clicking the object and, from the context menu, selecting Create and choosing your object. Only valid objects that can be created within the selected object will

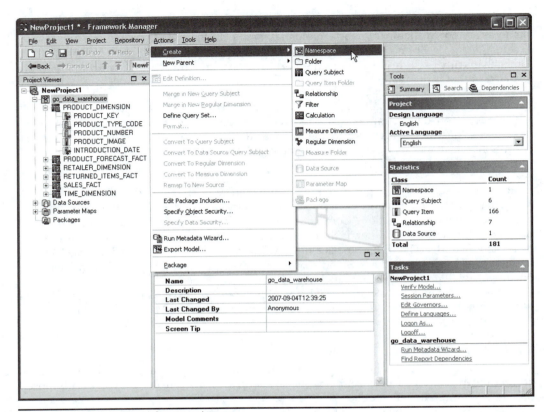

Figure 15-7   The Actions | Create submenu

show up in this context menu. For instance, when you right-click a Query Subject, you can choose only to create a Query Item Folder or a Relationship.

When you create an object manually, the information you will need to supply next depends on the class of the object. Creating a number of the objects will cause an associated wizard to start up to gather additional information. The following sections cover those objects and any associated creation wizards to help you understand what is necessary for creating them. Creating regular and measure dimensions are not discussed here, since those are related to the concept of dimensionally modeling a relational data source, which is covered in Chapter 16.

Creating Objects to Organize Your Model

Two objects are primarily used to organize your model: namespaces and folders. Both hold a number of objects, including query subjects, filters, and other namespaces and folders, so your ability to contain and organize objects in your model is seemingly limitless. See the section "Approaches to Model Organization" later in this chapter.

Creating a Namespace

Namespaces can be created only within existing namespaces or folders. To create a namespace, right-click the namespace or folder in which you wish to place your new namespace. To create a namespace, you simply need to supply a name, so there is no wizard. The new namespace is created immediately with the default name selected, allowing you to start typing the name you want. Technically, even that is optional, but we are figuring that you really do not want a namespace to keep the default name of New Namespace.

Once the namespace is created, you can move or copy existing objects into it, or you can create other new objects within it. As mentioned, the benefit of a namespace is that it allows you to organize your model and put a query subject or shortcut of the same name in two different namespaces. So, for example, you can organize your model based on subject area, with a namespace called Sales that has a shortcut to the Product query subject and another namespace called Inventory that also has a shortcut to the Product query subject, with both named Product. See the section "Star Schema Groupings and Reference Shortcuts" later in this chapter.

Namespaces give you a layer of protection from name collisions. However, namespaces can do this because the namespace becomes part of the path to the contained query subjects and their query items. It is important to know this, because changing the name of an existing namespace can result in problems if existing reports reference items in that namespace. When you try to run those reports, they will be looking for a namespace of the old name, which they will not find. The best approach is to give thought to the organization of your model and to choose names for your namespaces wisely when you create them. If you must change a namespace name, you should analyze the impact of publishing your package with the changes by choosing Tools | Package | Analyze Publish Impact.

Creating Folders

When you create a folder, the Create Folder Wizard appears, as shown in Figure 15-8. The only two things the wizard will ask you to supply is the name you want for the folder (again, the default name of New Folder is probably not what you want), and then what

Figure 15-8
The Create Folder Wizard - Select Data screen

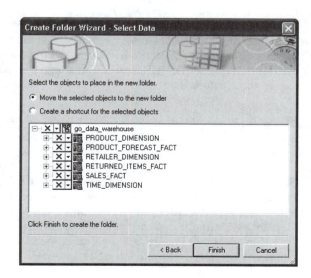

content from the model you want to move to this new folder, or, optionally, the content to which you want to create shortcuts in this new folder. If you select nothing, the folder will be empty. In either case, you can always drag-and-drop objects into the folder from within the Project Viewer pane after it is created.

Creating and Editing Query Subjects

Because query subjects are central to a model (a relational model without query subjects does absolutely nothing), there is a lot to cover in discussing how to create them. You can create three types of query subjects—data source, model, and stored procedure—in a few different ways. And a number of aspects of query subject behavior can be defined. We will start by going through the ways to create all of the query subject types, and then we will address completing the definition of your query subjects because a number of aspects of a query subject definition are common across types.

Creating Data Source Query Subjects

You have three paths to creating new data source query subjects in an existing model: You can choose to run the Metadata Wizard, or you can create one from the Create menu, using either the New Data Source Query Subject Wizard or going directly to the Query Subject Definition dialog. Note that a query subject definition can exist only within a namespace or folder, so select the appropriate namespace or folder within which you want to create your query subject before proceeding with any of the creation methods. This section reviews the Metadata Wizard creation method first since that should be fresh in your mind. Then the other two methods that use the Create menu are discussed, along with the differences between the data source query subjects created with the Metadata Wizard and those created by one of the Create menu methods.

> **TIP**   *A good start for organizing your relational model is to create a namespace called* Database View *that will hold all data source query subjects. Where you create model query subjects and relationships will depend on your approach as covered later in the section "Approaches to Model Organization." It is good practice to leave the naming of the data source query subjects and their query items the same as the source tables and columns when you can (aliases, an exception to that rule, are covered in the section "Aliasing"). This allows you to refer to the model and easily trace back to the source database.*

Running the Metadata Wizard Manually

The Metadata Wizard is an effective way to create a number of new data source query subjects at once, optionally with relationships among them. However, when you initially create a new model, you may not know all the tables in a source database that you will need to bring into your model. Fortunately, you can run the Metadata Wizard manually from within an existing model to add more data source query subjects based on source tables.

To invoke the Metadata Wizard, right-click a namespace or folder in your model and choose Run Metadata Wizard. Or you can highlight the desired namespace or folder and choose Actions | Run Metadata Wizard. All the data source query subjects that you create using this method will be placed into the selected namespace or folder.

From this point, the steps are the same as running the Metadata Wizard when you create a new model, which was covered at the beginning of this chapter. The only real difference will be when you reach the Generate Relationships screen, shown in Figure 15-5. One of the options in this screen is Both. This option tells the wizard to try to create relationships between the new query subjects that the wizard will create and also between those new query subjects and the query subjects that are already in the model, based on the criteria that you specify in the Generate Relationships screen. When you create a brand new model, this option is superfluous because no query subjects exist in the model. If you run the Metadata Wizard manually, chances are you already have some query subjects in the model. But the same warning about generating relationships still holds in this case: Make sure you do not create more work for yourself by letting the wizard automatically generate incorrect relationships. At most, we recommend that you generate relationships based on primary and foreign keys only.

Creating a Data Source Query Subject from the Actions Menu

When you create a query subject from the Actions | Create menu, the New Query Subject screen appears. Within this screen, shown in Figure 15-9, you can enter the name of the new query subject, and, more importantly, you can select the type of query subject you want to create: Model, Data Source, or Stored Procedure. The next screen you see will depend on your selection of the type.

NOTE   *You cannot change the type of a query subject once it is created, so make sure you select the right type for the query subject you are creating when prompted by the New Query Subject screen.*

Select the option to create a Data Source Query Subject. If you are following our convention on naming data source query subjects, you will want to name it the same as the table you are going to pull in, assuming it is a simple table.

FIGURE 15-9
New Query Subject
screen

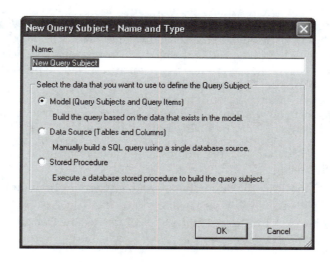

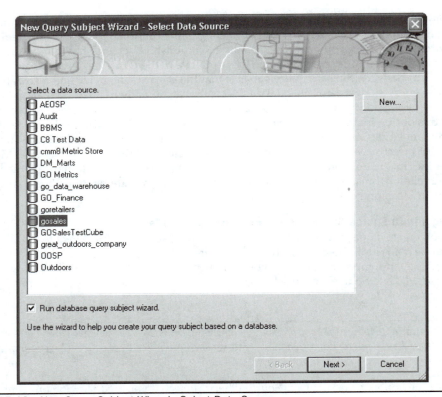

Figure 15-10   New Query Subject Wizard - Select Data Source

After you click OK, you need to select the data source. The screen in which you select the data source, shown in Figure 15-10, is similar to the screen that appears when you use the Metadata Wizard. Note that the Run Database Query Subject Wizard checkbox is checked. We will go through that wizard first, and then return to this screen to discuss clearing the checkbox and creating the new data source query subject without a wizard. Proceed by choosing the data source from which you want to pull the data and click Next, which opens the Select Columns screen.

In the Select Columns screen, shown in Figure 15-11, you can choose the tables or just the columns that you want from the Database Objects pane and put them in the Included Columns pane in one of the following, equivalent ways:

- Select the tables and/or columns, and then click the right arrow button in the middle of the dialog.

- Drag-and-drop the desired tables and/or columns from the Database Objects pane to the Included Columns pane.

- Double-click the desired tables and columns in the Database Objects pane.

To remove an included column, you can do one of the following equivalent operations:

- Select the columns you want to remove in the Included Columns pane, and then click the left arrow button in the middle of the dialog.

- Select the columns you want to remove and then press the DELETE key.

- Double-click an item in the Included Columns pane.

You can change the order that your included columns appear in the query subject by selecting an item and using the up and down arrows on the right of the dialog. Once you're finished choosing data, click Next to open the Select Joins screen.

In Figure 15-11, we selected columns from both the PRODUCT_LINE and PRODUCT_TYPE tables. Usually, we would select columns from only one table, but selecting from two related tables will better illustrate the subsequent screens. The Select Joins screen, shown in Figure 15-12 lets you define how the tables from which you selected the columns are related. If you selected columns from only one table, you would just click Next without defining any joins. However, in this case we need to relate the PRODUCT_LINE and

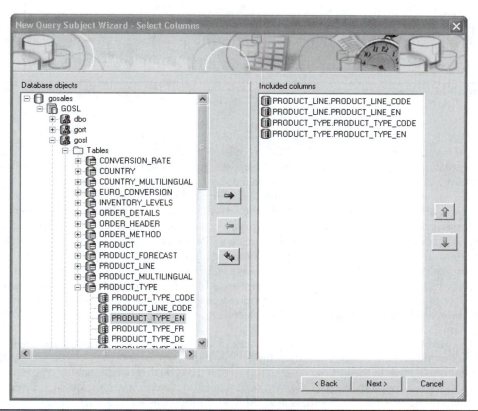

FIGURE 15-11 Select Columns screen

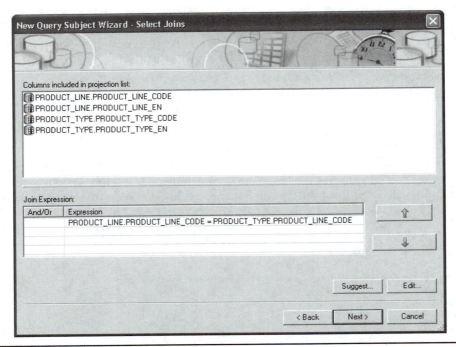

FIGURE 15-12   Select Joins screen

PRODUCT_TYPE tables. You can see in Figure 15-12 that the join expression is defined as being when the PRODUCT_LINE_CODE from each of the tables is equal. The New Query Subject Wizard suggested this join. The wizard attempts to detect which columns might relate from the source tables that are referenced.

You can manually create joins by double-clicking column names in the upper pane. This will automatically insert the columns into the Join Expression pane. You can type directly into the Expression line to complete an expression or to add a new one. Use the up and down arrows to arrange the individual expression lines and the And/Or part of the Join Expression to link each individual expression logically to create the full expression. Alternatively, you can click the Edit button to type in the entire join expression.

You can also have the wizard try to detect joins for you. If you click Suggest, you will see a list of likely joins. Select the checkbox next to each part of the expression that you want to include, as shown in Figure 15-13. The selected expressions will be included in the full Join Expression.

The purpose of the screens shown in Figures 15-12 and 15-13 is to help you write the join criteria that will be used only in the definition of the data source query subject you are creating. As mentioned, most of the data source query subjects that you create will include columns only from a single source table. In that case, you do not need to create joins in the query subject. Whether you determined your joins or just skipped through this section, click Next to continue to the Select Filters screen.

FIGURE 15-13
Select Suggested
Joins dialog

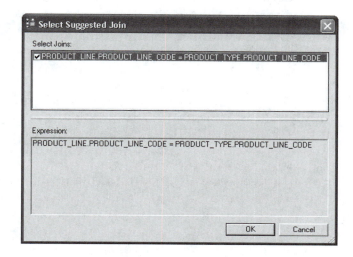

In the Filter Expression pane of the Select Filters screen, shown in Figure 15-14, you can enter a filter expression to limit the data that is provided to studio users from this query subject. For instance, if there are PRODUCT_LINE_CODES that are used only for testing that have values of zero or less, you might want to include a filter that brings in only the valid codes that are greater than zero. If you include a filter expression here, that filter will be used whenever any data is pulled from this query subject onto a report.

FIGURE 15-14
Select Filters
screen

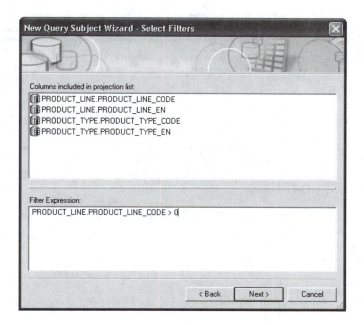

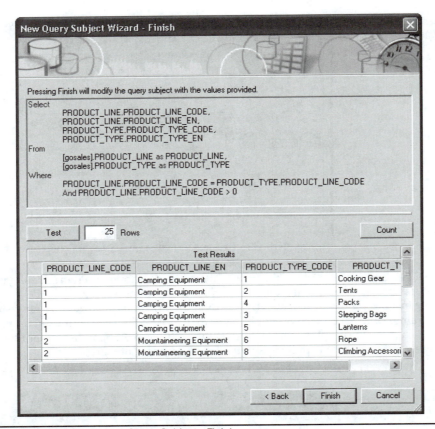

FIGURE 15-15 New Data Source Query Subject - Finish screen

The last screen of the New Data Source Query Subject Wizard is the Finish screen, shown in Figure 15-15. You can review the complete SQL expression that the wizard created for you. You can also test the query subject to see the results that are returned or find out how many records the query subject will currently return by clicking the appropriate button. Click Finish to exit the wizard, and your new query subject will be created—you can always edit it later if you need to make changes.

Creating a Data Source Query Subject Using the Definition Window

You may not be a fan of the wizard, or it may not be able to create the SQL you need. For instance, you might need to summarize some fields in the source table to get the desired query subject. In these cases, you can skip most of the wizard dialogs by clearing the Run Database Query Subject Wizard checkbox when you are asked to select the data source in the Select Data Source screen, shown in Figure 15-10. If that checkbox is cleared, when you click Next after selecting your data source, the Query Subject Definition window will open and you can enter the definition criteria directly.

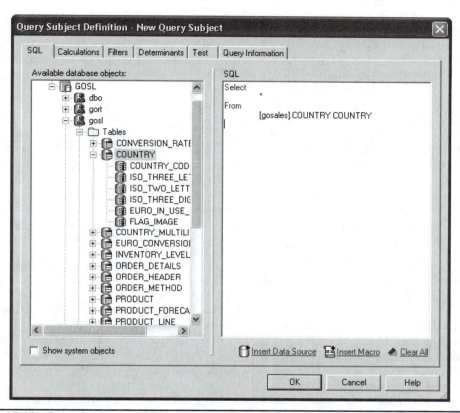

FIGURE 15-16   Query Subject Definition screen for data source query subjects

The Query Subject Definition window for data source query subjects, shown in Figure 15-16, has tabs for SQL, Calculations, Filters, Determinants, Test, and Query Information. At a minimum, you need to provide the SQL for the query subject definition on the SQL tab, so we will address that tab alone for now. We will talk about the rest of the tabs when we cover editing query subjects in the section "Completing Query Subject Definitions."

On the SQL tab, you can type in the SQL select statement that will return the result set that you need for your query subject. You can select tables and columns from the Available Database Objects pane on the left and drag them to the SQL pane on the right, but if you are doing anything more than just selecting a single table or just some columns from a single table, you will need to type in some of the SQL. It is beyond the scope of this book to get into a discussion about SQL and how to write a syntactically correct SQL statement that will return the desired result. If you need to create a query subject in this manner and you need help with the SQL, contact your database administrator.

Once you have the SQL entered, click OK to save your new data source query subject.

Which Method to Use to Create a Data Source Query Subject

You can create a data source query subject in three distinct ways: via the Metadata Wizard, the Data Source Query Subject Wizard, and the data source Query Subject Definition. So which one should you use? Chances are you will use at least two of them, and maybe all three, depending on the situation.

The Metadata Wizard is best when you want to bring in a number of tables at once. This makes it ideal to use when you create a new model, which is why it launches automatically when you do so. But it is also effective when adding one or more tables to an existing model. When you use the Metadata Wizard, the query subjects you create will have the following features by default:

- References only one table
- Named the same as the table it references
- The SQL is written as *Select * From …*, which means all columns in the table are brought in as query items.

In most cases, these are all good things. You generally want to keep the query subject references to the underlying tables simple so that Cognos 8 has the ultimate flexibility in generating the necessary query or queries when a report is run. We mentioned that it is good practice to name the data source query subjects the same as the underlying tables in most instances because it will be easier to trace back to the database, if necessary. You usually want all columns, or at least you can tolerate having them available as query items if you need them. And when the SQL is written as *Select * From …* it will be easier to update the query subject if new columns are added to the underlying table by choosing Tools | Update Object from the menu bar.

The Data Source Query Subject Wizard is a good choice if you are bringing in only one table. It is especially good if you want to bring in only selected columns from a table. That might be best if you have a source table with lots of columns that you know you will not need. Specifying only the columns you want will keep the other columns out of the model as query items, thus keeping the model a little tidier. When you use the Data Source Query Subject Wizard, the query subjects you create will have the following features by default:

- References one or more tables
- Named whatever name you give it
- Only the selected columns are brought in as query items
- The SQL specifies the column names

In reality, you will probably rarely, if ever, use the full wizard to create joins and filters in your query subject. You might, however, select your columns, and then just click Next through the rest of the wizard to create your query subject. Because the SQL specifies the columns that are brought in as query items, if you want to add columns, choosing Tools | Update Object will not add anything; you will need to edit the SQL in the definition manually to add new columns.

The Data Source Definition Dialog method is the choice if you have to generate complex SQL to get the query subject you want. By *complex*, we mean anything the other methods will not automatically do for you. You could always use this method, but for simple data source query subjects, the other methods are faster. Since you are in complete control of the query subject definition in this method, there are no default characteristics of the resulting Query subject.

Creating Model Query Subjects

A model query subject, unlike a data source query subject, does not allow you to pull tables and columns from a source database. Instead, it allows you to pull in existing query items from other query subjects. Why would you want to do that if you already have those query items in the model? Model query subjects are all about taking the model from the point of view of the data source, as reflected in the data source query subjects, and moving to the point of view of the business users. The source database layout is designed by data modelers to store the data most efficiently and effectively, adhering to the conventions of the database system. It is not necessarily (and not usually) designed to be friendly in organization and naming to the business user. You want the model that you will publish and the reports based on that model to be business-user friendly, with business names for the query items, organized as business entities such as products and customers. That is one of the top reasons you create a model query subject. You can pull query items from different data source query subjects, rename them to reflect the business terms, and organize them into business entities. You also might need to create model query subjects to solve issues such as those covered later in the section "Modeling Challenges."

NOTE *Depending on your approach to organizing your model, you might create model query subjects to present a business view after you create your relationships between your data source query subjects. Because much of the creation and definition of creating query subjects of any type is the same, it makes sense to address how to create a model query subject before covering relationships.*

As with creating data source query subjects, creating the model query subject definition starts from the Project Viewer pane by right-clicking the namespace or folder into which the query subject will be placed to reveal a context menu. Alternatively, you could choose Actions | Create. Once again, either will present the New Query Subject dialog that you saw in Figure 15-9. You can enter the name you want for the new query subject in this dialog. Choose to create a Model query subject then click Next, and you will proceed to the Query Subject Definition screen, shown in Figure 15-17. This is the same screen you will see if you later choose to edit the definition of the query subject, so creating and maintaining a model query subject are really the same process. Note that this screen has tabs for the Query Subject Definition, Filters, Determinants, Test, and Query Information.

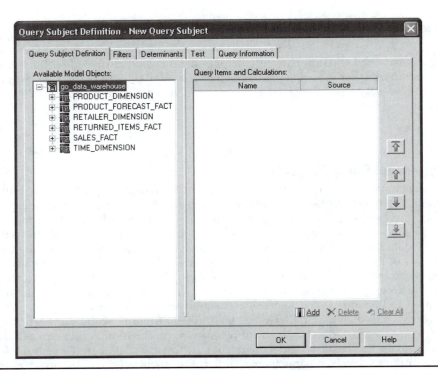

FIGURE 15-17 Query Subject Definition screen for model query subjects

The Query Subject Definition

For now, we will address only the Query Subject Definition tab in discussing the creation of a new model query subject. This tab allows you to select query items that exist in the model and bring them into this query subject. Furthermore, you can create calculations to create new query items that do not exist physically in the data source. These calculations can be created by applying operators and functions to one or more other query items or constants.

When viewing the Query Subject Definition tab, you can add Query items to the Query Items And Calculations pane in any of the following ways:

- Double-click the desired query items in the Available Model Objects pane on the left.

- Drag-and-drop the item from the Available Model Objects pane to the Query Items And Calculations pane.

- Click the Add link at the bottom right of the screen, as shown in Figure 15-18, and edit the definition in the Calculation Definition screen (Figure 15-19).

All these are equivalent operations if you are creating a simple reference to a single query item that is already in the model. Even the double-click and drag-and-drop methods create a calculation. Those methods assume the calculation is the simple reference and that

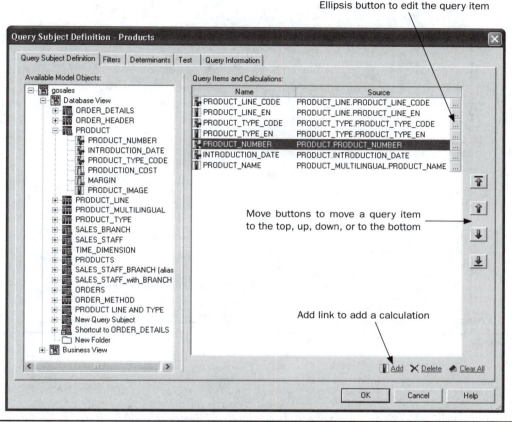

FIGURE 15-18   Model Query Subject Definition screen showing query items

the name of the referenced query item is a good default name for this new query item. If you are creating a calculation that is more complex than a simple reference, you will need to do so by clicking the Add link and using the Calculation Definition screen.

Regardless of which method you start with, you can always edit the calculation for the query item by clicking the ellipsis button to the right of the item in the Query Items And Calculation pane, as shown in Figure 15-18. Even if you started with a simple reference to a single query item and now need to complicate the calculation, you can do so in this manner. If you just want to rename the query item, do not edit the definition; it is easier to change the name property, which is covered in the section "Setting Properties" later in this chapter.

When you are editing the query item in the Calculation Definition screen, as shown in Figure 15-19, note that the Available Components pane has three tabs: Model, Functions, and Parameters. The Model tab lets you select existing query items from the model. Note that when they are dragged into the definition, they are referenced by a fully qualified name, which consists of the namespace name, the query subject name, and the query item name.

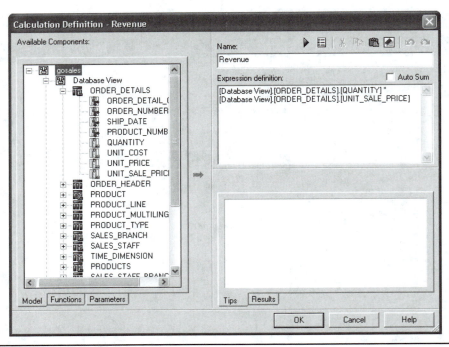

FIGURE 15-19 Calculation Definition screen

TIP *You need to understand the naming convention for references to the query items. Knowing the fully qualified name of any query item referenced in any calculation can ultimately help you understand which fields in the underlying database are being referenced. Consider the following reference: [go_data_warehouse].[RETAILER_DIMENSION].[RETAILER_NAME] This tells us that we are referring to the RETAILER_NAME query item in the RETAILER_ DIMENSION query subject in the go_data_warehouse namespace in the model. If we click that item in the Project Viewer and look at its properties, we will be able to verify the name of the database field to which it refers. If you followed the convention of keeping the data source query items and subjects named the same as in the source database, the database field name would be the same as the name of the data source query item.*

The Functions tab of the Calculation Definition screen lets you select operators and functions to modify your calculation value. The available functions are too numerous to list here, and the combinations are endless. To learn more about specific functions, you can refer to the product documentation or look at the Tips tab in the calculation definition when you select a function. Suffice it to say, a number of operators and functions are available for each of the basic data types (text, numeric, and date).

The Parameters tab lets you reference parameter maps, session parameters, and macros. Those are advanced topics, however, and we are still trying to get through the basics, so we will address those concepts in the "Macros" section in Chapter 16.

To create the calculation from the available components, you can double-click an object to move it into the calculation definition, or you can drag-and-drop it into the definition. Alternatively, you can just type your calculation in the Expression Definition pane.

TIP *While you can type the entire definition into a calculation rather than dragging in components, typing it in would require that you exactly and correctly type the fully qualified references to query items in the model, and that you correctly type the function, parameter, and macro references. It is a better practice to drag those parts of the definition from the available components rather than typing them in. Plus, dragging functions over also gives you the arguments of the function so that you can properly substitute for them to get the calling sequence correct. As for constants and simple logical or mathematical operators, it is often easier and faster just to type those in.*

We still need to talk about the other tabs in the Query Subject Definition screen: Filters, Determinants, Test, and Query Information. However, because those tabs are the same on both model query subjects and data source query subjects, we will cover them shortly in the section "Completing Query Subjects Definitions," after we look at the final query subject type.

Creating Stored Procedure Query Subjects

In some source systems, you need to employ stored procedures to apply the proper business logic to get the desired result set. Situations in which stored procedures are necessary are not covered here. Instead, this discussion will show how to pull data from a stored procedure into Cognos 8. It is likely that any store procedure you need to get the data you seek will already exist in your source database. All you need to know now is how to get the stored procedure into your model.

Any stored procedure you call in a stored procedure query subject must return a result set similar to a table or query, and the result returned must be consistent. That is, if the procedure can optionally return different result sets, then all possible result sets must have the same number and data type of the columns, and the column names must be the same. Framework Manager is going to treat the result of the stored procedure like a table, so the results must be consistent and predictable. If your stored procedure returns multiple result sets, Cognos 8 will take only the first one. If your procedure does not return results in table format, or if it can't return any results, Framework Manager will display errors when you try to test the query subject. Stored procedures that return scalar values cannot be used as a Cognos 8 query subject. And while you can pass parameter values into a stored procedure, return parameters from a stored procedure are not supported. You can, however, use this definition process to have a stored procedure act as a user-defined function that can be made accessible when creating a calculation, which will be mentioned briefly in the section "Turning a Stored Procedure Query Subject into a Function," later in the chapter.

TIP *You can model a stored procedure that modifies data in the source database. Data modification stored procedure query subjects can only be used by Cognos Event Studio and require that the database signon have write permission.*

As with creating data source and model query subjects, creating the stored procedure query subject definition starts with right-clicking the Project Viewer pane on the namespace or folder into which the query subject will be placed to open a context menu of options.

Alternatively, you could choose Actions | Create. Once again, doing either will present the New Query Subject dialog that you saw in Figure 15-9. Note that because stored procedure query subjects are accessing source data, they should be placed in the same namespace as your data source query subjects.

To create a stored procedure query subject, select Stored Procedure Query Subject from the New Query Subject dialog, and then click Next to open the Select Data Source dialog. Select the source database in which your stored procedure is defined and then click Next to display the Stored Procedure dialog. From this dialog, you need to navigate through the contents of your database to locate the stored procedure you want, select the procedure, and then click Next to open the Query Subject Definition dialog for stored procedures, shown in Figure 15-20.

The Query Subject Definition dialog for stored procedures offers a few options for configuring how the stored procedure should be called. Ellipsis buttons appear to the right of the stored procedure name, the data source, and the parameters. Clicking the ellipsis button next to any of these will allow you to change its value. You might want to use a macro to alter the stored procedure or data source name at runtime, allowing you to dynamically change the stored procedure you are calling based on session information. If you are not familiar with macros, don't panic; they are covered in Chapter 16. For the parameters, you can edit the value to pass in a particular value or use a macro, possibly to pass in a session parameter such as a language or to prompt the end user to provide a value.

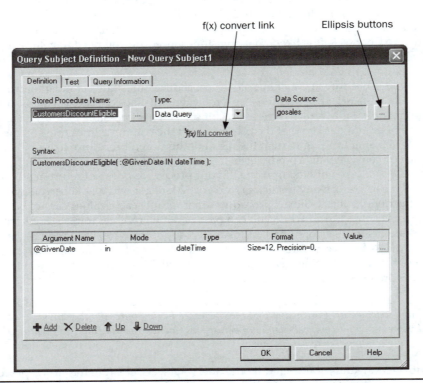

FIGURE 15-20   Query Subject Definition dialog for stored procedure query subjects

You can use the Type drop-down menu to select the type. This should usually be set to the default of Data Query, but if you are going to use the stored procedure query subject in Event Studio, you may need to change this setting to Data Modification. Refer to help for a more in-depth explanation of this setting.

Turning a Stored Procedure Query Subject into a Function

You can turn a stored procedure query subject definition into a function that can be called from a calculation. This can be handy if you have a stored procedure that encapsulates some complex business logic to return a scalar value or output parameter. To make that procedure available to you in the creation of calculations, click the f(x) convert link, which brings up the dialog shown in Figure 15-21. From this dialog, you can select the output parameter that should be used as the return value or specify that the scalar return value of the stored procedure be used as the return value for your function. You can optionally choose to delete the original stored procedure query subject definition, which you might want to do, because in this case it cannot be used as a query subject that returns a data result set.

If you want to see or delete the new function definition, go to the Search tab of the Tools pane and set the Class Type to Function. When the search reveals the function you created, you will be able to see information on it, or you can right-click it in the search results and choose Delete to get rid of it. Just make sure it is not referenced in any calculations before you delete it.

As mentioned, it is likely that all of the stored procedures that you need to access will probably already exist in your source database. If they do not, but you determine that a stored procedure is necessary in your application, you should contact your DBA to request a stored procedure that will conform to your needs.

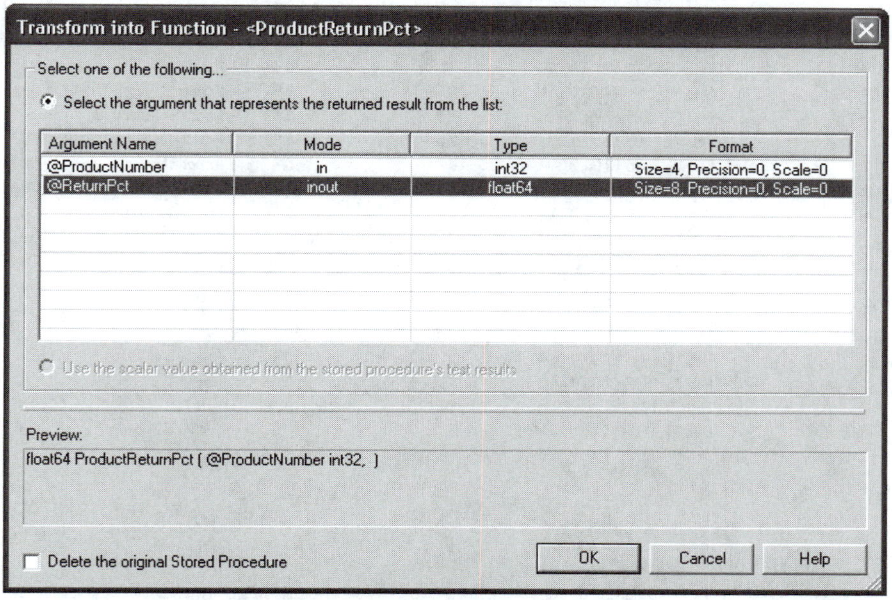

FIGURE 15-21   Transforming a stored procedure query subject to a function

Completing Query Subjects Definitions

Once you have created the type of query subject that you need, you can work with it by setting filters and determinants, by testing it to see your results, or by looking at query information. Let's start by looking at testing the query subject since that is something you should do right after creating one to make sure it works and returns the desired results.

Testing Query Subjects

Open a query subject definition by going to the Project Viewer tree and double-clicking the query subject you want to edit, or by right-clicking it and selecting Edit Definition. On the Test tab of the Query Subject Definition dialog, you have the option of running the query to return a sampling of rows so that you can verify the results. The number of rows returned by the test is configurable by accessing the Options link, which is addressed shortly. You can also run a related query to return the count of the total number of rows that the query will return given the current data in the database. The links for running either test and for accessing the options are at the bottom right of the Results pane, which shows the results of the test, as shown in Figure 15-22. The Test tab is available on the Query Subject Definition dialog for all three query subject types.

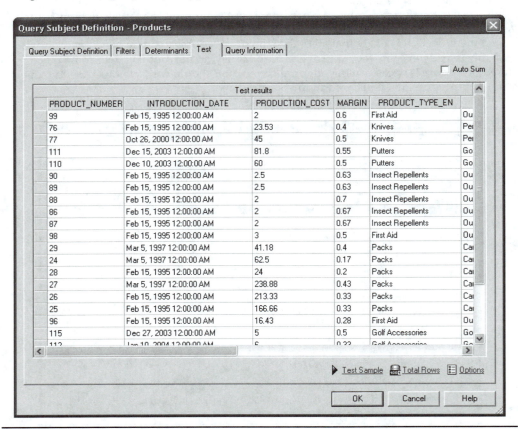

FIGURE 15-22   Testing a query subject

Getting Query Information

On the Query Information tab of the Query Subject Definition dialog, click the Test Sample link to return both the Cognos SQL and the native SQL that Cognos 8 will generate on your behalf when executing the query subject. If you get the query information for a data source query subject whose SQL is of the form *Select * From...*, you will notice that the SQL returned by the query information does not say *Select * ...*, but instead selects the specific columns. What is happening here is that Framework Manager sees the *Select * ...* notation when the query subject is created and queries the database to get the metadata for all the available columns. Having done that, Framework Manager stores the specific column names and types in the model. This helps Cognos generate efficient SQL at the time a report is run by including only the necessary columns, if possible. More on this topic in the next section, "Options for the Query and for Testing." Because the metadata for the columns is stored in the model, if columns are added to a table in the source database, you must select the related data source query subject and choose Tools | Update Object to tell Framework Manager to query the database again for the updated metadata to be able to see the new columns.

A convenient link is located in the upper-right corner of the Query Information tab to allow you to print the SQL if you need to do so to analyze the generated SQL. The Query Information tab is available on the Query Subject Definition dialog of all three query subject types.

NOTE *The Query Information tab shows both Cognos and native SQL. Two different SQL statements appear because Cognos 8 will first turn a query into Cognos SQL, and then it will determine what it can send to the source database server, which becomes the native SQL. You should be able to copy the native SQL out of the Query Information and use it as a query directly against your source database. The Cognos SQL will differ in some qualification naming, at least, and might include additional directives for things that cannot be passed to the data source, such as functions that may be used in calculations that are not available in the source database. Comparing the Cognos SQL to the native SQL can sometimes help you determine why a query might be running slowly.*

Options for the Query and for Testing

Both the Test tab and the Query Information tab display an Options link at the bottom-right corner. If you click the Options link, you will see the dialog shown in Figure 15-23.

On the Test Settings tab, you can change the number of rows you want to receive when you test your query subject. A number of other settings affect the test results, including setting session parameters, design mode filters, security filters, and prompt values. Those topics are addressed in the next section, "Putting Filters on Your Query Subject," and in Chapter 16.

On the SQL Settings tab, you can choose two options: the SQL Type and whether to Generate The SQL As A View Or Minimized.

The SQL Type defaults to Cognos SQL, which is a more standard version of SQL. You will usually want to leave this setting on Cognos SQL. You will absolutely need to leave it on Cognos SQL if you ever want to re-point your model from one database type, say Oracle, to another, say IBM DB2. One of your other options is native SQL, which you can use if you

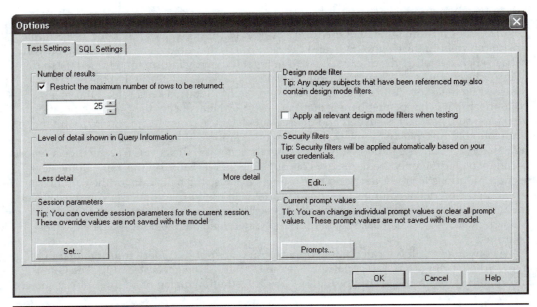

Figure 15-23   Query information and test options

need to write some SQL specific to your database type to get your desired result, though with two caveats: Cognos is still likely to modify it before passing it to the database, which may increase efficiency; and restrictions mean that not every Select statement valid in your source database can be set to native SQL. Your other option is Pass-Through SQL, which will be sent directly to the database as is, with no possibility of Cognos trying to optimize it, but you can write any SQL valid in your source database.

Our advice is to leave the SQL Type set at Cognos SQL unless you have a compelling reason to write database-specific SQL that is not valid in Cognos SQL. If that is the case, try Native. If that fails, then you probably have a bad SQL statement, so you might want to try running it through your source database tools outside the Cognos environment to show that it is not a Cognos problem. Try Pass-Through only as a last resort.

As for the Generate setting, your options are Minimized, which is the default, and As View. Leave this set to the default value of Minimized unless you have a compelling reason to change it. Minimized tells Cognos to pull into the final query only the fields that are needed to satisfy the report. So even if you have a data source query subject for the Product table written as `Select * From PRODUCTS`, if you report only on the PRODUCT_NAME, then the SQL passed to the database will be `Select PRODUCT_NAME From PRODUCT` rather than less efficiently selecting all columns. The Minimized setting will *always* be at least as efficient as, and usually *more* efficient than, running As View.

You can choose the As View setting in those limited cases where executing the query as a view would return the proper set of resulting rows, whereas trying to run it Minimized might return extra rows that you do not want. For instance, if a query subject combines columns from the PRODUCT_TYPE table and the PRODUCT table, and you have a new product type of Camper but no camper products have yet been introduced or assigned to it, you might not want to see *Camper* listed in your results. If you run a report to list the PRODUCT_TYPES, minimized SQL will return *Camper* with all of the other types because the SQL will be minimized to be `Select PRODUCT_TYPE from PRODUCT _TYPES`. However, if you run the same report with the query subject set to As View, the PRODUCT table will be included in the resulting SQL, which means the Camper product type will be dropped because there are no matching products of that type. It's a rare occasion, if ever, that you need to do this, which is why you should leave the SQL set at Minimized in most cases.

CAUTION *If you try to put too much logic directly into your SQL, such as calculated columns and WHERE clauses, the query subject may execute as a view,* regardless *of your Generate setting. Cognos will not likely be able to break down what you have hard-coded in the SQL to be able to minimize it. The result is that your query subjects might execute inefficiently and your reports might run more slowly. So, if your SQL coding skills are good, you might think that it is faster for you to type in the SQL you need, but you are probably creating a model that will produce sluggish reports. Often, when this happens, the modeler blames Cognos 8 for running slowly, but it is the modeler that limited the ability of the tool to optimize the report queries. Instead, you should use the constructs available to you in the query subject definition, such as the Calculation tab and the Filters tab discussed in the next sections, or model calculations, which are covered in the section "More Objects for Report Writers."*

Putting Filters on Your Query Subject

When you define a query subject, you sometimes need to restrict the rows that are returned by filtering out the unwanted stuff. You do that by creating one or more embedded filters for your query subject on the Filters tab of the Query Subject Definition dialog. Examples of filters you might need to include are the following: excluding inactive customers in a marketing model, limiting sales data to the prior five years to exclude poor data or data that is too old to be useful, or restricting the results based on which user runs the report. That last reason, security, is just a teaser. You will want to add a filter to do that, but we address data security in Chapter 16.

Selecting the Filters tab, which is available on data source and model query subjects, will show you the list of filters applied to the query subject, as show in Figure 15-24. Note that you can have multiple filters on a query subject. While you could just write one big filter with all of the clauses combined with AND statements, it is a better practice to write individual filters so you can easily change or delete them.

You can add a filter in one of two ways: You can drag-and-drop a model filter if one exists in the model. Creating stand-alone model filters is discussed in the section "Creating Filters for Users" a bit later; for now, just know that you can create filter criteria for users to drag-and-drop into their reports. You can use a model filter in an embedded query subject filter if the criteria meet your requirements. If so, drag the filter from the Available Model Filters pane on the left to the Filters pane on the right.

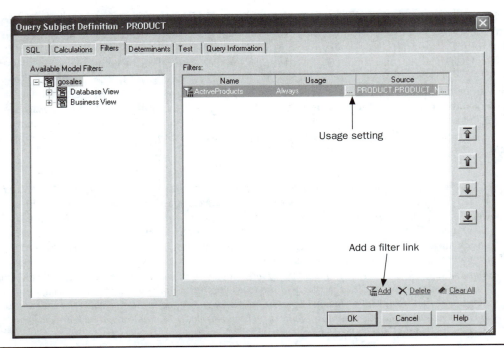

FIGURE 15-24 Filters tab of the Query Subject Definition dialog

The other, more usual method of creating an embedded query subject filter is to click the Add link at the bottom-right of the Filters tab. That will open the Filter Definition dialog, in which you can perform the following steps:

1. Name the filter. Make it a meaningful name, such as *Security Filter* or *Active Customers*.

2. Create the expression by dragging in any available query items from the Model tab of the Available Components pane on the left, along with any functions from the Functions tab, and parameters and macro functions from the Parameters tab. (Parameters and macros are discussed in Chapter 16.) Note that any columns you want to reference in the filter must already exist as query items in the model.

3. Click OK to complete the filter and return to the Filters tab. If you have an error in your filter, you will see a jagged red underline in the expression definition at or near where the problem is, and you will see an error dialog if you try to save the erroneous filter.

NOTE *Your filter criteria should not normally contain IF-THEN-ELSE logic. Modelers sometimes think of a filter as an IF condition, but the filter should only be the conditional test, such as [PRODUCT_NUMBER] > 1000 or [STATUS_FLAG] = 'A'. Any rows for which the condition or conditions are true are returned in the query subject.*

Once you return to the Filters tab, you can also set the usage for the filter. The default value for Usage is Always, which means that the filter criteria are always included when the query subject is executed. That makes sense most of the time. You would always want a security filter to be in use, or one that eliminates unwanted data. But there are two other Usage settings. The first is Optional, which only applies to filters with prompts. A *prompt* is a filter with a test value consisting of a prompt variable surrounded by question marks, like this:

```
? Start Date ?
```

A prompt in a filter will ask the user that runs the report to supply a value to be used in the filter criteria. A prompt can be used in a filter with Usage set to Always, but if the Usage is set to Optional, then the user can supply a value for the filter or the user can choose not to supply a value, in which case the filter will not be applied. While you can add a prompt filter in your query subject, remember that the report user will be prompted every time he or she runs a report that uses any item from that query subject. That is why we rarely put the prompt filter into the query subject. If necessary in a particular report, a prompt filter can be added in Report Studio, as was covered earlier in this book.

The third filter usage setting is Design Mode Only. Design mode filters can be used when testing a query subject by applying them on the Test Setting tab of the Options dialog, discussed earlier in this chapter. Also, the design mode filter can be employed in Query Studio or Report Studio to get only a test sampling of the results.

TIP   *If a query subject will return lots of rows and potentially be slow to respond, you can help your Query Studio and Report Studio users more rapidly develop their queries by applying a design mode filter. Determine the criteria that will limit the results and speed up the query, and put those criteria in your design mode filter. If the user accesses a query subject with a design mode filter, he or she can choose the Run With Limited Data option, which will activate the design mode filters. If there are no design mode filters, running the query or report with limited data will have the same effect as running it with all data.*

Setting Determinants

Before we get into how to set determinants on the Determinant tab of the Query Subject Definition dialog, available on data source and model query subjects, we need to explain what determinants do. The main purpose of determinants in a query subject is to specify the granularity at which other related query subjects might be joined. We will cover how to create relationships in the next section, but if you are creating query subjects in Framework Manager, you probably already understand enough about how tables are joined in a database query to understand determinants.

When you join from one table to another with a relationship in Cognos 8, you match one or more columns in one query subject with one or more columns in another. Sometimes, though, the data in one of the joined tables references a column that is not at the lowest level of granularity and can have the same value repeated. This would cause the joined table to match the same row to multiple rows, causing data to be over-counted.

The best way to illustrate this situation is by example, which will help to point out the necessity and effect of determinants. Say we have sales of products down to the product level, but we forecast only to the product type level. For instance, within our Golf Equipment product line, we might have two putters with sales in January: the Blue Steel Putter with $300 in sales and the Course Pro Putter with $200 in sales. Further, we might have a forecast during that same time period of $400 total for all putter sales. If our product query subject has all of our individual putters, then in the PRODUCT_TYPE column we will see the PRODUCT_TYPE of Putter for each putter in the PRODUCT table. In our example we have only the two putters to keep it simple (see the following tables). If we model the sales by joining the SALES table to the PRODUCT table, then we will have the sales of the Blue Steel Putter joined to the single row in the PRODUCT table that describes the Blue Steel Putter, and we will have each sales transaction for the Course Pro Putter joined to the single row in the PRODUCT table for that putter. However, since our forecast is for product types, if we joined our forecast table to the PRODUCT table by PRODUCT_TYPE, then our one row of forecast will be joined to two rows in the PRODUCT table because we have two items that are both classified as putters.

PRODUCTS Table

PRODUCT_LINE	PRODUCT_TYPE	PRODUCT
Golf Equipment	Putters	Blue Steel Putter
Golf Equipment	Putters	Course Pro Putter
Golf Equipment	Drivers	Blue Steel Max
Camping Equipment	Tents	Star Gazer
…	…	…

PRODUCT_FORECAST Table

PRODUCT_TYPE	DATE	FORECAST_SALES
Putters	January 2008	$400
Tents	January 2008	$2000
…	…	…

PRODUCT_SALES Table

PRODUCT	DATE	SALES
Blue Steel Putter	January 2008	$300
Course Pro Putter	January 2008	$200
	January 2008	$700
…	…	…

Results of Joining PRODUCT_FORECAST to PRODUCTS Table by PRODUCT_TYPE Without Correct Determinants

PRODUCT_LINE	PRODUCT_TYPE	FORECAST_SALES
Golf Equipment	Putters	$400
Golf Equipment	Putters	$400

The resulting query, if we were to report on the forecast, would over-count the forecast amount, giving us an incorrect forecast value, as shown in the preceding table. In other words, our $400 forecast for Putters would be joined to both the Blue Steel Putter row and the Course Pro Putter row in the PRODUCT table, and we would end up with $800 in total forecast for putters, which is incorrect.

Determinants let us properly reflect the situation in the model to avoid over-counting. In the definition of our product query subject, we need to specify that we have a *Unique determinant* for PRODUCT because each product is in the table only once. We also need to specify a *Group By determinant* for PRODUCT_TYPE. Specifying a determinant as Group By tells Cognos 8 that we first need to group the query subject by the determinant key—in this case the PRODUCT_TYPE column—before we join to tables that are joined on that column. In our example, we would group the PRODUCTS table by the PRODUCT_TYPE, ignoring the PRODUCT itself because we do not need it in our join to the forecast table. This would give us only one row that says Putters. Now, as shown in the next table, when we join to the forecast table by the PRODUCT_TYPE, only one row is returned, giving us the correct forecast of $400 for all putters.

Products Grouped by PRODUCT_TYPE

PRODUCT_LINE	PRODUCT_TYPE
Golf Equipment	Putters
Golf Equipment	Drivers
Camping Equipment	Tents

Correct Results of FORECAST Joined to the Grouped PRODUCTS

PRODUCT_LINE	PRODUCT_TYPE	FORECAST_SALES
Golf Equipment	Putters	$400
...	...	...

To set the determinants on the Determinants tab of the Query Subject Definition dialog, as shown in Figure 15-25, click the Add link under the Determinants pane. This will put a new determinant in the list with the default name of *New Determinant*. Right-click the name and choose Rename to give the determinant a more meaningful name. What you name the determinant is not important to the model, but you should name it something appropriate, such as Product Type in this example, to make it easy to understand what the determinant does. Next, select the appropriate checkbox to declare whether the determinant is Uniquely Identified or a Group By.

NOTE *You should always have a Uniquely Identified determinant set at the lowest level of granularity of the data in your table (the level of the primary key) if you need to add Group By determinants. If you set only a Group By determinant without any specified as Uniquely Identified, you will likely receive errors. Furthermore, you should have one and only one determinant specified as Uniquely Identified, with all others set to Group By. Do not create a determinant without properly setting either the Uniquely Identified or Group By setting, and do not create determinants with both settings.*

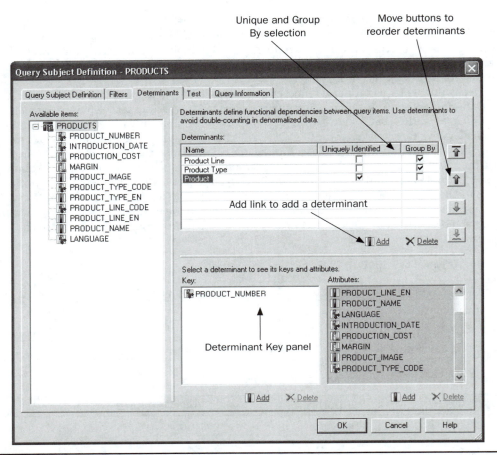

Unique and Group By selection

Move buttons to reorder determinants

Add link to add a determinant

Determinant Key panel

FIGURE 15-25   The Determinant tab of the Query Subject dialog

You will need to specify the key that drives your determinant. The query item or items on which you will define relationships using this determinant must be specified in the Key pane. With determinants selected in the Determinants pane, you can drag-and-drop them from the Available Items pane or highlight them in Available Items and click the Add link under the Key pane.

Next, you should specify any attributes that are associated with the key value. For instance, if you have a Group By determinant for Product Type with PRODUCT_TYPE_KEY as the Key value, you will want to put the PRODUCT_TYPE_NAME or any other query items associated specifically with the Product Type into the Attributes pane. Like adding the Key, you add Attributes by selecting the Determinant, then using drag-and-drop or the Add link to put the query items in the Attributes panel. For your Uniquely Identified Determinant, you will not need to set Attributes because all query items in the query subject are considered Attributes of the Unique Determinant, so all of them are listed and you cannot remove them.

Finally, you should order your determinants using the arrow buttons to the right of the Determinants pane. Determinants are not really hierarchical in nature. You can create separate determinants that are mutually exclusive and not hierarchical, such as one for Color and one for Introduction Year on your Products table, if that makes sense. But often the determinants do reflect a hierarchy, such as Product Line, Product Type, and Product. If the determinants reflect a hierarchy, put them in that order, top to bottom, to make them easy to understand, and *always* put your Uniquely Identified determinant at the bottom of the list. If the determinants are not hierarchical, order still might be important because the determinants are evaluated top to bottom until the attribute or key used in the query is found.

Determinants play other roles in your query subject when its items are grouped or aggregated for a key or attribute that is repeated. For instance, if you had a Product Type introduction date and you wanted to count the number of Product Types introduced by year, you would not want to count each product of that Product Type, only the Product Type itself. But by far, the most important reason to set determinants is for joining data at different granularities. Determinants can be set on data source and model query subjects, but not on stored procedure query subjects.

The Calculations Tab

The Calculations tab of the Query Subject Definition dialog is specific to the data source query subject because, if you recall, *all* query items in the model query subject are really calculations that are created from the Query Subject Definition tab, so there is no need for a separate tab to create calculations as there is for a data source query subject.

The Calculations tab allows you to create calculations for the data source query subject via the same Calculation Definition dialog you saw for the model query subject back in Figure 15-19. Since it is the same dialog, the method of creating the calculation is the same: drag-and-drop or double-click items from the Available Components on the Model, Functions, or Parameters tab, or type in your calculation. You can, of course, code a calculation in the SQL for the data source query subject definition, but that means you are now working somewhat outside the Framework Manager tool, which is not a practice we recommend for reasons of efficiency, maintainability, and potentially portability.

Creating Query Item Folders to Organize Query Subject Contents

We already looked at creating folders to organize your query subjects. It is also helpful at times to be able to organize the content within a query subject. While the query subject itself acts kind of like a folder, if it contains a lot of query items, it can be advantageous to organize them further. A query item folder will help you do that.

To create a query item folder, right-click a query subject in the Project Viewer tree and choose Create | Query Item Folder from the context menu, or select the query subject and choose Actions | Create | Query Item Folder. Much as in Microsoft Windows Explorer, the query item folder will be created and you will immediately have the opportunity to rename it. To organize the contents, simply drag-and-drop the items you want from the query subject to the appropriate query item folder. You can rearrange the query items in folders later without impacting existing reports that reference the query items, so organizing your model to the benefit of your users can be a continual improvement process.

TIP *Frequently, in large databases, a number of columns are not used often by report writers, but might be used on occasion. A handy way to keep these columns available as query items without cluttering your model is to create a query item folder named* Rarely Used *within each of your query subjects that warrants it. You can then move those rarely used query items to this folder, thus getting them out of the way while still making them available for reporting if necessary.*

Creating Relationships

You wouldn't have much of a relational model without relationships. A *relationship* in Cognos 8 defines how two query subjects relate, or refer, to each other. For instance, say you have a Product query subject that has a row for each product and includes the product number and the product name. Suppose also that you have an Order Details query subject that contains line items for sales orders, and each line refers to the ordered product by the product number, along with the quantity ordered and the amount of the sale. If you want a report that lists the product names and the quantities ordered, you will need to pull the product name from the Product query subject and the quantity ordered from the Order Details query subject. The way you tell Cognos 8 how orders relate to products is by defining a relationship between the product numbers in each of the query subjects, as shown in the following illustration. Those of you who understand SQL as it relates to querying will recognize a relationship as the join criteria between the underlying tables.

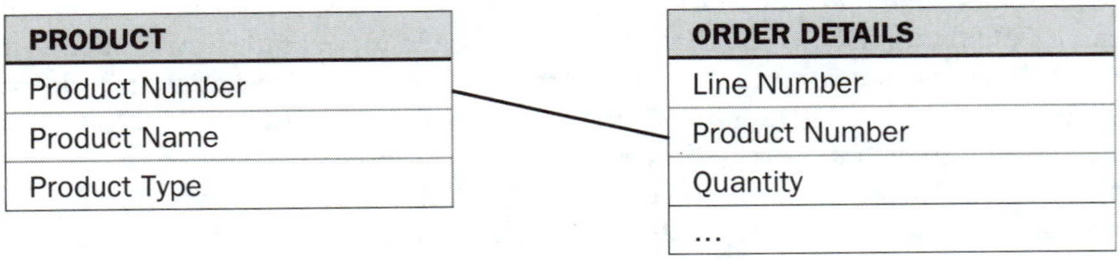

PRODUCT		ORDER DETAILS
Product Number		Line Number
Product Name		Product Number
Product Type		Quantity
		...

A component of the relationship is the *cardinality*, which tells the relationship how many rows from one of the query subjects defined in the relationship are expected to match a row in the query subject on the other side of the relationship. In our example, we would want to tell the model that many order details can refer to the same product.

Let's look at how you create relationships in Cognos 8. Relationships can be created in the same manner used to create other objects covered so far: by right-clicking an object in the Project Viewer tree—in this case a namespace, folder, or query subject—and choosing Create | Relationship from the context menu; or, by selecting the object and choosing Actions | Create | Relationship. Either way will bring up the Relationship Definition dialog. But there are more efficient ways to create relationships. You can CTRL-click to select the two query items that will define the relationship between the two query subjects. Then you can right-click and choose Create Relationship from the context menu, which will bring up the Relationship Definition dialog shown in Figure 15-27.

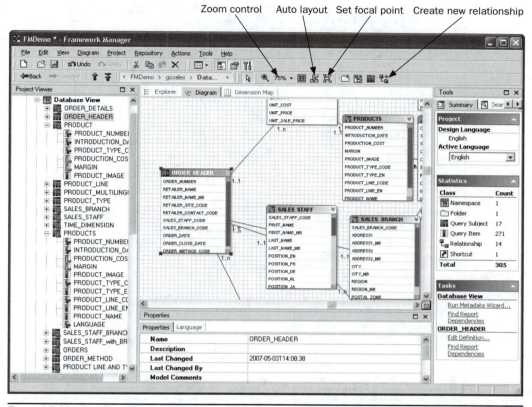

FIGURE 15-26   The Diagram toolbar with the relationship button on the right

Another efficient way to create relationships is to use the Diagram tab of the Project window. With the Diagram tab selected, you will notice a set of buttons, shown in Figure 15-26, that appear in the toolbar. The rightmost button is used for defining relationships in the diagram. You can also use this toolbar to create folders, namespaces, and query subjects, but the relative convenience of the buttons for those objects is nowhere near that of the relationship button.

Clicking the relationship button will change the cursor to indicate that it is ready to create a relationship. You can then drag-and-drop from one query subject to another in the diagram to establish the relationship. Doing so will also bring up the Relationship Definition dialog shown in Figure 15-27.

Because the relationship was created using one of the efficient methods, Framework Manager created the link between the selected query items and gave a useful default name, using the names of the two query subjects separated by the string <--> to signify the relationship between them. You can rename it if you wish, but you should stick with the names and the naming convention that these creation methods produce.

The components of the relationship are the two referenced query subjects, the link or links shown between the query subjects, the query items referenced by each link, and the

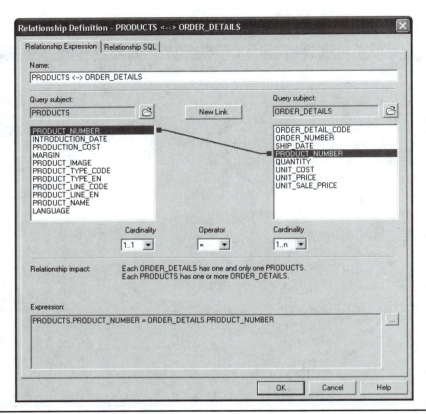

FIGURE 15-27   Relationship Definition dialog

operator that defines how the query items in a link are compared. All of those components are taken together to produce the expression shown at the bottom of the dialog. One more component of the relationship, the cardinality, controls the relationship impact, shown above the expression.

You can set or change anything on this dialog. You can change the referenced query subjects by clicking the folder button to the right of the query subject name. You can change a query item referenced in the link by clicking another query item under the appropriate query subject. You can change the operator or the cardinality using the drop-down boxes. You can even add a new link or edit the expression directly. Following are some guidelines for when you would need to do any of these things.

Relationship Links

When you create a relationship and work in the Relationship Definition dialog, you should check that the query subjects and query items on each side of the link are correct. If you need to change the referenced query item, simply click the correct query item and the link will change accordingly.

The operator tells the relationship how to compare the two query items. In nearly all cases, as in our simple example of product numbers in the product and order details query subjects, the link should be made when the value of the query items are the same; thus the default equals operator (=) will be correct. You will rarely need to change it. However, in some situations, you may need a different operator. For instance, you might need a link where the condition says that a date query item in a record in one query subject matches all of the records in another query subject with a date query item that has an earlier date. In this case, you would change the operator to less than (<).

Sometimes you need a compound link to establish the correct relationship. For instance, in an enterprise resource planning (ERP) system that covers multiple organizations, the condition on which you join the query subjects might be where both the product number and the organization code match. In this case, you would have one link match the product numbers, and you would need to add another link to accommodate the organization code. To do so, click the New Link button between the Query Subject areas. This will add a link, for which you can set the query items. Note that the query items and the operator can be set only for one link at a time. The selected link appears as a bold, blue line. To select and work with a different link, just click the link (the line) and then you will be able to modify it.

As you add or change links, you will notice the expression at the bottom of the dialog changing. You could edit the expression directly by clicking the ellipsis button to the right of the expression, but most everything you need to do to create a set of valid links can be done by adding links, changing operators, or adding calculations to the query subject before establishing the relationship. We recommend doing that rather than editing the expression if at all possible.

Cardinality

The cardinality setting tells the model what to expect in terms of matching records from the two query subjects. A cardinality setting is associated with each side of the relationship. Cardinality can be expressed as one of the following:

- **1..1**   One and only one record from this side of the relationship
- **1..n**   One or more records from this side of the relationship
- **0..1**   Zero or at most one record from this side of the relationship
- **0..n**   Zero or more records from this side of the relationship

Let's look at the 1..1 and 1..n settings first. In relational database terminology, we often refer to *one-to-one* and *many-to-one* relationships. In a one-to-one relationship, each record in one table has one and only one matching record in the other. That is modeled with a cardinality of 1..1 on both sides of the relationship.

More prevalent are many-to-one relationships, in which many records in one table refer to the same record in the other table. Sometimes these are referred to equivalently as *one-to-many* relationships; it is just a matter of which side you are mentioning first. Our simple example of the order details relating to the product information is such an example. Many order detail records refer to the same product because we sell the same product many times. To model this relationship, you will need to set 1..1 on the "one" side, like the product, and 1..n on the "many" side, like the order details.

If you think you may have a many-to-many relationship, you should think again. Most likely, you missed a table in your model, or perhaps an additional necessary link in the relationship, or a filter. Many-to-many relationships are usually established through a relationship table that provides the valid combinations. For instance, in an education model, you might have a table of teachers and a table of classes. And you might think there would be a many-to-many relationship because each teacher can teach multiple classes, and each class can be taught by multiple teachers. But there should be another table that would provide the valid combinations of teachers and classes. That table would be linked many-to-one to teachers, and many-to-one to classes. You would not have a many-to-many relationship in that model.

TIP   When you create a relationship by selecting the relationship toolbar button and dragging the relationship between the two query subjects in the diagram, you will save time if you do the following things: Make sure your query items are showing in the diagram (choose Diagram | Diagram Settings, and then select Query Items under Level of Detail); and drag from the query item in the query subject on the "one" side of the relationship to the related query item in the query subject on the "many" side of the relationship. If you create the relationship by selecting the query items and choosing Create Relationship from the context menu, select the query item on the "one" side of the relationship first. Framework Manager assumes that you are creating a one-to-many relationship, and it further assumes that the item you click first is on the "one" side of that relationship. It also assumes that the query items you clicked will be the items that define the relationship. So, just by clicking the right place, you should have most of your relationships defined correctly for you.

Inner Joins vs. Outer Joins

What about the 0..1 and 0...n cardinality settings? Let's review the difference between inner joins and outer joins.

When you join information from two query subjects by creating a relationship, you specify the join criteria; that is, you define which field or fields in one query subject should match which field or fields in the other query subject. An inner join is characterized by requiring that the information exists in both tables in order for it to be part of the result. Inner joins will use only the 1..1 and 1...n cardinalities.

An outer join says that the information should still be returned if it exists in one of the query subjects even if it does not have a match in the other. Outer joins are useful when the absence of information is itself informative. For instance, if you have a query subject of Employee information and another that returns Employee Reviews, you might not have a review in your query subject results for every employee. From a report perspective, it would be nice to know which employees have not been reviewed, as well as knowing the reviews that some employees have received. By specifying an outer join as a relationship with 1..1 cardinality on the Employee side and 0...n cardinality on the Employee Review side, when you report employee review information you will always get the full list of employees and their related review information, if any exist.

While it might seem beneficial always to model relationships using outer joins, be forewarned that execution of outer joins is usually less efficient than the execution of comparable inner joins. Sometimes it is much less efficient. Before you model something as an outer join, you should be certain that it is necessary to obtain the correct desired result in your reports.

If you need an outer join, you also need to know which side of the relationship you always want returned. If in some instances you want one side and in other instances you want the other side, you will need to alias the query subjects and model two separate relationships on two separate sets of query subjects.

You can also model a full outer join by specifying 0..n cardinality on both sides of the link, which would return all entities from both query subjects whether matches existed or not. If you are trying to model a full outer join involving two fact tables related through a common dimension table, note that Cognos 8 will handle such situations using a stitch query, which does not require that you model any of the relationships as an outer join. See the discussion on stitch queries in the next section.

How Cognos 8 Uses Relationships to Generate Queries

To provide the most predictable and correct results, Cognos 8 uses clues from the model to try to determine which tables in a query are likely to have fact information and which tables are likely to have dimensional, descriptive information. Fact information encompasses such things as sales quantities, forecast dollars, patient counts, and the number of days it took to close a help desk case. These are all numeric values that are usually aggregated in some fashion when reported. Dimensional information is the descriptive information that qualifies the fact amounts. Dimensional data encompasses such things as products, products lines, customers, dates, and locations. When you relate query subjects containing fact information to those containing dimensional information, the relationship will be many-to-one with the "many" side on the fact query subject. For example, many sales transactions in the Sales query subject will refer to one product in the Product query subject because you sell the same product over and over again. Knowing this, Cognos 8 will assume that the fact query subject is on the "many" side of the relationship.

Even if the model is more complex and the dimensional information is stored across multiple tables—say, for instance, a Product query subject, a Product Type query subject, and a Product Line query subject—Cognos 8 will try to trace the join paths to determine the fact table correctly. However, with some complex models, the query engine's attempt can result in incorrect determination of the fact query subjects or query subjects that can be treated as facts or dimensions in different situations, yielding slow queries and sometimes incorrect results. It is up to you, as the modeler, to understand the affect of cardinality on the resulting SQL. You must strive to create the model correctly, and you must test the model thoroughly to ensure that the results are predictable and valid. We cannot give you specifics for every eventuality that you might encounter in your modeling. We can only give you these guidelines, and a few more in the section is in this chapter now section on "Modeling Challenges."

Stitch Queries to Relate Facts

What happens if you write a report in Cognos 8 that pulls information from more than one fact query subject along with some dimensional information? If modeled correctly, Cognos 8 should be able to join the facts from the different query subjects through the dimension query subjects. It does this by querying the set of facts from one query subject joined to its relevant dimensions, separately joining the set of facts from the other fact query subject to its relevant dimensions, and then joining the resultant information in what appears to be a full outer join through the dimensions. This is known as a *stitch query*. Joining in this fashion allows the stitch query to accommodate situations in which one set of facts exists for a particular dimensional entity while another set of facts does not.

For example, if you have a forecast for a new backpack called the Day Hiker 3, you may not have any sales yet for that product. You might have some sales for an older backpack, say the Day Hiker 1, though you might not have forecast any sales for it because it is no longer being promoted. The Day Hiker 2 backpack might have both sales and forecast information. If you create a report for products, sales, and forecast, and if you have properly modeled the situation, the report will produce a stitch query. That stitch query will first retrieve the sales data for the Day Hiker 1 and the Day Hiker 2 backpacks, as well as the forecast information for the Day Hiker 2 and Day Hiker 3 backpacks. Stitching those two results sets together, Cognos 8 will display that you have only sales for the Day Hiker 1, sales and forecast for the Day Hiker 2, and only forecast for the Day Hiker 3. This is effectively a full outer join without having to model explicit outer joins in the relationships among these tables. You will notice a *coalesce* statement if you look at the generated SQL in a report that uses a stitch query.

Relationship SQL

In the Relationship Definition dialog's Relationship SQL tab, shown in Figure 15-28, Framework Manager will generate the SQL necessary to retrieve all of the query items from the two query subjects specified, joined by the link criteria in your relationship definition. You can check the SQL to verify the join criteria. You can also click the Test button to have Framework Manager execute the SQL to return a sampling of the rows in the result set. You can then look at the results to see if the relationship criteria return the expected results.

Viewing Relationships in Your Model

The easiest way to look at the relationships in your model is graphically. One way to do that, of course, is with the Diagram view in the Project window. If your model is relatively small, you might be able to see all the tables and relationships in the Diagram view. You can even use the zoom controls on the toolbar or choose Diagram | Zoom to try to make the entire diagram fit so you can see everything—though bigger models are difficult to see if you try to display the whole thing in the window. Fortunately, a few features are available to help you find and see what you need.

Locate in Diagram

If you want to find a particular table in the diagram, right-click the query subject in the Project Viewer tree and choose Locate in Diagram. The display in the Project window will automatically shift to move the selected query subject to the center of the view.

TIP *If you have located the query subject that you want to see, you can set it as the focal point of the diagram by selecting Diagram | Set Focal Point or by clicking the Set Focal Point button on the toolbar (see Figure 15-26). That will place the selected query subject on the left side of the diagram with all of the related query subjects branching off to the right, making them easier to see while the whole diagram is showing.*

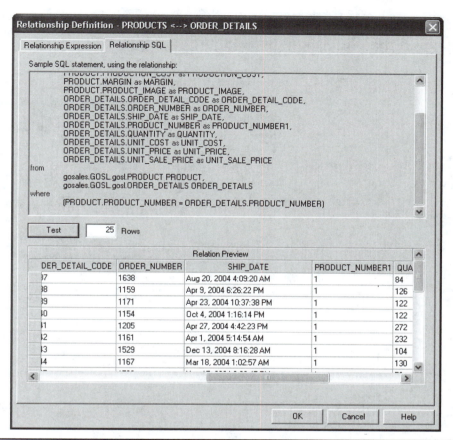

FIGURE 15-28   The Relationship SQL

Navigation Pane

Another way to focus the diagram on an area you want to see is to use the Navigation pane. When you click the Navigate button in the lower-right corner of the Diagram view, the Navigation pane appears, as shown in Figure 15-29. Within the Navigation pane is the visible area indicator, which shows the part of the diagram that is visible in the Project window. You can drag the indicator around the Navigation pane to change the visible part of the diagram. In versions prior to 8.3, the button works on a drag-and-drop principle: click the button to bring up the Navigator, but keep the mouse-button pressed while you drag around the visible indicator before releasing the button.

Navigation pane   Visible area indicator

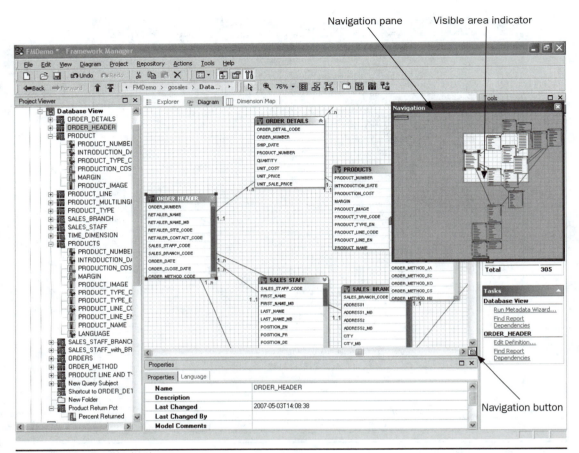

FIGURE 15-29   The Navigation pane

Context Explorer

A third way to make it easier to see your related tables is to use the Context Explorer, which focuses on selected query subjects and the query subjects to which they are related, as shown in Figure 15-30. Right-click the query subject or CTRL-click multiple query subjects and then right-click and choose Launch Context Explorer. The Context Explorer functions like a small-scale Diagram view, so you can double-click a query subject or relationship link to bring up the respective definition dialog. The Context Explorer has toolbar options to show query subjects that are related to or referenced by the query subject selected.

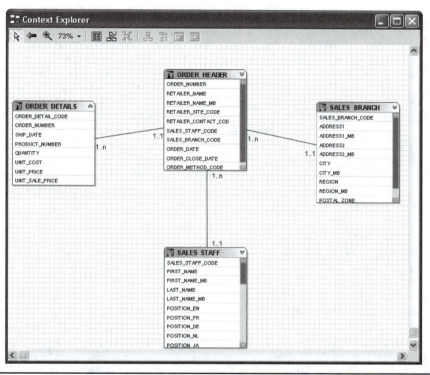

FIGURE 15-30   Context Explorer

TIP   When looking at the relationships between query subjects in the Diagram view of the Project window or in Context Explorer, you can view the cardinality in one of two different notations. Merise notation uses the min..max cardinality format like 1..1 and 0..n to mean 1 and only 1 and zero or more, respectively. Merise notation is good at explicitly conveying the cardinality. However, when your model starts to get complex with lots of joins, and when you are trying to get the big picture to identify facts with the "many" side of the relationships versus dimensional tables with the "one" side of the relationship, Merise notation starts to lose its value. It requires reading the values to understand the cardinality, and sometimes the values get obliterated in the diagram when many relationships are packed together. In this case, we recommend switching to Crowsfeet notation, which is shown in Figure 15-30. The graphical format of the many side of the relationship is easy to pick up, as is the circle on the relationship indicating an optional (outer join) relationship. To switch the cardinality notation, choose Diagram | Diagram Settings and select the appropriate radio button. On versions prior to 8.3, the menu selection Diagram | Notation.

Modeling Challenges

Creating a good model that produces valid results requires that you understand how to address modeling challenges. As mentioned in the section "How Cognos 8 Uses Relationships to Generate Queries," your relationships and cardinality settings dictate how queries are put together. If you are modeling a star schema data warehouse, relationships are straightforward, linking fact tables on the many side to dimension tables on the one side. Challenges arise when a straightforward modeling approach used on a normalized database results in ambiguity or incorrect joins. The cardinality of a relationship might not correctly indicate a fact table or a reference table. To remove ambiguities or *traps*, as Cognos refers to them, you might need to use model query subjects to make your model appear as if it was created on a star schema data warehouse. That will allow Cognos 8 to correctly identify fact query subjects and produce predictable queries. You also might need to alias query subjects to solve other challenges.

Approximating a Star Schema

To approximate a star schema model, create your data source query subjects. As you create relationships, consider how Cognos 8 will use a relationship to generate queries. If it is not obvious that the cardinality will properly indicate the usage of the table, you can create a model query subject from one or more related query subjects, preserving the relationships between them, and then create new relationships from the model query subject as if it were created from a single table in a star schema. For instance, you might need to create a single Products model query subject from the Product Line, Product Type, and Product data source query subjects. To do so, CTRL-click the query subjects that you want to merge and then right-click and choose Merge in New Query Subject from the context menu. You would then create relationships from this new Products model query subject to fact query subjects like Sales and Forecast, giving you a model that looks like a star schema.

The section on "The Model Advisor" later in this chapter covers how to use that feature to identify possible modeling traps.

Aliasing

Another modeling challenge is dealing with role-playing tables that can be used in multiple contexts, such as country or code tables. The country table might be related to the sales branch, the customer location, and the shipping address. A code table might be related to an address table for state codes, an inventory table for classification codes, and a sales order table for sales status codes. A role-playing table can even be referenced more than once by the same query subject. For instance, a date table might be related to a sales shipments table by the order date, requested date, and shipped date. To avoid providing join paths through a role-playing table or dropping rows in your results, you should alias the table for each specific role and create relationships to the aliases. Note that one alias might be used in two different relationships if the role is the same. For instance, an alias of the date table as order date would be related to both the sales order and the sales shipment tables if they both contained an order date.

To alias a table, create a single data source query subject for the role-playing table and then create a model query subject for each role that the table plays. Create your relationships using the model query subjects. Alternatively, you could create shortcuts as the aliases to the data source query subject and create your relationships to the shortcuts. To create an alias shortcut, right-click on the query subject it will reference and choose Create Alias Shortcut from the context menu.

NOTE *Prior to Cognos 8.3, a shortcut would be treated as an alias only if it was in the same namespace as the query subject on which it was based. If it was in a different namespace, it was treated as a reference. With Cognos 8.3, shortcut behavior can be set explicitly to alias or reference using the Treat As property.*

Using model query subjects as aliases is more flexible than using shortcuts because you can rename and selectively include query items. In a shortcut, the query items and their names come from the query subject on which the shortcut was based.

More Objects for Report Writers

In addition to the query subjects and their query items, you can include a couple more objects in your model for the benefit of report writers and to promote consistency across reports: filters and calculations.

Creating Filters for Users

We looked at creating filters on query subject definitions earlier in this chapter. Those filters are always applied to the generated SQL whenever something from the associated query subject is accessed. But what if you have optional filter criteria that a user may or may not want to include in a report? The user (report writer) can create his or her own filter in a report. But what if complex criteria need to be coded to get the proper filter or if arcane codes would need to be checked and may be too confusing for a user to understand? Certainly, as the modeler, you would want the model to support consistent results across all reports, such as what constitutes an open order or an active customer. Leaving a complex filter to be implemented consistently and correctly by all report writers might be too much to ask. In these situations, you can define the filter with the proper criteria and put it in your model. Users, then, would simply need to use the defined filter in their reports to get the desired, consistent results.

To create a user filter, right-click a namespace or folder in the Project Viewer tree and choose Create | Filter. Alternately, you could select the namespace or folder, and then choose Actions | Create | Filter. The Filter Definition dialog displays. You create this filter the same way that you create a query subject filter: drag-and-drop the available components from the Model, Functions, or Parameters tab into the expression definition. You can make compound logic by linking your expressions with *and* or *or* statements. For instance, you might have a filter for open orders look something like this:

```
[Orders].[Status] = 'O' or ([Order].[Status] = 'H' and [Order].[Close Date] is null)
```

Note that the logic resolves to a single true or false value. A common mistake when creating a filter is to try to make it an if-then-else statement. Do not fall into that trap. Code only the condition that will be true if you want to show the data and false if you do not.

Remember to give your filter a meaningful business name so that your users understand what it does. These user filters can be placed only in folders or namespaces, not in query subjects. We recommend that you organize them within a folder structure within the main namespace. If you only have a few filters, you can simply call the folder Filters or Business Filters. If you have a number of them, it is beneficial to create the top-level Filters folder and then organize them within subfolders, or to create folders within appropriate namespaces.

Creating Calculations

You can create a calculation outside of a query subject for use by a report writer. These calculations can be created within a namespace or folder the same way you create other objects within a namespace or folder: right-click it and choose Create, or select the object and choose Actions | Create | Calculation. Either method will bring up the same Calculation Definition dialog that you saw in Figure 15-19. Since it is the same dialog, the method of creating the calculation is the same: drag-and-drop or double-click items from the available components on the Model, Functions, or Parameters tab, or type in your calculation.

The only difference between these calculations and those in query subjects is the placement. Query subjects tend to be specific to a subject area, so placing a calculation within a query subject implies that the calculation is related to the query subject. If you would like to organize a number of business calculations in a folder for your users without implying that they are directly related to a particular query subject, or if you would like to keep your query subjects uncluttered for easier maintenance and portability, you can use this method to create your calculation within a folder or namespace of your choosing.

Setting Properties

Your model comprises a number of objects: query subjects, query items, relationships, data sources, and so on. Each object in your model has *properties*. These properties are attributes of the object that control everything from what the object is named, to the behavior the object will exhibit, to helpful hints for report writers using the object. Whenever you select an object in the model, either from the Project Viewer tree or from the Project window, the Properties pane will change to show you the list of properties for that object along with the current setting of those properties. Many of the properties can be changed to tune the object for the benefit of your users.

To modify a property setting, just click the current setting for the property in the Properties pane. While some properties are only for information and cannot be modified, those that you can modify use one of four methods:

- **Typing**   Properties such as Screen Tip or Description are free-form text and allow you to type in anything you like.

- **Drop-down button**   Properties such as Is Hidden or Usage that have a finite list of valid values present a drop-down arrow when selected. Click the drop-down arrow to reveal the list of valid values from which to choose your setting.

- **Ellipsis**   Properties that can have a more complex value that might include a macro (discussed in the next chapter), such as certain data source properties, present an ellipsis button when selected. Clicking the ellipsis will present a dialog in which you can construct the value you need.

- **<Click to edit>**   Some properties can have complex settings or multiple subproperties and cannot be displayed simply in the Properties pane. They also require a separate dialog from which to set them. Examples are the Format property of a query item, which has subproperties for configuring all aspects of the data presentation format, and the Security Filters property of a query subject, which can have more than one security filter defined, as you will see in the "Security" section of Chapter 16. To set any of these types of properties, click the <Click to edit> link to bring up the appropriate dialog.

If you do not see a <Click to edit> link, an ellipsis button, or a drop-down button, and typing does not change the value, then you have a read-only property, such as the Last Changed date, that Framework Manager controls on your behalf and which you cannot edit.

Important Properties to Set

The process of setting the properties is easy. Understanding which properties you should set is the real issue. You might never touch some of the properties, but some of them are critical and you must set them if you want to produce the most effective and complete model. Others are important to understand so that you can properly maintain your models.

Query Item Properties

For every query item that you have included in your model, you should review the following properties to make sure that the query item behaves the way you want it to when it is used in a report. If you take the time to set these properties on the query items in your data source query subjects, then all of the model query subjects that include those query items will inherit the settings you have made. You can always override those settings in your model query subjects, if necessary.

Usage   One of the most helpful features of reporting in Cognos 8 is that it will auto-summarize for you. This means that it will automatically summarize the numeric values while grouping by the descriptive information. For instance, if a report writer adds Product Line, Year, and Revenue to a report, Cognos 8 will assume that the desired result is to group by the product lines and the years, and to show the total revenue for those groupings, rather than show the detailed rows of every sale with the Product Line, Year, and Revenue of that sale. Normally, the summarized view is what a user wants, so this is good.

How does Cognos 8 know what to do when it tries to auto-summarize? The Usage property on the query items drives the behavior. More exactly, the Usage setting determines the default behavior of the query item when it is brought into a report. The report writer can always change the behavior, but it is best to have the properties set for the usual case to reduce the amount of work that needs to be done across all reports.

The Usage property can be set to one of the following values:

- **Identifier**   With this setting, a query item will be grouped when auto-summarizing. Dates and indexed values are set to identifier by Framework Manager by default.
- **Attribute**   As with identifiers, these query items will be grouped when auto-summarizing. Non-indexed character values are assigned this setting by default.
- **Fact**   This setting tells Cognos 8 to summarize the value. By default, non-indexed numeric columns in your source database are set as facts.

Based on the Usage property, Cognos 8 will also display the appropriate icon in the studios to help the report writer understand which columns are facts and which are likely to be indexed or not.

TIP   *The columns that you will want to concentrate on when checking and setting the Usage are the ones set to Fact, because these are the non-indexed numeric columns. Cognos 8 will try to summarize them when they are brought into a report. That's fine if the column is a quantity, but if it is a year or an order number, then you will want to make sure that you change the Usage property to Attribute so that Cognos 8 groups by it, rather than giving you a nonsensical sum of the years or order numbers.*

Regular Aggregate   The Regular Aggregate property works in conjunction with the Usage property to drive the behavior of the auto-summarizing feature of Cognos 8 reporting. For query items with a Usage of Fact, the Regular Aggregate property tells Cognos 8 how to summarize the values. The default is Sum, which most often makes sense for such things as revenue or quantity, but if your fact is a price or a percentage, Sum is probably not what you want. You can change the property setting to any of the supported aggregate types, such as Average, Count, or Maximum, for example. Remember that the report writers can change the default setting, so if you leave it at Sum and they want a report on the average order size, they can still create it. The goal here is to anticipate what the usual application of the query item will be and to set the property accordingly to save the most time for report writers.

You can set the Usage of a character field to Fact and the Regular Aggregate to Count or Count Distinct if you want to facilitate reporting on such things as the number of orders or the number of sales reps that meet certain criteria. Do not, however, set the Regular Aggregate property of a character field to aggregate types that do not make sense, such as Sum, because the database will not know how to sum a character field and you will receive an error when running a report that uses that field.

TIP   *Sometimes you want more than one aggregate method for the same query item to be easily accessible for your report writers. For instance, if you have a help desk application, you might want to report on both the maximum number of days that cases have stayed open as well as the average number of days that they stay open. In this case, put the same query item in the model query subject twice, setting the Regular Aggregate and the name of the query item appropriately.*

Format   You will likely have query items in your model that users will normally want to see in a particular presentation format. These could be revenue or profit amounts that you want to see as currency, index values that you want to see as a percentage, or dates that you want to see in a consistent format, such as *Jan 7, 2008*. Again, each report writer could format the data in his or her reports, but that would mean taking the time to do it on each of several reports, not to mention the possibility of inconsistency. Instead, set the Format property of the query item for the preferred presentation format.

Click the <Click to Edit> link in the setting to open the Data Format dialog shown in Figure 15-31. Choose the Format Type first, and then set the associated properties—such as decimal places and negative number formats, in the Properties pane. Report writers can override the default format that you set here in their reports.

Common Properties

Some properties apply to a number of different classes of objects. Those properties really have the same effect regardless of the object, so we can look at them in general.

Names   All objects have a Name property. Changing the Name property is equivalent to right-clicking an object and selecting Rename. Renaming some objects such as data source query subjects and data sources may not be necessary, but you should give a recognizable business name to any object that is published in the model that your end users will see. If you gave it some forethought, you probably already gave decent names to your model

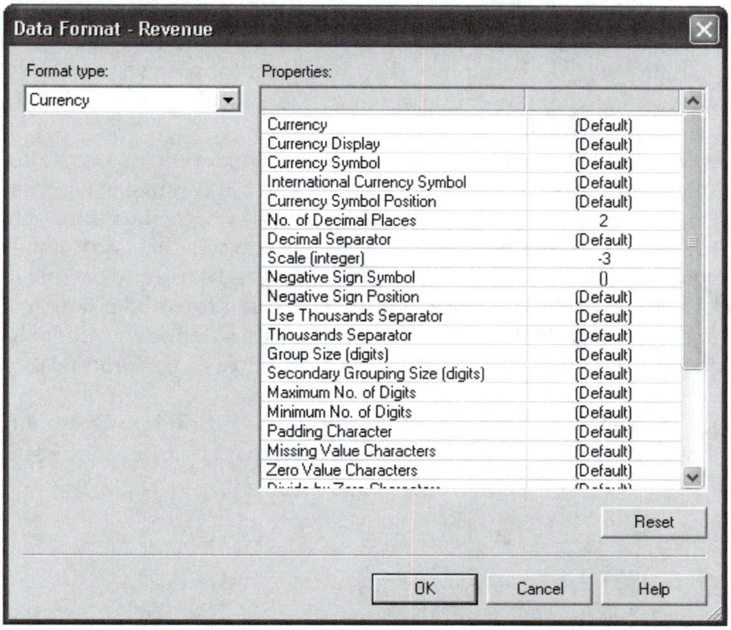

FIGURE 15-31   Data Format dialog

query subjects, namespaces, folders, and filters when you created them. The biggest group of objects you probably need to rename are the query items in your model query subjects, because they will keep the name of the query item they reference by default. This often means that they inherited some cryptic database column name. These need to be renamed to something that an end user, a report writer, would understand.

Descriptions   Objects that appear in the published model, including query subjects, query items, namespaces, folders, filters, and packages, have three properties that help you to describe what the object does or how it might be used: Description, Model Comments, and Screen Tip. Each has a slightly different use.

The Model Comments are to be used to document something about the object that a modeler working in Framework Manager might need to know. The Model Comments are not accessible by report writers using the model.

The Description is similar to the Model Comments, except that a report writer can access the Description of the object if it was published in the model by right-clicking the object in Report Studio and choosing Properties.

Finally, the most user-friendly of the three for report writers is the Screen Tip. A Screen Tip, sometimes referred to as Tip Text in other applications, is revealed to a report writer if he or she hovers the mouse over the published object. Use the Screen Tip for a helpful, short description of the object if its use is not obvious just from its name.

Data Source Properties

Three properties of a data source work in conjunction to point your model to the tables and columns in the source database. Those properties are Content Manager Datasource, Catalog, and Schema. When you create a new data source or reference one from Cognos Connection through the Metadata Wizard, these properties are all set for you, so you may not ever need to change them. However, in some circumstances, it is critical to know what these properties do so you can use them correctly.

The Content Manager Datasource property is an indirect pointer to a data source defined in Cognos Connection. The Cognos Connection data source is where the connection information for the source database is kept. No database type, connection, or sign on information is maintained in the Framework Manager model. This is advantageous if you ever need to re-point a data source in your model. You might need to do this if you are pointing to a test version of the database, but want to point the model now to a production version. You can simply have both data source connections defined in Cognos Connection, and then change the Content Manager Datasource property of your model data source from the test to the production connection.

The Catalog and the Schema properties work in conjunction to fully qualify the path of the source database tables. Simply put, the native SQL that is passed to the source database will be of this form:

```
[Catalog property setting].[Schema property setting].[Table name]
```

Knowing this can help you properly set those values if you receive errors when modeling that say a table or view cannot be found.

TIP *If you use two or more data sources in your model that reference databases that are on the same database server and can be accessed with the same signon, set the Content Manager Datasource property the same for all data sources. Only one connection to the database server will be used. If you created relationships across the data sources, the database server will perform the joins. Separate connections would result in separate queries that the Cognos 8 BI Server would need to join, which would be less efficient.*

The Easiest Way to Set Properties on Many Objects

When you are setting properties such as Name, Usage, Aggregate, and Format on a number of query items in your model, selecting each query item and setting each property individually can be tedious. Fortunately, Framework Manager provides a way to set properties on multiple objects at once.

If you select multiple objects in the Project Viewer tree (as is standard in many applications, you can SHIFT-click to select a range of objects or CTRL-click them individually), the Property pane will change from a list of properties for one object to a spreadsheet-like grid, with the selected objects down the left and the properties across the top, as shown in Figure 15-32.

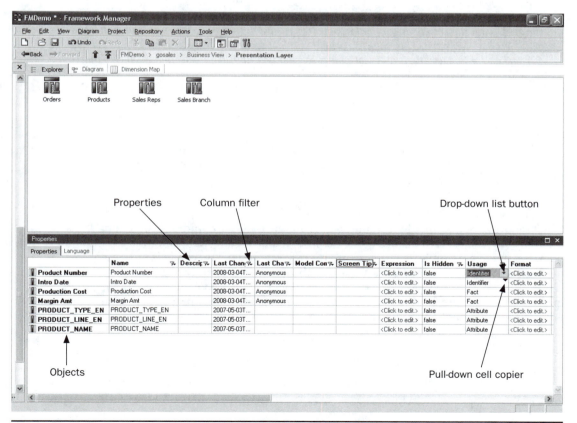

FIGURE 15-32   The Property pane for setting properties on multiple objects

This property grid will help you set properties much faster. First, let's say you are setting the Name property of a number of query items. You can just type in the name of the first query item in the list and then click the down arrow on your keyboard to move to the next to set its name. Another nice feature is the ability to copy cell values for a property by using the pull-down cell copier. If you set a value for a property in the first row, you can click and drag that control across the subsequent rows to copy the value from the first cell. This is very similar to how a spreadsheet works. This particular feature is helpful if you need to set the same usage or format for a lot of query items.

Another feature of the grid is the column filter, which is another spreadsheet-like feature. If you click the filter icon in the column header, you will see a drop-down list of all the values that the selected objects have for that property. If you select one of those values, only the objects that have that setting for that property will remain visible. This can be quite handy if you have a long list of query items. First, you can go through them all to set their names and their usages. Then you can filter only for those with a usage of Fact so that you can set the Regular Aggregate property for each of those.

NOTE *If you select multiple objects of different classes, such as a namespace, a query subject, and some query items, the property grid will still appear in the Properties pane. However, because different classes of objects have different sets of properties, the only properties that will appear in the grid—and the only ones you will be able to set—are the properties that are common across the object types selected. This might be okay if you just want to change a bunch of names or set the ScreenTips, but generally, it will make more sense if you limit your selection to objects that are all of the same type.*

Organizing Your Model

You should organize your model to suit your end users so they can easily find what they need and so they can present the data correctly in their reports. Some basic guidelines will help you organize your model.

Star Schema Groupings and Reference Shortcuts

What report writers generally want to see in a model in Report Studio is something organized by subject area in such a manner as to make obvious the relationships among the data. If you have a simple, single subject area in your model, you can loosely present the model query subjects in the business view of the data without much regard to organization. If, for instance, your model covers only product sales, you could have the following model query subjects in your Business View namespace, with the data source query subjects on which they are based in parentheses:

- Sales (from ORDER_HEADER, ORDER_DETAILS)
- Products (from PRODUCT, PRODUCT_TYPE, PRODUCT_LINE)
- Customers (from CUSTOMER, CUSTOMER_LOCATION, CUSTOMER_TYPE)
- Sales Reps (from SALES_STAFF, SALES_BRANCH)

Presenting all of these directly within the Business View would be fine. It would be obvious to your users that the information is all related. But what if your model included more than one subject area? For instance, let's add the following to the list:

- Inventory (from INVENTORY)
- Location (from PLANT, WAREHOUSE, INVENTORY_LOC)

If you publish all of these in a flat model, with no further organization, you present a problem to the report writers. Are they to assume that all of the information in the model is related? What happens if they want to look at inventory, and they choose to view it by customer? The point is that, while the results may be valid, it is difficult from a flat organization of the data for the report writers to understand that sales relates to products, customers, and sales staff, but not location; and inventory relates to product, and location, but not customer or sales staff. It would be better to organize the model to reflect the business.

You can use star schema groupings to provide organization in your model that will help your users understand how things are related. A star schema grouping is a namespace that contains shortcuts to query subjects. The idea behind a star schema grouping is that it contains a query subject with facts, such as Sales, and all of the related query subjects that contain information from the business entities, such as Product and Customer, often referred to as *dimension tables* (not to be confused with *dimensional modeling*, which is covered in Chapter 16). This appears to the report writers as a folder with the sales information and all the business entities that apply to it. Your users, then, can be instructed to stay within that folder when writing a sales report.

Because the star schema grouping is intended for the report writers, and if you are following our convention for organizing the model, you will want to create it based on the model query subject from the Business View namespace that contains the facts you want to present. To create a star schema grouping, CTRL-click to select all the query subjects that you want in your grouping: the Fact query subject and the related query subjects that contain the business entities. Then, right-click the selected query subjects and choose Create Star Schema Grouping from the context menu. Note that this is a separate option on the context menu than the Create option that you used to create other objects You will be presented with the Create Star Schema Grouping dialog shown in Figure 15-33.

FIGURE 15-33
Create Star
Schema Grouping
dialog

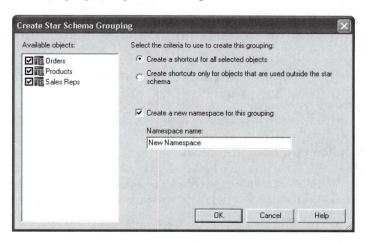

The dialog will show in the Available Objects pane your selected query subjects plus all query subjects to which they are related. If you base your star schema groupings on query subjects that have relationships, you can just select the Fact query subject and let Framework Manager find the related query subjects. Unfortunately, showing the related query subjects isn't as helpful as you might like if relationships are on the data source query subjects in the Database View namespace, but your groupings are based on your model query subjects, for which you do not have any direct relationships. Not to worry, though, as long as you know which query subjects belong in the grouping. The dialog still does a couple of things for you: it creates the new namespace for the grouping, which you should name accordingly, and it creates the shortcuts for the query subjects you selected. Do that for all of the subject areas in your model so that each central Fact query subject or set of closely related Fact query subjects (such as Sales Orders, Sales Invoices, and Sales Returns) has a star schema grouping, and you will have a model that is well organized for publishing.

If you later need to add a reference to a model query subject to an existing star schema grouping, you will need to add the shortcut manually. To do so, right-click the query subject, and choose Create Shortcut. A shortcut to the selected query subject, named with *Shortcut To* prefixed to the query subject name, will be placed in the same namespace as the query subject. Move that shortcut to your star schema grouping namespace and rename it by removing the *Shortcut To* from the name so it is named the same as the referenced query subject. Recall that you can name it the same because it is now in a different namespace. Your query subject is now added to your star schema grouping.

If you have modeled and organized correctly, reports that pull facts from multiple star schema groupings and include data from at least one common, related query subject, will normally generate a stitch query.

NOTE *The shortcuts used in star-schema groupings are reference shortcuts, which means that the shortcut is really just a pointer to the referenced query subject; it is not a stand-alone object like an alias shortcut would be. The benefit of a reference shortcut is that all references point to the same query subject. For example, suppose you have a Products query subject that is referenced by a shortcut in a Sales star schema grouping and is also referenced in an Inventory star schema grouping. If you want a consolidated sales and inventory report, you can pull data onto your report from Sales and Inventory, including Product information. Because the Product shortcuts refer to the same query subject, Cognos 8 will have a join path through Product. Because it appears to Cognos 8 that Product is a dimension table for the reasons we covered earlier in the chapter, Cognos 8 will produce a stitch query and you will get valid results. If the shortcuts in the star schema groupings are set as alias, they are treated as separate, individual objects, which means there would be no join path from Sales to Inventory, and your report would likely produce an error indicating that you are trying to do a cross-product join. Whether a shortcut behaves as a reference or alias is controlled by the Treat As property of the shortcut, so if you create the wrong one, you can always change the type by changing that property.*

Approaches to Model Organization

Knowing what to do, you may be wondering where to do it. You can organize your model a few different ways, and each way has its pluses and minuses. All approaches use top-level namespaces to create views, or layers, within which objects are organized. The difference in approaches lies in which layers query subjects, relationships, filters, and calculations are placed. We suggest names for the view namespaces, but you can use different names.

The simplest is a *two layer approach* with a Database View namespace and a Presentation View namespace. The Database View contains all data source query subjects and any model query subjects necessary to solve modeling challenges. It also contains all relationships, filters, and calculations. The Presentation View contains only star schema groupings based directly on the database view objects. You will need to give your data source query items business names so your users will not be exposed to cryptic database column names. This approach is fast to model, but possibly more difficult to maintain and to port to a different database type. It can work if your source is a data warehouse that will present few modeling challenges and will require little reorganization and renaming of query items.

An alternative is a three layer *isolation approach*, with a Database View, a Business View, and a Presentation View. The Database View namespace contains all the data source query subjects, but no model query subjects or relationships. In the Business View namespace, you create a model query subject for each data source query subject plus any that you need to resolve challenges, and you create the relationships between the model query subjects in this layer. The Business View also contains all filters and calculations. A Presentation View contains the star schema groupings based on the Business View. This approach is the most time consuming to create because you are creating redundant query subjects, but it is also the most portable because the Business View provides a layer of insulation between the source database and the reports based on the Presentation Layer.

The *consolidation approach* also uses three layers. The Database View namespace contains all data source query subjects, any model query subjects necessary to resolve challenges, and all relationships. Little or no renaming is done in the database view except when creating aliases. The Business View namespace contains model query subjects that organize the query items, all named for business users. For instance, you can put all customer related query items in one model query subject, and all inventory status indicators in another. Place filters and calculations in the Business View unless you need to place them in the Database View for maximum reuse. The Presentation View contains the star schema groupings based on the Business View. This is a compromise approach that provides some insulation between the reports and the data source, but does not require as much modeling effort as the isolation approach. It is a good place to start for most projects.

Validating Your Model

You should validate your model to make sure it is solid by testing it, verifying it, and running the model advisor on it. You should perform these tasks throughout the modeling process, but it is critical that you do so prior to publishing to your end users.

Testing

We already talked about testing single query subjects when you create them, and we looked at testing the results of relationships. One more test you can perform to validate your design further is to test multiple query items from multiple query subjects. Doing so can test multiple relationships and their cardinality. To perform a test of this nature, CTRL-click all the query items you want to include in the test to select them. With all the desired query items selected, right-click and choose Test. That will get you the Test Results dialog shown in

FIGURE 15-34
Test Results dialog

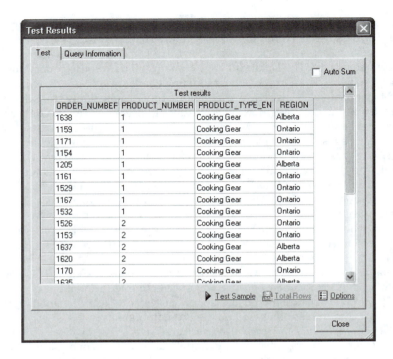

Figure 15-34. The query will immediately be generated and will execute, showing the results. You can check the results, or, as with testing a query subject, you can change test options or select Auto Sum and run the query again by clicking the Test Sample link. Another important way you can use the Test Results dialog to validate your model is to use the Query tab, on which you can see the SQL statement that was generated based on your selection and the way the model was built.

Though we are presenting this test method as something to consider prior to publishing, it is also a good method to use to troubleshoot should the reports built from your model return questionable results.

Verifying

You can verify your model at any time, but it is important to do so prior to publishing to reduce to likelihood of publishing a model with problems. Verifying is kind of like syntax checking for your model. It will not tell you if you have a well-designed model, but it will find things like incomplete determinant definitions and cardinality issues in relationships.

You can verify all or part of the model by selecting the object or objects in the Project Viewer tree that you want to verify. Verification will be done on that object and all of its child objects. To verify the entire model, select the top-level namespace. Right-click the object to verify and choose Verify Selected Objects from the context menu. You will have the opportunity on the Verify Model dialog, shown in Figure 15-35, to select both the severity and types of issues you want Framework Manager to look for. Until you get familiar with all that can be reported, we suggest you leave all options selected. Click the Verify Model button to start the verification.

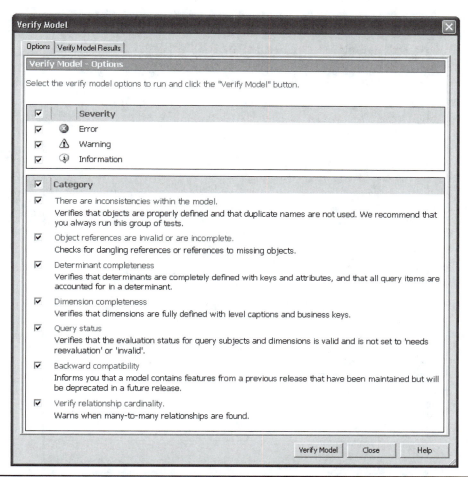

FIGURE 15-35   Verify Model options

The results of the verification appear as in Figure 15-36. Note that you can edit the object that has the problem or just find it in the Project Viewer tree by clicking the appropriate icon under Actions. You can also have Framework Manager try to repair some problems automatically. If a checkbox appears to the left of the issue, you can select that issue and click the Repair Selected link to have Framework Manager attempt the repair. Once the repairs are attempted, the model will immediately be verified again, so you will know if it worked.

The Model Advisor

The Model Advisor, new to Version 8.3, will attempt to point out design issues with your model, thus helping you to produce a model that is designed well and thus more likely to produce predictable, correct results for your users. Consider it validation as opposed to

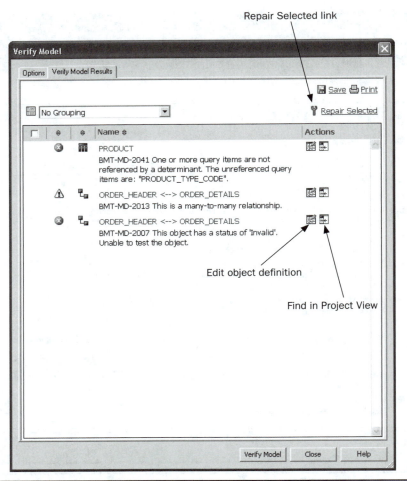

FIGURE 15-36   Verify Model results

verification. To run the Model Advisor, select the component you want to analyze in the Project Viewer tree by right-clicking it and choosing Run Model Advisor to reveal the Model Advisor options shown in Figure 15-37.

Select the options to tell the Model Advisor what to check. As with verifying your model, we suggest leaving all options selected until you are sure you need to focus only on certain issues. Click the Analyze button and the Advisor will run against the selected object and its related objects. This allows you to run the Model Advisor on a section of your model that you are about to publish without cluttering the results with issues in an area of the model that is not yet fully modeled. Your results will appear on the Model Advisor tab of the dialog, shown in Figure 15-38.

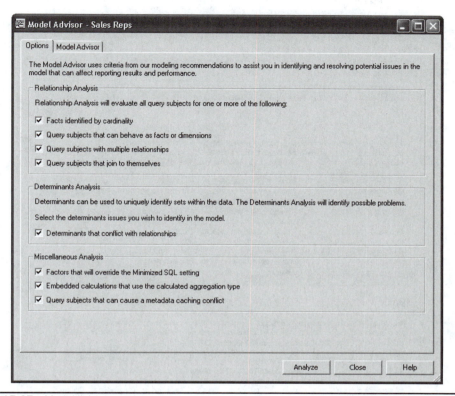

FIGURE 15-37   Model Advisor options

These results will show you your potential issues categorized by type. Note that not all issues are bad. Many are in fact desirable. For instance, if the Advisor says that the ORDERS query subject is identified as containing facts based on the cardinality of its relationships, then you know you have properly modeled that part because you want ORDERS to be treated as facts.

The Model Advisor has handy links to the Cognos documentation for further explanation of the issue types, as well as icons under the Action column that will link you to the Context Explorer for the referenced query subject so that you can easily check relationships if the issue does not appear to be desirable.

Publishing Your Model

If you made it through all the steps covered to this point, you have created a relational model that is probably ready to publish. Publishing is the act of making the model available in the Cognos 8 BI suite to support generating content, such as reports, based on your model. You can do other things in a model but before you get to that stuff in the next chapter, let's look at what you need to do to publish a model to Cognos Connection.

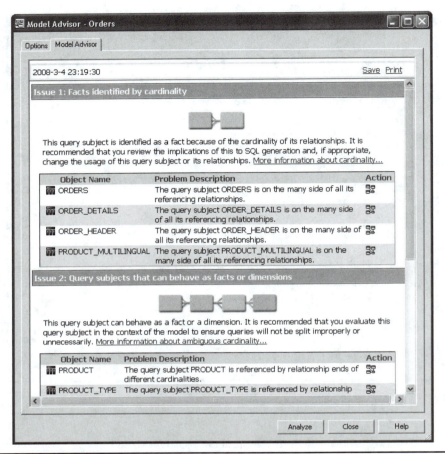

FIGURE 15-38   Model Advisor results

You do not publish the entire model. What you do publish is a package, which consists of the objects in the model that you choose to publish for use by your end users. While you can choose all the objects, most of the time a package is just the subset of objects in your model that you need to expose to the end users so that they can create their own content in reports and events, for example.

Creating a Package

To create a package, select the packages node at the bottom of the Project Viewer tree and then choose Actions | Create | Package; alternatively, right-click the packages node and choose Create | Package. The Create Package wizard appears. The first screen in the wizard asks for the name of the package and the description and Screen Tip. Remember that the package is for the end users, so name the package appropriately to convey the information that is accessible. Keep in mind that you might have more than one package from the same model, or you might have other packages that can overlap the subject area of your model, so take care in naming the package correctly. Once you've given it a good name and optionally given it a Screen Tip and description, you can click Next.

Defining Objects to Include in the Package

On the Define Objects screen of the wizard, shown in Figure 15-39, choose which objects from the model will be part of the package. Think of this tree in terms of what a report writer will see as available objects in the model in, say, Report Studio. For each object within the project namespace, from namespaces to folders, to query subjects, down to the query items, and including user filters and calculations, you choose to select (the green checkmark), hide (a green triangle with a small checkmark), or unselect (the red X) that object. Selected objects and their children appear to end users in the published package. Hidden objects are included in the package but do not appear to the end users. Unselected objects are not included, unless they are needed to support an included object, in which case Framework Manager will automatically turn them into hidden objects during the publish.

So what should you select for inclusion in your model? If you followed our suggested conventions, you will select the star schema groupings that you want the report writers to use. You can unselect the root of the project and then select each star schema grouping so the groupings appear as the root of the published package, making it easier for your users to navigate. Now is a good time to make sure that you like the way the published content will be named and organized. Once you have made your selections, click Next.

Figure 15-39
Create Package
Wizard - Define
Objects screen

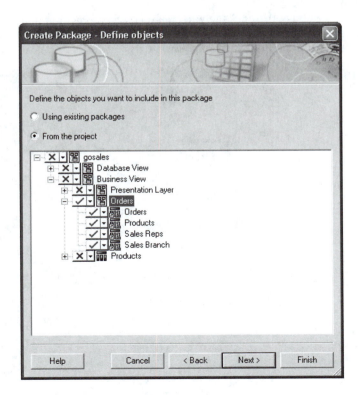

Function Sets

The last dialog in the Create Package wizard allows you to select function sets. Function sets define which functions will be available for report writers to use when they create reports from the package. The goal here is to match the function sets to the database type or types from which the model will pull its data. So if your source database is DB2, you will want to include the DB2 function set. You will not want to include function sets that cannot execute on your source database(s). Your selected function sets should appear in the right pane of the Create Package - Select Function Lists screen. Once you have selected them, you can click Finish. Another screen will pop up and ask if you want to publish the newly created model. If you choose not to do so, you can always publish it later.

TIP   *By default, all function sets will be included in the package, so you need to pull out those you do not want. You can change the default to pull in only the function sets for the types of databases that are accessed by the model. To change the default, choose Project | Project Function List. You will be able to set the default function lists based on the database types your models will access.*

Publishing a Package

You need to publish the package to make it available to end users. You will publish the package initially once you think it is ready for use or at least for testing by report writers. You will also publish the package after every time you make a change or addition to the model that needs to get to the end users.

You can publish the package you created by right-clicking it and selecting Publish Packages, or select the Package and choose Actions | Package | Publish Packages. Either way will get you the Publish Wizard shown in Figure 15-40.

FIGURE 15-40
Publish Wizard

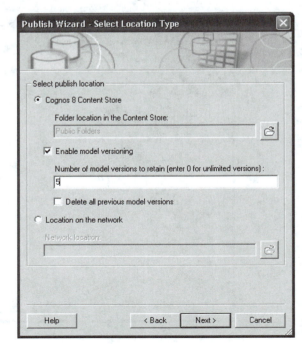

Through the wizard, you can select where you would like your model published. The choices are to the Cognos 8 Content Store or to a network location. The only way to publish it so that users of the Cognos 8 BI suite can access it is to publish it to the Cognos 8 Content Store, so this is normally what you want to do.

Model Versioning

When you publish your model to the Cognos 8 Content Store, you can specify how many versions of the model you want to keep available in the Content Store for the use of IBM Cognos 8 BI. Model versioning is a handy facility that enables you to publish a new version of the model without worrying about breaking existing reports. Reports and other content are written against the latest version of the model at the time that content is created. If changes to the model are published subsequently, the existing reports will continue to reference the version against which they were created, as long as that version exists. If that version is removed, the existing reports will try to run against the latest model version, which may or may not work.

Through versioning, then, you can publish your new version to support new reports as soon as possible. You can then go back and check reports against the latest model version, fixing them as necessary until all of your content is validated on that version.

TIP *To see which existing reports are impacted by changes to your model, select your package in the Project Viewer tree and then choose Actions | Package | Analyze Publish Impact. Framework Manager will look at the existing content based on that package and will tell you what content you need to check.*

You should specify a reasonable number of versions that will support your work. Remember that each publish action will create a new version, so if you publish a new version, find a problem, fix it, and then republish, that will take two versions. And remember also that if you do that enough times to clobber all saved versions, then your existing reports will be forced to use the latest version without the benefit of validation. Setting the number of versions to zero will let you keep unlimited versions, but that will just take up unnecessary space in your Content Store and will not promote discipline in managing your published model. If you manage the versions well, setting the number of saved versions to five or six should be sufficient.

You can also choose not to version, meaning you will only ever keep the latest version, and you can optionally choose to delete all previous model versions via the wizard. Again, just understand that if you do either of these, existing content will be forced onto the latest published version of the model.

Once you have selected the destination for the model and optionally the number of versions, you can click Next in the wizard.

Initial Model Security

In the next screen, the wizard will allow you to set the initial security for the published model. This can also be done or can be overridden by changing the access permissions in Cognos Connection. For a more in-depth discussion of your model security options, see Chapter 16. Click Next to advance the Publish Wizard.

Publish Options

You have a final couple of options before Framework Manager pushes the model out. You can choose to verify the model before publishing, which is a good idea unless you just verified it before you initiated the publish operation. You can also choose to externalize query subjects, which makes the resulting data available outside Framework Manager.

Choosing to externalize query subjects affects only those query subjects for which you have specified an Externalize method in their property settings. You can set that property to have the query subject produce a CSV (comma-separated value) or tab-delimited text file, or an IQD, which is the query definition file type that you will need if you are using IBM Cognos 8 BI as a data source for building Cognos PowerCube OLAP sources with a version of Cognos Transformer prior to 8.3.

Finalizing the Publish

After choosing your publish options in the wizard, you can click the Publish button to complete the publishing. Your model will now be available to you in Cognos Connection for use in creating content with the appropriate studios. One final task that you should complete as the modeler is to go into IBM Cognos 8 BI and test your new model in Query Studio or Report Studio to validate it further before you turn it over to users.

Remember that thus far we have covered only creating a relational model. Models of this type can be used to create reports in Report Studio or Query Studio, or events in Event Studio. But they cannot be used as a source for Analysis Studio. Chapter 16 will address how to extend your model through dimensional modeling to make it available in Analysis Studio.

Framework Manager II

In Chapter 15, you learned how to model your relational data using Framework Manager. This chapter discusses additional features found in Framework Manager that might be useful in your model, including macros, security, dimensional modeling of relational data sources, and features to help manage multi-user model development. Macros supply variable values at run time to customize objects based on the user accessing the content. Security can be applied to packages, objects in the model, or the data that is returned. Dimensionally modeled relational (DMR) data sources allow multidimensional exploration of data in Analysis Studio, as well as drill-down and drill-up capability in Report Studio and Query Studio. Model Branching, linking, and segmenting allow you to create shortcuts to your original models to reuse them within larger projects or to break models into segments for multiple developers.

Macros

Macros in Framework Manager are similar to those found in many other applications. Macros are small pieces of logic or code that can be inserted into many different objects in your model, such as model query subjects, data connection definitions, and filters. Any object that can make use of information that becomes available when the model is accessed by reports or other content from a Cognos 8 Studio can use a macro. Macros can include references to parameter maps, a user's session parameters, or parameters defined by the modeler called *Model Session Parameters*. Model session parameters are parameters that are either static values or macros. Using macros in a model session parameter allows you to create session parameters that can leverage all macro functions, other session parameters, and parameter maps. In other words, you can create your own dynamic model session parameters.

A common use of macros is to dynamically modify the filters being used by Cognos 8 when a report is run. For instance, suppose a report author wants to create a sales report that returns only records belonging to the user running the report. The report author knows that one column in the Sales_Staff table is called Staff_Name, so he could put a prompt in the report asking for the user name and then use Staff_Name as a filter—such as *[Staff name]* = ?P_Staff_name?. While this will limit the query results to those records that have the sales name entered by the person running the report, what if the person running the report enters someone else's name? What if someone has access to Query Studio and decides to look at the sales data for all sales staff? With Framework Manager, you could use a macro to filter records in the query based on the user's login information.

Also using macros, you can change the column names used during SQL generation. For example, if you have tables with multiple columns each containing descriptive information in different languages, one for each supported locale, the appropriate column could be selected at run time based on the user's runLocale session parameter. Users would see information in a report in their native language. This example is covered in detail in the Cognos documentation.

Macros can even be used to switch database connections at run time. Suppose you run a service company providing data collection and reporting for hospitals. Given the concern surrounding patient privacy, the hospitals that use your service want to be assured that their data is kept physically separate from your other customers' data. To address the data separation issue you create multiple databases to separate the data, one for each hospital, all of which use the same schema. Rather than create a Framework Manager model for each hospital, which would require separate development and maintenance, you would like to have one Framework Manager model and one set of reports that every hospital can use. By using parameter maps combined with session parameters and macro functions, you can automate selection of the database to use each time a report is run.

Creating a Macro

Before we go into the details of the examples, let's cover what a macro comprises, how a macro looks, and how to create macros.

Session Parameters

When working with macros, two types of session parameters are available: *Environment Session Parameters* and *Model Session Parameters*. The environment session parameters are set when the user signs on to Cognos Connection, opens a Cognos Studio, or opens Framework Manager. By default, when a user logs in through an authentication provider, the standard environment session parameters available for use in macros include runLocale, account .defaultName, and account.personalInfo.userName. Depending on your authentication source, additional parameters might be available as some authentication providers support custom session parameters. Additional environment session parameters are defined by your administrator through Cognos Configuration to make them available to Framework Manager. For example, you could have an additional attribute in your LDAP provider called City which is used to indicate the City in which a user works. This session parameter could be used in a macro to filter data on the user's city.

You define model session parameters within Framework Manager. These parameters are created using hard coded values, macro functions, query items, and other session parameters.

Note *When using a session parameter in a macro, the parameter is preceded with a dollar sign ($)*

Accessing and modifying session parameters will be discussed in "Macro Functions" later in the chapter.

Anatomy of a Macro

In its simplest form, a macro consists of *Delimiters* and *Expressions*. A delimiter is a character that is used to mark the beginning and end of the expression. In a Cognos 8 macro, the pound sign (#) is the delimiter used. So, a macro would look like:

```
#expression#
```

The expression part of the macro is more complex. An expression can comprise a macro function, a session parameter, a query item, text, and so on. What is in the expression depends on what you want the macro to do. Table 16-1 gives a few general examples of macro expressions.

Parameter Maps

The last example in Table 16-1 makes use of a *parameter map* called `Language_lookup{}`. Parameter maps are two-column look-up or substitution tables defined within your Framework Manager model. In our example, we pass the string *en-us* to the parameter map, which returns the string *EN* to the macro as the mapped value for the key *en-us*.

Parameter maps are used when your data sources and session parameters do not contain the exact information you need in your model. In the case of the `Language_lookup` parameter map, you know that people from different countries will be using this model. Each connection (or session) made to Cognos Connection could result in one of many `runLocale` values. At least 15 different `runLocales`; exist for English alone, including en, en-us, en-au, en-ca, en-gb, and so on. Each of those `runLocales` can use the same base language, English.

Macro	Expression	Result
#$runLocale#	$runLocale	en-us
#sb($runLocale)#	sb($runLocale)	[en-us]
#$runLocale + 'is my preferred language'#	$runLocale + 'is my preferred language'	En-us is my preferred language
#$Language_lookup {$runLocale}#	$Language_lookup {$runLocale}	EN

Table 16-1 Sample Macros

Instead of modeling every possible `runLocale`, you can create the `Language_lookup` parameter map to replace multiple language codes with a single, common code found in the data. As seen here, parameter maps are simple structures:

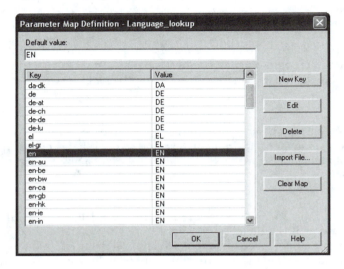

The parameter map has a key (the item to look up), and a corresponding value that is returned.

NOTE   *Parameter maps can contain any Key-Value pair that you need, but it is important to remember that as your map becomes larger it also becomes slower.*

We will return to parameter maps when we get back to our hospital example in the "Using Macros to Point to the Right Database" section of this chapter.

Make a Macro

Your location within Framework Manager determines exactly how you create a macro. When you are working with the Query Subject Definition for a model query subject, you can use macros in either the Filter tab or in a query item from the Query Items And Calculations pane, as shown next:

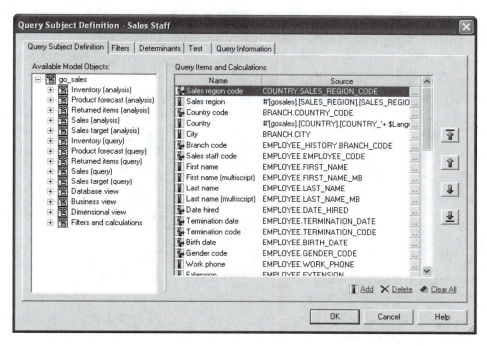

Access the Query Subject Definition dialog by right-clicking on a model query subject and choosing Edit Definition from the context menu, or you can double-click on the model query subject.

NOTE *While you can create macros in data source query subjects, we recommend that you only use macros in model query subjects. This follows the practice of leaving data source query subjects as clean as possible for maintenance reasons.*

The Filter Definition dialog and the Calculation Definition dialog both have a Parameters tab at the bottom of the Available Components pane, as shown next:

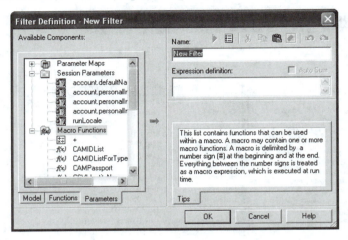

By using one or more of the items in the Parameters tab, you can create any macro you need. We will show you an example of how to use a macro to return the records from the Sales Staff model query subject for the person running the query.

Here's how to make a macro:

1. Double-click the model query subject to access the Query Subject Definition screen.

2. Click the Filters tab at the top of the screen.

3. Click the Add link at the bottom of the screen, as shown next:

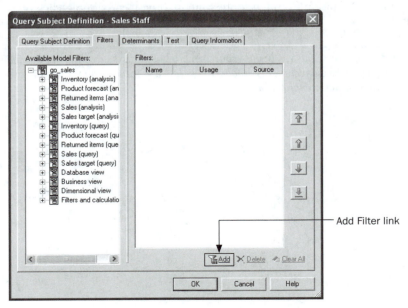

Add Filter link

4. Enter a name for the filter in the Name text box.

5. On the Model tab in the Available Components pane, navigate to the data item on which you want to filter. In this example, we use the Staff name from the Sales Staff model query subject.

6. In the Expression definition pane, add the Data item.

7. In the Expression pane, after the Data item, add the logical operator and the appropriate session parameter on which to filter. In this example we use the equal (=) and the `account.defaultName` session parameter.

At this point your filter will look something like the one shown next:

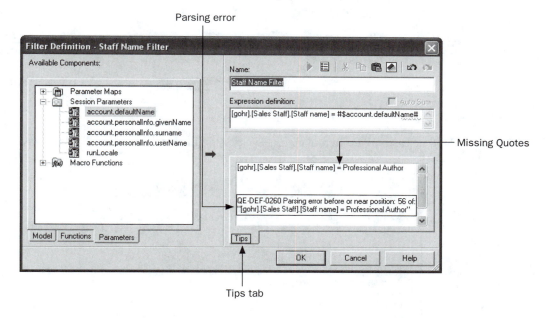

There are three items of which to take note in the previous illustration.

- The Parsing error seen in the Tips pane.
- Our default user name is missing quotes.
- The user name is listed as Professional Author, which is not a name found in the Sales Staff model query subject.

The missing quotes present an issue because when you use a string in a SQL statement, the string has to be enclosed in single quotes. We can fix the missing quotes using a *Macro Function*, which we will discuss in the "Macro Functions" section of this chapter.

As for the user name, Framework Manager provides us with the ability to set override values for any session parameter as shown in the next section.

Override Default Session Parameter Values

Overriding the default session parameter values makes developing and testing macros much easier by removing the need to setup multiple test users.

Here's how to override the default values of the session parameter:

1. From the toolbar in Framework Manager, click on the Project menu, as shown next:

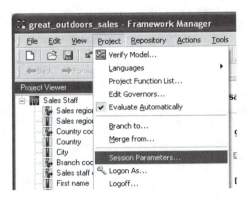

2. Click on the Session Parameters menu. The Session Parameters screen displays, as shown next:

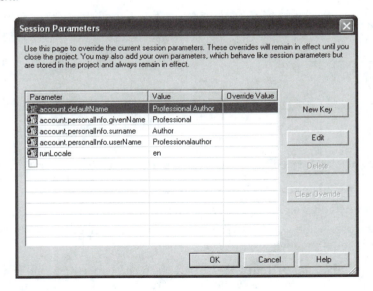

3. Select the parameter to be modified and click the Edit button. The rows for the selected parameter become text boxes in which you can enter data.

4. In the Override Value column for the selected parameter, enter the override value. In this example, we use the override value of **Sally White** because we know this is the name of one of our sales staff.

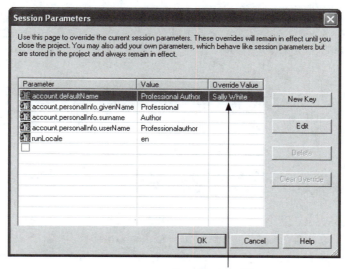

Override defaultName

5. Click OK. Framework Manager stores the override value and changes the result of the test, as shown next:

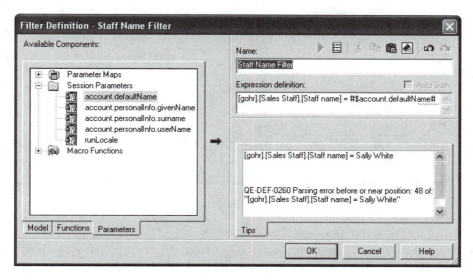

The user name is beginning to look better, but we are still missing the quotes. To fix that issue, we need to look at the built-in macro functions in the next section.

Macro Functions

Framework Manager provides different types of macro functions that you can use when building your macros. Selecting a macro function from the macro functions folder displays additional details about the function in the Tips pane, as shown next, such as to what the macro can be applied, how it works with your information, and what the current results are for that macro.

NOTE   *Framework Manager comes with a number of Macro Functions. Refer to the IBM Cognos 8 BI documentation for a complete list.*

Macro Functions folder

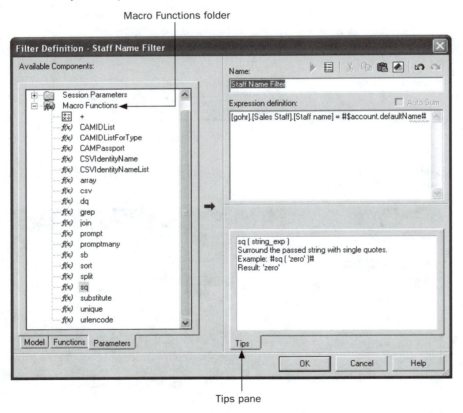

Tips pane

When working with different objects in Framework Manager, you use delimiters to tell the application with what type of object it is working. For example, when working with a query item or a Namespace, you must wrap the objects in square brackets so Framework Manager knows this is a data item. When you need to use a string, as in our example, you use the single quotes macro: `#sq( $account.defaultName)#` which, results in 'Sally White'. If you need square brackets, you can use the `sb()` function.

Let us finish the user filter example that we started in the "Make a Macro" section of this chapter. To do this, we need to use the `sq` macro function, and a filter like the one shown next:

```
[gohr].[Sales Staff].[Staff name] = #sq($account.defaultName)#
```

As a result, our Filter Definition updates, as shown next:

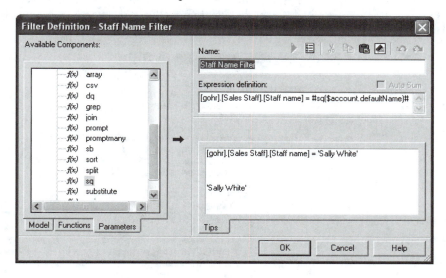

Click the Test Sample link to test the modified model query subject and make sure that the filter returns only records belonging to Sally White.

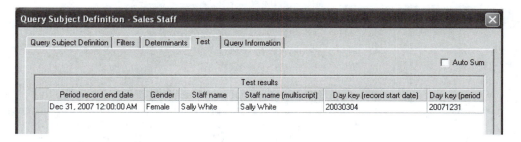

Additional Macro Examples

Macros have many applications for which they can be used when you need the flexibility to determine information at run-time in order to get the desired result. In the next two sections, we will cover two more examples to further illustrate how they can be used.

Using Macros in Multilingual Implementations

Our next example uses the `runLocale` session parameter to dynamically define a data item in a model query subject. Using the sample data that comes with Cognos 8.3 we continue with the Sales Staff model query subject. In this example, we will use the paragon of outdoor equipment providers, the Great Outdoors Company (GO). GO has customers in France, Italy, and the United States, but they do not want to maintain separate databases for each language. In this case, you, as the database administrator at GO, have decided to include a column for each supported language in any table that may hold information in multiple languages.

A good example of this is seen in the ORGANIZATION table. This table holds three pieces of information; the organization code, the organization parent, and the name of the organization presented in 23 columns, one column for each supported language.

When the modeler created the Sales Staff model query subject, he used a macro to dynamically select the appropriate language for the current user based on the `runLocale`. We want to edit the query item in the Query Subject Definition and use a Parameter Map to replace the default column, "ORGANIZATION_NAME_EN", with the following macro:

```
#'[gohr].[ORGANIZATION].[ORGANIZATION_NAME_'+ $Language_lookup{$runLocale}+ '] '#
```

When the macro is added, the Tips pane updates, as shown next:

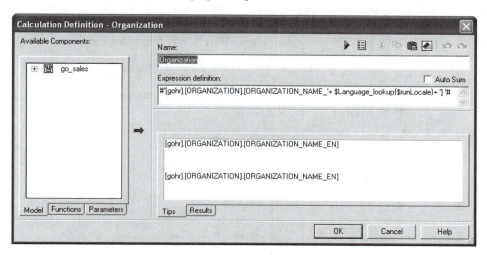

Click the Test button to test the macro with default session parameters to make sure that correct information has been accessed. The test results display in the Test Results pane, as shown next:

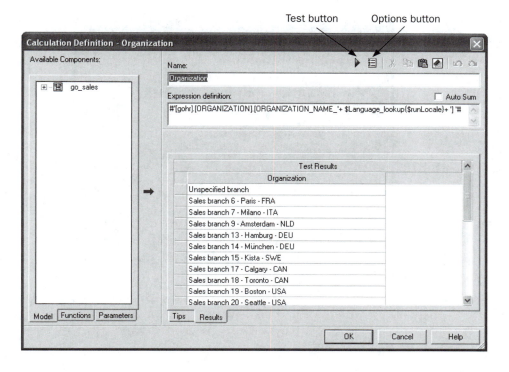

Click the Options button to override the current session parameters to test the macro with a different `runLocale`. The Options dialog displays, as shown next:

Session Parameters button ——→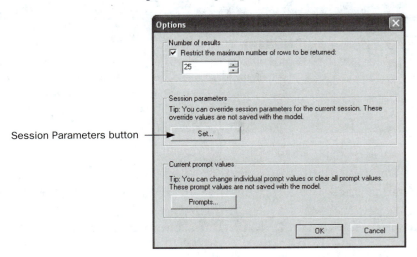

Click Set to open the Session Parameters screen to override the `runLocale` and set it to Italy (it), as shown next:

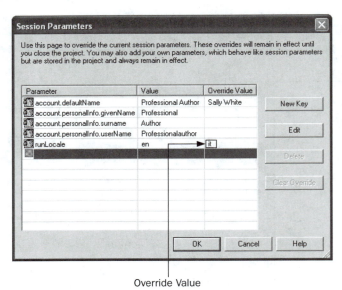

Override Value

Click OK. The Calculation Definition displays, and the Tips pane shows the modified query item, as shown next:

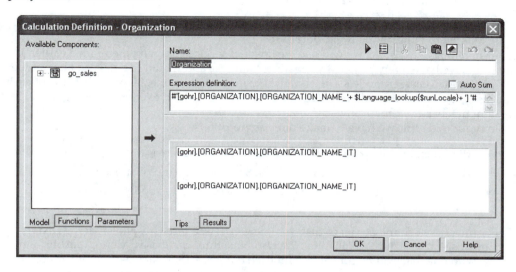

Test the new `runLocale` to make sure that the macro returns the desired results by clicking the Test Button. The results from the Organization column now display in Italian.

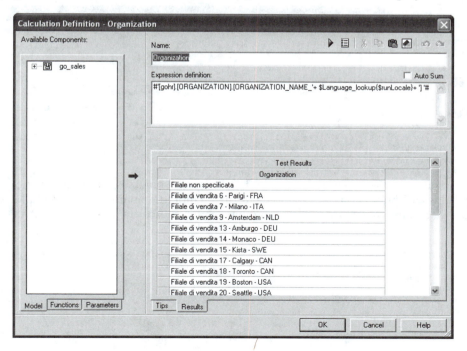

NOTE *Session parameters are for the current session and remain in effect until the user ends the session or manually overrides the setting.*

Using Macros to Point to the Right Database

In our final macro example, we will use the hospital service company mentioned earlier. If you recall, we have many physically separate databases and would like to keep our number of Framework Manager models low, somewhere in the area of one. Since the schema of each database is the same, the only real challenge that we face is how to connect the right user to the right database automatically.

In order to do this we have to make three assumptions:

- All of the databases exist and have the exact same schema.
- All of the databases are defined as Data Sources in Cognos Connection.
- We have some way to associate the person accessing the model with the correct data source.

For the sake of simplicity let us also assume we service three hospitals; Mercy Hospital, Lincoln Hospital, and Adams Hospital. We also have three databases; Mercy, Lincoln, and Adams with one data source connection for each database. Our database administrator has created the databases per our request and we have set up our data source connections, so conditions one and two are met.

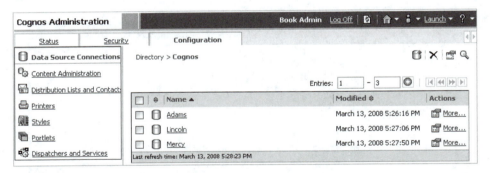

In order to meet our third condition we need to know something about our users; specifically, which users can see what data. In an attempt to keep this example simple, let's assume that all the sign-on names in our authentication source are unique and that any one signon is only permitted to see exactly one database. For our example, we manually create a *Parameter Map* to map a user to the appropriate database.

Create a Parameter Map   Before we can create a parameter map we need a project in which to put it. If we start from scratch using the Adams data source for our new project, our Hospital Framework Manager project would look like the illustration shown next:

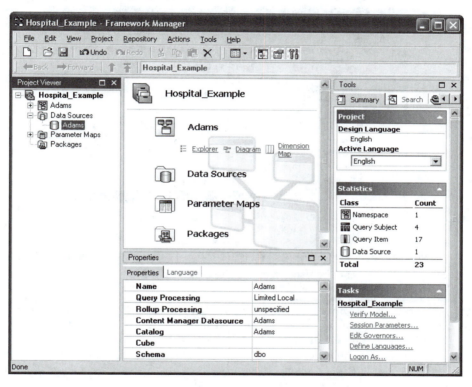

Now that we have a project to work in, we can create our parameter map. The easiest way to create a parameter map is to use the Create Parameter Map Wizard.

Here's how to create a parameter map using the Create Parameter Map Wizard:

1. Right-click on the Parameter Maps folder in the Project Viewer pane.

2. Select Create from the context menu and click Parameter Map. The Select Creation Map screen displays, as shown next:

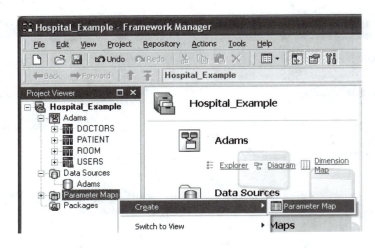

3. Enter the name of your Parameter Map.

4. Select the method to be used to create the map.

NOTE *In our example, we are creating our parameter map manually. However, you can also create a parameter map from an external file, or based on query items. This can be useful if you have an employee table that contains attributes about the people in your organization and you want to supply the parameter map values based on query items. One of those employee attributes could contain the database that the employee is able to access. We could use the Employee ID as the key and the database they can access as the value to populate the parameter map. For more information on using query items to populate a parameter map, refer to the Framework Manager documentation that came with your Cognos 8 installation.*

5. Select the Manual option for creating your map.

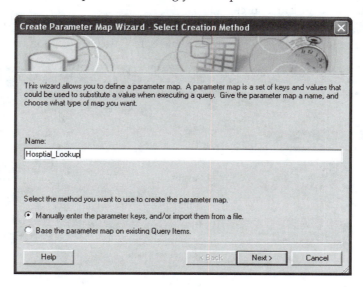

6. Click Next. The Parameter Map Definition screen displays, as shown next:

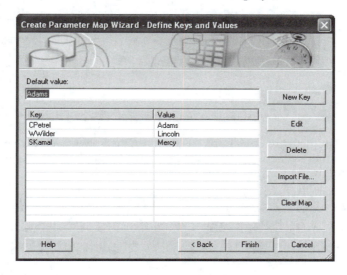

7. Enter a default value. This is the value returned if no key matches what is provided to the parameter map.
8. Click the New Key button.
9. Enter the keys for your map. In this example, we use individual user IDs.

10. Enter the value to which the key maps. In this example, we enter the name of the Content Manager Datasource.

11. Click Finish. The parameter map can be used to map users from our LDAP authentication provider to the appropriate data source connection name.

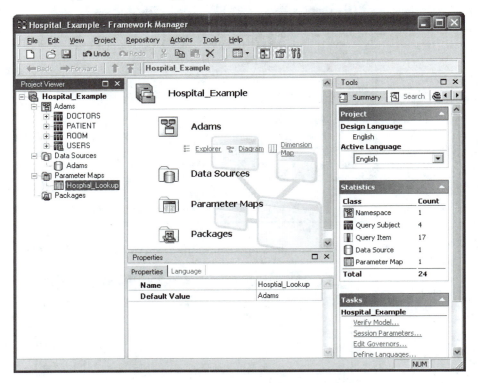

We know that there are more hospitals than Adams, so we need to make the name of our data source more generic, and we decide to use **Hospital.** When we rename Adams to Hospital, the following warning displays:

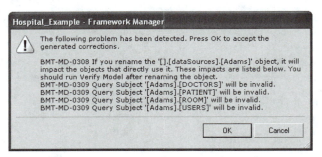

This warning notifies us that Framework Manager has also updated any data source query subject that was using Adams. This is a new feature in Cognos 8.3. For example, [Adams].[DOCTORS] table is now the [Hospital].[DOCTORS] table. The objective of this example is to have one data source that can point to any data connection based on the macro. As a result, this automatic renaming works to our advantage. Framework Manager did all the busy work of renaming the query subjects for us.

The table query definition for USERS displays, as shown next:

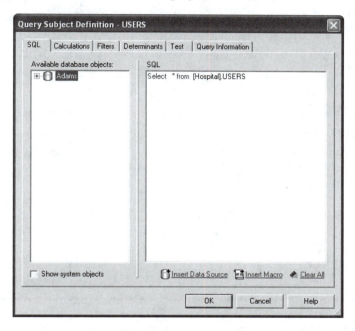

This example shows us that our query listed in the SQL pane looks correct. However, our Available Database Objects pane still displays Adams because we only renamed the Data Source. We did not change the data source connection.

We have renamed the data source to a more generic name. Now we need to add our macro. This example shows the Properties pane for our Hospital data source connection:

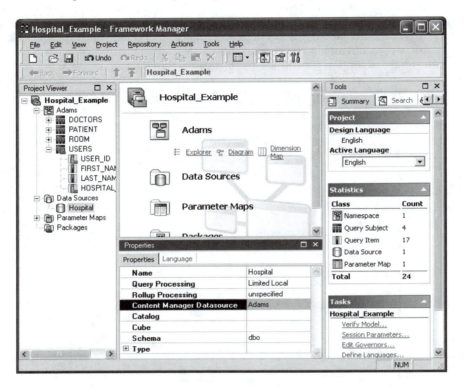

NOTE   *In this example the Catalog property of the data source can be blank because all the databases have the same catalog. If the database used different catalogs or schemas, you would need macros in those fields as well.*

The Content Manager Datasource is where we need our macro. Click in the field to the right of the Content Manager Datasource. Click on the ellipsis that display. The Edit Property Value dialog box displays, as shown next:

Insert Macro button

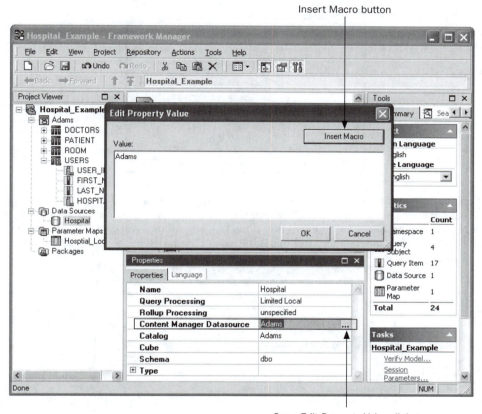

Open Edit Property Value dialog

Click on the Insert Macro button to open the Macro Editor dialog to build the macro.

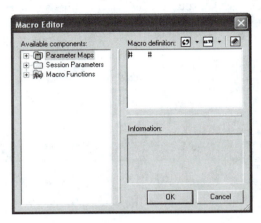

Our macro needs to determine who is trying to connect to which database. If we look at our session parameters, as shown next, we see that the `account.personalInfo.userName` is available. We can probably assume that this value will be unique as all of our users are defined in the same authentication source, and this is the session parameter that we want to edit:

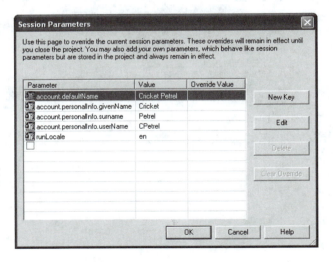

Click Edit. The Macro Editor screen displays, as shown next:

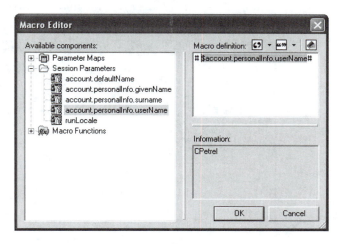

This example shows us the `userName` for the current session, and this gives us the key to our parameter map. We must next find the proper database, and we can modify our macro to do that, as shown next:

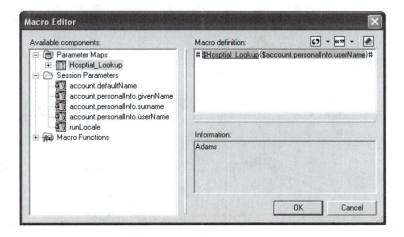

The session parameter is passed to the parameter map, which returns the database value associated with `CPetrel`. In this example, the database value is Adams.

We can see the SQL created when the user is `CPeterl` by clicking on the Query Information tab in the Query Subject Definition screen, as shown next, and clicking on the Test Sample link at the bottom right of the screen:

Adams database ———→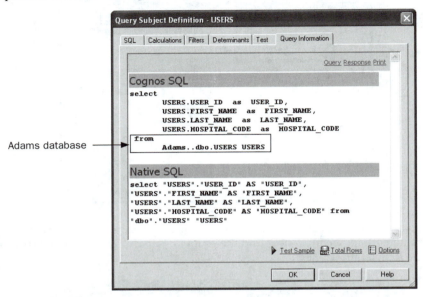

We can test query to make sure that each user is accessing the correct database by supplying a username from the Lincoln hospital as the parameter override value. In this example, we use `WWilder`. This user can access the Lincoln data source as seen below:

Lincoln database ———→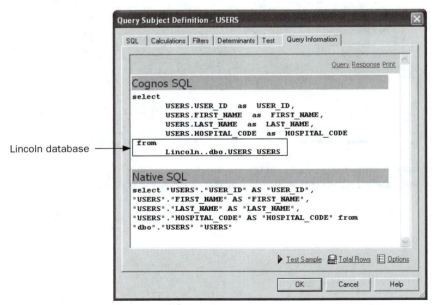

If we override the username in our session parameter list to SKamal, that user can access the Mercy data source, as shown next:

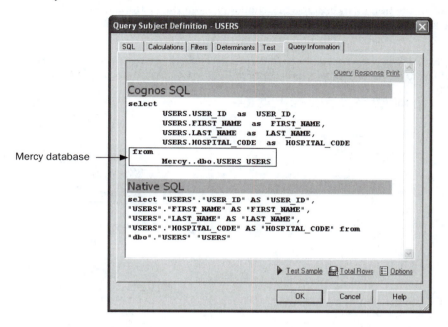

Mercy database

In each case, it is the same query subject referencing an entirely different database through the use of a macro that uses a parameter map and a session parameter.

Macros can be used to keep your models simple and flexible. Anytime you find yourself duplicating effort, take a step back, and ask yourself if a macro might be the solution.

Security

With Cognos 8 Framework Manager, you can specify *Package Security* which defines who can access the package to author and run reports, and who can administer the package to publish it and set permissions for it. You can specify *Object Security* which sets explicit allow or deny access to folders, namespaces, query subjects, query items, and so on. And finally, *Data Security* in which you apply security filters to restrict rows returned from a query.

Configure Package Access

You can configure access permissions on a package in order to give specific users, groups, or roles access to the contents of the package through the Cognos Studios. Permissions are added to a package using the users, groups, and roles found in the Cognos Namespace or your authentication provider.

Package access permissions can be applied when publishing the package the first time using the publish wizard, or at any time after that through Framework Manager or Cognos Connection. It is a personal choice as to when you apply package access permissions.

In our experience, it has been easier to apply package access after initially publishing the package and accessing its properties later. You can access the package's properties in Cognos Connection or in Framework Manager from the Actions menu where you select Packages and then click the Edit Package Settings submenu, as shown next:

NOTE *The package properties accessed from the Edit Package Settings in Framework Manager are identical to the package properties accessed in Cognos Connection (including the Permissions tab).*

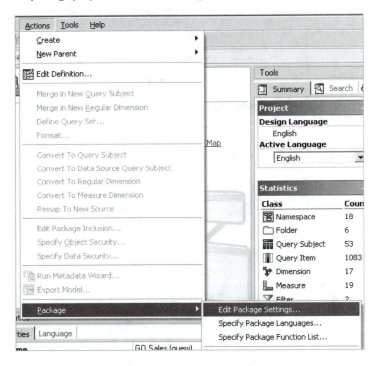

When you publish a package, and do not set the access permissions from the publish wizard, the package inherits the permissions from the folder to which it is published. By selecting the Permissions tab on the Edit Package Settings screen, seen next, we see what those default settings are, how they were applied to the package, and we have the opportunity to modify them. To specify package access permissions, you grant Read, Write, Execute, and Traverse permissions. To specify administrator access permissions, you grant Read, Write, Set Policy, and Traverse permissions.

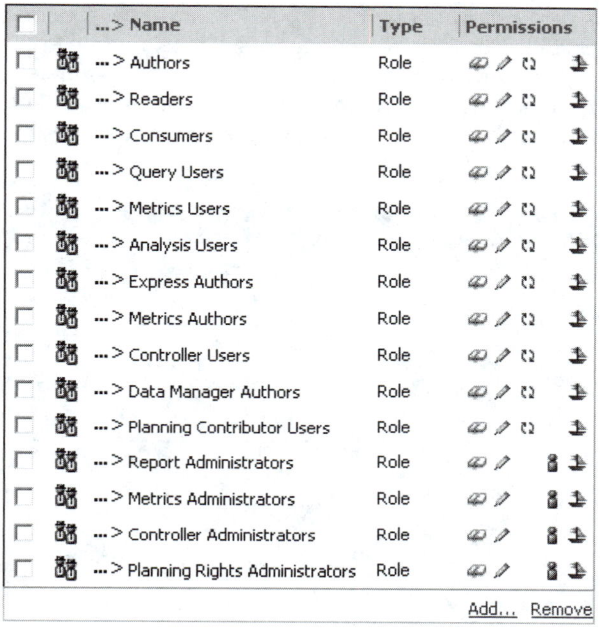

		...> Name	Type	Permissions
☐	🔍	...> Authors	Role	
☐	🔍	...> Readers	Role	
☐	🔍	...> Consumers	Role	
☐	🔍	...> Query Users	Role	
☐	🔍	...> Metrics Users	Role	
☐	🔍	...> Analysis Users	Role	
☐	🔍	...> Express Authors	Role	
☐	🔍	...> Metrics Authors	Role	
☐	🔍	...> Controller Users	Role	
☐	🔍	...> Data Manager Authors	Role	
☐	🔍	...> Planning Contributor Users	Role	
☐	🔍	...> Report Administrators	Role	
☐	🔍	...> Metrics Administrators	Role	
☐	🔍	...> Controller Administrators	Role	
☐	🔍	...> Planning Rights Administrators	Role	

Add...   Remove

If the inherited permissions do not meet the specific needs for the package, you can easily modify them from the Permissions tab. In this example, if we wanted to restrict access on this package to only Authors, we simply remove all the other users, groups, and roles from the permissions list.

NOTE *Setting permissions on Cognos Connection objects is discussed in Chapter 17.*

Specify Object Security

Object Security in Framework Manager allows you to apply security to individual elements in the model. This means that for any object in the model, you can specify which users, groups, or roles can access it. If they do not have access to the object, they will not see it in any of the studios.

Object Security is very strict in how it is applied. Basically, the second you secure one object, all other objects in the model are no longer visible to anyone in the Cognos 8 studios. To demonstrate, consider the following example. We take a few simple query subjects from the sample Cognos data and publish them as a test package called GO Sales (security). The next illustration shows the simple package created from the Sales model query subject folder:

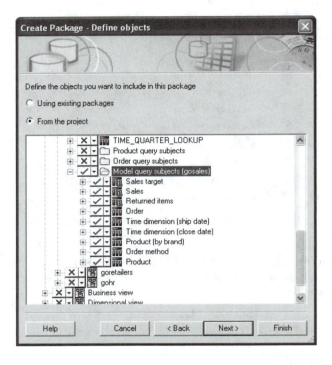

This example shows a simple report, with no object security, using the query items from the Sales Target model query subject:

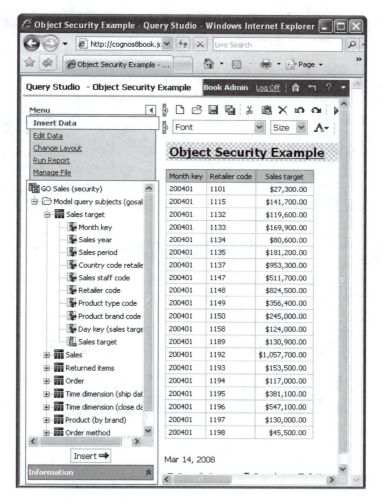

Management decides that only one sales manager, Sally White, should be permitted to see the Sales Target. You can apply object security to the Sales Target query item in the Sales

Target model query subject to accommodate their request. From the Actions menu, select Specify Object Security, as shown next:

Access the Specify Object Security screen, as shown next, and click the Add button:

Locate Sally White in the authentication provider and add Sally to the list of users permitted to access the Sales Target item, as shown next:

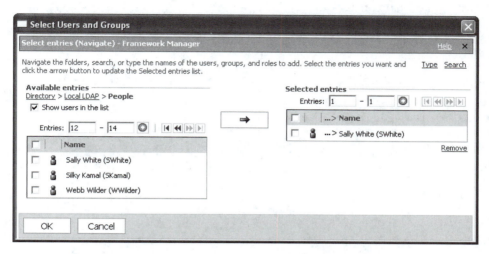

Click OK. The Specify Object Security screen displays, as shown next:

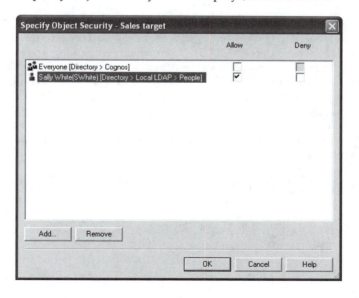

Just to show you how serious object security is, as soon as you click OK, Framework Manager displays a warning. Not only are you warned; but, you are also given instructions on how to undo what you just did!

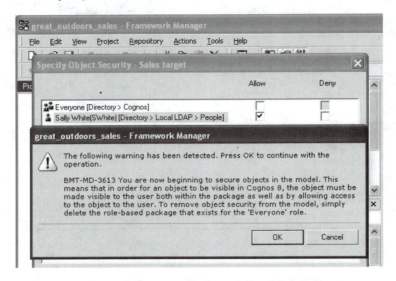

NOTE *The warning reads as follows: The following warning has been detected. Press OK to continue with the operation. BMT-MD-3613 You are now beginning to secure objects in the model. This means that in order for an object to be visible in Cognos 8, the object must be made visible to the user both within the package as well as by allowing access to the object to the user. To remove object security from the model, simply delete the role-based package that exists for the 'Everyone' role.*

When you publish the package and open the report again as an administrator, you see an error, as shown next:

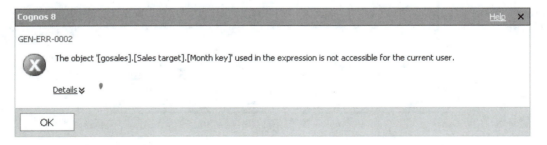

In Query Studio, click on the Insert Data option from the Menu, and you see only the name of the package and nothing else, as shown next:

If you log on to Cognos Connection as Sally White, the situation is not much better. Sally can only see one item from the entire package, as shown next, and anyone else who logs on cannot see any items from the package:

We went through all of that to demonstrate a point. The second you secure one item in an object, all other objects in that package are no longer visible to anyone until you do something about it.

You can quickly restore visibility by going to the root namespace or folder and allowing Everyone (or some other appropriate group or role) access to all objects, as shown next. This does not undo the security you set on the Sales Target object, but all other unsecured objects inherit the security from the root level and will be available to all users:

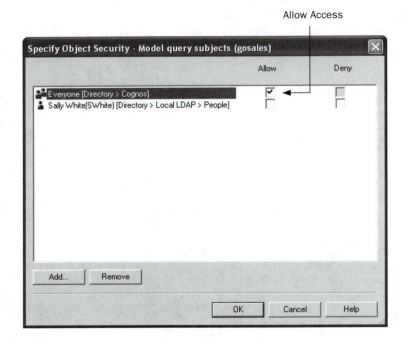

When applying object security, there are two approaches. First, you can lock down everything and then grant access, which requires going through all the objects to specify the appropriate security. This happens when you specify Object security on an object as in our example above. The other method is to grant access to everyone at the root level and then go in and specify object security on objects you want to hide from some users. We recommend the second method because you typically only want to hide a select set of items from all users; not your entire model.

NOTE *Use the Deny setting if you have a particular user or group that you do not want to see an object, but they belong to another group that has access to the object. Deny overrides the Allow setting users have in the other groups to which they belong.*

Data Security

In the "Macros" section of this chapter, we discussed how to build macros that can act as dynamic filters on query subjects. So far in the "Security" section, we have discussed how to set access permissions on entire packages in "Package Access," and how to grant or deny access to individual objects in the model in "Object Security." In this section we discuss how to specify *Data Security*.

Data Security is important because the goal of Cognos 8 is to enable your users to create their own reports and analyses while keeping certain information confidential. For example, suppose your sales force is divided along product brands. There is one sales person responsible for each given brand, and you want to apply data security so that the sales person running the report can only see his brand.

In order to make this work, we need to identify where in our model to apply data security. Using the sample data in Cognos 8, we see the model query subjects Products folder in the great_outdoors_sales Framework Manager project, as shown next. We decide that given the nature of our data security filter, this would be a good place to start:

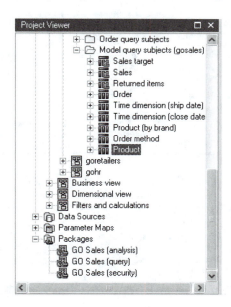

Click the Actions menu and then Specify Data Security, as shown next:

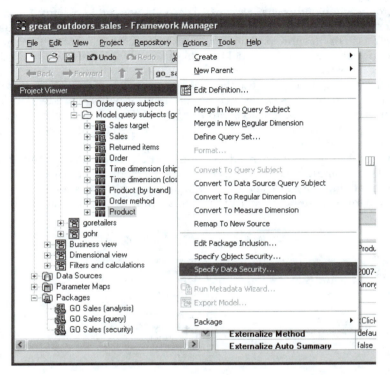

The Specify Data Security screen, as shown next, allows you to define one or more Groups. These data security groups are collections of user, groups, or roles from your authentication provider, to which you will be applying specific filters:

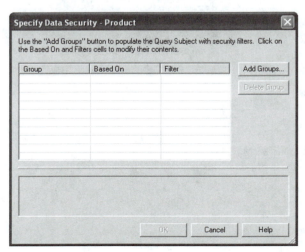

Continuing with our example, Sally White is responsible for the "Husky" product brand. We can restrict the data she sees by adding data security to the Product query subject, adding Sally to the data security group, and creating a filter that only returns Husky brand products.

We click the Add Groups button, find Sally in our authentication provider, and add her to the selected entries, as shown next:

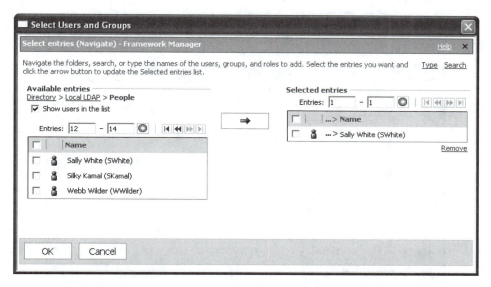

Now that Sally is in a group, we want to create a filter for her brand. We have the option of creating a new filter or using one that has already been defined in the model. For this example, we create a new filter, as shown next:

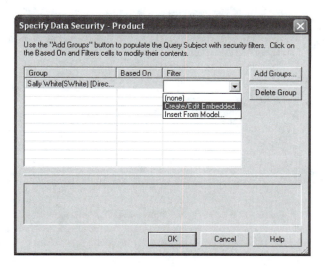

PART IV

NOTE *The Based On column in the Specify Data Security screen allows you to reuse groups that have already been defined and inherit their security. For example, if you added another user, Frank Bretton, to the Specify Data Security screen and he should only see the "Star Gazer" product brands as well as the Husky product brands, you can base Frank Bretton's security on Sally White's security to provide access to the Husky product brands. You would then create a filter for the Star Gazer product brands for Frank Bretton. This way you can leverage work already done in another security filter. Refer to your Cognos documentation for more details.*

We create a simple filter that restricts product brands to Husky, as shown next:

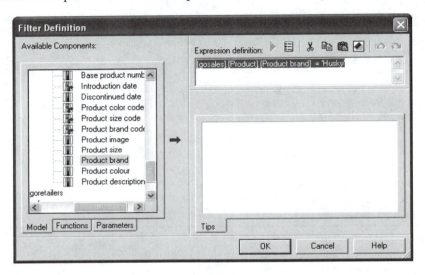

When we publish the package and log on as user other than Sally, we can see all product brands, as shown next:

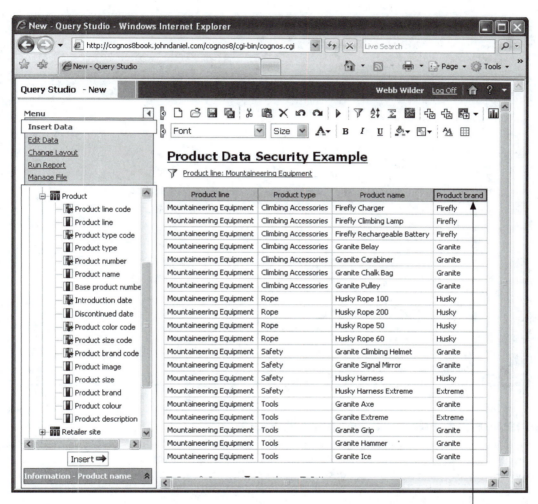

Product Brands

When Sally logs on and runs the exact same report, only Husky product brands display, as shown next:

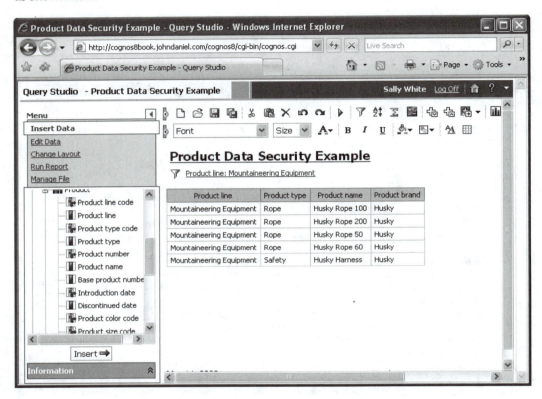

Dimensionally Modeled Relational Models

One of the most powerful, and cool, features of Framework Manager is its ability to model relational data so that the it appears dimensional to the Cognos 8 Studios and to your users. In this section we will discuss the basics of creating Dimensionally Modeled Relational models (DMR). Also, we will assume that you have read and digested, Chapter 15. This is an extremely important assumption because if the relationally modeled metadata being used to create your DMR is not correct, your DMR will be DOA. By way of explanation, DOA stands for "Dead on Arrival", a rather gruesome phrase but quite apropos, because a fundamental concept of DMR is that you have a solid relational model to use as a starting point.

Why Dimensionally Model Metadata?

Have you ever had one of your business users ask you for this: I want a report that shows me the gross sales of our widgets for the last month, by brand, by customer, and by region, and group the city under those regions while you're at it! Your business user is not, contrary to popular opinion, asking for a smack upside the head. He is, in fact, asking for dimensional data.

Anytime he says the word "by", you should hear dimension or a level in a dimension. The phrases "for the last…" and "for the next…" speak to a time dimension; and "show me the…" almost always refers to money or some other value to be measured. We will be discussing time and measure dimensions individually below.

NOTE *Dimensional data answers the questions: Who, what, when, where, and why. Who bought something? What, exactly, did they buy? When did they buy it? Where did they get it? Why did they return it?*

When the topic of Dimensional modeling is discussed, two other terms, usually, are not far behind; *OLAP* and *Cubes*. OLAP is an acronym for On-Line Analytical Processing, a methodology for presenting data in an optimized dimensional manner. While cubes (also called OLAP Cubes) are self-contained collections of data that have been optimized for dimensional reporting and analysis, they also contain a predefined set of data.

There is an important distinction to be made between OLAP Cubes and Dimensionally Modeled Relational metadata. OLAP Cubes are, by definition, dimensional in nature. OLAP Cubes are self-contained, limited sets of data that have been optimized for reporting, which makes them fast. OLAP Cubes also allow business users to look at data in smaller groups (drill-down), look at data in larger groups (drill-up), and look at data from a different perspective (slice and dice).

Dimensionally Modeled Relational metadata gives the user the ability to drill-up, drill-down, and slice and dice as well. The difference lay in *what* they are performing these operations on. In a DMR, the data comes from a relational database; not from an optimized OLAP Cube (a file). Of course, there are pros and cons. OLAP is faster but it is only as timely as the last build, where a DMR is slower but the data is up to the minute. OLAP models are easier to create, most of the time, where DMR modeling is more complex.

Regardless of which method you decide upon, business users think dimensionally, and if you want to be a hero in your organization, listen for the "bys" and turn them into dimensions.

NOTE *Cognos 8 Transformer is the tool used to create OLAP cubes. While Transformer is beyond the scope of this book, be sure to look into it.*

A Dimensional Primer

If you have never heard of, seen, or used a dimensional data source, you might be wondering what the fuss is all about. Dimensional data provides the report author and analysis user with the ability to quickly navigate through large amounts of data while, at the same time, exploring multiple aspects of that data.

Regular Dimensions

These "aspects of the data" are called *Regular Dimensions*. Regular dimensions can be things like product, customer, date, geography, sales person, or anything that groups and describes your data. Regular dimensions are layered objects; they have hierarchies, hierarchies have levels, and finally, levels have mandatory and optional attributes, as shown in the next illustration. At run time, this information is used to generate members, which are the data entities found in multidimensional sources and, at a minimum, consist of a business key and a caption.

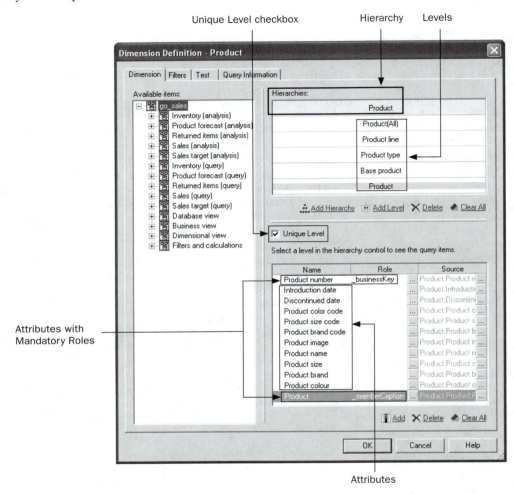

A Hierarchy defines how the levels in your regular dimension relate to each other. The previous illustration shows a product dimension from the Cognos 8 sample data. In this hierarchy there are 5 levels. From the lowest level to the highest these are: Product, Base product, Product type, Product line, and Product(All). A veteran dimensional modeler would read that hierarchy as: Products rollup to Base products, which rollup to Product types, which rollup to Product lines, and Product lines rollup to the artificial level of Product(All).

Levels in a dimension must contain an attribute that takes on the role of the businessKey; that is, it uniquely identifies a member for that level. In the previous illustration, the Product level has a business key of Product number. Levels also must contain an attribute that takes on the role of labeling the members for the level. This role is called the memberCaption.

The `memberCaption` is commonly a text description as opposed to the business key. The business key is usually a code of some sort, but in some cases the `businessKey` role and the `memberCaption` role can be applied to the same attribute. Levels can also contain an attribute that uses the `memberDescription` role or attributes that simply provide additional information about the items at a given level. For the Product level, a few of the non-role attributes are product color, product size, and introduction date.

Another important concept when talking about levels is uniqueness. How does Cognos 8 know which items in a level consists of the unique group for that level? Later on, you will see that the Dimension Definition screen contains a Unique Level checkbox. The Unique Level checkbox in regular dimensions must be checked for any level that has a business key that uniquely identifies the row of data, even if the key repeats in the data. This specifies that the level's key does not need the parent key to identify it. If it does, then you leave the box cleared. If it does not, you select it. The highest level has no parent, so you do not need to select it. For example, you would clear the checkbox if your month key is 1 through 12, you will also need the year keys 2005, 2006, to uniquely identify month 1-2005, 2-2005, 3-2005,…, 1-2006, 2-2006, 3-2006, and so on.

Attributes are the actual data items used to define the level. Attributes can take on roles such as `businessKey`, `memeberCaption`, and `memberDescription` or they can simply provide additional details about members in a level.

Measure Dimensions

Regular dimensions provide context to the measures in which users are interested. *Measures* are the items that we count, also called facts, metrics, or key figures. Sales dollars, quantities (such as sold, shipped, bought, and broken), and inventory levels are all examples of measures, as shown next:

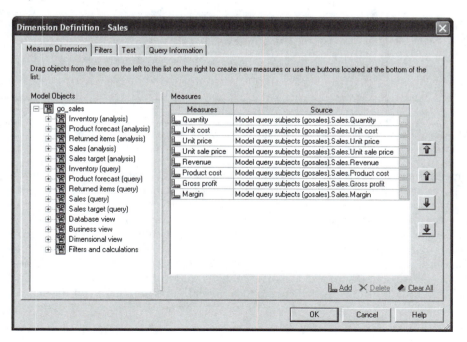

Measure dimensions are much easier to understand than regular dimensions because there are no hierarchies, levels, and so on. There are just numbers—plain, simple, numbers.

Time (Date) Dimensions

A *Time Dimension* is really just a regular dimension that gives your data chronological meaning, as shown next:

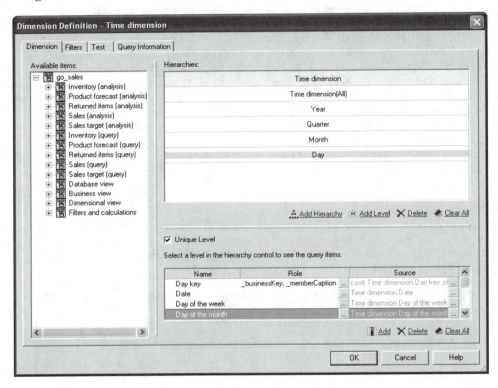

NOTE *Most Time Dimensions do not, in fact, have "time" in them. The lowest level of a time dimension is normally the Day.*

Time dimensions in an OLAP Cube normally include levels that are useful in analyses and reports, such as month, quarter, and year. These levels are not normally found in relational data sources, but we will talk about that in a bit.

One very nice feature of a time dimension is the ability to contain multiple hierarchies. This is very useful if your organization uses more than one calendar. For example, your organization may use a fiscal calendar for the financial department that runs from July to June, and a standard calendar for all other departments that run from January to December.

If a business user asks for a report of all widgets sold during the first quarter, which quarter is he talking about? Does he mean the one that starts in January, for the standard calendar, or the one that starts in July, for the fiscal calendar? In this example, you can create two hierarchies within the same time dimension. There would be a Fiscal Calendar Hierarchy and a Standard Calendar Hierarchy.

NOTE *If you need to report on both hierarchies at the same time, it's recommended to create a separate dimension for each hierarchy. Currently, accessing multiple hierarchies from a single dimension is not supported.*

Using Dimensionally Modeled Metadata to Answer the Second Business Question

Another reason that we use Dimensionally Model Metadata is to answer the *Second Business Question*. The second business question is the one that the user either meant to ask in the first place, or it is a question he was not even aware existed until he got the answer to the first.

A hypothetical conversation leading to the second business question might go like this:

"Who bought all of our blue widgets last month?" asks Mr. Business User.

"Armin bought them all," replies the Really Intelligent Report Author.

"What!" says Mr. Business User, "Sophia usually buys all of our blue widgets! What did Sophia buy last month since we were all out of blue widgets?"

The second business question is: "What did Sophia buy last month?"

If your data has been dimensionally modeled, the business user can quickly and easily answer the question himself using the drilling and slicing and dicing capabilities mentioned earlier. If it has not, you will probably spend some time writing a second report to answer the second business question. Oh, and did I mention the third business question?

Building the Dimensionally Modeled Relational Model

To reiterate, we assume that you have modeled your relational data using the practices described in Chapter 15, and that the relational model has been thoroughly and successfully tested.

When building a DMR model, it is helpful to consider the Star Schema design, as shown next. Star schemas are usually found in data warehouses, and in basic terms, they are simplified data structures that have been optimized for reporting and analysis:

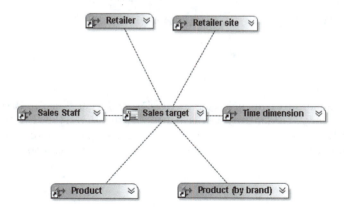

Star schemas are dimensional by nature in that they have one Measure table and a set of Dimension tables. In the illustration above, the Sales target table would be our measure dimension and the other six tables surrounding it would be regular dimensions. If you can model your relational data so that it resembles a star schema, you will have a good DMR model.

Build a Regular Dimension

Using the sample data and the great_outdoors_sales Framework Manager project, we start our DMR modeling by identifying the regular dimensions in the Database view namespace, as shown next:

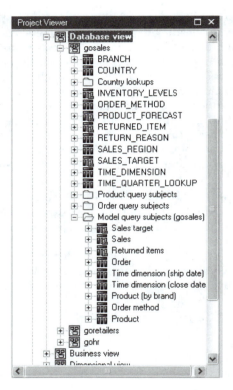

There are three measure dimension candidates: Sales Target, Sales, and Returned Items. The regular dimension candidates are: Order, TIME_DIMENSION, Product (by brand), Order method, and Product. In this example, we use Sales target as our measure dimension, Product as our regular dimension, and TIME_DIMENSION as our time dimension.

Once you have identified the query subjects to be used for your DMR objects, create your first regular dimension.

Create a new namespace to contain your DMR objects. Right-click on the new namespace, select Create then, and then select Regular Dimension, as shown next:

The Dimension Definition screen displays, as shown next:

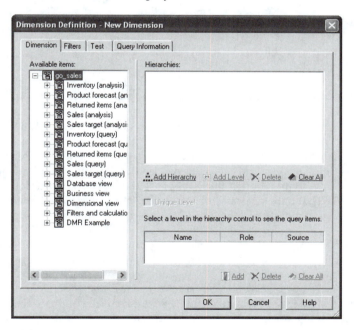

In the Available items pane, navigate to the Product model query subject, as shown next:

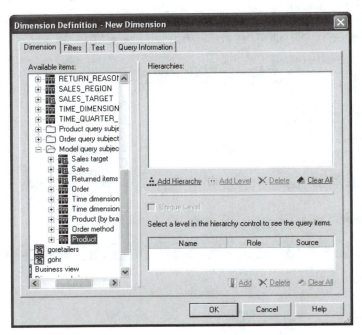

As with all of the Cognos tools, there is more than one way to get what you want, and the Dimension Definition tool is no exception. Before we start building our regular dimension, recall our discussion about what you need to make one: hierarchies, levels, and attributes. At this point, you should have a clear idea of what the new regular dimension should look like. How do members rollup? What are the levels? What uniquely identifies a member in a level? What data describes that member? What additional information do we want to include about a member in the level? You need all of this information before you start.

Continuing with the example from earlier, we know that Products rollup to Base Products, which rollup to Product Types, which rollup to Product Lines, and Product Lines rollup to the artificial level, Product(All), which allows you to easily see overall totals for a hierarchy. So, those are our levels. To create a level in the Dimension Definition tool, you first have to have a hierarchy in which to put it. With this tool, you have two options to create the new hierarchy: you can click on the Add Hierarchy button, or you can drag-and-drop a query item from your model query subject. The drag-and-drop option creates the hierarchy and adds the new level at the same time.

Product number is the query item that uniquely identifies a product. Since products are the lowest level of detail in our new dimension we can assume that this query item will play the role of businessKey in the Products level. Drag the Product number query item into the Hierarchies pane of the Dimension Definition dialog, as shown next:

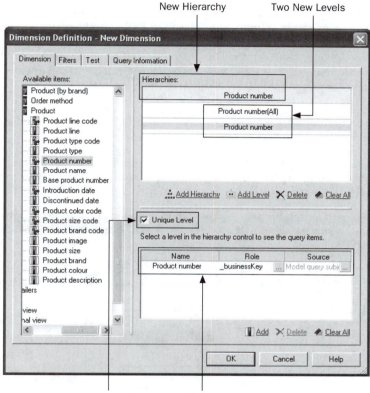

After our drag-and-drop, three things happen: a new hierarchy is created, two levels are added to the hierarchy, and a member with the role of businessKey is added to the level.

NOTE *To rename any object in the Dimension Definition, right-click on the item and select rename from the context menu.*

The two created levels take their names from the query item itself (Product number(All) and Product number). Because we started with the lowest level of our hierarchy, we can assume that at this level the business key is unique, and we need to select the Unique Level checkbox.

The hierarchy takes the name of the query item that was used in the drag-and-drop; you can right-click on the name of the hierarchy to rename it. It is good practice to keep your names on the generic side. Because our example dimension contains more than just the product number, it would be wise to rename the hierarchy to Product.

NOTE *The All level of a hierarchy is an automatic level that acts as a rollup of everything in the hierarchy.*

The Dimension Definition tool tries to guess what the newly added query item's role should be. If the query item is defined as an identifier in the model query subject, the Dimension Definition tool assigns it the role of businessKey. If the query item is defined as an attribute in model query subject, the Dimension Definition tool assigns it the role of memberCaption. Remember that if the tool guesses incorrectly, you can always reassign the role manually and/or assign more than one role to the query item.

NOTE *The tool only makes a guess for the first member added to the level, for all subsequent members you will be asked to identify the role.*

Because we added an identifier first, we must manually add the memberCaption to the Product level. Drag the Product name from the model query subject to the appropriate level, as shown next:

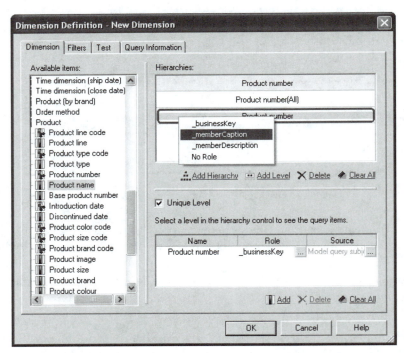

After adding the caption, the level displays, as shown next:

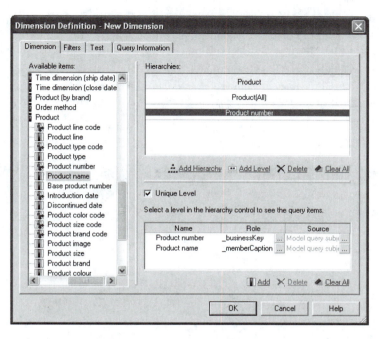

Drag the Base Product Number to its proper location in the hierarchy, in this case between Product and Product(All), as shown next:

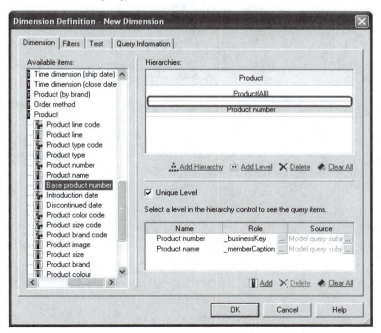

The Base Product Number is a bit of an exception, in that it does not have any query item that acts as a caption. Fortunately, members can be assigned multiple roles. For this level, the Base Product Number acts as both `businessKey` and `memberCaption`.

NOTE *Attributes filling the role of memberCaption must be character strings. If they are dates or numbers, you must convert them to strings in the Source definition of the attribute.*

Select the level you want to modify, and click the ellipsis next to the role to assign. The Specify Roles dialog displays, as shown next:

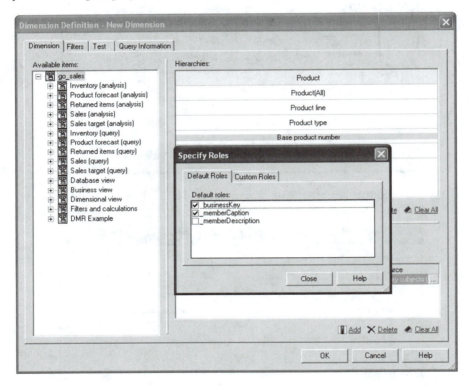

Continue building the levels in the hierarchy by adding the following:

- Product Type (level name), Product Type Code (business key), and Product Type (member caption).

- Product Line (level name), Product Line Code (business key), and Product Line (member caption).

The hierarchy displays, as shown next:

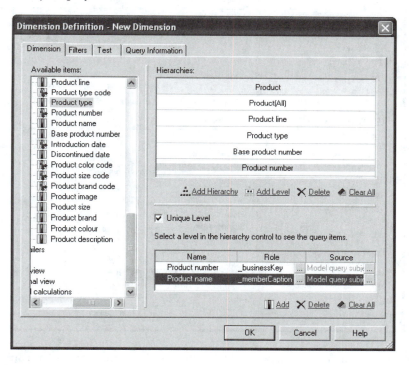

To complete this regular dimension, we add query items as attribute members to the Product level without assigning them any role, as shown next, and select the Unique Level checkbox for all levels that meet the criteria discussed above.

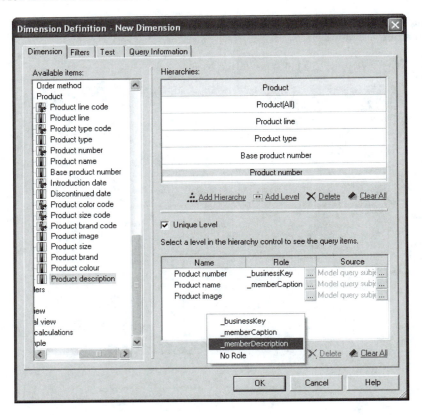

If available and required, you can assign an item to the `memberDescription` role. For example, you can specify Product Description.

NOTE   *Attributes can be added to any to level except the (All) level*

Build a Time Dimension

A time dimension is virtually the same as any other regular dimension. The only exception is the nature of the data. Dates are often used as an example of a hierarchy since days roll into weeks, which roll into months, and so on. As discussed above, relational data sources often do not include a table that specifically references time; but since they are so useful, you will want to include one in any DMR that you design. To do so, you have two options: 1) You can create a time model query subject and add calculated query items for the levels and attributes you would like, such as month, quarter, year, and so on. 2) You can create a new table in your relational data source that contains these items and join the time table to your

Date	Month	Quarter	Year	Fiscal Quarter	Fiscal Year
01/01/2008	January	Q1	2008	Q2	2007
06/12/2008	June	Q2	2008	Q4	2007

TABLE 16-2   Multiple hierarchies in a date dimension

measure dimension on the date. We prefer the second method, as it reduces the number of calculations that occur every time you use a date.

A common use of time dimensions is to make use of multiple hierarchies. A simple way to think of how a multiple hierarchy works is to consider our fiscal and standard calendars from above. One date can have different, and mutually exclusive, attributes. Table 16-2 demonstrates this ability.

Table 16-2 shows that one date, June 12, 2008, can be grouped in two different ways. In the standard calendar, this date is in the second quarter; in the fiscal calendar, it is in the fourth quarter.

If your data supports multiple hierarchies, you can add them to your time dimension by creating the dimension using the calendar dates, then adding the fiscal dates as an alternate hierarchy, as shown next. For example, we added Fiscal Year and Fiscal Quarter query items to the sample data provided by Cognos:

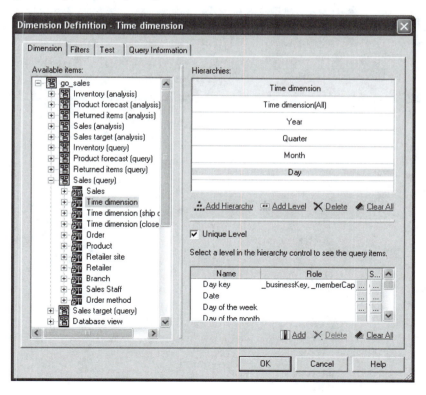

We add our alternate hierarchy by dragging a level of the new hierarchy to the right-hand side of the current hierarchy in our dimension, as shown next:

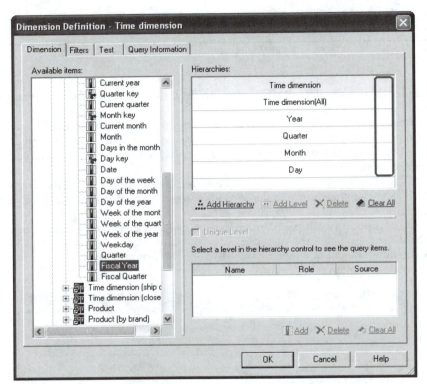

For our alternate hierarchy we use the Fiscal Year as the new level, as shown next:

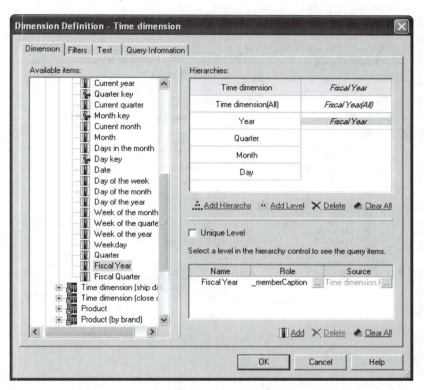

We manually set the `businessKey` and `memberCaption` for the new level and add the Fiscal Quarter, Month, and Date levels. Set the members and roles for each new level as appropriate, as shown next:

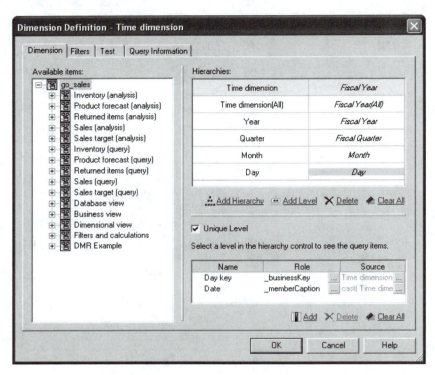

When we save our new time dimension, it contains both hierarchies, as shown next:

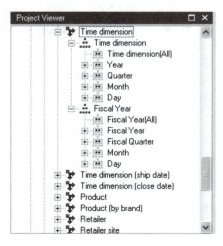

NOTE *Multiple hierarchies can be created in any regular dimension.*

Build a Measure Dimension

The measure dimension contains the items in which most business users are ultimately interested: how many and how much. The ideal measure dimension contains only measures. If you think you need something other than measures, you should re-examine your relational model to make sure it is designed properly.

NOTE *The theory and practice of how to model data is a very large area with many topics beyond the scope of this book. If you run into trouble while modeling your data, the first place to look for help is in the* Guidelines for Modeling Metadata *documentation that comes with your IBM Cognos 8 BI installation.*

Here's how to create a measure dimension:

1. Right-click on the namespace where you would like the measure dimension to reside.

2. Click on Create and then Measure Dimension, as shown next:

3. Navigate to the model query subject that contains the measure(s) you would like to include.

4. Drag the measure from the model query subject to the Measures pane of the Dimension Definition screen, as shown next:

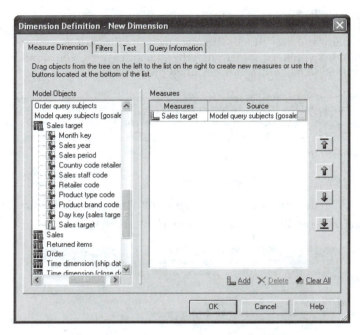

5. Click OK and examine the namespace. In this example, we now see two regular dimensions and one measure dimension, as shown next:

Scope Relationships

The *Scope Relationship* defines which measures are in scope for which dimensions and at which levels for a hierarchy. Consider the following example for an explanation. Suppose you sell widgets every day of the year and, of course, you are interested in how those widgets are selling. In this case, the widget sales measure is in scope down to the day level of the Time hierarchy. When you talk about widget sales per day, it makes sense. Suppose you set a sales target for widgets and your goal is to sell one million widgets per month. The widget sales target measure is in scope only down to the month level of the Time hierarchy, not the day level.

Scope is not limited to dates. Suppose the one million widget sales target is not for a specific type of widget, such as widget number 1337, but the target is for all widgets in the widget product line. In this case, our sales target is not only in scope to the month level of the time hierarchy, it is also in scope to the product line level of the product dimension, leaving all levels below product line out of scope.

Framework Manager provides you with a visualization of scope, as shown next, when you double-click on the namespace with your dimensions and then select the Dimension Map in Framework Manager:

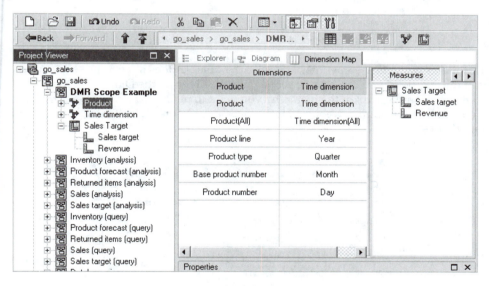

To see the scope of a measure, click on the measure of interest from the measures pane.

NOTE *You can apply different levels of scope for different measures within the same measure dimension if required.*

Framework Manager will examine the metadata for the selected measure and it will try to determine, based on the tables and joins, which levels make sense for the measure.

If a level is thought to be in scope, then the background color of the level changes from white to a kind of purplish, salmon color, as seen next:

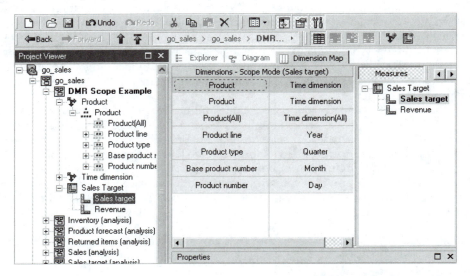

Despite its best effort, sometimes Framework Manager does not get the scope quite right. If this happens, you can change scope pretty easily from the Dimension Map.

Right-click on the level of the hierarchy you want to modify and select Set Scope, as shown next. In this example, we use Month since our measure, Sales Target, is only valid to the month level:

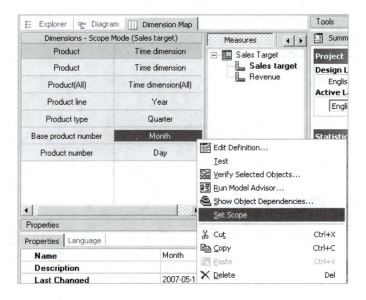

This defines the scope as ending at the selected level, as shown next. All levels below the selected one are now considered to be out of scope:

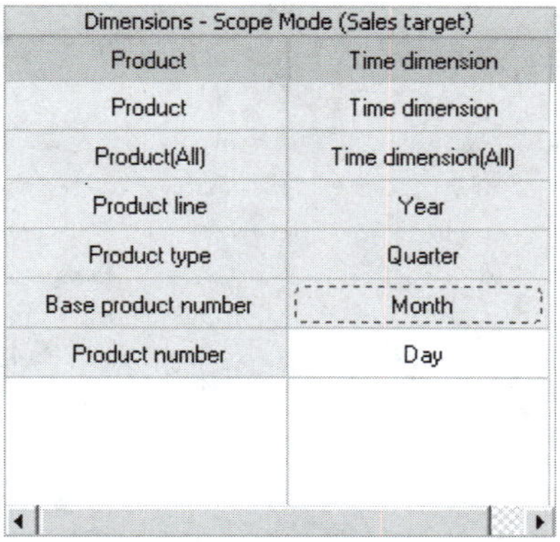

Dimensions - Scope Mode (Sales target)	
Product	Time dimension
Product	Time dimension
Product(All)	Time dimension(All)
Product line	Year
Product type	Quarter
Base product number	Month
Product number	Day

Now we can set the scope for the Base product number and for the Days in our Date hierarchy, as shown next:

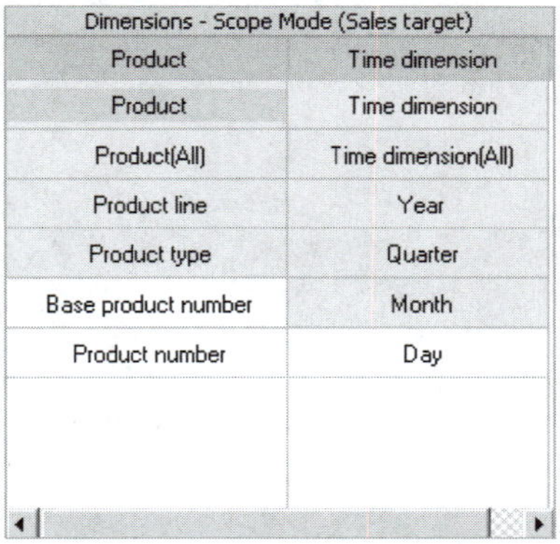

Dimensions - Scope Mode (Sales target)	
Product	Time dimension
Product	Time dimension
Product(All)	Time dimension(All)
Product line	Year
Product type	Quarter
Base product number	Month
Product number	Day

NOTE *When you publish a package, you must include all Namespaces that are referenced in the query subjects seen by the users. Objects that are not included in the package are not available for use in any of the Studios.*

After publishing the model and accessing the package in Analysis Studio, we:

1. Place the Time Dimension on the columns and drill-down to the month level.
2. Place the Product Dimension on the rows and drill-down to the Product Type.
3. Add Revenue and Sales Target as the measures.

PART IV

The result is an analysis showing the values for Revenue and Sales Target, since they are both in scope:

If we drill-down on the Time Dimension to the day, we see that Sales Target becomes null; this is because Sales Target *at the day level* is out of scope, seen here:

If we drill-down on the Product Dimension to the Base product number, we again lose the Sales Target because Sales Target at the Base Product Number is out of scope, as shown next:

Sales target	April		May		June		Q2
	Revenue	Sales target	Revenue	Sales target	Revenue	Sales target	Revenue
42	$1,155,656.00		$972,648.00		$995,296.00		$3,12
43	$760,085.50		$695,647.00		$701,062.00		$2,15
44	$2,276,328.96		$2,083,012.25		$2,133,399.74		$6,49
45	$1,548,015.82		$1,792,726.86		$1,655,076.90		$4,99
Rope	$5,740,086.28	$20,702,000.00	$5,544,034.11	$19,864,000.00	$5,484,834.64	$19,378,000.00	$16,76

Managing Projects in Framework Manager

If you've made it this far into the chapter, you probably realize that Framework Manager Projects can become very large, complex, and even confusing, objects. Fortunately, Cognos 8 provides you with some built-in tools to help you manage your projects.

There are a few different approaches to project management. You can have one large project that covers every area of your business and includes multiple packages. You can have many little projects, each of which addresses a very specific need in your business. You can have projects organized along functional or geographical areas. Finally, you can pretty much organize your projects in any way that you choose.

However, as the adage goes, just because you can do something does not mean that you should do it. For example, you can have one project that covers every area of your business; that does not mean you should. The same is true for many small projects. Like most things in life there is a happy medium, especially in Framework Manager project design.

When you start creating your projects, you should consider some of the items that might cause you to select one method over another. How many developers will be working on the project? What are the data sources for the project? Are those data sources going to change, and if so, how frequently? What business needs will be addressed by the project? Of those needs, can other areas of the business benefit from the project? How much time do I have to develop the project?

These factors, and more, determine which approach is best for you. However you decide to build your projects, keep in mind *manageability* and *scalability*. If you cannot manage your project, or if your project does not scale, you will want to find another approach. I can tell you that the idea of one large project or a lot of little projects should be taken off your list of options right now due to the manageability and scalability constraint.

Multi-user Development

One of the more important questions we ask is: How many developers will be working on the project? The size of the project and availability of resources is one of the largest factors in answering this question. If the answer is more than one, you have two options: *branching and merging*, or *segmenting and linking*.

Segmenting and linking allows the developers of Framework Manager projects to create, in effect, self-contained subprojects. The subprojects can be referenced by other projects through linking projects together. A link is a shortcut from one project to another. The process and practice of segmenting and linking projects is beyond the scope of this book. Refer to the Cognos 8 Framework Manager Guide for details on using this feature.

A Branching Scenario

The other tool that allows multi-user development is branching and merging projects. The following example illustrates just one of the ways you can use this tool. Suppose you have been working on a dimensionally modeled, sales area, Framework Manager Package, and you have been working on this for a few weeks. Management originally placed the project low on the priority list; you are not feeling any pressure. Despite this, you have done some work on it. The Framework Manager project has the data source connections defined, two or three data source query subjects, and maybe a few joins. Now it's month end and the sales goals have been missed by 50%. All of the sudden, management wants that sales package now, and to help you get it done faster, they assign another person to the task.

Taking stock of the situation, you write down everything you know about the task. You know you need two measure dimensions: (sales and orders), and three regular dimensions: (product, date, and organization). You have the date dimension done already, and do not want to throw it away. Your major concern is: How do you and a coworker develop the other items for the same project at the same time?

The short answer is: You don't! You use the branch function to create a copy, or branch, of the project in its current form. You continue to work on the project the same as you did before, and your coworker starts to work on the newly created branch of the original project.

When you are ready to bring the two projects together, you use the merge function to combine the changes made in one project into the other. The branch process creates a log of all the actions that have occurred in both projects and the merge process runs the log as a script to recreate the actions from the merge source. When the merge process is complete, you have a single project that includes the changes made to both projects.

TIP *You should be in constant communication and decide on what pieces they are going to work. It does not make sense for you both to be working on the same things. This just makes merging a headache. If you just work on your own specific portions, merging is a breeze.*

Branching   The branch process is very simple. With the source project open, click on the Project menu and select Branch to, as shown next:

The Create Branch Project screen displays, as shown next:

Enter the branch project name and location, click OK, and you are done. At this point your coworker can begin developing the items on his list and you can work on yours.

After working feverishly, you both have your projects ready. The next example shows your project:

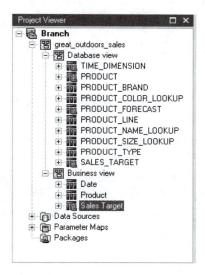

This illustration shows your coworker's project:

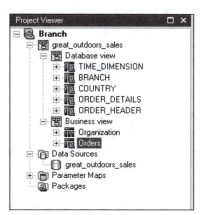

Merging   With both projects ready, click on the Project menu from either of the two projects and select Merge From, as shown next:

The Select Project to Merge From dialog displays, as shown next. This is where you navigate to the project to be merged into the current project:

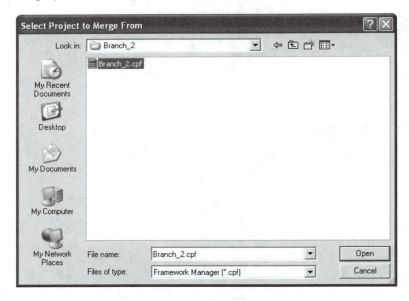

Select Open and the Perform The Merge screen displays with every transaction that took place in the merge source, as shown next:

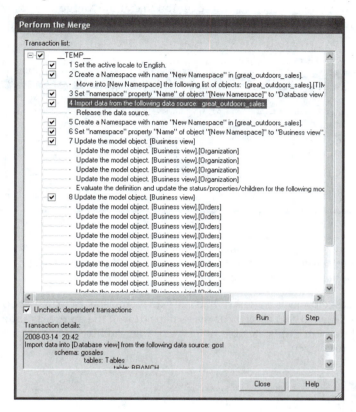

There are a few options from which to choose on the Perform The Merge screen. You can click the Run button, which applies all of the transactions selected in the Transaction list pane to the project to which you are merging. You can click on the Step button to execute one transaction at a time for each button click. You can clear the checkbox for a transaction if you do not want to include it in your project. If you clear a transaction checkbox, a Branch screen listing any other transactions that are dependent on the one you cleared displays, as shown next. Finally, you can click the Close button to exit the Merge process without processing any transactions.

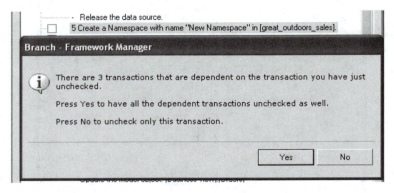

NOTE *When the merge process runs, any exceptions display as they occur with actions to address them. The actions available to you depend on the nature of the exception. Refer to the IBM Cognos 8 BI documentation for more details.*

When you merge projects that have had the same namespace created in both, Business View, be sure to clear the checkboxes for those steps during the merge, as shown next. If you do not, you end up with duplicate objects (namespace and namespace1) which results in additional work to correct:

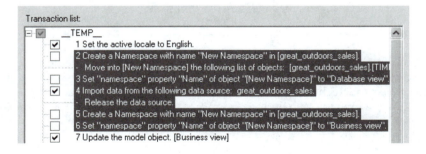

When the merge process is complete, you can either accept the results of the transactions or you can revert the project back to its original state, as shown next:

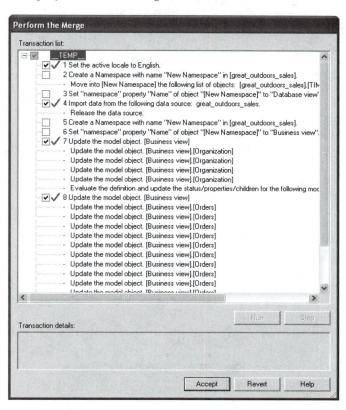

Once you accept the changes, you will not be able to run that particular merge process again. If you try, an information dialog displays, as shown next, with a message notifying you that there are no differences between the current project and the merge source:

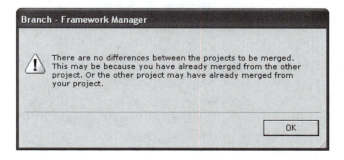

NOTE *You should review the Cognos 8 Framework Manager User Guide for additional examples, scenarios, cautions, and limitations relating to Branching and Merging.*

Other Items of Interest

As you become more familiar with Framework Manager you will, undoubtedly, come across interesting features not mentioned in this chapter. It is simply not possible to discuss all the features here; but, we would like to introduce you to a few that you can investigate at your leisure.

Document the Project

You can create XML or HTML based documentation of the project or any object within the project. From the Tools menu, select Model Report, as shown next:

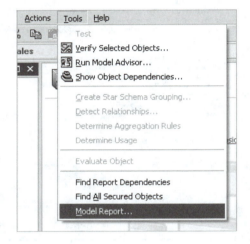

This illustration is a sample of the Product model query subject Model Report:

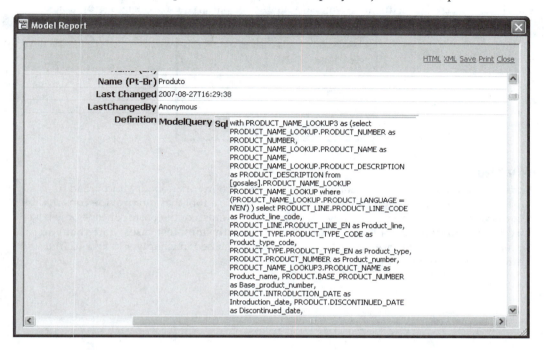

Diagram Copy and Paste

Another helpful feature, especially for those who like documentation, is the ability save a screen copy of the model diagrams to an image file. Arrange the model diagram to your liking, click on the Diagram menu, and then click Screen Capture:

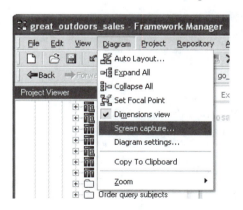

A Save A Copy Of The Diagram In An Image File dialog box displays. From here, you can select the size of the image to save and the file format (jpg, gif, or tif), as shown next:

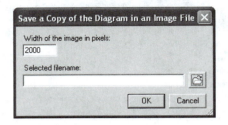

What Now?

Framework Manager is an extremely powerful tool, rich in functionality and broad in capability. It is not a tool you can master quickly, but it is a tool that can provide considerable returns with a small amount of study. Once you have a grasp of the basic concepts, the best way to truly understand this tool is to use it. Start with small test cases, data that you understand, and try the various strategies and tools discussed in Chapters 15 and 16. You will learn a lot and you might even have some fun.

Security

Having consulted with a large number of customers since the release of Cognos 8, we have found that security implementations tend to fall into one of two categories: not enough or too much. Not enough security occurs when the Cognos 8 default settings are left in place and security is relegated to the user logon or no security at all. The danger here is obvious: anyone with access to Cognos Connection can view or print any information that has been published. They can also delete any objects they find, such as reports, folders, and packages. Too much security occurs when the system administrator either does not understand the flexibility of Cognos 8 security, or, to be frank, the system administrator is paranoid. In this case, legitimate business users cannot access the information they need to make sound business decisions. The business users quickly become frustrated and the Cognos 8 installation is considered a failure by the people it is meant to help the most.

Every organization should be concerned both with information security (not allowing unauthorized user to access information) and content integrity (not allowing someone to remove or change content). Cognos 8 lets you apply a fine level of control over all of the features and content found in the Cognos 8 environment, ensuring that you can meet both of these objectives.

Authentication

Security is disabled by default. Your Cognos 8 installation team must configure and enable security before you can use it. If the security feature is not enabled, anyone who connects to Cognos Connection will have full access to everything in Cognos 8.

Cognos 8 security starts with *authentication*, the process of verifying that a user is who he or she claims to be, making sure he is authentic. This is done with user credentials (a username and password) that are stored in a secured authentication source. Note that Cognos 8 does not provide an authentication source or any means of authenticating users; therefore, this must be implemented using a third-party authentication provider. Cognos 8 supports a variety of authentication providers that can change over time, so be sure to check your Cognos 8 Installation Guide for the most recent list of supported providers.

NOTE *As of this writing, the authentication providers supported in Cognos 8 are Active Directory Server, Cognos Series 7, eTrust SiteMinder, Lightweight Directory Access Protocol (LDAP), NT LAN Manager (NTLM), and SAP.*

Cognos 8 allows the use of more than one authentication provider, which is helpful for distributed security models. For example, if your organization is multinational, you might use one authentication provider for the United States, a different one for Central Europe, and possibly a third for the Asia Pacific region. You can log on to as many authentication sources as needed to access your application.

Cognos 8 prompts you to select the provider you want to use at log on, as shown here:

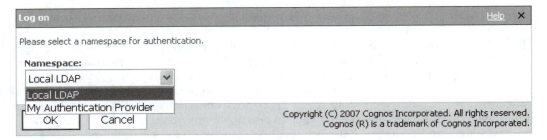

If you have a single authentication provider, you will go directly to the Log On screen with no prompting:

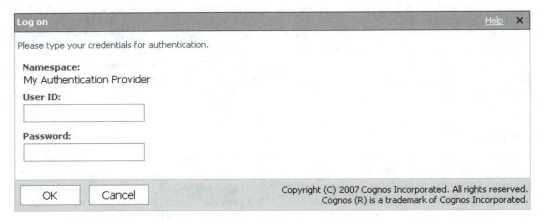

When a user attempts to log on to the Cognos 8 environment, the security mechanism first checks to see whether the user credentials are valid. Does the username and password entered match those stored in the authentication source? If the credentials are not valid, the user is prompted to try again. If the credentials are valid, the user is granted access to Cognos Connection. The next layer of security, authorization, comes into play.

Authorization

Now that Cognos 8 knows who you are, the next question is "What are you authorized to do?" *Authorization* defines the level of access that a user has to the Cognos 8 functionality and content. An installation of all the Cognos 8 studios results in a large number of tools being available to users, and not all users need to have access to everything. A lot of information is likely available in Cognos Connection, and again, not every user should have permission to see everything. It is the job of the Cognos administrator to assign specific permissions to specific users.

Users, Groups, and Roles

Managing individual user access and permissions can become extremely complex. To help simplify this effort, Cognos 8 allows you to combine users into groups and roles. *Users* are the individual people who have usernames and passwords and have permission to access the application. *Groups* are a collection of users that have the same access permissions—for example, everyone in the Sales group can see content related to sales. *Roles* are a collection of users that have the same access to functionality—for example, everyone in the Authors role can create reports.

If you have defined groups and roles in your current security model and you are using that security model as your authentication provider, you can easily apply the Cognos 8 permissions directly to your existing structure. If you have multiple authentication providers or your current security model does not meet your needs, you can use the predefined groups and roles found in the Cognos 8 namespace, create your own groups and roles, or do both. A *namespace* is a unique collection of items. In this discussion, a namespace refers to a collection of users, groups, and roles. Each of the icons used to represent these items is shown in Table 17-1.

Individual users are defined in your existing security model and can become members of groups, roles, or both. For all practical purposes, groups and roles behave in the same manner. The only technical difference is that groups limit their membership to users and other groups while roles can contain all three—users, groups, and other roles.

NOTE *For more on the difference between groups and roles, see "Groups and Roles: What Is the Difference?" later in the chapter.*

When a user belongs to more than one group or role, permissions for all of the groups and roles are merged into one set and applied to that user. So, for example, someone in the

Type	Icon
User	👤
Group	👥
Role	👥

TABLE 17-1 User, Group, and Role Icons

Sales group who has the Authors role will be able to see the sales content and edit reports. Another user can be in the Marketing group and also have the Authors role. This user will be able to edit marketing reports, but will not be able to see sales content.

The Cognos 8 namespace comes with predefined users, groups, and roles. The more frequently used default users, groups, and roles are discussed in the following sections.

NOTE   *A complete list of Cognos 8 users, groups, and roles is available in the IBM Cognos 8 documentation.*

Default Users

Anonymous is the only default user in the Cognos 8 namespace. This generic account is used when security has not been enabled or when content is available to anyone with access to Cognos Connection. By default, the Anonymous user has access to any items that have not been secured and to any items that members of the Everyone group can access. To disable the Anonymous user, the Cognos 8 installation team must configure an authentication provider and set the Allow Anonymous flag to False in Cognos Configuration.

Default Groups

Cognos 8 supplies two groups by default: All Authenticated Users and Everyone. These groups are provided so that you can begin to use your Cognos 8 application as quickly as possible by allowing every user to access almost everything.

All Authenticated Users

All Authenticated Users contains any user that has been granted access by an authentication provider. This group cannot be modified or deleted; it can only be included or excluded in another group or role.

Everyone

Everyone contains any user that has been granted access by an authentication provider, as well as the Anonymous user. This group cannot be modified or deleted; it can only be included or excluded in another group and role or disabled.

Default Roles

Along with default groups, Cognos 8 supplies a number of default Roles. These default roles define what capabilities are available to users and groups. By assigning a user or group to a role, you are granting those users the same capabilities that the role has.

System Administrators

The System Administrator is the *super user*. This is the most powerful role in the Cognos 8 security model because members of this role can access and change any item found in Cognos Connection. The System Administrator role requires at least one member.

Consumers

Consumers are the most commonly used roles. Users with the Consumers role can access Cognos Connection and read and execute previously created content such as reports. Consumers cannot access any of the authoring tools.

Query Users

Query Users have all the same access as Consumers. In addition, they can also use the Cognos 8 Query Studio, which lets them create and save basic reports in their personal folders and perform ad hoc queries using any published framework manager package.

Analysis Users

Analysis Users have all the same access as Consumers. In addition, they can use the Cognos 8 Analysis Studio, which lets them "slice and dice" OLAP cubes and dimensionally modeled data and to create and save reports in their personal folders.

Authors

Authors have the same access as Query Users and Analysis Users. Authors can use Report Studio, Analysis Studio, and Query Studio as well as save reports as public content that other users can access.

Report Administrators

Report Administrators can manage the content found in Public Folders. In addition, they can also use Cognos 8 Report Studio and Cognos 8 Query Studio.

Server Administrators

Server Administrators can manage the inner workings of the Cognos 8 environment. They can modify the settings of servers, dispatchers, and jobs.

Directory Administrators

Directory Administrators can manage the content of Cognos 8 namespaces. They can manage groups, accounts, contacts, distribution lists, data sources, and printers.

Securing the Default Roles

The first step in securing Cognos 8 is to define the membership of the roles in your environment. A good place to start is by deleting the Everyone group from roles, because, by default, it is found in a number of groups and roles. To delete this group, you must navigate to each role that includes the Everyone group by default. Your IBM Cognos 8 BI documentation provides the list of roles that contain the Everyone group by default.

Here's how to access users, groups, and roles in Cognos 8:

1. Log on to Cognos Connection.
2. Click Launch to display the drop-down list, and click Cognos Administration:

3. From the Cognos Administration screen, click the Security tab. The default Cognos 8 namespace displays, as well as any third-party authentication providers that have been configured, as shown next:

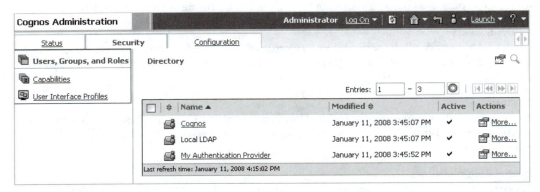

4. Click Cognos to access the Cognos 8 namespace, shown here:

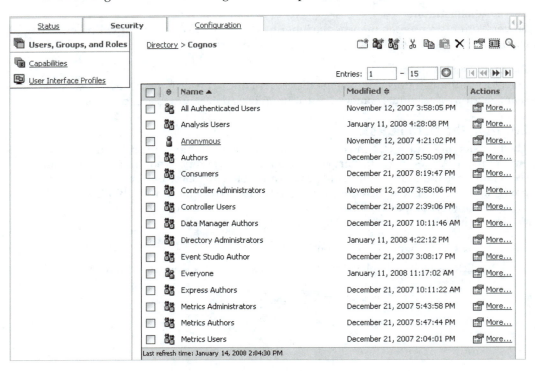

NOTE   *You can log on to as many authentication sources as needed to access your application. If more than one authentication provider is configured, all will be displayed on the Security tab. To work with a namespace other than the Cognos namespace and the one by which you are currently authenticated, you must log on against the applicable namespace.*

Remove the Everyone Group

As mentioned above, removing the Everyone group from your roles is a great place to start securing your Cognos 8 installation.

Here's how to remove the Everyone group from roles:

1. Navigate to a role.

2. Click the properties of the role.

3. Click the Members tab, as shown here:

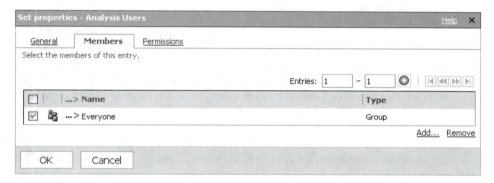

4. Select the checkbox next to the Everyone group, and then click the Remove link, and then click OK.

5. Repeat steps 1 through 4 to remove Everyone from other roles.

Adding Users, Groups, and Roles to the Cognos 8 Namespace

Suppose that you have decided to use the default Cognos 8 roles as a starting point in your security model. You want to add users from the marketing group, found in your authentication provider, to the default Authors role because everyone is excited to start writing reports.

Here's how to add a user to the Cognos 8 namespace:

1. Navigate to the role you want to modify.

2. Click the properties of the role.

3. Click the Members tab.

4. Click Add. The Select Entries (Navigate) - Authors screen displays, listing all of the configured namespaces (authentication providers), as shown next. Only the Cognos 8 namespace and the namespace you are authenticated against will be active:

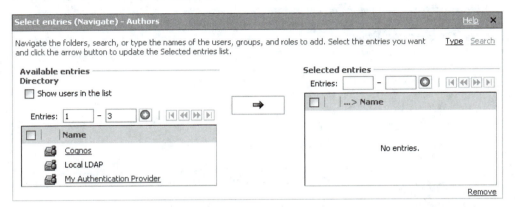

5. Because you are adding users from your authentication provider to the Cognos 8 namespace, click My Authentication Provider. The My Authentication Provider screen displays, listing the folders and groups in the namespace, as shown next. Using the group and role naming convention, the Users folder is the same as a group and the Root User Class is the same as a role:

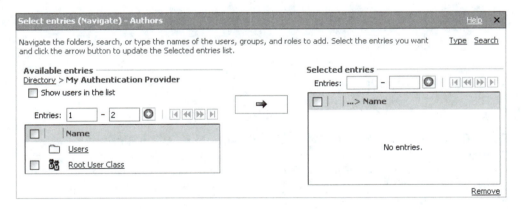

6. Click Users to examine the contents of the folder. The next screen displays:

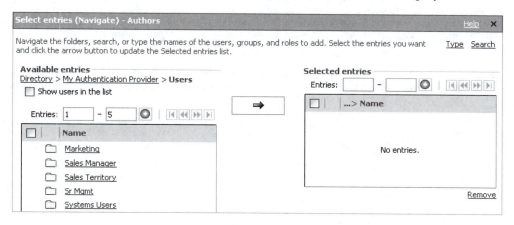

7. Click the Marketing folder. By default, Cognos 8 does not display the individual users within groups because large groups can take a while to load, as shown next:

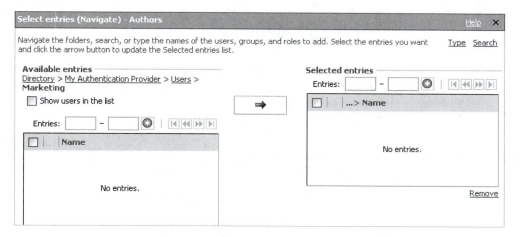

8. If you want to view the members of a group, select the Show Users In The List checkbox and the list will automatically refresh:

CAUTION *Groups with a large number of members can be slow to load if the authentication provider is not indexed.*

If you have a large list of users and you do not want to scroll through the entire list, you can use the Search feature to find a name.

9. Click the Search link in the upper right corner of the screen. By default, the Search feature looks for matches only in the names of groups and roles. The Search screen is shown next:

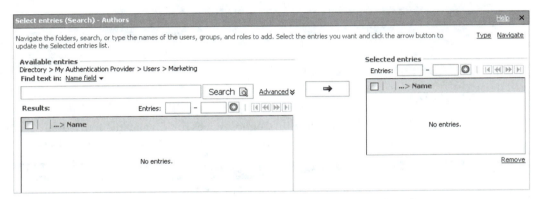

10. If you are looking for a specific User, click the Advanced link.

11. From the Type drop-down list box, shown next, select Any, Groups And Roles, or Users to change the type of entry for which you are looking. The Find Text In string located above the input region updates to identify the type selected:

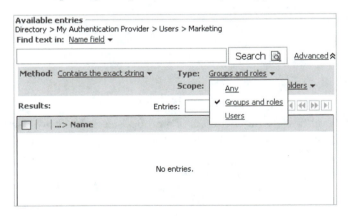

12. If you are looking for a user named Sherry Rowland, for example, you would type a segment of the name in the input region beneath the Find Text In text box.

13. Click Search. The matched entries are returned, as shown here:

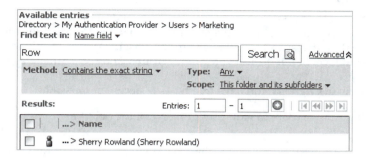

14. To add a user from your list to the role, select the checkbox next to the user name.

15. Click Add (the arrow in the center of the screen) to add the user to the Selected Entries list and then click OK at the lower-left corner of the screen. Your first user has been added to the Authors role, as shown next:

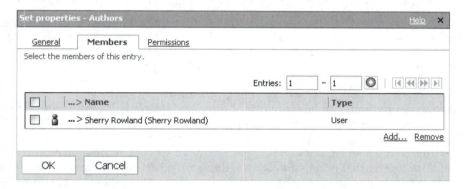

Add Groups and Roles from Your Authentication Provider

Adding groups and roles from your authentication provider follows the same steps used for adding a user.

Here's how to add groups and roles:

1. Search for the group or role that you want to add.

2. Select the checkbox next to the name of the group or role.

3. Click the Add button (arrow) to add it to the Selected Entries list, and then click OK.

Access Permissions

Groups allow you to organize your security structure and place users with common interests (for example, sales and marketing) together. Roles allow you to assign functionality (such as Authors, OLAP Analysis, and so on) to groups and users. Access permissions allow you to determine what level of interaction your users, groups, and roles can have with the objects in Cognos Connection.

Most objects in Cognos 8 can have five types of access permissions:

- **Read**   Allows users to view any property of the object as well as create shortcuts to the object.

- **Write**   Allows users to delete objects and modify the properties of an object, such as the name or description. When enabled on a folder, users can create new objects in that folder and save reports to that folder.

- **Execute**   Allows users to run reports and access data sources.

- **Set Policy**   Allows users to modify the security settings of an object.

- **Traverse**   Allows users to view the contents of an object and execute reports.

NOTE *Traverse permissions are needed when a drill-through report references another report in a different folder. If the report user does not have Traverse permissions on the folder that has the target report, the user will not be able to use the drill-through.*

The icons associated with each type of permission are shown in Table 17-2.

Access permissions can be set in one of three ways: Granted, Denied, or Not Set. If a user has a specific permission granted, the user can do whatever that permission allows. If the user has a specific permission denied, the user can never do whatever that permission allows (this is called an *Explicit Deny*). If the user has a specific permission Not Set, the user cannot do whatever that permission allows (this is called an *Implicit Deny*). The Not Set and Denied permissions sound the same, but there is an important difference between the two, which will be discussed in the "Access Permissions Interaction" section of this chapter.

Access Permission	Grant Icon	Deny Icon
Read		
Write		
Execute		
Set Policy		
Traverse		

TABLE 17-2   Permission Icons

Setting Access Permissions

To set the access permissions on an object, such as a report for example, you click the properties icon of the report and then click the Permissions tab on the Set Properties screen, as shown next:

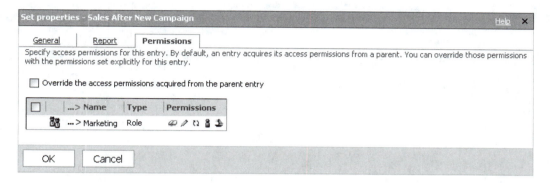

By default, Cognos 8 sets the access permissions of a report (or any other object) to the same access permissions set for the parent folder. This is a powerful tool when managing your security model. If the access requirements are the same for everything in a folder structure, you can set the access permissions at the top of the structure and anything you add in the folder will automatically inherit that folder's permissions.

In this example, a report named Sales After New Campaign is located in the Marketing folder created by a user assigned the Report Administrator role. Suppose you want to give the Sales Manager role permissions to the report even though the report is in the Marketing folder. You can change the access permissions.

Here's how to change the access permissions for a specific object:

1. In the Set Properties screen, select the Override The Access Permissions Acquired From The Parent Entry checkbox. The Access Permissions screen displays:

2. Click the Add link to add a role to the Permissions list. The Select Entries screen displays, seen next.

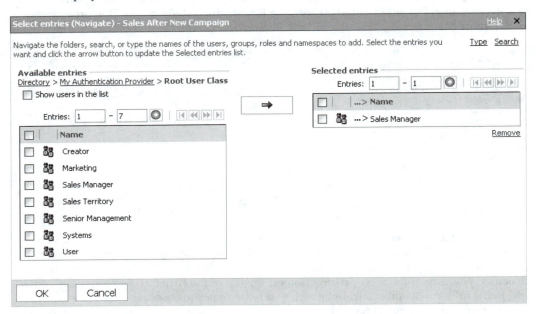

3. Navigate to the role in your authentication provider—Sales Manager, in this case.

4. Select the checkbox next to the role.

5. Click the green arrow to add the role to the Selected Entries list, as shown next, and then click OK. The Permissions tab of the report displays with the Sales Manager role available.

Grant or Deny Permissions for a Role

After you have changed the access permissions for a specific object, you will need to grant or deny permissions for the roles that you want to be able to access that object.

Here's how to grant or deny permissions for a role:

1. In the Permissions tab, select the checkbox next to the role name.

2. Select the Grant checkbox for all of the access permissions this role should be assigned.

3. Select the Deny checkbox for all of the access permissions this role should never be assigned.

4. Click Apply.

In this example, you want to allow members of the Sales Manager role to run the report, so you grant them Execute permission. The icon for the Execute permission is shown in the Permissions list for the Sales Manager role, as shown here:

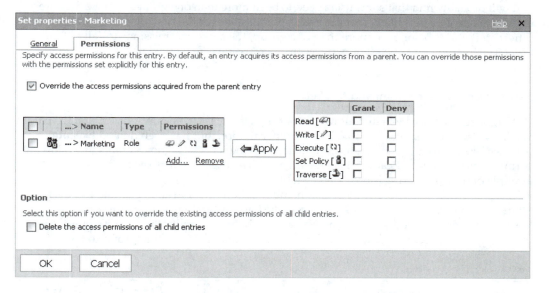

Because this report is in a folder, you have to confirm that the Sales Manager role can access the folder itself. If they can't see the folder, they won't be able to access the report inside of it. View the permissions of the Marketing folder, as shown next, to determine whether the Sales Manager role is in the Permissions list of the folder:

If someone from the Sales Manager role wanted to run the Sales After New Campaign report, he or she would not be able to do so. With the current permissions on the Marketing folder, members of the Sales Manager role do not have permission to view the folder (nor does the folder display). You will need to assign the Sales Manager role Traverse access permissions on the Marketing folder.

Here's how to allow Sales Managers to view the Marketing folder:

1. On the Permissions tab of the Set Properties screen, add the Sales Manager role to the Permissions list (as discussed earlier in the chapter).

2. Click the Traverse Grant checkbox to assign the role Traverse permissions, as shown here:

With this access permission, members of the Sales Manager role can access the Marketing folder and execute the Sales After New Campaign report. They cannot do anything else to the Marketing folder or to the report.

Access Permissions Interaction

You will probably find that some users need to be in more than one group. Because they are in different groups, it is likely that the access permissions for the two (or more) groups are different. If a user belongs to more than one group, the access permissions for all of their groups get merged into one set of permissions. Permissions are merged using one of two rules:

- Grant replaces Not Set.
- Deny replaces Grant and Not Set.

Suppose a report exists that allows two groups to access it. Group A has Write, Execute, and Traverse permissions. Group B has Read permission, but has been denied Execute permissions. If a user is in both groups and accesses the report, Cognos 8 grants the following permissions to the user: Read, Write, and Traverse. The user lost the Execute permission. An example of how this works is provided in Table 17-3.

As an example, suppose Cricket is a member of both the Marketing group and the Sales Manager group and she would like to access the Sales After New Campaign report. A Marketing user created the report and he has the ability to modify the permissions of the report (Set Policy Access Permission). The author wants the Marketing group to have Read,

Group	Read	Write	Execute	Set Policy	Traverse
A	Not Set	Granted	Granted	Not Set	Granted
B	Granted	Not Set	Denied	Not Set	Not Set
New Permissions	Granted	Granted	Denied	Not Set	Granted

TABLE 17-3 Access Permissions Interaction

Group	Read	Write	Execute	Set Policy	Traverse
Marketing	Granted	Granted	Granted	Not Set	Granted
Sales Managers	Granted	Not Set	Denied	Not Set	Denied
Cricket	Granted	Granted	Denied	Not Set	Denied

TABLE 17-4   Merged Access Permissions

Write, Execute, and Traverse permissions and only wants the Sales Managers to view the report. Not sure of how security works, the author decides to set the permissions in the following manner:

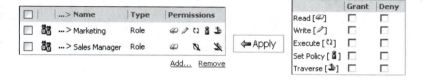

For Cricket, who is a member of both of the groups, the permissions are merged into the results shown in Table 17-4.

The author who set the permissions on these groups made two incorrect assumptions: First, the author assumed that the Read permission was needed to allow a user to run a report; however, Execute is the permission that is needed. The second assumption was that the Deny set on the Execute permission would affect only the Sales Manager group. Because of the merge rules, Deny always takes precedence over all other permissions. The result in this example is that anyone who is in both the Marketing and Sales Manager groups has lost the ability to Execute the report. The proper permission would be Traverse.

Cognos 8 Capabilities

Cognos 8 provides a fine level of control over the content users can see. Through access permissions and the ability to apply those permissions to the groups that you have defined, you are able to ensure proper access to information. Capabilities are another level of control provided by Cognos 8 that relate to what users can do as opposed to what they can see. A *capability* in Cognos 8 can have multiple functions contained within.

For example, in Report Studio, Authors have the ability to edit the SQL generated by the Cognos 8 report engine and run the report using the modified SQL; they can also embed HTML code in a report. With the scheduling capability, users have the ability to schedule reports to run at any time. This capability also allows users to change the priority of their scheduled jobs. In both of these examples, you might not want the users to have those specific abilities within the capability.

NOTE *The capabilities that are available in Cognos 8 can change over time. Check your IBM Cognos 8 BI documentation for a full list of current capabilities.*

The capabilities in Cognos 8 come with permissions assigned to default roles. In most cases, the default settings will be sufficient for your security needs. However, if you find that you need to modify the default settings, the process is the same as setting the access permissions on folders, reports, and other objects, as discussed earlier. Simply add or remove users, groups, or roles from the Permissions list of the capability or function within a capability that you would like to modify.

The capabilities in your installation of Cognos 8 will vary based on which components have been purchased and installed. Some of the more common capabilities and their additional functions are listed here.

Administration   Users are able to administer the Cognos 8 installation.

- **Capabilities and UI profiles**   Users can manage the secured functions and features and the Report Studio user interface profiles.

- **Administration tasks**   Users can administer exports, imports, index updates, consistency checks, and report updates.

- **Controller administration**   Users can use the administrative functions of Cognos 8 Controller.

- **Data source connections**   Users can add and remove data sources, as well as create sign-ins to data sources.

- **Distribution lists and contacts**   Users can create and maintain report distribution lists and contact information.

- **Metric Studio administration**   Users can create new metric packages with the new Metric Package Wizard in Cognos Connection and access the Tools menu in Metric Studio.

- **Activities and schedules**   Users can monitor the server activities and manage schedules.

- **Planning administration**   Users can access the Planning Contributor Administration console and the Planning Analyst to perform administration tasks.

- **Styles and portlets**   Users can manage styles and portlets in Cognos Administration.

- **Printers**   Users can add, remove, and modify printer connections.

- **System configuration and management**   Users can configure dispatchers and services and manage the system.

- **Users, groups, and roles**   Users can create, delete, and modify namespaces, users, groups, and roles.

Analysis Studio   Users can run Analysis Studio.

Cognos Viewer   Users can modify the behavior of the Cognos Viewer.

- **Context menu**   Users can use the context menus (submenus) in Cognos Viewer.
- **Run with options**   Users can modify the default run options of a report.
- **Selection**   Users can select and copy text from a report.
- **Toolbar**   Users can access the toolbar in Cognos Viewer.

Detailed Errors   Users can receive the full message text when they encounter an error.

Drill-Through Assistant   Users can access the Drill-Through Assistant.

Event Studio   Users can run Event Studio.

Metric Studio   Users can run Metric Studio.

- **Edit view**   Users can modify the default settings of Metric Studio.

Query Studio   Users can run Query Studio.

- **Advanced**   Users can use style formatting, multilingual support, advanced calculations, and create complex filters.
- **Create**   Users can use the Save As option.

Report Studio   Users can run Report Studio.

- **Bursting**   Users can create burst reports.
- **Create/Delete**   Users can create new reports and delete existing reports.
- **HTML items in report**   Users can include embedded HTML in reports.
- **User Defined SQL**   Users can directly modify the SQL created by the report.

Scheduling   Users can schedule activities.

- **Scheduling priority**   Users can modify the priority of new or existing activities.

Accessing Capabilities

Capabilities are located on the Security tab of the Cognos Administration screen. Your list of capabilities will look similar to those shown here:

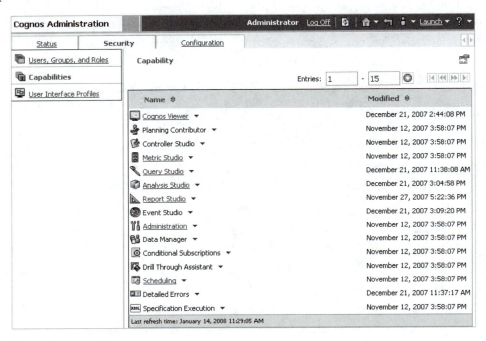

Links (underlined in blue) have multiple capabilities, each of which can have their permissions set individually. For example, the Administration capability is actually made up of a dozen capabilities, as shown here:

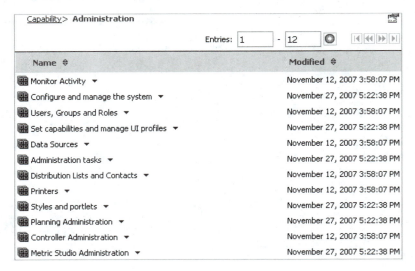

Capabilities You Might Want to Change

As mentioned earlier, in most cases, you will not need to modify any of the capabilities. However, the Detailed Errors capability is one exception.

By default, when an error occurs, Cognos 8 writes the error to a log file in the Cognos 8 installation folder on the server. This is normally a secure location that most users will not be able to access. In the event of an error during report execution, the user is presented with a message that informs him or her of the location of the error details within the log file. This makes Authors dependent on someone else to assist them with troubleshooting the problem. You can configure Cognos 8 to send the complete error message to the user by adding the appropriate group or groups to the Permissions list of the Detailed Errors capability. Normally, Authors and Consumers roles are added to this capability.

Here's how to modify the Detailed Errors capability:

1. Navigate to the Capability screen.
2. Click the down arrow next to Detailed Errors. A text box displays the Set Properties command:

3. Click Set Properties.
4. Click the Permissions tab.
5. Select the Override The Access Permissions Acquired From The Parent Entry checkbox.
6. Add the Consumers role.
7. Assign the Consumers role both Execute and Traverse permissions, and then click OK.

Anyone who now encounters an error during report execution will see the full error text.

Groups and Roles: What Is the Difference?

Earlier in this chapter, we talked briefly about the differences between groups and roles. The only technical difference between a group and a role is this: A role can contain users, groups and other roles while a group can *only* contain users and other groups. Other than that difference, groups, and roles can behave exactly the same. To keep life easier, we suggest you follow this rule of thumb: Use groups to define what Cognos 8 content a set of users can access, and use roles to define what capabilities a set of users has. By following this rule, you can use groups and roles to set default functionality. As an example, if you are in the Sales Manager group and you have not been assigned a role, you cannot perform any actions in that group because roles define what you can do. While in the Sales Manager group, if you are also assigned the Consumers role, you can do anything allowed by the Consumers role for any object for which the Sales Manager group has access permissions.

Once security has been applied and you have been assigned a role but not a group, you can perform the actions permitted by the role and will have limited access to the application.

If you have been assigned the Authors role, for example, but you have not been placed in a group, you will be unable to access a reporting source and, even if you could, you would be unable to save the report to a global folder. You could save reports to My Folder. But because no one else can see that folder, the organization would not benefit from reports authored by you.

NOTE *Membership in groups or roles is optional; however, you should use them. Administering permissions and capabilities for each user quickly gets out of hand and maintenance becomes a nightmare.*

Using Roles, Access Permissions, and Capabilities

The success level that you achieve with your security configuration will be determined to a great degree by how well you plan your strategy before you begin. It is vital that you understand how your content will be stored, which groups will have access to what content, and which users will have which capabilities.

For most users, content is organized along functional lines. Folders are created in Cognos Connection for operational areas (such as, Finance, Sales, Management, and so on). Each operational area can be split further as needed (for example, the Sales folder could contain regions or product lines). For multinational customers, a geographical organization might display first followed by a standard operational structure underneath. How your content is organized will ultimately be determined by what works best for you. No matter where you end up, you should start by mapping out on paper how you think you want your content organized and keep it handy.

When considering the access permissions you will need, start by thinking about what should be secured. In broad terms, you will need three security roles: Consumers, Authors, and Administrator. The Consumers role needs to navigate the folder structure that you have created and be able to execute reports. The Consumers role will contain the largest number of users and in general will usually need Traverse, Write, and Execute access permissions. Make a list of the users who will have only these permissions and label it *Consumers*.

Authors need to have the access permissions of Consumers, as well as the ability to access one or more studios. Make a new list of Authors and studios to which they will have access. Repeat this process for the roles that you will be using. You will end up with something similar to Table 17-5.

Consumers	Authors	Administrator
Janet	Dan	Susie
Rob	Sue	
Bryan		
Alicia		

TABLE 17-5 Sample Role List

The Administrator role can vary based on how you maintain your Cognos 8 installation. Typically, in centralized organizations, a small group of people have full administrative responsibilities. In larger organizations, individuals with a subset of the Administrator role are given responsibility for a functional area within Cognos Connection, while an overall Administrator is responsible for all of the functional areas.

You should have a clear idea of which users should be assigned to which roles, so now you can start on the content. Assuming you decide to use the functional method of organizing your content, make a list of the functional areas. This list will be the starting point of both your folder structure and, if not already defined, your groups. Assume that your functional areas, and by extension your groups, are Marketing, Research and Development (R&D), Senior Management, Sales Management, and Sales Territory. Use this list to make an Access Permissions grid. List the groups as columns and the top level Cognos Connection folders as rows. In each intersection, write what access permissions the group in the column has to the folder in that row. The resulting grid will look something like Table 17-6.

This grid provides you with a quick reference that you can use while setting up your security and for troubleshooting access permissions in the future.

How you decide to administer the security of your installation will depend on any number of factors: how many users, how much content, how widely distributed is your user base? All these factors and any others that are specific to your organization should be considered before you begin implementing a security strategy.

Business Case: Configuring Initial Security

The need for security sounds simple: Do not let people see or do things that they are not permitted to see or do. However, when you try to make that work with many different people having many different levels of access, that simple task becomes complex.

Suppose you work for a company that makes outdoor equipment, called The Really Good Outdoors Company, and you have just been given the responsibility of managing the security of the new Cognos 8 installation. Your existing authentication provider has already defined users and groups and the system is working well. Your groups consist of: Marketing, Research and Development, Senior Management, Sales Management, and Sales Territory. Senior management has decided that your first task is to ensure that members of each group can access only content belonging to their group. Assume a directory administrator has already

Access Permissions	Marketing	R&D	Sr. Mgmt	Sales Mgmt	Sales Territory
Marketing folder	RWET	ET	RET	ET	
R&D folder	ET	RWET	RET	ET	
Sr. Mgmt folder			RWET		
Sales Mgmt folder			RET	RWET	
Sales Territory folder			RET	RWET	RET

TABLE 17-6 Group and Folder Access Permissions Grid

created the folders that each group will use. After thinking about this request, you decide that you need to take the following actions:

1. Add a user to the System Administrator role so that once security is enabled, someone has the permissions needed to make changes later on.

2. Remove the Everyone group from all of the Cognos roles and add named users and/or groups so that they will have access to default functionality provided by these roles.

3. Set access permissions on the folders so that appropriate access is provided for specific users, groups, and roles.

These actions are described in the following sections.

Add a User to the System Administrators Role

This step has been missed in the past, resulting in the Administrator (and usually everyone else) being locked out of Cognos 8. It is possible to reset the default System Administrator access, but that needs to be done by a database administrator, and it would be best to avoid that situation.

Using the same steps from the "Adding Users, Groups, and Roles to the Cognos 8 Namespace" section, add a user, most likely yourself, to the System Administrators role.

Here's how to add a user to the System Administrators role:

1. From Cognos Connection, click the Launch link.

2. Click the Cognos Administration link.

3. Click the Security tab.

4. Click the Cognos link.

5. Scroll down to the System Administrators role.

6. Click the properties of the System Administrators role.

7. Click the Members tab.

8. Click the Add link.

9. Follow the same navigation method to find your login ID in your authentication provider.

10. Add that ID to the Members list.

NOTE *By default, Cognos Connection shows 15 items in a list at a time. You can change that default by editing your preferences.*

Set Access Permissions

Your Cognos 8 installation is not quite secure yet. By default, all objects that are added to Cognos Connection inherit the security properties of the folder in which they are placed, which is called the *parent* or *parent object*. Examine the properties of the Public Folders:

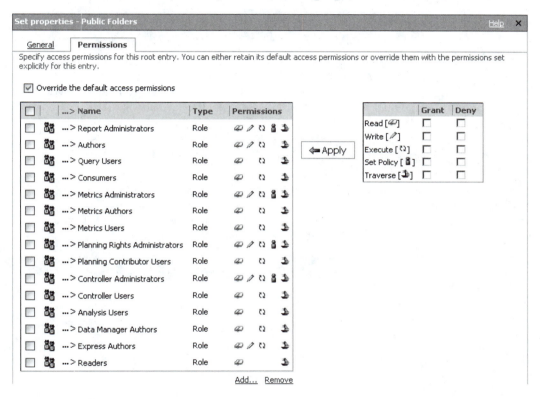

NOTE *By default, the Public Folders in Cognos Connection allows all the default roles to have Read and Traverse access permissions to anything in the folder. When creating new objects, make sure you set the access permissions to meet your needs.*

Complete the following steps to secure the folders found in the Public Folders. This ensures that only roles belonging to the operational area that correspond to a folder name can access the content of the folder.

Here's how to set access permissions:

1. Starting with the Senior Management folder, click the properties icon of the folder. By default, the folder inherited the permissions of its parent (in this example, the Public Folders).
2. Select the Override The Default Access Permissions checkbox.
3. Delete all of the roles that are defined by default.

TIP *Select the checkbox in the header of the list to select the entire list.*

4. Click Add.

5. Navigate to your authentication provider.

6. Select the checkbox of the role or group that you want to have access to this folder.

7. Click Add (the arrow in the center of the screen).

8. Click OK.

9. Because the Senior Management role owns this folder, assign the role or group Read, Write, Execute, and Traverse access permissions. When you are finished, the Senior Management permissions should look like this:

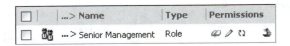

At this point, only members of the Senior Management role can access the Senior Management folder. In fact, users in other non-administrative roles cannot even see the Senior Management folder. If a member of the Marketing role were to log on to Cognos Connection at this point, he or she would see a screen similar to this:

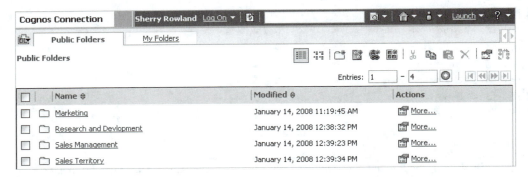

If a member of Senior Management were to log on, he or she would see a screen similar to this:

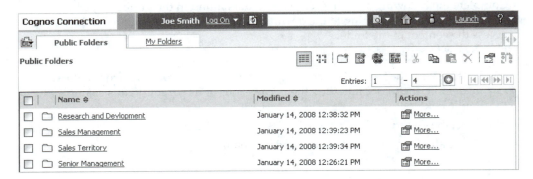

The Cognos Connection screen displays two differences in what Senior Management sees as compared to what Marketing sees. First, Senior Management can see the Senior Management folder, which is what you would expect. However, managers cannot see the Marketing folder because you changed the permissions on that folder earlier in this chapter.

Note *To finish the initial security of the Public Folders, you need to repeat steps 1 through 9 for each of the subfolders found in the Public Folders.*

Business Case: Wait! That Is Not What I Wanted!

You have successfully implemented the security strategy that Senior Management devised. When Senior Management members log into Cognos Connection, they call you in a panic because they cannot find the Marketing reports. After you reassure them that the reports have not been deleted, you ask for clarification on what they would like to see. Senior Management explains that users from each operational area should see only what is in that area's folders, but Senior Management needs to see everything.

Allowing multiple groups to have different access permissions to an object, be it a report, folder or anything else, is common. Having a Group and Folder Access Permissions Grid (as in Table 17-6) comes in handy. Look up the Senior Management group and the Marketing folder. The Senior Management group should have Read, Execute, and Traverse access permissions on the Marketing folder. When you look at the access permissions on the Marketing folder, however, you see that is not the case:

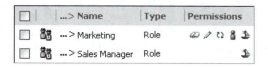

Senior Management is not on the Permissions list. Follow the steps from the "Access Permissions" section earlier in this chapter to add Senior Management to the Permissions list of the Marketing folder and assign that role Read, Execute, and Traverse access permissions. Your results will look similar to this:

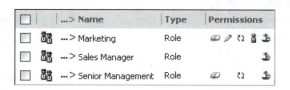

User Modes

Understanding how security in Cognos 8 works in a mechanical sense gets you half way to having a manageable and effective security configuration. To finish the job, you need to apply your security in such a way that you 1) are sure your Cognos 8 content is available to the proper users, 2) have a system that you can manage, and 3) are in compliance with your IBM Cognos 8 BI licenses. Chapter 3 discussed the many licenses that are available in

Cognos 8. A common question is "How do I configure my users and groups so that I am in compliance with my licenses?" This question is best answered through the combination of groups, roles, and capabilities. Earlier in this chapter, we touched on this concept, but we will now discuss it in more detail.

The largest percentage of your licenses will be Consumers. Imagine your user base as a pyramid. The foundation will be Consumers, Authors will make up the middle because you will have fewer Authors than Consumers, and Administrators, which are very few, will make up the top.

Configuring the Consumers Role

With the information you gathered for Table 17-5 you are ready to configure your Consumers role.

Here's how to ensure your consumer licenses are compliant:

1. Verify that you have a license for everyone on your list. This might sound silly, but if you did not purchase the licenses, you cannot assume that you have as many as you think.

2. In Cognos Administration, navigate to the Cognos Namespace screen and then click the properties of the Consumers role.

3. Locate each user from the Consumers list in your authentication provider and add them to the Consumers role. (For instructions on how to complete this action, refer to "Adding Users, Groups, and Roles to the Cognos 8 Namespace" earlier in this chapter.)

4. To complete the Consumers role, verify that the Everyone group has been removed from all roles with studios on them, included in your Cognos 8 installation.

If you have not modified the default settings of the capabilities, your Consumers role is now ready. If you have modified the default settings, you need to verify that each capabilities permissions are configured so that the Consumers role cannot access any of the secured studios.

Configuring the Authors Role

Configuring the Authors role is very similar to configuring the Consumers role. Your list from Table 17-5 contains all the users who will be creating new content. Follow the same steps as those in the "Configuring the Consumers Role" section, to add the users identified as Authors to the Authors role in the Cognos namespace.

If you have a set of users who will be using only Query Studio, make sure those users are in the Query User role and not the Authors role. By default, members of the Authors role can use Query Studio. However, members of the Query User role cannot use Report Studio.

Configuring the Administrator Roles

Cognos 8 offers multiple levels of default administration. How you approach the configuration of these roles will depend on how you plan to distribute the responsibility of maintaining your installation. If you have centralized control with one or two administrators managing everything, you can add the appropriate users to the System Administrator role and those users will have access to everything.

However, if you have a large installation, you might want to spread the responsibility of managing your installation across users. In this case, you have to identify which users will be responsible for which areas. If you want to have one person manage the reporting environment and another manage the directory structure, place the proper users in the respective Administration roles.

If the default roles provided with Cognos 8 do not meet your needs, you can create your own roles, be they Administrator, Authors, or others. The principles of setting up roles and access are the same for whatever roles you choose to create. The combination of roles and capabilities that you can define are nearly infinite, and keeping track of them can be difficult. Maintaining good records of what user belongs to which role will make managing this easier.

Troubleshooting and Testing

Applying security in Cognos 8 is not technically difficult, but it is challenging. As mentioned earlier in this chapter, the key to success is good planning. However, even the best plan will not account for every possibility. When problems are found with your security model, think about the groups and access permissions involved and start with the user and groups in question. If a sales person cannot see the Sales folder, make sure the user is assigned to the Sales group. Check the access permissions on the objects in question. Look for overlapping groups that might have an Explicit Deny. When someone cannot execute a report, check the access permissions on the object and the roles to which the user belongs. If someone is trying to use Report Studio to edit a report, is the user a member of the Authors role? Does he have access permissions to the folder or report?

Finally, the best thing you can do is try it yourself. Create test users for each group and set access permissions to make sure the security is working according to plan. Nothing can replace your ability to try it and see for yourself.

Cognos Connection Management

B y this point, you have packages, reports, queries, events, scheduled jobs, and more floating around your IBM Cognos 8 BI installation. What do you do with it all? You could let the content become cluttered like your workshop or garage, where you can never find that one tool that you need or the holiday decorations that you bought on sale at the end of the season. Or you could become an organizing guru like those on the home and garden TV shows, organizing your clutter and creating an inviting and functional workspace that allows you to function at peak performance. The beauty is that you won't have to work nearly as hard as that professional organizer. Cognos 8 and Cognos Administration provide all the organization tools for you. You just need to understand your system and the needs of your organization.

Introduction to Cognos Administration

Cognos Administration is the area from which you perform the majority of the functions outlined in this chapter. From this area, you create and manage data source connections, perform some aspects of content administration, manage schedules, maintain distribution lists, perform server administration, and manage status and monitoring. The task you are performing determines what section of the Cognos Administration area you use. The next three illustrations show the different sections of Cognos Administration.

When you access Cognos Administration, the Status, Security, and Configuration tabs display. By default, the Status tab with the Status menu displays first. Use the Status menu to view scheduled jobs; view past, current, and future activities; and access the system status and monitoring tools, as shown next:

Status menu

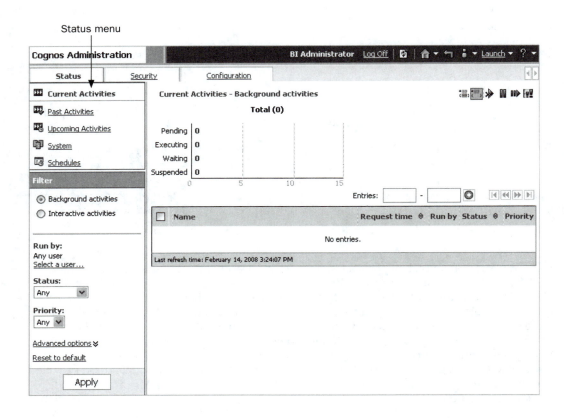

The Security tab displays the Security menu from which you can assign and modify permissions, assign and modify access to studios, and manage specific Cognos 8 capabilities, as shown next:

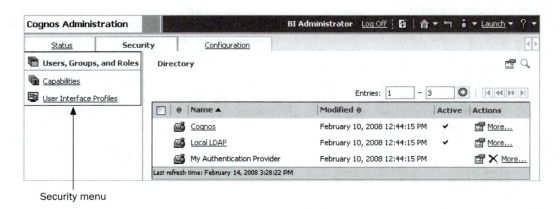

Security menu

The Configuration tab displays the Configuration menu from which you can manage your data source connections, distribution lists and contacts, portlets, and dispatchers and services, as shown next:

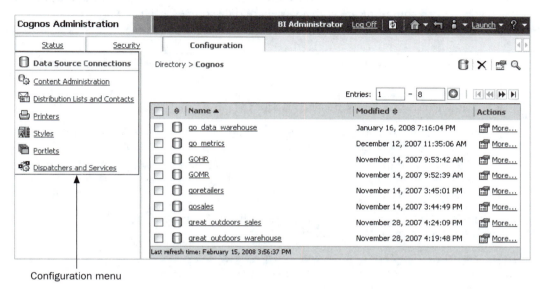

Configuration menu

NOTE *Review the preceding three illustrations prior to reading this chapter, and revisit them any time you have a question on a screen's appearance. These screens are referenced often throughout this chapter.*

Manage Data Source Connections

Data source connections provide the communication channel between Cognos 8 and your data sources. Cognos Administration makes it easy to create new data source connections and modify existing ones. Create a data source connection using the New Data Source wizard. If any of the parameters for the data source connection change, access Cognos Administration, make the changes, and save the modified connection.

A data source connection has three components: the data source, the connection that contains all of the details on how to access the external data in which you are interested, and the sign-on that contains the authentication (user name and password) for the external data source.

NOTE *When we refer to a* data source connection, *we are including all three components unless otherwise specified.*

Create a Data Source Connection

Cognos 8 needs to know how to communicate with your data source. The New Data Source wizard makes it easy for you to define the parameters by which this communication can occur. Cognos 8 can communicate with a variety of data sources, such as XML, relational data sources, or PowerCubes, to name a few.

NOTE You can also create a data source connection from Framework Manager. Cognos 8 launches the same New Data Source wizard, and the steps are identical.

Here's how to create a data source connection:

1. From the Launch menu, select Cognos Administration. Cognos Administration displays with the Status, Security, and Configuration tabs.

2. Click the Configuration tab. The configuration menu displays at the upper left of the screen with a list of existing data sources.

3. Click the New Data Source on the toolbar:

   The New Data Source wizard launches and displays the Specify A Name And Description screen, as shown next:

4. In the Name text box, type the name by which you want to reference your data source connection. The name should help users identify the data that is housed in the data source.

5. Optionally, in the Description text box, enter a description of the data source.

6. Optionally, in the Screen Tip text box, enter a ScreenTip that displays when the user moves the pointer over the database icon to the left of the data source name.

7. Click Next. The Specify The Connection screen displays:

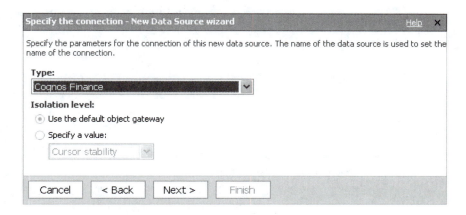

8. From the Type drop-down list, click the type of data source to which Cognos 8 is connecting. The type you choose depends entirely on your data source.

9. In the Isolation Level area, click the level of isolation. The isolation level is a database attribute that defines how the database secures and keeps records consistent in its system. The Use The Default Object Gateway option uses the connection as it is defined by the database. The Specify A Value option allows you to select an isolation value from a list. The available isolation levels for this option include Cursor Stability, Phantom Protection, Read Committed, Read Uncommitted, Reproducible Read, and Serializable.

TIP *Start with the default option unless otherwise instructed by your database administrator. You can modify this setting later if you decide it is needed.*

10. Click Next. The Specify The Data Source Connection screen displays with the data source–specific parameters that need to be completed. The next three illustrations show the three most common types of data sources used.

This example shows the parameters to be completed for a Cognos PowerCube:

The following key fields need to be completed:

- **Read Cache Size (MB)**   The amount of system memory that Cognos 8 has available for PowerCube access. This memory is used for specific actions such as sorting and aggregations. If you do not enter a value for this field, Cognos 8 uses 16MB. We recommend starting with 16MB and moving up to 32MB if PowerCube access seems to be slow.

NOTE *Your system performance can be affected by many factors. Changing one setting is not guaranteed to improve your overall system performance. If your system is not performing as well as you believe it should be, ask your system administrator to review the Architecture and Deployment Guide that comes with the IBM Cognos 8 BI documentation.*

- **Windows Location**   The actual location of the PowerCube on the server where the Cognos 8 application component is installed.
- **Unix Or Linux Location**   The actual path to the PowerCube on a Unix or Linux installation. You will use this field only if the cube is on a Unix or Linux server.
- The Signon area contains two regions and allows you to define the signon values:
  - **Select An Authentication Method**   Choose which namespaces are available for use as authentication sources. The All Applicable Namespaces (Including Unsecured PowerCubes) option is selected by default and uses all available namespaces. The Restrict PowerCube Authentication To A Single Namespace option allows you to choose a specific namespace with the PowerCube on which authentication can occur.
  - **Select Whether A Cube Password Is Needed**   Choose to require that the user accessing the data on the PowerCube enter the password for that cube. You may need to obtain that password from the PowerCube administrator.

The following example shows the parameters to be completed for a Microsoft SQL Server (Native Client) data source.

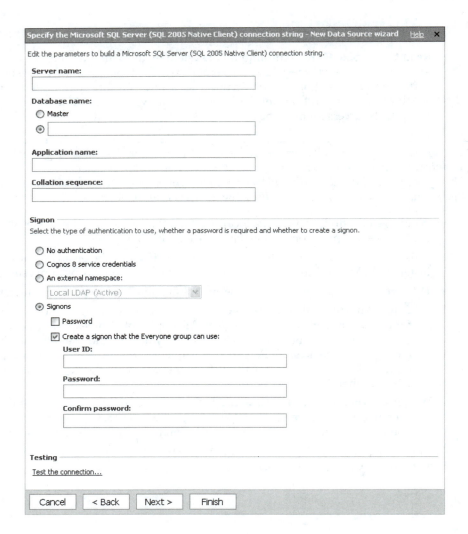

The following key fields need to be completed:

- **Server Name**   The actual name or IP address of the computer on which the database resides.
- **Database Name**   The actual name of the database for which you are creating the connection. The Database name contains the following two options:
    - **Master**   Uses the Master database that was installed with Microsoft SQL Server.
    - **Text box**   An option to name the specific database to be accessed. This is the recommended option.
- The Signon area contains the following four options for signon:
    - **No Authentication**   Users are not required to authenticate to access the data from the database.

- **Cognos 8 Service Credentials**   Users are not required to have individual signons, but all users authenticate using the logon they use when the Cognos 8 service starts.

- **An External Namespace**   Use one of the namespaces that has been defined in the Cognos Configuration.

- **Signons**   Requires that a specific user ID be entered for authentication. Additionally, you can select the Password checkbox to require a password. This is the recommended option.

This example shows the parameters to be completed for an Oracle database:

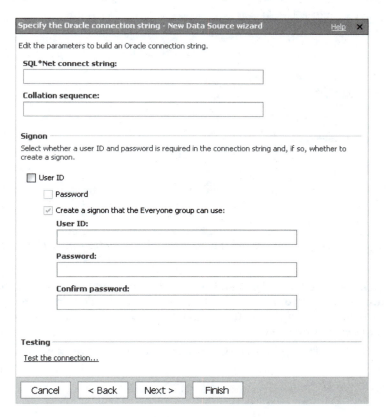

The following key fields need to be completed:

- **SQL*Net Connect String**   The actual string as defined by Oracle for the database to be used.

- **Signon**   This area requires that a specific user ID be entered for authentication. Additionally, you can select the Password checkbox to require a password. This is the recommended option.

11. Complete the appropriate parameters. The type of database that you selected determines the parameters that need to be completed.

12. Optionally, click Test The Connection. The Test The Connection screen displays:

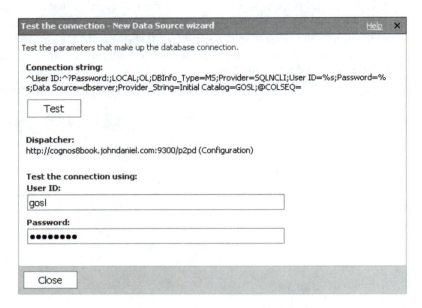

TIP *It is a good idea to test your connection to ensure that all of the parameters have been completed correctly.*

13. Click Test. The View The Results screen displays and identifies whether the test was successful or failed. If the test failed, you can click Failed under the Status column. A screen explaining the failure displays. Address the issues outlined in the error, and retest your connection.

14. Click Close. The Specify The Connection String screen displays again:

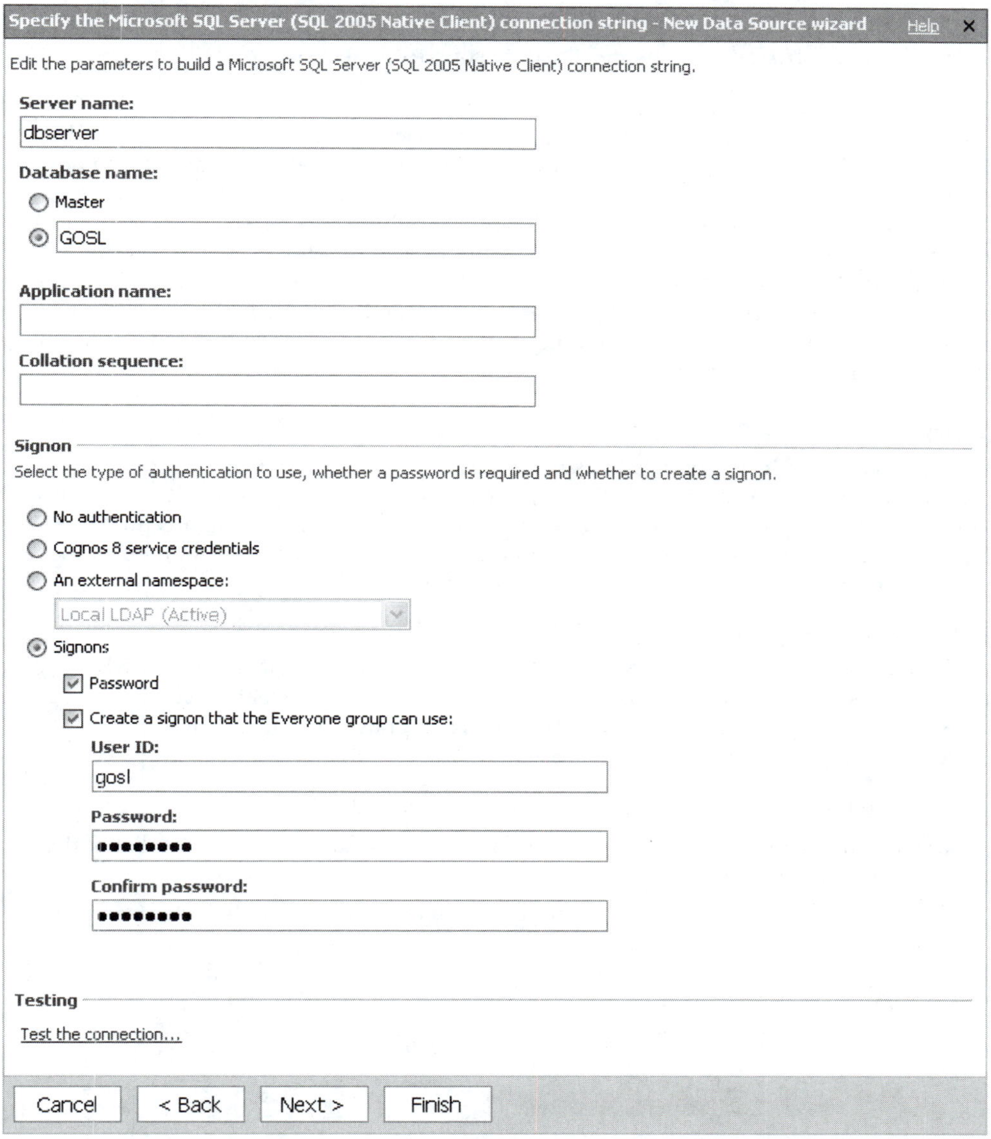

Specify the Microsoft SQL Server (SQL 2005 Native Client) connection string - New Data Source wizard   Help   ✕

Edit the parameters to build a Microsoft SQL Server (SQL 2005 Native Client) connection string.

Server name:

dbserver

Database name:

○ Master

◉ GOSL

Application name:

Collation sequence:

Signon

Select the type of authentication to use, whether a password is required and whether to create a signon.

○ No authentication

○ Cognos 8 service credentials

○ An external namespace:

Local LDAP (Active) ▼

◉ Signons

☑ Password

☑ Create a signon that the Everyone group can use:

User ID:

gosl

Password:

●●●●●●●●

Confirm password:

●●●●●●●●

Testing

Test the connection...

| Cancel | < Back | Next > | Finish |

PART IV

15. Click Next. The Specify The Commands screen displays a list of optional commands that a database executes when opening or closing a connection or session.

16. Optionally, click Set next to the command to be set. The Set The Commands screen displays with a text box in which you can enter the database command in XML.

17. In the XML Database Commands text box, enter the database command in XML format.

18. Click OK. The command has been set.

19. Click Finish. Cognos 8 creates the data source connection.

When you finish creating a data source connection using a Cognos PowerCube, Cognos 8 gives you the option of creating a package. To create the package, select the Create A Package checkbox. The New Package Wizard launches. For more information on creating a package, refer to Chapter 15.

When you finish creating a connection using a database supported by Metrics Studio, such as Microsoft SQL Server, DB2, or Oracle database, and you have Cognos Metrics Manager installed, Cognos 8 gives you the option of creating a metric package. To create a metric package, select the Create A Metric checkbox. The New Metric Package Wizard launches. For more information on creating metric packages, refer to the IBM Cognos 8 Metrics Manager Documentation.

Modify a Database Connection

Cognos 8 lets you modify your database connection parameters through Cognos Administration. This may be necessary if the connection string, sign-on values, database commands, general information about the data source, or type of data source to which Cognos 8 connects have changed. The following sections show you how to modify these different connection parameters using Cognos Administration.

Edit the Connection String

The connection string tells Cognos 8 where and how to find the data source to which you want to connect to generate reports and analyze data. If that information changes, Cognos 8 makes it simple to edit the connection string using Cognos Administration.

Here's how to edit the connection string:

1. From the Launch menu, select Cognos Administration.

2. Click the Configuration tab. The configuration menu displays with a list of the existing data sources.

3. Click the data source with the connection to be changed. The selected connection displays:

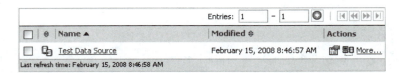

4. From the Actions column, click Set Properties. The Set Properties screen displays with the General, Connection, and Permissions tabs.

5. Click the Connection tab. Parameters for the connection display. The Connection String text box lists the connection string:

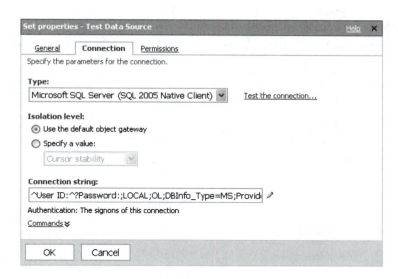

6. Click Edit The Connection String, the little pencil to the right of the connection string. The Edit The Connection String screen displays with the data source–specific parameters that can be edited:

7. Change the appropriate parameters.

8. Optionally, click Test The Connection. The Test The Connection screen displays.

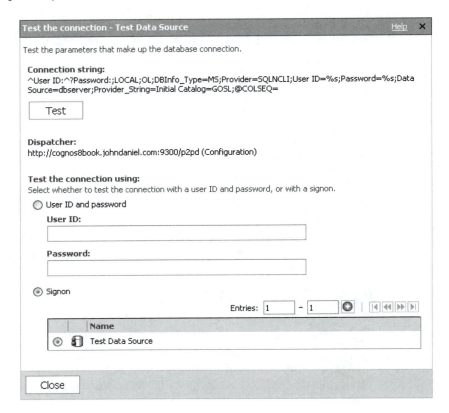

TIP *It is a good idea to test your connection to ensure that all of the parameters have been completed correctly.*

9. Click Test. The View The Results screen displays and identifies whether the test was successful or failed. If the test failed, you can click Failed under the Status column. A screen explaining the failure displays. Address the issues outlined in the error and retest your connection.

10. Click Close. The Test The Connection screen displays again.

11. Click Close. The Edit The Connection String screen displays again.

12. Click OK. The Set Properties screen displays again.

13. Click OK. The database displays and the connection string has been changed.

Edit Database Commands

Cognos 8 allows you to set database commands that execute when opening or closing a connection or session with a DB2, Oracle, or Microsoft SQL Server data source. For example, you can require that the database runs a stored procedure every time Cognos 8 makes a connection to it. For more information, refer to the IBM Cognos 8 BI documentation.

Here's how to edit database commands:

1. From the Launch menu, select Cognos Administration.

2. Click the Configuration tab. The configuration menu displays with a list of the existing data sources.

3. From the Actions column, select Set Properties for the data source for which you want the commands to be changed. The Set Properties screen displays with General, Connection, and Permissions tabs.

4. Click the Connection tab. The parameters for the child connections of the selected data source display:

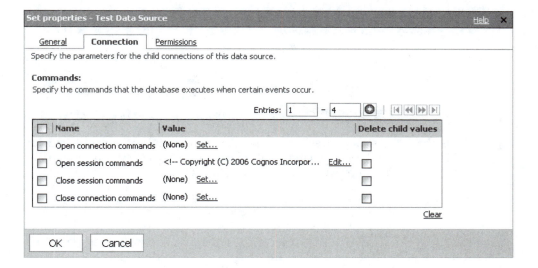

5. Click Edit next to the command to be edited or Set next to the command to be set. The Set The Commands screen displays.

NOTE *Edit will only display if a command was previously set.*

6. In the XML Database Commands text box, enter the database command in XML format.

7. Click OK. A portion of the database command displays under the Value column. The command has been set. Test the functionality of the command the next time you access the data source from Cognos 8.

Change the Signon

You can change the Signon credentials that users enter to access your data source using Cognos Administration. The signon credentials are the user ID and password. You may need to change the user ID or password if the credentials have been compromised, or based on organizational requirements.

NOTE *The Signon feature is not available for the XML data source.*

Here's how to change the signon:

1. From the Launch menu, select Cognos Administration. Cognos Administration displays with the Status, Security, and Configuration tabs.

2. Click the Configuration tab. The configuration menu displays with a list of the existing data sources.

3. Click the data source with the signon to be changed. The selected data source connection displays:

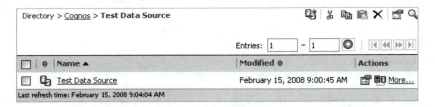

4. From the Actions column, select More in the row containing the data source for which you want the signon credentials to be changed. The Perform An Action screen displays and provides you with additional actions:

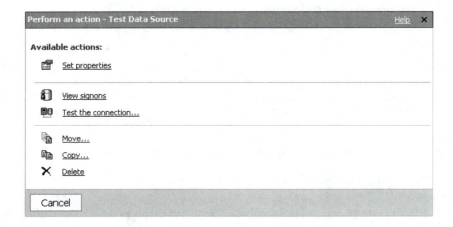

5. Click View Signons. The selected data source connection displays again.

6. From the Actions column, select Set Properties for the data source for which you want the signon credentials to be changed. The Set Properties screen displays with General, Signon, and Permissions tabs.

7. Click the Signon tab, as shown next, to display the Edit The Signon link. You can also add or remove users, groups, or roles that can use the signon.

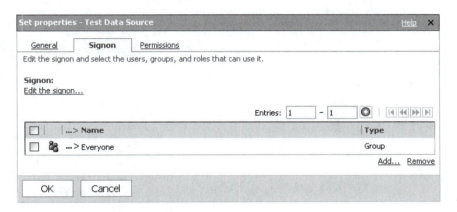

8. Click the Edit The Signon link. The Enter The Signon screen displays with User ID, Password, and Confirm Password text boxes.

9. Enter the changes in the appropriate text boxes. If you change the password, you must enter the same password in the Password and Confirm Password text boxes.

10. Click OK. Cognos 8 changes the signon credentials and the Signon screen displays.

Change General Information

You can edit the general information of a data source, which includes the display language, name of the connection, and icon—to name a few.

Here's how to change the general information for a data source connection:

1. From the Launch menu, select Cognos Administration. Cognos Administration displays with the Status, Security, and Configuration tabs.

2. Click the Configuration tab. The Configuration menu displays with a list of the existing data sources.

3. Click the data source with the general information to be changed. The selected data source connection displays:

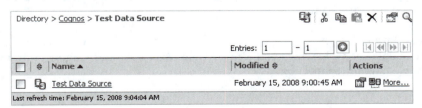

4. From the Actions column, select Set Properties for the data source for which you want the general information to be changed. The Set Properties screen displays with the General, Connection, and Permissions tabs. By default, the General tab is active and shows properties for the selected data source connection. Some general properties of the data source connection that display but cannot be modified include Type, Owner, Location on the server, creation date, and the last date the connection was modified, as shown here:

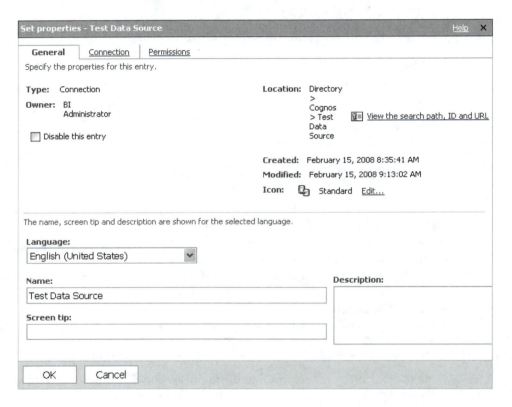

You can edit the icon that displays for the data source connection, the display language, and the name, description, and ScreenTip.

5. Make the desired changes.

6. Click OK. Cognos 8 updates the general information for the data source connection based on your changes.

Change the Database Type

If the type of data source to which you connect Cognos 8 to changes, Cognos Administration makes establishing the connection easy.

Here's how to change the database type:

1. From the Launch menu, select Cognos Administration. Cognos Administration displays with the Status, Security, and Configuration tabs.

2. Click the Configuration tab. The configuration menu displays.

3. Click the data source with the database type to be changed. The selected data source connection displays:

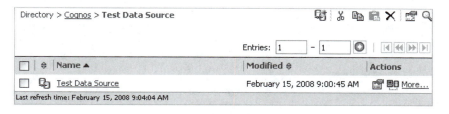

4. From the Actions column, select Set Properties for the data source for which you want the database type to be changed. The Set Properties screen displays with General, Connection, and Permissions tabs.

5. Click the Connection tab. The Connection tab displays with parameters for the selected data source connection:

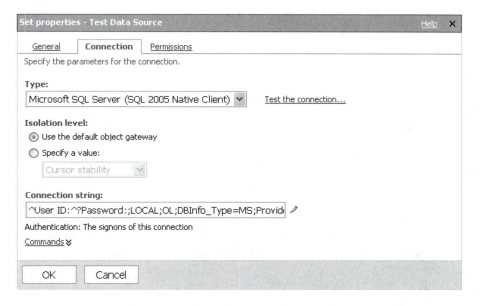

6. From the Type drop-down list, select the new database type. A message displays warning you that changing the connection string type results in the loss of the current connection string.

CAUTION *You should make sure that no users are on the system as this will terminate their database connection, and they may not be able to continue working with that data source in Cognos 8.*

7. Click OK. Complete the required parameters for the selected database type. The type of database that you selected determines the exact parameters that need to be completed.

8. Optionally, click Test The Connection. The Test The Connection screen displays:

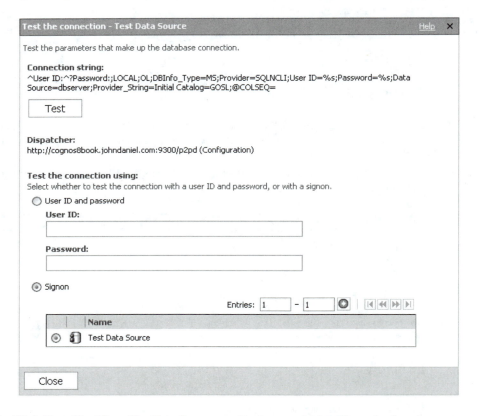

9. Click Test. The View The Results screen displays and identifies whether the test was successful or failed. If the test failed, you can click Failed under the Status column. A screen explaining the failure displays. Address the issues outlined in the error and retest your connection.

10. Click Close. The Specify The Connection String screen displays.

11. Click Next. The Specify The Commands screen displays a list of commands that an Oracle database executes when opening or closing a connection or session, or when a DB2 or Microsoft SQL Server session opens.

12. Optionally, click Set next to the command to be set. The Set The Commands screen displays with a text box in which you can enter the database command in XML.

13. In the XML Database Commands text box, enter the database command in XML format.

14. Click OK. The command has been set.

15. Click Finish.

Content Administration

Content Administration within Cognos 8 allows administrators to manage the content to which users have access by creating backups, moving items from one system to another (such as reports, queries, and packages), and moving items within a single system. You can complete this task in at least three ways: You can export your content into an archive; you can import content from an archive; and you can organize your content into folders to make it easier for a user to access.

The primary function of Content Administration occurs when your organization has more than one Cognos 8 environment in which users are working. For example, a large organization may have a development environment, a test environment, and a production environment, where the reports are created in the development environment, validated in the test environment, and finally promoted for release and consumption in the production environment. Cognos 8 makes promoting your content easy using export archives. Simply create an export archive of the content from the development environment and import that archive into the test environment and then repeat to go from the test environment to the production environment.

Create an Export Archive of Your Content

You can create an export archive of your content to transfer from one installation of Cognos 8 to another or when moving content from a test environment to a production environment. Creating an export archive is a great way to create a content backup. The archive is actually a .zip file that contains all of the XML definitions of the content that you have selected to export. Cognos 8 creates the .zip file with the same name of the export job and stores it in the `installation path/c8/deployment` folder on the server running the export. This .zip file can then be copied to another Cognos 8 installation and used as an input source to be imported. For more information on importing, refer to the "Import a Content Archive" section later in the chapter.

NOTE *The Cognos administrator can customize the default deployment folder location through the Cognos Configuration tool.*

Here's how to export content:

1. From the Launch menu, select Cognos Administration. Cognos Administration displays with the Status, Security, and Configuration tabs.

2. Click the Configuration tab. The configuration menu displays.

3. Click Content Administration. A list of the exports, imports, and content maintenance tasks display:

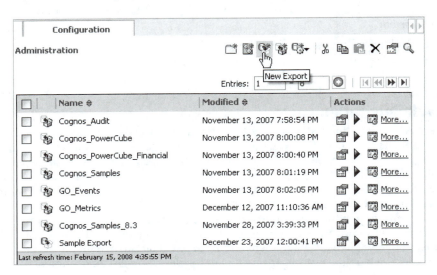

4. Click New Export. The New Export Wizard launches:

5. In the Name text box, enter a name for the export.

6. Optionally, in the Description text box, enter a description of the export.

7. Optionally, in the Screen Tip text box, enter a ScreenTip that displays when the user moves the pointer over the Export icon.

8. Click Next. The Choose A Deployment Method screen displays with two options, as shown next. You can choose the Select Public Folders And Directory Content option, which allows you to choose the content to be exported, or you can choose the Select The Entire Content Store Option, which creates a copy of all of the content within that store to move it to another system or to keep it as a backup. If you choose the latter option, you can include user account information. This information includes the individual user's personal folders and personal pages.

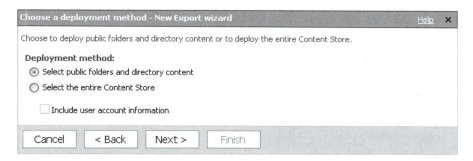

TIP   *The Select The Entire Content Store option is a great way to create a backup of your content.*

To use the Select Public Folders And Directory Content option, proceed to step 9.

To use the Select The Entire Content Store option, skip to step 28.

9. Click Next. The Select The Public Folders Content screen displays with a Public Folders Content area and an Options area. The Public Folders Content area displays everything that you have selected to be exported. If you are initially starting the export process, this area is blank.

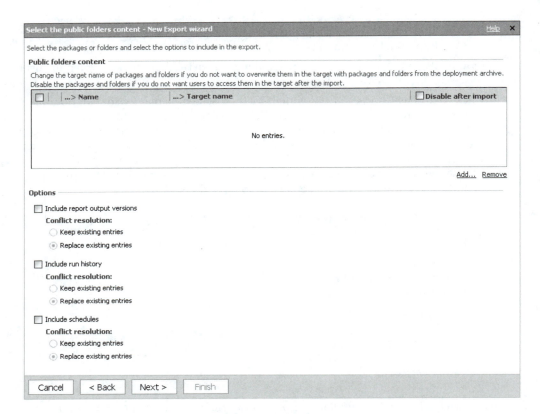

10. Click Add. The Select Entries (Navigate) screen displays with a Public Folders area and Selected Entries area. From this screen, you can choose a folder from the list or click a folder name to navigate to the content to be exported, as shown next:

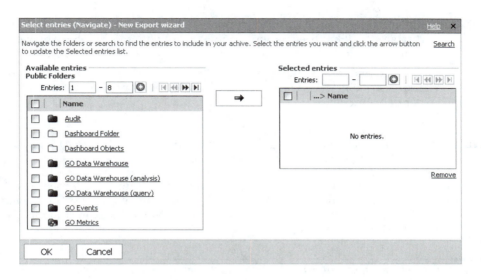

11. Select the checkbox next to the folder that you want to export.

12. Click Add (the green arrow). The selected folder displays in the Selected Entries area.

13. Click OK. The Select The Public Folders Content screen displays and lists the selected content in the Public Folders Content area:

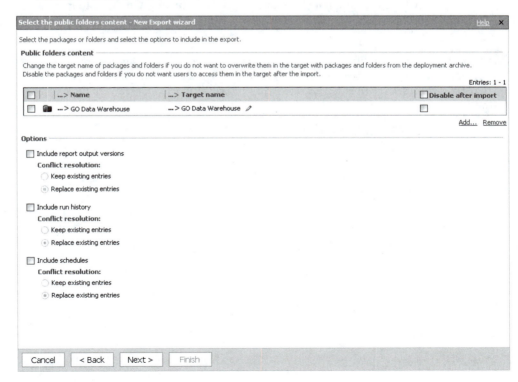

14. Optionally, select the Disable After Import checkbox for the content that you want to disable after it has been imported into the destination. Typically, you want the content to be enabled after it has been imported; therefore, this option is cleared.

15. Optionally, under the Options area, select the Include Report Output Versions checkbox to export the saved versions of any reports contained in the selected folder or package.

NOTE *Typically, when you are exporting from one environment to another you do not want to include versions of reports that you ran in the previous environment.*

16. Optionally, under the Options area, click the Include Run History checkbox to export all runs of the content. For example, if the content is a report, and you ran it six times in the test environment, and it was successful three times and failed twice, you can choose to export that history.

NOTE *Typically, when you are exporting from the one environment to another environment you do not want to include the run history from the previous environment.*

17. Optionally, under the Options area, select the Include Schedules checkbox to include any schedules you created with the content. For example, if the content is a report for which you have created a run schedule, you can choose to export that schedule. This may be an option that you want to select. If not, you will have to re-create the schedule in the target environment.

NOTE *If you select any of the checkboxes in the Options area, you also have the option to select Keep Existing Entries or Replace Existing Entries under Conflict Resolution. Selecting Replace Existing Entries overwrites any entries of the same content when imported to the new destination.*

18. Click Next. The Select The Directory Content screen displays:

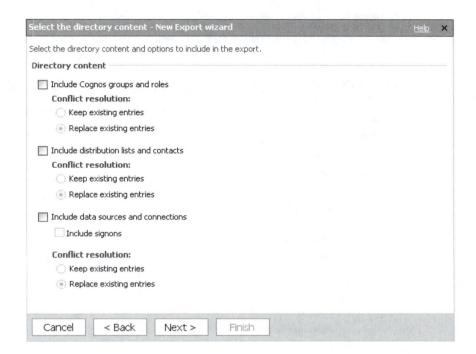

19. Optionally, select the Include Cognos Groups And Roles checkbox to include all groups and roles from the Cognos namespace except Everyone, All Authenticated, and Anonymous.

20. Optionally, select the Include Distribution Lists and Contacts checkbox to include any distribution lists or contacts that you created in the source environment. If you choose not to include new distribution lists or contacts, you will have to recreate them in the new environment.

21. Optionally, select the Include Data Sources And Connections checkbox to include any data sources that you created in conjunction with the content. If selected, you can include any signons created for the connections.

NOTE *If you select the Include Signons checkbox, Cognos 8 forces you to encrypt the export package as discussed in step 30 of this task.*

22. Click Next. The Specify The General Options screen displays with Access Permissions, External Namespaces, Entry Ownership, and Deployment Record areas:

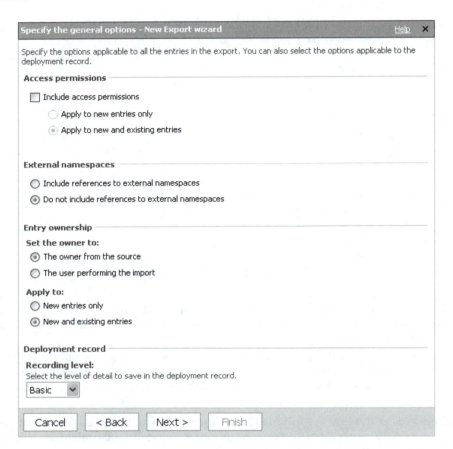

23. Optionally, in the Access Permissions area, select the Include Access Permissions checkbox to include any permissions associated with the content.

24. In the External Namespaces area, click the Include References To External Namespaces option or Do Not Include References To External Namespaces option. The Include References To External Namespaces option includes users that are found in a namespace other than the Cognos namespace. These users can be found in items such as distribution lists, contacts, group, roles, data source signons, and e-mail recipients. If a user is referenced in the source environment but not in the target environment, you will receive errors during the deployment.

25. From the Entry Ownership area, under Set The Owner To, set the creator of the source content as the owner by clicking the option The Owner From The Source, or set the user performing the export as the owner by clicking the option The User Performing The Import option.

26. From the Entry Ownership area, under Apply To, click the New Entries Only option or the New And Existing Entries option. The New Entries Only option sets the owner selected in the previous step as the owner only for new entries of the content. The New And Existing Entries option sets the owner selected in the previous step as the owner for new and existing entries of the content.

27. From the Deployment Record area, from the Recording Level drop-down list, select the level of detail to store in the deployment record. The options are Minimal, Basic, and Trace. By default, the Recording Level is set to Minimal. You can increase the amount of detail in the deployment record to check for errors if the export fails.

28. Click Next. The Specify A Deployment Archive screen displays:

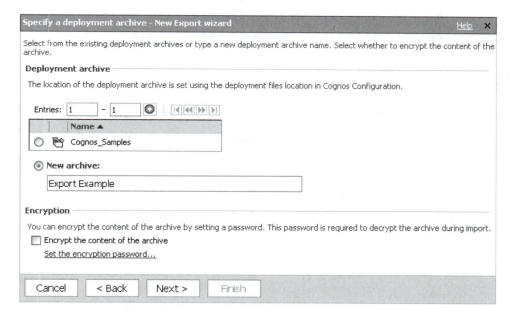

29. In the New Archive text box, enter the name for the deployment archive. The deployment archive is a .zip file stored in the Cognos 8 deployment folder on the server housing the Cognos 8 installation.

NOTE *If you selected the Select The Entire Content Store option in step 8, you must complete step 30.*

30. Optionally, under the Encryption area select the Encrypt The Content Of The Archive checkbox. This option is required if you chose to include signons in step 21 or if you are exporting the entire content store. If you choose to encrypt the content, click Set The Encryption Password to set the password.

NOTE Choosing to encrypt the archive requires a password to open the archive. Consider this option if your archive contains passwords or other sensitive information.

31. Click Next. The Review The Summary screen displays with the summary detail of the export settings:

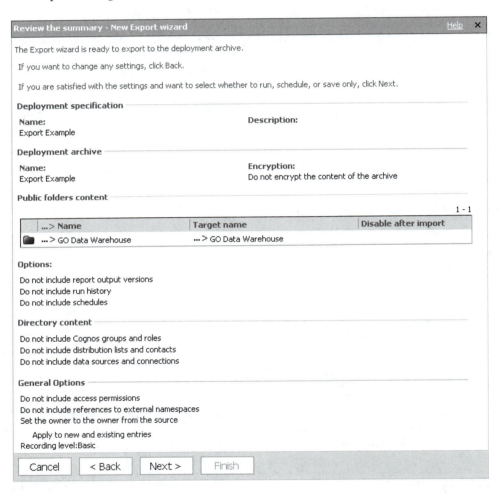

32. Review the settings summary.
33. Optionally, click Back to change any of the settings and make the desired changes.

34. Click Next. The Select An Action screen, shown next, allows you to choose what actions occur after you have saved the export. The Save And Run Once option saves the export and runs the content immediately. The Save And Schedule option saves the export and allows you to schedule the content to run at a later time. The Save Only option saves the export without running the content.

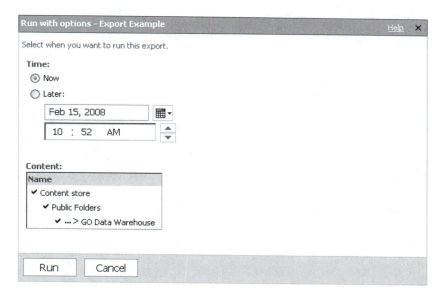

35. Click Finish. If you chose to Save Only, Cognos 8 saves the export, and your export archive has been created. If you chose to Save And Run Once, the Run With Options screen displays, as shown next. Proceed to step 36.

If you chose to Save And Schedule, the Schedule screen displays, as shown next. Skip to step 38.

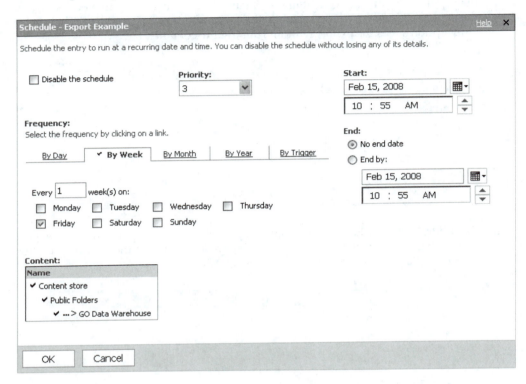

36. Click the Now option to run the content immediately, or click the Later option and select a date and time to run the content at a later time. If you choose Now, you can choose the View The Details Of The Export After Closing This Dialog checkbox.

37. Click Run. A screen displays with the View The Details Of This Export After Closing This Dialog checkbox. Skip to step 39.

38. Enter the appropriate information to create the schedule.

39. Click OK. If you selected to view the details, the View Run History Details screen displays:

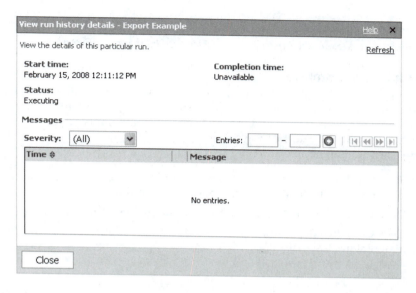

Depending on the size of the export and activity on the server, the screen shows a Status of Executing. The screen does not dynamically update. Periodically, click the Refresh link in the upper-right corner of the screen. The screen updates with the run history.

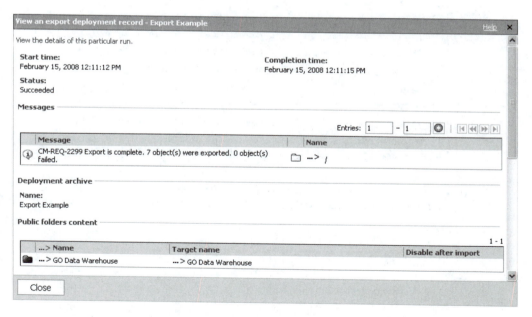

40. Click Close. A list of the imports and exports display. Your content has been archived and is ready to be imported to the destination server. For more information, refer to the "Import a Content Archive" section later in this chapter.

NOTE *A System Administrator is required to physically copy the .zip file from the source server to the target server before the export file can be accessed by the target server.*

Import a Content Archive

Before you can move content from one server to another you must first create an export archive as discussed in the "Create an Export Archive of Your Content" section. Once the export archive has been created and moved to the destination server, you are ready to import the archive on the destination server.

Here's how to import an export archive:

1. From the Launch menu, select Cognos Administration. Cognos Administration displays with the Status, Security, and Configuration tabs.

2. Click the Configuration tab. The Configuration menu displays.

3. Click Content Administration. A list of the exports, imports, and content maintenance tasks displays:

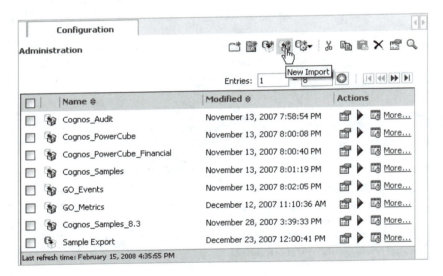

4. Click New Import. The New Import Wizard launches and displays the Select A Deployment Archive screen with a list of the content archives, as shown next:

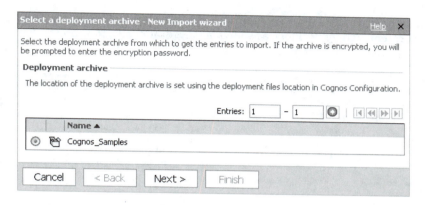

5. Click the archive to be imported.

6. Click Next. The Specify A Name And Description screen displays with the Name, Description, and Screen Tip with which the archive was originally created:

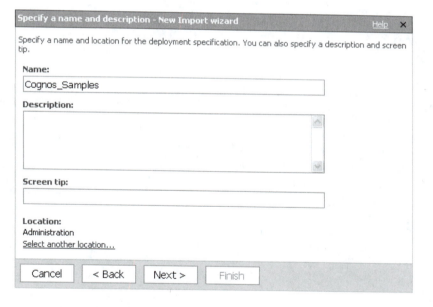

7. Optionally, change the Name, Description, or Screen Tip by entering new information in the appropriate text box(es).

8. Click Next. The Select The Public Folders Content screen displays with a list of the content archive's folders, as shown next. Additionally, the options defined during the creation of the archive display:

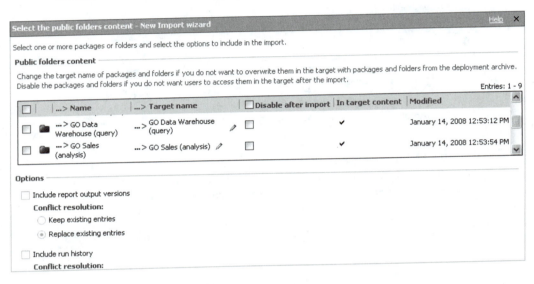

NOTE *You can clear any of the options defined during the creation of the archive. However, you can not add new options.*

9. From the list of folders, select the checkbox next to the folder(s) to be imported.

10. Optionally, select the Disable After Import checkbox. This option allows the content to be imported into the target environment but does not allow users to access it. This gives administrators the ability to test and validate the deployment before the users can see it.

11. Click Next. The Specify The General Options screen displays with the general options defined in the creation of the archive:

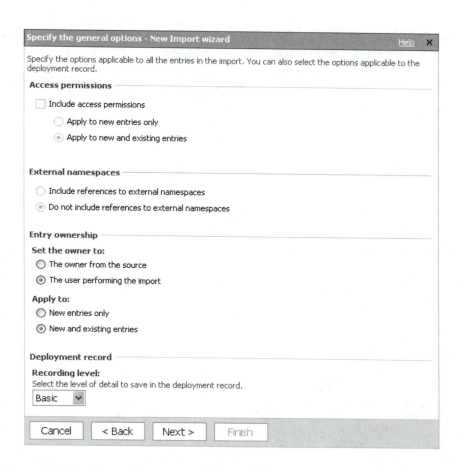

12. From the Entry Ownership area, select either The Owner From The Source or The User Performing The Import option. The Owner From The Source retains the ownership of the source with the initial creator, and The User Performing The Import option sets the owner of the deployed content as the user performing the import.

13. From the Entry Ownership area, select the New Entries Only or New And Existing Entries option. The New Entries Only option sets ownership of only new content created in the data source based on your selection in step 12, and the New And Existing Entries option sets ownership of all content based on your selection in step 12.

14. From the Deployment Record area, set the recording level to Basic (the default), Minimal, or Trace. Basic recording saves the progress and summary information. Minimal saves only the summary information. Trace saves all the details. You can use the Trace option to help identify problems if your deployment has errors. The Trace level of recording requires the most amount of memory out of the three options and has the largest performance impact.

15. Click Next. The Review The Summary screen displays with a summary detail of the import settings, as shown next:

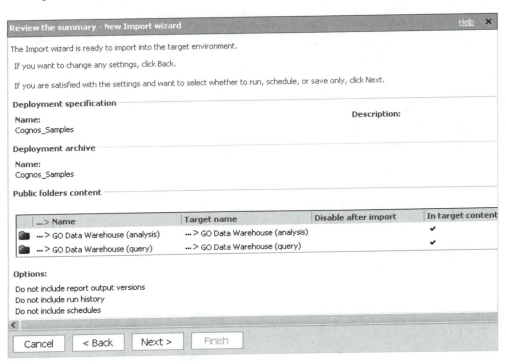

16. Review the settings summary.

17. Optionally, click Back to change any of the settings and make the desired changes.

18. Click Next. The Select An Action screen displays with action options that occur after you have saved the import. The Save And Run Once option saves the import and runs the content immediately. The Save And Schedule option saves the import and allows you to schedule the content to run at a later time. The Save Only option saves the import without running the content.

19. Click Finish. If you chose to Save Only, Cognos 8 saves the import task in the Administration folder. The task can either be scheduled or run manually at a later time. If you chose Save And Run Once, the Run With Options screen displays, as shown next. Proceed to step 20.

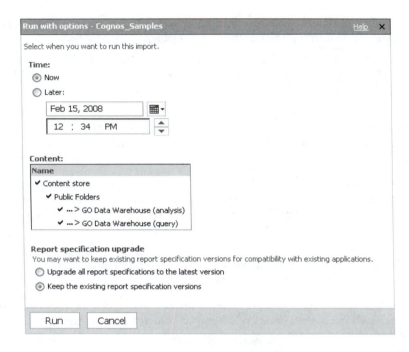

If you chose to Save And Schedule, the Schedule screen displays, as shown next. Skip to step 23.

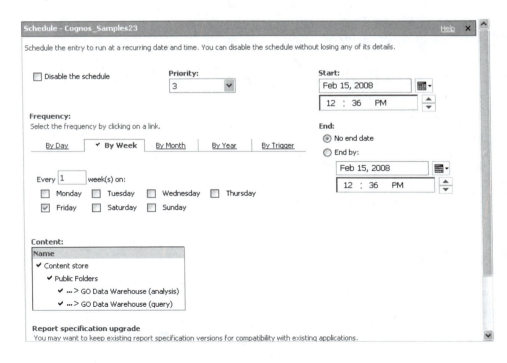

20. Click the Now option to run the content immediately, or click the Later option and select a date and time to run the content later.

21. Optionally, under the Report Specification Upgrade area, click the Upgrade All Report Specifications To The Latest Version option or Keep The Existing Report Specification Versions option.

NOTE *These options are extremely important for users moving content from a server running an older version of the Cognos application to a server running a newer version of the Cognos application.*

The Upgrade All Report Specifications To The Latest Version option attempts to upgrade your content to the newer version of the Cognos application running on the destination server. If the upgrade is not successful, you will have nonfunctional content in your target installation.

NOTE *This option is not recommended unless you are confident that all of your content will upgrade without errors.*

The Keep The Existing Report Specification Versions option keeps your report specifications in the version of Cognos in which it was created.

22. Click Run. A screen displays with the View The Details Of This Export After Closing This Dialog checkbox. Optionally, select the View The Details Of The Export After Closing This Dialog checkbox. Skip to step 24.

23. Enter the appropriate information to define the schedule.

24. Click OK. If you chose to view the details of the export, the View Run History Details screen displays:

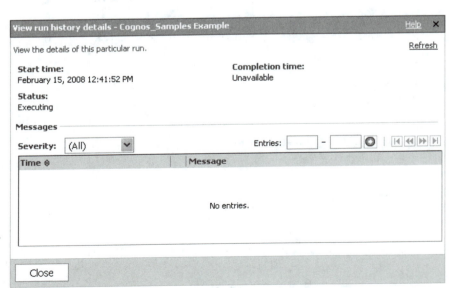

Depending on the size of the archive and activity on the server to which the archive is being imported, the screen shows a status of Executing. The screen does not dynamically update. Periodically, click the Refresh link. The screen updates with the run history:

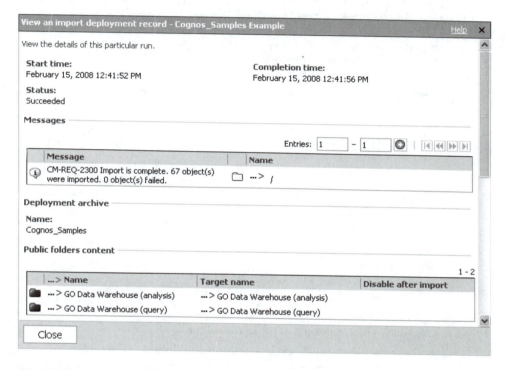

25. Click Close. Cognos 8 imports the archive to the destination server and a list of the imports and exports displays.

Organize Content

The administrator can organize content from Cognos Connection. When content is organized properly, it makes using Cognos Connection that much easier for the user. With Cognos 8, the administrator can create folders to house packages, content, or both. For example, the administrator can create a folder for the Accounting department that contains all the packages and content for Monthly Accounting, and another folder for Quarterly Accounting.

NOTE *The blue folders denote Framework Manager packages that may or may not contain package specific content. The slightly paler blue folders with the metric symbol on them are Metric packages. These folders contain links to the Metric Studio content. The yellow folders are created by a user and can have content and/or blue folders within them.*

After you create a folder, your next step is to organize content by moving packages, content, or both into the folder.

Here's how to organize content:

1. In Cognos Connection, click Create New Folder on the toolbar. The New Folder Wizard's Specify A Name And Description screen displays:

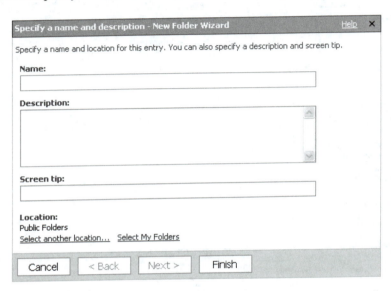

2. In the Name text box, enter the name of the folder.

3. Optionally, in the Description text box, enter a description of the folder.

4. Optionally, in the Screen Tip text box, enter a ScreenTip that displays when the user moves the pointer over the folder icon to the left of the folder name.

5. Optionally, click Select Another Location or Select My Folders to define where the folder should be saved. By default, Cognos 8 creates the folder in your current location.

6. Click Finish. Cognos 8 creates the folder.

7. Optionally, click Set Properties for the newly created folder to set the permissions on the folder. The Set Properties screen displays with the General and Permissions tabs.

8. Click the Permissions tab. A list of users with permission to access the folder displays.

9. Modify the permissions and then click OK. For more information on modifying permissions, refer to Chapter 17.

10. Select the checkbox(es) next to the content to be moved into the new folder.

NOTE *If you do not see all of the entries listed, click the right arrow next to the number of entries to advance to the next set of 15 entries. By default, Cognos 8 displays only 15 entries at a time. The default number of items displayed can be modified in your personal settings.*

11. Click Cut on the toolbar.

12. Open the newly created folder.

13. Click Paste on the toolbar. Cognos 8 pastes the selected content into the new folder. Repeat steps 10 through 13 to move additional content into the folder.

Schedule Management

Managing scheduled jobs is extremely important to system performance. This is especially true in large organizations with a large number of people scheduling large amounts of jobs (such as reports or event notifications). As the administrator, you were probably given a finite amount of resources with which to work. As a result, when too many jobs are scheduled to run at the same time, jobs with errors are running, or jobs are running at peak times that could be run after hours, your system can get bogged down. As administrator, you need to be able to review and modify schedules as necessary.

View Schedules

Viewing scheduled jobs is the first step in managing schedules. You need to determine what jobs are scheduled when and the properties dictating the jobs.

Here's how to view schedules:

1. From the Launch menu, select Cognos Administration. Cognos Administration displays with the Status, Security, and Configuration tabs.

2. Click the Status tab. The Status menu displays.

3. From the Status menu, select Schedules. The Schedules screen displays. A chart graphically depicting the number of scheduled items that are enabled and disabled appears in the center of the screen. Directly below the chart is a list of the scheduled jobs and the status of those jobs. The list shows the date that the schedule was last modified, who scheduled the job, the status, and the priority of when it should run.

4. Optionally, click Show Details, the list expands and shows you the location of the scheduled job.

5. Optionally, click Actions. A context menu displays with a list of options, as shown next. The options include Set Properties, Run The Schedule Once, Modify The Schedule, Remove The Schedule, View Run History, Enable The Schedule or Disable The Schedule (if the schedule is enabled), and Set Priority.

PART IV

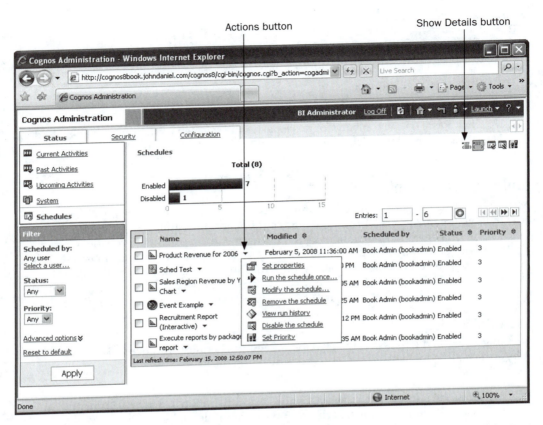

6. Optionally, from the context menu, select Set Properties to display the properties of the item. For more information on modifying the properties, refer to Chapters 5 and 6.

7. Optionally, from the context menu, select Run The Schedule Once. The Run With Advanced Options screen displays, as shown next. You can run the schedule now or later, or you can change the delivery options, format, language, and whether to prompt for values:

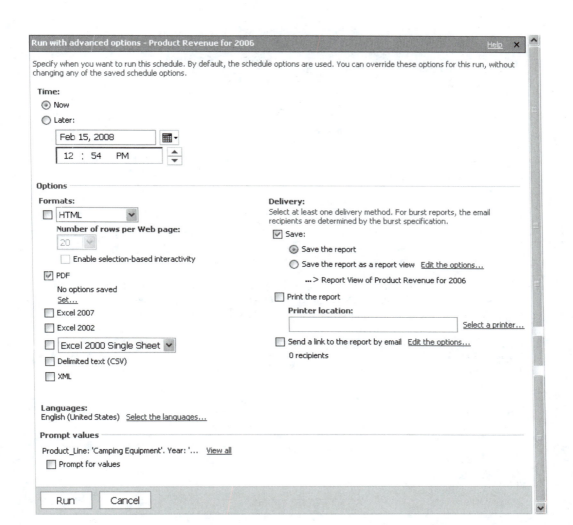

8. Optionally, from the context menu, select View Run History. The View Run History screen displays. For more information on run history, refer to Chapter 6.

9. Optionally, filter your schedules using the filter options, as shown next:

10. Optionally, under Filter, click Select A User to view schedules created by a specific user. The Select The User (Navigate) screen displays, as shown next. You can navigate to the user whose schedule(s) you want to view.

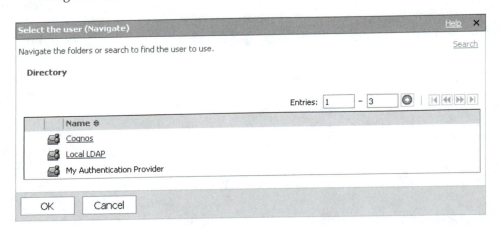

11. Optionally, from the Status drop-down list and/or the Priority drop-down list, click a status and/or a priority on which to filter.

Tip *Filtering by the status is useful when a user states that a scheduled job did not run. You can view the disabled job and determine whether a schedule was inadvertently disabled.*

12. Optionally, click Advanced Options. Advanced filtering options display and give you the ability to filter by the owner of a job, the type of job, or the scope. The owned by user options allows you to navigate to a user and filter for any jobs created by that user in the same way that you can filter by the user who scheduled the job. The Type drop-down list allows you to choose a job type from the list on which to base your filter. The Scope option allows you to define a specific folder in which to filter jobs.

13. Click Apply. Cognos 8 displays the schedule(s) based on the selected options.

14. Optionally, click Current Activities on the Status menu to view schedules that are currently running, as shown next. An option to apply filters on which to view current activities displays. The Current Activities filter options are the same as those for Schedules, with the additional options of filtering by Background Activities or Interactive Activities. Background activities are scheduled to run without any

human interaction. Interactive activities require that the user answer prompts to enter information. Additionally, you can choose to Suspend, Release, or Cancel a job by clicking the appropriate icon located in the upper-right of the screen.

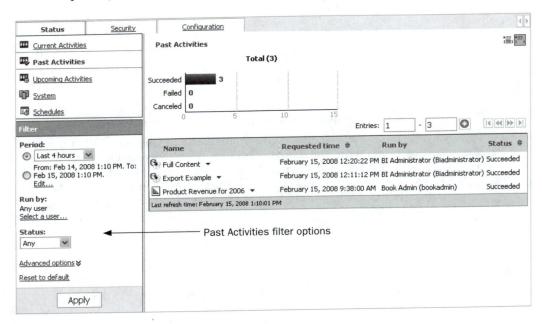

15. Optionally, click Past Activities on the Status menu to view schedules that have run in the past, as shown next. An option to apply filters on which to view past activities displays. The Past Activities filter options are the same as those for Schedules, with the additional option of choosing a general time period ranging from the last four hours to the last 365 days, or you can choose a more specific date and time frame on which to filter by clicking Edit under the Period area. Finally, under Advanced Options you can also choose to filter by a dispatcher.

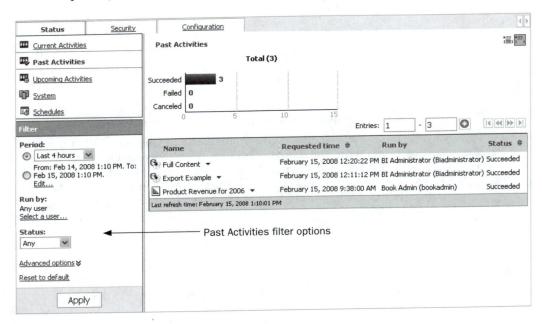

Past Activities filter options

16. Optionally, click Upcoming Activities on the Status menu to view schedules that will occur at a future time. An option to apply filters on which to view upcoming activities displays. Again the Upcoming Activities filter options are the same as those for Schedules with the additional option of choosing a specific day.

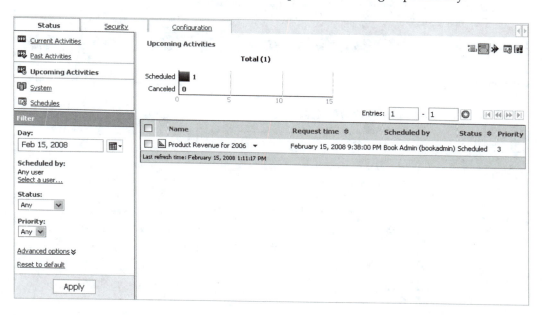

Modify Schedules

Users can create schedules for many different types of jobs. If a lot of users are accessing resources, you may end up with a large volume of scheduled jobs. Additionally, if several groups of users do not necessarily communicate with one another, through no fault of their own, you may end up with a large number of jobs scheduled to run at the same time, creating resource issues. Cognos Connection allows administrators to modify schedules created by other users at a variety of levels. You can modify the actual scheduling of a job, you can enable or disable a job, or you can change the priority of a job.

Modify the Schedule

One of the options available for freeing up valuable resources is to modify the schedule. As the administrator, you can modify schedules to move nonessential jobs to off-peak times. Here's how to modify the schedule:

1. From the Launch menu, select Cognos Administration. Cognos Administration displays with the Status, Security, and Configuration tabs.

2. Click the Status tab. The Status menu displays.

3. From the Status menu, select Schedules. The Schedules screen displays:

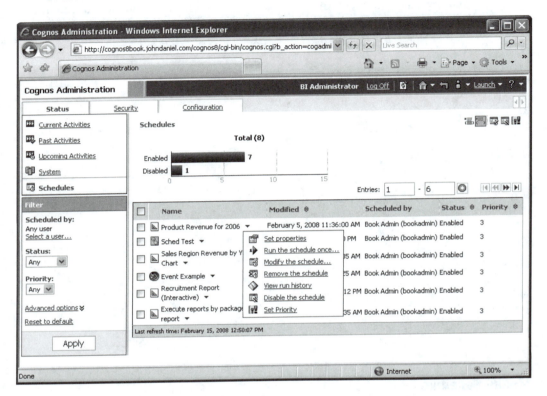

4. From the Actions context menu for the schedule to be modified, click Modify The Schedule. The Schedule screen displays:

Schedule - Product Revenue for 2006   Help   ✕

Schedule this entry to run at a recurring date and time. You can run using the default values or specify the options. You can disable the schedule without losing any of its details.

☐ Disable the schedule

Priority:
`3`

Start:
`Dec 21, 2007`   🔳▾
`9 : 38  PM`   ▲▼

Frequency:
Select the frequency by clicking on a link.

| ✔ **By Day** | By Week | By Month | By Year | By Trigger |

End:
◉ No end date
○ End by:
`Feb 15, 2008`   🔳▾
`1 : 15  PM`   ▲▼

○ Every `12` minute(s)
◉ Every `12` hour(s)
○ Every `12` day(s)

Options

☑ Override the default values

Formats:

☐ HTML ▾

Number of rows per Web page:
`20` ▾

☐ Enable selection-based interactivity

☑ PDF
No options saved
Set...

☐ Excel 2007

☐ Excel 2002

☐ Excel 2000 Single Sheet ▾

☐ Delimited text (CSV)

☐ XML

Delivery:
Select at least one delivery method. For burst reports, the email recipients are determined by the burst specification.

☑ Save:
   ◉ Save the report
   ○ Save the report as a report view   Edit the options...
       ...> Report View of Product Revenue for 2006

☐ Print the report
Printer location:

Select a printer...

☐ Send a link to the report by email   Edit the options...
0 recipients

Languages:
English (United States)   Select the languages...

Prompt values

☑ Override the default values

Product_Line: 'Camping Equipment'. Year: '...   View all
Edit...   Clear

[OK]   [Cancel]

5. Modify the scheduled job based on the system resources you have available. For more information on schedules, refer to Chapter 5.

6. Click OK. Cognos 8 updates the schedule.

Enable/Disable

Another option for freeing up valuable system resources is to disable a scheduled job. Again, as the administrator, you can perform this function. Additionally, you have the permissions to enable a job that you or someone else has disabled either inadvertently or with a purpose.

NOTE *Disabling a job does not delete it. It simply turns off the schedule.*

Here's how to enable/disable a schedule:

1. From the Launch menu, select Cognos Administration. Cognos Administration displays with the Status, Security, and Configuration tabs.

2. Click the Status tab. The Status menu displays.

3. From the Status menu, select Schedules. The Schedules screen displays:

4. Select the checkbox next to the scheduled job.

5. On the toolbar, click Enable to enable the job or Disable to disable the job, as shown next. A confirmation message displays.

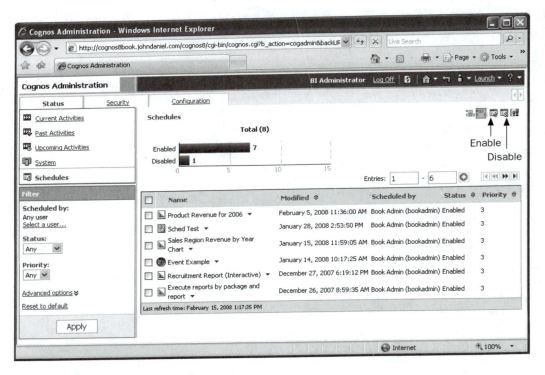

6. Click OK. The status of the item and the graphical depiction changes.

TIP *As an alternative method—from the Actions context menu for the schedule to be enabled or disabled, click Enable The Schedule or Disable The Schedule.*

Change Priority

When users create a schedule for a job, they are asked to set a priority for the job from 1 to 5, with 1 being the highest priority and 5 being the lowest priority. If numerous jobs have the same priority, let's say a priority of 1, then the job that was scheduled first is placed into the queue first and therefore runs first. The priority of a job is extremely important when you have a large number of jobs scheduled to run at the same time. Jobs with the higher priority run first. This can become an issue with system resources when you have a job that takes a long time to run set with a priority of 1 and placed in the queue first and is scheduled to run with numerous smaller jobs with the same priority. The smaller jobs may be more important to the organization than the larger job, but the larger job will run first and may delay the smaller jobs. As the administrator, you can change the priority of the larger job allowing the smaller jobs to run first.

Here's how to change the priority of a job:

1. From the Launch menu, select Cognos Administration. Cognos Administration displays with the Status, Security, and Configuration tabs.

2. Click the Status tab. The Status menu displays.

3. From the Status menu, select Schedules. The Schedules screen displays.

4. Select the checkbox next to the scheduled job.

5. Click the Set Priority button on the toolbar, as shown here:

   The Set The Priority screen displays:

   Set Priority button

Set the priority	Help ✕
Specify the priority for the selected entries. Entries with a value of 1 are processed first and entries with a value of 5 are processed last.	
Priority:	
3 ▾	
OK Cancel	

   As an alternative, from the Actions context menu for the schedule for which you want to change the priority, choose Set Priority.

6. From the Priority drop-down list, click the priority to which you would like to assign the job.

7. Click OK. The priority of the selected job changes. In the following example, the first job was chosen.

PART IV

	Name	Modified ⇕	Scheduled by	Status ⇕	Priority ⇕
☑	Product Revenue for 2006 ▼	February 15, 2008 2:45:09 PM	Book Admin (bookadmin)	Enabled	2
☐	Sched Test ▼	January 28, 2008 2:53:50 PM	Book Admin (bookadmin)	Enabled	3
☐	Sales Region Revenue by Year Chart ▼	January 15, 2008 11:59:05 AM	Book Admin (bookadmin)	Enabled	3
☐	Event Example ▼	January 14, 2008 10:17:25 AM	Book Admin (bookadmin)	Enabled	3
☐	Recruitment Report (Interactive) ▼	December 27, 2007 6:19:12 PM	Book Admin (bookadmin)	Enabled	3
☐	Execute reports by package and report ▼	December 26, 2007 8:59:35 AM	Book Admin (bookadmin)	Enabled	3

Last refresh time: February 15, 2008 2:45:36 PM

Maintain Distribution Lists

Distribution lists allow you to distribute content automatically to users. They can be used in conjunction with a scheduled job. Your distribution list can include members of your organization or recipients outside of your organization. Users can create distribution lists when initially scheduling a job or administrators can create a distribution list using Cognos Administration. This section covers how to create a contact for someone outside the organization, and how to create a distribution list using contacts both in and out of the organization.

Add a Contact

It may be necessary to share content with someone outside of the organization. Further, it may make sense to include that person in a distribution list if the content is shared on a regular basis. To accomplish this, Cognos 8 must have some contact information about this person–namely, a name and e-mail address. Cognos 8 refers to these individuals as *contacts*.

Here's how to add a contact:

1. From the Launch menu, select Cognos Administration. Cognos Administration displays with the Status, Security, and Configuration tabs.

2. Click the Configuration tab. The Configuration menu displays.

3. From the Configuration menu, select Distribution Lists and Contacts. The Directory screen displays with a list of the namespaces:

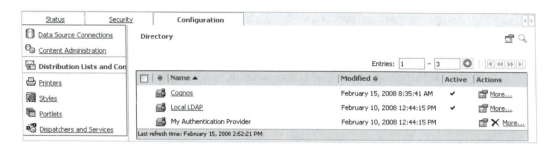

4. Click the Cognos namespace. The Cognos Namespace screen displays with a list of existing contacts and recipients:

NOTE *The Cognos namespace is the only namespace that you can use to store a contact.*

5. Click New Contact. The New Contact Wizard launches and the Specify A Name And Description screen displays.

6. In the Name text box, enter the name of contact.

7. Optionally, in the Description text box, enter a description for the contact.

8. Optionally, in the Screen Tip text box, enter a ScreenTip to display when the user moves the pointer over the contact icon to the left of the contact name.

9. In the Email Address text box, enter the e-mail address for the contact.

10. Optionally, click Select Another Location to designate a new location within the Cognos namespace to save the contact. By default, Cognos 8 saves the contact in the root of the Cognos namespace.

11. Click Finish. Cognos 8 adds the new contact to the list of contacts and recipients.

Create a Distribution List

Cognos 8 facilitates the creation of distribution lists using Cognos Administration. Distribution lists are a good way to have jobs such as reports, queries, or event notices sent to a group of users or contacts on a scheduled basis. This section discusses the creation of the distribution list.

Here's how to create a distribution list:

1. From the Launch menu, select Cognos Administration. Cognos Administration displays.
2. Click the Configuration tab. The Configuration menu displays.
3. From the Configuration menu, select Distribution Lists and Contacts. The Directory screen displays with a list of the namespaces:

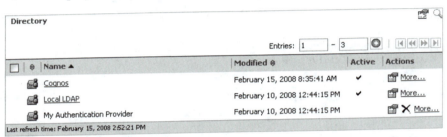

4. Click the Cognos namespace. The Cognos Namespace screen displays with a list of existing contacts and recipients:

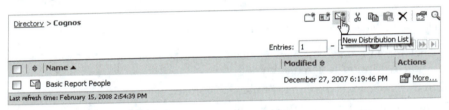

5. Click New Distribution List. The New Distribution List Wizard launches and the Specify A Name And Description screen displays:

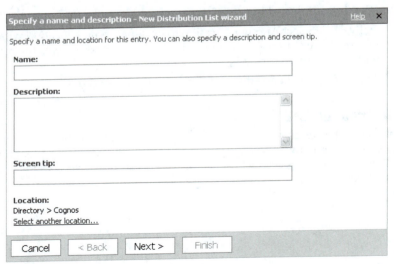

6. In the Name text box, enter the name of the distribution list.

7. Optionally, in the Description text box, enter a description for the distribution list.

8. Optionally, in the Screen Tip text box, enter a ScreenTip to display when the user moves the pointer over the distribution list icon to the left of the distribution list.

9. Optionally, click Select Another Location to designate a new location within the Cognos namespace to save the distribution list. By default, Cognos 8 saves the distribution list in the top level folder.

10. Click Next. The Select The Members screen displays, as shown next, showing a list of recipients. Initially, the list is blank as no recipients have been added:

11. Click Add. The Select Recipients (Navigate) screen displays, as shown next. The screen includes an Available Entries area, Selected Entries area, and the Show Users In The List checkbox. The Available Entries area lists the namespaces from which you can select recipients. The Selected Entries area shows the recipients selected as members of the distribution list. When selected, the Show Users In The List checkbox displays all of the users within a selected folder.

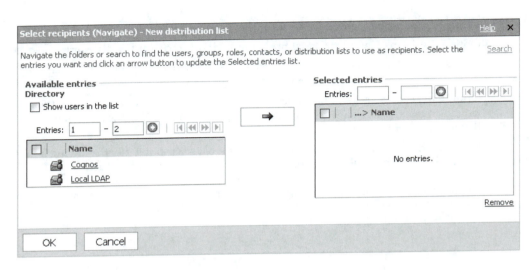

12. Select the Show Users In The List checkbox to make the user entries visible.

13. Click the namespace containing the recipients to be added to the distribution list.

14. Click the folder containing the recipients to be added to the list. The list of available users and contacts contained in the selected folder displays:

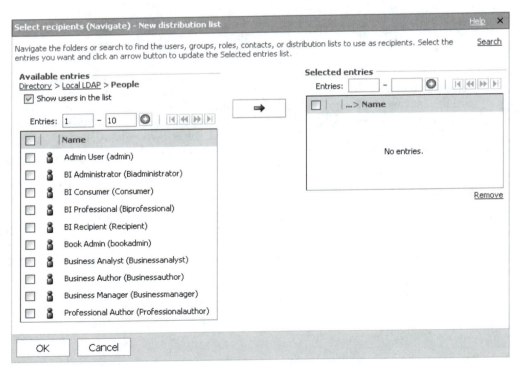

15. Select the checkboxes next to the users to be added.

16. Click Add (the green arrow). Cognos 8 adds the users to the Selected Entries area.

17. Click OK. The Select The Members screen displays with a list of the users you added.

18. Click Finish. A screen displays with the newly created distribution list added to the list of distribution lists.

Server Administration

Server administration is typically performed by the System Administrator. It involves maintaining all of the software and configuration settings that Cognos 8 uses to run. Normally, the software and configuration settings do not need to be modified out of the box, but given the many ways in which Cognos 8 can be installed and the wide range of hardware and operating systems supported, you may find that tuning your installation will increase performance.

CAUTION   *Before modifying any of the settings discussed in this section, be sure you have full knowledge of your system.*

The System Administrator can manage the metrics monitoring the system, manage the software and configuration properties, manage gateways, set logging levels, tune the system, view the status of jobs, and monitor the system.

Manage Metrics

The metrics that are available for the system are similar to those that are available when scorecards are created. The metrics monitoring the system allow you to set the thresholds that alert you when the system or a part of the system is functioning optimally or not functioning as designed. Three-point and five-point metrics are available. The three-point metric shows Bad, Goal, and Excellent, and the five-point metric shows Poor, Low, Target, Good, and Exceptional. Metrics are available for the servers, server groups, dispatchers, and services. This section discusses the way in which you manage those metrics.

Here's how to manage metrics:

1. From the Launch menu, select Cognos Administration. Cognos Administration displays.

2. Click the Status tab. The Status menu displays.

3. From the Status menu, select System. The Scorecard, Metrics, and Settings panes display. At the top of the Scorecard pane is a list from which you can choose to display All Servers, All Server Groups, All Dispatchers, and Services, as shown next.

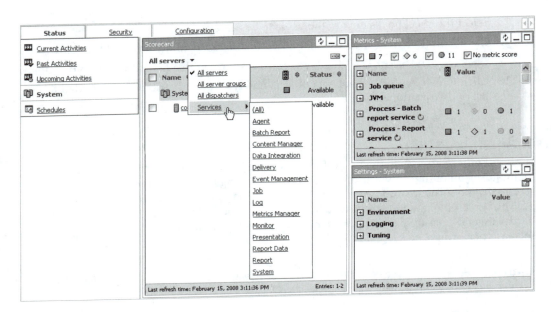

4. From the list, click System, Server, Server Groups, Dispatcher, or Services. A Scorecard pane, Metrics pane, and Settings pane display for the selection. The Metrics pane lists all the functions that can have metrics associated with them. The left half of the pane shows the name of the function and the right half shows the metric score:

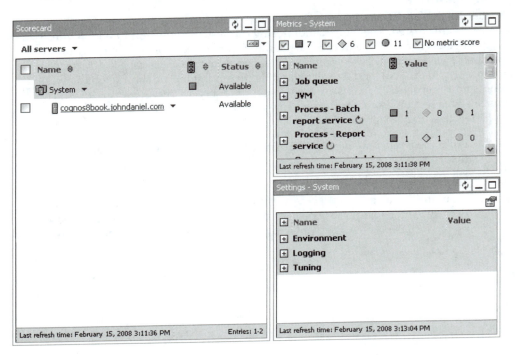

5. From the Metrics pane, click the plus sign to expand the function on which you want to modify the metrics. Specific information for the selected function displays:

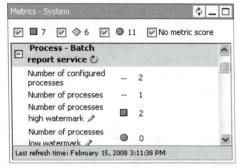

6. Click Edit (the little pencil), next to the item for which you want to modify the metrics. The Set Thresholds For Metric screen displays and contains a Performance Pattern area and a Threshold Values area. The Performance Pattern area provides four options on which you can base the performance of the metric, as shown next. The None option turns off the metric:

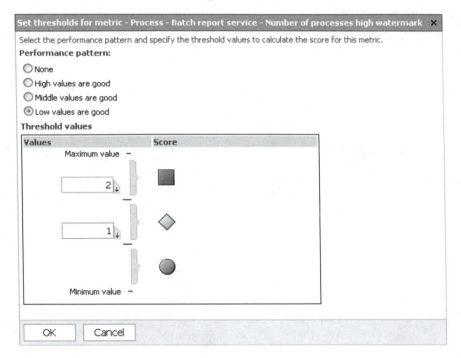

The High Values Are Good and Low Values Are Good options use a three-point metric. For the High Values Are Good option, values that exceed the defined threshold are good. For the Low Values Are Good option, values below the defined threshold are good.

The Middle Values Are Good option creates a five-point metric where values that are just below or just above the threshold are good. The Threshold Values area provides a place to set your threshold.

7. In the Performance Pattern area, click the desired option.

8. In the Threshold Values area, enter thresholds for the metric.

9. Click OK. Cognos 8 sets the threshold values for the metric. You can now monitor system performance.

Set Properties

In Cognos Administration, you can manage the properties for a variety of items. You can manage properties for servers, groups of servers, dispatchers, users, groups, roles, data source connections, distribution lists, and portlets, to name a few. The properties that can be modified include the owner, display icons, language, connections, and user permissions.

You access the Set Properties screen for all of the items for which this is an option similarly. The Set Properties screen contains any combination of four tabs: General, Settings, Connections, and Permissions. For example purposes, we show you how to access the properties for the system.

Here's how to set properties:

1. From the Launch menu, select Cognos Administration. Cognos Administration displays the Status, Security, and Configuration tabs.

2. Click the Status tab. The Status menu displays.

3. From the Status menu, select System. The Scorecard, Metrics, and Settings panes display. The following example shows the Set Properties icon. This icon is the same for all items in Cognos Connection.

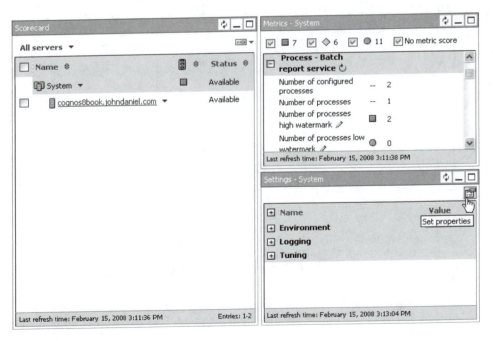

4. From the Settings pane, select Set Properties. The Set Properties screen displays with the General, Settings, and Permissions tabs.

5. Make the desired changes to the properties. This example shows the general properties that can be modified on the General tab:

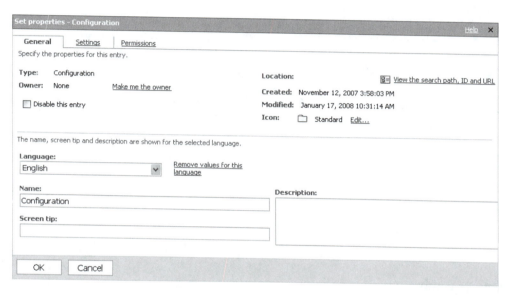

This example shows the settings that can be modified on the Settings tab:

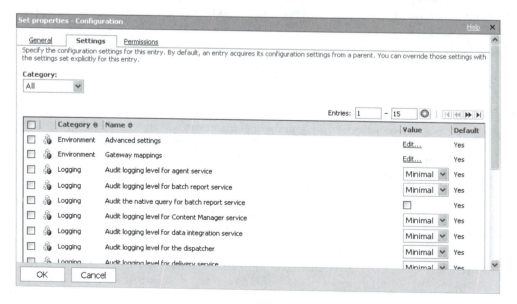

This example shows the permissions that can be modified on the Permissions tab:

6. Click OK. Cognos 8 saves the changes and the Set Properties screen closes.

Manage Gateways

If you have an installation of Cognos Series 7 and your users want to access data from that installation through Cognos 8 Go!, you will need to let Cognos 8 know how to locate and communicate with the earlier installation. This communication is done through the mapping of gateways. The gateway in this case is the URL of the Cognos Series 7 install.

NOTE *Configuring gateways to Cognos Series 7 is beyond the scope of this book. Refer to the section "Specify Advanced Dispatcher Routing" in Chapter 5 of the Cognos 8.3 Administration and Security Guide.*

Manage Logs

Logging records any occurrence you deem worth tracking and messages in a log file or in the log database. For example, suppose a user launches Query Studio, uses Query Studio for a period of time, and then closes the application. Depending on the logging level, you can view details about that usage of Query Studio.

Cognos 8 offers five levels of logging:

- **Minimal**   Shows system and service startup and shutdown and runtime errors.
- **Basic**   Contains the elements of Minimal plus user account management and usage, and use requests.
- **Request**   Contains the elements of Minimal and Basic plus service requests and responses.

- **Trace**   Contains the elements of Minimal and Basic plus requests to all components along with their parameter values and third-party queries to Cognos 8 components.
- **Full**   Contains the elements of all logging levels.

As a rule, you do not want to go beyond a basic log for day-to-day operations. Higher logging levels are going to impact system performance due to the amount of information being written to the log file. The more information that is being written to the log file, the slower the system runs; as a result, log levels other than Minimal or Basic should be used only for troubleshooting.

NOTE The default logging level is set at Minimal.

Here's how to manage logs:

1. From the Launch menu, select Cognos Administration. Cognos Administration displays.
2. Click the Status tab. The Status menu displays.
3. From the Status menu, select System. The Scorecard, Metrics, and Settings panes display. At the top right of the Scorecard pane is a list from which you can choose to display All Servers, All Server Groups, All Dispatchers, and Services.

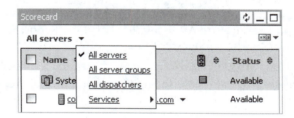

4. Choose All Servers, All Server Groups, All Dispatchers, or Services.
5. From the Settings pane, click Set Properties. The Set Properties screen displays.
6. Click the Settings tab. A list of configurations display (see following illustration). The list shows Category, Name, Value, and Default columns. The Category column shows the type of configuration and the Name column shows the specific configuration that can be modified.

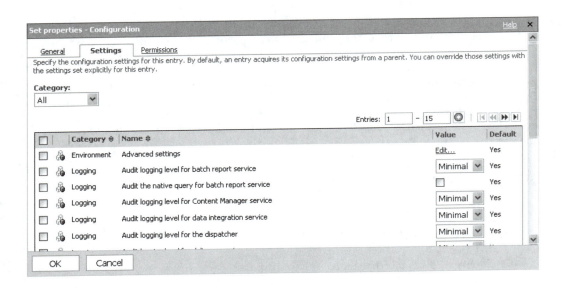

7. From the Category column, navigate to the Logging configuration categories.

8. From the Name column, navigate to the logging item to be changed. All but two of the logging items are modified using a drop-down list. The Audit The Native Query For Batch Report Service and Audit logging Level For Report Service are modified by selecting the checkbox under the Value column.

9. Modify the desired logging levels.

10. Click OK. Cognos 8 updates your logging items and the Set Properties window closes.

NOTE *The logs by default are written to a log file, as flat text files, in the logs directory on the server where the software is installed. You can configure the system to write the log information to a database. You can then run reports off of the database from the tables. This functionality is configured with the Cognos Configuration tool. The Cognos System Administrator can set this up.*

Manage Tuning

Tuning allows administrators to optimize system performance. Cognos 8 has various items that can be tweaked to help your system function more efficiently. Some examples include setting the report size limit (governor limit), PDF settings such as compression type and font embedding, and peak hour usage.

NOTE *The specifics on how to tune your environment are beyond the scope of this book. Refer to the "Tune Server Performance" section of Chapter 5 in the Cognos Administration and Security Guide for specific details.*

Here's how to manage tuning:

1. From the Launch menu, select Cognos Administration. Cognos Administration displays.

2. Click the Status tab. The Status menu displays.

3. From the Status menu, select System. The Scorecard, Metrics, and Settings panes display. At the top left of the Scorecard pane is a list from which you can choose to display All Servers, All Server Groups, All Dispatchers, and Services.

4. From the list at the top of the Scorecard pane, click All Servers, All Server Groups, All Dispatchers, or Services.

5. From the Settings pane, click Set Properties. The Set Properties screen displays.

6. Click the Settings tab. A list of configurations displays. The list shows Category, Name, Value, and Default columns. The Category column shows the type of configuration and the Name column shows the specific configuration that can be modified.

7. From the Category drop-down list, select Tuning.

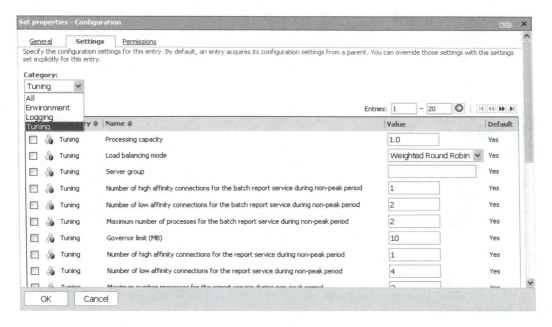

8. From the Name column, navigate to the tuning item to be changed.

9. Modify the tuning items by choosing values from a list or entering values in a text box.

10. Click OK. Cognos 8 updates your tuning items and the Set Properties window closes.

Manage Status and Monitoring

Status and monitoring allow you to keep an eye on the health of your installation by showing you where system performance is slowing. Here's a real-life scenario: One department in an organization decided to implement Cognos 8 and planned appropriately for the deployment for that department. After a few months, other departments saw the value of Cognos 8 and decided they wanted to deploy it as well. The Administrator starts adding licenses and the system that was originally designed for 20 or 30 people grew to 150 to 200 people. System performance started to go down the drain. To avoid a similar situation, you can stay ahead of the curve using status and monitoring.

View Status

Status shows you how your system is running. You can see current, past, and upcoming activities. The activities screen displays a bar chart showing jobs that have succeed, failed, and have been cancelled. You can apply filters to narrow down the amount of items for which you are viewing the status. You can view the run history or the history details. Status viewing is extremely useful for jobs that have failed, since you can view the run history and history details to determine why that job did not run and take corrective actions for that job so that it runs properly. For future events, you can view what is scheduled to occur to ensure that the system will not be overloaded with requests that would negatively affect system performance.

The "Schedule Management" section earlier in this chapter discusses how to view and modify schedules to alleviate demand on the system. The "Server Administration" section discussed other aspects of the system that can be modified to help diagnose issues and improve system performance.

Monitoring

Cognos 8 makes monitoring your system easy by using metrics. The thresholds that you set define target values that show you that your system is working as designed. If any part of your system displays a red light, you can address that portion appropriately to restore the system to peak performance. Additionally, you can use logging to evaluate how your system is performing. Metrics and logging offer a complete view of your system. Use metrics to determine what portion of the system is running poorly. Then you can you view the logs to determine the reason. Remember that you can choose from five levels of detail for your logs. For more information on metrics and logging, refer to the "Server Administration" section of this chapter.

Portlet Integration

Portals are used to display and organize their content inside a Web-based application. Cognos 8 supports third-party portlets that conform to Web Services for Remote Portlets (WSRP) standards (such as Plumtree, Oracle portlets, and Sun portlets). WSRP is a new standard for remote portlets and is still being implemented by many vendors. As a result, Cognos 8 cannot verify or support that all third-party portlets meet this standard. Speak with your IBM Cognos 8 BI representative for more information.

Index